THE AMERICAN FINANCIAL SYSTEM

ALLYN AND BACON, INC.   BOSTON, 1961

THE AMERICAN FINANCIAL SYSTEM: markets and institutions

JAMES B. LUDTKE

Professor of Finance, University of Massachusetts

332.0973
L947a

To MY WIFE AND FIVE CHILDREN

Preface

During the postwar period many colleges and universities adopted a financial institutions course. In the author's experience, this course was adopted as a replacement for money and banking in the junior core curriculum of our School of Business Administration. Nearly all students who enroll in this course have completed a year's work in economics and accounting and are required to take corporation finance. This book is an outgrowth of considerable experience in the development of a financial institutions course, and it is designed to serve as a text in money and banking courses as well as in financial institutions courses.

The basic objective of a financial institutions course is to provide a complete picture of our financial system. Compared with the more conventional money and banking course, the financial institutions course takes a broader point of view. The concept "money" is replaced by the broader concept "financial assets," and "banking" is replaced by "financial institutions."

In the process of experimenting with various approaches to the study of the structure and operation of our highly complex financial system, a flow-of-funds approach has proven to be the most successful because it provides an integrated, comprehensive framework. Attention can be focused on the major financial markets and the decision-making processes as they relate to the financial environment.

It is not the purpose of this text to be highly critical of the structure and operation of our financial system, but it does set the stage for lively discussion of deficient and misdirected flows of funds. Numerous tables help the student to develop a perspective of the magnitude and diversity of each of the sector's holdings and annual acquisitions of financial assets, and to recognize changes that are occurring in the financial markets. The majority of tables may be easily updated by referring to flow-of-funds data in current Federal Reserve bulletins.

The outline of this text is derived from the sector and financial transaction categories that comprise the flow-of-funds system of accounts. The structure of this system of accounting and its relationship to other forms of national accounting are examined in Chapters 2 and 3. The monetary standard and the issue and control of the various forms of money are the subject matter of Part 2. The main body of the book is organized according to four basic sectors: consumer and nonprofit organizations, business, government, and rest-of-the-world. These sectors are examined in relation to financial markets (financial transaction categories in the flow-of-funds system of accounts). The analysis of the flow of funds through financial markets begins with the consumer sector, because this sector is the ultimate or primary source of net national saving. Since a major portion of consumer saving is put to use by the acquisition of financial assets issued by financial institutions, almost all of the major financial institutions are introduced in the discussion of the consumer sector. The conditions under which funds flow into these institutions have an important bearing on the ultimate investment of the funds. In studying the other sectors, attention is focused primarily on the issue of equity and credit instruments by businesses and governmental units, and the acquisition of these instruments by financial institutions.

The ability and willingness of consumers, business enterprises, governmental units, and financial institutions to enter into financial transactions are reflected in the marketplace for goods and services as well as in the money and capital markets. Discretionary decision-making power in the management of funds flowing through financial institutions affects the level and composition of national output. Likewise, changes in the level and pattern of income, prices, and expenditures influence the level and composition of financial transactions. A flow-of-funds approach to the study of our financial system provides an excellent framework for the consideration of national economic objectives and for the analysis of financial measures to achieve these objectives.

The data provided by publications of the Federal Reserve System, National Bureau of Economic Research, congressional hearings, and various trade associations have been very helpful in the preparation of the manuscript. The author is particularly indebted to Professor Pao L. Cheng, who co-authored the first draft of Chapter 3 and reviewed critically the first draft of all chapters, and to Professor Maurice Unger for his encouragement in the early stages of the project and for his contributions to Chapter 14. Undergraduate and graduate students were very helpful in their criticisms. Special recognition goes to Tom Rogers, John Parker, and Donald Savage for their assistance in the construction of tables.

J.B.L.

Contents

PART 3 — CONSUMER, NONPROFIT ORGANIZATION SECTOR

THE
AMERICAN
FINANCIAL
SYSTEM

part 1: Introduction

PART 1 describes in a very general way the nature of our financial system and the relationships between financial flows and nonfinancial flows. The nature of our financial system is discussed in terms of the major influences that have affected its growth and development; financial flows and nonfinancial flows are discussed in relation to national economic accounting.

1

1: Nature and functions of financial institutions

THE prime objectives of the study of financial institutions are (1) to obtain a clear picture of the structure of our country's financial system and (2) a sound understanding of the relationships among financial institutions and between those institutions and other economic entities, including households, businesses, and governmental units. The term "financial institutions" is interpreted to include practices, laws, and customs having to do with finance as well as the business organizations and governmental agencies that specialize in carrying on financial activities. The institution of money and the practices relating to credit instruments are examples of financial practices; commercial banks and savings banks are examples of financial organizations. All are examples of financial institutions.

Today the major part of economic activity is carried on by transfers of money and credit or both. Funds flow into financial institutions under a variety of conditions and from a variety of sources. Financial institutions make loans to households, businesses, and governmental units and invest in securities of businesses and governments. They facilitate the exchange of goods, services, and financial assets, affect the level and composition of saving, and play a very important role in directing the flow of saving into investment. Fundamental relationships exist between financial institutions and the level of economic activity.

To explain the course of development of our financial system would be a monumental study in itself, and to predict the extent and duration of future changes implicit in our system would be hazardous. Rather than attempt either of these grandiose approaches, we shall focus our attention primarily on financial institutions as they exist today, realizing, of course, that the institutions are undergoing continuous change. Certain historical developments are pertinent to a clear understanding of the present status of nearly all financial institutions. Historical perspective is presented wherever it seems appropriate.

The financial system is dynamic. The over-all structure of the financial system and practices having to do with finance are undergoing continuous change. Established financial institutions sometimes fail to

3

respond to changing economic needs, and new financial institutions are developed. Sometimes, new forms fail to measure up to expectations and further changes occur. In most instances our financial institutions have developed, not by purpose or decision of constituted authority, but as expressions of relatively free relationships among individuals.

The development and growth of consumer credit illustrate the introduction of new financial institutions in response to changing economic needs. Almost all commercial banks either resisted the development of consumer credit or hesitated to adapt their lending operations to fit the credit needs of consumers. Sales finance companies and other specialized consumer credit institutions entered the scene and developed this new type of financing. Gradually, commercial banks reexamined previous policy decisions on this matter and decided that consumer credit could and should be a part of their lending operations. Other examples could be cited wherein legal restrictions prevented financial institutions from adapting their operations to meet new situations.

The state and Federal governments have established agencies to regulate various private financial institutions, to guarantee certain types of loans and investments made by private financial institutions, and to make direct loans and investments. The taxing, spending, and borrowing by state and local governments and the Federal Government are vital parts of our financial system. Public financial institutions receive attention throughout this study. For example, the functions of the Federal Housing Authority are considered in the chapter dealing with financing urban real estate expenditures; the Small Business Administration is treated in the chapters having to do with business finance.

INFLUENCES THAT HAVE SHAPED OUR FINANCIAL INSTITUTIONS

Financial institutions develop in response to the need to carry out finance functions that are vital to an economic system. Division of labor, specialization, and extensive use of capital goods, all of which are characteristics of modern economic systems, are dependent on the performance of certain basic finance functions. The structure of a financial system and the manner in which its functions are carried out depend on the over-all institutional arrangements that have been devised for carrying on economic activity. Influences that shape the general character of an economic system also affect the nature of its financial system. The primary determinant of the structure of our country's financial system is the institutional framework of free-enterprise capitalism.

All social groups must devise institutional arrangements or mechanisms for carrying on economic activity. Some sort of property arrangement must be devised; an incentive system is vital to all economic systems. For an economic system to be efficient, economic activity must be integrated and coordinated. There must be some arrangement for the distribution of goods and services. The institutional structure within which economic decisions are made and economic functions carried out comprise an economic system.

Unique Institutions of our Economic System

PRIVATE OWNERSHIP OF PROPERTY. In our economic system persons have the right to own and control property, including the means of production. Applied to our financial system, almost all of the financial institutions are, therefore, privately owned.

The three basic forms of business organization are the sole proprietorship, the partnership, and the corporation. Considering the size and nature of most of our financial institutions, almost all of them are incorporated.

The basic procedure in forming a corporation to serve the financial needs of the economy is very similar to that followed in establishing any other corporation. States have general corporation laws under which a group of qualified persons (incorporators) is permitted to form a corporation by making and filing a certificate of incorporation in proper form and paying required fees. A certificate of incorporation is the legal instrument through which a proposed corporation obtains and possesses its legal being or existence.

Concomitant with the development of many of our financial institutions, states adopted special sets of laws pertaining to their formation and operation. Generally, financial institutions are required to satisfy more stringent incorporation laws than are other corporations. Relatively large minimum capital requirements, for example, are specified for many types of financial institutions. Initial regulation of financial institutions is achieved through the charter; regulation of their operation and liquidation is achieved through various governmental agencies that have been set up to supervise them.

The dual system of charter is another major difference between incorporating a financial institution and incorporating another type of business. At various times Congress has passed legislation giving incorporators the right to incorporate certain types of financial institutions under Federal charter; the incorporators of certain types of institutions therefore have a choice between a charter issued by the Federal Government and a charter issued by a state government. This arrangement is referred to as the dual system of charter. Commercial banks are an example: a commercial bank may be chartered by either the Federal Government or a state government. In the former case, the bank is known as a national bank; in the latter case, a state bank. Credit unions, savings and loan associations,

5

and small business investment companies also operate under a dual system of charter.

Some of our financial institutions are established by governmental agencies. Even in these cases, the stock of the financial institutions may be privately owned. For example, the member commercial banks of the Federal Reserve System own the capital stock of the Federal Reserve banks. However, it should be pointed out that the stock of the Federal Reserve banks and similar corporations do not have the normal attributes of corporate stock. Dividends may be fixed by law and control may be very limited.

A corporation may be either a stock or non-stock corporation. Both types are prevalent in finance. A stock corporation is one that has its capital stock divided into shares and issued to stockholders. The capital fund of the corporation is subscribed to by the stockholders, who, in turn, hope to receive dividend income or realize capital appreciation. A private non-stock corporation is a form of cooperative enterprise owned by the organization's customers. Mutual savings banks and mutual insurance companies are organized as private non-stock corporations.

PROFIT MOTIVATION. Profit motivation underlies the formation and operation of business firms in our economy, and financial firms are no exception. It is a fact that the motive underlying the formation of some of our financial institutions of the mutual type, such as mutual savings banks and mutual insurance companies, is something other than profit, but, once the institutions are established, their motivation and operation are very much the same as that of the non-mutual types. Profits represent the residual return to those who have invested ownership capital, and in theory, financial firms operate so as to maximize financial returns to owners.

The major determinants of the per cent return on a firm's ownership capital are turnover of assets, net operating margin, and the use of non-ownership capital.* For nonfinancial firms, turnover refers to net sales or revenues divided by total assets. This definition is equally applicable to some of the financial institutions, such as investment banking firms and commercial paper houses, but for the majority of financial institutions, the definition is not applicable, because they are in the business of "renting" funds rather than selling products or services. To state that a financial firm has carried on a certain volume of loans and investments during an annual period is equivalent to stating that it has maintained its assets at a given level during the period. If one were to stretch the term "sales" to mean "loan and investment volume," the turnover would be equal to one.

---

* The rate of return on assets of financial and nonfinancial institutions may be stated in terms of an equation: R is net sales or revenue, P is operating profit, and A is total assets. Relationships include: turnover (t) is R/A, Margin (m) is P/R, and percentage return on total assets (r) is the product of tm. To restate: $P/R \times R/A = P/A$.

The operation of a hypothetical investment banking firm serves as a good illustration of those financial firms for which turnover of assets is more than one and is therefore important in achieving maximum profits. Assume that an investment banking firm has total assets of $1,000,000, and that all of the funds are supplied by the owners of the firm. Assume further that each month the firm purchases and resells $1,000,000 of newly issued corporate securities at a price differential of 2 per cent. Over a 12-month period, the total transactions would amount to $12,000,000 and the gross revenue would equal $24,000, the latter of which represents a gross return of 24 per cent on capital (12 months times 2 per cent per month equals annual return of 24 per cent). After deducting costs of operation, the residual return must still represent a satisfactory return on the $1,000,000 of invested ownership capital. Other financial firms carry on similar types of operations, and thereby obtain respectable rates of return on invested capital even though the margin on each transaction is very small.

For nonfinancial firms net operating margin refers to net operating profit divided by net sales. The per cent return on total assets is calculated by multiplying the net operating margin times the turnover of assets. For the majority of financial firms, the calculation is much more direct. If total assets are substituted for net sales, and turnover is one by definition, the net operating margin for financial firms is net operating profit divided by total assets, giving the percentage return on total assets. Net operating profit is the difference between total revenue and total cost. As noted above, a nonfinancial firm's revenue results from the sale of goods and services. In the financial segment of the economy, revenue consists of fees, interest, and dividends. Costs consist primarily of expenses relating to receiving, managing, and disbursing funds and interest on borrowed funds. The basic types of expenses can be broken down into fixed and variable costs, just as they are broken down in nonfinancial firms.

The net operating margin realized by financial firms is much lower than that realized by nonfinancial firms. The gross revenue, expressed in terms of a gross yield on assets, may average less than 4 or 5 per cent, the exact yield depending on the uses of funds and the level and structure of yields on financial assets. Expenses and interest on borrowed funds are subtracted from gross yields to determine the net operation margin, which may be as low as 1 or 2 per cent. To attract ownership capital, the return on ownership capital must be much higher than 1 or 2 per cent; it should range somewhere between 10 and 15 per cent. With a gross yield of only 4 or 5 per cent, how do financial firms achieve, say, a 10 per cent return on ownership capital?

Almost all financial institutions, including those which emphasize turnover of assets, secure a major portion of their funds from nonownership sources, and these funds are secured at a cost lower than the gross yield on the firms' uses of funds. The following hypothetical case may serve as a good illustration of how borrowed capital can improve the return on ownership capital. Assume that XYZ Commercial Bank has $1,000,000 of assets; owners of demand deposits supply $600,000; owners of savings deposits supply $300,000; and stockholders supply the residual, $100,000. Assume that the cost of handling the checking accounts is offset by service charges and that depositors are paid 3 per cent per year on savings deposits. Assume further that the bank is able to earn a 2 per cent return on total assets. After subtracting the 3 per cent interest paid on savings deposits ($9,000), there is a residual of $11,000, which represents an 11 per cent return on invested ownership capital. Although the bank had a low gross operating profit margin, the use of relatively large amounts of low-cost borrowed capital (deposits, in this case) permitted the owners to realize a fairly respectable return on ownership capital. The very low operating margins on financial transactions explain why many financial institutions rely very heavily on borrowed funds.

COMPETITIVE PRICING. Another unique characteristic of our economic system is competitive pricing. It is not a pricing system that is unique in our economy, but rather the environment within which the pricing system operates. Some financial markets operate under conditions that closely approximate the conditions associated with pure competition. Securities trading through the facilities of the New York Stock Exchange is probably the best example of such a market.

Financial transactions are carried out by telephone, wire, and mail, obviating personal visits for many types of financial transactions. Geographical location no longer presents an effective barrier to competition. Firms and households have many choices when making deposits. The price or interest rate paid on such deposits will depend primarily on the type of financial institution in which the funds are deposited. Similar institutions are likely to pay identical rates. A savings deposit in the XYZ Commercial Bank is much like a savings deposit in the ABC Commercial Bank, and if rates varied among commercial banks, shifts in deposit balances would probably bring about readjustments until the rates were once again uniform. Fear of the consequences of such cut-throat competition among commercial banks in seeking funds has led to the adoption by supervisory authorities of maximum rates of interest to be paid on deposits. Some of the more specialized savings institutions are able to offer relatively more attractive rates to depositors, but with some product differentiation.

There is not the same degree of competition among financial institutions in their role as suppliers of funds to households and firms. Personal contacts are generally necessary in arranging loans, and there are definite limits to both the number and location of financial institutions that can be considered by a household or firm in a loan transaction. Many of the smaller financial institutions are unable to compete for the large-sized loan. Obviously, there are elements of monopolistic competition and oligopoly in some financial markets. However, there is sufficient mobility (shiftability) of funds from one market to another to prevent rates in one segment of the market from getting far out of line with the general level and structure of interest rates.

FUNCTIONAL DISTRIBUTION OF INCOME. A price or cost system is applied to the factors of production as a means of achieving rational allocation of economic resources. In our economic system, the prices of the factors of production (land, labor, and capital) are determined in the market and prices are paid to the owners of these resources. The income a person receives is related to the monetary importance (value) of his functional contribution to the production of goods and services. This relationship is referred to as functional distribution of income.

Under a functional distribution of income, persons are encouraged to acquire ownership of income-producing assets such as land, stocks, and bonds to supplement wages and salaries. The basic desire on the part of individuals to acquire such assets has led to the adoption and operation of many of our financial institutions.

There is not complete identity between functional distribution of income and personal income. Some persons and firms receive transfer payments, which consist of monetary income receipts for which no services are rendered currently. Social security and unemployment benefits are prime examples of transfer payments. Many of the transfer payments are handled through either private or public financial institutions.

The system of income distribution also affects the level and composition of savings. If personal income were equally distributed, the amount of savings would probably be smaller and the uses to which the savings were put would also be different. The present distribution of income is such that a relatively large amount of personal saving is done by the middle-income groups, and these persons rely very heavily on savings and thrift institutions. Persons in higher income groups have tended to invest their savings directly in securities, mortgages, and real estate.

FREE CONSUMER CHOICE. In our economic system, consumers have considerable freedom as to how they use their available funds. The function of free consumer choice is to place in the hands of the ultimate users of economic resources the power of deciding what goods are to be produced, and in what quantities.

In the absence of overt restrictions, free consumer choice has been partly responsible for the adoption of specific financial practices and the organization of some of the specialized financial institutions. Freedom of

9

action in the consumer sector has enabled consumers to utilize credit in many of their transactions, including consumer durable goods, home financing, and security investment. These practices have led to the development of many specialized institutions. Where there have been abuses, some restrictions have been introduced. The stock market crash of 1929, for instance, was partly blamed on the amount of credit used to finance stock market transactions, with the result that in 1934 Congress gave the Federal Reserve Board the power to regulate the maximum amount of credit that could be extended on certain types of securities transactions. During World War II, overt restrictions were placed on nearly all types of credit transactions.

Free consumer choice affects the level and pattern of savings. Consumers are free to decide whether to spend or not to spend. Obviously, some persons with low incomes do not actually have a choice, for all of their income must be spent in order to survive; but given an adequate level of income, there is freedom to decide. Savers desire to make funds available to others under such a variety of conditions that numerous types of thrift and investment institutions have been established.

Division of Labor, Specialization, and Capital Formation

To complete an introduction to the environment in which finance and financial institutions operate, it is necessary to describe some of the common practices relating to production in a modern economic system and show how they influence the structure and operation of a financial system.

All advanced economies have achieved division of labor, specialization, and intermediate means of production. Russia has demonstrated that a high level of production can be achieved under a set of economic institutions very much different from our own. One of the reasons for this success is that the Russians are able to employ basic economic practices such as division of labor, specialization, and extensive application of intermediate means of production. Division of labor and specialization, which refer to concentration by persons and firms on particular productive activities, have been used to some extent in all but the very simplest economic systems. Another common characteristic of modern economic systems is the degree to which intermediate means of production, such as buildings, machinery, and semifinished goods are employed in almost all industries. In both Russia and the United States, for example, the production of capital goods requires a relatively large proportion of total productive activities. Extensive systems of exchange and savings-investment processes, both of which directly involve a country's financial system, are basic to division of labor, specialization, and extensive application of intermediate means of production. However, it should be mentioned that the Russians employ a program of forced savings.

DIVISION OF LABOR AND SPECIALIZATION. Man has discovered that division of labor and specialization increase the total amount of production of goods and services from a given amount of resources. The automobile assembly line provides a striking illustration of the application of division of labor. As the body frame of the automobile moves along the assembly line, the many different components of the automobile are attached. The production line workers are assigned specific tasks, such as placing the wheel on the axles or tightening the nuts after the wheels are placed in proper position. Such minute division of labor permits the automobile companies to turn out a larger quantity of automobiles than would otherwise be possible. The prospects of higher wages encourage or motivate workers to accept assignments of specialized tasks, even though they may lose individuality, sacrifice opportunities to be creative while on the job, and probably experience monotony, fatigue, and insecurity. Proper utilization of increased leisure time may tend to offset some of these job disadvantages.

Specialization by business firms also contributes to a higher level of production of goods and services. Today, no one firm produces all types of goods or provides all types of services. Instead, firms specialize in the production of a relatively few goods or services. Larger firms, each of which may be involved in the production of a hundred or more products, have many specialized plants. Product specialization by business firms permits greater efficiency in the use of economic resources.

Many stages of production may be involved in moving resources from the raw material stage to final consumption. Firms not only specialize in the production of certain goods, but also tend to restrict productive activities to either one or only a few stages of production. The production of a loaf of bread may serve as an illustration of this point. Involved in the total process are wheat farmers, elevator operators, millers, warehousemen, bakers, and retailers. Each type of firm is specializing either in one or only a few stages of the total productive process; each firm is probably using division of labor in its production set-up. In addition, the materials and much of the equipment used in these various firms are supplied by other specialized firms. The geographical dispersion of the many firms requires an elaborate net of transportation and communications. There is also product specialization by geographical areas, such as wheat in Kansas and automobiles in Detroit. Obviously, division of labor and specialization impose interdependence among all economic units.

The extent to which division of labor and specialization can be carried out depends on the amount of trade or exchange, the state of technology, and the amount of capital goods or intermediate means of production. Large buildings, complex and expensive machinery, and training programs are needed to realize fully the potential economies involved in division of labor and specialization. To cover the costs of these programs, the large amounts of production flowing out of such processes must be sold in the market, and exchange is therefore a necessary condition. To realize capital formation, savings must be encouraged and transferred from those who do not use savings for this purpose to those who do.

EXCHANGE. Individuals and firms would not be willing to concentrate on particular productive activities unless they were reasonably confident that the goods or services they were producing could be exchanged for other goods and services. The employees of the automobile companies desire food, clothing, shelter, and many other goods and services; yet they concentrate their productive activities on the production of automobiles. The automobile firms assemble many more automobiles than there are auto workers. The persons directly involved expect to exchange the "excess" automobiles for the "excess" goods and services of other firms and individuals who concentrate their productive activities on the assumption that the automobile firms will produce automobiles. Interdependence is concomitant with specialization. The total output of goods and services is increased, but the system becomes more complex and interdependent.

Division of labor and specialization can be carried on in a simple barter economy. Families or households could concentrate their productive activities on the basic consumption goods and exchange the goods without the use of money. One family could concentrate on the production of food, another on clothing, another on providing shelter, and still another on fuel. Except in the most simple barter economy, it would be difficult and perhaps impossible to assess accurately the relative values of the factors of production and output. Man would discover and has discovered that barter imposes severe limits on the extent to which specialization and division of labor can be carried out. Eventually, barter trading leads to the general acceptance of something as a standard of value and something as a medium of exchange. Trade would be served best, perhaps, by adopting the same thing to serve both functions. The term "money" refers to that which is generally accepted as a means of payment. In modern economic systems money also serves as the measure of value and the standard of deferred payment.

Another major difficulty in carrying on trade in a barter economy would be the need for double coincidence of wants. For illustration, Mr. Brown, who has concentrated his productive activities on the growing of turnips, must find persons who not only want turnips, but who also have goods to exchange that are attractive to Mr. Brown. If two persons' disposable "excesses" are not mutually suited to each others' needs, exchange is not possible in a barter economy. An escape from this impasse is to introduce some good generally acceptable to all persons and firms that could be used in the exchange process. If Mr. Brown were willing to accept the good in exchange for his turnips, then double coincidence of wants would be unnecessary. Man has discovered that two transactions based on the use of a generally accepted good (money) are much simpler than one transaction based on double coincidence of wants.

The use of money introduces a common measure of value for factors of production and the goods and services that are produced. Money exchange, as opposed to barter exchange, facilitates comparison of values. Furthermore, the expression of all economic activities in terms of a common denominator makes record keeping possible. Accurate record keeping delights the business man, the household manager, and the tax collectors.

Credit also facilitates production and consumption. A credit transaction is one in which a person or firm receives money, goods, or services in the present in exchange for a promise to pay in the future. Money, in addition to serving as a medium of exchange and common measure of value, also serves as the standard of deferred payments in credit transactions.

Credit facilitates the formation and operation of business firms, including financial institutions. The amount of funds required to launch a new firm may exceed the funds of the owner or owners and if it were not possible to raise additional funds through a variety of credit arrangements, the promotion of many new firms would never reach fruition. Furthermore, many individuals desire to avoid the risks commensurate with ownership status. Many suppliers of funds, especially many of the savings and thrift institutions, are required by both law and prudence to supply credit rather than ownership capital. Through credit transactions a considerable portion of funds is transferred from savers to prospective users.

Widespread application of intermediate means of production and the use of many stages in the productive process require many transfers of goods prior to final sale. One firm's sales do not necessarily represent final or ultimate sales of that firm's product. The product may simply represent the materials to be used in later productive stages. The use of credit facilitates the continuous flow of goods and services from firm to firm and from firm to ultimate consumer. To require cash payment prior to the actual release of goods and services would not only be cumbersome, but would actually preclude the operation of many firms.

Through the use of credit, manufacturers, wholesalers, and retailers are able to increase inventories in preparation for expected peak sales. As inventories are worked down to more normal levels by sales, proceeds of such sales can be used to retire the debts which had made possible the increase in inventories. The use of borrowed funds tends to generate the funds for repayment of loans. If permanent funds were used to finance such temporary needs, the funds would be largely idle during the periods of off-peak inventories. Idle funds produce little or no income and their presence tends to lower the average return on total invested capital.

Credit is also used by consumers. Some purchases involve such large amounts of money that by the time a consumer could accumulate the funds necessary for full cash payment, few years would remain during which the purchased item could be enjoyed. The residence is a good case in point. The same basic philosophy has been applied to many durable consumer goods. Furthermore, many purchases would not make sense if they were placed on a cash basis, such as the daily consumption of water, electricity, and gas.

Firms specialize in money and credit just as other firms specialize in manufacturing, wholesaling, and retailing. In fact some financial institutions are known as wholesalers of credit and some are known as retailers of credit. The financial institutions play a crucial role in carrying on specialization and division of labor.

CAPITAL FORMATION. The intermediate means of production, such as buildings, machinery, and semi-finished goods must be produced. It is imperative that a portion of total output be allocated to the intermediate means of production. Residential and apartment construction are also vital to our economic system.

Since 1952, expenditures on new plants and equipment by United States business have been exceeding $30 billion annually. In 1959, manufacturing corporations had invested over $100 billion in property, plant, and equipment after deduction of the reserve for depreciation and depletion. Billions of dollars of raw materials, semi-finished goods, and finished goods are on their way through the productive process at all times. In 1959, inventories of all manufacturing corporations exceeded $50 billion; inventories of wholesalers exceeded $12 billion; and inventories of retailers exceeded $24 billion. Residential construction exceeded $15 billion.

Capital goods are subject to wear and tear, deterioration, and obsolescence. The goal of sustained economic growth, which is a goal common to all modern economic systems, requires not only replacement of capital goods but a net increase in the total stock of capital goods. Manufacturers, wholesalers, and retailers hold billions of dollars worth of goods in inventory so that they will be able to maintain uninterrupted production and delivery to customers. Economic growth requires an increase in inventories as well as a net increase in plant, equipment, and residences.

Gross national product may be viewed in terms of either a flow of income or a flow of output. The flow of income represents the income earned in the productive process and the charges against existing capital goods. The flow of output represents the value of goods and services produced. If the total income were spent on consumption, then no part of the productive process would be devoted to the production of capital goods. Not even the worn-out capital goods would be replaced. The system would be typed as a disinvesting or decaying economy. Obviously, all income should not be spent on consumption. Income not spent for consumption is referred to as savings. There must be savings and savings must be transferred into investment.

A considerable portion of total savings is done by business through depreciation and retention of earnings, and given profitable investment opportunities, business saving will be reinvested in business. Individuals also save. In recent years, personal saving has been about 50 per cent of business saving. If the persons who save do not plan to invest the funds directly in capital goods, then the funds should be transferred to those who will invest the funds. If planned savings were to exceed planned investment the flow of spending would be adversely affected, and national income would fall to a level at which planned savings and planned investment would be more in line with each other. If planned savings were less than planned investment, then some investment would have to be postponed unless the banking system created additional funds to sponsor all of the planned investment. In the latter case, if the economy were operating at or near full. employment, the total demand for goods and services would exceed total output at current prices and the price level could be expected to rise.

One of the major characteristics in the present economic stage of development in the United States is that one group of persons does the personal saving, whereas in large measure a completely separate group does the investing. Given the goal of economic stability at a high level of income, and given the additional fact that a high level of personal savings accompanies a high level of income, a high level of investment is essential. At the same time, however, it is also important to guard against excessive investment financed by bank credit because of its effects on prices and economic stability.

Financial institutions encourage savings, receive savings, and transfer savings into investment. Financial institutions assist households, business firms, and governments in raising funds to finance various forms of investment. Financial institutions provide market facilities that are attractive to savers and investors. Persons and firms are willing to purchase and hold securities because they expect to be able to exchange securities for cash by shifting them to other holders, whenever cash is needed or desired. Although the purchase of outstanding securities may not represent real investment, additional funds are allocated to the capital markets, providing conditions favorable to the issue of new securities. Proceeds from the sale of new securities will probably be used to acquire additional plant, equipment, and inventories, all of which are part of total capital formation.

Financial institutions are important in directing the flow of saving into investment and they may also influence the magnitude of saving and investment. There is a fundamental relationship between our financial system and the rate and pattern of economic growth.

FUNCTIONS OF FINANCIAL INSTITUTIONS

On the basis of our introductory remarks, it is now possible to outline briefly the major functions performed by financial institutions.

Provide an Adequate Stock of Money

One of the prime functions performed by financial institutions is to provide an adequate stock of money. Financial institutions that are directly involved in performing this function are referred to as monetary financial institutions, and they constitute the core of the financial system. Financial institutions not directly involved in performing this function are referred to as non-monetary financial institutions. The monetary financial institutions can actually increase and decrease the stock of money; the non-monetary financial institutions can only transfer money. Inasmuch as total spending is affected by both the stock of money and its transfer, the activities of both monetary and non-monetary financial institutions affect employment, production, and income.

Persons, firms, and governmental units must hold cash balances (money) to enable them to meet their obligations as they become due. The stock of money required for this purpose or function depends primarily on the following factors: (1) the total money volume of transactions in goods, services, and securities; (2) the frequency, regularity, and coincidence of money flows for persons, firms, and governmental units; (3) transportation and communication facilities relating to money transfer; and (4) the availability and volume of credit. Change in any one of these factors affects the demand for money.

Conceivably, the total demand for money and thus the required stock of money could be explained solely in terms of the need for money as a means of payment or a medium of exchange. However, the likelihood of this explanation being adequate is remote, for money may also be held as a store of value. For example, persons and firms may attempt to build up their present cash balances (money) in order to take advantage of expected near-term price reductions of goods, services, or securities. Some investors may build up cash balances, thinking that interest rates will rise in the future. Persons who believe that their incomes will cease or taper off in the future may also attempt to build up cash balances. Like the medium-of-exchange function, the store of value function directly affects the demand for money. The demand for moneny to serve as a store of value is as unstable as the state of expectations.

Money is generally defined in terms of one or more of its functions. It may be defined as that which is generally used to make payments for goods and services and to make payments on debts. The definition specifically refers only to the medium-of-exchange function. Other definitions could be formulated, the phrasing depending on the particular function(s) to be emphasized. The definition given here is the one generally used because it points up the existing importance of demand deposits in modern economic systems, especially in the United States. On the basis of the definition, money consists of coins, paper currency, and demand deposits (checking accounts in commercial banks).

There have been periods in American history when the stock of money proved grossly inadequate for the needs of the times. During the Colonial period and most of the 18th century, scarcity of sound money tended to curb the rate of economic growth. At times, overly rapid contraction in the stock of money contributed to financial panics, such as those of 1837, 1873, 1897, and 1907. At other times, excessive amounts of money resulted in a general increase in the level of prices. Experience demonstrates that the provision of an adequate stock of money is a necessary part of any over-all program aimed at maintaining economic stability and promoting sound economic growth. If the stock of money is excessive, it is likely to contribute to a rate of spending that exceeds the rate of production of goods and services at prevailing prices, rocketing the economy into the never-never land of inflation. If the stock of money is contracted or expanded too slowly, it might be a mournful prelude to a lower level of production and increased unemployment.

Today, the monetary financial institutions consist of the United States Treasury, Federal Reserve banks and agencies, and commercial banks. The demand for coins and paper currency is registered with commercial banks, which, in turn, request shipments of currency from district Federal Reserve banks. Shipments of currency are likely to consist of all forms of currency: coins, silver certificates, United States notes, and Federal Reserve notes. The demand for money in the form of demand deposits is also registered at commercial banks, and depending on their reserve positions, commercial banks may increase the amount of demand deposits. The Federal Reserve agencies are able to affect the cost, availability, and volume of money by influencing the reserve positions of commercial banks.

Money and credit and monetary financial institutions are basic to the operation of the total economy. Therefore, these matters are treated early in this text. The mechanics of coin and currency issue, the deposit and loan functions of commercial banks, and the nature of credit transactions constitute the subject matter of Part 2.

Provide Liquidity

Liquidity is the ability to meet maturing obligations and adjust the composition of assets. In the case of commercial banks, liquidity also refers to the ability to increase the volume of assets through new loans and investments. Inability to meet maturing obligations may force premature liquidation of assets and may lead to bankruptcy. Inability to adjust the composition of assets precludes immediate response to market developments. For example, an inadequate liquidity position may prevent a non-financial firm from building up inventory in spite of once-in-a-lifetime bargain prices. Had the firm been holding money or other liquid financial assets, it would have been able to adjust quickly to the change in market developments. Numerous other examples could be cited to illustrate the importance of liquidity to nonfinancial firms. Liquidity is an even more important consideration in the management of financial firms, especially in the case of commercial banks. Commercial banks must not only stand ready to meet possible deposit withdrawals, but must also be able to shift assets into loans if the demand warrants. Successful financial management calls for *minimum* liquidity which is or should be true for all firms. When the liquidity positions of firms are below desired minima, our system is much less flexible and adjustments are more difficult.

The need for liquidity is met by holding money and other financial assets that possess a high degree of "moneyness." The basic determinants underlying the demand for liquidity are nearly identical to those which underlie the demand for money, and to the extent that the need for liquidity can be met by holding assets other than money, the stock of money can be that much smaller. The division between money and near-money assets depends primarily on the level and structure of interest rates. If the level of rates is very low, the loss of interest income from holding money is not very great. At a higher level of interest rates, the possible loss in interest income prompts individuals, firms, and governmental units to hold a greater portion of their liquidity in the form of interest-earning assets. The structure of the rates will affect the selection among the various short-term credit instruments that serve liquidity needs.

Money is the most liquid of all assets. Some of the other financial assets possess a high degree of "moneyness" in the sense that they may be converted into money within a very short time at little or no loss in value. Assets that satisfy these criteria include time deposits, shares in savings and loans associations and credit unions, United States Government savings bonds, short-term Federal obligations, bankers' acceptances, and commercial paper. Some of these assets are liquid by design, such as the first three types noted above, and the others are liquid because they are actively traded in national markets. Obviously, if all holders of such assets attempted to convert them into money at the same time, the assets would turn out to be illiquid, unless monetary authorities provided the demand for financial assets. In the process of doing so, the stock of money would be increased. However, in the normal course of events, as depositors withdraw funds, others deposit funds; as some holders of short-term Federal obligations decide that the time has come to convert their assets into money, others believe that the time has come to add to their holdings of Federal obligations. By having an adequate supply of such assets, individuals, firms, and governmental units are able to move into and out of cash as their needs determine. The existence of such assets and their active trading allow individual economic units considerable flexibility in adjusting liquidity positions and allow a given volume of economic activity to be carried out with a much smaller stock of money. In other words, the circulation or turnover of money is directly related to the stock of and turnover of financial assets that possess a high degree of "moneyness."

Financial institutions are of considerable importance in meeting the economy's liquidity needs. The banking system provides the stock of money, and it has the potential ability to increase it. Ability of the commercial banking system to add to the stock of money is directly related to the system's own liquidity position. If the system's liquidity position is under pressure to the extent that it cannot increase the volume of loans and investments, the monetary officials have it within their power to relieve the strain and make it possible for the banking system to expand loans and investments. The non-banking financial institutions add to the over-all liquidity of the economy by creating financial assets that serve as very close substitutes for money. For example, an individual sacrifices only a slight degree of liquidity when he exchanges money for a savings account. The institution receiving this deposit transfers money to an economic unit that requires the most liquid type of asset. Large money market banks and government securities dealers provide liquidity by making markets for short-term credit market instruments. This market structure also provides a mechanism through which short-term loans can be arranged.

At times the over-all liquidity position of the economy may be inadequate. Possible reasons for this condition might include any one of the following: (1) an arbitrary reduction in the total stock of liquid assets; (2) imposition of barriers to the turnover of money and other liquid assets; (3) an increased need for liquidity has not been met by an increase in either the stock or turnover of liquid assets. Assuming that the reaction to inadequate liquidity is an attempt on the part of individual economic units to build up their respective liquidity positions, their actions might influence adversely the level of economic activity. A higher level of interest rates makes liquidity more expensive to all economic units. To the extent that a high cost of liquidity discourages economic units from maintaining adequate liquidity, a tight-money policy reduces the degree of economic flexibility and may tend to obstruct economic growth and make it more difficult to maintain stability in the economy. If there is excessive liquidity in the system, individual economic units are likely to shift to less-liquid assets, and in the process increase the aggregate demand for goods and services. An increase in the level or value of production will generate an increase in the demand for liquidity, which will tend to absorb the previously existing excess liquidity.

Inasmuch as short-run changes in the degree of liquidity may be both a cause and an effect of changes in production, income, and employment, liquidity is a vital consideration in the formulation and application of monetary, credit, and debt management policies.

Transfer of Savings into Investment

Sound economic growth is not automatic. Savings must be encouraged, and savings must be transferred into investment. Financial institutions play important roles in the savings-investment process. As noted above, financial institutions provide market facilities enabling persons and firms to shift their assets from cash to securities and back to cash, thus creating conditions conducive to the ownership of financial assets. Persons and firms who do not wish to hold securities are able to shift from cash to various types of savings deposits. In the development of the modern industrialized economy, a dominant factor has been the increase in savings and its embodiment in plant, equipment, and other capital goods. The mobilization and allocation of personal saving required by the advance of research and technology are accomplished primarily through financial institutions.

During the last few decades, our financial institutions have played a relatively more important role in the savings-investment process. The evolution of a strong middle class and its capacity to do the bulk of personal saving in our economy have channeled the major portion of personal saving through savings and thrift institutions, and these financial institutions have intelligently met the pressing need for the allocation of personal saving to the various needs of households, businesses, and governmental units.

The increasing importance of the savings and thrift institutions is a major factor accounting for a shift in emphasis in the study of the financial system. The non-monetary financial institutions presently hold the major portion (60 per cent) of all assets held by financial institutions; at the turn of the century they held only about 40 per cent of the total assets. Commercial banks, the major monetary financial institution, have also become more active in promoting savings and thrift through their savings departments.

Minimize Risk

Persons, firms, and governmental units are subject to many possible financial losses. "Risk" refers to the uncertainty of a financial loss. Risk is universal; excessive risk is undesirable, and there is a psychological propensity to seek security through reduction or avoidance of excessive risk. All risks cannot be eliminated and profit represents owner-investor compensation for voluntarily assuming irreducible risks.

Risk exerts a retarding influence on economic activity. If it were not for the activities of some of our financial institutions in the management of risk, a considerable portion of economic activity would be considered too risky in view of prospective gain.

Some forms of risk are insurable, and financial institutions have been established to provide insurance facilities. Insurance carriers handle only those risks which meet certain broad tests. The more important tests are: (1) a large group of homogeneous exposure units so as to predict losses by the use of the law of large numbers; (2) the occurrence of a loss in each individual case is accidental or fortuitous; (3) the cost of insuring is economically feasible; and (4) a majority of the insured are unlikely to incur loss at the same time. If a risk meets these and other tests, private insurance companies strive to combine a sufficiently large number of exposures to make particular types of losses predictable. Insurance carriers also provide facilities through which the insureds are able to share the predictable loss(es) proportionately. By means of insurance, persons and firms are able to substitute relatively small premium outlays for much larger, but uncertain financial losses. Insurance carriers actually reduce risk in the sense that they predict within satisfactory limits the probable losses resulting from specified perils. Satisfactory limits refer to the fact that capital stock companies, motivated by profit, are able to offer insurance to persons and firms.

A recent example of the relationship between insurance and economic activity is found in our atomic reactor program. Private enterprise hesitated to proceed with tests on nuclear reactors or work on atomic power plants until there was assurance that there would be financial protection against the possibility of huge financial losses in the event of a major nuclear accident. Both private and government insurance protection are now available.

Insurance is of prime importance in loan decisions by financial institutions. If a firm is not adequately insured, it may not be able to repay a loan if a loss occurs. In fact, an uninsured loss may cause a firm's failure. To the extent that insurance enables a firm to continue intact after a loss, insurance contributes to greater over-all business stability.

Another example of the way in which financial institutions reduce risk is the operation of commodity exchanges. Commodity prices are unstable and holders of title to commodities and contracts or both involving the future use of such commodities are subject to possible financial losses as a result of future price changes. In response to the economic needs of persons and firms, commodity exchanges were established to provide facilities through which persons and firms may trade in contracts calling for immediate or future delivery of many different commodities. By trading in future contracts, persons and firms are able to minimize the adverse effects of possible price changes.

Fortunately, there are some persons who believe that they can realize gain by voluntarily assuming the risk of price changes. These persons are referred to as speculators and they create very active markets for future contracts. As for the role of financial institutions, the commodity departments of large broker-dealer houses assist both persons and firms in executing orders to be completed through the facilities of the organized commodity exchanges. Also, commercial banks provide considerable financing to those who trade in future contracts.

Many functions are performed by the commodity exchanges. Their operations lead to competitive price determination, greater over-all stability of commodity prices, equality of trading privileges, and a guarantee to traders that contracts will be fulfilled. All of these functions are related to the reduction of risk.

QUESTIONS

1. What is meant by "financial institutions"?
2. The financial system is dynamic. Explain.
3. Trace the origin and development of the dual system of charter.
4. If a financial institution has a low per cent return on total assets, how is it possible to attract ownership capital?
5. What are the unique institutions of our economic system and how has each affected the structure and operation of our financial system?
6. Describe the relationships between the common characteristics of all modern economic systems and the financial system.
7. List and explain the importance of each of the major functions performed by our financial system.

ADDITIONAL READING

Readings from other books and periodicals are suggested in footnotes or at the end of each chapter; that is, titles appearing in footnotes are not repeated at the end of each chapter. Because basic texts in the various fields of finance provide additional reading in many areas, these texts may pertain to more than one chapter of this book. However, in subsequent bibliographies, rather than repeating titles, reference will be made only to those chapters in which such texts are completely listed. For example, each of the following books contains chapters dealing with most of the subjects covered in this book, and students are encouraged to refer to them for supplementary reading. These titles are not repeated at the end of other chapters.

Dauten, Carl A., and Merle T. Welshans. *Principles of Finance.* Cincinnati: South-Western Publishing Co., 1958.
Prochnow, Herbert V. (ed). *American Financial Institutions.* Englewood Cliffs, N.J.: Prentice-Hall, Inc., 1951.
Robinson, Roland I. (ed.), Erwin W. Boehmler, Frank H. Gane, and Loring C. Farwell. *Financial Institutions* (3rd ed.). Homewood, Ill.: Richard D. Irwin, Inc., 1960.

The latter two texts contain lengthy bibliographies, and reference to them provides many leads to additional reading.

Adams, George P., Jr. Competitive Economic Systems. New York: Thomas Y. Crowell Co., 1955.

Bowen, Howard R. Toward Social Economy. New York: Rinehart & Co., Inc., 1948. Chaps. 1-6 present a concise treatment of an economic system in terms of basic economic institutions and institutional arrangements. Specific topics include the following: the economic system, economic relativity, social institutional development, and economic institutions.

Goldsmith, Raymond W. Financial Intermediaries in the United States Since 1900. (NBER Study.) Princeton, N.J.: Princeton University Press, 1958. Describes and explains the position of financial intermediaries in the American economy, and provides a partial foundation to a theory of financial institutions.

Gurley, John G., and Edward S. Shaw. Money in a Theory of Finance. Washington, D.C.: The Brookings Institution, 1960. A theoretical study of how debt, financial assets, financial institutions, and financial policies shape, and are in turn shaped by, general levels of prices and output; attempts to develop a theory of finance and a theory of financial institutions.

Halm, George N. Economic Systems. New York: Holt, Rinehart, & Winston, Inc., 1951.

Loucks, William N. Comparative Economic System. (5th ed.) New York: Harper & Bros., 1960.

Moulton, H. G. Financial Organization and the Economic System. New York: McGraw-Hill Book Co., Inc., 1938.

Oxenfeldt, Alfred R. Economic Systems in Action. New York: Holt, Rinehart, & Winston, Inc., 1952.

Sikes, Earl R. Contemporary Economic Systems. (Rev. ed.) New York: Holt, Rinehart, & Winston, Inc., 1951.

2: National economic accounting, I

NATIONAL economic accounting may be defined as the systematic arrangement of statistics that describes the operation of the nation's economy during a year (or a shorter period) in much the same way as business accounts describe the operations of an enterprise.* National economic accounting may also be described as a process of combining and consolidating accounts of individual economic units into sector and national accounts. The current forms of national economic accounts include the following: national income and product accounts, international balance of payments, flow-of-funds accounts, input-output tables, and national balance sheets. The first three provide data on both a quarterly and an annual basis; input-output tables and national balance sheets are constructed only occasionally. Students who have studied the principles of economics are probably most familiar with national income and product accounts and international balance-of-payments statements. For the purpose of this study of financial institutions, it is important at the outset to expand the knowledge of national economic accounting to include flow-of-funds accounts, because this system of accounts deals with the sources of funds received by various sectors, including financial institutions sectors, and the uses these sectors make of these funds.

National economic accounts, and in particular the flow-of-funds accounts, are considered early in the text because the outline for Parts 3-7 and almost all of the data obtained therein are derived from flow-of-funds accounts. As a prelude to a cursory review of national economic accounting, the two fundamental business accounting statements are reviewed briefly. At the end of Chapter 3, a series of hypothetical transactions are considered in terms of their effects on both national income and product accounts and flow-of-funds accounts.

*U. S. Subcommittee on Economic Statistics of the Joint Economic Committee, *The National Economic Accounts of the United States,* Hearings, Appendix: A Report of the National Accounts Review Committee of the National Bureau of Economic Research, 85th Cong., 1st Sess. (Washington, D.C.: Government Printing Office, 1957), p. 109. This report is also available as General Series 64, National Bureau of Economic Research, Inc.

ACCOUNTING STATEMENTS

Generally, accounting is the double-entry recording of quantitative data. The term "double entry" means that a transaction is recorded or reflected in a transactor's accounts by at least two entries. To illustrate, take the sale of goods by Firm A to Firm B; and the terms of sale are cash. In the seller's accounts, the transaction is recorded as a reduction in inventory and an increase in cash; in the buyer's accounts, the transaction is recorded as an increase in inventory and a reduction in cash. Very small economic units or transactors, such as some small business firms and many consumer units, use a simple single-entry method of accounting, but from the overall point of view, double-entry recording is by far the most important method of accounting. Complex transactions may involve many entries. The accounting method underlying national economic accounting is similar to that of most business firms, that is, the multitude of transactions are classified into accounts and actual transactions are reflected in a set of double-entry accounts. In cases in which individual economic units do not actually keep a set of accounts, social accountants attempt to estimate or build up accounts that would have been available if those economic units had maintained double-entry accounting records.

The purposes or functions of accounting include the provision of a continuous record of operations, a periodic indication of financial position, and a statistical framework for analysis. The two fundamental business accounting statements are the profit-and-loss statement (or income statement) and the balance sheet. In addition to these, many other statements may be constructed to assist management in the operation, planning, and control of operations. Many persons and agencies outside of a particular unit are also interested in the statements. Comparable statements may be constructed for non-business economic units.

On the basis of actual or estimated statements for individual economic units, social accountants are able to construct many types of combined or consolidated national economic statements, including income statements and balance sheets for major sectors of the economy and for the total economy. At the present time, national economic accounts are basic considerations in the formulation of both government economic policy and business policy.

Inasmuch as accounting statements are most easily understood in terms of a given business firm, the explanation in this section is couched primarily in terms of business accounting. A firm's balance sheet states the dollar value of the firm's tangible and intangible assets and an equal dollar value of the firm's liabilities and residual ownership interests, the latter of which is referred to as net worth. An example of a typical balance sheet is deferred to the following chapter, in which we shall consider business accounting statements in greater detail. It is theoretically possible to construct a balance sheet at the end of each transaction, day, month, or year. The majority of firms actually construct balance sheets at the end of each month or quarter. It is important to note that the balance sheet portrays conditions at a particular point of time. With the passage of time, the balance sheet undergoes change, and the changes reflect the economic unit's net sources of funds and net uses of funds during a given accounting period.

A firm's income statement or profit-and-loss statement summarizes the revenues received and the costs incurred during a given accounting period. The statement may cover as short a time as it takes to conduct one transaction to a period as long as a year. As noted above, the majority of firms summarize their activities in terms of financial statements on a monthly or quarterly basis. Computers have enabled some firms to maintain a nearly continuous flow of financial statement data. As the name of the account indicates, the income statement shows whether an economic unit has operated at a loss or a profit during the preceding accounting period. It should be noted that considerable accounting judgment enters into the construction of financial statements, and the results as reported in the statements reflect these judgments.

The major link between these two fundamental accounting statements is the change in net worth, and specifically the change in earned surplus. For example, if a firm makes a profit during a certain period, the net worth of the firm must be higher at the end of the period than at the beginning, assuming that an equal amount of funds is not drawn out or paid out as dividends during the period. If the firm incurs a loss, its net worth must be less than what it was at the beginning of the period. Since net worth appears only in the balance sheet, the change in net worth during an accounting period must be equal to the profit retained or the loss sustained during that period. In other words, since net worth is equal to total assets minus total liabilities (or net assets), an increase (or decrease) in net worth must not only equal the profit (or loss) made for that period, but must also equal the change in net assets. The change in net worth or net assets constitutes the vital link between a firm's income statement and its balance sheet.

NATIONAL ECONOMIC ACCOUNTS

In this section we shall review briefly the five forms of systems of national economic accounts, and shall note the relationships between the flow-of-funds and the other four systems of accounts. Obviously, the scope of this study precludes a rigorous review of the definitional and statistical problems that have been and continue to be involved in the structure and presentation of national economic accounts. Students are referred to basic sources for each of the accounts; these sources are referred to in footnotes to each of the headings in this section of the chapter.

National Income and Product Accounts*

National income and product accounts provide a conceptual accounting framework for recording current economic activity. Specifically, the accounts provide dollar measures of total national output of finished goods and services, of final uses of finished goods and services, of incomes flowing to various groups as a result of their contribution to the productive process, and of certain transactions with the rest of the world.

The modern economy is a highly complex structure of institutions and relationships, and one of the first steps in the construction of any system of national economic accounting is to break down and classify the millions of transactors and transactions. National income and product accounts incorporate a functional sector approach in order to focus attention on behavior and motivation of broad economic groups. The major groups or sectors are consumers, businesses, governmental units, and the rest of the world. The various sets of accounts summarize the current economic process in terms of the interrelated transactions of the four sectors. The accounts place measurements of national output against the background of transactions that underlie production, distribution, and consumption.

National income, and product accounts summarize current economic activity in terms of a flow process, in the sense that total output is measured as the summation of both the costs incurred in production and the final product flows. The accounts for 1959 are summarized in Table 2–1. The top half of the table shows the nature and amount of costs incurred in the production of finished goods and services. The costs are broken down in terms of factor costs, capital consumption allowances, and other charges. Factor costs consist of employee compensation, income of unincorporated enterprises, rental income of persons, and corporate profits. It should be noted that inventory valuation adjustments are made to the income of unincorporated enterprises and corporate profits. Since it is customary in business accounting to include inventory profit or loss in final income or profit, inventory valuation adjustments must be made so that only the value of the real change in inventories is counted as current output. Capital consumption allowances reflect the value of capital used up during the accounting period in the production of goods and services. Other charges include indirect business taxes and non-tax liabilities, business transfer pay-

---

* United States Department of Commerce, "National Income, 1954 Edition," A Supplement to the Survey of Current Business (Washington, D.C.: Government Printing Office, 1954); United States Department of Commerce, "U. S. Income and Output," A Supplement to the Survey of Current Business (Washington, D.C.: Government Printing Office, 1958); Studies in Income and Wealth, Vols. 1, 1937 to 23, 1959 (New York: National Bureau of Economic Research, Inc.).

ments, adjustments for subsidies and current surplus of government enterprises, and statistical discrepancy.

TABLE 2–1
NATIONAL INCOME AND PRODUCT ACCOUNTS, 1959
(BILLIONS OF DOLLARS)

Charges Against Gross National Product

Compensation of employees
Wages and salaries	$257.8	
Supplements	19.6	$277.4

Income of unincorporated enterprises and inventory valuation adjustments		46.3
Rental income of persons		12.0

Corporate profits and inventory valuation adjustments:
Corporate profits tax liability	$ 23.3	
Dividends	13.2	
Undistributed profits	11.3	
Inventory valuation adjustment	— 0.6	47.2

Net interest	15.6
Capital consumption allowances	40.2
Other charges against gross national product [1]	40.8

Total	$479.5

Purchases of Gross National Product by Sectors

Personal consumption expenditures
Durable goods	$ 43.0	
Nondurable goods	147.9	
Services	120.7	$311.6

Gross private domestic investment
New construction	40.2	
Producers' durable equipment	26.1	
Change in business inventories	4.8	71.1

Net foreign investment	—0.8

Government purchases of goods and services:
Federal:
National security	$45.8	
Other	8.1	
Less: Government sales	—0.4	$ 53.5

State and local	44.1	97.6

Total	$479.5

[1] Includes indirect business tax and nontax liabilities, business transfer payments, statistical discrepancy, and adjustment for subsidies and current surplus of government enterprises.

Source: *Survey of Current Business*, May 1960.

The bottom half of Table 2-1 shows the final flows in terms of purchases of the four major sectors. The flow of aggregate spending consists of personal consumption expenditure, gross private domestic investment, net foreign investment, and government purchases of goods and services. Net foreign investment reflects, in general, the net purchases of goods and services from abroad. The broad classifications under each of these aggregate flows do not require explanation.

The following quotation from a United States Department of Commerce publication summarizes the construction of this national economic accounting system in a very simple and concise manner.*

> A national income and product account is first established. This account provides measures of total national output, which is the sum of the outputs produced by the four sectors of the economy.
>
> Next, accounts are set up for the sectors. In addition to showing the portions of national output originating in each of them, they are designed to depict the economic structure in terms of the interrelated transactions of the four major economic groups.
>
> Specifically, four current accounts are shown, one each for business, consumers, government, and the rest of the world. These trace the transactions determining the current income of each of the sectors, and what part of that income is used up and what part is devoted to saving. The sector account for business is in essence a consolidated profit and loss account for the business system as a whole. For the other sectors, the accounts represent current receipt and expenditure accounts, in conformance with the nonprofit-making character of their transactions.
>
> Most of the current transactions that appear in the account of one sector are matched by corresponding entries in another. However, this is not so with respect to the items of saving or investment. With these, the corresponding entry is found in the capital or gross saving and investment account, which shows on a consolidated basis the saving and investment for the economy as a whole. This is the sixth account in the [system of national income and product accounts].

From this brief description, it might be noted that national income and product accounting utilize the double-entry method of accounting.

NATIONAL INCOME AND PRODUCT AGGREGATES. There are five fundamental national income and product aggregates: gross national product or expenditure, net national product or expenditure, national income, personal income, and disposable income. Each of these is defined below and the definitions are those of the Department of Commerce.†

> National income is the aggregate earnings of labor and property which arise from the current production of goods and services by the Nation's economy. Thus, it measures the total factor costs of the goods and services produced by the economy. The nation's economy in this

*"National Income, 1954 Edition," op. cit., p. 28.
† Ibid., p. 58.

context refers to the labor and property supplied by residents of the Nation. Earnings are recorded in the forms in which they accrue to residents of the Nation, inclusive of taxes on those earnings. As such, they consist of the compensation of employees, the profits of corporate and unincorporated enterprises, net interest, and the rental income flowing to persons.

Gross national product or expenditure is the market value of the output of goods and services produced by the Nation's economy, before deduction of depreciation charges and other allowances for business and institutional consumption of durable capital goods. Other business products used up by business in the accounting period are excluded. Gross national product comprises the purchases of goods and services by consumers and government, gross private domestic investment, and net foreign investment.

Net national product or expenditure is the market value of the net output of goods and services produced by the Nation's economy. All business products used up by business in the accounting period are excluded.

Personal income is the current income received by persons from all sources, inclusive of transfers from government and business, but exclusive of transfers among persons. Not only individuals (including owners of unincorporated enterprises), but non-profit institutions, private trust funds, and private pension, health, and welfare funds are classified as "persons." Personal income is measured on a before-tax basis, as the sum of wage and salary disbursements, other labor income, proprietors' and rental income, interest and dividends, and transfer payments, minus personal contributions for social insurance.

Disposable income is the income remaining to persons after deduction of personal tax and non-tax payments to general government.

Input-Output Accounts*

Input-output or interindustry accounts provide a quantitative structure within which to analyze interrelationships among a multitude of industries. The accounts show the production of each industry against its consumption from every other industry. Economic activity is classified or grouped into major categories of production, distribution, transportation, and consumption and set up on a matrix. Horizontal rows of figures show the distribution of a given industry's output among other industries; the vertical columns show each industry's sources of input. Obviously, the double-entry method of accounting underlies the construction of input-output tables or accounts. This system of national economic accounts portrays in

*Suggested readings on the topic of input-output accounts include the following: W. Duane Evans and Marvin Hoffenber, "The Interindustry Relations Study for 1947," *The Review of Economics and Statistics*, 34, No. 2, May 1952, pp. 97-142; W. W. Leontief, *The Structure of the American Economy, 1919-1929* (New York: Oxford University Press, 1951); W. W. Leontief, "Input-Output Economics," *Scientific American* 185, No. 4, October 1951, pp. 15-21; "Input-Output Analysis, An Appraisal," *Studies in Income and Wealth*, Vol. 18 (National Bureau of Economic Research, Inc.; Princeton University Press, 1955).

fine detail the nature of and degree to which industries are woven together by the flow of goods and services. The brief description of the input-output accounts indicates that these accounts focus attention upon the flow of goods and services. In contrast with the national income and product accounts, the input-output accounts reveal the flow of raw materials and semi-finished goods at each stage of production, as well as the flow of finished goods.

International Balance-of-Payments Accounts*

The international balance-of-payments accounts provide a statistical summary of all transactions between the residents, firms, and governmental units of the United States and individuals, firms, and governmental units of the rest of the world. A transaction is considered to be an international transaction and so recorded in the balance-of-payments accounts if it involves a transfer of something that has an economic value measurable in monetary terms from a "resident" of one country to the "resident" of another country.

Like other systems of accounting, transactions must be classified into a relatively small number of categories. In the design of international balance-of-payments accounts, an attempt has been made to achieve considerable uniformity with terminology and classification embodied in national income and product accounts. The major international categories are merchandise, services, investments, and gifts. The first two categories comprise the current accounts of a balance of payments and investment comprises the capital account of a balance of payments. Investment consists of financial claims, monetary gold, and immovable property. Transactions in the nature of gifts are designated as "unilateral transfers." To the extent that transactions do not give rise to an actual flow of payments and receipts, the title of this system of social accounting is somewhat misleading. However, most of the transactions do give rise to a flow of payments and receipts, and the use of the concept "balance of payments" is firmly established. Inasmuch as a simple form of an international balance-of-payments account is presented in the following chapter, no attempt is made at this time to develop the balance of payments in any detail.

A double-entry method of accounting is used in the construction of balance-of-payments accounts. For instance, assume that for a merchandise export of the United States the terms of sale are payment in cash in the form of a check drawn on a demand deposit account held in a commercial bank in the United States. The export is recorded in the export merchandise account and the offsetting entry is a reduction in foreign claims

*For an excellent discussion of the international balance-of-payments accounts, including their relation to business accounting statements and other social accounting statements, see Charles N. Henning, *International Finance* (New York: Harper & Brothers, 1958), pp. 15-41.

on the United States (investment accounts). It must be pointed out that a balance of payments is not the same thing as a balance sheet. As noted above, the balance of payments is a record of transactions through time, whereas a balance sheet is a summary of assets and liabilities and net worth at a particular moment in time. Actually, the balance of payments is a summary of changes in assets and liabilities during an accounting period as these accounts are affected or related to international transactions. The balance-of-payments accounts are vital in appraising a country's role in international trade and its foreign exchange position.

National Balance Sheet*

The meaning of "national balance sheet" is self-evident. It states for various sectors or groups and for the nation as a whole the dollar value of tangible and intangible assets and an equal dollar value of liabilities and net worth. Restricting such a statement to tangible assets, makes it a statement of wealth. To the extent that holdings of tangible and intangible assets and the extent and nature of liabilities influence economic decisions, national balance sheets are of considerable value in the formulation of both business and government policy. Unfortunately, national balance sheets are not integrated into the other systems of national economic accounting, and such balance sheets are not available on a regular periodic basis. Various forms of sector and subsector balance sheets are available, but the problem is one of consolidating inconsistent accounts and estimating accounts that are not available.

Flow-of-Funds Accounts †

The flow-of-funds accounts, which are sometimes referred to as money-flow statements, measure and trace the flow of funds received by various groups or sectors and the uses made of these funds. Accordingly, the flow-of-funds accounts deal with all transactions effected by a transfer of

*Raymond W. Goldsmith, "Measuring National Wealth in a System of Social Accounting," Studies in Income and Wealth, Vol. 12, Part 1 (National Bureau of Economic Research, Inc.; Princeton University Press, 1950); Raymond W. Goldsmith, A Study of Savings in the United States, Vol. 3 (Princeton University Press, 1956), pp. 3-119.
† The first fully developed flow-of-funds statements are set forth in Morris Copeland, A Study of Moneyflows in the United States (National Bureau of Economic Research, Inc., Princeton University Press, 1952). Additional references dealing with basic features of the accounts or providing actual data for the flow of funds include the following: Board of Governors of the Federal Reserve System, Flow of Funds in the United States, 1939-1953, 1955: "A Flow-of-Funds System of National Accounts, Annual Estimates, 1939-1954," Federal Reserve Bulletin, October 1955: "Summary Flow-of-Funds Accounts, 1950-1955," Federal Reserve Bulletin, April 1957: "A Quarterly Presentation of Flow of Funds, Saving and Investment," Federal Reserve Bulletin, August 1959; S. J. Sigel, "A Comparison of the Structures of Three Social Accounting Systems," Studies in Income and Wealth, Vol. 18 (National Bureau of Economic Research, Inc., Princeton University Press, 1955).

money or credit, or by a combination of the two. Specifically, this system of national economic accounting, in contrast with national income and product accounts, focuses attention on transactions pertaining to existing physical assets as well as currently produced goods and services. There are continuous interactions of financial and nonfinancial processes, and they are important elements in the determination of the level and composition of national output. The flow-of-funds accounts facilitate the recognition and analysis of patterns of financial and nonfinancial flows of funds through the economy and patterns of saving and investment. Like the construction of other systems of national economic accounts, the flow-of-funds accounts are based upon a firm statistical foundation and an appropriate statistical framework, providing a systematized and quantitative basis on which to study the strategic role of our financial system. The economy is divided into major sectors, and a system is devised to identify and classify all transactions effected by a transfer of money or credit, or by a combination of the two.

The flow-of-funds system of accounts incorporates a functional sector breakdown; that is, the sectors reflect groups of economic units that are similar with respect to function and institutional structure or both. In a sense, each sector may be viewed as an aggregate decision-making unit in the flow of funds. Inasmuch as the purpose of this system of national economic accounting is to record credit transactions as well as income payments and purchases of final goods, it is necessary to use many more sectors than are used in national income and product accounts. Accordingly, transactions or individual economic units are classified into five major sectors, three of which are further subdivided into additional sectors. The five major sectors are: financial sectors, nonfinancial business sectors, government sectors, the rest-of-the-world sector, and consumer and nonprofit sector. Given improvement in the data, it is likely that the latter sector will be further subdivided, especially in order to reflect the importance of personal trusts.

As noted in Chapter 1, the functions of finance include the creation and transfer of money, the transfer of savings into investment, the reduction of risk through insurance, and the facilitation of special types of financial transactions. The four financial institutions sectors in the flow-of-funds accounts fit these four functions very closely: commercial banking, savings institutions, insurance, and finance (not elsewhere classified). The commercial-banking sector is designed to reflect our monetary system, so it includes the Federal Reserve System and certain Treasury monetary functions as well as the commercial banks. The savings-institutions sector consists of mutual savings banks, saving and loan associations, and credit unions. The insurance sector includes self-administered pension and retirement plans as well as what is normally considered insurance. Financial institutions not otherwise classified comprise the finance not-elsewhere-classified sector. Institutions in this sector tend to be highly specialized and are involved primarily in facilitating the flow of credit and financial instruments rather than in supplying funds directly.

Nonfinancial business units are broken down into three separate nonfinancial business sectors, reflecting the fact that the financial requirements and the means of meeting them are not the same for all types of business. The flow-of-funds accounts draw a distinction between non-farm and farm businesses and between non-farm corporate and non-farm non-corporate businesses. The unique nature of farming and the development and operation of specialized financial institutions to serve the needs of farm businesses are two reasons for treating farm businesses as a separate sector. Similar reasons explain the division of non-farm businesses into the corporate and non-corporate business sectors.

Government is broken down into two sectors: the Federal sector and the state and local sector. There are various reasons for making such a distinction. First, the Federal Government's annual flows of receipts and expenditures are considerably larger than those of state and local governments. Second, the nature and magnitude of the Federal obligations are very different from state and local obligations. Third, a large amount of state and local borrowing is done to finance specific capital outlays, whereas much of the borrowing of the Federal Government simply reflects the fact that cash expenditures exceed cash receipts. Fourth, the Federal Government supplies funds to all other sectors, whereas the state and local governmental units do not.

The purpose of the rest-of-the-world sector is to reflect transactions that occur between the United States and the rest of the world. The sector is comprised of residents and governments of countries outside the United States and its territories and possessions. International organizations, including international financial institutions, are included. The sector account is on a consolidated basis and does not show transactions with and among other countries.

The consumer and nonprofit organization sector covers the following: (1) persons in their capacity as members of households, (2) personal trusts; and (3) non-profit organizations serving individuals. The business activities of individuals are excluded from this sector and are placed in the appropriate business sector. For example, the business activity of an individual who is a proprietor of an unincorporated non-farm business is included in the nonfinancial, non-corporate farm business sector, and the lessorship activity of an individual who is a landlord is included in the non-financial, non-corporate, non-farm business sector. With respect to personal trusts, it may be noted briefly that a trust is a legal agreement under which the ownership of property is transferred to another party for the benefit of a beneficiary or beneficiaries, and personal trusts are those created primarily for natural persons. Nonprofit organizations include foundations, private schools and hospitals, labor unions, and charitable, welfare, and religious organizations.

A set of interlocking, internally consistent sources and uses of funds statements for the major sectors constitute the core of the flow-of-funds accounts. To achieve internal consistency, all transactions of the various sectors are classified in a standard way throughout all sector accounts. The basic idea underlying this form of national economic accounting has been summarized as follows:*

> Each payment by one economic unit is also a receipt of another, and each debt of one also a financial asset of another; with both sides of each transaction or claim classified similarly, the transactions of one sector can be related to those of other sectors, and transaction accounts can be set up showing the amounts various sectors put into, and receive from, various broad markets. In the financial area, standardization of transaction classification provides a consistent structure of all financial flows. Estimates of outstanding amounts of financial assets and liabilities similarly provide an over-all picture of the structure of debt relationships.

Compared with the double-entry method of accounting used in national income and product accounts, the flow-of-funds accounts require a quadruple-entry method of accounting. For example, take a typical consumer transaction entailing the use of cash. Assume that a college student purchases a textbook from the college bookstore. Four bookkeeping entries would be made to reflect this transaction: (1) acquisition of the book by the student; (2) sale of the book by the store; (3) reduction in cash balances of the student; and (4) increase in cash balances of the store. In summary, two bookkeeping entries were made to reflect the transfer of the physical good, and two bookkeeping entries were made to reflect the transfer of cash between the student and the store. If the student had paid partly in cash and agreed to pay the balance in the future, eight entries would have been recorded in these accounts.

The term "flow of funds" is applied to transactions that are effected with money and credit or both, and all of these transactions are viewed in terms of "uses of funds" and "sources of funds." The textbook transaction may be used to illustrate this idea. From the student's point of view, purchase of the textbook was a "use of funds" and the reduction in his cash balances was a "source of funds." From the bookstore's point of view, sale of the book was a "source of funds," and the increase in the store's cash balance was a "use of funds." Statements of sources and uses of funds reflect current income of all types, current expenditures, capital expenditures, borrowing and lending, and the acquisition of various types of financial assets. Statements of sources and uses of funds are developed in detail in the following chapter.

*A *Quarterly Presentation of Flow of Funds*, op. cit., p. 830.

On the basis of flow-of-funds data, various sets of tables are published in the *Federal Reserve Bulletin*. The most basic set of tables consists of sector statements of sources and uses of funds. The other sets of tables represent primarily various rearrangements of the data. Tables are constructed showing a summary of principal financial flows: currency and demand deposits, fixed-value redeemable claims, savings through life insurance and pension funds, and credit and equity market instruments. Totals of savings and investment for each domestic sector and for the nation as a whole are also set forth in separate tables.

> Placing savings and investment totals within the framework of the flow-of-funds system of accounts provides perspective for these totals in terms of sector transactions and in terms of financial market developments that are important both as determinants and as consequences of the patterns of savings and investment. Similarly, the explicit recording of saving and investment totals in the accounts provides convenient summaries of current flows and of capital flows in terms of concepts that are often used as strategic elements in analyzing the levels and fluctuations of total demand, income, and employment, as well as growth in income and productive capacity.*

One of the most revealing tables summarizes the flow-of-funds accounts in terms of a matrix. Sector accounts are shown vertically and market or transaction accounts are shown horizontally. Horizontal rows of figures trace particular types of flows, vertical columns summarize the uses and sources of funds of each sector. Such tables are presented at the end of the following chapter.

The usefulness of this system of national economic accounts has been summarized by Chairman Martin of the Board of Governors of the Federal Reserve System as follows: †

> The flow-of-funds accounts contribute to an understanding of differential impact of monetary factors by presenting a broad historical record of credit flows to and from various major sectors in competing credit markets. The grouping of data for the various sectors and for the various financial markets of the economy and the regrouping of these data into sector and transaction categories that are analytically useful has made possible the systematic examination of the financing activities of each group in the perspective of what else is happening in the economy in general and in the credit markets in particular.
>
> The availability of the flow-of-funds accounts has improved our ability to analyze each type of credit flow to each major sector simultaneously in terms of (1) the total credit flow of that type, (2) the whole pattern of capital market flows, (3) the other sources of financing utilized by the sector, and (4) the sector's need for funds in relation both to its income and its expenditures. As a result, the flow-

Ibid., p. 829.

† U. S. Joint Economic Committee, "Employment, Growth, and Price Levels," Hearings, Part 6C, 86th Cong., 1st Sess. (Washington, D.C.: Government Printing Office, 1959), p. 1776.

of-funds accounts are a convenient vehicle for analyzing the mutual impact of the various financial and non-financial groups in the economy and of the mutual adjustment process among the various financial markets.

It would appear from the description of the flow-of-months accounts and from the above statement by Chairman Martin that the structure of flow-of-funds accounts provides an ideal framework within which to study the structure, operation, and functions of financial institutions. Such an approach allows full integration of all sectors and markets, and provides a common source of data. Furthermore, the accounts "are designed to provide a statistical framework appropriate to the analysis of problems involving relationships among financial and nonfinancial developments and to permit the tying together of sector and financial market analysis into an integrated analysis for the economy as a whole."*

Relationships Among National Economic Accounts

Inasmuch as the flow-of-funds accounts serve as the basic framework for this study of financial institutions, relationships among national economic accounts are examined in terms of relationships between the flow of accounts and the other national economic accounts. Almost all of the discussion in this section of the chapter is based on the findings of the National Accounts Review Committee of the National Bureau of Economic Research.†

The main points of dissimilarity between the flow-of-funds accounts and the national income and product accounts are: (1) a system of quadruple entry is used to construct flow-of-funds accounts as compared with the use of the double-entry system in national income and product accounts; (2) the flow-of-funds accounts incorporate a large number of private sectors as compared with the use of only two private sectors in national income and product accounts; (3) the flow-of-funds accounts provide sector and market data on the net purchases and sales of many types of financial assets that are excluded from national income and product accounts; (4) the flow-of-funds accounts do not show imputed income, while national income and product accounts do show some forms of imputed income; (5) the flow-of-funds accounts provide data on the holdings of claims and liabilities of each sector, whereas such data are not part of the national income and product accounts. Other differences between the two systems involve degree of netting, scope of consolidating, timing of some transactions, method of valuation, estimating procedures, and sources of data. Greater integration of the two accounts can be expected in the future. Both systems of national accounts are available on both a quarterly and an annual basis.

*Quarterly Presentation of Flow of Funds, op. cit., p. 829.
† Op. cit., pp. 236-238.

The flow-of-funds accounts are loosely related to the idea of a national balance sheet. As noted above, the flow-of-funds data include partial balance sheets for all sectors. The balance sheets are partial in the sense that tangible assets and net worth are excluded from the accounts. A true national balance sheet would contain tangible assets and net worth. Both of these systems of national economic accounts permit able analysts to compare flows with related stocks, and to evaluate the importance of net changes in holdings of assets and liabilities. The National Accounts Review Committee summarized the relationship between flow-of-funds and input-output accounting as follows:*

> Neither in theory nor in practice is there a close relationship between flow-of-funds statements and input-output tables. Indeed these two aspects of a comprehensive national accounting system are about as removed conceptually and statistically as is possible within that system. The flow-of-funds statement emphasizes financial flows and collects all its data on an enterprise basis. Input-output tables omit financial transactions altogether, concentrate on flows of goods and services among producers, and must be derived from very detailed data collected on a plant and preferably even on a process basis.

There is considerable similarity between flow-of-funds accounts and international balance-of-payments accounts. Both systems of accounts show the sources of funds received by individuals, firms, and governmental units, and the uses made of these funds. The flow-of-funds accounts indicate sources and use of funds for all domestic and international transactions, but the balance-of-payments accounts cover only international transactions. The export of merchandise and services to the rest of the world, and investment by the rest of the world in the United States constitute the "sources of funds," and the imports of merchandise and services from the rest of the world and foreign investment by residents, firms, and governmental units of the United States constitute "uses of funds."

QUESTIONS

1. Define national economic accounting.
2. What is a balance sheet? What is an income statement?
3. List five forms of national economic accounting.
4. Summarize the construction of national income and product accounts in terms of its six basic accounts.
5. List and define the five fundamental national income and product aggregates.
6. Summarize the construction of input-output accounts.

*Ibid., p. 238.

7. Summarize the construction of an international balance of payments.
8. Summarize the construction of flow-of-funds accounts.
9. Relate the system of flow-of-funds accounts to other system of national economic accounting.

ADDITIONAL READING

Your attention is called to the numerous readings cited in the footnotes. See the additional reading at the end of Chapter 3.

Goetz, B. E., and F. R. Klein. *Accounting in Action*. Boston: Houghton Mifflin Co., 1960. Recommended to those who require additional accounting background; emphasizes the managerial approach and the relation between accounting and social sciences.

3: National economic accounting, II

N this chapter, we shall review briefly financial statements of individual economic units in terms of their relationships with national economic accounts. In theory, national income and product accounts are based primarily on income statements, whereas flow-of-funds accounts are based on both income statements and balance sheets. The vital link between national income and products accounts and flow-of-funds accounts is very similar to the link between a firm's income statement and its balance sheet; it is the change in "net worth" or "net assets" of the nation's economy. The problem of combining and consolidating individual statements into sector and national statements is considered briefly in the closing section of the chapter. The major part of the discussion here is based on a hypothetical firm's accounting statements, because almost all students are or should be familiar in a general way with such statements. After discussion of non-financial business firms and consumers, attention is turned briefly to the other major sectors. Although the conceptual underpinnings with respect to these other sectors are similar to those of the business sector, there are some unique aspects that need to be stressed to explain fully the structure of national income and product accounts and flow-of-funds accounts.

A NONFINANCIAL BUSINESS FIRM'S ACCOUNTING STATEMENTS

National income and product accounts and a firm's income statement are similar in that each purports to show the income- and output-generating activity of the economic unit in question. National income and product accounts depict the national economy as an aggregate economic unit, whereas the firm's statements depict only a component of the nation's economy. To derive or construct a national income statement, it is necessary to consolidate the income statements of millions of individual economic units.

To illustrate the relationships between financial statements of individual economic units and national economic accounts, an income statement of a hypothetical nonfinancial business firm, hereafter referred to as the ABC Company, is shown below (data in thousands of dollars):

Net sales		$10,000
Less: Cost of goods sold		
Beginning inventory	$1,000	
Purchases	4,000	
Labor cost, or wages	2,000	
Depreciation	1,000	
	$8,000	
Minus: Ending inventory	2,500	
Cost of goods sold		5,500
Gross profit		$4,500
Selling and administrative expenses:		
Salaries	$1,000	
Supplies	1,000	2,000
Profit before income taxes		$2,500
Income taxes at 50%		1,250
Profit after income taxes		$1,250
Dividends		500
Retained profit or earnings		$ 750

This income statement embodies statistical data useful to both the firm's management and to students of national economic accounting. For the firm's management, the statement facilitates analysis of the firm's operating performance during the accounting period. Students of national economic accounting find in the data the firm's contribution to income and output generation during the accounting period.

The quantitative contribution of this firm can be measured either by the dollar amount of income generated by the factors of production employed by the firm or by the dollar value of output produced by the firm. The amount and composition of income generated by the ABC Company during the year are as follows (data are shown in thousands of dollars, and may be considered as income or nonfinancial flows):

Wage income (or labor cost)	$2,000
Salary income to selling and administrative personnel	1,000
Income to invested capital, but taxed away by income taxes	1,250
Income to invested capital, but paid out to owners as dividends	500
Income to invested capital, but retained in business	750
Total income generated	$5,500[1]

[1] It is mere coincidence that this figure is equal to the cost of goods sold. There is no inherent reason for their equality.

In terms of national economic accounting, the dollar value of output produced by the firm during the year is not the same as the firm's net sales, because the sales do not all represent production of that firm. Net sales include the value of what was produced by other firms and exclude the value of goods produced by the firm but not sold during that accounting period. In other words, raw materials and supplies are included in the final products but an increase in inventory is not shown. By subtracting the value of raw materials and supplies from net sales and by adding the change in inventory to net sales, the value of output produced by the firm during the year figures out to $6.5 billion.

It should be noted that the value of output produced by the firm is $1 million larger than the income generated by the firm. The difference between output produced and income generated arises from depreciation or capital consumption allowances. Assume for the moment that the firm did not make any capital expenditures during the year; that is, the firm did not spend funds for either replacement or additions to plant and equipment. The income statement shows that the firm charged to the cost of goods sold $1 million for depreciation. This amount of depreciation is an ingredient of the $6.5 million value of output, but it actually represents past productive activity that was brought forward to and made a part of the value of output produced in the current year. So far as the current year is concerned, the firm did not produce the $1 million ingredient; it only produced a net output of $5.5 million, no more and no less.* In summary, the firm's contribution to gross national product during the year is $6.5 million, and its national income contribution or net national product contribution is $5.5 million.†

On the basis of the data and comments made thus far, the following observations may be made. First, the income flow of $5.5 million generated by the firm does and must equal the net output flow of the firm. Second, out of the income generated by the firm, the firm saved $750,000, which was labeled in the income statement as income to invested capital, but retained in business. Hereafter this form of income is referred to as earnings retained. Three, the amount the earnings retained represents the increase in the firm's net worth, and this saving constitutes an internal source of funds.

To illustrate the effect of earnings retained, assume that all of the firm's transactions are on a cash basis and all of the transactions affect the income statement. On the basis of the firm's hypothetical income state-

---

*If all of the plant and equipment had been purchased at the beginning of the year, the $1 million depreciation is still not part of product of that firm. What if the firm, itself, produced all of its own plant and equipment? Students are encouraged to think these cases out for their own benefit.

† By inserting a figure for excise taxes in the income statement, net national product and national income would differ by that amount.

ment shown above, the firm's cash receipts and cash expenditures are listed below (data shown in thousands of dollars):

Cash Receipts		Cash Expenditures	
Net sales $10,000		Purchases of materials ....$ 4,000	
		Purchases of supplies 1,000	
		Payment of wages 2,000	
		Payment of salaries 1,000	
		Payment of income taxes 1,250	
		Payment of dividends 500	
Total $10,000		Total ....$ 9,750	
		Excess of cash receipts ....$ 250	

The difference between total amount of cash receipts and total amount of cash expenditures represents the increase in the firm's cash balance. In this case, the firm's cash balance increased by $250,000. Cash is a financial asset, and it can be stated that the firm made a net financial investment of $250,000 during the year.

The firm's investment in nonfinancial assets also changed. The investment in plant and equipment was down by $1,000,000 and investment in inventory was up by $1,500,000. The firm's net nonfinancial investment was $500,000. The firm's combined net financial and nonfinancial investment was $750,000. It should be recalled that the summation of earnings retained and depreciation was the same amount. It may be stated that earnings retained and depreciation were used to finance the firm's additional investment in cash and inventory.*

Additional observations are appropriate at this point. First, the increase in net assets was matched by an equal increase in net worth. Second, analysis of the income statement revealed the firm's saving. If the firm had incurred a loss, the statement would have revealed the firm's dissaving. Third, the net saving of the firm was equal to the summation of its net financial investment and nonfinancial investment. Fourth, depreciation represented a reduction in the stated value of the firm's plant and equipment and it was noted as a non-cash expense. Fifth, depreciation and earnings retained financed the net increase in cash and inventory. Sixth, the gross saving of the firm may be defined as the summation of net saving and capital consumption allowances.

To make the example more realistic, assume that the ABC Company

---

*It is generally acceptable to refer to depreciation as a source of funds, and this usage is adopted for the purpose of this study. However, it is important to realize that all internal financing is from revenue. In the illustration above, depreciation merely explains why only $750,000 of the firm's revenue must be regarded as assets provided by this year's earnings. Depreciation is merely recovery of a previous committment of cash in plant and equipment or other nonfinancial investment. The recovery is accomplished because revenues were sufficient, not because "depreciation" occurred or was recorded.

also enters into transactions that have no immediate effect on the income statement. Such transactions do not change either the saving and investment link between the income statement and balance sheet or the amount of the firm's saving and investment. Barring any change in net worth other than that resulting from the retention of earnings, changes in financial assets, nonfinancial assets, or liabilities do not alter the change in net worth as foretold by the income statement. Net worth can be affected directly by transactions involving change in the amount of owners' contributed capital. An increase in net worth brought about by payment of funds into the firm by old or new owners represents a form of owners' saving and investment. An increase in the firm's liabilities represents a form of financial saving and investment by creditors. To the firm, both types of saving represent sources of funds to finance an increase in financial and nonfinancial assets or both.

Some of the previous observations may now be restated in more complete form. The firm's net investment is equal to the difference between the increase in the firm's uses of funds and the increase in the firm's liabilities and contributed capital. The firm's net saving is equal to the difference between the increase in the firm's sources of funds and the increase in the firm's liabilities and contributed capital. The firm's net saving remains stated as the amount of profit retained by the firm.

The financial statements of the ABC Company are now re-examined in terms of the combined effects of all transactions. To facilitate the analysis, two exhibits are presented below. The first summarizes the changes in the balance sheet between the beginning and the end of the year (amounts are shown in thousands of dollars).

Financial Assets	Jan. 1	Change	Dec. 31	Liabilities	Jan. 1	Change	Dec. 31
Cash	700	−500	200	Bank loans	800	−200	600
A/C Rec.	900	+900	1,800	A/C Payable	400	−50	350
Notes Rec.	900	+600	1,500	Bonds Payable	500	+2,500	3,000
Total	2,500	+1,000	3,500	Total	1,700	+2,250	3,950
Nonfinancial Assets				Net Worth			
Inventory	1,000	+1,500	2,500	Capital	5,000	+500	5,500
				Earned			
Plant & Eq.	5,000	+1,000	6,000	Surplus	1,800	+750	2,550
Total	6,000	+2,500	8,500	Total	6,800	+1,250	8,050
				Total Liabilities and			
Total Assets:	8,500	+3,500	12,000	Net Worth	8,500	+3,500	12,000

It is customary to classify assets under the following headings: current, intermediate, fixed, and intangible; and it is customary to classify liabilities under similar headings: current, intermediate, and long-term. How-ever, for the purpose of this discussion, it is much more appropriate to classify assets into two broad categories, financial and nonfinancial, and to show lia-bilities as a group. The terminology relating to net worth is customary — contributed capital and earned surplus.

The other exhibit is a statement of uses and sources of funds (the amounts are shown in thousands of dollars).

Net Uses of Funds		Net Sources of Funds	
Net increase in financial assets, or financial investment	$1,000	Net increase in liabilities or creditors' saving	$ 2,250
Net increase in nonfinancial as-sets, or nonfinancial investment	2,500	Net increase in capital, or own-ers' saving	500
		Net increase in earned surplus or firm's net saving	750
Total	$3,500	Total	$3,500

Gross Uses of Funds		Gross Sources of Funds	
Current and nonfinancial, or transactions affecting income statement:		Current and nonfinancial, or transactions affecting income statement:	
Purchases of material for sales	$ 2,500	*Receipts from sales	$10,000
Supplies purchased	1,000		
Wages paid	2,000		
Salaries paid	1,000		
Income taxes paid	1,250		
Dividends paid	500		
Total outflow	8,250	Total remaining $1,750	
Purchase for inventory increase	1,500	Depreciation 1,000	
Cash increase (qua income statement)	250	Retained profit 750	
Total	$10,000	Total	$10,000
Capital and financial, or trans-actions not affecting income statement:		Capital and financial, or trans-actions not affecting income statement:	
Increase in accounts receiv-ables	$ 900	Reduction in cash	$ 750
Increase in notes receivables	600	Increase in bonds	2,500
Purchases of plant and equip-ment	2,000	Increase in contributed capital	500
Repayment of bank loans	200		
Reduction of accounts pay-able	50		
Total	$ 3,750	Total	$ 3,750
TOTAL	$13,750	TOTAL	$13,750

* It is assumed that there are no receipts from non-operating income.

The statement of uses and sources of funds of the ABC Company is broken down into four major sections: net uses of funds, gross uses of funds, net sources of funds, and gross sources of funds. Each of these sections is further broken down into two types of transactions, "current and nonfinancial" and "capital and financial." Transactions affecting the income statement are current and nonfinancial, and transactions not affecting the income statement are capital and financial. The reader is asked to make frequent reference to the balance sheet changes and the statement of uses of and sources of funds in the discussion that follows.

The existence of transactions that do not affect the income statement breaks down the consistency between a firm's income statement and its balance sheet. The ABC Company's transactions illustrate this situation. The income statement shows a reduction of $1 million dollars in plant and equipment; the balance sheet shows an increase of $1 million in plant and equipment. The statement of sources and uses of funds provides the key to understanding the underlying forces affecting these accounts. The company invested $2 million in plant and equipment; the $1 million depreciation represented disinvestment and contributed to the gross sources of funds; the $2 million acquisition of plant and equipment was part of the gross uses of funds; and the $1 million increase in plant and equipment was part of the net uses of funds.

Reconciliation must also be made with respect to the cash account. In earlier discussion, it was pointed out that the income statement indicated an increase of $250,000 in the cash balance. The balance sheets presented above show that the actual change in cash balance was a reduction of $500,000. The difference is explained in terms of the firm's capital and financial transactions, which amounted to $750,000.

The balance sheet at the end of the year shows the firm's earned surplus to be $2,550,000, and previous analysis has indicated that this year's operations contributed $750,000 to this total. The remainder represents the previous year's contributions from operations. The earned surplus may be viewed as the firm's accumulated saving from the time it started operations to the present.

Net financial investment by a firm is defined as the difference between the increase in financial assets and the increase in creditors' claims and owners' contributed capital. Net cumulative financial investment is defined as the summation of total liabilities and contributed capital minus total assets. Applying these concepts to the ABC Company, it may be noted that the firm's net financial investment during the year was a negative $1,750,000, and the firm's net cumulative financial investment at the end of the year was a negative $5,950,000. It is normal for business firms to show a negative financial investment. The firm's nonfinancial investment during the year was $2,500,000, and the firm's net cumulative nonfinancial investment at the end of the year was $8,500,000.

Net cumulative investment is the summation of net cumulative financial investment and net cumulative nonfinancial investment. In the case of the ABC Company, net cumulative investment is $2,550,000, which represents the summation of a minus $5,950,000 and a plus $8,500,000. It should be noted that $2,550,000 is also the amount of the firm's earned surplus at the end of the year.

It is possible for the level and composition of a firm's balance sheet at the end of a year to be identical to the level and composition of the firm's balance sheet at the beginning of the year. In this case, a statement of uses and sources of funds based on changes in the balance sheet would reveal very little. However, it does not follow that the firm did not engage in capital and financial transactions during the year. The firm might have borrowed funds to finance a seasonal increase in inventory and might have repaid the loan prior to the end of the year. Many other transactions might also have occurred during the year, but the circuit flow was started and completed within the year. Quarterly statements of uses and sources of funds might have revealed many of these transactions. Quarterly statements are vital in the analysis of seasonality. The shorter the accounting period, the smaller the proportion of cancellation between inflows and outflows.

One of the weaknesses of the flow-of-funds system of accounts is that gross flows of financial transactions are not shown. For example, during a year the gross purchases and gross sales of financial assets and the gross extensions and gross repayments of credit amount to billions of dollars, but the flow-of-funds accounts show only the net flows in these accounts. For the most part, the net flows are derived from the net changes in quarterly and annual balance sheets or both. The Report of the National Accounts Review Committee recommended that "transactions in different types of securities (excluding short-term Treasury and similar securities for which gross flows are of less significance) by the various sectors should in principle be presented on a gross basis, showing separately issues and retirements by issuers and purchases and sales by each of the other sectors. The same principle should apply to mortgages, separating new loans from repayments; to term loans by commercial banks, and to installment loans — in short to all assets and liabilities with an original maturity of more than approximately one year."* The flow-of-funds accounts do show gross flows for almost all current and nonfinancial transactions, and such presentation is one of the main basic attractions of the flow-of-funds accounts for the economic and financial analyst. It should be obvious from this brief discussion that statements of uses and sources of funds and flow-of-funds accounts do not show the actual total of gross money flows. Furthermore, the consolidation of individual economic units into sector accounts removes the intrasector flows, which also involve flow of funds. However, it should

*Op. cit., pp. 239-40.

be noted that by placing sectors on a consolidated basis, the data are more significant in terms of relations among sectors.*

The absence of gross flow data not only reduces the amount of information available to analysts but is likely to lead to uncertainties and errors in the calculation of net flows whenever there are realized capital gains and losses or revaluations, and this is the common situation not only for stocks but for long-term fixed-interest-bearing securities. In that situation specific adjustments to the net flow estimate calculated from balances at the beginning and end of the period must be made, using the profit and loss statements of the institutions involved in the transactions. Since these statements are rarely available in sufficient detail (to social accountants), rough estimates usually must be resorted to. Because of these difficulties, adjustments to the net change in holdings as shown by opening and closing balance sheets are made only for some sectors and assets in the Federal Reserve Board's flow-of-funds statements.

A CONSUMER'S ACCOUNTING STATEMENTS

To facilitate comparisons with the data presented above, the financial or accounting statements of a hypothetical consumer unit are tailored to fit the formats used in presenting the individual firm's accounting statements. The income statement of John Doe and Family is as follows:

"Net sales"		$10,000
(or income from selling his labor service and/or property service)		
Less cost of goods sold:		
Purchase (or consumption) of non-durable goods	$4,000	
Depreciation	500	4,500
"Gross Profit"		$ 5,500
Income tax (or tax on "net sales")		1,500
Other taxes		500
"Profit" after taxes or "earnings retained"		$ 3,500

Compared with the ABC Company's income statement, two important differences may be noted. First, John Doe's income tax is based on his "sales" rather than his "profit." His costs and expenses are not tax-deductible. In the case of ABC: its income tax was based on its profits rather than its sales. Second, inventory is not shown in the "cost of goods sold" section of John Doe's income statement. It may be assumed that either non-durable goods are consumed immediately upon purchase or the beginning inventory is practically the same as the ending inventory. Under either assumption there would be no change in inventory of non-durable goods. In practice neither assumption is true but there is no way to measure

*Ibid., p. 240.

change in consumers' inventories of non-durable goods. With respect to the inventory of durable consumer goods, it is assumed that they either last beyond the current accounting period or are fully accounted for by depreciation. John Doe's net addition to his stock of "plant and equipment" (homes and durable consumer goods) is a form of capital expenditure and does not appear in the income statement. However, it is possible to restate the "cost of goods sold" section so as to include inventory, and this statement is illustrated below:

"Cost of goods sold"	
Beginning inventory of durable goods	$ 9,000
Purchases of non-durable goods and services	4,000
Purchases of durable goods	2,000
	$15,000
Minus	
Ending inventory of durable goods	10,500
Equals	
Cost of goods sold	$ 4,500

The changes in John Doe's balance sheet between the beginning and the end of the year are as follows:

Financial Assets	Jan. 1	Change	Dec. 31	Liabilities	Jan. 1	Change	Dec. 31
Cash	$ 200	$ +100	$ 300	Consumer credit	$ 500	$ −150	$ 350
Fixed-value r.c.	500	+200	700	Mortgage credit	4,000	−500	3,500
Credit and equity mkt. instr.	500	+1,050	1,550				
Total	$1,220	$+1,350	$2,550	Total	$4,500	−650	$3,850
Nonfinancial Assets				Net Worth			
Durables	1,000	+ 500	1,500	Accumulated saving	5,700	+3,500	9,200
Home	8,000	+1,000	9,000				
Total	$ 9,000	$+1,500	$10,500	Total	$5,700	$+3,500	$9,200
Total Assets	$10,200	$+2,850	$13,050	Total liab. and N.W.	$10,200	$+2,850	$13,050

The consumer's accumulated saving represents net worth, and is equal to the summation of the consumer's net financial investment and nonfinancial investment. Two of the items included under financial assets were not included in the ABC Company's balance sheet; namely, fixed-value redeemable claims and credit and equity market instruments. The former includes time deposits, savings shares, and United States savings bonds; the latter includes Federal obligations, corporate and foreign bonds, corporate stock, state and local government obligations, one- to four-family mortgages, other mortgages, and security credit.

The principles underlying the construction of the statement of uses and sources of funds of the ABC Company are fully applicable to John Doe's financial statements. John Doe's statement of uses and sources of funds for the year is shown below:

Net Uses of Funds

Net increase in financial assets, or financial investment	$1,350
Net creditors' dissaving, or financial disinvestment	650
Net financial investment	$2,000
Net increase in nonfinancial assets, or nonfinancial investment	1,500
Net investment	$3,500

Net Sources of Funds

Net increase in net worth; or net saving	$3,500
Net saving	3,500

John Doe's net saving of $3,500 is equal to the summation of his $2,000 of net financial investment and his $1,500 of nonfinancial investment. In this case, net financial investment is derived by adding the $650 of debt reduction to the $1,350 increase in financial assets. If John Doe had increased his liabilities, the increase in the liabilities would have been deducted from the increase in financial assets. Nonfinancial investment simply represents the net increase in John Doe's nonfinancial assets.

GOVERNMENT SECTORS

Theoretically it is possible to construct balance sheets for the government sectors, but statistical problems have been too great, especially those pertaining to nonfinancial assets and net worth. Governments treat all expenditures as current expenditures. The absence of capital expenditures data precludes calculation of the government sectors' nonfinancial investments. Therefore, investment by government sectors by necessity is restricted to net financial investments, which by necessity must equal the government sectors' net saving.

With respect to the Federal Government sector, gold could be treated as either a commodity or a financial asset. Functionally, gold ¹ ·· a direct bearing upon the stock of money in our economic system and is used as a means of payment in international transactions. Therefore, for the purpose of constructing the most meaningful flow-of-funds accounts, the gold account of the Federal Government is considered part of the commercial banking and monetary authorities sector.

Since the major purpose of the accounting statements presented above was to illustrate principles underlying the construction of the flow-of-funds accounts, it is not necessary to present additional statements. It is enough to mention that the government sectors' budget surpluses represent net saving, and the sectors' budget deficits represent dissaving. The government sectors' gross inflow of funds are their receipts, and the sectors' gross outflow of funds are their disbursements.

COMMERCIAL BANKING AND MONETARY AUTHORITIES SECTOR

The commercial banking and monetary authorities sector consists of three basic elements: (1) commercial banks in the United States; (2) the Federal Reserve System; and (3) Treasury monetary funds. Commercial banks are profit-making institutions, and the treatment of their accounting statements in the construction of flow-of-funds statements does not differ substantially from the way nonfinancial business firms' accounting statements are treated. The treatment of Federal Reserve banks' accounting statements is also very similar to the treatment accorded nonfinancial firms' statements, even though the Federal Reserve System is not operated for profit. Treasury monetary funds consist of a selection of Treasury accounts, including the gold account, the silver account, an account constructed from various Treasury data to record currency liabilities of the Federal Government and the assets underlying these liabilities, and the Exchange Stabilization Fund. The sector statements are on a consolidated basis, meaning that certain claims among the elements comprising the sector cancel out. A few examples are cited to illustrate cancellations. Gold certificates held by Federal Reserve banks offset the outstanding gold certificates liabilities of the United States Treasury. Reserve deposit liabilities of Federal Reserve banks are offset by reserve deposits held by commercial banks. Deposits held by commercial banks in other commercial banks, which are called interbank deposits, also cancel out. As a result of these cancellations or offsets, the net amount of currency and demand deposit liabilities of the commercial banking sector is equal to the total currency and demand deposits in circulation. Subsector accounts for commercial banks and monetary authorities are also contained in flow-of-funds statements.

Compared with the flow-of-funds statements of nonfinancial business sectors, the commercial banking and monetary authorities sector's liabilities bear a disproportionate relationship to both net worth and the holdings of nonfinancial tangible assets. The same is also more or less true for the other sectors representing financial institutions.

Although the commercial banking and monetary authorities sector is similar to all other sectors in the sense that expansion in the sector's uses

51

of funds must be accompanied by an equal increase in the sector's sources of funds, this sector literally creates its own sources of funds. The sources of funds consist mainly of increases in demand deposits, currency, and time deposits. The legal reserve requirements against such liabilities sets an upper limit to the expansion in these liabilities. The sources of funds of this sector are unique in relation to the sources of funds of all other sectors in the sense that the sources of funds are mainly in the form of money.

Hypothetical loan transactions may be used to illustrate the significant differences between the commercial banking and monetary authorities sector and other sectors.* In the examples, the loan is $1,000 and sectors are viewed as aggregate operating units. The term "commercial banking sector" is used throughout in place of the longer title "commercial banking and monetary authorities sector." Assume in the first instance that the commercial banking sector makes a loan to the nonfinancial business sector. The sectors' accounting statements are affected as follows: the commercial banking sector's financial assets (loans) and the sector's liabilities (demand deposits) each increase by $1,000; the nonfinancial business sector's assets (cash balance in the form of demand deposit) and liabilities (bank loans evidenced by notes payable) each increase by $1,000. The effective supply of and the demand for financial assets increase by $2,000. Now assume that some other sector, say the savings institutions sector, makes the loan to the nonfinancial business sector. In this instance, the sectors' accounting statements are affected as follows: the savings institutions sector's financial assets remain unchanged, because the increase in loans is offset by a reduction in the sector's holdings of demand deposits; the nonfinancial business sector's statement is affected in the same way as before. In the first instance, the supply of and the demand for financial assets increased by $2,000, but in the second instance, the effective supply of and demand for financial assets increased by only $1,000.

The loan transactions may be restated in the form of a set of principles. An increase in liabilities constitutes an increase in the demand for funds, and an increase in non-cash financial assets and the stock of money constitutes an increase in the supply of funds. An increase in the commercial banking sector's non-cash financial assets constitutes an increase in the effective supply of funds to other sectors. An increase in the effective demand for funds by other sectors is equal to the increase in the sectors' liabilities and holdings of cash balances, and an increase in the stock of money. An increase in the commercial banking sector's non-cash financial assets leads to an increase in the supply of money to all other sectors, whereas an increase in other sectors' non-cash liabilities leads to a transfer of the existing stock of money.

---

*The loan transactions of all types of financial institutions are considered in detail in later chapters.

FINANCIAL INTERMEDIARIES SECTOR

The financial intermediaries sector is comprised of financial institutions not included in the commercial banking and monetary authorities sector. The major difference between the two sectors is that the financial intermediaries sector cannot add to the total stock of currency and demand deposits; that is, the sector cannot create money. However, the sector can and does create a multitude of non-cash financial assets, such as shares and time deposits.* For example, savings and loan associations and credit unions issue additional shares (non-cash financial assets) to the public in exchange for money. Very little expense is incurred in transactions of this type, and nearly all of the money so received can be loaned out to others almost immediately. It is not surprising that financial institutions have become known as financial intermediaries.

The potential amount of funds supplied by the commercial banking sector depends upon that sector's cash and legal reserve position, whereas the potential amount of funds supplied by the financial intermediaries sector depends only upon its cash position. Of course, loan demand is a sufficient condition in both instances. The commercial banking sector is said to be "loaned up" when its legal and cash reserve positions do not warrant additional loans and investments. When this condition exists, the sector must first acquire additional legal reserve before it can increase its loans and investments and thereby increase its deposit and currency liabilities. When the financial intermediaries sector is "loaned up," it has merely to build up its cash position before it can increase its loans and investments. Monetary authorities can obstruct an increase in commercial banks' legal reserves, but they cannot, under existing regulations, obstruct shifts of funds among financial institutions. Financial returns to holders of liabilities issued by the financial intermediaries sector can serve as an inducement to promote such shifts, especially if commercial banks are not permitted to pay competitive rates to their creditors (holders of time deposits in commercial banks). The difference between the commercial banking sector and the financial intermediaries sector in relation to the effectiveness of monetary measures is examined in greater detail in the closing chapter of this book.

The financial intermediaries sector, with the cooperation of economic units in other sectors, particularly consumer savers, are able to increase the efficiency of a given stock of money by encouraging economic units to shift out of liabilities issued by the commercial banking sector and into the liabilities issued by the financial intermediaries sector. Much of the increase in the velocity of circulation of money in the postwar period has been

---

*See John G. Gurley, "Liquidity and Financial Institutions in the Postwar Period," Study Paper No. 14, Prepared in connection with the study of Employment, Growth, and Price Levels, 86th Congress, 1st Sess. (Washington, D.C., Government Printing Office, 1960).

accomplished through such shifts. This aspect of the financial intermediaries sector may be referred to as its "monetary effect."

The same effects occur when economic units exchange existing cash balances for newly issued credit and equity market instruments, such as securities and mortgages, but many holders of liabilities issued by the financial intermediaries sector may not want to make direct exchanges for market instruments because of the risks associated with holding marketable financial assets. To the extent that the condition exists, the financial intermediaries sector provides a "market place" and related financial facilities that bring together the suppliers and users of funds. This aspect of the financial intermediaries sector may be referred to as its "marketing effect."

From the point of view of an individual economic unit, the liabilities of the financial intermediaries sector have many of the same characteristics as demand deposits. They are fixed in price and redeemable into currency on demand. This raises a very fundamental question: Should fixed-value redeemable claims of the financial intermediaries sector be considered part of the stock of money? In Chapter 1 the term "money" was defined as that which is currently accepted as a means of payment. In terms of this definition, fixed-value redeemable claims would not qualify as money because such claims are not generally accepted as a means of payment. However, for the purpose of analysis, it would be possible to formulate a definition of money that would include such claims. For example, any asset that satisfied a certain degree of liquidity could be considered as money, or at least considered as "idle money." Many of the fixed-value redeemable claims are regarded by their holders as part of their "funds" available for expenditure. Most of the intermediaries' liabilities offer the same degree of "moneyness" to savers, as do inactive and idle demand deposits at commercial banks. In the absence of financial intermediaries and time deposits at commercial banks, there would be a much larger volume of inactive demand deposits. If inactive demand deposits of this nature are considered money, why should not their close substitutes also be considered money? If they were, the total loans and investments made by the intermediaries minus cash reserves (their demand deposits at commercial banks) would be considered the effective supply of funds to the rest of the economy, and the intermediaries' liabilities would be considered part of the money supply, instead of being considered as intermediaries' demand for funds.

In summary, an increase in the financial intermediaries sector's sources and uses of funds is directly related to the decisions of economic units that are part of other sectors. The sector is loaned up immediately at the time economic units in other sectors cease to acquire the sector's liabilities. An increase in the commercial banking sector's sources of funds is directly tied in with the sector's loans and investments. Assuming unfilled demand for funds, the sector has the ability to add to the supply of funds if its legal reserves exceed minimum legal required reserves. As noted above, these two sectors are compared in relation to monetary measures in the closing chapter of the text.

REST-OF-THE-WORLD SECTOR

Transactions of the rest of the world with the domestic sectors of our economy are recorded in both national income and product accounts and the flow-of-funds accounts. In fact, the format of the international balance-of-payments account is often used in explaining the format of the flow-of-funds system of accounts. For example, "the flow-of-funds accounts can be visualized as a set of interlocking balance-of-payments statements, each of which, in major respects, is similar in format to balance-of-payments statements that have been developed to record the flow of international payments."* This similarity has prompted an attempt to apply balance-of-payments methodology to the formulation of a set of integrated accounts.†

To illustrate the basic flow-of-funds concepts as applied to the rest-of-the-world sector, a hypothetical balance-of-payments statement or a uses and sources of funds statement is presented below (the statement covers a one-year period, and amounts are shown in billions of dollars):

Transactions	Uses of Funds	Sources of Funds
Nonfinancial and current:		
Purchases and sales of goods and services ...	$23	$21
Income payments	2	1
Private remittances	1	2
	$26	$24
Financial and capital (acquisition of financial assets):		
Credit and equity market instruments	5	3
Fixed-value redeemable claims	2	2
Currency and demand deposits	1	3
Gold import and export	2[1]	1[1]
	$10	$12
Total	$36	$36

[1] The net gold movement is the difference between the gold imports and the gold exports. In this example, there is a net gold import of $1.

*Board of Governors of the Federal Reserve System, *Flow of Funds in the United States, 1939-1953*, 1955, p. 2.

† This subject is beyond the scope of this chapter. For information on such a project see the following: Poul Høst-Madsen, "The Integration of Sector Finance and National Income Accounts," *Staff Papers*, International Monetary Fund, Vol. VII, No. 3, April 1960, pp. 327-348; *Report of the National Accounts Review Committee*, *op. cit.*, pp. 139-158.

The statement shows the sector's gross uses and sources of funds in relation to transactions involving the domestic economy. Transactions among economic units making up the rest-of-the-world sector are not recorded. Saving and investment are restricted to financial saving and financial investment.

The nonfinancial flows reveal a "loss" or "deficit" of $2 billion. This dissaving of the sector is analogous to the dissaving of nonfinancial firms, and must be matched by an equal amount of disinvestment, which must occur in the financial and capital flows. In the example, the sector's financial assets increased $1 billion, and the sector's liabilities increased $3 billion. The sector's net financial disinvestment was $2 billion. National investment in the rest-of-the-world sector increased $2 billion.

SAVING AND INVESTMENT

This section will establish the relationship between the flow-of-funds and national income accounts with respect to saving and investment. The specific definitions of saving and investment differ between the accounts. For example, the purchase of consumer durables is treated as investment in the flow-of-funds accounts, but in the national income accounts, it is treated as consumption. For this and other reasons the amount of investment recorded in the flow-of-funds accounts is larger than that recorded in national income accounts. In the flow-of-funds accounts, the saving of a sector is always equal to the investment of the sector, and the investment may take the form of either nonfinancial investment or net financial investment, or both. A sector may also dissave and disinvest. Furthermore, a sector may be disinvesting in financial assets while it is at the same time investing in nonfinancial assets. However, the sector's net investment or disinvestment must equal its net saving or net dissaving. In the national income accounts, investment is broken down into two major components: private domestic investment in the form of tangible assets, and net foreign investment in the form of export surplus. Net financial investment is not incorporated in national income accounting.

In the flow-of-funds accounts, the net financial investment of any sector is equal to the increase in the sector's financial assets minus the summation of the increase in the sector's liabilities and capital. Since all financial assets are either debts* or capital of other sectors, the following relationships or identities can be set forth as follows:

A. Total net financial investment of all sectors
= Total increase in financial assets — (total increase in liabilities + total increase in capital)

*Cash, which is defined to include Treasury currency, Federal Reserve notes, and demand deposits, represents debt of the United States Treasury, Federal Reserve banks, and commercial banks.

Since the total increase in financial assets must be equal to the summation of the total increase in liabilities and total increase in capital, relationship (A) can be restated:

B. Total net financial investment of all
   sdectors   = 0

C. Total net investment of all sectors   = Total net saving of all sectors

   Since the total net saving of all sectors must be equal to the summation of total net financial investment of all sectors plus the total net nonfinancial investment of all sectors, and since total net financial investment of all sectors is zero, the relationship (C) can be restated:

D. Total net nonfinancial investment
   of all sectors   = Total net saving of all sectors

E. Total net saving of the domestic   Total net saving of all sectors — total
   sectors (net national saving)   = net saving of the rest-of-the-world sector
                                     or
                               Total net savings of all sectors + total
                               net dissaving of the rest-of-the-world
                               sector

Since the total net saving of the rest-of-the-world is equal to the United States import surplus, and the net dissaving of the rest-of-the-world sector is equal to the export surplus, relationship (E) can be restated:

F. Net national saving   = Total net saving of all sectors — the
                               United States import surplus
                               or
                               Total net saving of all sectors + the
                               United States export surplus

G. Net national investment   = Net private domestic investment + net
                               foreign investment

Since net foreign investment is equivalent to the United States export surplus, relationships (F) and (G) can be set equal to each other.

H. Net private domestic investment = Total net saving of all sectors

I. Net foreign investment   = United States export surplus

J. National income   = Consumption + Government purchases
                               of goods and services + net private
                               domestic investment + net foreign in-
                               vestment (or — net foreign disinvest-
                               ment)

K. Net national saving   = National income — (consumption +
                               Government purchases of goods and serv-
                               ices)

L. Net national saving   = Net private domestic investment + net
                               foreign investment

Note that (G) and (L) are identical.

Students are asked to figure out for themselves the following:

M. Net national financial investment = Rest-of-the-world financial disinvestment

N. Net national investment   = Net national nonfinancial investment +
                               Net national financial investment

O. Net national investment   = Net private domestic investment + ex-
                               port surplus (or net foreign investment)

P. Net national investment   = Net national saving [see (G)]

EXERCISE

Statistical treatment of a series of typical transactions that affect the flow-of-funds and national income accounts

This exercise illustrates the theories and relationships that were introduced in the body of the chapter. Various nonfinancial and financial transactions are recorded in the appropriate sector accounts. Upon conclusion of all transactions, the net totals are summarized in a master flow-of-funds table and are also restated under the following headings:

> Consumption
> Gross private domestic investment
> Government purchases of goods and services
> Net foreign investment (investment in the United States by the rest-of-the-world sector)
> Gross national product

> Capital consumption allowances
> National income, distributed as follows:
> > Wages and salaries after income taxes
> > Nonfinancial business profit retained
> > Financial business profit retained
> > Income to governments

> Current expenditure
> > Consumer
> > Business
> > Government

> Net national saving, distributed as follows:
> > Consumer saving
> > Business saving
> > Government saving

> Net financial investment of all sectors
> Net nonfinancial investment of domestic sectors
> Net acquisition of financial assets of all sectors
> Net increase in liabilities and capital of all sectors
> Export surplus (same as net foreign investment or dissaving of the rest-of-the-world sector)
> Net national investment

> Increase in the money supply (same as increase in liabilities of banking sector)

Assume the following:

1. All transactions are handled through demand deposits.
2. All costs and incomes (current transactions) are handled through earned surplus accounts. This method avoids the necessity for setting up income statements for each of the sectors.
3. The final totals reflect only the effect of the assumed transactions.
4. The rest-of-the-world sector holds demand deposits at United States domestic banks.

NATIONAL ECONOMIC ACCOUNTING, II

5. The commercial banking sector is broken down into its three major components or subsectors: commercial banks, Federal Reserve Banks, and United States Treasury gold account.
6. All the transactions take place within a given accounting period.
7. All figures are in billions of dollars.

The following 24 transactions are recorded in the appropriate sectors. Each entry is identified by its assigned number, and its effect is indicated by either a plus or a minus.

1. Nonfinancial business firms pay $24 in wages and salaries for production.
2. Nonfinancial business firms purchase $5 worth of machinery; the "cost of goods sold" of this machinery is $4.
3. Nonfinancial business firms borrow $10 from commercial banks.
4. Consumers pay $2 in income taxes.
5. Consumers purchase $7 worth of nondurable consumer goods from nonfin. business firms; the "cost of goods sold" of these goods is $6.
6. Builders (nonfinancial business firms) construct and sell $5 worth of buildings to nonfinancial business firms. In construction process, builders purchase and use $1 worth of material, pay out $3 in wages and salaries. The firms selling the material realize neither profit nor loss on the sale of material.
7. Nonfinancial business firms pay $2 in interest to commercial banks.
8. Commercial banks pay $1 in salaries.
9. Consumers borrow $5 from commercial banks; consumers borrow $4 from financial intermediaries.
10. Nonfinancial business firms pay $2 in income taxes.
11. Federal Reserve Banks purchase $5 of Federal obligations from commercial banks.
12. Consumers purchase $8 worth of durable goods from nonfinancial business firms; the "cost of goods sold" of these goods is $6.
13. The Federal government purchases $2 worth of goods from nonfinancial business firms; the "cost of goods sold" of these goods is $1.
14. Local governments pay $1 in salaries.
15. Nonfinancial business firms purchase $2 worth of coffee from Brazil.
16. Japan purchases $3 worth of goods from nonfinancial business firms; the "cost of goods sold" of these goods is $2.
17. Japan exports $1 worth of gold to the United States.
18. Germany purchases $2 worth of Federal obligations from commercial banks.
19. Builders construct and sell $5 worth of family residences to consumers, who increase their mortgage debt by $4, all of which is payable to intermediaries. In construction, builders purchase and use $1 worth of material and pay out $3 in wages and salaries. The firms selling the material realize neither profit nor loss on the sale of the material.
20. Nonfinancial business firms charge $1 depreciation on their plant and equipment.

21. Consumers charge $1 depreciation on their durable goods.
22. Nonfinancial business firms issue $5 worth of stock, consumers purchase all of the new issues.
23. Consumers invest $2 in savings and loan associations' shares.
24. Steel-using non-financial business firms purchase on credit $3 worth of steel from the steel-making nonfinancial business firms; the "cost of goods sold" of the steel is $2.

SECTOR ACCOUNTS

Consumer Sector

Assets

Demand deposits
(1)	+24	(4)	−2
(5)	−7	(6)	+3
(8)	+1	(12)	−8
(9)	+4,+5	(19)	−1,+3,−4,+4
(14)	+1	(23)	−2
(22)	−5		+16

Corporate stocks (22) +5 | +5

S & L Assns. shares (23) +2 | +2

Consumer durable goods (12) +8 ; (21) −1 | +7

Family residences (19) +5 | +5

Liabilities:

Loans payable to commercial banks (9) +5 | +5

Loans payable to other financial institutions (9) +4 | +4

Mortgage loans (19) +4 | +4

Net worth
(1)	+24	(4)	−2
(5)	−7	(6)	+3
(8)	+1	(14)	+1
(19)	+3	(21)	−1
			+22

Nonfinancial Business Sector

Assets

Demand deposits
(1)	−24	(3)	+10
(5)	+7	(6)	−2
(7)	+2	(10)	+2
(12)	+8	(13)	+3
(15)	+2	(16)	+5
(19)	+5,−3	(22)	+5
	+4		+3

Trade credit (24) +3 | +3

Inventory
(1)	+24	(2)	−4
(5)	−6	(6)	−1
(12)	+6	(13)	−2
(15)	+2	(16)	−2
(19)	−1	(24)	−2,+3
			+6

Plant and equipment (2) +5 ; (20) −1 | (6) +5 | +9

Liabilities:

Bank Loans (3) +10 | +10

Trade credit (24) +3 | +3

Net Worth:

Contributed capital (22) +5 | +5

Earned surplus
(2)	+1	(5)	+1
(6)	+1	(7)	−2
(10)	+2	(12)	+1
(13)	+1	(16)	+1
(19)	+1	(20)	−1
(24)	+1		+4

State, Local, and Federal Government Sector

Demand deposits					Surplus or deficit				
(4)	+ 2	(10)	+ 2		(4)	+ 2	(10)	+ 2	
(13)	− 2	(14)	− 1		(13)	− 2	(14)	− 1	
				+ 1					+ 1

Commercial Banking Sector
(excludes Federal Reserve System and Treasury gold account)

Assets

Reserve deposits	(11)	+ 5	(17)	+ 1		+ 6
Loans:						
To business	(3)	+10			+10	
To consumer	(9)	+ 5			+ 5	
Investments:						
Federal obligations	(11)	− 5	(18)	− 2		− 7

Liabilities

Liabilities:					
Demand deposits	(3)	+10	(7)	− 2	
	(8)	+ 1	(9)	+ 5	
	(15)	− 2, +2			
	(16)	+ 3, −3			
	(17)	+ 1	(18)	− 2	
					+13
Net worth:					
Earned surplus	(7)	+ 2	(8)	− 1	
					+ 1

Federal Reserve Banking Sector

Gold certificates	(17)	+ 1			Reserve deposits (member bank deposits)	(11)	+ 5	(17)	+ 1		+ 6
Federal obligations	(11)	+ 5									
				+ 1							
				+ 5							

United States Treasury Gold Account

Gold	(17)	+ 1		+ 1	Gold certificates	(17)	+ 1		+ 1

Other Financial Institutions Sector

				Liabilities and net worth:		
Demand deposits	(9) (23)	− 4 + 2	(19) − 4	S & L shares	(23) + 2	+ 2
Loans to consumers	(9)	+ 4	− 6			
Mortgage Loans	(19)	+ 4	+ 4 + 4			

Rest-of-the-World Sector

				Surplus or deficit		
Gold	(17)	− 1	− 1		(15) (16)	+ 2 − 3
Demand deposits	(15) (17)	+ 2 + 1	(16) (18) − 3 − 2			− 1
Federal obligations	(18)	+ 2	− 2 + 2			

SUMMARY OF FLOW-OF-FUNDS ACCOUNTS FOR THE ASSUMED PERIOD [1]
(BILLIONS OF DOLLARS)

Transaction Category	Consumer U	Consumer S	Nonfinancial business U	Nonfinancial business S	Government U	Government S	Commercial banking[2] U	Commercial banking[2] S	Other U	Other S	Rest of the world[3] U	Rest of the world[3] S	All sectors U	All sectors S	National saving and investment
Gross saving		23		5		1		1				-1		29	30
Capital consumption		1		1										2	2
Net saving		22		4		1		1				-1		27	28
Gross investment	23		5		1		1				-1		29		30
Private capital expenditures															
Consumer durable goods	8												8		8
Nonfarm residential construction	5														5
Plant and equip.			10										10		10
Change in inven.			6										6		6
Net financial investment	10		-11		1	1	1				-1		0	1	1
Net acquisition of financial assets	23		4				14		2				43		44
Net increase in liabilities		13		15				13		2	-1			43	43
Gold and treasury currency							1				-1		0		+1
Currency and demand deposits	16		4				13	13	13	-6	-2		13	13	+2
Fixed-value redeemable claims	2									2			2	2	0
Credit and equity market instruments	5	13		15			13		8		2		28	28	-2

[1] For purposes of illustration, the summary of flow-of-accounts of the Board of Governors of the Federal Reserve System has been simplified in many ways. However, the basic format is the same.

[2] Savings and investment of all sectors is equal to private domestic savings and investment.

[3] Consolidated for Federal Reserve System, United States Treasury gold account and commercial banks.

**ESSENTIAL RESULTS DUE TO
NONFINANCIAL AND FINANCIAL TRANSACTIONS
(BILLIONS OF DOLLARS)**

Charges against G.N.P.	Dept. of Comm.	Flow of Funds
Wages and Salaries	$30	29 [1]
Income of financial firms	4	4
Income of nonfinancial firms	1	1
Tax receipts of government	4	4
Capital consumption allowances	1	2 [1]
Total	$40	$40

Purchases of G.N.P. by sectors	Dept. of Comm.	Flow of Funds
Personal consumption expenditures	$15	$ 7 [2]
Gross private domestic investment:		
Residential construction	5	5
Consumer durables		8
Producers' plant and equipment	10	10
Change in business inventories	6	6
Net foreign investment	1	1
Government purchases of goods and services	3	3
Total	$40	$40

[1] Reflects the capital consumption allowance on consumer durable goods.
[2] Durable consumer goods considered a form of consumer tangible investment.

Net saving of domestic Sectors:	Dept. of Comm.	Flow of Funds
Net consumer saving	$15	$22
Net business saving	5	5
Net government saving	1	1
	$21	$28

Flow-of-funds aggregates:

Net acquisition of financial assets of all sectors ($43) = Net increase in liabilities of all sectors ($43)

Net financial investment of all sectors = 0

Net saving of domestic sectors ($28) = Net investment of domestic sectors ($28)

Export surplus ($1) = Net foreign investment ($1) = Dissaving of rest-of-the-world sector ($1) = Net financial investment of U. S. ($1)

Increase in money supply ($13) = Increase in liabilities of banking sector ($13).

QUESTIONS

1. In what way is a firm's income statement related to its balance sheet? In what way are national income accounts related to flow-of-funds accounts?

2. Differentiate between nonfinancial and financial flows.

3. In what sense is depreciation a source of funds?

4. What major categories are included in net uses and net sources of funds?

5. Compared with nonfinancial firms, list and explain briefly two unique characteristics of the commercial banking sector.

6. Explain some of the more important differences between commercial banking and noncommercial banking financial institutions.

7. What is meant by the "monetary effect" of financial intermediaries? What is meant by the "marketing effect" of financial intermediaries?

8. Set forth and explain some of the basic relationships or identities relating to national income and flow-of-funds accounts.

9. Explain how the financial and nonfinancial transactions of the rest-of-the-world sector influence or affect net national saving and investment.

10. Describe briefly the structure of the "summary of flow-of-funds accounts."

11. Work out the problems in the Exercise to Chapter 4, and check your results with the sector accounts and the summary of flow-of-funds accounts.

12. Is the net result of the transactions shown in the Exercise inflationary or deflationary? Explain.

ADDITIONAL READING

Your attention is called to the numerous readings cited in the footnotes to Chapters 2 and 3.

Biggs, R. M. *National Income Analysis and Forecasting.* New York: W. W. Norton & Co., Inc., 1956.

Dahlberg, Arthur O. *National Income Visualized: A Graphic Portrayal of How Economic Activity Is Measured.* New York: Columbia University Press, 1956.

Fei, John C. H. "The Study of the Credit System by the Method of Linear Graph," *The Review of Economics and Statistics,* Vol. XLII, No. 4, November 1960, pp. 417-428. The author sets up a method that may be used to identify and classify all transactions from credit structure models.

Ruggles, Richard, and Nancy D. Ruggles. *National Income Accounts and Income Analysis.* (2nd ed.) New York: McGraw-Hill Book Co., Inc., 1956. Part I deals with the origin, collection, and adjustment of national income and product data; accounts and aggregates are built up in terms of basic accounting statements; approach is very similar to that used in Chap. 3; related systems of national economic accounting treated in authors' Chap. 9. Part II traces the process of economic change in terms of national income and product accounts and aggregates.

Siegel, Barry N. *Aggregate Economics and Public Policy*. Homewood, Ill.: Richard D. Irwin, Inc., 1960.

Studenski, P. *The Income of Nations — Theory, Measurement, and Analysis*. New York: New York University Press, 1958.

part 2: Currency and demand deposits

THE importance of an adequate stock of money was established in Chapter 1. Some of the relationships between financial flows and non-financial flows were noted in Chapters 2 and 3. The next three chapters set forth the basic framework within which changes occur in the level and composition of the stock of money. Accordingly, three major topics are considered: the United States monetary standard, the issue and retirement of coins and paper currency, and the expansion and contraction of demand deposits.

4: The monetary standard

HE monetary standard constitutes the basic framework within which monetary financial institutions operate. The purposes or functions of a monetary standard are to select a monetary unit, to define and maintain its value in terms of a standard, to equalize the value of all types of money in terms of each other, and to establish controls over the total volume of money. In this chapter we examine these four functions of a monetary standard in terms of our own experience in the United States.

FUNCTIONS OF A MONETARY STANDARD

Selection of the Dollar as the Monetary Unit

One of the purposes or functions of a monetary standard is the selection of a monetary unit. Historically, the American colonies under British rule were not allowed a national coinage. Rather the people in the colonies used whatever coins happened to reach them in the course of trade. This led to confusion because the trade relationships between the colonies and the rest of the world brought coins from many different countries into domestic circulation. Among the many different coins were the Spanish dollar and its subdivisions; British pounds, shillings, and pence; the French guinea and pistole; and the Portuguese moidore and johannes, to mention a few.* These coins, oddly enough, circulated freely until as late as 1857, at which time Congress repealed the statutes permitting the circulation and legal tender status of foreign coins.

The free circulation of coins of many countries provides evidence of a protracted period of specie shortage. Included in the list of major reasons for the specie shortage are the following: (1) colonists did not bring with them any significant amount of specie; (2) there were no gold or silver mines on our eastern seaboard; (3) much of the specie available was needed to finance foreign trade.

*Barton Hepburn, *History of Coinage in the United States* (New York: The Macmillan Co., 1930), pp. 11-13.

The Spanish dollar and its subdivisions constituted the major medium of exchange in most of the colonies. Heavy use of the Spanish dollar as the monetary unit is explainable in terms of our trade relationships with other countries.* Britain was the primary source of capital goods; however, Britain was not the most important market for the exports of American colonies. Therefore, our imports from Britain greatly exceeded our exports to her. British pounds gained through trade were quickly used to finance needed imports from Britain. Trade with the West Indies was just the opposite: our exports to the West Indies exceeded our imports from there, with the result that Spanish dollars flowed into the country. Some Spanish dollars earned in our trade with the West Indies were used to finance the excess imports from Britain; other Spanish dollars passed into general circulation. During much of this period, records of the colonists were kept in pounds, shillings, and pence. During the colonial period, one monetary unit served as a measure of value and another served as a medium of exchange.

Habits and customs are basic determinants in monetary affairs, just as they are in almost all other relationships. When the time came for formal adoption of a monetary unit in the United States, the dollar was chosen over the pound. After all, many more people used the dollar as a medium of exchange than used the pound as a measure of value. The first official recognition of the dollar came in 1775, when the Continental Congress authorized the issuance of notes payable in dollars. Ten years later a Congressional resolution decreed that " the money unit of the United States be one dollar." A few years later, Congress passed an act authorizing the establishment of a mint and the regulation of coins of the United States. The act also stated "that money of account of the United States shall be expressed in dollars." The dollar was officially designated the medium of exchange and the unit of account.

Definition of the Dollar

It is one thing to declare that the monetary unit of the United States is the dollar, and another thing to state what is meant by the dollar. Therefore, another function of a monetary standard is to define precisely the monetary unit, i.e., what is a dollar? Regardless of the colonial trade relationships, which led to the adoption of our particular monetary unit, it would have been defined in terms of a metal. Although many commodities have been used to perform the functions assigned to money, some good(s) will usually be selected as money par excellence by custom or force of circumstance. By the time of the founding of the American colonies, money had evolved to such a degree that it was generally defined in terms of a metal. The circulating media were in metallic form.

In 1786, the first mint act defined the United States dollar in terms of

*D. R. Dewey, *Financial History of the United States*, 10th Ed. (New York: Longmans, Green and Co., Inc., 1928), pp. 18-21.

both gold and silver, thus establishing a bi-metallic monetary standard for our newly created government. However, the act never became fully operative because no coins were actually struck under the law. Later, in the Act of 1792, the dollar was redefined, but again the definition was in terms of both gold and silver. The Spanish dollars then in existence varied considerably because Spain had degraded or changed its definition of the dollar at different times in the past. Alexander Hamilton recommended to Congress that the silver content of the United States dollar be based on the silver content of the actual average value of Spanish dollars in circulation. Congress followed the recommendation and defined the dollar as containing 371.25 grains of pure silver. The prevailing gold-silver commodity relationship was such that the dollar in terms of gold was defined to contain 24.75 grains of pure gold.

Defining a monetary unit in terms of a commodity, including rare metals such as gold and silver, does not imply the existence of something of fixed value. The value of a monetary unit depends on its actual use as a means of payment, i.e., how much does a dollar purchase in the market? The physical volume of goods and services that can be purchased with the monetary unit is subject to constant variation. Defining the monetary unit in terms of a metal means simply that a uniform unchangeable substance, such as so many grains of pure gold, has been chosen in terms of which all ratios of exchange are expressed or calculated. The definition of the dollar makes it equivalent or equal to a fixed quantity of metal. Many persons believe that the choice of a rare metal such as gold or silver makes it less difficult to control the total stock of money, making it possible to maintain relative stability in the purchasing power of the monetary unit.

Equalization of Value of all Types of Money

Money is defined as that which is generally used to make payments for goods and services and to make payments on debts. On the basis of this definition, money consists of coins, paper currency, and demand deposits (checking accounts in our commercial banks). However, during the 18th and 19th centuries, demand deposits were not considered money; rather the use of the term " money " was restricted to circulating gold coin and paper currency that was freely convertible into gold. The use of demand deposits as a generally accepted means of payment has increased considerably in the last fifty years; so much so that the present volume of demand deposits is more than three times the volume of coins and paper currency in circulation. The modern definition of money is generally stated in terms of the medium of exchange function to point up the existing importance of demand deposits.

If the many forms and types of money are to serve the functions of money simultaneously there must be equalization of value of all types of money in terms of each other. Generally, this standardization has been accomplished by redemption or the assignment of legal-tender status to all forms of currency.

If standard money (gold coin, for example) were allowed to circulate freely, there would have to be some method of insuring that the other forms of money would not depreciate in terms of the standard. Ideally, people should be indifferent to receiving a five-dollar gold piece or paper currency with a stated value of five dollars. In fact, for the standard to work best, people should actually prefer the paper currency over the gold coin, thus conserving gold. Under the conditions noted above, a government could maintain equalization of value of all types of currency by assuring the public that all types of coin and paper currency could be freely convertible or redeemed into gold or gold money on a dollar-for-dollar basis. If the banks were to do the same for demand deposits, then all types of money would circulate at par.

If the government and the banks were to refuse the right of redemption or if the public believed that such a step was likely in the near future, the public would tend to hold on to standard money and use the other forms of money for transactions. In other words, the public would come to believe that forms of money other than the standard money were overvalued in terms of the standard. The obvious result of these expectations would be the disappearance of the standard money from circulation. Paper currency and demand deposits would depreciate in terms of the standard. The results are so certain that the proposition has been stated in terms of a law: bad money drives out good money. This law has been named after an Englishman, Sir Thomas Gresham, who clearly perceived its operation more than three centuries ago. A more refined version has been stated as follows: " bad (overvalued) money is attracted into monetary use and good (undervalued) money into non-monetary use."*

Today, only limited convertibility of currency into gold is permitted. If the purpose for which a person or firm wants gold bullion satisfies the government, existing currency can be converted into gold bullion at par. Although the purpose of this arrangement is not to maintain domestic interconvertibility, it is a fact that our money can be converted into a fixed quantity of gold. The major method used to achieve domestic interconvertibility is the legal right of lawful holders of coins and currencies of the United States to exchange them, dollar for dollar, for other coins and currencies that may be lawfully acquired and are legal tender for public and private debts.

Legal tender is the other factor contributing to equalization of values. The applicable law provides: " All coins and currencies of the United States (including Federal Reserve notes and circulating notes of Federal Reserve banks and national banking associations) heretofore or hereafter coined or

*W. H. Steiner and Eli Shapiro, Money and Banking, 4th Ed. (New York: Holt, Rinehart, and Winston, Inc., 1958), pp. 32-33.

issued, shall be legal tender for all debts, public and private, public charges, taxes, duties, and dues."*

The Act of June 19, 1934 specifically provided the same for silver certificates. Legal-tender money serves as valid payment of all debts. If a creditor refuses to accept legal tender, the debt is not cancelled, but interest will not accrue from the date that payment was tendered.

Demand deposits fit into the above picture through the right of the depositors to receive from appropriate depository banks legal-tender money on demand. Commercial banks are legally obligated to redeem their demand deposit obligations on demand in legal-tender money. Many regulations are imposed upon the commercial banks so as to maintain the public's confidence that the banks will be able to redeem deposit liabilities on demand.

Control Over the Stock of Money

As noted previously, there have been periods in American history when the stock of money was grossly inadequate, and other times when it was excessive. The influence of the stock of money and its velocity of circulation on prices of goods and services requires some sort of control mechanism consisting of rules and discretionary powers of responsible public officials. Probably both types of control are necessary, and the latter is undoubtedly the more important of the two.

Deliberate control over the composition of the stock of money is not necessary in the United States, for the public has a fairly ready means of rejecting an over-issue of coins and paper currency through conversion into demand deposits. However, control over the volume of demand deposits is necessary because lack of control may lead to destructive runaway inflation and ruination of our monetary system. The destructive elements that history and economic analysis show to be necessary for such catastrophes to occur are as prevalent in the United States as they were in those countries which have gone through such an experience. If lack of control over our monetary system led to a rise in prices, and if the public believed that no change in policy were likely, the public's reaction would be to shift out of cash and other fixed-dollar financial assets into goods and equity types of securities in an attempt to offset future price increases or benefit by them. The increased flow of funds into equity types of securities would push their prices to higher levels and lead to expectations of further increases in securities prices. The increased flow of spending on goods would lead to higher commodity prices, especially if existing resources were being utilized to near capacity. If total saving were being done by economic units that were willing to assume the risks connected with direct investment in equities or physical goods, such conditions might lead to a greater volume of planned

*Section 43 of the Act of May 12, 1933, as amended by Section 2 of the Joint Resolution approved June 5, 1933.

savings and investment, unless the public were convinced and sick of hyperinflation. If the economy were comprised primarily of small shopkeepers and farmers, perhaps a large number of individuals could build up inventories as a hedge against future price increases, but this is not the condition in the United States. Furthermore, a large portion of personal saving in the United States is done by individuals who have demonstrated in the past an unwillingness to assume the risks connected with direct ownership of equity types of securities. A possible reaction of this group of savers to a protracted rise in prices might be to increase their consumption of goods and services. In economic terminology, hyperinflation might lead to an increase in the marginal propensity to consume, that is, a greater proportion of each additional dollar would be spent on consumption. With an unlimited expansion in the stock of money, planned investment would be satisfied with new money creation in the event that planned investment exceeded planned saving, and further inflation would occur. If prices were not rising at the same rate in other major trading countries, an unbearable strain would be exerted on our gold reserves. Eventually, the nation's monetary system would be ruined, and the administration of the government would probably be discredited. To restore a sound monetary system, it would probably be necessary to impose more rigorous controls throughout the economic system. It is interesting to note that inflation in China and Hungary facilitated the eventual establishment of communist regimes.

One of the objectives of monetary controls is to provide a stock of money adequate to support a flow of total spending that will maintain a high level of production and employment and at the same time not lead to inflation. If the stock of money is allowed to become excessive, it will contribute to a rate of spending exceeding the supply of available goods and services at prevailing prices, rocketing the economy off into the direction of runaway inflation. On the other hand, if the stock of money were allowed to contract too rapidly or not permitted to expand in a pattern commensurate with the needs of the economy, it might lead to a lower level of production and serious unemployment. In our economic system Treasury and Federal Reserve officials pursue discretionary actions within a broad set of rules laid down by Congress.

VARIATIONS IN THE MONETARY STANDARD

Choice of Metal

The financial history of the United States reveals that many variations have occurred in the monetary standard. One type of variation has been the choice of metal(s) in terms of which the dollar has been defined. Originally, the dollar was defined in terms of both gold and silver. Gradually, gold overshadowed silver, and in 1873 Congress indicated its intention of deserting a bi-metallic standard for a mono-metallic standard by declaring that a gold "one-dollar piece" should be the "unit of value." The provision for a standard silver dollar was omitted. Later legislation did permit the coinage of silver dollars, but the government was not obligated to purchase unlimited amounts of silver and was permitted to pay a price lower than its monetary value.

Metallic Content

When the silver dollar was adopted in 1792 as one of the two monetary units of the United States, its metallic content was fixed at 371.25 grains of pure silver, and the gold dollar was fixed at 24.75 grains of pure gold. The proportionate mint ratio of the two metals was 15 to 1 (371.25 divided by 24.75). However, definition of the gold dollar had to be changed when it became obvious that the Act of 1792 had undervalued gold. Recalling Gresham's Law, overvalued money is attracted into domestic monetary use and undervalued money into non-monetary use, the overvalued silver circulated and the undervalued gold was exported. To remedy the situation, the Act of June 28, 1834 reduced the content of the gold dollar from 24.75 to 23.20 grains of pure gold. The metal content of silver was left unchanged and the mint ratio between gold and silver became 1 to 16.0002. Three years later, a further change was made in the gold dollar; its weight was increased slightly to 23.22 grains of pure gold. Since both the acts of 1834 and 1837 undervalued silver in terms of gold, silver was exported.

The silver content of the silver dollar remains at 371.25 grains of pure silver. However, it should be noted that the market price of this amount of silver is less than one dollar. In other words, the commodity price of silver is less than its value for monetary purposes. As for the gold content of the dollar, it remained unchanged between 1837 and 1933. In May, 1933, the President was granted the power to reduce the gold content of the dollar. The Gold Reserve Act of 1934 provided that the weight of the gold dollar be fixed at not more than 60 per cent and at not less than 50 per cent of its previous weight (23.22 grains of pure gold). It was fixed at 13.71 grains of pure gold by Presidential Proclamation on January 31, 1934, and it has not been changed again. Congress would have to authorize any further change.

Right of Redemption

The third type of variation that has occurred in our monetary standard pertains to the right of redemption. An important feature of a monetary system is the maintenance of parity among all types of money. To accomplish this objective some countries permit the public to redeem the various forms of money into standard money. Standard money is that "money in which the central authority is in fact making its final payments."*

*D. H. Robertson, Money, Rev. Ed. (New York: Harcourt Brace, 1929), p. 73.

When the public cannot legally or practically convert various types of money into standard money at par, or not at all, the monetary standard is known as an inconvertible paper standard.

During much of the time between 1792 and 1861, paper money was not in practice kept redeemable at par, and the United States was on an inconvertible paper money standard even though the laws at the time provided for a bi-metallic standard. During the Civil War and for some years following, both the government and the banks officially refused to redeem paper currency in specie (metal). The government did offer to buy silver and gold at the legally established mint prices, but understandably none was offered under these terms. Again Gresham's Law explains the phenomenon: overvalued money had driven out the undervalued money.

Between 1879 and 1933, the United States, legally and in practice, was on a gold-coin standard. The various forms of money were freely convertible into gold money at par. However, during World War I there was a slight departure from complete freedom. In view of the need to expand the stock of money and to avoid the possible effects of gold exports, Congress permitted the President to prohibit gold exports. Gold could be exported only under license from the Federal Reserve Board. The restriction was lifted in 1919.

During the post-World War I period, especially in the late 1920's and early 1930's, world conditions were not conducive to the maintenance of the right of redemption in many of the major trading countries. By 1933 the gold standard had become inoperative in nearly 50 major countries. In anticipation that the United States would also depart from the gold standard, foreigners withdrew funds in the form of gold, and domestic residents preferred gold over deposits and paper currency. During the early 1930's, prices of goods and services were falling; business firms, including commercial banks, were failing in large numbers. Pessimism mounted and led to an increase in the demand for gold. Gold was being sought as a store of value, not as a medium of exchange. Deposit withdrawals from our banks became so great that some states declared bank holidays, and on March 6, 1933, President Roosevelt proclaimed a nationwide banking holiday. Gold constituted only a small part of the stock of money, and it was impossible for all paper currency and demand deposits to be converted into gold. Official action by the state and federal authorities was necessary.

Between 1933 and 1937 many important changes were made in the monetary system of the United States. The gold standard's demise was close at hand on March 6, 1933 when, by Presidential Proclamation, banks were prohibited from paying out or exporting gold or dealing in foreign exchange or transferring credits from the United States to any place abroad. Government offices were prohibited from paying out gold except under license. On April 5, 1933 an Executive Order required that gold coin, gold bullion, and gold certificates be surrendered, and on December 28 of that same year, an order of the Secretary of the Treasury required every person subject to the jurisdiction of the United States to deliver to the Treasurer of the United States all gold coin, gold bullion, and gold certificates situated in the United States. No longer could grandsons and granddaughters receive gold coins for Christmas. The final blow came January 31, 1934, with the passage of the Gold Reserve Act. It stated that no gold should thereafter be coined into United States coin, nor should any such coin be paid out or delivered by the United States. Under the Gold Reserve Act, the existing gold was reduced to bars, and in the process the United States established a limited gold bullion standard. It was limited in the sense that the United States did not permit either a free gold market or unrestricted redemption of money into gold bars (bullion). The uses of gold in industry, the professions, and the arts and the importation and exportation of gold became subject to Treasury restrictions. Within these limits, money is convertible into gold, but from the point of view of all domestic residents, the United States has an inconvertible gold bullion standard. At the same time, however, the standard cannot be referred to as a fiat standard, because our monetary unit is kept equal to a specific quantity of gold.

Control

As noted previously, one of the functions of a monetary standard is control over the total volume of money, especially control over the specie or reserve that is the ultimate support for the total stock of money. A metallic standard such as the gold coin standard discussed in the previous section incorporated a set of rules by which the monetary game was to be played. The rules were designed to allow the standard to function automatically (provided they were being followed to the letter). To play the game of the automatic gold standard, the following rules were to be followed: (1) The value of the monetary unit should be defined by the government as equal to a fixed quantity of gold; (2) Coinage should be unlimited and there should be no mint charge; (3) The government should agree to buy and sell gold in unlimited amounts and at a fixed price; and (4) There should be no restrictions on the import and export of gold.

During the 19th and early 20th centuries, the leading commercial nations generally lived up to the rules, and the standard took on a strong international flavor. Exchange ratios of the various monetary units were determined by the relative amounts of gold contained in each country's monetary unit. Given the right to export and import gold, exchange rates or ratios would fluctuate within very narrow limits. For illustration, if the exchange ratio between the United States and England were $4 to £1, and if the cost of shipping the equivalent amount of gold between England and the United States were only $0.04 in American money, then the exchange ratio would not exceed $4.04 or be less than $3.96. These amounts are referred to respectively as "gold export" and "gold import" points.

The similarity of rules brought about close interrelationships among the price levels of the countries that adhered to the rules of the gold standard. If Country A's prices were high in relation to prices in other countries, domestic residents would tend to purchase goods from other countries. The imports of Country A would be very large. Country A's goods would not be attractive to foreigners for the same reason, and the exports of Country A would be very small. Country A would have an unfavorable balance of trade, and gold would have to be exported to settle the adverse balance of trade. The loss of gold would also be a loss in monetary reserves. The reduction in monetary reserves would require contraction in the stock of money, which, in turn, would lead to lower prices in Country A. Eventually, the price level of Country A would adjust downward until it was in line with the price levels of other countries. The opposite effects were expected to occur in a country whose prices were low in relation to prices in other countries.

Automatic adjustments under the gold standard caused rather painful and long-drawn-out economic effects. Sometimes, when price level adjustments tended to turn against some countries, they were likely to fudge on the rules in order to moderate their adverse effects. A high price level country might devalue its monetary unit rather than allow imports to exceed their exports and lose gold to other countries. A low price level country might adopt a domestic economic program aimed at accelerating the rate of economic growth, and impose various types of trade restrictions, including restrictions on foreign exchange transactions.

Tinkering with the valuation of the monetary unit and restricting trade are examples of deliberate monetary management. The rub is that when most of the countries individually and in their own self-interest violated the rules of the game, the total volume of trade among nations fell off sharply.

Defense programs during World War I required modification in the strict rules of the gold standard. The purpose of most of the rule changes was to facilitate the accomplishment of domestic policy, especially monetary policy. When the fighting was over, the restrictions were relaxed and trade among nations was expected to proceed on the basis of the same rules that prevailed prior to the outbreak of the war. However, during World War I, many countries suffered varying degrees of inflation, and the pre-World War I rates of exchange did not reflect these changes. Resumption of trade under these conditions was destined to fail. Given the automatic adjustments inherent in the international gold standard, some countries suffered heavy losses of gold reserves. Fearing the consequences of continued heavy losses of reserves, monetary authorities in many countries obstructed the free flow of gold. The game was not worth the candle in terms of possible adverse effects on employment and production. The adjustments were believed to be too severe.

World War I controls were either reinstated or not relinquished at all. Monetary management became well-established in nearly all countries. The Federal Reserve and the Treasury, or both, can insulate our domestic monetary system and price level against the effects of international gold flows. The normal effects of gold imports and newly mined domestic gold are increases in deposit liabilities and primary reserves of the commercial banking system. Assuming that the Treasury issues gold certificates to the Federal Reserve banks, the ultimate reserves of Federal Reserve banks are also increased. To offset the normal effects, either the Federal Reserve or the Treasury can withdraw an equivalent amount of primary reserves out of the banking system. The actual techniques to accomplish this withdrawal are described later. Since the action of the Federal Reserve and the Treasury aims to sterilize the normal effects of gold movements, the policy is referred to as gold sterilization.

OUR PRESENT MONETARY STANDARD

Our present monetary standard is a hybrid. It is not a gold standard in the strict sense of the term, because the basic rules are not followed. Neither is it an inconvertible paper standard, because the dollar is kept at a constant value in terms of a fixed amount of gold, and paper currency can be converted into gold under specified conditions. Our present monetary standard could properly be titled a managed limited gold bullion standard. A brief explanation of each term provides clarity to the title.

Managed

The word " managed " recognizes the important role played by Federal Reserve and Treasury officials in the formulation and implementation of monetary, credit, and fiscal policies. Officials have considerable discretionary power with respect to the operation of the monetary system.

Limited

" Limited " refers to the limitations upon the right of redemption. The Gold Reserve Act of 1934 provided that gold should be held by the government as a monetary reserve and that it should not be available for private use for other than legitimate industrial, professional, or artistic purposes. The basic principle is that the most important use of gold is for the domestic and international monetary functions of government. Persons and firms desiring gold for legitimate industrial, professional, or artistic purposes are permitted to convert paper currency into gold at par.

Gold

Gold is used in the title because it is the metal in terms of which the dollar is defined. Furthermore, the Secretary of the Treasury is required by statute to maintain all forms of United States money at a parity with the gold dollar. The Treasury maintains the price of gold at $35 an ounce in the legal gold market in the United States.

Bullion

Bullion is the form in which gold is held. Since coins are no longer allowed to circulate, there is no need to mint the gold into coins.

Future Change

Debate continues as to whether our present monetary standard should be modified so that gold could play a more important and sensitive role in the formulation and implementation of monetary, credit, and fiscal policies. Suggested modifications range from merely removing the limitations on the right of redemption to the readoption of a circulating gold coin standard. In general, the arguments for change boil down to one simple proposition: If the public has the right to hoard gold, officials responsible for policy will be more careful to avoid extremes. Otherwise, the public might be tempted to hoard gold, thus threatening the financial structure of our economy. It is assumed that the potential threat would force public officials to make sound economic decisions.

The arguments against change boil down to the assertion that the ultimate success of monetary, credit, and fiscal policy depends largely on the quality of the public officials responsible for recommending and implementing policy. Internal gold convertibility is not considered an essential condition for good decision making. If the public wishes to protest the action of its duly elected officials, the ballot box is preferable to the collapse or near collapse of our monetary system.

In the future, gold will probably play a less important role in the domestic economy, but it will continue to be important in international payments. Here are some of the possible changes:* (1) Prohibiting residents of the United States from holding gold in the rest-of-the world sector, just as they are now prohibited from holding gold in the domestic sector. (2) Repealing the reserve of 25 per cent in gold against the liabilities of Federal Reserve banks, thereby making all our gold holdings available

*See Henry C. Alexander (Chairman of the Board, Morgan Guaranty Trust Company of New York), "Of Men and Money," an address delivered at the annual meeting of the Investment Bankers Association of America, Hollywood, Florida, November 28, 1960. (Reproduced in the *Morgan Guaranty Survey*, December 1960.) Change (1) was effected by an Executive Order issued by the President on January 14, 1961. The Order prohibits the purchase and holding of gold outside the United States by U.S. private citizens and U.S.-owned corporations. Present gold holdings must be sold by June 1, 1961.

for making international payments; under the present arrangement gold is held against nonredeemable liabilities, and in the process reduces the effective supply of international reserves. (3) Shifting all gold reserves to an international central bank; this change is examined in greater detail in the chapter dealing with international finance.

The major safeguard against overexpansion of the money supply is the adoption of sound monetary, credit, and fiscal policies. The Federal Reserve officials have the power to curb excessive increases in the total stock of money. Congress has the power to control expenditures and taxes. However, if both the public and Congress believe that a rising price level supported by a rising stock of money are essential to the maintenance of a high level of employment and a reasonable rate of economic growth, the rising price level becomes something to be desired rather than dreaded. The question of goals and the effectiveness of national policy are considered in greater detail near the end of this study.

QUESTIONS

1. Define what is meant by "monetary standard" in terms of its functions.

2. Explain the importance of each of the functions in our present economic system.

3. Trace briefly the changes in our monetary standard since 1800.

4. Explain the term "automaticity" as it relates to gold standards.

5. Label and explain our present monetary standard.

6. What are the arguments for and against a return to a gold coin standard; to a gold bullion standard?

7. State and defend your position on the proposition: "The United States should adopt a gold bullion standard." Be certain to define carefully what is meant by "gold bullion standard."

ADDITIONAL READING

The standard college texts on money and banking that have been published in recent years provide additional reading on the topics covered in this and many other chapters. Chapter titles and indexes reveal the appropriate chapters and pages. Twenty such texts are listed below:

Chandler, Lester V. *The Economics of Money and Banking.* (3rd ed.) New York: Harper & Bros., 1959.

Day, A. C. L., and S. T. Beza. *Money and Income.* New York: Oxford University Press, Inc., 1960.

Foster, Major B., Raymond Rodgers, Jules I. Bogen, and Marcus Nadler. *Money and Banking.* (4th ed.) Englewood Cliffs, N.J.: Prentice-Hall, Inc., 1955.

Halm, G. N. *Economics of Money and Banking.* Homewood, Ill.: Richard D. Irwin, Inc., 1956.

Hart, Albert G. *Money, Debt, and Economic Activity.* (2nd ed.) Englewood Cliffs, N.J.: Prentice-Hall, Inc., 1953.

Jome, H. L. *Principles of Money and Banking.* Homewood, Ill.: Richard D. Irwin, Inc., 1957.

Kent, Raymond P. *Money and Banking.* (3rd ed.) New York: Holt, Rinehart, & Winston, Inc., 1956.

Klise, Eugene S. *Money and Banking.* Cincinnati: South-Western Publishing Co., 1955.

Lindholm, Richard W., John J. Balles, and John M. Hunter. *Money and Banking.* W. W. Norton & Co., Inc., 1954.

Money and Banking, Compiled by a committee on money and banking; a collaborative writing group of 59 money and banking professors. New York: Pitman Publishing Corp., 1957.

Prather, Charles L. *Money and Banking.* (7th ed.) Homewood, Ill.: Richard D. Irwin, Inc., 1960.

Pritchard, Leland J. *Money and Banking.* Boston: Houghton Mifflin Co., 1958.

Ritter, L. S. (ed.). *Money and Economic Activity.* (A Selection of Readings in the Field of Money and Banking.) Boston: Houghton Mifflin Co., 1952.

Smith, Lawrence. *Money, Credit, and Public Policy.* Boston: Houghton Mifflin Co., 1959.

Steinter, W. H., Eli Shapiro, and Ezra Solomon. *Money and Banking.* (4th ed.) New York: Holt, Rinehart, & Winston, Inc., 1958.

Stokes, Milton L., and Carl T. Arlt. *Money, Banking, and the Financial System.* New York: The Ronald Press Co., 1955.

Thomas, Rollin G. *Our Modern Banking and Monetary System.* (3rd ed.) Englewood Cliffs, N.J.: Prentice-Hall, Inc., 1957.

Whittlesey, Charles R. *Principles and Practices of Money and Banking.* (Rev. ed.) New York: The Macmillan Co., 1954.

————(ed). *Readings in Money and Banking.* New York: W. W. Norton & Co., Inc., 1952.

Woodworth, George W. *The Monetary and Banking System.* New York: McGraw-Hill Book Co., Inc., 1950.

Other Reading

Bell, James W., and Walter E. Spahr (eds.). *A Proper Monetary and Banking System for the United States.* New York: The Ronald Press Co., 1960.

Bloomfield, A. I. *Monetary Policy Under the International Gold Standard, 1880-1914.* New York: Federal Reserve Bank of New York, 1959.

Brown, A. J. *The International Gold Standard Reinterpreted.* New York: National Bureau of Economic Research, 1940.

Currie, Lauchlin. *The Supply and Control of Money in the United States.* Cambridge, Mass.: Harvard University Press, 1934.

Dewey, D. R. *Financial History of the United States.* (12th ed.) New York: Longmans, Green & Co., Inc., 1934.

Hammond, Bray. "Historical Introduction," *Banking Studies.* Washington, D.C.: Board of Governors of the Federal Reserve System, 1941. Provides a concise review of American banking history.

Hawtrey, R. G. *Currency and Credit.* (3rd ed.) New York: Longmans, Green & Co., Inc., 1928.

Jevons, W. S. *Money and the Mechanism of Exchange.* New York: Appleton-Century-Crofts, Inc., 1896.

Keynes, J. M. *Treatise on Money*. 2 vols. New York: Harcourt, Brace & Co., 1930.

Nussbaum, A. *A History of the Dollar*. New York: Columbia University Press, 1957. Traces the development of the American monetary system from Colonial days to the 1950's; emphasizes underlying political and economic factors.

Olivecrona, D. K. *The Problem of the Monetary Unit*. New York: The Macmillan Co., 1957.

Studenski, Paul, and Herman Kroos. *Financial History of the United States*. New York: McGraw-Hill Book Co., Inc., 1952.

Sutherland, C. H. V. *Gold: Its Beauty, Power, and Allure*. McGraw-Hill Book Co., Inc., 1959. Provides considerable descriptive material and historical background to gold.

"The Monetary System of the United States," *Federal Reserve Bulletin*, February, 1953. Available as a reprint from the Division of Administrative Services, Board of Governors of the Federal Reserve System.

U.S. Senate Subcommittee on Banking and Currency. *Gold Reserve Act Amendments*. Hearings on S. 12, S. 2332, S. 2364, and S. 2514, to permit the sale of gold, to resume the redemption of gold, to permit the free marketing of newly mined gold, to establish a sound monetary system, and for other purposes, 83rd Cong., 2nd sess. Washington, D. C.: Government Printing Office, 1954.

5: Issue and control of coins and paper currency

IN view of the legal and economic differences among the three forms of money, each is discussed separately. Coins and paper currency are considered in this chapter; demand deposits, in the following chapter.

COINS

Many commodities have served as media of exchange, but precious metals have proved far superior to all others. In our economic system, the use of coins is now confined to a relatively small volume of transactions in which they retain convenience. Coinage of metal has made its circulation very convenient. It consists of shaping metal into uniform flat pieces, the shape of which may be circular, square, hexagonal, or otherwise, and impressing designs upon both sides and on the edges. Intricate processes of minting and exactness of design discourage and prevent counterfeiting, simplify recognition or identification of valid coins, and minimize both intentional and unintentional loss of metal from the coin. Generally, coinage is handled directly by government instead of being placed in the hands of private firms. It is not surprising, therefore, that Article 1, Section 8 of the Constitution of the United States states: " the Congress shall have the power . . . to coin money, regulate the value thereof, and of foreign coin."

Classification of Coins

Coins may be classified in various ways. One possible classification is based on the relationship between a coin's metallic value and its monetary value. Coins, whose value as a commodity for nonmonetary purposes is equal to its value as money, are referred to as full-bodied coins. The Act of April 2, 1792 authorized the minting of both gold and silver coins. The weight and fineness of the coins were specified by law, and the weight of the smaller coins was made exactly proportional to the weights of the larger. For example, the dime contained one-tenth of the amount of silver contained in the standard silver dollar.

Under the rules of the metallic standard, persons had the unrestricted right to present unlimited amounts of metal to the mint for coinage, free of expense, to melt down coins in unlimited amounts, and to export and import the metals. Since the metal was free to flow back and forth between monetary and commodity uses, the two values were kept equal by the integration of market forces. The supply of full-bodied coins was dependent upon the supply of metal for monetary purposes.

Full-bodied gold coins were a part of our total circulating media until mid-1933, at which time they were removed from circulation. It might be noted that at that time such coins constituted only a small percentage of the total stock of money.

A coin with a commodity value lower than its assigned monetary value is referred to as a token coin. All the coins circulating in the United States today are token coins. The commodity value of token coins cannot be entirely disregarded. If their monetary value greatly exceeded their commodity value, counterfeiting might present a problem. If their monetary value were equal to their commodity value, a slight rise in the metal's market value might prompt persons to melt coins and sell the metal at a profit in the commodity market. The disappearance of token coins from the monetary system would cause serious inconvenience in "making change." The melting down of coins in the 1850's prompted Congress to make fractional coins token coins.

People are willing to accept token coins for several reasons. First of all, many transactions require the use of coins. Second, token coins are struck only on government account, and their supply can be restricted to the needs of the public. Third, the government has made token coins legal tender. Fourth, the government permits their redemption into other forms of money. All of these factors help to explain why token coins circulate at their assigned monetary values.

Another classification of coins relates to the metal used in coinage. The Act of April 2, 1792 authorized both gold and silver coins. Gold coins included eagles, half eagles, and quarter eagles. An eagle was equivalent to ten dollars. Silver coins included dollars, half dollars, quarter dollars, dimes and half dimes.

Another classification relates to the monetary value of the coins. In our monetary system, a coin with a monetary value of less than one dollar is called a fractional or minor coin. At the present time, fractional coins consist of half dollars, quarter dollars, and dimes; minor coins consist of the nickel and the penny. As noted above, fractional coins were once full-bodied coins; now all our coins are subsidiary or token coins. In most countries, the base metals have mostly replaced the precious metals in circulating coins.

History of Coins in the United States

FOREIGN COINS. As noted briefly in the previous chapter, the protracted shortage of coins required the circulation of foreign coins for a number of years. In 1857, Congress provided for their retirement from circulation and repealed their legal tender status. Up to that time, foreign coins had been legal tender at rates proportional to their respective gold and silver contents.

GOLD COINS. As provided in the Act of April 2, 1792, the ten-dollar gold piece, referred to as the eagle, became the standard denomination of our gold coin. Gold pieces of smaller dollar amounts, the half eagle ($5) and quarter eagle ($2.50), were also authorized under the law. The various coin denominations were of proportionate weight and of the same fineness as the eagle. If the gold content of a coin were below the standard weight, it was legal tender only in proportion to its actual weight. The pure gold content of the coins was changed in 1834 and 1837. In March 1849, the double eagle ($20) and the one-dollar gold piece were also authorized; in 1853 a three-dollar gold piece was added. The smaller gold pieces did not work out very well; the one dollar and three dollar pieces were discontinued in 1890; the quarter eagle, in 1930.

In 1933, all gold coins had to be surrendered to the government. However, the United States Treasury continues to buy and sell gold in transactions with domestic producers and users, foreign governments, and central banks at a fixed price of $35 an ounce. Although gold coins are no longer minted, gold continues to play an important role in our monetary system. Gold is the statutory reserve for almost all of our paper currency and Federal Reserve deposit liabilities, and it continues to be used as a residual means of settling foreign balances.

SILVER COINS. The silver dollar was also provided for in the Act of April 2, 1792, and its metal content was fixed at 371.25 grains of pure silver. Its weight in terms of standard silver (.8924 fine) was set at 416 grains. In 1837, the standard for both gold and silver coins was changed to 0.9000 fine, so the standard silver weight became slightly less (412.25 grains). Since 1837, neither the weight nor the fineness of the silver dollar has been changed.

Although the weight and fineness of the standard silver dollar have remained constant since 1837, there have been numerous changes in the laws pertaining to actual coinage of silver dollars. In 1873, an act revising the coinage laws omitted provision for the coinage of the silver dollar. The silver interests referred to the Act of 1873 as the "crime of 1873." However, the act authorized the coinage of silver trade dollars that were intended for export to the Orient in exchange for goods. The trade dollar contained more pure silver than the standard silver dollar (378 grains of pure silver as compared with 371.25 grains), and their coinage was restricted by the Secretary of the Treasury to an amount believed sufficient to meet the export need. In 1887, coinage was discontinued and the outstanding trade dollars were either purchased as bullion or exchanged for standard silver dollars.

The Act of 1873 was modified in 1878 with the passage of the Bland-Allison Act, which provided for the restoration of coinage of the standard silver dollar. However, the rules pertaining to their coinage were changed considerably. Previously, coinage of silver dollars was free for the account of the depositor at a mint price of $1.2929+ per fine ounce. The Bland-Allison Act directed the Secretary of the Treasury to purchase each month, at the market price, not less than $2,000,000 nor more than $4,000,000 worth of silver bullion and to coin the bullion so purchased into standard silver dollars. The Treasury would not pay more than $1.29 per fine ounce, and might pay less, depending on the market value of silver in the commodity market. In other words, the Treasury would not pay more than one dollar and might pay even less for 371.25 grains of pure silver. Therefore, it was possible for the Treasury to issue more dollars in the form of coins than it was paying out for the metal. The profit that the Treasury makes in minting coins is referred to as " seigniorage," and it is treated as a miscellaneous receipt of the government.

A further change in the silver purchase policy was made in 1890 by the passage of the Sherman Silver Purchase Act, which required a monthly purchase of 4,500,000 ounces of silver bullion per month at the market price. The silver bullion was to be used either for coinage or for the backing of paper currency. The paper currency was to consist of Treasury Notes of 1890. Three years later the purchasing clause of the Act of 1890 was repealed.

Not much more was done for the silver interests until the Pittman Act of 1918, which authorized the limited conversion of standard silver dollars into bullion. The purposes of this action were to enable the sale of a large quantity of silver bullion to Great Britain and to provide additional bullion for the coinage of subsidiary silver coins. Under this Act, nearly 300,000,000 standard silver dollars were converted into bullion, and approximately 11,000,000 standard silver dollars were used for coinage of subsidiary coins. The Act required that the quantity of silver so used was to be replaced by purchasing an equivalent amount from the output of American mines, at a fixed price of $1 per ounce.

Further action to benefit the silver interests was taken in the 1930's. In accordance with the terms of the London Economic Conference (Senator Pittman was a delegate), the President by proclamation directed the mints to receive for coinage into standard silver dollars, silver mined subsequent to December 21, 1933, from natural deposits in the United States or any place subject to our jurisdiction. Under this action, silver producers initially received 64.64 cents per ounce. Supplemental proclamations raised the amount to 71 cents.

In June, 1934 another silver purchase act was passed. This act sets forth the present policy of the United States as it pertains to silver:

It is hereby declared to be the policy of the United States that the proportion of silver to gold in the monetary stocks of the United States should be increased, with the ultimate objective of having and maintaining one-fourth of the monetary value of such stocks in silver.

The act originally authorized and directed the Secretary of the Treasury to purchase silver at such rates, at such times, and upon such terms and conditions as he deemed reasonable and most advantageous to the public interest. Actually, Presidential proclamation did place a floor on the price of silver. Legislation in 1939 modified the policy to the effect that the Secretary of the Treasury was ordered to buy at 71.11 cents per ounce all newly mined domestic silver offered him. This floor price continued until July, 1946, when the minimum price was raised to 90.5 cents per ounce. The floor price remains set at 90.5 cents per ounce.

The Act of April 2, 1792 also authorized silver coins for the fractional parts of the dollar. Originally, their weight and silver content were proportional to those of the silver dollar; their coinage was free; and the coins had full legal tender status. In 1853 the government had to reduce the gross weight and fine content of the fractional silver coins to prevent melting of the coins. At the same time, their legal tender status was limited and free coinage was discontinued. Since 1853, fractional silver coins have been token coins and are coined only for government account. At various times in the past, denominations other than the half dollar, quarter dollar, and dime were coined. Included among these were the half dime and the three-cent silver coin.

Silver plays a relatively small role in our monetary system. At the present time silver is used in the coinage of subsidiary coins and silver dollars and is the statutory reserve of silver certificates. In terms of the total face value of United States currency in circulation, that based on silver amounts to about $3.6 billion. Most of the action pertaining to silver has been primarily for the benefit of silver producers, rather than for improvement in our monetary system. United States producers sell silver to the Treasury only when the market price of silver is below the established mint price of 90.5 cents or when it is more convenient to sell to the Treasury than it is to make delivery in the free market.

As for minor coins, their metal contents have included primarily copper, nickel, and bronze. Their denominations have included the five-cent piece, three-cent piece, two-cent piece, one-cent piece, and the half-cent piece.

Issue of and Control over the Supply of Coins

Among the specific duties performed by the Treasurer of the United States are the procurement, manufacture, storage, and redemption of United States currency. All coins of the United States are struck at the United States mints. Three mints are now in operation: Philadelphia, San Francisco, and Denver.

The Treasury puts coins into circulation through the facilities of the Federal Reserve banks. The Treasurer of the United States maintains deposit accounts at the various Federal Reserve banks, and upon receipt of coins from the Treasury, the Federal Reserve banks credit these deposit accounts. The Treasury replenishes its supply of coins by purchasing metals and having the mints strike additional coins.

The Federal Reserve banks stand ready to provide coins to commercial banks upon request. A shortage of coins in a given city or region is made noticeable by a reduction in the currency held by commercial banks. When commercial banks find it necessary to replenish their vault cash, they request shipments of currency from their respective Federal Reserve banks. In some instances, smaller banks may request shipments from larger commercial banks. Directly or indirectly, the need for additional currency is registered with the appropriate Federal Reserve banks. They simply ship bags of currency, including coins, and debit the deposit accounts of the banks receiving shipments.

When commercial banks hold currency in excess of their needs, the excess is shipped back to Federal Reserve banks. Cash is a non-earning asset, and commercial banks have no reason to hold large amounts of idle cash. The major limitations to possible over-issue of token coins are the inconvenience arising from having an excessive volume of coins in circulation and the administrative responsibility of Treasury officials.

PAPER CURRENCY

Inconvenience and uncertainty involved in using commodity money, including coins, led to the adoption and widespread use of paper currency. The development of paper currency in 15th- and 16th-century Italy provides a good illustration. There was considerable variation among the circulating coins and people hesitated to accept either coin or bullion without first ascertaining true weight and fineness. The money changers in Italy provided assay facilities to assist in handling this function, and evolving out of this function was the actual deposit of coins and bullion with the money changers. The public discovered that it was convenient to leave their coins and bullion in the possession of the money changers and to withdraw coins and bullion only when needed. Under these circumstances, there was little question as to weight and fineness since they had been determined at the time of deposit. The money changers issued a receipt or deposit credit at the time of deposit. Gradually, the public became willing to accept the receipts of the money changers as means of payment. After all, paper receipts were much more convenient than coins. Promissory notes or receipts represented a given amount of gold, and as long as the public had confidence in the money changer and the person from whom the promissory note was received, the receipt was as good as the gold. Those notes were, in effect, an early form of paper currency.

A similar evolutionary development of paper currency took place in 17th-century England. The deposit of coins and bullion for safekeeping led to the adoption and use of paper currency. The public sought out the facilities of the goldsmiths to meet its needs for safe custody of funds, and the goldsmiths acknowledged receipt and possession of coins and bullion by issuing receipts. As it had in Italy, it became common practice to transfer the ownership of these receipts rather than to transfer the gold physically. To facilitate transfer of receipts, goldsmiths shifted away from issuing personalized receipts to issuing formal promissory notes. Eventually the goldsmiths issued notes payable to bearer, thus obviating the need of endorsement to effect transfer. The prototype of the modern bank note (one form of paper currency) had thus been created.

An illustration of an early form of paper currency in this country may be found in the Colony of Virginia where, during the 18th century, tobacco was employed as a means of payment. In transactions involving large dollar accounts, the actual transfer of tobacco was very inconvenient to both parties. To avoid the inconvenience, negotiable warehouse receipts, which represented a certain amount and grade of tobacco, were transferred. The negotiable warehouse receipts served the same monetary purpose as the promissory notes of the money changers in Italy and the goldsmiths in England.

Government may either monopolize the issue of paper currency, as it does coinage, or it may allow private and quasi-public banking institutions to assume the function in its entirety. The function might also be shared between the government and the commercial banks. In the United States, note issue was originally handled entirely by commercial banks; now, however, all of our paper currency constitutes obligations of the United States Government and Federal Reserve banks, or of both.

History of Paper Currency in the United States

The history of paper currency in the United States may be broken down into four periods: (1) prior to the Civil War; (2) the Civil War period; (3) after the Civil War and prior to the Federal Reserve Act (1913); and (4) since the Federal Reserve Act.

PRIOR TO THE CIVIL WAR. The disappointing experiences with paper money issued by the colonies and the notes issued by the Continental Congress were important factors in limiting the power of the new Federal Government with respect to the issue of paper money. Authority to issue paper money was given solely to private banks. Therefore, prior to the Civil War, the supply of paper currency in the United States consisted of notes issued by private banks. With the exception of some Treasury debt that was used temporarily as circulating currency, there was no Federal or national currency. The Constitution specifically prohibited the States from either coining money or emitting bills of credit (paper money), so there has never been any state currency. It was not until after the Civil War that the Supreme Court decided that Congress had the constitutional power to authorize the Treasury to issue paper money.

During the operation of the Bank of the United States (1791-1811) and the Second Bank of the United States (1816-1836), the greater part of the currency in circulation consisted of notes issued by these banks. These notes were accepted by the government in payment of taxes and were redeemable in specie (coins and bullion or both). Both the First and Second Bank of the United States attempted to establish uniform standards with respect to paper currency by regularly presenting State bank notes for redemption. The Suffolk Bank in Boston did the same in the New England region by offering to hold deposits of other banks for the purpose of redeeming at par any of their banks' notes that were presented to the Suffolk Bank. The Suffolk Bank accumulated the notes of the banks that did not cooperate and presented them at one time at those banks for redemption. Measures such as these prompted considerable cooperation among bankers in the New England States, and resulted in a generally acceptable currency system for the region.

Failure to secure a new charter for the Second Bank of the United States left the note issue function solely in the hands of the state-chartered banks. With a few exceptions, such as New England, New York, and Louisiana, the quality of the paper currency issued by State chartered banks left much to be desired. The states' banking laws and supervision of commercial banks were considerably below today's standards. Many of the state banks issued notes with little consideration for the responsibility of redeeming them on demand. Many of the bank notes issued by state banks circulated at values below par and some became worthless. The lack of uniformity in design and related features made counterfeiting a serious problem. It is not surprising to discover that securities of the United States Government circulated as money during this period. The chaotic currency system was bound to lead to national reform. The problems relating to financing the Civil War brought the issues into focus. Reform was not only desirable but was also necessary.

CIVIL WAR PERIOD. Legislation in 1861 authorized the Government to issue non-interest bearing Treasury notes that were legal tender and were receivable for all public debt. Shortly thereafter, Congress created United States notes (greenbacks) as a substitute for Treasury notes. Greenbacks were non-interest bearing, payable to bearer, and legal tender for nearly all types of debts. The distinguishing characteristic of these new notes was that they were not redeemable into specie. This action placed the United States officially on an inconvertible paper standard. Many issues of these notes were authorized and as the amount outstanding increased, their value in terms of specie declined. At the peak of their issue, nearly $450,000,000 was outstanding at one time. United States notes still comprise a part of the total supply of paper currency; the amount outstanding is now fixed at $346,681,016.

The suspension of specie payments in 1862 caused subsidiary coins to disappear largely from circulation. The "bad" money drove "good" money out of circulation. Various substitutes were devised to facilitate "making change," culminating in the issue of fractional paper currency (shinplasters) in denominations corresponding to the denominations of subsidiary silver coins. Approximately $50 million of fractional currency circulated during and after the war. Legislation in 1876 provided for the eventual redemption of this form of paper currency. The records show that about $2 million is still outstanding.

In 1863, Congress authorized the Secretary of the Treasury to receive gold coin and bullion and to issue gold certificates therefor in denominations of not less than $20. Obviously, the disparity between the monetary value of gold and its commodity value both during and after the war precluded the issue of gold certificates during this period. Gold certificates still form a part of the total stock of money, but only the Federal Reserve banks are permitted to hold them.

The National Bank Act of 1863 was the major currency reform during this period. The act provided for the organization of national banks, i.e., commercial banks chartered by the Federal Government. Either state banks or newly organized banks were eligible to apply for a Federal charter. National banks were given the right to issue circulating notes. To make the note issue privilege attractive, Congress eliminated state bank notes from the stock of money by imposing on state bank notes a prohibitive tax of 10 per cent. For the first time the Federal Government was able to exercise exclusive regulation over currency. At just about this time, however, demand deposits had become as important as currency as a form of money, and so the Federal Government did not achieve control over the total stock of money.

The National Bank Act required the newly chartered national banks to transfer title and deliver to the Treasurer of the United States interest-bearing registered bonds of the United States Government in amounts relating to their respective amounts of paid-in capital. In return for pledging the·bonds as security, the national banks were entitled to receive from the Comptroller of the Currency federally engraved circulating notes equal in amount to 90 per cent of the current market value of the bonds. The notes were demand promissory notes of the issuing bank, and the law permitted the notes to be used for settlement of nearly all transactions. The law restricted the note issues of an individual bank to an amount not in excess of its paid-in capital and restricted the aggregate volume of notes to $3 billion. (National bank notes are in the process of being removed from circulation; occasionally they are used in transactions, but when they pass through commercial banks, they are removed from the monetary system.)

AFTER THE CIVIL WAR (1866-1913). Immediately after the Civil War the policy was to retire the United States notes. However, after the policy was in effect for only two years, and after only $44,000,000 was retired, the policy was suspended, and the amount then outstanding continued to circulate. During the Panic of 1873, which was the first of four full-fledged banking panics that were to occur before the passage of the Federal Reserve Act, the government reissued about $26,000,000 of United States notes. In 1875 a policy of gradual retirement was reinstituted, but the amount outstanding was not to be reduced below $300,000,000. Again the policy was short-lived, for in 1878 it was again suspended. At that time $346,681,016 in United States notes was in circulation, and this amount remains outstanding.

Congress declared in the Credit-Strengthening Act of 1869 that it was the policy of the United States to provide for the right of redemption of United States notes into coin. Seven years later the Secretary of the Treasury was directed to prepare and provide such redemption on and after January 1, 1879. In line with the policy, the Federal Government issued during the intervening years $95,500,000 in bonds for gold, the proceeds of which were placed in a fund for the redemption of notes. The law restricted the issue of gold certificates in the sense that none could be issued if the gold reserve fund for United States notes was less than $100,000,000. Later, the minimum size of the fund was set at $150,000,000.

In 1878, Congress authorized the issue of silver certificates and directed the purchase of silver bullion and its coinage into standard silver dollars. Silver certificates could be issued in return for the deposit of silver dollars with the Treasurer of the United States. The certificates were redeemable in standard silver dollars on demand.

The Treasury notes of 1890, the other new currency issued during this period, were issued in payment for the silver bullion presented to the Government under the terms of the Sherman Silver Purchase Act. These notes were redeemable on demand in either gold or silver coin at the discretion of the Secretary of the Treasury. The total amount outstanding was directly related to standard silver dollars coined from the bullion and held in the Treasury. In 1900, Congress directed the cancellation and retirement of Treasury notes and authorized the issue of silver certificates against the silver dollars coined under the silver purchase agreements.

Many changes were made in the laws relating to the issue of national bank notes. The more significant changes included the right to issue notes up to par value rather than just 90 per cent of par and elimination of the ceiling on the maximum amount of national bank notes. Beginning in 1908, the law was amended to permit the issuance of additional national bank notes if emergency conditions warranted. Just prior to the organization of the Federal Reserve banks, nearly $400,000,000 of national bank notes were in circulation.

The major defect of the currency system as it existed during most of this period was that the supply of currency was not directly related to the public's need. The supply of currency was arbitrarily limited by factors such as the stock of monetary gold, the amount of Federal securities outstanding that were eligible as security for the issue of national bank notes, and the amount of silver purchased by the Federal Government. Elasticity of note issue had been unduly sacrificed for safety of note issue. The inability of banks to respond to currency needs led to financial panics.

SINCE THE ORGANIZATION OF FEDERAL RESERVE BANKS. One of the express purposes of the Federal Reserve Act was " to furnish an elastic currency." The Act created a new form of currency that could be issued at the discretion of the Board of Governors of the Federal Reserve System. The security or collateral behind the currency was directly related to business conditions. Originally, the collateral was to consist of notes and bills accepted for discount by the Federal Reserve banks. The idea was that commercial banks would acquire eligible collateral in their loans and investments, and by transferring such assets to the Federal Reserve Banks, the Federal Reserve banks could in turn pledge these as collateral and issue additional Federal Reserve notes to satisfy the public's need for additional currency. However, when it became obvious that there was no dependable relationship between the Federal Reserve banks' holding of eligible paper and the demand for currency, the definition was broadened. Eligible collateral now includes drafts, acceptances, gold, gold certificates, and direct obligations, as well as notes and bills for discount.

The effective limit to the issue of Federal Reserve notes was the requirement that each Federal Reserve bank maintain a reserve in gold of not less than 40 per cent against its Federal Reserve notes in circulation. No Federal Reserve bank was permitted to pay out notes issued by another bank, and the notes of one bank received by another were returned to the issuing bank. The gold reserve requirement has now been lowered to 25 per cent, gold certificates have replaced the gold; and a Federal Reserve bank is now permitted to pay out notes issued by other Federal Reserve banks.

The Federal Reserve notes are obligations of the United States and are a first lien on all assets of the issuing Federal Reserve bank. At the time of their inception and until 1933, Federal Reserve notes were redeemable in gold at the United States Treasury or in gold or lawful money at a Federal Reserve bank. The present law provides only that they shall be redeemable in " lawful money," which means that the holder of a note has a legal right to demand in return only that which may be lawful money. The general definition of lawful money is any medium of exchange that circulates under sanction of law. Prior to 1933, it was necessary to draw a distinction between the broader term "lawful money," and "legal tender," for neither silver certificates nor Federal Reserve notes were legal tender, but they were lawful money. Now, however, the law specifically provides that "all coins and currencies of the United States . . . shall be legal tender for all debts, public and private." Accordingly, a holder of a Federal Reserve note has no legal right to demand any particular type of currency. He is obligated to accept any lawful money in circulation. Lawful money now includes coin, United States notes, silver certificates, and Federal Reserve notes.

Federal Reserve notes are issued through Federal Reserve agents, who are located at the various Federal Reserve Banks and serve as representatives of the Board of Governors. A Federal Reserve bank applies to its Federal Reserve Agent for a specified amount of notes, including with the application a tender of collateral in an amount equal to the requested amount of Federal Reserve notes. The notes are advanced to the Federal Reserve bank, and are placed in circulation through the commercial banks.

The Federal Reserve Act also authorized the issuance of Federal Reserve bank notes, a form of currency very similar to the national bank notes, except that the amount issuable was not limited to the capital stock of the issuing Federal Reserve bank. Between 1914 and 1920, their volume increased to about $185,000,000, but in 1920 steps were taken for their retirement, and these are still in the process of retirement.

The Federal Reserve Act provided national banks the opportunity to retire the whole or any part of their respective circulations of national bank notes. Eventually, the outstanding bonds carrying the circulation privilege were called for redemption. Provision for the issuance of national bank notes was cancelled in 1935 and provision was made for their retirement. National banks transferred their liability on these notes to the Federal Government by depositing required amounts of lawful money with the Treasury.

The original intent of the Federal Reserve Act was to supplement the existing forms of currency, but as it worked out, Federal Reserve notes became the primary form of currency within a matter of six years. Federal Reserve notes now account for about 85 per cent of the total supply of currency in domestic circulation outside the Treasury and Federal Reserve banks.

During the 1933-1934 monetary reform, the outstanding gold certificates were cancelled and retired when received by the Treasury. Under the provisions of the Gold Reserve Act of 1934, a new form of gold certificate was issued to Federal Reserve banks against appropriate credits that had been established on the books of the Treasurer of the United States. The Treasury maintains, as security for these gold certificates, gold bullion of a value equal to the face amount of such gold certificates. Gold certificates

TABLE 5–1
KINDS OF UNITED STATES CURRENCY OUTSTANDING AND IN CIRCULATION, DEC. 31, 1959*

Kinds of currency	Total out-standing Dec. 31, 1959	Held in the Treasury			Held by F. R. Banks and agents	Currency in Circulation[1] Dec. 31, 1959
		As security against gold and silver certificates	Treasury cash	For F. R. Banks and agents		
Gold	19,456	19,194	261[1]	16,348	......	31
Gold certificates	19,194	......	......	......	2,816	31
Federal Reserve notes	29,448	......	91	......	1,710	27,647
Treasury currency — total	5,311	2,406[3]	39	......	359	4,913
Standard silver dollars	488	155	27	......	8	298
Silver bullion	2,251	2,251	......	......	......	......
Silver certificates and Treasury notes of 1890	2,406[3]	......	......	......	271	2,136
Subsidiary silver coin	1,517	......	3	......	45	1,468
Minor coin	546	......	2	......	6	538
United States notes	347	......	6	......	29	312
Federal Reserve Bank notes	106	......	([4])	......	1	105
National Bank notes	57	......	([4])	......	([4])	56
Total — Dec. 31, 1959	([5])	21,601	391	16,348	4,885	32,591
Nov. 30, 1959	([5])	21,688	401	16,462	4,471	......
Dec. 31, 1958	([5])	22,404	683	17,135	4,815	......

* On basis of compilation by United States Treasury. In millions of dollars.

[1] Outside Treasury and Federal Reserve Banks. Includes any paper currency held outside the continental limits of the United States.

[2] Includes $156,039,431 held as reserve against United States notes and Treasury notes of 1890.

[3] To avoid duplication, amount of silver dollars and bullion held as security against silver certificates and Treasury notes of 1890 outstanding is not included in total Treasury currency outstanding.

[4] Less than $500,000.

[5] Because some of the types of currency shown are held as collateral or reserves against other types, a grand total of all types has no special significance and is not shown.

Source: *Federal Reserve Bulletin*, February 1960, p. 171.

comprise part of the reserve (at least 25 per cent) against deposit liabilities and note liabilities of Federal Reserve banks.

Summary of U. S. Currency Outstanding and in Circulation

Table 5-1 shows the kinds of United States currency outstanding and in circulation as of December 31, 1959. On that date the Treasury held approximately $19 billion in gold for monetary purposes. The gold is held in the form of bars and constitutes security for gold certificates, reserve for United States notes and Treasury notes of 1890, and funds for stabilization purposes. Silver monetary stock consists of standard silver dollars, silver bullion held in the Treasury, and subsidiary silver coins. The monetary value of silver held as reserve against currency amounted to about $2.4 billion. Standard silver dollars in circulation outside the Treasury and Federal Reserve banks amounted to approximately $300 million. The combined total of subsidiary silver coins and minor coins was approximately $2 billion.

Paper currency outstanding and in circulation includes gold certificates, Federal Reserve notes, and Treasury currency. The latter classification includes silver certificates, Treasury notes of 1890, United States notes, Federal Reserve bank notes, and national bank notes, but of these only silver certificates and United States notes are being issued currently; the other forms of Treasury currency are slowly disappearing from circulation. Federal Reserve notes comprise the major portion of our paper currency outside the Treasury and Federal Reserve banks.

All outstanding coins and currencies of the United States are legal tender for all public and private debts, and lawful holders of coins and currencies of the United States are entitled to exchange them, dollar for dollar, for other coins or currencies that may be lawfully acquired and are legal tender.

The following brief statements summarize the method of issue and reserve relating to the various kinds of currency and coin.*

FEDERAL RESERVE NOTES

Method of Issue. Issued through local Federal Reserve agents on request of local Federal Reserve Bank to agent.

Reserve. Secured by a like amount of gold certificates, eligible discounted or purchased paper, or direct Federal Government obligations, but at least 25% of this collateral must be gold certificates. "Gold certificates" include credits with the Treasury payable in gold certificates.

SILVER CERTIFICATES

Method of Issue. Issued by the Treasury and placed in circulation through the Federal Reserve Banks. Silver certificates must be issued to match the cost of silver purchased by the Treasury (which must be at not less than 90.5 cents an ounce). Additional certificates

*From *Readings on Money*, Federal Reserve Bank of Richmond, pp. 16-17. Reprinted by permission.

may be issued up to the monetary value of the silver stock, $1.29+ an ounce.

Reserve. Silver bullion or silver dollars of equal monetary value.

UNITED STATES NOTES

Method of Issue. New notes may be issued by the Treasury to replace worn-out notes, but the total amount outstanding may not be increased. Circulation held constant at $347 million.

Reserve. $156 million of gold bullion (which includes gold backing for Treasury notes of 1890).

TREASURY NOTES OF 1890

Method of Issue. No new notes may be issued. Currently being retired on receipt.

Reserve. Silver bullion or silver dollars of equal monetary value. Also shares reserve of $156 million of gold bullion with United States Notes.

FEDERAL RESERVE BANK NOTES

Method of Issue. No new notes may be issued. In process of retirement.

Reserve. Deposits of lawful money of equal monetary value to redeem outstanding notes. When last authorized to be issued, the reserve was: (a) any direct obligation of the United States or (b) any notes, drafts, bills of exchange, or bankers' acceptances acquired by the Federal Reserve Banks.

NATIONAL BANK NOTES

Method of Issue. No new notes may be issued. In process of retirement.

Reserve. Deposits of lawful money of equal monetary value to redeem outstanding notes.

GOLD CERTIFICATES

Method of Issue. Issued by the Treasury and paid to Federal Reserve Banks only. These certificates are not permitted to enter the currency circulation of the country. The small amount now shown as outstanding is an overhang from pre-1934 days when gold coins and certificates circulated freely.

Reserve. Gold bullion of equal monetary value.

STANDARD SILVER DOLLARS

Method of Issue. Issued by the Treasury and paid to Federal Reserve Banks in lieu of silver certificates if desired.

Reserve. No reserve. Total weight of coin is 412.5 grains, 90% silver and 10% copper alloy.

SUBSIDIARY SILVER COINS

Method of Issue. Issued by the Treasury and paid to Federal Reserve Banks to accommodate public demand.

Reserve. No reserve. The weights of the coins (which are 90% silver and 10% copper alloy) are — Half dollar: 192.9 grains; Quarter: 96.45 grains; Dime: 38:58 grains.

MINOR COINS

Method of Issue. Issued by the Treasury and paid to Federal Reserve Banks to accommodate public demand.

Reserve. No reserve. Nickel: 77.16 grains, 75% copper and 25% nickel. Penny: 48 grains, 95% copper and 5% tin or zinc.

Historical precedent has saddled the United States with unnecessary complications and overlapping authorities in connection with the issue of money, and there is not much chance of eliminating them. The country's currency system is now adequate in the sense that the volume of currency is responsive to the changing needs of the public. Furthermore, the public has demonstrated confidence in our currency and has not demanded that the United States return to a gold coin standard. In the United States, the unrestricted right of redemption is a thing of the past, and many economists believe that that is where it should remain.

QUESTIONS

1. Define coinage. List and illustrate four different classifications of coins.

2. Trace briefly Federal legislation relating to silver. What is the present role of silver in our monetary system?

3. Where do our coins come from and how do they get into circulation?

4. Trace briefly the development of paper currency.

5. Explain why the issue of paper currency was taken out of the hands of commercial banks.

6. What major defects in our currency system were corrected by the establishment of the Federal Reserve System?

7. What are the defects in our present currency system?

8. Explain how Federal Reserve notes are placed in circulation.

9. Identify the three major type of paper currency, and indicate their method of issue and reserve.

ADDITIONAL READING

Nearly all of the books listed at the end of Chapter 4 contain one or more chapters dealing with the history and present status of our currency system.

Kemp, A. *The Legal Qualities of Money.* New York: Pageant Books, Inc., 1956.

Longstreet, Victor M., "Currency System of United States," *Banking Studies.* Washington, D. C.: Board of Governors of the Federal Reserve System, 1941.

6: Demand deposits

MANY individuals and some firms continue to pay their bills with currency and occasional purchases of money orders, but the largest part of the total flow of money payments in the United States is made by checks drawn against the demand deposits in commercial banks. Demand deposits account for approximately three-quarters of the money supply and are used as a means of payment in 90 per cent of total money transactions. The number of checking accounts exceeds 50,000,000 and the number of checks written annually approaches 10,000,000,000.

NATURE AND ORIGIN OF DEMAND DEPOSITS

A demand deposit is a liability of a commercial bank payable on demand. When a bank advertises that its deposits are a certain dollar amount, the bank is, in effect, informing the public that the bank owes that sum of money to the public. Of course, a large and growing volume of deposits indicates that the public has faith and confidence in the bank.

Since demand deposits are spent by writing checks, those deposits are referred to as checkbook money as compared with coins and currency, which are referred to as pocketbook money. In non-legal terms, a check may be defined as an order, addressed by a depositor, ordering his bank to pay on demand a certain sum of money to the order of either a certain party, which may be himself, or the bearer.

The reasons for the introduction and eventual widespread use of the check as a means of payment are very similar to those underlying the earlier introduction and eventual widespread use of coins and paper currency. Greater convenience and safety are high on the list of favorable conditions. Checks may be drawn for any amount, obviating the necessity of making change. The size of the check is limited only by the size of the depositor's account. One of the largest checks ever drawn was a Treasury check for $7,500,000,000, which was used to transfer funds between two government accounts. Depositors are reasonably certain that banks will be able to pay out lawful money on demand; depositors believe that it is safer to hold money in the form of deposits than in the form of coin and paper currency. Check writing also provides safety, for if a check is lost or mistakes discovered, the drawer of the check may order his bank to stop payment on the check. If a check is drawn and endorsed to the order of a certain party, there is little or no risk in sending it through the mails.

Check writing is not of recent origin. Records show that checks in the form of mud tablets wree used as long ago as the 9th century, B.C. Romans and Syrians used checks in some of their transactions. To illustrate conditions conducive to the adoption and widespread use of the check as a means of payment, assume a situation in which two persons maintain deposit accounts in the same bank. In the previous chapter dealing with currency, it was pointed out that the receipts of the bank (bank notes) could be used as a means of payment. It is also possible for one depositor to order the bank to transfer on the books of the bank a certain sum from his account to another depositor's account. The liabilities of the bank remain the same; only the ownership of the bank's liabilities is altered. The same thing occurs in the transfer of bank notes. Book transfers are also possible among banks that have deposits in the same bank. For illustration, Bank A deposits in Bank C $100,000 of checks drawn on Bank B; Bank B deposits in the same bank $75,000 of checks drawn on Bank A; Bank C offsets deposits against each other and transfers $25,000 from Bank B's account to Bank A's deposit account. Deposit transfers have developed to such a degree that nearly 90 per cent of the total volume of money transactions are settled by checks.

One of the major differences between demand deposits and the other forms of money is that checks are not legal tender and may be refused as a means of payment. However, if the financial condition of both a drawer and a drawee bank are known to be financially sound, and there is no doubt about the genuineness of the drawer's signature, generally a check is as acceptable as lawful money. A person receiving a check generally deposits it in his commercial bank, increasing his deposit account by that amount. However, he may demand the bank to pay him the amount in lawful money. He may not successfully enforce his demand without delay. The bank might require him to wait until the check is cleared. It is impossible for the public to be informed fully on the financial condition of all banks, depositors, and endorsers. There is always the possibility that signatures may not be genuine. For all of these reasons, hand-to-hand circulation of checks is severely limited as compared with hand-to-hand circulation of coins and paper currency.

Instead of circulating, checks are deposited in commercial banks as soon as possible after receipt, thereby building up depositing customers' balances and reducing drawers' accounts. Depositors who have realized increases in their accounts are now in a position to write additional checks. Old checks are replaced by new checks. In other words, demand deposit accounts turn over by check writing, currency turns over by hand-to-hand circulation. The turnover rate of demand deposits is derived by dividing annual volume of payments by check by the average level of demand deposits during the year. Since New York City payments are affected more by financial transactions than are payments in other areas of the country, it is customary to exclude New York City figures from the computation. Using this measure, the money supply in the form of demand deposits was turning over at an annual rate of 25 times in mid-1959. During the period 1951-1958, the annual rate of turnover ranged from 18.4 to 23.0 times. In New York City, the annual rate of turnover exceeded 50 times in 1958. During the postwar period, there has been a definite upward trend in the turnover rate of money. Also, the ratio of Gross National Product to the total money supply (defined to include currency and demand deposits) has risen during the postwar period. As noted previously, the turnover rate of money is a vital factor in the execution of monetary and credit policies. The monetary authorities have to consider present and future rate of turnover in adjusting the money supply.

Checks drawn on one bank and deposited in another are viewed by the latter bank as items for collection, and banks advise their depositors to delay drawing checks against new deposits until sufficient time has elapsed to enable depository banks to present checks to drawee banks. Depository banks do not realize additional available funds until the checks are cleared. If depositors had to delay withdrawal for many days to allow for clearing, the size of their bank balances would have to be very large. Assume a business has its entire daily receipts in the form of checks drawn against banks located in other parts of the country. If clearing required ten days, the business would have to maintain an idle bank balance equal to at least ten days' receipts. A large investment in idle cash depresses the rate of return on invested capital. Furthermore, long delays in clearing also increase risk, for the goods would probably be delivered prior to the completion of clearing.

The widespread use of demand deposits requires elaborate check-clearing facilities. A check may pass through as many as 30 separate operations from the time it is drawn to the time it is cancelled and returned to the drawer. In a city with many banks a local clearing house may be set up to facilitate the clearing of checks drawn on and deposited in local commercial banks. The collection of out-of-town checks requires some form of cooperative arrangement among banks located in different towns and cities.

The nature of a country's regional and national check-clearing arrangements depends on the structure of its commercial banking system and the existence of central banking facilities. Although the American banking system consists of unit, branch, group, and chain banking, it has always been a unit banking system on both a regional and national basis, because state statutes have been the controlling factor. There is a definite trend toward branch banking, but until it is permitted to cross state lines, the structure of our banking system on both a regional and national basis will continue to be based on unit banking. Except for the First and

Second Banks of the United States during the early 1800's, the United States was void of central banking until the establishment of the Federal Reserve System in 1914.

Before examining the relationship between the structure of the banking system and check clearing, the various forms of banking mentioned above are described briefly. Unit banking refers to banks that maintain only one place of business. In a pure unit banking system, the number of banking offices is equal to the number of banking corporations. The adoption and predominance of unit banks in the United States may be attributed to fear of concentration in finance, local pride, and the protracted shortage of money during the 19th century. The relationship between a unit banking system and safety of deposits in commercial banks is examined in a later section of the chapter.

Branch banking refers to banks that maintain two or more places of business. Under branch banking, the number of banking offices is greater than the number of banking corporations. Branch banking facilitates the establishment of additional bank offices, speeds up the transfer of funds to points of greatest need, enables an individual banking office to make larger loans and offer more services than comparable unit banking, and provides conditions favorable to the training of bank management. The development of branch banking in the United States has been determined by state banking statutes. Until 1927 national banks were prohibited from forming branches. Between 1927 and 1933 the establishment of branches by national banks was permitted, but contingent on state legislation. Furthermore, branches were limited to the city of the parent bank. Since 1933 national banks have been permitted to establish branches on a state-wide basis if states permit such branches. State-chartered, member banks must receive approval of Federal Reserve authorities before establishing branches outside the city of the parent bank. Approximately one-third of the states permit state-wide branch banking, approximately one-third permit branches, but not on a state-wide basis, and the other states either prohibit branches or have no legislation dealing with them. The banking system in California is basically branch banking with the four largest banks accounting for almost all of the state's commercial banking activity. The numerical importance of branch banking at the end of 1959 is indicated by the following data:* 805 national banks operated 4,769 branches; 383 state-chartered, member banks operated 2,490 branches; and 956 insured, nonmember banks operated 2,087 branches.

Group banking refers to the use of the holding-company device to control three or more banks. Depending on state law, the holding company may be an operating bank. Both unit and branch banks may be associated through group banking. The advantage of group banking is the provision of common services for the associated banks, including accounting, purchasing,

*Federal Reserve Bulletin, April 1960, p. 441. See pp. 440 and 441 for additional information on banks and branches.

training, and coordination of loan and investment policy. With some exceptions, group banking has developed in those states which either prohibit or restrict branches to a relatively narrow geographical area. Group banking has permitted the association of banks in different states, and to some extent has provided regional banking services. Approximately one out of every 17 banking offices is affiliated with a bank holding-company system, and approximately 7.5 per cent of total commercial bank deposits are held in such banks. The Firstamerica Corporation, Marine Midland Corporation, and the Northwest Bankcorporation are the three largest group banking systems. New York has the largest number of bank holding companies. The Bank Holding Company Act of 1956 requires the approval of the Board of Governors of the Federal Reserve System before a bank holding company is permitted to acquire an additional bank. If the bank to be acquired is outside the state of the holding company's principal operations, acquisition is legal only if the state in which this bank is located specifically authorizes such an acquisition. The Act also requires bank holding companies to divest themselves of non-banking interests.*

Chain banking is very similar to group banking. The major difference is the means used to achieve control of three or more banks. Generally, control requires common ownership of voting stock by an individual or group of individuals. In some cases control can be achieved through interlocking directorates, obviating the need for majority ownership. Chain banking systems are less important than branch and group banking systems.†

Federal approval is required for merger, consolidation, asset acquisition, and deposit assumption transactions between banks subject to Federal control. The Comptroller of the Currency acts when the resulting bank is to be a national bank or a bank located in the District of Columbia. The Board of Governors of the Federal Reserve System acts when the resulting bank is to be a state member bank. The Federal Deposit Insurance Corporation acts when the resulting bank is to be a nonmember insured bank. In granting or withholding consent to any such transaction, the appropriate agency must consider the general banking factors and the effect of the transactions on competition.

A branch banking system provides built-in connections between the commercial banks located in the larger cities and the banking offices located in the smaller cities and towns. The head office of a branch system can clear off claims against its branches. Check clearing involving two or more banks can be handled through the banks' head offices, all of which might be located in the major financial center of the country. In a pure branch

---

*See *Federal Reserve Bulletin,* June 1960, p. 697, for a list of bank holding companies. See the law department section of the Federal Reserve bulletins for frequent discussions of holding-company developments. For further detail on group banking, see the list of additional reading for this chapter.

† The pros and cons of the different banking systems are a subject in themselves; readers are referred to the list of additional reading for Chapter 6.

banking system, there may be less than ten major banks. The branches also provide built-in, out-of-town banking services for both customers and bank office managers.

A unit banking system does not provide built-in banking connections between the commercial banks located in the larger cities and the commercial banks located in the smaller cities and towns. However, the need for out-of-town banking services is just as great in a unit banking system as it is in a branch banking system. Unit banks tend to associate themselves voluntarily with larger banks in major trading areas. The system of voluntary interbank relationships is called correspondent banking. In the absence of central banking, check clearing in a unit banking system is accomplished through correspondent banking systems. Each system is held together by a network of interbank deposits, with the deposits centralized in the larger commercial banks. A large city bank may hold deposits of hundreds of other banks. Commercial banks forward out-of-town checks to their respective correspondents for collection. The banks in the larger cities may clear checks through a clearing house, each bank presenting the checks deposited for collection by out-of-town correspondent banks.

Except for the First and Second Banks of the United States, there was no central banking in the United States until the establishment of the Federal Reserve System in 1914. Prior to that time check clearing was accomplished through correspondent banking relationships and numerous local clearing houses. One of the early major tasks of the Federal Reserve System was to improve regional and nationwide check clearing. The Federal Reserve System has been very successful in providing the commercial banking system with a very efficient check clearing system. However, the Federal Reserve System has not replaced all check-clearing facilities. Local bank clearing, such as that by the New York Clearing House, is still important.

The process of check clearing through the Federal Reserve System is similar to that of the large correspondent banks, although the System's rules and regulations are naturally more strict and exacting. Member banks are required to maintain at their district Federal Reserve bank their respective reserve deposit accounts, and check clearing is accomplished by entering net changes in reserve deposit accounts. The district Federal Reserve banks are integrated through what is called an Inter-District Settlement Fund. Net amounts due or to be received by the various Federal Reserve banks are made daily in the banks' balances, which are maintained in the fund. The superimposition of the Federal Reserve banks upon the commercial banking system and recent improvements in communications and transportation have increased the speed and efficiency of check clearing. At the present time, a check drawn on a bank in San Francisco and deposited in a New York bank is cleared in two days, i.e., the New York bank's deposit account at the Federal Reserve Bank of New York is increased, and the depositor of the New York bank is free to write checks on the new deposit.

Automation in processing bank checks is another factor accounting for the speed and efficiency in bank clearing. Further progress is needed along these lines. By 1970, banks will probably have to process more than 20 billion checks, and each check is handled between 10 and 20 times by the banks involved in collecting. The use of new electronic equipment enables banks to process checks automatically almost from the point of receipt until they are posted to individual accounts in the drawee banks and customers' statements are placed in the mail. A system that is currently in its early stages of development uses magnetic ink to print a series of code numbers on the bottom of checks identifying the drawee bank, the drawer's account number, the amount of the check, and the type of transaction. The latter two code numbers are printed on the check by the depository bank. Electronic equipment reads the numbers and processes the checks automatically.*

There is a possibility that the introduction of expensive electronic equipment — perhaps as much as a million dollars for a completely integrated system — will bring about some changes in the structure of the banking system as it relates to check clearing. For example, service agencies may be organized to accommodate the needs of the smaller banks that cannot support or afford the costs of an automated check-clearing assembly line.

Expansion and Contraction of Demand Deposits

When commercial banks make loans to persons and firms, the banks receive promissory notes from the borrowers and credit the borrowers' checking accounts. In essence, the banks exchange deposit liabilities to the public for the public's liabilities to them. Bank lending permits the conversion of the public's promissory notes into demand deposits. Therefore, commercial banks create money (demand deposits) by making loans. The same principles apply when banks invest. The volume of demand deposits expands when commercial banks expand their loans and investments, and contracts when bank loans and investments decline.

Deposits that come into being when a bank makes a loan or an investment are referred to as derivative deposits; other deposits, such as those resulting from the deposit of currency or claims to currency (checks) are called primary deposits. However, the checks that are written on the two types of deposits cannot be distinguished. When a bank makes a loan and credits the borrower's account, it is allowing the borrower to use the bank's credit standing as his own. The bank exchanges its credit worthiness for a borrower's promise to pay. The major difference between a credit transaction with a commercial bank and a credit transaction with, say, a department store is that bank credit is a generally accepted means of payment whereas the use of department store credit is restricted to certain stores.

Loans give rise to newly created deposits, and these deposits along
*See the American Bankers Association's Bank Management Publication No. 147 for further information about the system.

with other deposits tend to be transferred continuously among the commercial banks. Therefore, newly created deposits are a prelude to the loss of deposits and reserves by lending banks and a gain in deposits and reserves by other banks. Considering a two-way flow of deposits among banks, nearly all banks gain deposits during periods of bank loan expansion. Borrowers repay loans by drawing checks against existing checking accounts. Therefore, when bank loans are contracted, the demand deposits are also contracted.

The securities transactions of commercial banks also affect the volume of demand deposits. When non-bank investors sell securities to commercial banks, they receive payment in the form of either deposit credits or cashiers' checks. A cashier's check is simply a check drawn by the cashier of a bank on the bank itself. Deposit of such checks will result in a higher level of deposits. In making a loan, a bank adds the borrower's promise to pay to its loan assets; in making an investment a bank adds the security to its investment assets. In both instances, demand deposits increase by the same amount. If securities were purchased from Federal Reserve banks, then demand deposits would not be increased; rather, the banks' deposit accounts at the Federal Reserve bank would be reduced by the same amount. Only the asset composition would be changed.

In summary, then, bank loans and investments tend to increase the total volume of money, and the reduction of bank loans and investments tend to reduce the volume of money. It is not difficult to understand that demand deposits are the most volatile component of the total stock of money.

Deposits and Reserves

Failure to exercise control over the total stock of money may create conditions conducive to greater economic instability. In the previous chapter it was pointed out how the stock of coins and paper currency is controlled. Since demand deposits account for the major portion of the stock of money, control over the volume of demand deposits is vitally important. When there is a need for expansion in the total stock of money, commercial banks should be encouraged to create these deposits through loans and security investments. When there is a need for a contraction in the total stock of money or at least retardation in the rate of increase in the stock of money, commercial banks should be encouraged to restrict their loans and purchases of assets held by non-bank investors.

In the United States, commercial banks are required to have legal reserves equal to a certain proportion of their deposits. The requirement places a legal limit upon the expansion of demand deposits. For illustration, if the reserve requirement were 20 per cent, total deposits could not exceed five times the volume of reserves. If deposits were already five times the reserves, additional reserves would have to be built up if commercial banks were to increase further the volume of demand deposits. By controlling marginal changes in reserve accounts, the volume of demand deposits can be effectively controlled.

It is one thing to have a system of reserve requirements, but quite another thing to design the system. At least three important decisions must be made: (1) per cent of reserve required; (2) base against which to impose reserve requirements; and (3) composition of reserves. A reserve requirement may range from only a fraction of 1 per cent to 100 per cent. If the requirement were as high as 100 per cent, commercial banks could not create money as they do today. Present reserve requirements against demand deposits average about 15 per cent. This requirement means that banks must have $15 in legal reserves for every $100 in checkbook money of their depositors. The long-run trend in the requirement is downward; eventually the requirement may be as low as 10 per cent. Our system of reserve requirements is called a fractional reserve system inasmuch as the legal requirements are only a fraction of deposits.

The Federal Reserve System's reserve requirements are based on a bank's classification and the nature of the bank's deposits. Bank classification has its roots in the National Bank Act of 1864, which classified banks on the basis of size and location into three categories: central reserve city banks, reserve city banks, and country banks. This system of classification was retained in setting up the structure of the Federal Reserve System. Much criticism has been directed toward this segment of the Reserve System.* In July, 1959 Congress passed legislation to correct certain inequities in the structure of reserve requirements. The legislation provided for the abolition of the classification "central reserve city" by July 28, 1962. In conjunction with this change, the legislation increased from 20 to 22 per cent the maximum reserves that reserve city banks may be required to maintain on net demand deposits, reduced from 26 to 22 per cent the maximum reserves that central reserve city banks may be required to hold, and reduced from 13 to 10 per cent the minimum that central reserve city banks may be required to hold. These changes made the maximum and minimum requirements the same for both central reserve city banks and reserve city banks. In carrying out the reclassification of banks, the Board of Governors is authorized to classify banks in central reserve cities as reserve city banks or country banks, and to classify banks in reserve cities as country banks if their banking activity resembles that of banks in the lower classification more closely than that of banks in their particular location. The nature of deposits refers to the distinction between demand deposits and time deposits. Demand deposits are payable on demand; time deposits are payable upon 30 days' notice. In practice, banks generally waive their right to notice and do pay depositors on demand. However, the time deposits are in practice a

*U.S. Senate, Committee on Banking and Currency, *Member Bank Reserve Requirements*, Hearings on S. 860 and S. 1120, 86th Cong. 1st sess. (Washington, D.C.: Government Printing Office, 1959).

more stable form of deposit. The reserve requirements against time deposits are much lower than those imposed upon demand deposits.

Prior to December 1, 1959 the Federal Reserve System required each member bank to keep all of its legal reserve on deposit at all times with its district Federal Reserve bank. Legislation enacted in July, 1959 authorized the Board of Governors of the Federal Reserve System to let member banks count all or part of their vault cash as reserves. In December, 1959, holdings of vault cash were made eligible to meet reserve requirements, to the extent they exceeded 4 per cent of net demand deposits in the case of country banks, and 2 per cent in the case of central reserve and reserve city banks. In 1960, on August 25 and September 1, respectively, the relevant percentages were reduced to 2½ per cent for country banks and 1 per cent for city banks. Effective November 24, 1960, member banks were permitted to count all their holdings of coin and currency in meeting required reserves against deposits. The counting of vault cash as part of legal reserve does not represent a radical change. Under the National Banking Act of 1864 and under the Federal Reserve Act up to 1917, banks were permitted to count vault cash as legal reserve. The change in 1917 was prompted by the need to prevent commercial banks from depleting the gold supply by withdrawals of gold to hold as reserve in their vaults. With the passage of the Gold Reserve Act of 1934, the original reason for ceasing to count vault cash as reserves was eliminated.

There is considerable variation in the provisions of state laws relating to the composition of bank reserves for state banks. Some states permit reserves to be held in many different forms, including vault cash, deposits with other banks, United States Government securities, and obligations of political subdivisions of the State in which the bank is located. This difference in the reserve requirements is one of the reasons why some state banks do not choose to become member banks of the Federal Reserve System.

The member bank reserve requirements in effect in December 1960 are shown in the tabulation below:

| | Net Demand Deposits [1] | | | Time Deposits | |
	Central reserve city banks	Reserve city banks	Country banks	Central reserve city and reserve city banks	Country banks
In effect 1960	16½	16½	12	5	5
Statutory minimum	10	10	7	3	3
Statutory maximum	22	22	14	6	6

[1] Demand deposits subject to reserve requirements: total demand deposits minus cash items in process of collection and demand balances due from domestic banks.

Deposit Expansion

The commercial banking system is permitted to hold deposit liabilities in an amount equal to a multiple of its reserves. Therefore, the banking system, as a whole, is enabled to expand demand deposits by a multiple of an increase in reserves and to maintain the increased volume of deposit liabilities as long as the increase in reserves is maintained. Assuming that there is a demand for bank credit, loans are the principal means through which demand deposits are created or increased. Commercial bank loans do not, in themselves, reduce the total reserves of the banking system, but rather they absorb an increase in reserves. Checks drawn on newly created deposits shift deposits and reserves from bank to bank. Since a dollar of reserve is able to support many more dollars of demand deposits, reserve dollars are often referred to as " high-powered money."

A brief review of the interrelationships among commercial banks aids in understanding the manner in which a unit banking system expands demand deposits by a multiple of an increase in reserve. It will be recalled that in making loans, banks generally credit borrowers' accounts and borrowers draw checks on the newly created deposits to pay for goods and services. Many of the checks drawn by borrowers on newly created deposits will be deposited in banks other than the ones on which the checks are drawn. The discussion of check clearing brought out the fact that the major portion of out-of-town checks are cleared through the Federal Reserve System. Federal Reserve banks make net changes in the respective deposit accounts (reserves) of each member bank. Reserve accounts of drawee banks are charged and reserve accounts of depository banks are credited.

On the basis of these few principles, a commercial bank's loan transaction and its effects on the deposits and reserves of other banks may be analyzed. However, before proceeding, certain simplifying assumptions are made: (1) Banks are required to hold 20 per cent reserve against demand deposits; (2) Banks' liabilities consists wholly of demand deposits; (3) Existing reserves are fully utilized, i.e., no reserve is available to support additional new deposits; (4) There is a demand for additional bank credit; (5) Additional deposit expansion will not require banks to put additional currency into circulation; and (6) Only member banks are considered.

Assume the management of Bank A sells some of the bank's holdings of United States Government securities and the buyer is the Open Market Committee of the Federal Reserve System, which is buying on behalf of Federal Reserve banks. Bank A receives payment in the form of an increase in its deposit account at its district Federal Reserve bank. Bank A has changed the composition of its assets: an increase in its deposit at the Federal Reserve bank has been substituted for some of its United States Government securities. Both the assets and liabilities of the Federal Reserve banks are increased: they own a larger volume of United States Government securities and owe a larger deposit liability to Bank A. The Federal Reserve banks have created some " high-powered money " by the purchase of the United States Government securities from Bank A.

Bank A is now in a position to increase its deposit liabilities. If there is an unsatisfied demand for bank credit, Bank A may increase its deposit liabilities either by making loans or by purchasing securities held by non-bank investors. For the purpose of this illustration, a loan transaction is assumed.

Assume that the bank sold $100,000 of United States Government securities. Although it is a fact that the additional reserves of $100,000 may support an additional $500,000 of new deposits, Bank A is not able to loan such a large amount for the simple reason that a major portion of any newly created deposits will be checked away to other banks. As noted above, loans give rise to newly created deposits (derivative deposits). These deposits, from the point of view of the lending bank, are a prelude to the loss of reserves and deposits through adverse clearings. If Bank A expects the total amount of newly created deposits to be checked away to other banks, Bank A has to restrict its additional loans to the initial increase in reserve, $100,000. If Bank A did not hold excess reserve adequate to cover the expected adverse clearings, its reserve account would be pulled down below its minimum requirement.

A general statement of principle is set forth: a unit bank can loan an amount approximately equal to its excess reserve, which is the difference between its actual and required reserves. The statement is qualified to cover the possibility that all of the newly created deposits are not checked away from the lending bank. In actual practice, borrowers do not draw down their balances to zero, and some checks are redeposited in the same bank. Since the adverse clearings are not as large as the loan, the bank can loan an amount larger than its excess reserves.

To continue the illustration, let us assume that Bank A loses deposits and reserves to other banks. What were derivative deposits from Bank A's point of view become primary deposits to other banks. Assume that all of the $100,000 is checked away, and the checks are deposited in Bank B. Bank A has lost both its newly created deposits and an equivalent amount of reserves to Bank B. Bank B's reserve balance is increased by $100,000, but its required legal reserve is increased by only a fraction of the deposit (1/5 of $100,000). The improved reserve position of Bank B makes it possible for the management of Bank B to make additional loans. Applying the principle stated above, Bank B may increase its loans by at least $80,000, i.e., new reserve ($100,000) minus additional required legal reserve ($20,000) equals excess reserve ($80,000). Assume a demand for additional bank credit in the community and an increase in loans by Bank B. New loans give rise to more deposits, against which checks are drawn. Deposits and reserves of Bank B are shifted to other banks. If the process continues to its conclusion with each bank lending amounts equal to its excess reserve, loans and deposits for the banking system as a whole may be increased until the original amount of excess reserve ($100,000) is fully absorbed. In this instance, loans and deposits could be increased by $500,000. In terms of a mathematical formula, loans and deposits may be increased by an amount equal to the reciprocal of the reserve ratio (1/0.20 equals 5) times the excess reserve, i.e., 5 times $100,000 equals $500,000.

The bank credit expansion process is summarized below by recording the same series of transactions on a set of hypothetical abbreviated balance sheets (the amounts are in thousands of dollars).

Bank A

	Before sale	After sale		Before sale	After sale
Loans	400	400	Deposits	1000	1000
Investments	400	300			
Reserves	200	300			

Federal Reserve Banks

	Before purchase	After purchase		Before purchase	After purchase
Gold Certificates	2000	2000	Deposits	2000	2100
Investments	2000	2100	Currency	2000	2000

Bank A

	Before loan	After loan		Before loan	After loan
Loans	400	500	Deposits	1000	1100
Investments	300	300			
Reserves	300	300			

Bank A

	Before withdrawal	After withdrawal		Before withdrawal	After withdrawal
Loans	500	500	Deposits	1000	1100
Investments	300	300			
Reserves	300	200			

Bank B

	Before deposit	After deposit		Before deposit	After deposit
Loans	400	400	Deposits	1000	1100
Investments	400	400			
Reserves	200	300			

Bank B

	Before loan	After loan		Before loan	After loan
Loans	400	480	Deposits	1100	1180
Investments	400	400			
Reserves	300	300			

Rather than carry the example any further in terms of balance sheets, the additional expansion is summarized as follows:

Bank	Deposits received	Reserves retained	Loans made
Bank A			$100
Bank B	$100	$ 20	80
Bank C	80	16	64
Bank D	64	12.8	51.2
Bank E	51.2	10.24	40.96
Other banks (in turn)	204.8	40.96	163.84
	$500.0	$100.00	$500.00

If there were only one bank in the country, it would constitute the banking system. In this situation the single bank would be able to loan out a multiple of its excess reserve because the single bank would not lose deposits and reserve.

Even though an individual unit bank can loan and/or invest only an amount equal to its excess reserve, the balance sheet of an operating bank will show that its deposit liabilities are a multiple of its reserves. How can this be? Part of the explanation is found in the interrelationships among banks. Bank A, in the example above, increased its loans only by an amount equal to its newly created excess reserves, but the effects of Bank A's loans filtered throughout the entire banking system. Other banks subsequently made loans, and customers of Bank A probably received checks drawn on other banks and thus built up their deposit balances with Bank A. The constant turnover in commercial bank loans is also an important factor. Near the end of a loan period, borrowers build up their deposit accounts and draw checks against these deposits in repaying their loans. In other words, there is a tendency for newly created deposits that are checked away to return eventually to the bank that created them. Therefore, even though many individual deposit accounts are very volatile, the over-all volume of deposits remains relatively constant. Since only a minor portion of a bank's deposits may represent newly created deposits, the bank does not expect that a major portion of its existing deposits will be checked away at the same time.

Deposit Contraction

Large banks have loans and investments maturing daily, and if they are not replaced by new loans and investment, earning assets and deposit liabilities of commercial banks are contracted. Issuers of maturing obligations and borrowers whose loans are approaching maturity build up bank deposits prior to the due dates and repay loans by drawing against these deposits. If new securities are to be issued or if loans are to be renewed, then the build-up in deposits would not be necessary.

115

Assume that the management of Bank A decides to reduce its volume of loans by $100,000, and the customers of Bank A are either unsuccessful in arranging new loans elsewhere or do not make the effort to do so. Although the decision to contract loans is initiated in Bank A, other banks are affected. As a prelude to loan repayments, borrowers from Bank A build up their deposit accounts in Bank A, thereby contracting deposit liabilities and reserves of other banks. If other banks do not have excess reserves at the time, they have to make adjustments, either by building up their reserves or by reducing their deposit liabilities. To reduce their deposit liabilities, they have to contract their loans and/or investments.

Assume that $100,000 of deposits and reserves are shifted to Bank A from other banks. With a reserve requirement of 20 per cent, other banks are now deficient $80,000 in required reserves, and either the reserves have to be restored or the deposits reduced.

The fractional reserve requirement and the interrelationships among banks provide the key to understanding the multiple contraction of demand deposits. Deposits must be contracted by five times the deficiency, i.e., five times $80,000 equals $400,000. Including the initial action of Bank A, the total contraction in deposits is $500,000, which is the same amount that was previously created.

After Bank A contracts its loans by $100,000, it holds an equal amount of excess reserves, which is a non-earning asset. Assume that Bank A purchases an equivalent amount of United States Government obligations, and that the seller is the Open Market Committee of the Federal Reserve System. The net effect is that Bank A's financial position is restored to what it was before the loans were made. Also, the excess reserves have been removed from the banking system.

Although the Federal Reserve System was involved in the above explanation, this connection should not imply that either multiple credit expansion or multiple credit contraction are dependent on the System. The system of commercial banks carried out multiple credit expansion before the introduction of the System. The essential point is the fractional reserve requirement. The Federal Reserve System was superimposed on the existing system of commercial banks. The new element was the ability of the system to create additional legal reserves, and thus provide the basis for additional multiple credit creation. By making the commercial banks dependent on the Federal Reserve System for marginal additions to legal reserves, the system is able to control the marginal change in reserves, and thus control marginal changes in the creation of new deposits.

Some people are disturbed by the fact that all commercial banks are not members of the Federal Reserve System. Such concern is unwarranted if it pertains to control over the volume of demand deposits, for if monetary officials can influence the loan and investment policies of banks accounting for 85 per cent of total banking activity, the other 15 per cent of banking activity must adjust automatically to what is being done in the larger group. To achieve either multiple credit expansion or contraction, banks must " keep in step " with each other. If a few banks attempt to increase loans and investments at the same time that almost all other banks are attempting to build up excess reserves or at a time when monetary officials are deliberately wiping out legal reserves, the banks initiating the loans will not receive a counterflow of deposits as described above. Their loans will be restricted to their excess reserve, and that is the end of it. Multiple credit expansion will not materialize.

Expansion and Contraction of Demand Deposits

The factors influencing the expansion and contraction of demand deposits may be broken down into two major groups: (1) those on the demand side, and (2) those on the supply side. The demand for bank credit depends primarily on seasonal factors, the level of income, output, and employment, and the state of expectations as to future business conditions. The supply of bank credit depends upon the reserve positions of commercial banks and bankers' attitudes toward future loan requests. Although public policy aims to affect both demand and supply, public policy measures are relatively more effective on the supply side.

Factors tending to increase or decrease members' bank reserves may be broken down into categories: (1) operating or technical transactions; and (2) direct or discretionary Federal Reserve credit transactions.

FEDERAL RESERVE FLOAT. Federal Reserve Float is one of the operating transactions affecting member bank reserves. " Float " refers to the temporary additions to bank reserves resulting from time lags in the clearing of checks. If in the clearing of checks the accounts of depository and drawee banks are changed at the same time, the total amount of deposit balances at the Federal Reserve banks remain constant and only the ownership pattern of deposit balances is changed. However, in actual practice the accounts of depository banks are often credited prior to the time checks are actually presented to the drawee banks. To illustrate, assume a check is drawn on a San Francisco bank and deposited in a New York bank. According to the time schedule used by the Federal Reserve System, the New York Federal Reserve Bank credits the reserve account of the depository bank at the end of two days. If the check is not physically handled by the Federal Reserve bank at San Francisco by the end of a two-day period, the reserve account of the San Francisco commercial bank is not charged at the end of the two-day period. Total reserves of commercial banks are increased until the drawee bank's account is charged. Over a long period of time, the size of the float does not vary considerably, but within a short period of time, say within a week or two, the effect of float on reserve may be as much as $500 million.

117

CURRENCY IN CIRCULATION. Variation in the volume of currency in circulation is another operating factor affecting the reserve positions of commercial banks. It is recalled that member banks meet the public's demand for additional currency by drawing down their reserve balances at Federal Reserve banks. If the public, for one reason or another, demands a larger volume of currency, its procurement by commercial banks from Federal Reserve banks reduces the reserves of commercial banks. The return of currency to the Federal Reserve banks increases the reserves of commercial banks.

TREASURY OPERATIONS. Another factor influencing reserve positions of commercial banks is Treasury operations. As will be explained later in a chapter dealing specifically with financing government, the Treasurer of the United States Government maintains deposit accounts in Federal Reserve banks and commercial banks. With few exceptions, the checks that are drawn by the government and payable to the public are drawn on the balances in the Federal Reserve banks. To replenish its accounts, the government transfers funds from commercial bank accounts to Federal Reserve bank accounts, thereby reducing reserves of commercial banks. A decrease in Treasury deposits with reserve banks has an opposite effect; it adds to the deposits and reserves of commercial banks.

INTERNATIONAL TRANSACTIONS. Transactions with other countries also affect deposit liabilities and reserves of commercial banks. Trade relationships with other countries may affect the *level of foreign deposits in Federal Reserve banks* as well as the *gold holdings by the Treasury*. In either situation, deposit liabilities and reserves are affected. For example, suppose foreigners or foreign countries desire to build up bank balances in the United States. One way for them to accomplish this increase is to sell more to the United States than they buy from the United States, and use the net proceeds to build up their deposits at the Federal Reserve banks. This procedure requires a shift in deposits previously owned by Americans and held in commercial banks to foreign ownership and eventual deposit in Federal Reserve banks. The clearing of checks causes a reduction in the reserve accounts of the member banks and an increase in Federal Reserve banks' deposit liabilities owed to foreigners. If foreign-held deposits are converted into gold, the gold will be purchased from the Treasury. The Treasurer's account will increase by the amount of the purchase, but it also has to be reduced, since gold certificates held by Federal Reserve banks will have to be retired. In either case, demand deposits in our commercial banks and the reserves of commercial banks are reduced.

DISCRETIONARY OR DIRECT FEDERAL RESERVE CREDIT TRANSACTIONS. As a means of offsetting the effects of technical or operating transactions and as a means of initiating changes in reserves, Federal Reserve officials carry out discretionary or direct Federal Reserve credit transactions. The Federal Reserve officials aim to promote economic stability by avoiding both unnecessary credit stringency and credit looseness. Therefore, discretionary or deliberate action is taken to offset the day-to-day and month-to-month variations in reserves resulting from the operating or technical transactions discussed above. To promote sound economic growth, reserve requirements will have to be decreased over the long run in order to provide additional reserves to support the needed increase in the stock of money. An expanding economy requires a larger and larger stock of money to finance the larger and larger output of goods and services. As noted previously, the long-run trend in reserves may result in a reserve requirement as low as 10 per cent.

Later in this text, monetary, credit, and fiscal policies will be examined in detail in terms of their effects on financial institutions and their customers. At this stage of the study, the three discretionary transactions used by monetary officials to affect reserves are described only for the purpose of understanding the expansion and contraction of demand deposits. The timing and the *modus operandi* of each of these transactions are discussed later.

One of the most frequently used discretionary transactions to affect reserves is the purchase and sale of United States Government securities by the Open Market Committee. It will be recalled that Bank A increased its reserve by selling securities. Buying and selling of government securities are at the discretion of Federal Reserve officials. If securities were bought from non-bank investors, such as life insurance companies and individual investors, both deposit liabilities and reserves of commercial banks would be increased. New deposits as well as new reserves are introduced into the monetary system. These transactions are referred to as open-market transactions.

Commercial banks are allowed to borrow and to receive advances from the Federal Reserve on the basis of acceptable collateral. What they are borrowing is bank reserve. The process is little different from any other type of loan transaction. The commercial bank's reserve account is credited in exchange for a promissory note. To repay the loan, the commercial bank simply authorizes the Federal Reserve to debit its deposit account at the Reserve bank. This transaction is discretionary in the sense that the Federal Reserve officials are able to vary the rate at which such loans are made and to refuse requests. The rate is referred to as the rediscount rate, and the practice of borrowing is called rediscounting. The prefix "re" denotes " again," and is used in this instance to denote repetition of discount. Many of the notes, drafts, and bills of exchange are acquired at discount by commercial banks, which means that the credit instruments are acquired at values less than their maturity values. For example, a commercial bank may acquire a 90-day, $100 note from a customer and credit the customer's deposit account for only $98. This is a discount loan because the bank has charged interest at the beginning of the loan period. Had interest been charged at maturity, it would have been a straight loan. Generally, open-market instruments do not specify rates of interest, and they are traded at discounts. The difference between maturity value and discount value represents interest income at maturity. Federal Reserve banks discount eligible paper. Since much of the paper was originally acquired by banks at discount, there is a repetition of discount, and thus the practice is referred to as rediscounting and the discount is referred to as the rediscount rate.

Federal Reserve officials may adjust reserve requirements within ranges set by Congress and change provisions relating to vault cash. In the first case legal reserves are changed, and in the second case actual reserves are changed. In both cases the level of excess reserves is affected. Assume that Bank A's actual and required reserves are the same. Assume that its deposit liabilities are $100 and its actual reserves are $20. If the reserve requirement is reduced to 10 per cent, required reserves become $10. The other $10 is still in the reserve account, and it becomes excess reserve. Assume Bank A's vault cash amounts to $4, and the bank is permitted to count as reserve vault cash in excess of 4 per cent of deposit liabilities. If the vault cash provision is changed to 2 per cent, $2 of bank vault cash can be counted as part of actual reserves, and the bank now has an additional $2 of excess reserves. An increase in the reserve requirement and vault cash percentage would reduce excess reserves.

The subsequent effect on loans and investments will depend on many factors, including the extent of the change, the level of free reserves at the time of the change, the manner in which banks adjust to changes in reserve requirements, and the demand for bank credit.

SAFETY OF BANKS DEPOSIT LIABILITIES

The title of this section makes no distinction between demand deposits and time deposits because from an operational point of view the funds are commingled. No specific asset is related to any specific capital account or liability. Therefore, to discuss the safety of demand deposits, one is obliged to discuss the safety of deposit liabilities.

The original purpose of bank reserves was to assure safety of deposits and outstanding bank notes, i.e., to assure the public of the bank's ability to redeem its obligations. In today's banking system, legal reserves on deposit with Reserve banks are not available to meet withdrawals. Nevertheless, a legal reserve requirement is directly related to safety of a bank's liabilities, because it limits the creation of deposit liabilities, thereby affecting the bank's ratio of capital accounts to deposit liabilities. The capital-deposit ratio indicates the degree to which a bank may suffer loss in asset value and still be able to show asset value equal to or in excess of liabilities. It must be realized that capital accounts are not assets and the existence of capital accounts does not imply that funds are available to meet withdrawals. The adequacy of a given capital-deposit ratio depends on the composition and quality of assets. Generally, a ratio of 10 per cent is specified as desirable, but actual ratios tend to be lower. In the absence of reserve requirements, the banking system might expand deposit liabilities and so lower capital-deposit ratios that the public would lose confidence in the banks' ability to meet withdrawals. These expectations would be based on the belief that the banks would not be able to absorb future losses. In this sense, bank reserves do play an important role in promoting safety of deposits.

For a bank to satisfy the demand for currency, it must hold either a large amount of vault cash or assets that can be readily converted into currency with little or no loss in principal value. Cash is a non-earning asset, and, therefore, banks desire to minimize their holdings of cash. Liquidity is provided primarily through the holding of assets that banks consider as primary and secondary reserves. An individual bank's primary reserves consist of cash on hand, its deposit accounts with other commercial banks, and its deposit account with the Federal Reserve bank. As a source of funds to meet depositors' demands, only a fraction of its deposit account with the Federal Reserve bank is available. If the reserve account is equal to the required legal reserve, and the legal reserve is 20 per cent, then for every deposit withdrawal of $100, only twenty dollars can be thought of as coming from the account at the Federal Reserve bank. If a bank's management believes that it cannot reduce further its cash in vault, deposits with other banks, and its deposit at the Federal Reserve bank, then it must turn to other assets that can be readily converted into cash without serious loss. Assets of this nature are considered secondary reserves; they are characterized by liquidity, marketability, and earning power. Assets that satisfy these criteria include bankers' acceptances, commercial paper, and short-term government securities. The characteristics of these specific assets are examined later in this text. However, there are many factors in addition to the various types of reserves that are important in providing safety to depositors.

The over-all structure of the banking system and internal factors such as caliber of management, size of capital accounts in relation to deposit liabilities, percentage and quality of assets at risk, and deposit insurance are all important factors bearing upon the safety of deposit liabilities. A unit bank has the responsibility of looking out for itself; the fiduciary relationship between the bank and its depositors points up the importance of character among management personnel; the excess asset value provided by capital accounts provides a buffer; the nature of the contractual relationship between a bank and its depositors requires that the bank emphasize safety, liquidity, and marketability in the loans and investments; and the existence of deposit insurance tends to minimize the possibility of financial panic and large-scale runs on our banking system.

Banking Structure and the Safety of Deposit Liabilities

From the viewpoint of safety of deposit liabilities, the over-all structure of the banking system in the United States leaves much to be desired. Neither the banking structure nor the dual system of bank charter is conducive to strength. The failure of one bank has repercussive effects throughout the banking system. The promotion of a large number of independent banks is bound to lead to the organization of some weak banks, causing weak links in the chain relationship among banks. If the present volume of banking were to be conducted by a few banks with thousands of branches, common sense suggests that the few banks would be strong banks.

A group of people desiring to start a bank may apply for a charter from either the Comptroller of the Currency or their respective state authority. The charter is the document through which the corporation obtains and possesses its legal entity, and the issuing authority has control over the corporation, including the right to set down certain requirements to which the proposed banking corporation must adhere. The dual system of bank charter results in as many sets of rules and supervisory agencies as there are sovereign powers to issue charters. Naturally, rules vary from state to state and, not surprisingly, the rules of most states are less stringent than those of the Comptroller of the Currency. Weak state banks and poor state supervision allow potentially unsound banks to operate, setting the stage for possible bank failures. Considering the interrelationships among banks, failure of one bank or a few banks can also weaken stronger banks. Some of the bank failures during the 1920's and early 1930's can be traced directly to inadequate regulation and poor supervision. States have tightened up their laws and supervision, and the scope of the Federal Deposit Insurance Corporation has brought almost all banks under some form of Federal statutory control.

Actually, there are 53 agencies actively engaged in setting down rules and supervising commercial banks. In addition to the 50 individual states, there are the Comptroller of the Currency, the Federal Reserve System, and the Federal Deposit Insurance Corporation (F.D.I.C.), each of which has its own set of statutory controls and supervisory agency. The tabulation below summarizes the classification of banks based on membership in the Federal Reserve System and insured status as of December 31, 1959.*

	All commercial banks	All member banks	All insured commercial banks
Number of commercial banks	13,474	6,233	13,107
Total deposits in commercial banks (in millions of $)	$219,903	$184,706	$218,474

*Federal Reserve Bulletin, June 1960, pp. 649, 651.

The statutory controls of the Federal Reserve System are more restrictive than those of the F.D.I.C., with the result that fewer banks have become affiliated with the Federal Reserve System than with the F.D.I.C. National banks are required to be both a member bank and an insured bank.

Almost all the commercial banks are subject to regulation and supervision by more than one authority. To avoid duplication in bank examination there is a working arrangement among the various agencies. For example, National banks are examined by the staff of the Comptroller of the Currency, and the audit reports are forwarded to both the Federal Reserve Board and the F.D.I.C. Federal Reserve examiners conduct examination of state member banks. It is the policy of the F.D.I.C. to make an annual examination of each insured bank not a member of the Federal Reserve System. In many instances, state bank examiners participate with both Federal Reserve and F.D.I.C. examiners.

The primary purpose of bank examination is to discover unsafe or unsound banking practices and violations of laws and regulations, and to initiate corrective action as soon as possible. The Federal Reserve authorities also consider the process of bank examination as one of the means of promoting economic stability. Needless to mention, the timing of these examinations is unannounced to bank management.

Regulations Over Loans and Investments

Sound loans and investments combined with diversification contribute to the safety of deposit liabilities. This section lists a few of the more important regulations over bank loans and investments. The discussion is restricted to the regulations under which national banks operate, and neither interpretation of nor exceptions to the regulations is considered.

The major types of loans made by commercial banks include the following: commercial and industrial, agricultural, securities, real estate, and loans to individuals. The nature of these loans is developed throughout this book. They are mentioned at this time only to indicate the diversity in commercial bank loans.

Diversification in a bank's loans is promoted by the requirement that a bank loan no more than 10 per cent of its capital and surplus to one party. However, it should be noted that the law allows exemptions for about 15 types of persons or industries, permitting loans up to 25 per cent of capital and surplus. An officer of a bank is permitted to borrow not more than $2,500 from his bank, and this loan requires the approval of the bank's board of directors. Loans secured by real estate are permitted upon compliance with specified conditions: Obligations evidencing the loan must be secured by a mortgage or similar instrument; the amount of the loan is limited to a certain percentage of the property's appraised value; the maturity of the loan may not exceed a certain number of years; and the aggregate of real estate loans made or purchased by a bank may not exceed the greater of either the total amount of capital and surplus or 60 per cent of time deposits. This requirement relates the nature of the loan to the source of funds.

The laws relating to investments are similar to those pertaining to loans. For example, in no event may the total amount of investment securities (marketable obligations evidencing indebtedness) of any one obligor or maker, held by the bank for its own account, exceed at any time 20 per cent of its capital and surplus. Furthermore, regulations generally restrict the investments to the four upper classes of securities as determined by leading investment rating services. A national bank is severely limited in its purchase or acquisition of corporate stock for its own account. It may acquire stock to protect itself against loss on a debt owed to the bank, to control an affiliated safe deposit company, to control the corporation that owns the bank's premises, to control a small business investment company, and to control foreign banking corporations. The latter two organizations are described in later chapters. As a member of the Federal Reserve System, it is required to hold some Federal Reserve Bank stock.

Bank Management

In the final analysis, safety of deposit liabilities of commercial banks depends on management's abilities to bring into equilibrium various forces acting concurrently in different directions. To assure maximum financial returns to stockholders, the holdings of non-earning assets are stressed in making loans and investments. Safety of principal is important because the excess of assets over liabilities is relatively small (e.g., 7.5 per cent); liquidity is important because deposit withdrawals may force liquidation of assets when market conditions are not favorable. Inasmuch as commercial banks are the primary source of short-term funds and one of the more important sources of intermediate-term funds, bankers should also recognize their banking obligations in their respective communities. The relationship between loans and investment on the one hand and the money supply on the other also makes it imperative that commercial bankers consider the effects of their decisions on the economy as a whole.

Various laws and regulations and the credit and monetary policies keep bankers alert to the concurrent forces, and tend to encourage — force in some cases — equilibrating actions.

Fortunately, the American Bankers Association has recognized the importance of high caliber bank management, and has long had a sincere interest in the development of educational programs having to do with banking. The Association has encouraged the development and expansion of related programs in higher education, and has organized its own American Institute of Banking.

Commercial banks encourage bank personnel at all levels to participate in the various educational programs, especially in those of the American Institute of Banking (A.I.B.) and the Graduate School of Banking. The curricula of A.I.B., including that of the Graduate School, include courses in orientation in banking, a set of courses designed to improve certain banking skills, and a fairly complete listing of college-level courses, including graduate courses in specialized fields. Wherever possible, the activities of the Institute are carried on through local organizations of banks, called chapters. If these arrangements are not possible, individuals may receive education through correspondence enrollment. The formal educational programs culminate with the granting of a diploma, issued jointly by Rutgers University and the Graduate School of Banking, to those students who attend three resident sessions, satisfactorily complete the graduate courses, submit acceptable theses, and pass the oral examinations. Some state banking associations have set up executive development programs to supplement the already existing educational activities described above. Similar educational programs have been established by other types of financial institutions. In addition, large financial institutions have their own executive development programs.

Continuation and expansion of the educational and executive development programs are probably the soundest, long-run means of achieving a more efficient and sound financial system.

Deposit Insurance

The Banking Act of 1933 established the Federal Deposit Insurance Corporation, and provided for deposit insurance to go into effect on January 1, 1934. The immediate goal was to rebuild depositor confidence. The continuing purposes of the F.D.I.C. are " to protect depositors, to maintain the confidence of depositors in banks, to raise standards of bank management, to increase the soundness of the banking system, and to aid in protecting the circulating medium."*

The interrelationships among banks cause bank failures to spread throughout the banking system if not checked in the bud. Loss of confidence in a bank usually shows up in heavy withdrawals, panic, and may lead to eventual failure of the bank. In the absence of a nationwide deposit insurance program, depositors are likely to carry on a competitive struggle for self-protection. Depositors will tend to shift funds from bank to bank, and as loss of confidence spreads, depositors may attempt to withdraw funds permanently from the banking system. Obviously, the attempt to convert all deposits into currency is a self-defeating effort in the search for safety, for the attempt will force strong banks as well as weak banks to fail.

The idea of deposit insurance was not initally conceived in 1933, for

*U.S. Subcommittee on General Credit Control and Debt Management of the Joint Commitee on the Economic Report, *Monetary Policy and the Management of the Public Debt*, Hearings, 82nd Cong., 2nd Sess., Statement of H. Early Cook, a director of the F. D. I. C. (Washington, D.C.: Government Printing Office, 1952), p. 868.

as early as 1886 a bill providing for deposit insurance was introduced in Congress, and from 1886 to 1933 at least 150 such bills were considered by Congress. During the same period, there were sporadic efforts by some states to protect depositors. The progressive deterioration of depositor confidence during the 1929-33 period culminated in near-total collapse of the banking system. Opposition to a Federal program of deposit insurance became futile, and the F.D.I.C. was established.

In the absence of deposit insurance, each bank was dependent upon its own resources and abilities to maintain confidence of depositors. Under the present program of deposit insurance, depositors do not have to rely solely upon the individual bank for safety; they know that their accounts are protected at least up to $10,000, and if the F.D.I.C. uses its power to reorganize a bank, or to merge a bank's sound assets and deposits with those of another bank, no loss will be suffered, regardless of the size of the deposit. Although deposit insurance is not a permanent solution to the problem of bank instability, the psychological effects of the program cannot be ignored.

The alternative techniques available under the law for the protection of depositors in failed or insolvent banks, and the criteria by which the F.D.I.C. handles each case were well summarized in the following official statement:*

The Federal Deposit Insurance Act of 1950 provides three general methods or techniques for the protection of depositors in failed or insolvent banks:

(1) Under the receivership method, the Corporation pays to each depositor of an insured bank which has been closed on account of inability to meet the demands of its depositors, the amount of each depositor's claim to a maximum of $10,000 as soon as the claim has been verified. The payment may be in cash or in the form of a deposit payable on demand transferred to another insured bank, or as a deposit in a new bank in the same community. If the Corporation finds it advisable, it may organize a new national bank to assume the insured deposits of the closed bank. A period of 2 years is provided by statute for disposing of the affairs of such a national bank.

(2) Section 13 (c) of the act provides that:

In order to reopen a closed insured bank or, when the Corporation has determined that an insured bank is in danger of closing in order to prevent such closing, the Corporation, in the discretion of its Board of Directors, is authorized to make loans to, or purchase the assets of, or make deposits in such insured bank, upon such terms and conditions as the Board of Directors may prescribe, when in the opinion of the Board of Directors the continued operation of such bank essential to provide adequate banking service in the community. Such loans and deposits may be in subordination to the rights of depositors and other creditors.

*U.S. Subcommittee on General Credit Control and Debt Management of the Joint Committee on the Economic Report, Monetary Policy and the Management of the Public Debt, Replies to questions and other materials. 82nd Cong., 2nd Sess., Reply of Maple T. Harl, Chairman of F.D.I.C. (Washington, D.C.: Government Printing Office, 1952), pp. 950-951.

(3) The Corporation may provide financial aid to facilitate a merger or a consolidation of an insured bank in financial difficulty with another insured bank. According to secton 13 (e) of the act:

Whenever in the judgment of the Board of Directors such action will reduce the risk or avert a threatened loss to the Corporation and will facilitate a merger or consolidation of an insured bank with another insured bank, or will facilitate the sale of the assets of an open or closed insured bank to and assumption of its liabilities by another insured bank, the Corporation may, upon such terms and conditions as it may determine, make loans secured in whole or in part by assets of an open or closed insured bank, which loans may be in subordination to the rights of depositors and other creditors, or the Corporation may purchase any such assets or may guarantee any other insured bank against loss by reason of its assuming the liabilities and purchasing the assets of an open or closed insured bank. . . .

The Federal deposit Insurance Act of 1950 specifies the circumstances wherein certain methods are appropriate for aiding depositors in failed and insolvent banks. A formula to determine applicability does not accompany each method. Nor does the act furnish any specific criteria for selecting the appropriate method. However, in exercising the discretion authorized by law, the Board of Directors assembles and takes into consideration all of the pertinent facts and circumstances available at the time of decision. For example, if a careful study of the total situation is convincing to the Board of Directors that the continued operation of an insured bank in difficulties is essential to provide adequate banking services in the community, then the Board may exercise its statutory discretion and rehabilitate the bank. Likewise, action to facilitate the merger or consolidation of an insured bank with another insured bank is an appropriate method for protecting depositors whenever the available facts support the judgment of the Board of Directors that each action will reduce the risk or avert a threatened loss to the Corporation.

When the Corporation pays depositors in a closed insured bank (a receivership case), protection is limited to a maximum of $10,000 for each depositor. By contrast, the rehabilitation of an insured bank in financial difficulties or its merger or consolidation with another insured bank results in the protection of all deposits. Thus, there is in fact a difference in the amount of protection afforded depositors under these alternatives which is an incident of the Federal Deposit Insurance Act of 1950 and inherent in its provisions. The same was true under the Banking Act of 1935 which established the first permanent Federal deposit insurance law.

From the establishment of the Federal Deposit Insurance Corporation through the end of 1959, 439 insured banks were involved in financial difficulties warranting some form of financial assistance from the F.D.I.C. In 257 of these cases, the banks were placed in receivership and their depositors were paid directly by the F.D.I.C. By the end of 1959, less than 5,000 depositors had not recovered the full amount of their deposit balances. In the other cases, the F. D. I. C. either made loans or purchased assets from the distressed banks to facilitate assumption of these banks' deposit liabilities by other insured banks. In these latter cases, all deposit liabilities, regardless of amount, were assumed by other banks and no loss was incurred by depositors.* Since 1943 not more than 5 insured banks have failed in any single year.

The F.D.I.C. is financed through assessments upon insured banks and interest income. Approximately one-fourth of total sources of funds has come from interest and other income, and the remainder from assessments. The statutory assessment rate is 1/12 of 1 per cent annually of total deposits less certain authorized exclusions and deductions. Under the provisions of the Federal Deposit Insurance Act of 1950, a credit amounting to 60 per cent of the prior year's net assessment income is allowed against current assessments. Net assessment income reflects the deduction of insurance losses and operating expenses. Since 1950, credits have reduced the effective assessment rate to approximately 1/27 of 1 per cent annually of deposits.* Retained investment income and other funds are invested principally in United States Government securities.

In 1960 the President approved a bill providing for a simpler method of determining assessments and for a higher credit of the net assessment income. Effective in 1961, assessments will be based on the average deposits shown in the reports of condition in each semiannual assessment period, and deductions of 16⅔ per cent of demand deposits and 1 per cent of time deposits will be permitted. The credit to insured banks will be computed at 66⅔ per cent of the net assessment income instead of 60 per cent.

QUESTIONS

1. Describe the nature of a demand deposit.
2. What are the major differences between demand deposits and other forms of money?
3. How is the turnover rate of demand deposits computed?
4. Why is speed important in the clearing of checks?
5. Explain how loans and investments of commercial banks affect the level and composition of the stock of money.
6. Describe the present system of commercial banks' reserves.
7. "The banking system is able to expand demand deposits by a multiple of an increase in reserves." Explain.
8. "An individual commercial bank can loan and/or invest an amount equal to its excess reserves, but the balance sheet of an individual bank

---

*Annual Report of the Federal Deposit Insurance Corporation for the year ended December 31, 1959, pp. 5, 6.

† Ibid., p. 16.

shows deposit liabilities as a multiple of the bank's reserves." How can this be?

9. List and explain three factors that influence the amount of commercial banks' reserves.

10. How is the structure of the commercial banking system related to the safety of deposit balances.

11. Describe the role and operation of the Federal Deposit Insurance Corporation.

ADDITIONAL READING

Nearly all of the books listed at the end of Chapter 4 contain one or more chapters dealing with demand deposits, clearing of checks, regulations of loans and investments, supervision of banks, deposit insurance, and management functions. Most of the readings listed below deal with specific topics rather than the entire field of banking.

Alhadeff, David A. Monopoly and Competition in Banking. Berkeley: University of California Press, 1954.
Berkhart, B. J. Banking Systems. New York: Columbia University Press, 1954.
Bell, J. W., and W. E. Spahr (eds.). A Proper Monetary and Banking System for the United States. New York: The Ronald Press Co., 1960.
Cagle, C. E. "Branch, Chain, and Group Banking," Banking Studies. Washington, D.C.: Board of Governors of the Federal Reserve System, 1941.
Dunbar, C. F. The Theory and History of Banking. (4th ed.) New York: G. P. Putnam's Sons, 1922.
Horbett, John E. "Banking Structure of the United States," Banking Studies. Washington, D.C.: Board of Governors of the Federal Reserve System, 1941.
Lent, George E. The Changing Structure of Commercial Banking. Hanover, N.H.: The Amos Tuck School of Business Administration, Dartmouth College. Contains a list of additional readings on the same subject.
Leonard, Robert F. "Supervision of the Commercial Banking System," Banking Studies. Washington, D.C.: Board of Governors of the Federal Reserve System, 1941.
Livingston, Homer J. Management Policies in American Banks. New York: Harper & Bros., 1956.
National Banking Laws and Related Statutes, December 31, 1959. Prepared by R. M. Gidney, Comptroller of the Currency. Washington, D.C.: Government Printing Office, 1959.
Paulger, Leo H. "Policy and Procedure in Bank Examination," Banking Studies. Washington, D.C.: Board of Governors of the Federal Reserve System, 1941.
Phillips, Chester A. Bank Credit. New York: The Macmillan Co., 1924. Part I provides a classic explanation of multiple credit expansion.
Robinson, Roland I. The Management of Bank Funds. New York: McGraw-Hill Book Co., 1951.
Rodkey, Robert G., Sound Policies for Bank Management, New York: The Ronald Press Co., 1944.

U.S. House of Representatives Subcommittee No. 5 of the Committee on the Judiciary. *Bank Mergers and Concentrations of Banking Facilities.* A staff report, 82nd Cong., 2nd Sess. Washington, D.C.: Government Printing Office, 1952.

U.S. Senate Subcommittee on Monopoly of the Senate Committee on Small Business. *Concentration of Banking in the United States.* A staff report of the Board of Governors of the Federal Reserve System. Washington, D.C.: Government Printing Office, 1952.

Note: Hearings of and reports to both the Senate and House Committees on Banking and Currency provide a wealth of data on the banking system.

Wingfield, B. Magruder. "Deterrents to Membership in the Reserve System," *Banking Studies,* Washington, D.C.: Board of Governors of the Federal Reserve System, 1941.

Current data are available in the monthly issues of the *Federal Reserve Bulletin,* and in the annual reports of supervisory agencies; namely, the Comptroller of the Currency, the Federal Deposit Insurance Corporation, and the Board of Governors of the Federal Reserve System. The district Federal Reserve Banks' monthly reviews of business and credit contain data relating to the respective districts.

part 3: Consumer and nonprofit organization sector

IN the flow-of-funds system of accounts the consumer and nonprofit organization sector covers the following: (1) persons in their capacity as members of households; (2) personal trusts; and (3) nonprofit organizations serving individuals. The latter groups include foundations, private schools, private hospitals, labor unions, and charitable, welfare, and religious organizations. The business activities of individuals are excluded from the sector. For example, the business activities of individuals as proprietors of unincorporated businesses are included in the farm non-corporate business sector. The same holds true for the lessorship activities of individuals acting as landlords.

The analysis of the flow of funds and the structure and operation of financial institutions begins with the consumer and nonprofit organization sector because this sector constitutes the major source of funds of financial institutions. The conditions under which funds flow into financial institutions are among the more important determinants of the ways in which the institutions loan and invest. The early chapters of Part 3 are concerned with the flow of funds from this sector to the financial institutions sectors, and the later chapters deal primarily with the flow of funds from the financial institutions sectors to the consumer and nonprofit organization sector. By using this approach, the structure of our financial system is gradually developed in terms of basic functions, and the fundamental relationships between and among these sectors are clearly revealed.

7: Consumer saving and investment

IN this chapter we shall establish a meaningful frame of reference within which each of the various forms that saving takes can be examined. To accomplish this organization, the following topics are considered in this chapter: definitions; level and composition of consumer saving and investment; systematic financial investment; shifts in consumer saving and investment; and level and composition of financial assets and liabilities of the consumer and nonprofit organization sector. The structure and operation of those financial institutions which are directly involved in consumer saving and investment are discussed in the remaining chapters of Part 3.

DEFINITIONS

For the purpose of this study, saving and investment are defined in the same way as the Federal Reserve defines the terms in the flow-of-funds accounts: "Saving is defined in terms of current transaction, that is, as the excess of current receipts over current expenditures . . . . Investment is defined in terms of capital transactions, that is, as the sum of net purchases of tangible assets (expenditures for both newly produced and previously existing tangible assets less sales of tangible assets) and net acquisition of financial assets less net increase in liabilities."* Consumer saving and consumer investment are equal. Saving represents the current sources of funds in consumers' capital transactions, and investment represents consumers' capital uses of funds.

A transaction is either financial or nonfinancial; a transaction is either current or noncurrent (capital). Both of these statements are tautologies and neither requires verification. However, it is necessary to specify the conditions under which a transaction is financial or nonfinancial and the conditions under which a transaction is current or capital. Since all the concepts are interrelated, it is only necessary to specify the coverage of capital transactions, and to break these transactions down into nonfinancial and financial.

*"Quarterly Presentation of Flow of Funds, Saving, and Investment," *Federal Reserve Bulletin*, August 1959, p. 832.

Investment in Tangible Assets

A nonfinancial transaction is one that involves a tangible asset. The guiding criterion used by the Federal Reserve in determining whether a nonfinancial transaction is investment or not is the "acquisition of an asset that yields services over time, that is, beyond the current accounting period." This definition is not so clear-cut that an individual transaction can be classified automatically. Rather, there remains the need to make certain arbitrary decisions on some types of transactions. For example, distinction can be made between assets that yield services in production for sale and assets that yield services in households, but in the flow-of-funds accounts, both types of transactions are considered investment. To cite an additional example, there are some services, such as education and clothing alterations, that yield their "services" over time, but in the flow-of-funds accounts all such expenditures are considered current rather than capital.

The decisions are even more difficult with respect to goods. Many types of consumer goods yield services over time. However, the Federal Reserve has arbitrarily limited the consumer tangible investment to purchases of consumer durable goods and residential housing. It could be argued that change in consumers' inventories of consumer goods represents a form of consumer investment, but the flow-of-funds accounts do not treat such inventory changes as consumer investment. One of the major reasons for restricting consumer tangible investment to purchases of consumer durable goods and residential housing is the associated problem of calculating the capital consumption that must be related to investment. If it is assumed that the acquisition of a tangible asset is a capital expenditure, it must be further assumed that the asset will depreciate as it yields services over time. Applied to the consumer and nonprofit organization sector, it is both possible and necessary to estimate depreciation on consumer durable goods, residential housing, and plant and equipment used by nonprofit organizations.

To the extent that data are available, transactions in existing tangible assets, including land, are also included in the data for individual sectors. However, such transactions do not affect the total of national investment because both the purchase and sale of such assets are recorded in capital transaction accounts of the sectors involved, and so in the measure of tangible national investment, the two transactions cancel out.

Investment in Financial Assets

The various forms of financial investment are indicated by the structure of accounts and the number of and description of financial categories. There are nine basic categories, some of which contain sub-categories. The nine basic categories are: gold and Treasury currency, demand deposits and currency, fixed-value redeemable claims, saving through life insurance, saving through pension funds, credit and equity market instruments, trade credit, proprietors' net investment in noncorporate business, and miscellaneous financial transactions. Three sub-categories are included under fixed-value redeemable claims, and ten sub-categories are included under credit and equity market instruments. As explained in Chapter 3, the net acquisition of financial assets less the increase in liabilities represents financial investment, which is very important in the consumer and nonprofit organization sector. However, it should be recalled that in the measure of total national investment, financial claims owed and financial claims held within the domestic economy cancel out, and the only financial component of national investment consists of the increase in net financial claims on foreigners. The decisions on measurement of financial investment within the individual sectors affect individual domestic sector totals, but do not influence the measures of national investment. Although much of consumer financial investment cancels out in calculating national investment, it should not be assumed that consumer financial investment is unimportant. On the contrary, it is vital to an understanding of the decisions relating to ultimate investment. The uses to which consumers put their savings, the decisions of financial intermediaries, and the state of the markets for equity and credit market instruments have important effects on ultimate decisions pertaining to national investment.

Stating that certain types of financial flows represent consumer saving does not eliminate the need to make certain arbitrary assumptions. A few examples are cited to illustrate some of the more important arbitrary decisions connected with consumer financial investment. The decisions of the Federal Reserve as to the treatment of life insurance and pension plans influence the level and composition of consumer investment. In measuring consumer claims on life insurance companies, the Federal Reserve selected policy reserves as the better of four possible measures. The saving through life insurance during an accounting period represents the estimated change in reserves against life policies, including individual annuities and supplementary contracts, and dividend accumulations.* All of these claims are attributed to consumers, although some of the contracts are held by businesses. The difference between the net addition to life insurance companies' assets and the total of these items plus saving through insured pension plans provides a measure of the saving and investment of the life insurance companies themselves. Government insurance is handled in a similar manner. With respect to pension plans, the treatment varies according to the type of plan. Private pension plans and government employee retirement plans are treated as investment transactions, whereas social security transactions in connection with old age, survivors insurance, and unemployment compensation programs are treated as current transactions. The flow-of-funds accounts

---

*The meanings of these terms are set forth in the chapters dealing specifically with insurance and annuities.

show the saving through pension plans as being done by the ultimate beneficiaries (consumers) rather than by the funds themselves. For plans administered by life insurance companies, this form of consumer saving is measured by the change in pension fund reserves; for noninsured pensions and government funds, by the change in total assets.

Another arbitrary decision affecting the level and composition of consumer saving and investment is the treatment accorded non-corporate business savings. It is not currently possible to define operationally and to measure actual current income withdrawals by proprietors, so the Federal Reserve treats total net income of unincorporated businesses as equal to income withdrawals by proprietors. This approach has the effect of defining away retained income of unincorporated businesses. Therefore, the flow-of-funds data show no net saving for the non-corporate business sectors. The only saving attributed to these sectors is capital consumption charges. If the unincorporated businesses' acquisitions of tangible and financial assets exceed their capital consumption charges and their increase in liabilities, the excess is defined as proprietors' net investment in their businesses for that accounting period.

There are important differences between consumer saving and investment in the flow-of-funds accounts as compared with consumer saving and investment in national income and product accounts. The flow-of-funds figures are much larger than Commerce data because the former set of figures contains many items not included in national income and product data. Specifically, these items are: purchases of consumer durable goods net of depreciation on such goods; saving through government life insurance; and saving through government employee retirement and railroad retirement funds. However, there are some small items that the flow-of-funds data do not show as consumer saving, but which are shown in Commerce data, such as internal saving of life insurance companies and of mutual financial institutions. As noted above, the Federal Reserve reports this saving as occurring in the financial institutions sectors. There are also statistical differences, but the agencies involved in reporting consumer saving and investment are attempting to eliminate as many of these differences as possible.

LEVEL AND COMPOSITION
OF CONSUMER SAVINGS AND INVESTMENT

The importance of consumer saving and investment in relation to net national saving, capital consumption, gross national saving, and gross national investment are shown in Table 7-1. The major headings making up this section are based directly on those shown in the table.

Net National Savings

The data in Table 7-1 show that the consumer and nonprofit organization sector accounts for the major portion of net national saving. In fact, in 1958 the net saving of the sector was greater than net national saving. The explanation for this difference lies in the treatment accorded government saving. Unresolved theoretical problems involved in drawing the line between current and capital expenditures of the government sectors require the exclusion of government tangible investment from the data. Until these problems are resolved, government investment covers only the financial transactions of government. In 1958, both the state and local sector and the Federal Government sector borrowed more than they loaned, so that the

TABLE 7–1
SAVING AND INVESTMENT, 1958
(BILLIONS OF DOLLARS)

Net national saving		$18.5
Consumer and nonprofit	$25.1	
Other sectors [1]	—6.6	
Capital consumption		74.9
Consumer and nonprofit	41.6	
Consumer durable goods	37.0	
Owner-occupied homes	4.0	
Plant and equipment (nonprofit)	.6	
Other sectors	33.4	
Gross national saving		93.4
Consumer and nonprofit	66.7	
Other sectors	26.7	
Gross national investment		92.9
Consumer durable goods	37.6	
Other gross private domestic investment:		
Consumer and nonprofit		
Non-farm residential construction	14.7	
Plant and equipment (nonprofit)	3.4	
Other sectors	40.6	
Change in inventories	—3.8	
Net financial investment	.4	
Consumer and nonprofit		
Net acquisition of financial assets	23.6	
Net increase in liabilities	12.1	
Statistical discrepancy		.5

[1] "Other sectors" is negative because of negative saving of Federal and state and local government sectors. Unresolved conceptual problems involved in drawing the line between the current and capital expenditures of the government sectors require the exclusion of government tangible investment. Until these problems are resolved, government investment covers only financial transactions. In 1958, the government sectors' net borrowing exceeded net lending.

Source: "A Quarterly Presentation of Flow of Funds, Saving and Investment," *Federal Reserve Bulletin*, August 1959.

Government sectors had a negative saving of $12.8 billion in 1958. In 1956, the Federal Government sector had net national saving of $5.8 billion and the state and local governments sector had negative net national saving of $2.7 billion. In that year the total net national saving was $41.3 billion, and the consumer and nonprofit organization sector share was $29.2 billion. In both years, the consumer and nonprofit organization sector accounted for the major share of net national saving.

Capital Consumption

The consumer and nonprofit organization sector accounts for more than one-half of total capital consumption. Most of the sector's capital consumption relates to the stock of consumer durable goods. The remainder represents mostly depreciation of owner-occupied homes.

Gross National Saving

Gross national saving is equal to the summation of net national saving and capital consumption. Since the consumer and nonprofit organization sector accounts for the major share of each of these measures, it must also account for the major share of gross national saving. The data show that this sector accounted for more than 70 per cent of gross national saving in 1958, and in no year during the period 1954-1958 was this sector's share of gross national saving below 60 per cent.

Gross National Investment

The importance of the consumer and nonprofit organization sector in gross national investment is shown at the bottom of Table 7-1. The data show that the sector acquired $37.6 billion of consumer durable goods, $14.7 billion of non-farm residential construction, and $3.4 billion of plant and equipment to be used in nonprofit organizations. These three items totaled $55.7 billion and accounted for 60 per cent of gross national investment. The data show that in 1958 the sector transferred $10 billion of its gross national saving to other sectors through financial transactions. Also, it should be noted that a considerable amount of the investment in the consumer and nonprofit organization sector was financed by financial transactions within the sector.

Net Financial Investment

The net financial investment of the consumer and nonprofit organization sector for the year 1958 is broken down in Table 7-2. The top half of the table shows the net acquisition of financial assets and the bottom half shows the net increase in liabilities. The difference between these two categories represents net financial investment. Although none of these categories enters directly into national saving and investment, the data do show the financial uses to which the sector's saving is put.

TABLE 7–2
NET FINANCIAL INVESTMENT OF THE CONSUMER AND NONPROFIT
ORGANIZATION SECTOR FOR THE YEAR 1958
(BILLIONS OF DOLLARS)

Net acquisition of financial assets:
Currency and demand deposits .... $ 2.5
Fixed-value redeemable claims
   Time deposits $7.7
   Savings shares 6.5
   U. S. savings bonds .... —.5   13.6

Saving through life insurance 3.4
Saving through pension funds 6.5

Credit and equity market instruments:
   Federal obligations .... —2.9
   State and local obligations 1.5
   Corporate and foreign bonds 5
   Corporate stock 1.7
   Mortgages 1.8   3.0

Net investment in non-corporation business .... —5.5

   Total net acquisition of financial assets $23.6

Net increase in liabilities
   Mortgages 10.1
   Consumer credit 3
   Security credit 7
   Other [1] 9

   Total net increase in liabilities $12.1

Net financial investment (net acquisition of financial assets minus net increase in liabilities) $11.5

[1] For consumers: loans on insurance policies; for nonprofit organizations: bank loans, loans from government, and trade debt.
Source: "Quarterly Presentation of Flow of Funds, Saving and Investment," *Federal Reserve Bulletin*, August 1959.

CURRENCY AND DEMAND DEPOSITS. Only a small portion of the sector's saving flows into cash balances. The turnover of demand deposits and currency indicates that the purpose or motive underlying cash balances is different from those underlying other forms of financial investment. The major portion of cash balances held by this sector is explained by the necessity to hold minimum cash balances to facilitate spending. Over the long run, this sector, as well as all other sectors, needs to build up larger cash balances to carry on a larger volume of transactions. The increase of $2.5 billion in 1958 was a relatively large annual increase, and probably reflects stronger precautionary and speculative motives arising out of the recession in 1958. Cash balances were built up to serve as a cushion against possible loss of income in the future and to have purchasing power ready at hand to take advantage of expected lower prices of goods, services, and credit and market instruments.

FIXED-VALUE REDEEMABLE CLAIMS. Approximately 60 per cent of the sector's net acquisition of financial assets was in the form of fixed-value redeemable claims. A large number of consumers desire the liquidity and dollar safety provided by fixed-value redeemable claims. In response to the needs of consumers, many outlets have been developed, including time deposits, savings shares, and United States savings bonds; the last of which are redeemable at the option of the holder. The financial institutions providing such outlets include commercial banks, mutual savings banks, the Postal Savings System, savings and loan associations, and credit unions. United States savings bonds are issued by many of these same institutions as well as by government agencies.

Issuers of Fixed-Value Redeemable Claims

The intermediaries that provide fixed-value redeemable claims developed primarily in response to the economic needs of the small saver. The nature of our economic and political system prevented the development of a single national saving system. The public desired that financial institutions be independent units chartered under state laws. The establishment of the Postal Savings System in 1910 was the first departure from this principle. Then, in the 1930's, Federal charters were introduced for some of our savings institutions. The trend at the present time is in the direction of a national saving system, but there is considerable distance to travel before it will ever be realized.

The economic conditions that prompted the development of our saving institutions were not peculiar to the American economy. England, Scotland, and other countries had undergone a similar stage of economic development years before, and many of our financial intermediaries had their origin in those countries.

The shift of population from farms to factories and the growth of the wage-earning group prompted the formation of specialized saving and thrift institutions. Saving facilities for the small saver are not very important in an agricultural economy. The income that farmers do not spend for consumption is reinvested in their farms. In other words, self-use of saving is primary. Wage earners have no businesses in which to reinvest their savings. Instead, the savings of wage earners serve as a cushion to absorb loss of income during periods of unemployment.

The early commercial banks did not provide saving facilities, and small savers generally entrusted their savings with someone who had a strongbox. This type of saving was very risky for the individual and detrimental to the economy. If saving is placed in strongboxes, the total flow of spending is adversely affected. The saving that flows into financial intermediaries is not put in vaults; rather it is invested in the capital markets. The creation of specialized thrift and saving institutions was good for wage earners, good for the communities, and good for the economy.

The basic ideas underlying the organization and operation of specialized saving and thrift institutions originated in the countries that had first faced the problems associated with industrialization. The first mutual savings bank was established in Scotland in 1810, and the idea spread rapidly throughout Scotland and England. In 1817, Parliament adopted a measure legalizing savings banking in England. Word of the new savings banks spread to America, and in 1816 mutual savings banks were established in Philadelphia and Boston. The basic idea or philosophy of mutual savings banking is reflected in the charter of the Philadelphia Saving Fund Society, which was the first mutual savings bank established in the United States. Among other things, the charter stated that the bank was "established for the sole purpose of receiving and investing . . . . such small sums as may be saved from the earnings of tradesmen, mechanics, laborers, servants, and others, and of affording to industrious persons the advantages of security and interest."

The incorporators of mutual savings banks were not motivated by profit. The financial returns on the assets of mutual savings banks, after deducting operating expenses, inure wholly to the benefit of the mutual savings banks' depositors. For the most part, the incorporators of mutual savings banks were public-spirited men who sought to improve their communities' saving facilities. It should also be remembered that the incorporation of financial institutions creates the need for managers, which also provided motivation.

The deplorable housing conditions in factory towns inspired a strong desire among many wage earners to get out of the overcrowded tenements and into their own homes. The financial institutions that prevailed in the early 1800's failed to provide adequate real estate financing for wage earners. Commercial banks provided neither saving facilities nor home financing. Mutual savings banks provided saving facilities, but did not grant home loans to wage earners.

Wage earners in England had faced similar problems and they responded by establishing "building societies" to accept savings of wage earners and to finance their purchase of homes. The basic idea of the early "building societies" was to collect weekly sums from shareholders, and when sufficient amounts were accumulated, to allow members of the societies the privilege of bidding for funds to finance their homes.

The first such institution established in the United States was the Oxford Provident Building Association, which was established in 1831 in the Philadelphia area. Within a few years building societies were established in many other communities. The institutions are now known generally as savings and loan associations, and they operate in every state.

Mutual savings banks provided saving facilities for wage earners, but did not loan funds to them. Savings and loan associations provided saving facilities, but restricted loans to real estate financing. A serious gap remained. Wage earners required personal loans as well as real estate loans. The credit union introduced cooperative credit in the form of personal loans. Credit union members provided the major source of loanable funds.

As with other institutions discussed in this section, the basic idea underlying the credit union became widespread in the countries of Europe. Credit unions were especially popular in Germany and Italy, and it was not until the idea had spread to India and Canada that the first credit union was established in the United States in the early 1900's. In 1909, Massachusetts formalized the cooperative credit associations by passing the first credit union law. A credit union restricts its membership to persons who have a common bond of interest. The flow of saving into credit unions is evidenced by shares, similar to those issued by savings and loan associations.

One of the strong backers of the credit union movement in the United States was Mr. Edward A. Filene, a prominent Boston merchant. In 1921, Filene financed the establishment of a Credit Union National Extension Bureau to get credit union laws enacted and to promote the creation of credit unions. Now there is a nation wide system of credit unions.

The term "industrial bank" refers to institutions that operate under various corporate titles, such as: industrial banks, industrial loan companies, industrial savings and loan companies, finance and thrift companies, discount companies, and Morris Plan banks. These institutions were developed to serve the same need as credit unions, i.e., to provide a source of funds for consumer loans. They are similar to savings and loan associations and credit unions in that consumer saving is their major source of funds.

Industrial banks were patterned after similar institutions that had been developed in Europe. The first such institution was established in the United States in 1901. Later, in 1910, Arthur J. Morris established an institution of this type in Virginia and actively promoted the creation of similar institutions in many other states.

There is considerable diversity among state laws pertaining to this type of financial institution. Some states have industrial bank laws that give these institutions bank status and permit them to use the word "deposits." Many other states have industrial loan laws that neither recognize them as banks nor permit them to call their savings accounts "deposits." In these states, industrial loan companies sell investment certificates on the installment plan and pay interest on the certificates. In the absence of specific laws, industrial banks or similar financial institutions are incorporated under either general corporation laws or general banking statutes.

In comparison with the other institutions discussed in this section, industrial banks are relatively unimportant in the aggregate. Federal Reserve authorities no longer report separate data for industrial banks.

Congress established the Postal Savings System in 1910. The weakness of many of the state-chartered commercial banks, the specialized character of savings and loan associations, and the failure of mutual savings banks to expand outside the New England and Middle Atlantic seaboard states prompted Congress to act in the national interest of the small saver.

Inasmuch as the postal system was widely dispersed throughout the country, it was a simple matter to establish a national system of saving through the existing post-office facilities. Since Congress was creating saving facilities in direct competition with private financial institutions, it established a relatively low rate of interest on postal savings and made provision for the redeposit of funds in local banks. At the time the Postal Savings System was established it tended to close a gap in our financial system. Today, however, the need for postal savings is very much in doubt. The recent downward trend in the level of such savings deposits reflects this decline.

United States savings bonds were not introduced until the mid-1930's. The bonds were introduced to absorb and activate idle cash balances held by consumers, to encourage additional savings, and to secure a wider distribution of the Federal debt. The securities were tailored to fit the investment requirements of small investors.

The ultimate investment of the savings that flow into fixed-value redeemable claims become the responsibility of financial intermediaries. Only in the cases of highly specialized financial intermediaries, such as the savings and loan associations, are individuals reasonably certain of the manner in which their savings will ultimately be invested. If the saving flows into savings and loan associations, the funds will probably be invested in residential mortgages. The variety of investment available to other financial intermediaries is so great that individuals cannot be certain of the ultimate investment of their savings. As a matter of fact, very few consumers either know or concern themselves with the investment policies of financial intermediaries. They know only that the institutions are subject to rules and regulations that should ensure both safety and liquidity of their claims. The final allocation of such savings depends on the relative proportions flowing into the various institutions and the investment decisions of these institutions.

In some communities nearly all the financial institutions mentioned above compete for consumer saving and investment. To a lesser extent, they also· compete in the lending and investing of funds. The competition has now reached a point at which the institutions are becoming or are attempting to become more like each other. As noted above, many industrial banks are now considered part of the commercial banking system. Mutual savings banks are striving for greater flexibility and more lending power with respect to home financing. Savings and loan associations are striving for more flexibility of investment power so that they may continue to invest consumer saving even when housing demand is not strong. Gradually, mutual savings banks and savings and loan associations are developing similar characteristics, and perhaps in time there will be a single national system of savings institutions. One suggested means to accomplish this objective is to introduce a Federal charter for mutual savings banking, which would be attractive to both state-chartered mutual savings banks and Federal and state-chartered savings and loan associations. Some institutions, such as credit unions and industrial loan companies, would probably remain outside such a national savings system.

SAVING THROUGH LIFE INSURANCE AND PENSIONS. The annual saving through life insurance and pension funds is approaching $10 billion. In the recession year of 1954, saving through life insurance and pensions was only $2 billion less than that through fixed-value redeemable claims. In 1958, the gap between the two was slightly less than $4 billion. However, in the not-too-distant future, saving through life insurance and pensions will probably exceed that in the form of fixed-value redeemable claims.

The accumulation of funds to meet the contingenices of death, disability, and retirement represents one of the most rapidly growing forms of consumer saving. The need to provide protection against premature death and disability is continuous, and protection against loss of income during retirement requires long-range planning. Protection against all of these contingencies is provided through group and individual programs. An important characteristic of saving through life insurance and pensions is that much of it is of a contractual nature. Individuals may allow life insurance policies to lapse, but the decision is difficult, for many persons regard life insurance premiums as obligations. Group retirement plans are highly formalized and the contributions are of a contractual nature.

Just as with the group of institutions issuing fixed-value redeemable claims, there is also considerable diversity among the institutions receiving saving through life insurance and pensions. Saving through life insurance and insured pension plans is invested in credit and market instruments by life insurance companies. The saving through private non-insured pensions is invested in credit and equity market instruments by trust departments of commercial banks and by specialized trust institutions. The saving through government pensions is invested by government agencies or boards. The ultimate investment of the saving through life insurance and pensions is directly related to the laws, regulations, and investment policies of these various institutions and the relative proportions of such saving that each type of institution receives.

The protracted rise in the price level has had considerable influence on both the flow and the management of saving related to insurance, annuities, and pensions. Saving through life insurance has lost some of its appeal. Non-insured pension plans have become more important than insured pension plans. Trustees of the non-insured plans have followed more aggressive investment policies than life insurance companies. In the long run, the more aggressive investment policies should lead to higher investment returns. From the point of view of both the employers and employees, this result is desirable.

CREDIT AND EQUITY MARKET INSTRUMENTS. In 1958, the consumer and nonprofit organization sector's net acquisition of credit and equity market instruments amounted to only $3 billion. This total was considerably less than net acquisitions in the three previous years. In 1955, 1956, and 1957, such acquisitions totalled respectively $8.0, $7.9, and $9.7 billion. The low total in 1958 reflects the effects of the 1958 recession. An even greater contraction occurred in 1954, during which year the sector's net acquisitions were less than $1 billion.

Credit market instruments consist of Federal obligations, state and local obligations, corporate and foreign bonds, and mortgages; equity market instruments consist of corporate stock. Generally, the prospect of greater financial returns prompts consumers and nonprofit organizations to invest part of their funds directly into credit and equity market instruments. Generally, not more than one-third of the sector's net acquisitions of credit and equity market instruments is in the form of corporate stock, and most of this total represents the acquisition of investment companies' shares. Investment companies combine the investments of many investors by selling their own securities, and the companies reinvest the funds in other credit and equity market instruments. The rationale behind investment companies is that they offer diversification and professional management to small investors. They enable small investors to minimize risks associated with market instruments, particularly equity market instruments. Since investment companies' shares are such an important investment medium and the investment company industry is so complex, all of Chapter 13 is devoted to investment companies.

In addition to the role played by investment companies, other financial institutions perform many functions relating to the acquisition of credit and equity market instruments. Financial institutions assist investors in formulating investment policies; they conduct studies to determine the investment quality of individual securities; and they create securities markets. Many functions are performed by the securities markets, including the valuation of securities, issuance of new securities, and trading in outstanding securities. The structure and operation of broker-dealer firms, investment banking firms, and securities markets are discussed in later chapters.

NET INVESTMENT IN NON-CORPORATE BUSINESS. The flow-of-funds treatment of net investment in non-corporate business was discussed in the early part of the chapter, where it was pointed out that it is assumed that net income of unincorporated business is completely withdrawn by proprietors and constitutes part of the consumer and nonprofit organization sector's current receipts. Whether or not this condition leads to consumer saving depends on other factors. As pointed out earlier, if the acquisition by unincorporated businesses of tangible and financial assets exceeds their capital consumption charges and their increase in liabilities, then the proprietors will have made a net investment in non-corporate businesses. In 1958, the opposite was true, and so Table 7-2 shows a negative net investment of $5.5 billion.

NET INCREASE IN LIABILITIES. During a given accounting period, there are continuous but changing flows of debt repayment and debt expansion. During 1958, there was a net increase of $12.1 billion in the liabilities of the consumer and nonprofit organization sector. Some consumers increase their holdings of financial assets during the same period in which they increase their liabilities. For example, security credit is used to finance the acquisition of securities. Some consumers borrow against their life insurance policies, and save at the same time through life insurance. Mortgage and consumer credit are directly related to investment in tangible assets, for most consumers use credit to finance the purchases of durable consumer goods and family housing. It might also be noted that repayment of liabilities represents a form of saving from the point of view of the individual consumer unit. A consumer's debt pattern is probably one of the more important factors determining the consumer's level and pattern of saving.

SYSTEMATIC FINANCIAL INVESTMENT

Various types of plans have been developed to encourage systematic financial investment. Payroll savings plans have been developed to encourage systematic investment in United States savings bonds and equity market instruments. Almost all of the financial institutions issuing fixed-value redeemable claims have introduced systematic methods of saving. Much of the saving through life insurance and pensions is systematic. Most of the liabilities of the consumer and nonprofit organization sector require periodic repayment. These plans tend to create greater over-all stability in consumer saving and investment.

Payroll Savings Plans

The payroll savings plan for investment in United States savings bonds is the most widespread plan for systematic investment. During World War II the Federal Government secured the assistance of employers to promote the sale of United States savings bonds through regular payroll deductions. Many of the plans have been continued. In 1960 nearly 45,000 separate businesses operated and managed payroll savings plans for the benefit of their employees as a public service without charge, and more than eight million persons employed in industry and government were signed up on the payroll savings plan. Experience has shown that the payroll savings plan is the most effective method of channeling regular systematic savings into the Series E savings bonds. Campaigns are carried on throughout the country to enlarge the number of plans and participants.

Some larger businesses have supplemented payroll savings plans for investment in savings bonds with plans to promote investment in common stock. The plans of Dupont and General Electric are cited as examples.* Under the Dupont plan, which is entirely voluntary and is available to employees with two years or more of service, the employees specify monthly payroll deductions of not less than $12.50 or more than $37.50 for the purchase of Series E savings bonds. For every dollar thus deducted, Dupont pays to a trustee 25 cents. The trustee buys Dupont stock for the employees' accounts and applies dividends to the purchase of additional stock. To obtain sustained savings, restrictions are imposed on premature redemption of savings bonds.

Under the General Electric plan, the company may be authorized by employees to deduct up to 6 per cent of their wages, and the company matches the deductions in the amount of 50 per cent. At least one-third of the combined amount is invested in Series E savings bonds and the remainder may be invested at the discretion of employees in either General Electric stock or additional savings bonds.

Some corporations do not want to encourage their employees to buy company stock. Rather, they want employees to have the freedom to invest in stocks of their own choosing. Therefore, some corporations have combined payroll deduction savings plans with the monthly investment plan operated by member firms of the New York Stock Exchange. Through this device, the employers shift the function of selection of investment media to employees and broker-dealer houses that specialize in investments.

Monthly Investment Plan

Member broker-dealer firms of the New York Stock Exchange provide a Monthly Investment Plan, which is designed to encourage the public to invest in securities that are listed on the New York Stock Exchange. The plan permits an individual to invest monthly or quarterly any amount from $40 to $999. Money is paid to a broker-dealer firm, which credits to the individual's account a certain number or fraction of shares of a specified stock. The plan may also be set up so that dividends received are automatically reinvested in the same securities. The individual may quit the plan, sell the stock accumulated under the plan, and skip some of the regular payments. A broker-dealer firm does reserve the right to terminate

*For a description of the American Telephone and Telegraph Company's payroll deduction plan see the monthly publication of the New York Stock Exchange, The Exchange, July 1960, pp. 10-13.

the account. Therefore, if there were excessive skipping, the option to terminate the account might be exercised.

The Monthly Investment Plan came into existence on January 25, 1954, and is now a well-established institution. The New York Stock Exchange summarized the first five years as follows:*

> Some 163,000 MIP plans were started. Of these 82,400 have been completed or terminated and 80,600 are still in force.
>
> Shares purchased aggregate 2,850,000, and the amount of money invested totals $112,600,000.
>
> More than 87 per cent of all plans now in effect call for reinvestment of all dividend income.
>
> MIP has enjoyed steady growth in its short history.
>
> Shares purchased in 1954 amounted to 300,504, from which point annual purchases rose to 402,937 in 1955; to 535,090 in 1956; to 754,596 in 1957 and to 797,339 in 1958.

The analysis of stocks acquired under M.I.P. indicates that investors have a decided preference for common stocks of well-known, long-established corporations whose reputations and products or services are well and favorably known.

Mutual Fund Plans

Open-end investment companies, also referred to as mutual funds, have developed various plans relating to systematic investment. Many mutual funds provide for the automatic investment of all dividends, immediately upon payment. As with the M.I.P., small amounts are not disregarded, for funds can be invested to the last penny in fractional shares.

Mutual funds have also developed accumulation plans under which the public can invest small amounts regularly from its current income. Broker-dealer firms and mutual funds have been successful in developing and promoting the idea of "budgeted investing." About one-fifth of all persons holding mutual fund shares invest under some form of an accumulation plan. In 1958, over 500,000 shareholder accounts for the regular purchase of mutual fund shares were on the books of investment companies. In recent years, the accounts have been growing at the rate of about 12,000 per month. Annual payments into accumulation plan accounts have been in excess of $250 million. The various types of plans that are used to promote systematic investment in mutual funds shares are discussed in the chapter that deals specifically with investment companies.

Life Insurance

Almost all life insurance is paid for by level premium payments rather than by single lump-sum payments. Level premium payment plans make it possible to sell larger face-value policies, which, in turn, provide greater dollar

*The Exchange, March 1959, p. 11.

protection to insureds and higher dollar commissions to insurance salesmen. One cannot wait to buy insurance until he accumulates a large lump sum, for he may die in the interim. Also, the period of saving may be so long that he will not need life insurance protection at the end of the period. Level premium insurance provides built-in budgeting for the insured.

Other Plans

Time deposits and savings shares are also built up through systematic investment. Many consumers who have mortgage loans outstanding from financial institutions make periodic investments with these financial institutions to cover property taxes. As noted in the discussion of industrial banks some consumers accumulate deposits and shares, or both, for payment of personal loans. Many of the institutions provide Christmas Club and similar accounts. In all instances, the saver is encouraged to invest funds with the institutions on a regular basis.

Payments Toward Liabilities

Most of the outstanding consumer debt is of the installment type, which means that the debt is reduced by periodic repayments. Generally, payments are made monthly. Almost all the outstanding mortgage debt is amortized, which means that it is reduced by periodic repayments, usually monthly. With respect to the repayment of mortgage debt, the monthly payment is uniform, but with the passage of time, the proportion that represents repayment of principal gets larger and larger. The practice of periodic debt repayment tends to establish habit patterns in consumer saving and investment. In many instances, consumers continue to save and invest regularly following elimination of installment debt.

SHIFTS IN CONSUMER SAVINGS AND INVESTMENT

Long-Run

Before commenting on the long-run shifts in consumer saving and investment, some observations on the secular trend in volume and composition of national saving are appropriate.* Adjusting 1897-1949 saving data for changes in the price level and population growth, the annual rate of growth in national saving averaged about 1.75 per cent, which was about the same as that of the previous century. During the same period, neither the ratio of consumer saving to total national saving nor the ratio of consumer saving to consumer income after taxes showed a marked trend either upward or downward.

*Raymond W. Goldsmith, A Study of Saving in the United States, Vols. I-III, Princeton University Press, 1955. The comments in this section are based on findings that are reported in Volume I.

During the first half of this century, marked shifts occurred in the structure of personal saving and investment. Dr. Goldsmith has observed that except for the two wars and the Great Depression, the shifts were "characterized by a considerable increase in the share of saving through consumer durables, life insurance, and pension and retirement funds, and by a decline in the share of saving through corporate stocks and bonds, mortgages, and real estate. The shares of relatively illiquid forms of saving, of contractual saving, and of saving through financial intermediaries . . . . [showed] an increasing trend. Saving transferred directly from savers to ultimate users of funds, primarily in the form of purchases of securities and mortgages . . . . [showed] a tendency to decline in relative importance. The share of saving to be used in the saver's own household or business . . . . [did not change] significantly."*

Short-Run

In the short run, there are marked shifts in the leval and structure of national saving. To illustrate the degree of variability, it can be noted that during the first half of this century, one year's national saving was in at least one-half of the cases 50 per cent higher or lower than that of the preceding or the following year. The ratio of consumer saving to disposable income also showed considerable variation. The ratio tended to rise during periods of prosperity and tended to fall during periods of depression. To illustrate some of the sharper declines, the ratio declined from 20 per cent in 1918 to only two per cent in 1921. Between 1929 and 1932, the ratio declined from a positive 14 per cent to a minus 8 per cent. The ratio during "normal periods" was about one-ninth or about 11 per cent.

Although consumers have many rational saving motives, the most important factor influencing shifts in consumer saving is change in current income. Almost all consumers have strong motivations to save, but first they must feed and clothe themselves and their dependents. They must subsist. Eventually, a consumer's income reaches a level that permits some saving to occur, but when that income falls, the level of saving will have to be adjusted to the new conditions. Dr. Goldsmith reports that "variations in current income alone account for more than two-thirds of the year-to-year changes in current personal saving (consumer saving) for the entire period, 1897-1949." † Much of saving is of a residual nature; it depends primarily upon the level of employment, income, and output, and the state of expectations as to future employment, income, and output.

To illustrate the effect of business conditions on the level and structure of consumer saving and investment, 1957 and 1958 quarterly financial data of the consumer and nonprofit organization sector are briefly analyzed. (See Table 7-3.) A rather sharp but short-lived recession occurred during

*Ibid., p.10.
† Ibid., p.12.

1957-1958; the downturn occurred in the summer of 1957, and ended in the spring of 1958. Consumers' net saving was $1 billion less in the first quarter of 1958 than it was in the first quarter of 1957; it was $2 billion less in the second quarter of 1958 than it was in the second quarter of 1957. Consumers' net saving in the fourth quarter of 1958 exceeded that of the fourth quarter of 1957.

The level of capital expenditures in each of the first two quarters of 1958 was about $200 million less than that in the corresponding quarters of 1957. These changes are relatively small and reflect the strong upward trend in housing construction that prevailed throughout 1957 and 1958. Capital expenditures on consumer durable goods were affected much more; quarterly expenditures were down by about $1 billion in each of the first two quarters in 1958. Capital expenditures for consumer durable goods during the first quarter of 1959 were up considerably. The plant and equipment expenditures of nonprofit organizations evidently were not affected by the recession.

The structure of consumer financial investment also underwent considerable change during the recession. Comparing the first two quarters of 1957 and 1958, the following observations can be made: net consumer investment in time deposits and savings shares increased; net liquidation of United States savings bonds slowed down; saving through life insurance and pension funds increased; net consumer investment in credit and equity market instruments fell off very sharply; and the net increase in consumer liabilities was down. The changes in liabilities were not uniform. The increase in mortgage liabilities in 1958 was nearly the same as that in 1957, reflecting the continuation of residential construction. A strong recovery in residential construction had started in 1957, and its momentum was sufficient to withstand the negative effects of the short-lived 1957-1958 recession.

During the first quarter of 1958, consumers reduced their credit liabilities by $2.3 billion, nearly twice the size of the reduction in the first quarter of 1957. Although consumers increased their credit liabilities in the second quarter of 1958, the increase was $1 billion less than the increase that occurred in the second quarter of 1957. The changes in consumer credit liabilities were directly related to the reduction in capital expenditures in durable consumer goods. Security credit increased $1.2 billion during the first half of 1958, compared with a $100 million increase in the first half of 1957. Expectations with respect to future changes in the level of interest rates and corporate stock prices prompted some consumers to borrow heavily to finance speculative transactions in credit and equity market instruments.

On the basis of these limited observations, a few tentative conclusions may be drawn. During a downturn, consumers' capital expenditures and investment in credit and equity market instruments are adversely affected. Once a recession sets in, existing durable goods and family residences are made to last longer. Consumers tend to postpone some of their previously

TABLE 7–3
CONSUMER AND NONPROFIT ORGANIZATION SECTOR'S SAVING
AND INVESTMENT, FIRST QUARTER, 1957 THROUGH FIRST QUARTER, 1959
(BILLIONS OF DOLLARS)

Category	Quarterly totals								
	1957				1958				1959
	1	2	3	4	1	2	3	4	1
Net saving	7.6	6.4	8.4	5.3	6.6	4.4	8.0	6.0	8.2
Gross saving	17.4	16.3	18.4	15.5	16.9	14.8	18.5	16.5	18.7
Gross investment	18.2	14.9	18.4	18.0	17.4	12.3	18.5	19.0	18.6
Capital expend. (net of sales)	13.7	14.2	14.3	16.2	12.7	13.1	13.4	16.6	14.5
Residential construction	3.8	3.3	3.8	4.0	3.6	3.1	3.6	4.3	4.3
Consumer durable goods	9.2	10.1	9.7	11.3	8.3	9.1	8.8	11.4	9.4
Plant and equip. (nonprofit)	.7	.8	.9	.9	.8	.8	.9	.9	.9
Net financial investment	4.5	.7	4.0	1.7	4.7	—.7	5.1	2.4	4.1
Net acquis. of finan. assets [1]	5.9	4.8	6.8	5.4	5.1	3.1	7.0	8.3	6.6
Currency and demand deposits	—2.5	—.6	1.0	1.3	—1.3	—.8	2.4	2.2	—1.3
Fixed-value redeem. claims	2.6	2.9	1.4	2.9	3.3	3.7	3.0	3.6	2.3
Time deposits	2.2	1.6	1.3	1.4	2.1	2.0	2.1	1.5	1.1
Savings shares	1.0	1.8	.6	1.8	1.3	1.8	1.0	2.3	1.4
U. S. savings bonds [2]	—.6	—.5	—.5	—.4	—.1	—.1	—.2	—.2	—.2
Saving through life insurance	.7	.7	.7	.7	.8	.7	.9	1.0	.8
Saving through pension funds	1.5	1.6	1.3	1.5	1.8	1.4	1.6	1.7	1.6
Credit and equity mkt. instr. [3]	4.7	1.3	3.5	.2	2.0	—.6	.5	1.1	4.5
Federal obligations	2.2	—.3	1.5	—1.0	—.3	—1.6	—1.1	.2	2.6
State and local obligations	.8	.3	.8	.4	.7	—.2	.6	.4	.6
Corporate and foreign bonds	.6	.2	.6	—.3	.8	—.3	*	—.1	—.1
Corporate stock	.5	.6	.1	.5	.3	.8	.4	.2	.5
Mortgages	.6	.6	.5	.5	.3	.6	.5	.4	.8
Net invest. in noncorp. bus.	—1.1	—1.1	—1.1	—1.1	—1.4	—1.4	—1.4	—1.4	—1.4
Net increase in liabilities	1.4	4.1	2.7	3.6	.4	3.9	1.9	5.9	2.5
Mortgages [4]	2.6	2.0	2.1	2.1	2.3	2.1	2.5	3.2	3.0
Consumer credit	—1.2	1.6	.7	1.6	—2.3	.6	.1	1.9	—.9
Security credit	—.2	.3	—.2	—.3	.2	.9	—.9	.5	.2
Other [5]	.2	.2	.2	.2	.3	.2	.2	.2	.2
Discrepancy	—.9	1.4	.1	—2.4	—.5	2.5	*	—2.5	.1

*Less than $50 million.
[1] Includes miscellaneous deposits with Federal Government not shown separately.
[2] Includes net accruals of interest.
[3] Includes net free credit balances with brokers not shown separately.
[4] Mainly consumer debt on one- to four-family properties.
[5] For consumers, loans on insurance policies; for nonprofit organizations, bank loans, loans from government, and trade debt.

Source: "A Quarterly Presentation of Flow of Funds, Saving and Investment," *Federal Reserve Bulletin*, August 1959.

planned capital expenditures, and the flow of credit extensions is reduced. The level of consumer credit liabilities declines because the rate of repayments on previous purchases is greater than the rate of new credit extensions. The postponement of capital expenditures has a direct impact upon the rate of redemption of fixed-value redeemable claims. For example, the change in the level of savings deposits depends on the relationship between new deposits and deposit withdrawals. If the rate of deposit withdrawals falls off and is not offset by a corresponding reduction in the rate of new deposits, then the rate of increase in net deposits will rise. The same basic relationship underlies the net change in the value of savings shares and United States savings bonds. During the first two quarters of 1958, there was a reduction in the rate of redemption of fixed-value redeemable claims, resulting in larger quarterly net increases in the volume of fixed-value redeemable claims.

The reduction in net acquisition of credit and equity market instruments reflects the uncertainty that accompanies a business downturn. The lower level of interest rates that prevailed during the recession made investment in credit market instruments less attractive. During the first two quarters of 1957, consumers' net acquisitions of credit and equity market instruments exceeded $6 billion, but during the corresponding quarters in 1958, consumers acquired only $1.4 billion of such instruments. A rather abrupt change also occurred in the net acquisitions of state and local obligations. Consumers liquidated such obligations in each of the first three quarters of 1958, compared with net acquisitions of $3.4 billion during the corresponding period in 1957. The net acquisitions of corporate and foreign bonds were also down in 1958. Only net acquisitions of corporate stock deviated from this over-all pattern. Consumers' net acquisitions of stock were down slightly in the first quarter of 1958 compared with the first quarter of 1957, but the pattern was reversed in the second quarter. During this recession, the stock market was a lead factor, that is, the market turned upward prior to general recovery. Investors believed that recovery was near and invested in corporate stock during the bottom of the recession to realize capital gains in the expected rising market.

LEVEL AND COMPOSITION
OF ASSETS AND LIABILITIES

Before considering in detail the various forms of consumer investment, it is appropriate to present very briefly the level and composition of the sector's holdings of financial assets and liabilities. The data are summarized in Table 7-4.

The sector's financial assets are about five times larger than the sector's total liabilities. If the data included the value of the sector's physical assets as well as the proprietors' net investment in non-corporate business for which no amount outstanding is available, the net worth position of the sector would be much larger. Corporate stock is the sector's most important financial asset, accounting for nearly 45 per cent of the total. The major portion of such value reflects the effects of rising stock prices rather than

TABLE 7–4
CONSUMER AND NONPROFIT ORGANIZATIONS SECTOR'S HOLDINGS
OF FINANCIAL ASSETS AND LIABILITIES, END OF 1958
(BILLIONS OF DOLLARS)

Category	Dollars	Per cent
Total financial assets [1]	867.9	100.0
Currency and demand deposits	60.9	7.0
Consumers	56.7	6.5
Nonprofit organizations	4.2	.5
Fixed-value redeemable claims	191.0	22.0
Time deposits	92.1	10.6
Savings and loan association shares	47.3	5.4
Credit union shares	3.8	.4
U. S. savings bonds	47.7	5.5
Savings in life insurance	83.4	9.6
Private	77.2	8.9
Government	6.2	.7
Savings in pension funds	64.8	7.5
Private	36.8	4.2
Government	28.0	3.2
Credit and equity market instruments	467.5	53.9
Federal obligations	16.4	1.9
Direct and guaranteed	14.9	1.7
Nonguaranteed	1.6	.2
State and local obligations	25.4	2.9
Corporate and foreign bonds	9.6	1.1
Corporate stock [2]	386.8	44.6
1- to 4-family mortgages	11.3	1.3
Other mortgages	16.6	1.9
Security credit	1.4	.2
Total liabilities	171.4	100.0
Credit market instruments	169.6	98.9
1- to 4-family mortgages	111.3	64.9
Other mortgages (nonprofit)	.9	.5
Consumer credit	45.1	26.3
Security credit	5.5	3.2
Bank loans, n.e.c. (nonprofit)	2.0	1.2
Other loans [3]	4.8	2.8
Trade credit (nonprofit)	1.8	1.1

Note: Details may not add to totals because of rounding.

[1] Includes miscellaneous deposits with Federal Government not shown separately; excludes proprietors' net investment in noncorporate business for which no amount outstanding is available.

[2] At estimated market price.

[3] Predominantly loans on insurance policies.

Source: "A Quarterly Presentation of Flow of Funds, Saving and Investment," *Federal Reserve Bulletin*, August 1959.

large annual net acquisitions of corporate stock. The sector's holdings of currency and demand deposits and fixed-value redeemable claims are three times larger than the sector's holdings of credit market instruments, indicating the importance that consumers attach to dollar safety and convenience.

The tremendous importance of savings in life insurance and pension funds is clearly revealed in the data. These forms of saving totaled nearly $150 million at the end of 1958, a figure not much lower than the sector's investment in fixed-value redeemable claims.

With respect to the sector's holdings of credit market instruments, mortgages and state and local obligations are the two most important instruments. Mortgage investment incorporates periodic repayment of principal as well as a flow of investment income. These features plus the relative attractiveness of mortgage yields account for the importance of mortgages in the sector's holdings of financial assets. State and local obligations are attractive because their income is exempt from the Federal personal income tax.

The data show that the sector's liabilities are concentrated in one to four-family mortgages and consumer credit. These two liabilities account for over 90 per cent of total liabilities, and reflect the need of consumers to finance capital expenditures.

The basic outline for the remainder of Part 3 follows very closely the order of listing in Table 7-4.

QUESTIONS

1. How are consumer saving and consumer investments defined in the Federal Reserve system's flow-of-funds accounts?

2. What criterion is used to determine whether a nonfinancial transaction is investment or not? Demonstrate the application of the criterion.

3. "Although much of consumer financial investment cancels out in calculating national investment, it should not be assumed that consumer financial investment is unimportant." Why not?

4. Illustrate two arbitrary decisions affecting the level and composition of consumer saving and investment.

5. What are the conceptual differences between consumer saving and investment in the flow-of-funds accounts and the United States Department of Commerce national income and product accounts?

6. Summarize briefly the development of intermediaries that provide fixed-value redeemable claims.

7. Compile a list of the many forms of consumer financial investment, and indicate which two are the most impotrant.

8. Summarize briefly systematic financial investment plans.

9. During the first half of this century, what changes occurred in the volume and composition of national saving? What shifts occurred in the structure of consumer investment?

10. What effects did the 1957-1958 recession have on the level and structure of consumer saving and investment?

11. In round figures, what is the magnitude of the consumer and nonprofit organization sector's holdings of financial assets and liabilities?

ADDITIONAL READING

Bigelow, Howard F. *Family Finance*. (Rev. ed.) Philadelphia: J. B. Lippincott Co., 1953.

Bradley, Joseph F., and Ralph H. Wherry. *Personal and Family Finance*. New York: Holt, Rinehart, and Winston, Inc., 1957.

Donaldson, Elvin F. *Personal Finance*. (2nd ed.) New York: The Ronald Press Co., 1956.

Friend, Irwin, with the assistance of Vito Natrella. *Individuals' Saving: Volume and Composition*. New York: John Wiley & Sons, Inc., 1954.

Hanson, A. W., and J. B. Cohen. *Personal Finance*. Homewood, Ill.: Richard D. Irwin, Inc., 1954.

Heller, W. W., F. M. Boddy, and C. L. Nelson (eds.). *Savings in the Modern Economy — A Symposium*. Minneapolis: University of Minnesota Press, 1953.

Jordan, David F., and Edward F. Willet. *Managing Personal Finances*. (3rd ed.) Englewood Cliffs, N. J.: Prentice-Hall, Inc., 1951.

Ketchum, Marshall D., and Leon T. Kendall (co-editors). *Conference on Savings and Residential Financing*, Sponsored by the United States Savings and Loan League. This conference was inaugurated in 1958, and many of the topics covered in the 1958 and 1959 conferences relate to material presented in Chap. 7. In the 1958 conference, Raymond W. Goldsmith discussed "The Supply of Saving"; Jules I. Bogen, "Trends in the Institutionalization of Savings"; and a panel considered the topic, "Inter-Institutional Competition in the Supply of Funds for Residential Housing." In the 1959 conference John G. Gurley and Ezra Solomon discussed the topic "Financial Institutions in the Saving-Investment Process."

Lasser, J. K., and Sylvia F. Porter. *Managing Your Money*. New York: Holt, Rinehart, and Winston, Inc., 1953.

Morgan, James N., *Consumer Economics*. Englewood Cliffs, N. J.: Prentice-Hall, Inc., 1955.

Troelstrup, A. W. *Consumer Problems*. New York: McGraw-Hill Book Co., Inc., 1957.

Current saving estimates may be obtained from the following: Flow-of-funds saving data are reported regularly in the monthly issues of the *Federal Reserve Bulletin*; the Annual Surveys of Consumer Finances provide comprehensive data on the financial position of the consumer and results are reported in various issues of the *Federal Reserve Bulletin*; the volume and composition of individuals' saving are reported by the Securities and Exchange Commission in both their *Statistical Series* and *Statistical Bulletins*; personal saving estimates of the Department of Commerce are reported in the monthly issues of the *Survey of Current Business*; a complete reconciliation of the Securities and Exchange Commission and Commerce Department series appears annually in the July issue of the *Survey of Current Business* and the July issue of the *Statistical Bulletin*.

8: Time deposits, postal savings deposits, and United States savings bonds

![G]IVEN the broad framework within which savings and insurance institutions operate, we shall examine in this and the following three chapters the structure and operation of commercial banks as they pertain to "time deposits," mutual savings banks, the Postal Savings System, United States savings bonds, savings and loan associations, credit unions, industrial loan companies, insurance companies, and trust institutions as they relate to pension and retirement plans. The numerous services provided by these financial institutions are useful to business and governments as well as to consumers.

COMMERCIAL BANKS

Individuals, business, and governments make deposits for a variety of reasons. To attract the maximum volume of deposits, commercial banks, acting in their own self-interest, have offered the public various types of deposit accounts: demand deposits, savings deposits, time deposits, and time certificates. In commercial banking statistics the term "time deposits" refers to all deposits other than demand deposits. Deposits that are legally withdrawable on demand and against which checks may be drawn are referred to as demand deposits. They are used as working balances and account for approximately 70 per cent of total deposits in commercial banks. Checks cannot be drawn against time deposits; they must first be converted into either currency and demand deposits. Although only 30 per cent of total deposits in commercial banks are time deposits, they represent a very important share of total fixed-value redeemable claims because of the size of the total deposits in commercial banks.

During the period that commercial banks added time deposits to their banking services, other banks, such as mutual savings banks, stock savings banks, and industrial banks were in the process of development. Mutual savings banks have remained separate from commercial banks. Stock savings banks were organized as savings institutions, owned by stockholders and operated for profit. Gradually, they added commercial banking services with the result that they have become virtually indistinguishable from commercial banks. It should be noted that statistics on time deposits in commercial banks include the deposits in stock savings banks and some industrial banks. The title of a financial institution may not reveal its nature and operation, especially in commercial banking.

Nature of Time Deposits

To open a savings account at a commercial bank, the bank issues to the savings depositor a savings passbook in which deposits, withdrawals, and interest earnings are recorded. Commercial banks reserve the right to require a waiting period of 30 to 60 days prior to honoring withdrawals from savings accounts. In practice, commercial banks rarely invoke the requirement, with the result that some savings depositors make frequent withdrawals. Commercial banks also accept time deposits and issue time certificates. A time deposit is an open-account deposit that is made on the basis of a contract between the depositor and the bank to the effect that the deposit will not be withdrawn prior to a certain date. A time certificate is issued as evidence of the receipt of funds that are to be held by the bank for a stated period of time. The rate of interest paid on time deposits and time certificates depends on the length of time they are to be held: 30 to 90 days, 90 days to 6 months, and 6 months and over. The rates that were in effect in 1959 are listed in the next section. Savings deposits are designed mostly for consumers, while time deposits and time certificates are designed for business and government. Approximately three-fourths of total time deposits are in the form of savings deposits.

Payment of Interest on "Time Deposits"

Prior to Federal legislation in the middle 1930's, commercial banks paid interest on all types of deposits. Since the legislation was passed, member banks and insured banks have not been permitted to pay interest on demand deposits, and the Federal Reserve Board and Federal Deposit Insurance Corporation have been empowered to regulate the maximum rates of interest paid on time deposits. Permissible top rates were established January 1, 1936 and they remained unchanged until January 1, 1957, at which time the authorities raised by $\frac{1}{2}$ of 1 per cent the maximum interest rate that member banks and insured banks can pay on savings and time deposits of 90 days or longer. No change was made in the rates as they applied to time deposits and time certificates of less than 90 days. The schedule of rates as of August, 1960 was:

Savings deposits .... 3.0 per cent
Time deposits and certificates of 6 months or more .... 3.0 per cent
Time deposits and certificates of 90 days to 6 months .. 2.5 per cent
Time deposits and certificates of less than 90 days .... 1.0 per cent

Many of the state banking authorities also regulate the interest rates that can be paid on savings. Under the National Banking Act, nationally chartered institutions are required to adhere to maximum rates set in the states in which they do business. Therefore, if state authorities impose lower ceilings than those shown in the tabulation, the lower ceilings prevail. The volume of time deposits and certificates is very sensitive to changes in the structure of interest rates. When business and government are able to obtain more attractive yields by investing directly in the low-risk securities, such as Federal obligations, they tend to draw down time deposits and time certificates.

Regulation of the payment of interest on deposits in commercial banks is defended on the ground that it tends to promote a strong banking system. It is asserted that in the absence of regulation, there would probably be excessive rate competition among commercial banks. Unless the higher cost of funds were offset by additional interest income, the profit margins in commercial banking would shrink, preventing needed additions to the capital accounts of commercial banks. As noted earlier, the size of capital accounts in relation to deposit liabilities is a measure of safety of deposits. The objective of additional interest income might lead some banks to make a large volume of high-interest, low-quality bank loans and investments, creating conditions conducive to bank failures. This line of reasoning was used to explain some of the bank failures that occurred prior to rate regulation.

It is highly unlikely that the laws will be changed to permit either the payment of interest on demand deposits or unlimited payment of interest on time deposits. Many commercial banks desire to avoid rate competition; they prefer the status quo. Since a change in the laws would probably lead to a higher level of interest rates, Congress is also opposed to change. However, it should be noted that the more competitive banks do favor relaxation of regulation, since it would enable them to compete more effectively for interest-bearing accounts. Under the present set of regulations, the non-commercial banking institutions have an "unfair" competitive advantage. In the absence of rate competition, commercial banks have resorted to other means to attract depositors, including the practice of charging lower interest rates on loans made to large depositors and providing accounting and bookkeeping services to large depositors.

Solicitation of Time Deposits

A new deposit account in a commercial bank is viewed by the depository bank as a primary deposit, an actual lodgment of cash or items for collection.

As noted earlier, primary deposits are desirable because they increase the reserves of the depository bank. Primary deposits may consist of demand deposits, savings deposits, time deposits, and time certificates. Given the partial reserve requirement imposed on deposits, the receipt of primary deposits puts the depository bank in a position to lend and invest. Given the capital accounts an increase in earning assets tends to increase the margin of profit on capital accounts.

The nature of the primary deposit is important because the legal required reserve against "time deposits" is less than it is against demand deposits. As pointed out in an earlier chapter, the reserve requirement for member banks on time deposits may be set by the Board of Governors as low as 3 per cent and as high as 6 per cent. In 1960, the requirement was 5 per cent. Prior to the Federal Reserve Act, national banks were required to maintain the same reserve against both time deposits and demand deposits. During the same period state banking laws made a distinction between deposits. State chartered commercial banks were required to hold smaller reserves against time deposits than against demand deposits. Under these conditions it is not surprising that prior to 1914 almost all of the time deposits in commercial banks were held in the state-chartered commercial banks. The Federal Reserve Act permitted national banks to make a distinction among deposits in computing reserve requirements. The percentage reserve against time deposits was set at a figure considerably lower than those imposed on demand deposits. Since 1914, both national banks and state banks have been interested in attracting and holding time deposits.

Some commercial banks do not actively solicit time deposits because they do not want to pay the maximum or near-maximum rates on such deposits. It is a fact that some persons and businesses hold time deposits in commercial banks in spite of relatively unattractive interest returns. Ignorance of alternative outlets and the convenience of commercial bank facilities probably account for the sizable time deposits in these commercial banks. To solicit actively for additional time deposits, these banks would have to meet the competition in their respective communities and increase the rate of interest paid on deposits. To avoid discrimination, the banks would have to increase the rate of interest paid on existing deposits. It might very well be that the income earned on additional loans and investments after deduction of added interest expense would not be worth the effort to build up deposits. Also, some bankers believe that a high level of interest on deposits is difficult to maintain over the long run, and rather than face the problem of having to reduce rates in the future, they prefer not to raise them at all.

Effect of Time Deposits on the Loan and Investment Policy

As a general rule, commercial banks commingle all funds received, so that it is nearly impossible to match up specific assets with specific liabilities. Only in those states which require that commercial banks segregate funds

161

received in the form of time deposits and invest the funds according to special rules is it possible to match up a group of assets with a group of liabilities. Whether funds are commingled or segregated, the effect of time deposits on the loan and investment policies of commercial banks is evident.

A national bank's aggregate real estate loans may not exceed an amount equal to its total capital and surplus or 60 per cent of its time deposits, whichever total is the greater. Generally, the latter figure exceeds the former, which means that the build-up in time deposits has permitted banks to increase their real estate loans. Except for the deposits of foreigners, business, and governments, the turnover of time deposits is much lower than the turnover of demand deposits. Other things being equal, a large percentage of deposits in the form of time deposits permits the banks to make more intermediate and long-term loans and investments.

Although the receipt of time deposits by commercial banks permits banks to consider seriously long-term investments, it is not necessarily true that the funds will flow into long-term uses. Commercial banks deal in both the short-term and long-term markets for funds. Commercial banks may allocate funds received in the form of time deposits to short-term uses. Essentially, that is what happened in 1957. The increase in maximum rates paid on time deposits and active solicitation of funds by commercial banks led to an increase of approximately $5.3 billion in time deposits. However, only about one-third of the funds so received was channelled into long-term uses. Therefore, an increase in time deposits in commercial banks should not be associated immediately with long-term investment. The funds may be temporarily diverted to short-term uses. When considering the market for long-term funds, the loans and investments of commercial banks are much more meaningful than the flow of funds into commercial banks. This distinction is not as important for some of the other institutional forms of savings, for the specialized savings and thrift institutions tend to restrict their loans and investments to long-term uses.

Growth in Time Deposits

The growth in time deposits in commercial banks is shown in Figure 8-1, which is plotted on semi-log paper in order to make the rate of change more evident. In 1900, time deposits in commercial banks were slightly less than $1 billion; in 1960, time deposits exceeded $70 billion. Between 1900 and 1930, the growth in time deposits proceeded at a steady rate. Beginning in the early 1930's, time deposits began to decrease and did not turn upward until 1934. The rate of growth during the latter part of the 1930's did not match that of the earlier period. During World War II time deposits in commercial banks increased very rapidly, but leveled off abruptly at the end of the war. Since 1950, the rate of growth in time deposits has increased. The gain in time deposits in commercial banks during 1957 and 1958 was considerably greater than the average rate of growth for the 1950-1957 period.

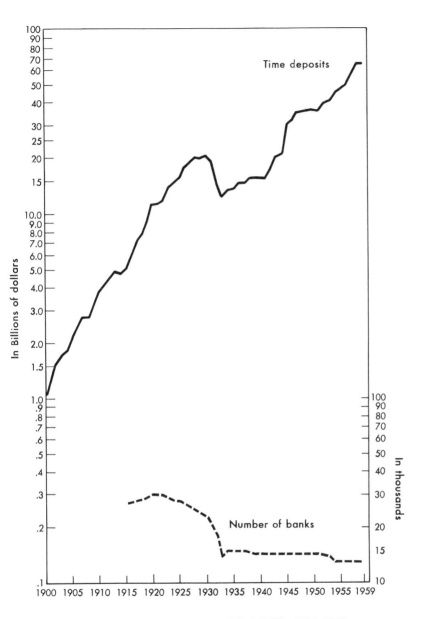

FIGURE 8-1   TIME DEPOSITS IN COMMERCIAL BANKS, 1900-1959

Source: Data derived from "All Bank Statistics — United States, 1896-1955," Board of Governors of the Federal Reserve System, April 1959; *Federal Reserve Bulletin*, September 1960.

MUTUAL SAVINGS BANKS

Mutual savings banks are banks of deposit; the regular savings deposits are their principal source of funds. With the exception of some mutual savings banks located in the states of New Jersey, Indiana, and Ohio, mutual savings banks are not permitted to accept checking accounts. Almost all such banks offer services in addition to regular savings deposits. Included among the other services are special purpose deposits, savings deposits for school children, safe deposit boxes, savings bank money orders, tellers checks, travelers checks, sale and redemption of United States savings bonds, savings bank life insurance and home financing. Some of the smaller mutual savings banks do not offer all of these services. Only those which are located in the states of Massachusetts, New York, and Connecticut are permitted to issue savings bank life insurance.

In the words of the Supreme Court of the United States a mutual savings bank is "an institution in the hands of disinterested persons, the profits of which, after deducting the necessary expenses of conducting the business, inure wholly to the benefit of the depositors, in dividends, or in a reserved surplus for their greater security." It is a non-stock corporation, chartered by the state in which it operates. Inasmuch as the services and operations of a mutual savings bank are governed by its charter, by-laws, and the laws of the state in which it is chartered, mutual savings banking is not completely uniform. However, there is sufficient uniformity among the operating policies of mutual savings banks to permit discussion on an over-all basis.

Organization and Administration

To secure a charter for a mutual savings bank, an organizing group, called the incorporators, follows a procedure very similar to that followed in establishing a state-chartered commercial bank. The incorporators file a petition with the appropriate state official, who, upon determining the qualifications of the incorporators and the need for such an institution in the specific locality, issues a charter. Many of the mutual savings banks established in the 1800's did not use the term "savings bank" in their corporate titles; instead, they used descriptive phrases such as "institution for savings" and "savings fund society." Also, it was not unusual for some of the early chartered mutual savings banks to use the words "five cent" and "dime" in their corporate titles, suggesting to the public that the institutions were designed for the small saver. Many mutual savings banks have retained their original corporate titles.

Like almost all other corporations, the power of administration in a mutual savings bank is vested in a board of directors, which may also be known as a board of managers or board of trustees. The board prescribes general policy and appoints operating officials, who are responsible for carrying on the day-to-day banking operations. There is an important difference between a board of directors of a mutual savings bank and a board of directors of a commercial bank or savings and loan association. The board of directors of a mutual savings bank is comprised of "disinterested persons." Board members receive no personal profit from the earnings of the bank and their membership on the board is not dependent on the will of the depositors. The board is a self-perpetuating group with board members serving either fixed terms or remaining on the board until resignation. Replacements are appointed by the existing board; they are not elected by depositors.

Branch banking is practiced to a limited extent in mutual savings banking. On June 30, 1959, 178 of the 519 mutual savings banks had branches totaling 425. Accordingly, there were 944 mutual savings banking offices in the United States on the same date.*

Nature of Deposits

Savings deposits in mutual savings banks resemble closely savings deposits in commercial banks. Both types of banks may require that depositors give notice of withdrawal before honoring or paying withdrawals. However, in some states the by-laws of a mutual savings bank may allow a bank's board of directors to extend the stipulated time period. In New York the banking officials have the power to regulate withdrawals from mutual savings banks if conditions warrant such action. In practice neither commercial banks nor mutual savings banks impose the notice of withdrawal requirement. The practice of allowing depositors to withdraw funds at any time has led to the use of savings accounts to accomplish relatively short-term savings goals. Some persons use savings accounts in lieu of checking accounts by requesting withdrawals in the form of tellers checks. When they do so, the depositors not only receive interest-dividends on relatively active deposit accounts, but are using checks free of charge in some cases.

Neither time deposits in commercial banks nor deposits in mutual savings banks can be used directly as a means of payment; both must be converted into either currency or demand deposits prior to their use as a means of payment. The use of a tellers check may make it appear that a deposit in a mutual savings bank can be used as a means of payment, but close examination reveals that a demand deposit account in a commercial bank is directly involved in the transaction. A teller at a mutual savings bank draws a check against the bank's demand deposit account. Assuming that the tellers check is eventually deposited in a commercial bank, the demand deposit liabilities of commercial banks remain unchanged; only ownership and location are changed. The withdrawal reduces the mutual savings bank's deposit liabilities and demand deposit account. If the mutual savings bank replenishes its demand deposit account, the total demand deposit liabilities of commercial banks will be increased. The same chain of events occurs

*Mutual Savings Banking, Annual Report, May 1960, p. F-7.

when a "time depositor" in a commercial bank withdraws funds in the form of a cashiers check. The deposit of the check causes an increase in demand deposit liabilities. In both instances commercial banks and demand deposits are involved.

One of the differences between deposits in mutual savings banks and time deposits in commercial banks concerns the limitations that mutual savings banks impose on the size of deposit accounts. In eight states, the maximum size of deposits is stated in the laws; in the other eleven states in which mutual savings banks operate, size limitations are imposed as a matter of policy rather than law. However, the limitations do not prohibit a person from holding accounts in more than one savings bank. Therefore, from the point of view of the depositor, there is no effective limit on the amount of savings deposits he may have in mutual savings banks.

Payment of Interest-Dividends on Deposits

Although there are many similarities between savings deposits in commercial banks and in mutual savings banks, there are also some major differences. It may be noted in the definition of a mutual savings bank that the profits "after deducting the necessary expenses of conducting the business, inure wholly to the benefit of the depositors, in dividends, or in a reserved surplus for their greater safety." The rate of return on a deposit in a mutual savings bank depends on the earnings of the bank and is expressed in terms of a dividend. In the case of a commercial bank, the rate of return on a savings deposit is stated at the beginning of each deposit period and is stated in terms of an interest rate. Any profits, after the expenses associated with these accounts are deducted, inure wholly to the benefit of the stockholders in the form of dividends and an increase in capital accounts.

Since all mutual savings banks are state-chartered, the regulation of rates paid to savers by mutual savings banks is the responsibility of each state. Generally, state authorities impose ceilings on the rates. For example, in 1959, the New York State Banking Board fixed a ceiling of 3.5 per cent on the regular annual rate that mutual savings banks in the state could pay to savers after October 1, 1959. Effective January 1, 1960, an additional dividend of .25 per cent could be paid on deposits that had been held in the bank for at least two years. The Pennsylvania Department of Banking authorized mutual savings banks to pay up to 3.5 per cent on savings accounts, effective October 1, 1959. Prior to that, the ceiling was 3.0 per cent.

The dividends on mutual savings bank deposits are calculated in a manner closely resembling the computation of interest on time deposits in commercial banks. The dividend rate is applied to both the volume and the length of time the deposit has been on a bank's books. Therefore, the payment to mutual savings bank depositors is often referred to as interest-dividend. No attempt is made here to explore the methods of computing interest or interest-dividends, for there are probably more than 100 different methods in use. It is sufficient to mention that the financial return on a deposit is significantly affected by the method that a bank uses in computing interest or interest-dividend.

Until January, 1957, at which time commercial banks were permitted to increase the rates of interest paid on various types of time deposits, the interest-dividend rate on deposits in mutual savings was generally .5 per cent higher than the rate of interest paid on savings accounts in commercial banks. During 1957 and early 1958 the average spread between the rate of return on the two types of deposits narrowed slightly. However, at the end of 1960, 3.5 per cent or more was being paid on 80 per cent of total deposits in mutual savings banks. An interest rate of 3 per cent or less was being paid on only 3 per cent of total deposits in mutual savings banks.* The data indicate that mutual savings banks have been able to maintain a competitive rate advantage over commercial banks.

Alert depositors tend to shift funds to financial institutions that pay the highest financial returns, assuming that all other things are equal. As noted in the discussion of commercial banks, many depositors shifted funds to commercial banks in 1957 and 1958 in response to the payment of higher rates of interest on time deposits in commercial banks. Some of the mutual savings banks also increased their interest-dividends in order to stay in line or stay slightly ahead of commercial banks. However, all banks did not change their rates. In metropolitan areas such as New York City there was considerable shifting of deposits. Some of the accounts that were shifted could not be considered permanent because the funds would probably be shifted again if other financial institutions offered more attractive rates. To discourage shifting, many mutual savings banks have adopted a split-dividend policy, paying the higher dividend only on year-old accounts. Therefore, if a depositor in one institution wanted to take advantage of a higher rate of return in another institution, he would have to wait one year following the transfer of funds before the higher rate would be paid on his deposit. If the depositor did not plan to hold the deposit in the second institution for at least one year, the shift would not be advantageous. In other words, depositors who do not plan to maintain deposit accounts longer than a year would be discouraged from shifting deposits from one bank to another. The split-dividend policy may also be used to discourage excessive turnover of time deposits.

Safety of Deposits

Prior to the establishment of the Federal Deposit Insurance Corporation, mutual savings banks had a competitive advantage over commercial banks in terms of safety of deposits. Deposit "runs" were less severe in mutual savings banking states, and mutual savings banks were not under pressure to meet demand deposit withdrawals. In New Jersey, there has not been an

*Ibid., p. F-23.

instance since 1888 in which a depositor in a mutual savings bank failed to get his funds back with interest-dividend in full. The same safety record has stood in New York since 1901. Impressive records of safety have been achieved in many of the other mutual savings banking states. Since 1933, only two mutual savings banks have had to liquidate or scale down deposits. In these two cases, the depositors were repaid at the average rate of $94.10 per $100 on deposit. In our present financial system, the deposits of the small saver are equally safe in insured commercial banks and mutual savings banks. In fact, more than 50 per cent of the mutual savings banks are insured by the F.D.I.C.

Safety of deposits in mutual savings bank was and continues to be achieved through relatively conservative and diversified loans and investments, the provision of strong surplus reserve positions, and the use of deposit insurance. Massachusetts, Connecticut, and New Hampshire had successful deposit insurance programs many years before the development of the F.D.I.C. Mutual savings banks in these states continue to rely on the statewide insurance plans. The F.D.I.C. insures savings deposit accounts in many of the statewide insurance plans and in many of the mutual savings banks that are not protected by state insurance funds. As of March, 1959, only 13 mutual savings banks carried no deposit insurance, either with the F.D.I.C. or with a state fund.

Conservative and diversified loans and investments also promote safety of deposits in mutual savings banks. Although the laws governing mutual savings banks vary from state to state, the basic ideas are the same. The laws prescribe specific requirements that must be met by securities in order to make them eligible for savings bank investment. Specific requirements are also imposed on real estate loans. The statutes prescribe conservative loan-to-value ratios and limit real estate loans to a certain percentage of total assets, such as 60 per cent.

The strength of the surplus position of mutual savings banks is measured by relating surplus to total assets and to assets other than cash and Federal obligations. At the end of 1958, the aggregate surplus and reserves of mutual savings banks were 8.6 per cent of aggregate assets. Deducting from total assets the non-risk assets of cash and Federal obligations, the aggregate surplus and reserves of mutual savings bank were 11 per cent of the residual or risk assets. The ratio means that mutual savings banks could absorb this percentage loss in principal value of their risk assets and still be able to cover deposit liabilities in full. The ratio of general reserve accounts to deposits was 9.5 per cent.

Assets of Mutual Savings Banks

Knowing the purpose of mutual savings banking and the nature of the deposits let us examine the banks' investment policies and their loans and investments in the postwar period.

The goal of investment management is to maintain the proper degree of safety and liquidity of assets and within these limits to assure maximum financial returns. Since most of the deposits originate with small savers, primary consideration must be given to safety. As noted above, the emphasis on safety is reflected in the state laws that regulate the investments of mutual savings banks. In general, the following types of investments are permitted: Federal obligations, state and local obligations, corporate bonds, and mortgages. Some states permit very limited investment in corporate stocks. The state laws specify that all of these credit and equity market instruments satisfy stipulated investment requirements. To promote diversification, the state laws limit the percentage of assets that may be held in the form of mortgages and corporate stocks.

Liquidity of assets is important in view of the general practice of allowing depositors to withdraw funds with little or no notice. Liquidity is also desirable because it permits bank management additional flexibility in the investment of funds. It allows banks to take advantage of unusual investment opportunities. Cash and short-term credit instruments are used to provide the necessary degree of liquidity.

Mutual savings banks cannot ignore the rate of return on assets because the banks are competing with alternative outlets for consumer saving. Although the over-all level of interest rates may not influence the total volume of consumer saving and investing, the structure of rates does affect the allocation of consumer saving. Mutual savings banks must pay an interest-dividend rate that is high enough to attract and hold deposits. In recent years, mutual savings banks have felt the pressure of the higher rates paid on savings and loan and credit union shares. As a result, restrictions on the investments of these banks have been relaxed slightly in order to give mutual savings banks an opportunity to improve the rate of return on total assets and to increase the interest-dividend rate. The more safe and liquid assets yield the lowest returns, and to reach out for higher yields, a certain degree of safety and liquidity must be sacrificed. Mutual savings banks have increased their investments in mortgages, a form of investment that is less liquid than bonds. Some mutual savings banks have invested limited amounts of funds in equity market securities. Equities are not as safe as the debt securities of the same issuing companies, but with careful selection and diversification the banks are not sacrificing unduly the safety of assets as long as equities do not exceed 5 or 10 per cent of total assets. The banks assume that the higher yields on mortgages and equities compensate for the assumption of greater risk and sacrifice of liquidity.

A change in the tax status of mutual savings banks has also influenced their investment policy in the postwar period. Since January 1, 1952 mutual savings banks that have surplus accounts as great as 12 per cent of their deposits are required to pay the regular corporate income tax on the investment income not paid out to depositors in the form of interest-dividend. If the ratio of surplus accounts to deposits is less than 12 per cent, all investment income, whether paid out as interest-dividends or added to surplus, is exempt from the corporate income tax. Therefore, the Federal corporate income tax is an important consideration to some mutual savings banks and unimportant to others. Generally, surplus accounts are less than 12 per cent of deposits. However, in banks having surplus accounts of at least 12 per cent of deposits, tax considerations tend to lead to higher interest-dividend payments and to investment in tax-exempt securities. The increased holdings of state and local obligations by mutual savings banks reflects the change in tax status of such banks.

The manner in which mutual savings banks balance safety, liquidity, and profit is reflected in the distribution of their assets, which is shown in Table 8-1. Liquidity needs are met through their holdings of cash (2.1 per cent of assets) and Federal obligations (20.3 per cent of assets). The importance attached to safety is made evident by the fact that nearly all of their assets are held in the form of credit market instruments. A much better measure of safety requires appraisal of the quality of their mortgages and corporate bonds. It is sufficient to mention that the quality is very high. The heavy

TABLE 8–1
FINANCIAL ASSETS AND LIABILITIES OF MUTUAL SAVINGS BANKS, END OF 1958
(BILLIONS OF DOLLARS)

	Dollars	Per cent
Financial Assets		
Credit and equity market instruments	36.5	97.4
Mortgages on 1- to 4- family properties	15.7	41.9
Other mortgages	7.6	20.3
Federal obligations	7.6	20.3
Corporate bonds	3.8	10.1
Corporate stocks	.9	2.4
State and local obligations	.7	1.9
Other loans	.2	.5
Consumer credit	.1	.3
Fixed-value redeemable claims — time deposits	.2	.5
Cash balances — currency and demand deposits	.8	2.1
Total assets	37.5	100.0
Liabilities		
Fixed-value redeemable claims — deposits	34.0	90.7
Surplus and reserve accounts	3.5	9.3
Total liability, surplus, and reserve accounts	37.5	100.0

Note: Details may not add to totals because of rounding.

Source: "A Quarterly Presentation of Flow of Funds, Saving and Investment," *Federal Reserve Bulletin,* August 1959.

concentration of assets in mortgages (62.2 per cent of assets) and corporate bonds (10.1 per cent of assets) reflects the importance attached to the yield on investments. Although the amount invested in state and local obligations is relatively small, the greatest percentage change in assets in the postwar period has occurred in this form of investment.

Investments in the Postwar Period

There was considerable variation in mutual savings banks' investments during the postwar period. For purposes of analysis, the period is broken down into three shorter periods. During the years 1946-1949, mutual savings banks invested approximately equal amounts of funds in mortgages and securities. One of the unique characteristics of their investments during this period was the net acquisition rather than liquidation of Federal obligations. During this period mutual savings banks did not have legal authorization to acquire mortgages outside of their own areas. Inasmuch as mutual savings banks were not located in states that were experiencing the more rapid rates of growth, the banks were unable to acquire as many mortgages as they would have preferred. Also, the rate differentials between corporate bonds and Federal obligations were not very large, and many mutual savings banks did not believe that the slightly higher yields offset the additional risk.

During the years 1950-1953, the net acquisition of mortgages nearly equaled the net increase in deposits and surplus in mutual savings banks. The holdings of Federal obligations were reduced by slightly more than $2 billion. Approximately $5 billion was invested in corporate bonds and about the same amount was invested in state and local obligations. It was during this period that mutual savings banks in New York and Massachusetts were authorized by their respective state authorities to make F.H.A. and V.A. mortgage loans on a nationwide basis. The nature of these mortgages is examined in the chapter that deals specifically with home financing.

Another factor underlying the portfolio changes during this period was the increase in yields on long-term securities. Securities became relatively more attractive to many institutional investors who had previously been investing heavily in mortgages. When these investors diverted funds from mortgages to securities, it became easier for the mutual savings banks to acquire a large volume of mortgages. The changes in the level and structure of interest rates encouraged mutual savings banks to shift out of low-yield Federal obligations into higher-yield corporate bonds. The change in the tax status of mutual savings banks in 1952 induced many mutual savings banks to invest funds in the tax-exempt state and local obligations.

Investments during the 1954-1958 period resembled closely the investments of the previous period. The liquidation of Federal obligations was continued, but at a reduced rate. The net acquisition of mortgages continued to exceed the net increase in deposits in mutual savings banks. However, the

TABLE 8–2
NET ACQUISITION OF FINANCIAL ASSETS BY MUTUAL SAVINGS BANKS, 1950-1958
(BILLIONS OF DOLLARS)

	1950	1951	1952	1953	1954	1955	1956	1957	1958
Total net acquisitions	.7	.9	1.7	1.8	2.0	2.1	1.9	1.8	2.5
Credit and equity market instruments: Mortgages on 1- to 4- family properties ...	.9	1.0	.9	1.2	1.6	2.1	1.9	1.1	1.6
Other mortgages	.6	.6	.6	.4	.4	.4	.4	.3	.5
Federal obligations ...	—.6	—1.0	—.4	—.2	—.5	—.2	—.4	—.3	—.3
Corporate bonds	—.1	.1	.3	.2	.1	—.3	.1	.6	.6
Corporate stocks	*	*	.1	.1	.1	.1	*	.1	.1
State and local obligations	*	.1	.2	.1	.2	*	*	*	*
Fixed-value redeemable claims [1]	—.1	*	*	*	*	*	—.1	*	*
Cash balances — currency and demand deposits..	*	.1	*	*	*	*	*	*	*

*Less than $50 million.
Note: Details may not add to totals because of rounding.
[1] Mainly time deposits.
Source: "A Quarterly Presentation of Flow of Funds, Saving and Investment," *Federal Reserve Bulletin*, August 1959.

net acquisition of mortgages did not match the increase in both deposits and surplus. In 1957, the net acquisition in corporate bonds was greater than the previous net acquisition of bonds for the entire period 1950-1956.

Table 8-2 shows a summary of financial flows through mutual savings bank for the years 1950-1958. This table and the table showing the assets and liabilities of mutual savings for the year ended 1958 demonstrate the importance of mutual savings banks in the mortgage market, especially concerning the mortgages on the one- to four-family properties. Depending on the level and structure of interest rates, mutual savings banks may also supply an important share of funds that flow into corporate bonds. The data indicate clearly the banks' ability and willingness to adjust their acquisition of assets in response to changes in the level and structure of long-term interest rates. In a later chapter the shift of funds among various types of mortgages will be noted.

As a result of postwar changes in the pattern of savings bank investment, mortgages as a percentage of total assets increased from less than 25 per cent to nearly 60 per cent. The percentage of assets invested in Federal obligations declined from 60 per cent to less than 20 per cent. The percentage of assets invested in state and local obligations increased from 0.4 per cent to 1.9 per cent; assets invested in corporate bonds, from 9.1 per cent to 10.1 per cent.

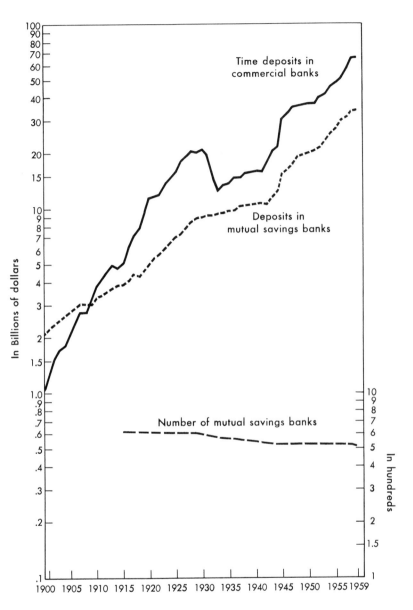

FIGURE 8-2   DEPOSITS IN MUTUAL SAVINGS BANKS AND TIME DEPOSITS IN COMMERCIAL BANKS, 1900-1959

Source: Data derived from "All Bank Statistics — United States, 1896-1955," Board of Governors of the Federal Reserve System, April 1959; *Federal Reserve Bulletin*, September 1960.

Growth in Mutual Savings Banking

The growth in the number of mutual savings banks and the growth in the volume of deposits held in mutual savings banks are plotted in Figure 8-2. The chart portrays a gradual decline in the number of savings banks and a rather steady rate of growth in the volume of deposits. The decline in the number of savings banks is more than offset by the establishment of branches. Deposits increased from approximately $1.5 billion in 1892 to over $33 billion in 1958. Although savings bank deposit growth declined in 1959, deposits increased $946 million. In 1960, the total assets of mutual savings banks passed the $40 billion mark.

Although the chart does not show the increase in the number of banks prior to 1900, it was during the period between the Civil War and 1880 that mutual savings banks experienced their most rapid rate of growth in terms of numbers; there was a net increase of 351 banks during the period. Between 1880 and 1900 there was a net increase of only 23 banks. After the turn of the century there was a decrease in the number of banks, and today the number is nearly the same as it was in 1880. It may be recalled that the peak in the number of commercial banks was nearly 30,000 and it occurred in 1920. Since that time, the number of commercial banks has fallen off by over 50 per cent.

The principal reason for the leveling off and eventual decline in the number of mutual savings banks was the failure of this type of institution to become firmly established outside of the New England and Middle Atlantic seaboard states. Mutual savings banks are located in only 17 states, and over, 90 per cent of total deposits in mutual savings banks is concentrated in five-states, with New York banks accounting for nearly 60 per cent of total deposits. Mutual savings banking is firmly established in New England and the Middle Atlantic seaboard states because it became firmly entrenched before the development of other savings and thrift institutions. By the time other sections of the country experienced economic and social conditions fostering the creation and development of specialized savings and thrift institutions, commercial banks and savings and loan associations were active competitors for consumer saving. In recent years, attempts have been made to establish additional mutual savings banks, but the efforts have not been successful. Today, mutual savings banking must compete directly with time deposits in commercial banks, savings and loan shares, credit union shares, savings through life insurance, pension funds, and United States savings bonds. Since savings banks cannot rely on conventional financing in the organization of newly chartered savings banks, there is an attempt under way to obtain contributions from existing savings banks to be used as a revolving capital fund to help organize new mutual savings banks. These funds would supplement the funds raised locally by civic-spirited citizens.

There has been a sustained rate of growth in total deposits in mutual savings banks. It was not until 1909 that time deposits in commercial banks exceeded savings deposits in mutual savings banks. The protracted depression in the 1930's did not affect savings deposits in mutual savings banks as much as it affected time deposits in commercial banks. In recent years commercial banks and mutual savings banks have experienced about the same rates of growth in time deposits.

POSTAL SAVINGS SYSTEM

The Postal Savings System was instituted in 1910 to encourage thrift and to provide a safe depository for savings. Thrift was encouraged by providing saving facilities on a nationwide basis through the existing post offices. Safety was achieved by the fact that the faith of the United States was solemnly pledged to the payment of the deposits with accrued interest. The Postal Savings System provides the means for depositing savings at interest with the security of the Federal government for repayment.

Nature of Deposits

An account may be opened either in person or by mail and deposits may be made in person or by mail by any competent person without regard to the residence of the depositor. However, a postmaster is not required to open an account if it is evident that the depositor desires merely to leave his funds in a safe place for a few hours or to make unreasonable use, otherwise of postal-savings facilities. Certificates ranging in value from one dollar to $2,500 are made out in the name of the depositors and serve as receipts. They are neither negotiable nor transferable, and in the event one is lost, stolen, or destroyed, it will be replaced. No postal savings depositor may have to his credit in the total Postal Savings System more than $2,500 exclusive of accumulated interest. All or a part of a postal savings deposit may be withdrawn either in person or by mail at any time, with any interest payable thereon, from the post office in which the deposit was made. The appropriate certificate is surrendered at the time of withdrawal. To discourage short-term accounts, a service charge of 10 cents is imposed on each certificate that is surrendered within one month from date of issue. Advance notice of withdrawal may be necessary if the amount of the withdrawal is very large, so as to allow the postmaster to secure the necessary currency.

Payment of Interest on Postal-Savings Deposits

Postal savings deposits earn interest at the rate of 2 per cent compounded annually. A deposit made on any day of the month begins to earn interest on the first day of the next succeeding month. For each complete quarter-of-a-year, a fourth of a year's interest is collectible. If a depositor desires to collect only the accrued interest on a postal savings deposit, he must exchange certificates. In an exchange, a depositor should exchange during the

TABLE 8–3
POSTAL SAVINGS SYSTEM FOR FISCAL YEARS 1911-1958

June 30	Total depositories	Number of depositors (in thousands)	Amount to credit of depositors (in millions)
1911	400	11.9	$ .6
1912	10,170	243.8	20.2
1913	12,820	331.0	33.8
1914	10,347	388.5	43.4
1915	9,546	525.4	65.6
1916	8,421	602.9	86.0
1917	7,161	674.7	131.9
1918	6,656	612.1	148.4
1919	6,439	565.5	167.3
1920	6,314	508.5	157.2
1921	6,300	466.1	152.3
1922	6,774	420.2	137.7
1923	6,802	417.9	131.6
1924	6,758	412.5	132.8
1925	6,655	402.3	132.1
1926	6,623	399.3	134.1
1927	6,672	411.3	147.3
1928	6,683	412.2	152.1
1929	6,770	416.5	153.6
1930	6,795	466.4	175.2
1931	7,459	770.8	347.4
1932	7,549	1,545.1	784.8
1933	7,888	2,342.1	1,187.1
1934	8,059	2,562.0	1,197.9
1935	8,111	2,598.3	1,204.8
1936	8,103	2,705.1	1,231.6
1937	8,068	2,791.3	1,267.6
1938	8,050	2,741.5	1,251.7
1939	7,964	2,767.4	1,262.2
1940	7,980	2,816.4	1,293.4
1941	8,038	2,882.8	1,304.1
1942	8,063	2,812.8	1,315.5
1943	8,060	3,064.0	1,577.5
1944	8,057	3,493.0	2,034.1
1945	8,050	3,921.9	2,659.5
1946	8,089	4,135.5	3,119.6
1947	8,141	4,196.5	3,392.7
1948	8,183	4,111.3	3,379.1
1949	8,195	3,964.5	3,277.4
1950	8,235	3,779.7	3,097.3
1951	8,247	3,529.5	2,788.1
1952	8,261	3,339.3	2,617.5
1953	8,247	3,162.1	2,457.5
1954	7,872	2,934.7	2,251.4
1955	7,750	2,711.1	2,007.9
1956	7,622	2,482.0	1,765.4
1957	7,369	2,200.5	1,462.2
1958	6,871	1,925.8	1,213.6

Source: Annual Report of the Postmaster General, 1958.

first month of an interest quarter to avoid loss of more than one month's interest. Assume that a deposit is made in February, 1961; interest begins on March 1, 1959. To minimize loss of interest he should exchange his certificate (s) in March, June, September, or December.

Investments

The funds due postal savings depositors on June 30, 1958 totaled approximately $1.3 billion, including interest. These liabilities were offset by: (1) deposits of sligthly more than $24 million in depository banks; (2) Federal obligations with a face value of more than $1.2 billion; and (3) cash in possession of the System and other net assets of about $69.5 million. The data show that practically all of the funds are invested in Federal obligations.

Growth in the Postal Savings System

The number of offices in operation, the number of depositors, and the size of the balance to the credit of depositors are shown in Table 8-3. The peak in the number of offices in operation occurred two years after the establishment of the Postal Savings System. After World War I and up to the beginning of the Great Depression, the number of offices in operation ranged around six and seven thousand. The number of offices increased by approximately 1,000 during the early years of the depression, and the number did not decline significantly until the early 1950's.

Little change occurred in the number of depositors until the Great Depression, during which time the number of depositors increased fivefold, reflecting the reactions of consumers to widespread bank failures. During World War II there was a steady increase in the number of depositors because the 2 per cent rate on postal savings deposits was higher than the rate being paid by many banks. After World War II the 2 per cent rate became very unattractive and the number of depositors declined.

The changes in the balance to the credit of depositors have followed a pattern very similar to the changes in the number of depositors. There was a sizeable increase in total balances between 1930 and 1933, and then the balance leveled off. Beginning in 1942 and continuing through 1950, the total balance increased steadily, reaching a peak of more than $3 billion in 1950. Since 1950, the balance has declined steadily. The turning point in the level of deposits coincides with the increase that occurred in long-term interest rates. Other savings and thrift institutions began to offer relatively more attractive rates of interest on deposit accounts.

The decline in the operations of the Postal Savings System is a prelude to its eventual elimination from our financial system. The decline indicates that the conditions that gave rise to the System no longer prevail, at least not to the same degree as they did in 1910 or the 1930's. There is no reason to expect a reversal in the present trend in Postal Savings deposits. Furthermore, deposits and withdrawals in the Postal Savings System are time-consuming processes compared with similar transactions in other savings and thrift institutions.

UNITED STATES SAVINGS BONDS

United States savings bonds were introduced in the early part of 1935 and were tailored to fit the investment requirements of the small investor. The savings bonds were introduced into the Federal debt structure to absorb and activate consumers' idle cash balances, to encourage additional consumer saving, and to secure widespread ownership of Federal debt. It is assumed that widespread ownership promotes greater interest in public affairs. In 1959, the underlying theme was that the purchase of savings bonds is a practical way for every American to help guard against the threat of inflation, thus protecting the buying powers of the dollar.*

Nature of Savings Bonds

United States savings bonds are fixed-value redeemable claims. They are non-marketable securities that can be redeemed at the holder's option. Since 1935, ten different series of savings bonds have been issued: Series, A, B, C, D, E, F, G, H, J, and K. Many changes have been made in the rate of return, schedule of redemption values, length of maturity, eligible investors, and the maximum amount that can be purchased in a single year. No attempt is made to summarize the many different series and changes. The discussion is primarily restricted to the Series E and Series H savings bonds, which are the only series that have been issued since February 1957, and detailed descriptions of these bonds are based on those series issued on or after June 1, 1959.

Savings bonds are issued in two forms: appreciation bonds and current income bonds. An appreciation bond (Series E) is issued at a discount basis and is not redeemable at par (face value) until maturity. For example, the $100 Series E denomination is issued at a price of $75. Between the date of issue and date of maturity, the bond is redeemable at various redemption values, the exact value depending on the length of time the bond is held. The increase in redemption values reflects the accrual of interest earnings on the investment. A current income bond (Series H) is issued at face value. Its issue price, maturity value, redemption value, and face value are identical. Interest checks are mailed out semi-annually to registered owners of Series H bonds.

United States savings bonds are issued only in registered form and registration is restricted to include only persons (whether natural persons or others) who are: (1) residents of the United States, its territories and possessions, the Commonwealth of Puerto Rico, and the Canal Zone; (2) citi-

*Excerpt from a message of Treasury Secretary Anderson in addressing savings bond workers.

zens of the United States temporarily residing abroad; (3) civilian employees of the United States or members of its Armed Forces, regardless of their residence or citizenship; and (4) other natural persons as co-owners with, or beneficiaries on death of, natural persons of any of the above classes. The value of savings bonds of each series, issued in any one calendar year, which may be held by any one person at any one time is limited to $10,000 maturity value. As will be explained later in the chapter, this rule does not apply to investors who are now entitled to exchange matured Series F and G savings bonds for Series E and H bonds. Savings bonds are not transferable; they are payable only to the owners named thereon. Various limitations apply to judicial proceedings involving savings bonds, and the bonds may not be hypothecated, pledged as collateral, or used as security for the performance of an obligation. The provisions pertaining to loss, theft, mutilation, deface-ment, or destruction are very liberal. In comparison with other types of se-curities, savings bonds have some very attractive aspects.

As of June 30, 1959 savings bonds were being issued by 22,501 issuing agents, including 1,120 post offices, 16,178 banks, 1,778 savings and loan associations, 336 credit unions, 2,401 companies operating payroll plans, and 688 that are classified as "all other."* During World War II, there were over 55,000 issuing agents. Most of the decline is accounted for by the withdrawal of post offices from the sale of bonds. On December 31, 1953 the sale of Series E savings bonds was discontinued at post offices, except in localities where no other public facilities for their sale were available. In 1950, over 25,000 post offices issued bonds; in 1960, approximately 1,100 post offices issued bonds. Declines have also occurred among savings and loan associa-tions, credit unions, and companies operating payroll plans.

Interest on Savings Bonds

The interest on a Series E savings bond is represented by the increment in redemption value and is payable only on redemption of the bond, whether before, at, or after maturity. The investment yield on the Series E bond is dependent on the length of time that the security is held. If held to maturity, which is 7 years and 9 months from date of issue, the investment yield is 3.75 per cent. The investment yield ranges from 0.00 to 3.75 per cent if the bond is redeemed prior to maturity. The redemption values and investment yields for Series E bonds bearing issue dates beginning June 1, 1959 are shown in Table 8-4.

Interest rates on savings bonds have been increased three times. In 1952, the rate was raised to 3.0 per cent from the original 2.9 per cent. In 1957, the interest rate was increased to 3.25 per cent. In 1959, the interest rate was boosted to 3.75 per cent. In each case, the increase was effected through a shortening of maturity: from ten years to nine years and eight

*Annual Report of the Secretary of the Treasury, for the fiscal year ended June 30, 1959, p. 118.

months; then to eight years and eleven months; and then to seven years and nine months.

TABLE 8–4
UNITED STATES SAVINGS BONDS — SERIES E
TABLE OF REDEMPTION VALUES AND INVESTMENT YIELDS FOR BONDS
BEARING ISSUE DATES BEGINNING JUNE 1, 1959
(BASED ON $100.00 BOND — COST $75.00)

Period after issue date	Redemption value [1]	Approximate on purchase price [3]	Investment Yield [2] on current redemption value [4]
First ½ year	$75.00	0.00	3.75
½ to 1 year	75.64	1.71	3.89
1 to 1½ years	76.76	2.33	3.96
1½ to 2 years	78.04	2.67	4.01
2 to 2½ years	79.60	3.00	4.01
2½ to 3 years	81.12	3.16	4.03
3 to 3½ years	82.64	3.26	4.05
3½ to 4 years	84.28	3.36	4.06
4 to 4½ years	86.00	3.45	4.06
4½ to 5 years	87.80	3.53	4.04
5 to 5½ years	89.60	3.59	4.03
5½ to 6 years	91.44	3.64	4.02
6 to 6½ years	93.28	3.67	4.01
6½ to 7 years	95.16	3.70	4.01
7 to 7½ years	97.08	3.72	3.99
7½ years to 7 years & 9 months	99.00	3.74	4.06
Maturity Value (7 years and 9 months from issue date)	$100.00	3.75	

[1] Shows increase in redemption value during successive half-year periods following issue. The values increase on the first day of period shown.
[2] Yields are expressed in terms of rate per cent per annum, compounded semiannually.
[3] From issue date to the beginning of each half-year period.
[4] From the beginning of each half-year period to maturity.

Source: *Annual Report of the Secretary of the Treasury*, for the fiscal year ended June 30, 1959, p. 225.

The interest on the Series H savings bond is payable semiannually beginning six months from its issue date and is paid on each interest payment date by check drawn to the order of the person or persons in whose name (s) the bond is inscribed and mailed to the address of record. The interest due at maturity is paid with the principal. If the Series H savings bond is held to maturity (10 years), the investment yield is the same as that earned on the Series E savings bond, 3.75 per cent. The ammount of interest paid on Series H savings bonds, bearing issue dates beginning June 1, 1959, on each interest payment date following issue and the approximate investment yield on the face value from issue date to each interest payment date are shown in Table 8-5. For both the Series E and Series H savings bonds,

TABLE 8–5
UNITED STATES SAVINGS BONDS — SERIES H
TABLE OF CHECKS ISSUED AND INVESTMENT YIELDS FOR BONDS
BEARING ISSUE DATES BEGINNING JUNE 1, 1959
(BASED ON $1,000.00 BOND) [1]

Period after issue date	Amount of interest checks [2]	Approximate from issue date to each interest payment date	Investment yield [3] from each interest payment date to maturity
½ year	$ 8.00	1.60	3.88
1 year	14.50	2.25	3.95
1½ years	16.00	2.56	4.00
2 years	20.00	2.91	4.00
2½ years	20.00	3.12	4.00
3 years	20.00	3.26	4.00
3½ years	20.00	3.36	4.00
4 years	20.00	3.44	4.00
4½ years	20.00	3.49	4.00
5 years	20.00	3.54	4.00
5½ years	20.00	3.58	4.00
6 years	20.00	3.61	4.00
6½ years	20.00	3.64	4.00
7 years	20.00	3.66	4.00
7½ years	20.00	3.68	4.00
8 years	20.00	3.70	4.00
8½ years	20.00	3.71	4.00
9 years	20.00	3.72	4.00
9½ years	20.00	3.74	4.00
10 years (maturity)	20.00	3.75	4.00

[1] Face value is equal to maturity value, redemption value and issue price. A bond is not redeemable during first six months.

[2] Amounts of interest checks paid on each interest payment date following issue.

[3] Yields are expressed in terms of rate per cent per annum, compounded semiannually based on face value.

Source: *Annual Report of the Secretary of the Treasury*, for the fiscal year ended June 30, 1959, p. 228.

the bonds must be held more than two years before the investment yield exceeds 3 per cent.

Redemption of Savings Bonds

A savings bond may not be called for redemption by the Secretary of the Treasury, but may be redeemed in whole or in part at the option of the owner prior to maturity under certain terms and conditions. A Series E savings bond will be redeemed at any time after two months from the issue date without advance notice. A Series H savings bond will be redeemed after six months from the issue date, on one month's notice in writing to the Bureau of the Public Debt, Division of Loans and Currency Branch, a Federal Reserve bank, or the Treasurer of the United States. Payment will be made as of the first day of the first month following by at least one full calendar month the date of receipt of notice. Assume that the notice is received June 2; payment will be made on August 1.

The redemption values for the Series E savings bonds and the size of the interest checks paid on Series H savings bonds tend to encourage retention of the bonds. The last columns in the tables referred to above show the approximate investment yields on current redemption values from the beginning of each half-year period to maturity. It can be seen that after the bonds are held for six months, the investment yield from that time on to maturity is 3.89 per cent, a relatively attractive investment yield. Savings bond investors would have to earn nearly 4 per cent on alternative investments to match the investment yields that could be earned on savings bonds.

A summary of sales and redemptions of savings bonds by series, through June 30, 1959, is shown in Table 8-6. Total sales at issue price plus accrued discount for all series exceeded $150 billion, but with redemptions of nearly $100 billion, the amount of savings bonds outstanding on June 30, 1959 totaled only $50,833 million. Individuals own approximately 90 per cent of outstanding savings bonds.

TABLE 8–6

TOTAL SALES AND REDEMPTIONS OF SAVINGS BONDS BY SERIES, THROUGH JUNE 30, 1959

(MILLIONS OF DOLLARS)

	Series A-D	Series E and H	Series F and J	Series G and K	Total
Total sales at issue price plus accrued discount	$5,003	$112,018	$7,069	$26,021	$150,111
Redemptions (including redemptions of matured bonds) at current redemption value	4,975	69,302	5,297	19,703	99,278
Amounts outstanding	$ 28	$ 42,716	$1,772	$ 6,318	$ 50,833

Source: *Annual Report of the Secretary of the Treasury*, for the fiscal year ended June 30, 1959, p. 535.

Growth in Savings Bonds

Table 8-7 presents a summary of the sales and redemptions of savings bonds for the fiscal years 1935-1959. Looking first at the sales column it can be observed that savings bonds caught on rapidly with the American public, with annual sales exceeding $500 million within three years from the date the bonds were first introduced. During World War II a combination of factors resulted in large annual sales. Consumer saving was exceptionally large because of the shortage of goods and services; patriotism was associated with the purchase of savings bonds; over 55,000 issuing agents were established throughout the country; payroll deduction plans were developed on a mass scale; and intensive savings bond sales campaigns were launched. During the peak of World War II financing, annual sales of savings bonds plus accrued discount exceeded $15 billion.

TABLE 8-7
SALES REDEMPTIONS OF SAVINGS BONDS, FISCAL YEARS 1935-1959
(MILLIONS OF DOLLARS)

Year	Sales at issue price plus accrued discount	Redemptions at current redemption values	Amount outstanding
1935 (March-June 30)	$ 62.6	$ 0,000.5	$ 62
1936	265.2	11.2	316
1937	519.7	36.2	800
1938	504.7	66.6	1,238
1939	712.5	82.0	1,868
1940	1,150.8	114.3	2,905
1941	1,557.4	148.1	4,314
1942	6,081.6	207.4	10,188
1943	11,916.3	848.3	21,256
1944	15,720.9	2,370.9	34,606
1945	15,277.8	4,298.4	45,586
1946	10,184.2	6,717.1	49,035
1947	7,898.7	5,544.9	51,367
1948	7,039.1	5,112.9	53,274
1949	8,067.6	5,067.4	56,260
1950	6,717.8	5,422.1	57,536
1951	6,292.3	6,137.1	57,572
1952	5,132.4	5,109.3	47,685
1953	5,790.7	5,620.9	57,886
1954	6,727.4	6,514.9	58,061
1955	7,704.2	7,250.6	58,365
1956	7,059.9	7,845.8	57,497
1957	6,097.4	8,958.2	54,622
1958	5,896.1	8,543.5	51,984
1959	5,734.0	7,249.2	50,833
Totals	$150,111.2	$99,277.7	

Source: Annual Report of the Secretary of the Treasury, 1950 (figures for 1935-1950), 1954 (figures for 1951), 1959 (figures for 1952-1959).

After the war sales fell off sharply, dropping by over $5 billion in fiscal 1946 and over $2 billion in fiscal 1947. The conditions that prevailed in the postwar period were not favorable to the sale of savings bonds. The Treasury faced a real problem. Sales were falling off and redemptions were increasing. Savings bonds that were purchased in the earlier period were beginning to mature. To maintain a large volume of outstanding savings bonds, the Treasury permitted the holders of matured Series E savings bonds to reinvest the proceeds in savings bonds by simply holding onto the matured bonds for an additional period.

Savings bonds were up against stiffer competition in the postwar period. The Treasury offered higher and earlier interest returns and increased the amount of the annual purchase limit. New series of bonds were introduced to tap additional sources of funds. The new series of bonds were designed for "investors" rather than "small savers." The attractiveness of the new series of bonds was short-lived; investors who purchased these and the larger denominations of the Series E bonds tended to shift funds among alternative uses, the specific investment being largely determined by their desire to attain maximum investment yields. As the level and structure of interest rates changed, the new series of bonds became relatively unattractive, and in time the issue of the new series, except for Series H, was discontinued. The Treasury stopped issuing the Series F and G bonds in 1952. These bonds had a maturity of 12 years and carried a 2.50 per cent interest rate. The Treasury stopped issuing the Series J and K bonds in 1958. These bonds were referred to as investment types of securities and paid an annual average rate of 2.76 per cent if held to their 12-year maturity. The Treasury now permits individuals and personal trust holders of Series F and G bonds to exchange their entire F and G matured issues for a like amount of Series E and H bonds. The idea behind this change in policy is that investors who have held Series F and G bonds for the full 12 years have demonstrated that they are a stable class of investors in savings bonds. By giving them the opportunity of moving into the more attractive Series E and H bonds, the Treasury will encourage them to stick with savings bonds and it will avoid the necessity of redeeming their matured issues for cash.

Another recent change designed to maintain sales is the opening of Series E and H bonds to those classes of investors who were originally attracted to the now discontinued Series J and K bonds. In recent years the Series E and H bonds could be purchased by any investor other than commercial banks. Small institutional investors, such as labor unions, fraternal, civic, service, patriotic, and veterans organizations, and local and state governmental bodies have need for savings bonds in their portfolios. Except for the exchange provisions, the annual limit of $10,000 applies to all investors, which means that the Series E and H bonds are available to large investors only in a limited amount.

Looking at the redemption column in Table 8-7, it can be observed that there has been a steady rise in the volume of redemptions, in spite of the measures referred to above. During the period 1949-1956, redemptions were about the same amount as sales plus accrued interest, with the result that the amount of savings bonds outstanding hovered between $56,260 million and $58,365 million. To appreciate the full extent of the problem that the Treasury faced during the postwar period, it must be realized that at the end of the war over 40 million people held savings bonds that were in reality demand obligations.

Beginning in 1956, the level of redemptions moved higher than the level of sales plus accrued discount, with the result that the amount of savings bonds outstanding dropped from $57,497 million to $50,833 million. Much of the decline was due to large redemptions of Series F, G, J, and K savings bonds, both matured and unmatured. However, the amount of Series E and H bonds outstanding (including accrued interest) reached an all-time peak of almost $43 billion in early part of 1959. The excess of redemptions of Series E and H bonds over sales during the fiscal year was more than offset by the automatic accrual of interest on the Series E bonds.

The rise in interest rates in 1959 complicated the Treasury's problems relating to savings bonds. In September, 1959, Congress empowered the President to raise interest on savings bonds as high as 4.25 per cent. Shortly thereafter, the President directed the Secretary of the Treasury to increase the rate of interest from 3.25 per cent to 3.75 per cent on all Series E and H savings bonds sold on or after June 1, 1959. The yields on Series E and H bonds outstanding on that date were also increased, but the higher rates were effective only from June 1, 1959, on. Generally, the bonds that had carried a 3.0 or 3.25 per cent interest rate received a 0.5 per cent boost, and those which carried a 2.9 per cent interest rate received a 0.6 per cent boost. If outstanding bonds had not been so treated, there would have been large-scale switching.

By comparing the trend in the volume of savings bonds with the trend in time deposits, it is obvious that savings bonds have lost ground. The Treasury has had a difficult time holding the present volume of savings bonds. In fact, it failed to meet this objective during much of the postwar period. In trying to stimulate sales and to discourage redemptions, the Treasury has become more dependent on the "investor" than on the "small saver." The implication of this change in emphasis is that the savings bond program in the future must be sufficiently flexible to allow the Treasury to offer a competitive financial investment. The savings bond program has become more sensitive to the threat of inflation because large investors are more likely to shift out of credit instruments into equities than are the small savers.

QUESTIONS

1. Describe and justify the regulation of the payment of interest on deposits held in commercial banks.

2. What effect do time deposits have on the loan and investment policy of commercial banks?

3. Describe briefly the purpose and organization of a mutual savings bank.

4. Trace the growth in the number and location of mutual savings banks.

5. Compare savings accounts in commercial banks with those in mutual savings banks.

6. Construct a simple aggregate balance sheet for mutual savings banks, showing the relative importance of each balance sheet item, and explain the asset composition in terms of investment policy.

7. Trace briefly the investments of mutual savings banks in the postwar period.

8. Explain the expansion and subsequent contraction in postal savings deposits.

9. What are the two basic forms of United States savings bonds? Describe briefly the current series of each form. How do they compare with savings accounts in commercial banks and mutual savings banks?

10. Trace the growth in United States savings bonds outstanding. In what ways has our savings bond program changed in the postwar period?

ADDITIONAL READING

Almost all of the money and banking tests listed at the end of Chapter 4, and almost all of the personal finance and consumer economics texts listed at the end of Chapter 7, treat the topics covered in Chapter 8; the investment texts listed at the end of Chapter 12 discuss the nature and the role of United States Government savings bonds.

Lintner, John. *Mutual Savings Banks in the Savings and Mortgage Markets.* Boston: Harvard University, Graduate School of Business Administration. Division of Research, 1948.

National Association of Mutual Savings Banks. *Mutual Savings Banks Annual Report.* See reports 1958 through 1960; they provide both data and analysis; beginning with the report dated May 1960, a lengthly statistical section is included with the report.

Sutcliffe, Wm. G., and Lindley A. Bond. *Savings Banks and Savings Department Management.* New York: Harper & Bros., 1930.

Welfing, Weldon. *Savings Banking in New York State.* Durham, N. C.: Duke University Press, 1939.

9: Savings and loan and credit union shares

OUR approach to the study of savings and loan and credit union shares is very much the same as that used in the previous chapter. The major points covered with respect to each of the financial institutions are: organization and administration, nature of savings and investment accounts (shares), dividends, safety and liquidity of savings and investment accounts, assets, investment in the postwar period, and long-run growth. We begin with savings and loan associations because they have been established for a much longer period and their aggregate operations are on a much larger scale than those of credit unions.

SAVINGS AND LOAN ASSOCIATIONS

Savings and loan associations are specialized savings and home financing institutions. They are not banks, and their savings and investment accounts cannot be referred to as deposits. However, in practice, many consumers do not distinguish between savings accounts in savings and loan associations and time deposits in banks. Many of the early chartered institutions did not use the words "saving and loan" in their corporate titles. Some of the state-chartered institutions in New England were incorporated as cooperative banks; some in Louisiana were incorporated as homestead associations; in many states the institutions were called building and loan associations. Regardless of the specific corporate title, all of them are specialized savings and home financing institutions and they constitute the savings and loan system. In this chapter, the institutions are referred to as savings and loan associations.

Organization and Administration

Like almost all other financial institutions, savings and loan associations adopt a corporate form of legal organization. Approximately 93 per cent of the associations are organized as non-stock corporations; the other 7 per cent, as stock corporations with permanent capital stock outstanding. The non-

187

stock associations are organized on a mutual basis with ownership and power of control vested in the holders of the various types of savings and investment accounts. The owners of savings and investment accounts are legally shareholders and part owners. For this reason the accounts are referred to as shares rather than as deposits. Most advertising of savings and loan associations emphasizes the concept of "savings and investment accounts" rather than that of "share capital." Regardless of the terminology, the holders of the accounts are members and are entitled as members to vote on general corporate matters and to elect directors who, in turn, appoint the officers and delegate responsibilities. In practice, the majority of association members behave like stockholders in large- and medium-sized corporations; they are relatively inactive and assign their voting power to management. However, the ultimate authority in a non-stock association rests with its members, and if they become disturbed about the manner in which the association is being directed and managed, they have the power to do something about the situation, and on occasion they have done so.

Permanent capital stock associations were set up to provide greater safety and a guaranteed rate of return to the holders of savings accounts. Unfavorable experience led to the abandonment of the guaranteed rate of return, but many of the associations continue to operate as permanent capital stock associations. Eleven states in the West and Midwest permit the establishment of state-chartered, stockholder-owned savings and loan associations. The permanent capital stock is not redeemable, as are the savings and investment accounts held in non-stock savings and loan associations. An investor holding permanent capital stock must find a buyer other than the issuing association to convert his stock into money. In this sense, his legal position is identical to that of a shareholder in any other corporation.

Like the other institutions studied, savings and loan associations secure a charter granted by government and function under the laws of the chartering authority. In the early stage of development of the savings and loan system, associations were chartered under the general corporation laws of the respective states. This common origin accounts for the features that are found in all corporations, whether they are financial or nonfinancial. For many years now, the states have had specific laws pertaining to the organization, administration, supervision, and liquidation of savings and loan associations.

During the period 1831-1932, savings and loan associations operated solely under state laws. The diversity in state laws led to considerable diversity among savings and loan associations. Some states promoted the development of savings and loan associations through constructive legislation or good supervision; other states established highly restrictive legislation or lax supervision. The variation in laws among the states reflects the fact that financial institutions compete in legislative bodies as well as in the market place for funds.

In recent years many associations have been acquired by savings and loan holding companies.* The holding company device has permitted innovations otherwise denied to savings and loan associations. For example, it offers a means of raising new capital. In most of the eleven states permitting stockholder-owned savings and loan associations, the laws make it very difficult for existing individual associations to raise new capital. States' laws generally limit an association's loans to a certain geographical area, such as a 50-mile radius of its office. Through a holding company, a certain management group can legally cover a much larger area. Furthermore, a holding company can shift resources among associations to take advantage of the 12 per cent tax rule. As indicated in earlier chapters, Congress has opposed concentration in the financial community. In 1959, the President signed into law a bill "to promote and preserve local management of savings and loan associations by protecting them against encroachment by holding companies." †Specifically the bill bars a holding company from acquiring any additional associations whose savings accounts are insured by the Federal Savings and Loan Insurance Corporation. Any newly formed holding company could acquire only one association whose accounts are insured. All other acquisitions would have to be restricted to the uninsured associations.

Savings and loan associations have been expanding their branch operations steadily. At the close of 1959, it was estimated that approximately 642 associations were operating one or more branches and that branches numbered around 1,200.**

Structure of the Savings and Loan System

The Great Depression dramatized many weaknesses in our financial system, including some within the savings and loan system. Congress responded by adopting various measures to improve the savings and loan system. In 1932, it established the Federal Home Loan Bank System; in 1933 it provided for the issue of Federal charters for savings and loan associations; in 1934, it set up the Federal Savings and Loan Insurance Corporation.

The Federal Home Loan Bank System is a reserve credit system designed to assist institutions that specialize in home financing. Therefore, almost all the members of the Federal Home Loan Bank System are savings and loan associations. A few mutual savings banks and life insurance companies are also members of the System. The System consists of eleven Federal Home Loan Banks which are owned by the member institutions. The Federal Home Loan Banks advance funds to member institutions in order to promote greater stability in home financing. Discussion of the

*Some of the holding companies are: San Diego Imperial Corporation (listed on the N.Y.S.E.); First Charter Financial Corporation of Beverly Hills, California; Great Western Financial Corporation of Los Angeles (listed on the American Stock Exchange).

† Public Law 86-374, approved September 23, 1959.

**Savings and Loan Fact Book, 1960, p. 72.

detailed operation of the Federal Home Loan Banks is delayed until Chapter 14, which deals specifically with home financing.

The Federal Home Loan Bank Board is the issuing authority of Federal charters for savings and loan associations. Congress created a dual system of charter, something that had prevailed in the commercial banking system for nearly 70 years. The purpose of the Federal charter was to encourage the development of nationwide uniform operating techniques and practices. Much progress has been accomplished in this effort.

The Federal Savings and Loan Insurance Corporation was set up to restore confidence among investors who had placed their funds in savings and loan associations. Like the Federal Deposit Insurance Corporation, which insures deposits in commercial banks and mutual savings banks, all federal-chartered savings and loan associations are required to be members of the Federal Savings and Loan Insurance Corporation. The members are assessed a premium rate of 1/12 of 1 per cent against total insurable accounts and creditor liabilities. The state-chartered savings and loan associations have a choice, with membership contingent on the association's ability to satisfy certain requirements. Individual savings and investment accounts in insured associations are insured up to $10,000, which is the same maximum that applies to deposits insured by the Federal Deposit Insurance Corporation. The state-chartered institutions in Massachusetts are insured by the Co-operative Central Bank of Massachusetts.

The structure of the savings and loan system is nearly as complicated as that of the commercial banking system. There are many classifications of associations: member or non-member of the Federal Home Loan Bank System; insured or non-insured by the F.S.L.I.C.; federal- or state-chartered savings and loan association. Federal-chartered associations are required to be members of both the F.H.L.B. System and the F.S.L.I.C. State-chartered associations may or may not be members of the F.H.L.B. System and the F.S.I.C. An association does not have to be insured to be a member of the F.H.L.B. System. In recognition of the importance of membership in both the System and F.S.L.I.C., many states now require newly chartered associations to be members of both. Also, for all practical purposes at the present time, an association seeking F.S.I.L. insurance must be a member of the F.H.L.B. System.

The organizational structure of the savings and loan system is summarized in Table 9-1, which shows the number and total assets of all associations, F.H.L.B. member associations, F.S.L.I.C. insured associations, Federal-chartered associations, and state-chartered associations. The total assets of the member associations of the F.H.L.B. System represent about 97 per cent of all savings and loan assets; the total assets of the F.S.L.I.C. insured associations represent nearly 94 per cent of all savings and loan assets. Including the Massachusetts program of insurance, nearly 95 per cent of the assets are insured by government. There has been a steady gain in the membership of both the F.H.L.B. System and the F.S.L.I.C. Non-members and non-insured savings and loan associations consist mostly of relatively small state-chartered associations.

Savings and Investment Accounts (Shares)

There is much variation in the terminology used by savings and loan associations to describe their accounts. Essentially, there are three basic types: savings accounts, bonus savings accounts, and investment accounts. Some savings and loan associations refer to their savings accounts as regular savings accounts in order to make the distinction sharper between savings accounts and investment accounts. A regular savings account or savings account in a savings and loan association is closely similar to a savings deposit in a commercial bank or a mutual savings bank. A passbook is issued to the savings account holder and dividends are added to his book at regular intervals. The amount and timing of either an addition to the savings account or a withdrawal from the account are at the discretion of the holder of the account. As noted in the previous chapter, many consumers make no distinction between a time deposit in a bank and an addition to a savings account in a savings and loan association.

TABLE 9–1
STRUCTURE OF THE SAVINGS AND LOAN SYSTEM, END OF 1959
(MILLIONS OF DOLLARS)

	Number	Per cent	Total Assets	Per cent
All associations	6,230	100.0	$63,472	100.0
Members, F.H.L.B. System ...	4,599	73.8	61,622	97.0
Insured by F.S.L.I.C.	3,979	63.9	59,550	93.8
Federal-chartered	1,841	29.6	34,362	54.1
State-chartered	4,389	70.4	29,110	45.9

Source: *Savings and Home Financing Source Book*, Federal Home Loan Bank Board, June 1960, Washington, D. C.

A bonus savings account is one form of systematic savings. Under a bonus savings account, the holder agrees to a definite plan of saving on the understanding that upon completion of the plan the association will pay a bonus dividend in addition to the regular dividend. Upon completion of a plan, the holder of the account either withdraws or transfers the funds to another form of savings account. Also, the holder of a bonus savings account may withdraw from a plan before it is completed. Savings and loan associations offer systematic plans of savings under other titles such as serial shares, serial savings accounts, and installment savings. Some associations impose a system of fines to encourage holders of systematic savings accounts to stick to their original plans, but this gimmick is used much less often than it was some years ago. Regardless of the terminology, nearly all savings and loan

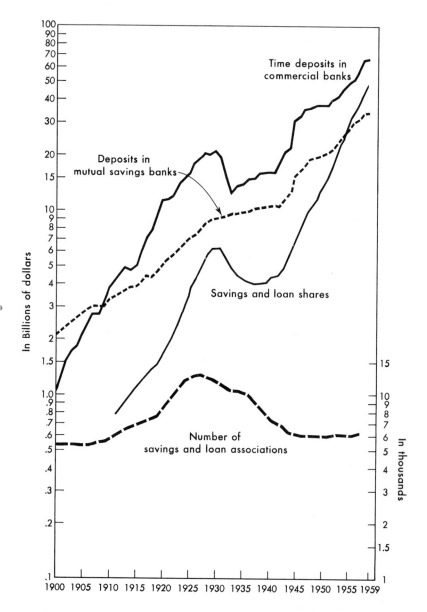

FIGURE 9-1   SAVINGS AND LOAN SHARES AND TIME DEPOSITS IN BANKS, 1900-1959

Source: Data for commercial banks and mutual savings banks derived from Board of Governors of the Federal Reserve System, "All Bank Statistics — United States, 1896-1955," April 1959; *Federal Reserve System*, September 1960. Data for savings and loan associations derived as follows: 1914-1919, annual reports, Secretary, United States Savings and Loan League; 1920-1959, Federal Home Loan Bank Board.

associations offer savings accounts designed to encourage systematic saving.

Investment accounts, which may be referred to as paid-up savings certificates by some savings and loan associations, are designed for investors who have accumulated a sum of money. Certificates or shares are issued to evidence the investment of funds. Depending on the association, the certificates or shares are issued in denominations of $100 and $200. The face value of the certificates or shares does not change, and they are cashable or redeemable at the option of the holder. Dividends on the accounts are either mailed to the registered owners of the certificates or applied directly to other savings accounts that are held in the associations.

Legally, savings and loan associations can require written notice of withdrawal before making payment to the holder of any one of the three types of accounts, but in practice the associations, like other savings and thrift institutions, do not impose the requirement. Technically, funds are not withdrawn; instead, the associations redeem or repurchase the members' shares.

In time of emergency, savings and loan associations, mutual savings banks, and commercial banks would have the legal right to require notice of withdrawal from their customers. However, consumers have become so accustomed to the freedom of withdrawal that these institutions would hesitate to impose the requirement for fear of offending their customers. As long as the majority of savings and thrift institutions prefer to suspend the notice of withdrawal, others must either waive their rights or suffer a competitive disadvantage.

If savings and loan associations do impose the requirements pertaining to withdrawal, there are technical withdrawal provisions that are unique to savings and loan associations. Generally, savings and loan associations would not be required to pay out the full amount of savings and investment accounts even at the end of a notice period. The provisions would permit them to stretch out the repayment period so that withdrawals could be paid in an orderly manner. The specific procedure that would be followed by a savings and loan association if it imposed the notice requirement would depend on whether it was state-chartered or Federal-chartered. If it were state-chartered, the procedure would depend on state law. The withdrawal procedure that might be followed in a Federal-chartered association is flexible in the sense that the Federal Home Loan Bank Board can tailor the procedure to fit the needs of a particular savings and loan association.

Generally, in a state-chartered savings and loan association the withdrawal requests are numbered as received, and after the end of the notice period the requests are honored in sequence up to a given dollar amount, say $1,000. The limit would depend on the availability of funds. Assume that the withdrawal requests were honored up to $1,000. If a savings account exceeded $1,000, the unsatisfied portion or residual would remain subject to withdrawal, but the request for the additional amount of withdrawal would have to be placed at the bottom of the list. The procedure would continue for as long as customers requested additional withdrawals and the association had sufficient assets. Insurance coverage would not come into the picture until the association was placed in receivership.

New York passed a law in 1958 requiring that state-chartered savings and loan associations pay out savings left with them on 60 days' notice, and that if they failed to make payments in full at the end of the notice period, the associations would be closed and insurance coverage made effective. This piece of legislation has removed in the State of New York one of the few distinctions that remained between savings and investment accounts in savings and loan associations and time deposits in banks. The legislation reflects the tendency of savings and loan associations to become more like savings banks. It is likely that other states will follow the action taken in New York.

Dividends on Savings and Investment Accounts

Except for the permanent stock savings and loan associations, the associations' policies and practices relating to dividends are closely similar to those of mutual savings banks. The dividend depends on the earnings of an association and the dividend policy of the association's board of directors. An association receives interest on its investments. From this interest the association must deduct the expenses of operations and must allocate a portion of net income to reserves and surplus. The remainder is used to cover dividend payments. The dividends are calculated like interest. The dividend rate is applied to both the volume and the length of time that an account has been on the books of an association. Like the situation that prevails in mutual savings banking, there are many methods of computing dividends and it is worth the time of an investor to be familiar with the methods and to invest his funds where the total dividends are the greatest, all other things being equal.

At the end of 1959, the Federal Home Loan Bank Board had no direct authority over the dividend rates that could be paid by Federal savings and loan associations. However, if the Board believed that a Federal savings and loan association was paying a rate that endangered its reserve and liquidity position, the Board could step in and warn the association. The absence of a Federal policy precludes many states from regulating the dividends paid by state-chartered associations.

During much of the postwar period the dividend return on savings and investment accounts not only exceeded the rate of return on time deposits in banks but also exceeded the yields that were obtainable on marketable Federal obligations. The ability of the associations to pay relatively attractive dividends is directly related to their investments in mortgages. During the postwar years there was a housing boom and a consequent strong demand for mortgage funds. The associations were in a favorable position. They held a large amount of Federal obligations that could be liquidated very easily because of the postwar policy of the Treasury and Federal Reserve System, which supported the market for Federal bonds. The increased earnings permitted increased dividends, which, in turn, attracted additional consumer saving.

A large number of savings and loan associations have dividend rates 1 per cent or more above rates paid by commercial banks on savings accounts, and ¼ to ½ of 1 per cent above rates paid by mutual savings banks. Associations were paying the following dividend rates in the dividend period ending December 31, 1959:* 3 or 3¼ per cent, 12 per cent of the associations; 3½ or 3¾ per cent, 44 per cent of the associations; 4 per cent, 38 per cent of the associations; and over 4 per cent, 6 per cent of the associations. Dividend rates continued to rise in 1960 and 4 per cent became the commonest rate. The relative attractiveness of the associations' dividend rates and their aggressive solicitation of new savings and investment accounts have contributed in a very important way to the rapid rate of growth of savings and loan assets.

Liquidity of Savings and Investment Accounts

Liquidity is important to savings and loan associations for two reasons. First, their savings and investment accounts are fixed-value redeemable claims, which are, in practice, payable on demand. Like other savings and thrift institutions, the associations cannot be absolutely certain as to either the timing or amount of withdrawals. They must gear their operations to accommodate withdrawals. Second, there is a tendency among many of the associations for the annual trough of net savings receipts to coincide with the annual peak in loan demand. Liquidity permits the associations to adjust their cash flows to accommodate both the holders of savings and investment accounts and borrowers.

Liquidity is provided in various ways. The first line of defense, as it were, is to hold cash and other assets that can be readily converted into cash at little or no loss in value. In addition to holding cash in vaults and demand deposit accounts in commercial banks, the associations hold Federal obligations and deposits in Federal Home Loan banks. In recent years the amount of assets held in the form of Federal obligations has been nearly the same as the amount of assets held in the form of cash and deposits.

Members of the Federal Home Loan Bank System are required to hold liquid assets equal to at least 6 per cent of total savings and investment accounts. In practice, member associations, in the aggregate, tend to hold approximately twice this percentage. It should be recalled that over 97 per cent of the savings and loan assets are owned by member associations.

Another first line of defense consists of the privileges of borrowing from other financial institutions, particularly Federal Home Loan Banks. Technically, a Federal Home Loan Bank can lend to a member savings and

*Savings and Loan Fact Book, 1960, p. 22.

loan association an amount equal to 50 per cent of the association's total savings and investment accounts. The Federal Home Loan Banks are discussed in greater detail in Chapter 14.

A substantial amount of built-in liquidity is provided by the type of loan that is made by savings and loan associations. Amortized home financing loans require that borrowers repay their loans by making equal monthly repayments consisting of interest on the unpaid balance and partial reduction of principal. The repayments provide a continual inflow of funds. Recalling the procedure of regulated withdrawals in the event that notice is imposed on the holders of savings and investment accounts, it should be noted that the continual inflow of funds could be used to pay withdrawals.

Another source of liquidity is the secondary mortgage market, in which mortgage lenders can dispose of Federally underwritten mortgages. Generally, approximately 20 per cent of associations' home financing loans are eligible for resale in the secondary mortgage market.

Safety of Savings and Investment Accounts

The soundness of mortgage lending practices, the adequacy of reserves and surpluses, and insurance are among the more important factors contributing to safety of savings and investment accounts. All of these factors are probably more important to savings and loan associations than they are to other savings and thrift institutions because the associations' loans and investments are not very diversified. Generally, the following mortgage lending practices are developed: (1) the associations tend to be very selective in making loans; (2) the associations deal directly with borrowers and are alert to changes in risk; (3) almost all their loans are secured by first mortgages on owner-occupied property; (4) their loans are amortized.

The aggregate reserves, surplus, and undivided profits is slightly in excess of 7 per cent of total assets. The goal of the savings and loan system is to build the percentage up to 10 per cent of total assets. Until that goal is reached, savings and loan associations will probably continue to allocate approximately one-fourth of their income after operating expenses to reserves. Approximately 10 per cent of the associations have attained or surpassed the 10 per cent goal.

In the event that an association fails to provide safety, insurance coverage may come into the picture. Holders of savings and investment accounts in insured savings and loan associations can look to the Federal Savings and Loan Insurance Corporation for protection to the extent of $10,000. The law provides that:

> In the event of a default by any insured institution, payment of each insured account in such insured institution which is surrendered and transferred to the Corporation shall be made by the Corporation as soon as possible either (1) by cash or (2) by making available to each insured member a transferred account in a new insured institution in the same

community of an another insured institution in an amount equal to the insured account of each insured member.

The total resources of the F.S.L.I.C. including its authority to borrow up to $750 million from the United States Treasury, exceed $1 billion. The F.S.L.I.C. has experienced net losses of only $5.5 million since its inception in 1934.

With the exception of the non-insured, non-member associations, savings and investment accounts are probably as safe as deposits in commercial banks and mutual savings banks. Some of the non-insured, non-member savings and loan associations are well managed and safety is adequate. However, in some of the non-insured, non-member associations safety is not on a par with that found in mutual savings banks and commercial banks.

Assets of Savings and Loan Associations

The assets of savings and loan associations reflect their underlying purpose, which is to make first mortgage loans on owner-occupied homes located in their respective communities. If the flow of funds into savings and loan associations exceeds the local demand for mortgage loans, the excess funds are generally invested in Federal obligations. The major part of the savings and loan associations' home financing is accomplished through conventional mortgages as opposed to Federally underwritten mortgages. Conventional mortgages require direct, personal contact with the mortgage borrower, and the associations are in a position to provide such service.

For various reasons the Federally underwritten mortgages are not particularly attractive to many savings and loan associations. First, the problem of liquidity is not so great that the associations have to rely on the secondary mortgage market. Second, Federally underwritten mortgages require of the lender special skills and patience in handling the paper work. Since many of the associations are relatively small financial institutions, they are not equipped to handle these loans. Last, the yields on conventional mortgage loans are generally more attractive than the yields on Federally underwritten mortgages.

The manner in which savings and loan associations balance safety, liquidity, and financial return is reflected in the distribution of their assets, which is shown in Table 9-2. The format of the table is identical to that used in the discussion of mutual savings banks. Liquidity needs were being met in 1958 by cash balances (3.3 per cent of total assets) and Federal obligations (7.7 per cent of total assets). At the same time, mutual savings banks held approximately 22.4 per cent of their assets in cash and Federal obligations. The importance attached to safety is made evident by the fact that almost all assets are held in the form of credit market instruments. The quality of these assets has already been discussed. The emphasis on financial returns and the specialized nature of their operations are reflected in the large percentage of assets in mortgages.

Investments in the Postwar Period

The postwar period is broken down into the same three shorter periods that were used in the previous chapter. During the 1946-1949 period savings and loan associations' net investment in mortgages exceeded the net inflow of funds from savings and investment accounts and the increase in capital accounts. The growth of the associations during this period required a substantial increase in cash balances. The liquidation of Federal obligations and an increase in idebtedness provided the additional funds. At the end of 1949, the ratio of cash and Federal obligations to savings and investment accounts stood at 18.8 per cent. The comparable ratio for the mutual savings banks was 63.8 per cent.

During the period, 1950-1953, the investment pattern was slightly different. The net increase in mortgages was equal to the net inflow of savings and investment accounts (savings capital). The associations increased

TABLE 9–2

ASSETS AND LIABILITIES OF SAVINGS AND LOAN ASSOCIATIONS, END OF 1958

(BILLIONS OF DOLLARS)

	Dollars	Per cent
Assets		
Financial assets	54.5	100.0
Credit and equity market instruments	51.3	94.1
Federal obligations	4.2	7.7
Mortgages on 1- to 4-family properties	43.2	79.3
Other mortgages	2.4	4.4
Consumer credit	.7	1.2
Miscellaneous financial transactions (F.H.L.B. stock)	.8	1.5
Fixed-value redeemable claims:		
Miscellaneous deposits (Home Loan Banks)	.8	1.5
Cash balances — currency and demand deposits	1.8	3.3
Liabilities and Reserves		
Liabilities and reserves	54.5	100.0
Credit and equity market instruments	1.5	2.8
Bank loans, n.e.c.	.2	.4
Other loans	1.3	2.4
Fixed-value redeemable claims:		
Savings and loan shares	47.9	87.9
Reserves and undivided profits [1]	5.1	9.4

Note: Details may not add to totals because of rounding.
[1] Includes loans in process.
Source: Flow-of-Funds/Savings worksheets, Board of Governors of the Federal Reserve System.

their holdings of Federal obligations by $500 million; cash balances by $600 million; and other assets by $700 million. The ratio of cash and Federal obligations to savings capital fell from 18.8 per cent to 15.3 per cent. Capital accounts increased $800 million and indebtedness increased $500 million. During the same period, the ratio of cash and Federal obligations to savings deposits in mutual savings banks declined from 63.8 per cent to 41.7 per cent.

A nearly identical pattern of operations was repeated during the years 1954-1958. The net increase in mortgages was slightly less than the increase in savings capital. The ratio of cash balances and Federal obligations to savings capital continued to decline, falling from 15.3 per cent to 13.3 per cent. The ratio of cash and Federal obligations to savings deposits in mutual savings banks declined from 41.7 per cent to 24.2 per cent.

During each of the periods the net inflow of savings capital was the major source of funds: $5.1 billion, $10.3 billion, and $20.6 billion. The next most important source of funds over the entire period was the $3.2 billion increase in capital accounts. For a few years after the war, the liquidation of Federal obligations provided an additional source of funds, but beginning in 1948 Federal obligations became a use of funds rather than a source of funds. The rapid growth and the need to maintain an adequate liquidity position required the reversal in policy with respect to Federal obligations. Another source of funds throughout the entire postwar period was the increase in indebtedness owed to Federal Home Loan Banks and other financial institutions. The loans were used to expand permanent lending power as well as to meet temporary needs. The associations' holdings of cash increased by $1.7 billion. A statistical summary of financial flows through savings and loan annual associations for the years 1950-1958, is presented in Table 9-3.

Growth

Figure 9-1 traces the changes in total savings capital since 1911 and in the number of associations since 1900. Also included on the chart are the changes in the time deposits in banks. The chart shows that the greatest rate of growth in the number of associations occurred during the early 1920's. Between 1920 and 1925, 4,615 additional savings and loan associations were established. The largest number of associations in operation at any one time occurred in 1927, when there were 12,804 associations. It may be recalled that the peak in the number of mutual savings banks occurred around the turn of the century, and the peak in the number of commercial banks, in 1920. The number of associations began to fall off in 1928, and the decline continued until 1950, at which time there were 5,992 associations. The trough in the number of associations has probably been reached and some additional growth in the number of associations can be expected. It is likely that the trough in the number of mutual savings banks has also been reached. The decline in the number of commercial banks will probably continue, reflecting a continuation of the merger movement and the establishment of branch offices.

The first peak in total savings capital occurred in 1930, when it totaled nearly $6.3 billion. Up to that time, the rate of growth in savings capital was greater than the rate of growth in number of associations. The chart portrays clearly the effects of the Great Depression on savings capital invested in savings and loan associations. During the period 1930-1935, savings capital declined very sharply, falling by about $400 million annually. Between 1936 and 1940, it fluctuated between $4.3 and $4.1 billion. From 1929 through 1940, 1,914 savings and loan associations failed and the estimated loss was $209,367,000.*

Since 1940, failures have fallen off very sharply and there has been a steady rise in total savings capital. At the end of 1948 total savings capital was more than two and one-half times greater than in 1940; at the end of 1953, twice what it was in 1948; at the end of 1958, the savings capital had doubled again. In 1959 savings capital increased by nearly $7 billion.

*Annual Reports of the Secretary, United States Savings and Loan League, Chicago, 1946.

TABLE 9–3
NET ACQUISITION OF FINANCIAL ASSETS BY SAVINGS AND LOAN ASSOCIATIONS, 1950-1958
(BILLIONS OF DOLLARS)

	1950	1951	1952	1953	1954	1955	1956	1957	1958
Total net acquisitions	2.2	2.2	3.4	4.1	5.0	6.0	5.2	5.2	6.9
Credit and equity market instruments:									
Federal obligations	*	.1	.2	.1	.1	.4	.6	.6	.6
Mortgages on 1- to 4-family properties	2.0	1.7	2.8	3.4	4.0	5.0	4.0	4.0	5.2
Other mortgages	*	.2	*	.2	.2	.3	.3	.3	.4
Consumer credit	.1	*	.1	.1	.1	.1	.1	.1	.1
Misc. financial transactions (F.H.L.B. stock)	*	.1	*	.1	.1	.1	.1	.1	.1
Fixed-value redeemable claims:									
Misc. deposits [1]	*	*	.2	.1	.2	—.1	*	*	.2
Cash balances — currency and demand deposits	.1	.1	.1	.1	.3	.2	.1	.1	.3
Memorandum:									
Net increase in liabilities......	1.9	2.1	3.1	3.7	4.4	5.4	4.7	4.8	6.1
Bank loans, n.e.c.	*	*	*	*	*	.1	*	*	*
Other loans	.4	*	.1	.1	—.1	.5	—.2	*	*
Savings and loan shares....	1.5	2.1	3.1	3.6	4.5	4.8	5.0	4.8	6.0
Reserves and undivided profit.	.3	.1	.3	.4	.6	.6	.2	.4	.9

Note: Details may not add to totals because of rounding.
[1] Trust and deposit liabilities of the Federal Government Sector (Home Loan Banks).
Source: "A Quarterly Presentation of Flow of Funds, Saving and Investment," *Federal Reserve Bulletin*, August 1959.

Savings and loan associations are firmly entrenched and it is probable that the association will continue to attract a large share of consumer saving. Some of the changes that may occur in the not-too-distant future are: (1) greater expansion through branches; (2) ability to attract funds flowing into public and private pension and retirement funds; (3) more flexibility in investment policy; and (4) the assumption of a more important role in urban renewal. If these changes come about, savings and loan associations might be able to attract a larger share of consumer saving. Also, the changes are in the direction of making savings and loan associations more nearly similar to other savings and thrift institutions.

CREDIT UNIONS

Credit unions are specialized savings and consumer financing institutions. Like savings and loan associations, credit unions are not banks and are not generally permitted to refer to their accounts as deposits. Members' savings are expressed in terms of shares. Credit unions' consumer financing includes both consumer credit and real estate credit. In addition, many credit unions cash checks, offer advice to members, and provide for the purchase of low-cost life insurance. The total assets of credit unions are much lower than the total assets of the other major savings and thrift institutions. At the close of 1959 there were nearly 20,000 credit unions, over 11 million credit union members, and nearly $5 billion in credit union assets.* The data indicate that the majority of credit unions are small.

Organization and Administration

A credit union is organized and operated as a non-profit cooperative association, with its membership restricted to persons who belong to a particular group. Credit unions are organized to serve occupational, residential, and associational groups. Nearly three-fourths of all credit unions are set up to serve occupation groups; consequently, the majority are located in the more heavily industrialized states. The motivation underlying the establishment of a credit union may originate with the employer, the employees, or a combination of the two. The important thing is that a properly managed credit union offers many advantages to both the employer and employees.

Credit unions may be chartered under state or Federal laws. Almost all of the states have enacted legislation providing for the chartering of credit unions. State-chartered credit unions are under the supervision of state authorities. Since 1934 it has been possible to charter an association under Federal law. At the present time Federal credit unions are chartered and supervised by the Bureau of Federal Credit Unions, an agency affiliated with the Department of Health, Education, and Welfare. Federal chartered

*Credit Union Yearbook, 1960, p. 8.

credit unions account for approximately one-half of the total number and total assets of credit unions. Perhaps in the near future a Federal program of credit union insurance will be established and regulations will become more uniform.

The members of a credit union elect the board of directors and may also elect members of various committees, including a credit and a supervisory committee. A credit committee has the responsibility of screening loan requests and expressing approval or disapproval. A supervisory committee has the responsibility of maintaining a close watch over operations and examining the affairs of the credit union. Each credit union member has one vote, regardless of the size of his share holdings. As in other formal associations, the board of directors appoints the officers.

The Federal Credit Union Act of 1959 increased the scope of Federal credit union operations and placed greater powers and responsibilities on Federal credit union officials. The changes were also intended to promote greater efficiency in operations. Some of the changes included in the Act are:* (1) the supervisory committee, previously elected by the members, will henceforth be appointed by the board of directors; (2) credit committees may appoint loan officers, authorized to approve certain loans that had previously required approval by the credit committee; (3) more than one vice president may be elected; (4) the board of directors may appoint an executive committee to act for the board in making investments; and (5) the board of directors, instead of the members, is now responsible for declaring dividends, with the added authority to declare semiannual or annual dividends. The 1959 Act also permits a credit union operating under a Federal charter to convert to operation under a state charter, and vice versa.

In the small credit union the treasurer may be the only active, salaried manager or officer. His responsibilities include keeping records, making financial reports, and handling funds. Other officers in these credit unions donate their services. The quality of a particular credit union rests heavily on the caliber of its officers, and particularly on that of its treasurer.

Nature of Shares

Members of credit unions do not make deposits in their credit unions; instead, they purchase shares in the association. Credit unions have the right of requiring that members give written notice prior to redemption of shares, but like many other savings and thrift institutions, they do not enforce their right. If a credit union did enforce it and failed to redeem outstanding shares at the end of the time period, the members would have to choose between a general scale-down of share values or liquidation of the credit union's assets. Many industrial credit unions arrange payroll deductions for members, thereby facilitating systematic purchase of shares and repayment of debt. The attractiveness of this form of financial investment is evidenced by the fact that the majority of those eligible for membership are actually members.

Dividends on Shares

Compared with commercial banks and mutual savings banks, the dividend rates paid by credit unions tend to be higher. In 1959, approximately 70 per cent of the credit unions paid dividends of 4 per cent or more, and around one-third of these paid 5 per cent or more. However, some credit unions paid very low rates or no dividends at all. This fact is brought out in Table 9-4 which groups Federal credit unions according to rate of dividends paid in 1959. Approximately 11 per cent of the Federal credit unions did not pay dividends. No Federal credit union paid higher than 6 per cent, because that is the legal maximum rate. The relatively high dividend rates paid on credit unions' shares reflect the combination of low cost of operations and high yields on consumer credit loans.

Safety of Shares

State and Federal laws require credit unions to establish reserves or guaranty funds. Additions to reserves are related to the level of earnings and delinquent loans. Some credit unions also establish contingency reserves voluntarily. Compared with the institutions already studied, the credit unions' reserves as a percentage of total assets is relatively low, approximately 4.5 per cent in 1959, and failures are more frequent.

TABLE 9–4

FEDERAL CREDIT UNIONS GROUPED ACCORDING TO RATE OF DIVIDENDS PAID, 1959

	Number	Per cent
Rate of dividend		
All Federal credit unions	9,447	100.0
Credit unions paying no dividends	1,050	11.1
Credit unions paying dividends	8,397	88.9
Less than 1 per cent	1	...
1 to 1.9	46	.5
2 to 2.9	264	2.8
3 to 3.9	1,763	18.2
4 to 4.9	4,042	42.8
5 to 5.9	1,782	18.9
6	539	5.7

Source: Federal Credit Unions, Report of Operations, 1959, U. S. Department of Health, Education, and Welfare, p. 7.

The record of liquidation of Federal credit unions for the period 1934-1959 is shown in Table 9-5 to illustrate magnitude and nature of liquidations. During that period 3,100 Federal credit unions were liquidated, and approximately one-fourth of these paid less than 100 per cent to their members. In recent years, over 200 credit unions have been liquidated annually, with most of it limited to the small credit unions.

*Federal Credit Unions, Report of Operations, 1959, p. 1.

TABLE 9–5
LIQUIDATION OF FEDERAL CREDIT UNIONS, 1934-1959

Item	Liquidations completed in:	
	1934-1959	1959
Number of Federal credit unions	3,100	242
Paid 100 per cent or more	2,424	176
Paid less than 100 per cent	676	66
Number of members	327,256	28,006
Received 100 per cent or more	263,127	22,073
Received less than 100 per cent	64,129	5,993
Amount of shares $27,677,998		$4,082,592
Repaid 100 per cent or more [1]	24,712,918	3,780,270
Received less than 100 per cent [2]	2,965,080	302,322

[1] In addition, dividends were paid on some of these shares as follows: 1934-1959, $1,536,497; 1959, $360,940.

[2] The losses on these shares were as follows: 1934-1959, $647,495; 1959, $45,191.

Source: Federal Credit Unions, *Report of Operations*, 1959, U. S. Department of Health, Education, and Welfare, p. 3.

Approximately 2 per cent of outstanding Federal charters are cancelled annually. Among the reasons cited for cancellation are failure to complete organization, merger with another credit union, conversion to state charter, and liquidation. The latter factor accounts for the major share of cancellations. The causes of liquidation may be internal or external or both. Internal factors include lack of interest and poor financial condition. External factors refer to those beyond the control of the credit union, such as severe production cutbacks and closing of plants. Where external factors are the cause of liquidation, members generally receive 100 per cent.

Credit union officials are bonded to protect members should an officer abscond with funds, but there is no insurance scheme comparable to those of the F.D.I.C. or the F.S.L.I.C. The Executive branch of the Federal Government recently requested that Congress consider the merits of share-account insurance and other measures that might be adopted to protect savings in credit unions, but up to the close of 1960, no insurance program had been established. The proponents of credit union insurance include the very large credit unions and other savings and thrift institutions, the latter of which are concerned with reducing the competitive cost advantages of credit unions. A credit union share account insurance plan would add to the costs of credit union operation and tend to narrow the cost differential. Many of the large credit unions are in a position to carry the cost of a Federal insurance plan, whereas many of the smaller credit unions are not in such a position. A few states do have limited programs of share-account insurance. Some form of Federal credit union insurance will probably be adopted within the next few years.

Assets of Credit Unions

The diversity in state and Federal credit union laws and variation in the size and age of credit unions make it very difficult to generalize on the use of funds by credit unions, except to state that about three-fourths of the funds are returned to members in the form of loans. The other funds are invested in government obligations and savings and loan shares. The majority of states restrict loans to short- and intermediate-term consumer credit, and restrict investments to U.S. Government obligations and share accounts in other institutions. Some states are more liberal. In Massachusetts, for example, credit unions may loan up to $12,000 on real estate loans secured by real estate located within the state.

TABLE 9–6

ASSETS AND LIABILITIES OF CREDIT UNIONS — END OF 1958

(BILLIONS OF DOLLARS)

	Dollars	Per cent
Assets		
Financial Assets	4.0	100.0
Credit and equity market instruments	3.1	78.0
Federal obligations	.1	2.5
Mortgages on 1- to 4-family properties	.4	10.0
Consumer credit	2.7	67.5
Fixed-value redeemable claims:		
Savings deposits, shares, and bonds	.6	15.0
Cash balances: currency and demand deposits	.3	7.5
Liabilities		
Liabilities	3.8	100.0
Fixed-value redeemable claims:		
Credit union shares	3.8	100.0

Note: Details may not add to totals because of rounding.
Source: Data derived from Flow of Funds/Savings Worksheets, Board of Governors of the Federal Reserve System.

Federal credit unions are much more restricted in their loans and investments than are some of the state-chartered credit unions. However, the restrictions have been liberalized five times, the latest time being the Credit Union Act of 1959. The following restrictions are based on this Act: (1) unsecured loans to members cannot exceed $750; (2) secured loans to any one member may not exceed $200, or 10 per cent of the credit union's paid-in unimpaired capital and surplus; (3) maturity of loans may range up to 5 years; (4) the maximum rate of interest on loans to members is 1 per cent a month on the unpaid balance, inclusive of all charges incidental to making the loan; and (5) refund of part of the interest paid by borrowing members during a calendar year is permitted.

The distribution of total assets and liabilities of credit unions is set forth in Table 9-6. The data show the extent to which credit unions specialize in consumer credit, holding nearly two-thirds of their financial assets in that form of credit. More than three-fourths of the funds received by credit unions are returned to members in the form of consumer and mortgage loans. Savings and loan shares and Federal obligations are the major forms of credit union investment.

During the early part of the postwar period, credit unions drew down the share of total assets in investments and shifted a larger percentage of funds to loans to members. Like other savings and thrift institutions during the war, credit unions invested heavily in U.S. Government obligations and then during the postwar period reduced the share of assets in such investments. From 1954 through 1959, the proportion of assets in loans continued to increase, but at the expense of their holdings of cash balances. Though the proportion of assets in investments remained constant, there were marked shifts in the investment pattern toward insured savings and loan shares and loans to other credit unions.

Growth of Credit Unions

The growth of credit unions is plotted in Figure 9-2, which shows the change in number of credit unions since 1931 and the change in total assets since 1937. It is sufficient to mention that in 1921 there were only 190 such institutions, and total assets of credit unions did not pass the $100 million mark until 1937. Though credit union assets are not very large in relation to almost all other financial institutions, credit unions have the distinction of being the most numerous and fastest-growing of all savings and thrift institutions.

In contrast with other savings and thrift institutions, credit unions continue to show a very rapid rate of growth in numbers of associations, but it should be noted that the rate of growth is decreasing. During World War II, the number of institutions fell off, reflecting the controls on consumer credit and the introduction of payroll savings plans. The need for additional credit unions was not very great during the war years. Total assets continue to increase at a more rapid rate than the deposits and deposit-types of accounts that have been plotted in previous charts.

As for future growth, it is likely that the size of total assets will continue to increase. It is estimated that more than half of those eligible to be members of Federal credit unions now belong to Federal credit unions, indicating possible growth within existing groups. The rate of growth in terms of numbers shows that there must be many groups that have no organized credit unions. Whether or not these groups constitute fertile ground for the creation of additional credit unions is uncertain. The limitations placed on the use of credit union funds tends to restrict growth in the sense that some credit unions may accumulate funds faster than they can lend funds to members. If a large portion of the funds were invested, the rate of dividend would be adversely affected and the credit union would lose one of its competitive advantages. If the laws and regulations were modified to allow credit unions more freedom in making loans and investments, they would be in a position to grow even faster, but at the same time they would tend to depart from the initial aims of the credit union movement. Imposing

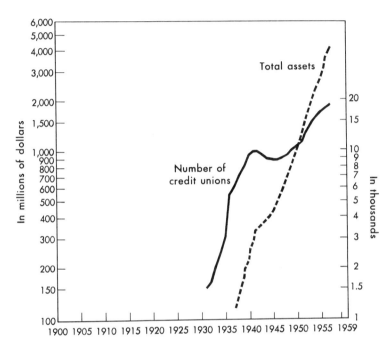

FIGURE 9-2   NUMBER AND TOTAL ASSETS OF CREDIT UNIONS, 1931-1959

Source: Credit Union National Association, *Credit Union Yearbook*, 1959 and 1960.

some form of insurance on credit unions would add to costs and tend to lower the dividend rates. The share accounts would become more attractive in terms of safety, but less attractive in terms of rate of dividend. In summary, credit unions are well entrenched and are in the process of change. The direction of change is such that credit unions are becoming more like other savings and thrift institutions.

QUESTIONS

1.   Compare the organization and administration of a savings and loan association with that of a mutual savings bank.

2.   What prompted the formation of savings and loan holding companies?

What action did Congress take to curb future growth in such holding companies?

3. Describe the structure of the savings and loan system, and compare it with that of mutual savings bank system and the commercial banking system.

4. Compare a share account in a savings and loan association with a savings account in a mutual savings bank. Is either type of account considered to be money? Explain.

5. Compare the interest or dividend rate on the savings and share accounts in your local community.

6. Discuss the factors affecting the liquidity and safety of savings and loan shares.

7. Construct a simple aggregate balance sheet for savings and loan associations, showing the relative importance of each balance-sheet item. Explain the asset composition in terms of the loan and investment policies.

8. Compare the growth rate of time deposits in commercial banks, savings deposits in mutual savings banks, and shares in savings and loan associations. Why have the growth rates varied?

9. Describe briefly the organization and administration of a credit union.

10. How do dividends paid on credit union shares compare with the interest or dividends paid on other savings accounts? What accounts for the difference?

11. Construct a simple aggregate balance sheet for credit unions, showing the relative importance of each balance-sheet item. Explain the asset composition in terms of the loan and investment policies.

12. What are the prospects for future growth in the number of credit unions and in the volume of credit union assets?

ADDITIONAL READING

Almost all of the personal finance and consumer economics texts listed at the end of Chapter 7 treat the topics covered in Chapter 9.

Bodfish, Morton, and A. D. Theobald. *Savings and Loan Principles.* Englewood Cliffs, N. J.: Prentice-Hall, Inc., 1938.

Credit Union National Association. *Credit Union Yearbook.* See latest report. Madison, Wisc.: International headquarters, Filene House, 1617 Sherman Avenue.

Croteau, J. T. *The Federal Credit Union — Policy and Practice.* New York: Harper & Bros., 1956.

Federal Home Loan Bank Board. *Savings and Home Financing Source Book.* See latest source book. Issued annually and emphasizes the institutions affiliated with the Federal Home Loan Bank System and the Federal Savings and Loan Insurance Corporation. The Federal Home Loan Bank Board also publishes periodic reports to provide current data for the series contained in the *Source Book*.

Ketchum, Marshall D., and Leon T. Kendall. *Conference on Savings and Residential Financing*. Sponsored by the United States Savings and Home League. Among the many topics covered in the 1958 and 1959 conferences, only one paper is cited at this point: "The Relevance of the Conference to the Savings and Loan Business," a panel discussion at the 1959 Conference.

U. S. Department of Health, Education, and Welfare, Social Security Administration, Bureau of Federal Credit Unions. *Federal Credit Unions — Report of Operations*. See latest annual report.

U. S. Savings and Loan League. *Savings and Loan Fact Book*. A compilation of statistics embracing all aspects of thrift and home financing in America; see latest report.

U. S. Senate Committee on Banking and Currency. *Savings and Loan Holding Companies*. Hearings, 86th Cong., 1st sess. Washington, D. C.: Government Printing Office, 1959.

10: Insurance, annuities, and pensions, I

HERE are many events that may cause considerable financial loss: (1) expense and loss of income associated with illness, accident, death, and old age; (2) loss or damage of property or both; and (3) liability arising out of injury to other persons and the property of others. The uncertainties of financial loss involved in these situations are universal and undesirable, and in most instances consumers, business, and governments cannot manage them alone. Group action is necessary. By pooling a sufficiently large number of individual risk situations, and by applying the law of large numbers, it is possible to predict within rather narrow limits the total losses of the group. The pooling of uncertainties averages out to near-certainty, allowing financial institutions to provide a system of sharing of losses by all those who participate. Essentially, insurance, annuities, and pensions are social devices for sharing various types of uncertainties.

In the next two chapters we shall examine the structure and operation of the financial institutions directly involved in managing funds that are related to insurance, annuities, and pensions. These financial institutions serve the needs of business and governments, as well as the needs of consumers, but the major share of funds flowing into the institutions flow directly from consumers, and much of the remainder of the flow is for the benefit of consumers. In the flow-of-funds system of accounts, life insurance, government as well as private, is reflected in the financial assets of the consumer sector. Also, both private pension plans and government employee retirement and railroad retirement plans are reflected in consumer investment in financial assets. Therefore, it is appropriate in this part of our study to focus attention on the insurance institutions sector of the economy. The insurance sector, as described in the flow-of-funds system of accounts, consists of all domestic insurance companies (life and nonlife), self-administered pension and retirement plans, and the insurance activties of fraternal orders. In these chapters we shall also consider government insurance and retirement programs. In the flow-of-funds sector structure, these are reflected in the liabilities of the government.*

*Life insurance and pension transactions enter the flow-of-funds accounts in several

ORGANIZATION, ADMINISTRATION, REGULATION OF INSURANCE COMPANIES

For the purpose of these chapters, all domestic insurance companies are broken down into two broad classifications: life and nonlife. Life insurance companies sell life insurance, annuities, accident and health coverage, and administer pension programs. Nonlife insurance companies sell policies that relate to fire, marine, casualty, and surety lines. Prior to 1947 the different types of nonlife insurance companies were restricted to writing only certain lines of insurance. Since 1947 the states have introduced multiple-line underwriting, which permits the individual nonlife insurance companies to write nearly all of the nonlife lines of insurance. Accident and health insurance is the only major line of insurance that is sold by both life and nonlife insurance companies. Nonlife insurance companies may be involved in life insurance only through subsidiary companies, i.e., by holding the controlling interest in the outstanding voting stock of life insurance companies.

The trend toward multiple-line underwriting and the sale of insurance through corporate subsidiaries of nonlife insurance companies demonstrate that there are basic insurance principles that underly all lines of

---

ways. The following explanation is quoted from "A Quarterly Presentation of Flow of Funds, Savings, and Investments," *Federal Reserve Bulletin,* August 1959, pp. 849-850: "Premiums and benefits in connection with life insurance, individual annuities, private pension plans, government employee retirement funds, and railroad retirement funds have characteristics of both capital transactions and current transactions. On the one hand, they can, in large part, be considered financial flows representing increased claims (or liquidation of claims) on insurance, pension, and retirement funds. On the other hand, they can also, to a great extent, be considered current outlays (many of them on a payroll deduction basis) and current income to consumers.

The present treatment recognizes the ambivalent nature of these transaction complexes and they are reflected in both current and capital transactions. Total premiums (including payroll deductions) and total benefits are included in the pertinent transaction categories as current flows in the consumer, Federal Government, State and local government, and insurance sectors. The net accrual of equity in insurance and pension funds is imputed as a current flow from these funds to consumers in the category "credits imputed to consumers in connection with life insurance and pension plans." As a counterpart to these income credits, consumers are shown as investing these accrued values back into the funds through the financial transaction categories "saving through life insurance" and "saving through pension funds." The net accrual flows, "credits to consumers, etc." differ from the net of the corresponding premium and benefit flows, being larger by the amount of the investment income of the funds and employer contributions to the funds and smaller by the amount of the operating expenses of the funds (including the pertinent internal saving of life insurance companies).

Saving of the insurance sector consists of the following: for life insurance companies and fraternal orders, change in surplus and other reserves except legal reserves on life insurance and pension plan contracts; and for nonlife insurance companies, total change in surplus and other reserves, since no financial claim against the companies is recorded for policyholders' prepayments of premiums. (Saving of nonlife insurance companies thus equals the subsector's net acquisition of assets, plus the subsector discrepancy.) No saving is recorded for the noninsured pension plans subsector since consumer claims against the subsector are estimated as equal to its total assets."

insurance. The purpose of this section is to set forth some of the features of insurance that are common to both life and nonlife insurance.

Legal Form of Organization

Some private insurance companies are organized on a proprietary basis and some are organized on a cooperative basis. The major theoretical difference between the two is that the former represents a company that is organized for profit, and the latter represents a company that is organized on a non-profit basis. In the latter situation, the members of insurance organizations offer insurance to one another at cost. Nearly all insurance companies are incorporated. The proprietary corporations are known as stock companies. The cooperative insurance carriers that are incorporated are known as non-stock or mutual companies. The major share of nonlife insurance is issued by stock companies; the major share of life insurance is issued by mutual companies.

The organization of stock and mutual companies is accomplished in accordance with the state insurance laws. The incorporators do not have to justify the incorportaion of an insurance company. As long as the incorporators have satisfied the requirements set forth in a state's insurance laws, and the appropriate official is satisfied that the incorporators are of good repute and intend in good faith to operate the company, the corporate charter will be issued. Generally, the name of the corporation must contain the word "insurance" and if the corporation is organized on the mutual plan, it must also contain the word "mutual." The paid-up capital requirements for an insurance company tend to exceed the paid-up capital requirements for other types of financial institutions.

Insurable Risks

If a risk situation satisfies certain broad tests then, in theory, it is insurable. Insurance companies collect and analyze much technical and economic data in order to arrive at a basis for prediction of loss experience in the future. Engineers, physicians, meteorologists, economists, statisticians, actuaries, and many other highly skilled pepole assume important roles in this process. For a risk situation to be insurable, it must satisfy certain requirements. One, the insurance industry must be able to apply the "law of large numbers" or the "law of averages." To do so, it must deal with a large group of closely similar risk situations. Two, the loss that is involved must be one that is definite—one that cannot be faked. This requirement implies that the loss must also be accidental or fortuitous. A faked or fraudulent loss is not accidental. Three, the loss must be large enough to make insuring economically feasible. Many expenses are involved in operating an insurance business, and if the loss that is being insured against is a very small one, the selling and administrative expenses may approach the size of the expected loss. Four, the loss should not be expected to occur to a very large number at the same time. In more technical language the chance of loss must be small, which means that the probable number and severity of losses out of a given number of risk situations must not be very great. This is the major factor accounting for the high cost of flood insurance.

The accuracy of prediction in most lines of nonlife insurance is not nearly as good as that obtained by life insurance companies. As a result, the ownership equity or policy holders' surplus, expressed as a percentage of an insurance company's obligations, is much greater for nonlife companies than it is for life companies.

The Insurance Policy

If a risk situation can be analyzed statistically and underwriting requirements are satisfied, then insurance policies and related forms or endorsements are designed and sold to the public. An insurance policy may be defined as "a document containing the contract between the insured and the insurer. Its anatomy is made up of declarations, insuring agreements, exceptions, and conditions. The declarations describe the nature of the risk, the insuring agreements indicate in broad terms the nature of the coverage, the exclusions cut the coverage down to size, and the conditions set forth the ground rules of the transaction."* State regulations require that the rates included in insurance contracts must not be excessive, inadequate, or unfairly discriminatory. The data used to draw up policy contracts and the actual experience under the contracts determine how satisfactorily the broad tests of an insurable situation are satisfied.

Selling of Insurance

Although insurance is very beneficial to almost all consumers and business, experience demonstrates that it must be sold and that an aggressive insurance sales force is necessary. The multiplicity of contracts and forms, technical terminology, and claims and counterclaims of competing companies and agents present many problems to insurance buyers. Within this maze, insurance buyers tend to rely on local insurance sales agencies to serve their needs. However, buyers must be alert, for state regulations are not so strict as to guarantee either that all agents are competent or that all companies are strong financially. At any given moment there are agents who are incompetent and some companies that are at the brink of financial failure. Therefore, insurance buyers must exercise care and judgment in the selection of agencies, companies, policies, and forms.

An insurance sales organization is very important. Prediction of loss is based on the law of large numbers, and if experience is to approach what was predicted, companies must strive for a large volume of sales. Insurance needs must be pointed out to many insurance buyers, and there are many

*Robert I. Mehr, and Emerson Cammack, *Principles of Insurance*, Rev. Ed., Richard D. Irwin, Inc., 1957, pp. 148-149.

other persons who are not motivated unless they are contacted. Operating economies are related to both volume and composition of sales.

Insurance is sold primarily through agents and brokers. Agents are persons who are authorized by companies to create, modify, and terminate contracts between companies they represent and the public. Brokers solicit and negotiate contracts for insurance buyers. The important difference is that agents represent companies, and brokers represent insureds. Some companies sell directly to the public, employing company operated branch offices and salaried representatives.

Agents enter into contracts with the companies they represent. The sales organizational structure within which agents function include general agency, branch office, and direct reporting. Under a general agency organization, the agency contract authorizes a person (general agent) to represent a company in a given geographical area, and he controls personnel and operations within the area. In some instances a general agency may perform so many functions in addition to sales that it is virtually an insurance company. The primary source of income to both general agents and their agents is commission on sales. In a branch office organization, the person in charge is under direct supervision of the home office; the insurance salesmen are agents, but they are the employees of the company rather than employees of the branch office manager. In a direct-reporting organization, agents deal directly with the home office instead of working through a general agency or a branch office.

Government Regulation

All types of insurance companies operate within a complicated network of governmental regulations. Except for taxes, most of it is state regulation. Until 1944, the courts had ruled that insurance was not interstate commerce and was not subject to Federal regulation. However, in the South-Eastern Underwriters Association case the United States Supreme Court held that the business of insurance was subject to federal regulation under the Commerce power. Congress reacted to the decision by passing the McCarran Act, which stated among other things that "the continued regulation and taxation by the several States of the business of insurance is in the public interest, and that silence on the part of the Congress shall not be construed to impose any barrier to the regulation or taxation of such business by the several States." The act also stated that the Sherman Act of 1890 and the Clayton Act of 1914 shall be applicable to the business of insurance to the extent that such business is not regulated by state law. The net effect of the McCarran Act and other Federal legislation is that insurance is regulated almost entirely by the various states. One of the few exceptions to the general statement is the variable annuity. In 1959, the United States Supreme Court held that the issue of the variable annuity by life insurance companies is subject to two Federal acts, the Securities Act and the Investment Company Act. The nature of the variable annuity is discussed in the next chapter.

Considering the nature of insurance, it is imperative that the public be protected from incompetent and fraudulent insurance operations. Furthermore, excessive competition among insurance carriers can lead to the failure of some companies, just as excessive rate competition among commercial banks may lead to the failure of some commercial banks.

An insurance company must satisfy not only the requirements of the state in which it is organized, but also the licensing requirements of those states in which it desires to solicit insurance by means other than mail. Inasmuch as many insurance companies transact business in the same states, such as New York and Massachusetts, there is more over-all uniformity in state regulation than first meets the eye. Fortunately, the regulations of New York and Massachusetts are very good, and as long as those and other states continue to administer effective regulation, the Federal government will more than likely continue to play a minor role in the regulation of private insurance companies.

The broad aim of regulation is the assurance of reliable insurance. The areas of state regulation are: the organization of domestic companies and the admission of out-of-state insurers; the establishment of a standard of solvency for setting up and maintaining minimum reserves; the reporting of financial conditions and the making of periodic examinations; overseeing the equitable treatment of policy holders by prescribing and appraising contracts; by licensing and regulating the conduct of agents and brokers; and by broad supervision of investments. Life insurance company investments are more closely supervised than are the investments of nonlife insurance companies. Specific insurance regulations are very extensive, and no attempt is made to enumerate them.

NONLIFE INSURANCE COMPANIES

Nonlife insurance companies write or sell many lines of insurance: fire, ocean and inland marine, casualty, fidelity and surety, and accident and sickness. The accident and health coverages are written by casualty insurance companies, life insurance companies, and special firms. The latter category refers to companies that sell only accident and health coverages and the various hospital and medical surgical plans, such as Blue Cross and Blue Shield. As noted earlier in the chapter, the modern trend is toward multiple-line writing and the industry divisions within the nonlife category are beginning to overlap. Assuming that certain financial requirements are satisfied, an individual nonlife insurance company may write or sell almost all coverages included in the nonlife branch of insurance.

Inasmuch as the field of nonlife insurance is very heterogeneous, the discussion of policies, premiums, reserves, and other financial data must be very general in nature. No effort is made here to indicate the exceptions.

Need for Nonlife Insurance Coverages

A survey of the physical properties of households, the activities of persons, and the financial losses that could result from any one of many causes, points up the need for the many coverages offered by nonlife insurance companies. Similar needs exist in the business and government sectors of the economy. In response to needs, nonlife insurance companies have been formed to administer plans of insurance related to loss of and damage to property and liability resulting from injury to other persons and their property. An almost endless number of specific types of coverages is available. In most instances, if insurance buyers can name it, insurance companies either have it or will make it available. There is a company and a policy for almost any conceivable type of risk situation.

Policies and Premium Payments

One of the differences between life and nonlife insurance is the length of time for which contracts run. In life insurance many contracts run for a long and indefinite period; many life insurance contracts remain in force until the death of the insured. In nonlife insurance, the policies generally run from less than one year up to five years. Policies that are written for a one-year period are called "annual policies." Premiums are based on annual policies. If a policy runs for a period less than one year, it is called a short-term policy and the rate is slightly higher, in the sense that per-day cost of insurance is higher. If a policy runs for a period of two to five years, it is called a "term policy." The rate of a term policy is slightly lower in the sense that a discount is allowed. To illustrate, a five-year policy may be written at four times the annual premium.

The cost of insurance is stated in terms of a premium, which is expected to cover selling and administrative expense, claims expense, and losses. As a general rule, premiums are paid in advance. With a few exceptions, the insured is permitted to cancel a policy before the end of a contract period and receive from the issuer a refund of premium. To offset the costs involved in putting a policy on the books, the company is not obligated to return a proportionate amount. Instead, the company refunds an amount based on the short rates, which are the rates that would have applied if the policy had been issued for less than one year. However, if the company cancels the policy, the company is obligated to return the proportionate amount of premium.

Reserves

Since nonlife insurance companies collect premiums in advance, there must be some way of assuring insurance buyers that the companies will have funds on hand to cover the payment of future losses, to pay future expenses involved in adjusting claims, and to return unearned premiums in the event of cancellations. State insurance laws require nonlife insurance companies to set up reserves to cover expected losses, expected claim expense, and cancellations. The setting up of reserves increases liabilities, and unless capital and surplus accounts are reduced, an increase in liabilities must be matched by an equal increase in asset values. Reserves tend to force the retention of funds in the business. Obviously, the funds are not held in the form of cash, but are invested in credit and equity market instruments. The unearned premium reserve is based on gross premium. However, expected losses and expected claim expense, on the average, are expcted to total only about 60 to 70 per cent of gross premium. Therefore, to base the reserve on gross premiums, a margin of additional safety is provided. If the premium on an annual policy were $100, the unearned premium reserve at the beginning of the policy would be $100; at the end of six months, $50; and at the end of the policy, zero. Since there is a continuous turnover of policies, the aggregate unearned premium reserve may remain relatively stable.

Another required reserve is the claim and claim expense reserve. Experience demonstrates that there are delays between the time insureds actually incur losses and the time that settlements are completed. Delays may arise because of slow reporting and the time necessary to investigate claims. In some lines of insurance, and especially in accident and sickness insurance, claims may not be fully paid for many years. If the unearned premium reserves were written down and no allowance was made for these factors, a nonlife insurance company may be short of funds in the future. The reserves for claims and claim expense provide reasonable assurance that companies will have sufficient asset values to cover the losses that have occurred and have not been reported and to cover the reported but unsettled claims.

The other reserves of nonlife insurance companies are not as important as those noted above and are very similar to the reserves that are used in other businesses.

Capital and/or Surplus Accounts

The capital and/or surplus accounts represent the excess of assets over liabilities; they indicate the extent to which asset values could decrease but still be adequate to cover liabilities. The exact nature of these accounts for any individual company depends on the company's lines of insurance and its legal form of organization. Stock companies have capital stock and surplus accounts; companies organized on a nonprofit basis have only surplus accounts. The surplus accounts consist of both paid-in surplus and earned surplus. Capital stock and paid-in surplus originate at the time an insurance company is organized. Additions to these accounts occur infrequently; for instance, when a capital stock carrier seeks additional funds through stock issue, or when an insurance carrier capitalizes some of its surplus. Earned surplus originates and continues as a result of successful operations.

Compared with many other financial institutions, the capital and/or surplus accounts of nonlife insurance companies are fairly large in relation to stated liabilities. At the end of 1958, the ratio of capital and/or surplus accounts to liabilities was nearly 60 per cent. The state of prediction for many nonlife insurance lines is far from perfect. As a result, there is much uncertainty of obligations under existing contracts. The stated obligations are only as reliable as the assumptions on which they are based, and assumptions are only expectations. The unearned premium reserves and claim and claim expense reserves may prove to be grossly inadequate in some years. To assure insurance buyers that insurance companies will be reasonably prepared to meet the contingency of adverse loss experience, the state insurance laws specify rather sizeable capital and/or surplus accounts. To prevent the capital and/or surplus from falling below specified minima, companies tend to maintain them at levels in excess of minima. Furthermore, if an insurance company is expanding its volume rapidly, the requirement that unearned premium reserves be based on gross premium may demand that the company draw down surplus to maintain balance.

Financial Pattern of Operations

Generally, management expects that premiums will cover losses and expenses and provide a reasonable return on capital stock and/or surplus accounts. If losses and claim expense are no greater than assumed in premium determination, and if the company is successful in holding down general expenses, then the company is in a position to realize a profit in its insurance operations. Underwriting profits are retained in order to build up surplus accounts, for in some years the companies are likely to experience underwriting losses, and may draw down surplus accounts. In some years, the companies do not expect to have underwriting gains because the states have not approved higher rates. In these years the companies' main objective is to minimize underwriting losses.

Investment income also contributes to the total financial returns of nonlife insurance companies. Unlike premium determination in life insurance, the investment income is not figured in the determination of premiums on nonlife insurance lines. In many instances, the investment income is adequate to offset underwriting losses, which means that earned surplus may actually increase during the same year that nonlife insurance companies incurred underwriting losses. Dividends paid on the capital stock of nonlife insurance companies are based on investment income. The investment income not distributed to owners and policy holders tends to build up surplus accounts. The word "tends" indicates that underwriting losses might be greater than retained investment income.

Figure 10-1 shows the variation in underwriting profits of nonlife

Per cent

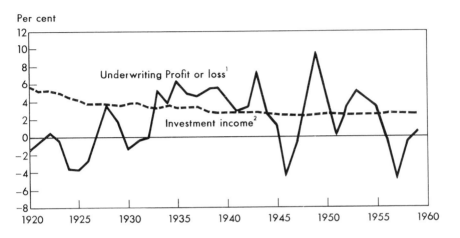

FIGURE 10-1   STOCK NONLIFE INSURANCE COMPANY INVESTMENT INCOME AND UNDERWRITING RESULTS, 1920-1959

[1] Underwriting profit or loss stated in terms of a percentage to earned premiums.
[2] Investment income stated as a percentage to assets.
Source: Best's Fire and Casualty Aggregates and Averages, 1959, (New York: Alfred M. Best Co.). Reprinted by permission.

stock insurance companies for the period 1920-1959. Over the long run, nonlife insurance companies have been able to realize underwriting profits, although during this period there were twelve years in which the companies in the aggregate suffered underwriting losses. Investment income shows little cyclical variation and a gradual downward trend.

Many nonlife insurance companies are closely similar to investment companies in the sense that nonlife insurance companies obtain their capital from the public sale of stock and reinvest the funds in securities of other businesses. At the end of 1958, the capital stock and surplus accounts of non-life stock insurance companies were about 38 per cent of total assets. If the reserve for unearned premiums were adjusted downward to reflect the 30 to 40 per cent excess margin, the buffer or excess assets· values would be approximately 50 per cent. Therefore, nearly 50 per cent of the assets represent stockholder investment; the other 50 per cent represent funds that are directly related to insurance operations. From an investment point of view, the analyses of nonlife stock insurance companies is broken down into insurance operations and investment operations. Investors in nonlife stock

219

insurance companies have the possibility of realizing favorable investment results over the long run because of the cumulative effects of reinvesting the funds representing retained underwriting profits and increased reserves.

Aggregate Balance Sheet of Nonlife Insurance Companies.

A statement of condition for nonlife insurance companies as of the end of 1958 (Table 10-1) reveals the relative importance of capital and/or surplus accounts and reserves, and also sheds light on the investments of nonlife insurance companies. Figures of individual companies differ from the percentages shown in the statement because individual companies neither write identical lines nor operate under identical financial circumstances.

In the event of exceptionally large losses, the nonlife companies must be prepared to pay out large amounts within a short time. Federal obligations are one of the most liquid earning assets, and the data in Table 10-1 show that the companies held 22.7 per cent of their assets in this form. The effect of taxation can also be observed by noting the importance of state and local obligtions (21.7 per cent of assets). The stock nonlife insurance companies are taxed at the rate of 52 per cent. Therefore, the tax-exempt state and local obligations are attractive investment outlets compared with corporate bonds. Corporate bonds have to yield nearly twice what state and local obligations yield for their after-tax yields to be the same. Corporate bonds account for only a very small percentage of total assets. (8.8 per cent of assets.)

The relative size of capital stock and/or surplus accounts and the margin of safety included in the unearned premium reserves permit nonlife insurance companies to adopt investment policies that are much more aggressive than those of, say, mutual savings banks and life insurance companies. The degree of excess asset values and the ability to assume loss of investment income permit nonlife insurance companies to invest rather heavily in equity market securities. The data show that the companies in 1958 had invested 29.2 per cent of their assets in corporate stocks. It is not difficult to understand why nonlife insurance companies are compared with investment companies. Corporate stocks are an attractive investment outlet for various reasons. First, in the long run the investment performance of a carefully selected group of common stocks is better than the performance of a carefully selected group of bonds. Second, under the Federal tax laws, a corporation need not pay taxes on all dividend income, but only on 15 per cent of that income. The result is that the effective tax on dividend income is approximately 7.8 per cent (.52 times .15 equals .078).

Investments

The investment pattern of nonlife insurance companies during the period 1950-1958 is shown in Table 10-2. In comparison with other institutions studied in earlier chapters, there are significant differences. Except for 1955 and 1956, nonlife insurance companies increased their holdings of Federal obligations each year. The data show that the companies invested a major portion of their funds in state and local obligations. In some years the nonlife insurance companies supplied nearly 20 per cent of the total net flow of funds into state and local obligations. During the period the net investment each year in corporate bonds tended to decline. In 1956 and 1957 the net acquisition of corporate bonds was less than $50 million. Throughout the period the companies invested between $100 and $200 million in corporate stocks.

TABLE 10–1

ASSETS AND LIABILITIES OF NONLIFE INSURANCE COMPANIES, END OF 1958

(BILLIONS OF DOLLARS)

	Dollars	Per cent
Assets		
Financial Assets		
Credit and equity market instruments:		
Federal obligations	6.7	22.7
State and local obligations	6.4	21.7
Corporate bonds	2.6	8.8
Corporate stocks [1]	8.6	29.2
Mortgages	.8	2.7
Other loans	.1	.3
Trade credit (premium balances)	1.6	5.4
Cash balances — currency and demand deposits	1.5	5.1
Physical Assets	1.2	4.1
Total Assets	29.5	100.0
Liabilities [2]		
Reserve for losses and adjusting expenses	7.4	25.0
Reserve for unearned premium	9.1	31.0
Other liabilities	2.1	7.0
Total liabilities (excluding capital accounts)	18.6	63.0
Capital stock and/or surplus	10.9	37.0
Total liabilities and capital accounts	29.5	100.0

[1] Based on market value.
[2] Liabilities and capital accounts estimated by author.
Source: "A Quarterly Presentation of Flow of Funds, Saving and Investment," *Federal Reserve Bulletin*, August 1959.

Growth

The growth in total assets of the stock nonlife insurance companies since 1910 (Figure 10-2) is used to indicate the growth in this segment of the financial system. Compared with the charts presented in previous chapters, the nonlife insurance companies' assets show a slightly faster rate of growth.

TABLE 10-2
NET ACQUISITION OF FINANCIAL ASSETS BY NONLIFE INSURANCE COMPANIES,
1950-1958
(BILLIONS OF DOLLARS)

	1950	1951	1952	1953	1954	1955	1956	1957	1958
Total net acquisitions	1.0	1.0	1.6	1.6	1.3	1.3	.6	1.0	1.1
Credit and equity market instruments:									
Federal obligations	.4	.2	.4	.3	.2	—.1	—.3	—.2	.1
State and local obligations	.3	.3	.4	.7	.7	.7	.7	.7	.7
Corporate bonds	.1	.2	.3	.1	.1	.2	.1	.2	.1
Corporate stocks	.1	.1	.2	.2	.2	.2	.1	.1	.1
Mortgages	*	.1	.1	.1	*	.1	*	*	*
Other loans	*	*	*	*	*	.1	*	*	*
Trade credit	*	.1	.1	.1	.1	.1	.1	.2	.1
Cash balance — currency and demand deposits ...	.1	*	.1	.1	*	*	—.1	*	*

*Less than $50 million.
Source: "A Quarterly Presentation of Flow of Funds, Saving and Investment," *Federal Reserve Bulletin*, August 1959.

The pattern within the nonlife insurance sector has not been the same for all lines of insurance. For example, the average annual rate of growth of casualty companies has been about 9 per cent. Fire insurance companies' assets have increased at an average annual rate of growth of about 6 per cent. As for the future, nonlife insurance companies' assets should continue to grow, at least as fast as property value and population do.

QUESTIONS

1. Define multiple-line underwriting. Is it possible for an insurance company to issue both life and nonlife insurance contracts? Explain.

2. Compare the incorporation of a life insurance company with the incorportaion of a savings and loan association.

3. Enumerate some of the individual requirements of an insurable risk.

4. Describe two types of insurance sales organizations. Distinguish between an insurance agent and an insurance broker.

5. To what extent are insurance companies regulated?

6. Identify two types of required reserves of nonlife insurance companies. What is the function of such reserves?

7. Compare the relationship between capital acocunts and stated liabilities for nonlife insurance companies and commercial banks.

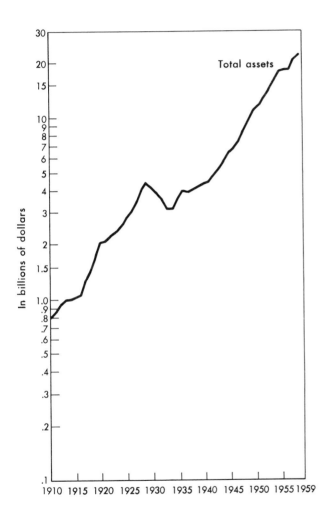

**FIGURE 10-2   GROWTH IN TOTAL ASSETS OF STOCK NONLIFE INSURANCE
COMPANIES, 1910-1959**

Source: *Best's Fire and Casualty Aggregates and Averages, 1958,* (New York: Alfred
M. Best Co.). Reprinted by permission.

8. With respect to stock nonlife insurance companies, which is more steady, investment income or underwriting profit? Explain.

9. Construct a simple aggregate balance sheet for nonlife insurance companies, showing the relative importance of each balance sheet item. Explain the asset composition in terms of the nonlife insurance companies' investment policies.

10. Review briefly the investment pattern of nonlife insurance companies for the period 1950-1958.

ADDITIONAL READING

All of the basic textbooks on personal finance listed at the end of Chapter 7 discuss insurance.

Basic college textbooks on general insurance:

Ackerman, S. B. *Insurance.* (3rd ed.) New York: The Ronald Press Co., 1951.

McGill, Dan M. (ed.). *All Lines Insurance.* S. S. Huebner Foundation for Insurance Education — lectures. Homewood, Ill.: Richard D. Irwin, Inc., 1960.

Magee, John H. *General Insurance.* (5th ed.) Homewood, Ill.: Richard D. Irwin, Inc., 1957.

Mehr, Robert I., and Emerson Cammack. *Principles of Insurance.* (Rev. ed.) Homewood, Ill.: Richard D. Irwin, Inc., 1957.

Mowbray, A. H., and Ralph H. Blanchard. *Insurance, Its Theory and Practice in the U. S.* (4th ed.) New York: McGraw-Hill Book Co., 1955.

Pfeffer, Irving. *Insurance and Economic Theory.* Homewood, Ill.: Richard D. Irwin, Inc., 1956.

Riegel, R., and J. S. Miller. *Insurance Principles and Practices.* (4th ed.) Englewood Cliffs, N. J.: Prentice-Hall, Inc., 1959.

Willet, Allan H. *The Economic Theory of Risk and Insurance.* Homewood, Ill.: Richard D. Irwin, 1951. A classic in its field.

Basic books on nonlife insurance:

Dickerson, O. D. *Health Insurance.* Homewood, Ill.: Richard D. Irwin, Inc., 1959.

Huebner, S. S., and Kenneth Black, Jr. *Property Insurance.* (4th ed.) New York: Appleton-Century-Crofts, Inc., 1957.

Kulp, C. A. *Casualty Insurance.* (3rd ed.) New York: The Ronald Press Co., 1956.

McCahan, David (ed.). *Accident and Sickness Insurance.* S. S. Huebner Foundation for Insurance Education –– lectures. Homewood, Ill.: Richard D. Irwin, Inc., 1954.

Magee, John H. *Property Insurance.* (3rd ed.) Homewood, Ill.: Richard D. Irwin, Inc., 1955.

Snider, H. Wayne (ed.). *Readings in Property and Casualty Insurance.* Homewood, Ill.: Richard D. Irwin, Inc., 1959.

11. Insurance, annuities, and pensions, II

I N this chapter we shall examine three closely related topics: life insurance companies, self-administered pension plans, and public pension and retirement plans.

LIFE INSURANCE COMPANIES*

Life insurance companies sell three types of coverage: life insurance, annuities, and accident and health insurance. The purpose of life insurance is to create an estate upon the death of the insured. Generally, life insurance involves the building up of an estate with a life contingency factor. In the event of the insured's premature death, the face value of the policy is paid to the beneficiary or beneficiaries. In the event the insured lives for a number of years, he tends to accumulate an estate through policyholder's saving. An annuity also involves the life contingency factor, but in this case, the policy provides for a systematic paying out of an estate. When a person lives beyond his earning period, he may have to draw on his accumulated funds to meet living expenses. Since he does not know how long he may live, he does not have any idea as to the rate at which he can draw on principal. Through the life contingency factor, the annuity provides for a periodic payment until death. Accident and sickness insurance is designed to provide for the payment of medical and hospital expense and income.

At the close of 1959, there were 127 million individual life insurance policyholders, and the face amount of their holdings was approximately $600 billion, 90 per cent of which was issued by legal reserve life insurance companies. The remaining 10 per cent was issued by fraternal and assessment organization, savings banks, and the Federal government's veterans insurance programs. In 1959, the aggregate income of life insurance companies from premiums, investment earnings, and other sources was $21.8 billion. Premiums on life insurance policies were $11.5 billion; on annuities, $1.5 billion; and on accident and health coverage, $3.6 billion. Net investment

*Unless otherwise indicated, statistical data relating to life insurance are taken from *Life Insurance Fact Book*, 1960. (New York: Institute of Life Insurance.)

earnings were $3.9 billion and other income, consisting mostly of policy proceeds left with insurance companies to be paid out in the future, was $1.3 billion. The total assets of life insurance companies passed the $100 billion mark in 1957, and at the end of 1959, reached $113.6 billion.

On June 30, 1960 there were 1,439 life insurance companies in the United States, of which 1,285 were stockholder-owned and 154 were mutually owned. Though the number of mutuals is relatively small, they account for more than 60 per cent of the face amount of insurance. In 1960, six life insurance companies reported assets in excess of $4 billion, and all were mutuals; 12 life insurance companies reported assets in excess of $2 billion, and nine of these were mutuals. The number of firms has increased by 995 since 1940; 789 since 1950; and 379 since 1955. In the most recent 12-month period, ending June 30, 1960, there was a net increase of 28 companies. Almost all of the companies formed in recent years have been organized as capital stock companies. In fact, the number of mutual companies declined by 12 between 1955 and 1960. Much of the increase in the number of life insurance companies has taken place in Texas and Arizona. In 1960, 300 life insurance companies were operating in Texas, and 108 companies were operating in Arizona. In the case of Arizona, it is interesting to note that not one domestic life insurance company was operating in the state in 1940, and only three were operating in 1950. Much of the growth in the number of life insurance companies can be attributed to the nature of states' regulations. In recent years, Texas has tightened up its regulation of life insurance companies, and growth in the number of companies in that state has been reversed.

Basic Types of Life Insurance

On the household level, life insurance is used to cover expenses incurred because of death, to retire debts outstanding at the time of death, to provide lump sum payments or income to beneficiaries, and to provide funds for other specified purposes. Life insurance is used by businesses to protect against financial loss resulting from the death of a key man and to facilitate the purchase of a small business, partnership interest, or stockholder interest upon the death of an owner-manager or major partnership interest. Life insurance also improves the insured's credit position because a policy's cash value may be assigned as security for a loan.

Considering the many uses of insurance, it is not surprising that there are many forms of life insurance policies. It is not unusual for a life insurance company to offer as many as 30 different policies. However, there are only three basic types of life insurance: term, whole life, and endowment insurance. Any particular policy is representative of one or a combination of these basic types.

Term insurance. Term insurance offers a plan of insurance payable at death, provided death occurs within a specified period. If the insured does not die during the specified period, the contract expires and there are no further benefits available under the contract. Inasmuch as term insurance provides only protection and does not incorporate policyholders' saving as do other plans of insurance, the premium outlay for a given face value is less for term insurance than for other forms of life insurance.

There are various forms of term insurance. Straight term terminates automatically at the end of a specified period. Renewable terms allow an insured to renew without taking another physical examination. Under both of these forms of term insurance, the original period may be a year or longer, but in most instances there is an age or time period beyond which term insurance will not be sold. To meet the needs of those who cannot afford initially policies incorporating policyholders' saving as well as protection, life insurance companies have designed convertible term, which allows an insured to convert his contract at any time during the specified period into a permanent form of insurance. Permanent insurance provides lifelong protection and incorporates policyholders' saving.

WHOLE LIFE INSURANCE. Whole life insurance provides a plan of insurance for the whole of life, payable at death. Whole life insurance provides protection as well as policyholders' saving. Under the terms of a whole life contract the insured has the right to surrender his policy and claim its cash surrender value, which represents his accumulated saving. The combination of saving and protection appeals to many people. If an insured should live so long that his family is no longer dependent on him, and the major problem is that of providing an adequate retirement income, the accumulated saving in his life insurance policies may be used to provide retirement income. Whole life insurance is a compromise between living for too short a time and living beyond income-earning years.

Various premium-paying arrangements are available in the purchase of whole life insurance. On straight life, premiums are payable until death. On limited-payment life, premiums are payable for a specified number of years, or until death if death occurs before the end of the specified period. Whole life insurance may also be paid for in one lump sum. All other things being equal, the shorter the premium paying period, the higher the premium. As far as permanent life insurance is concerned, straight life insurance provides the greatest dollar amount of protection per premium dollar.

ENDOWMENT INSURANCE. Endowment insurance is a plan of insurance providing for payment of a definite sum of money to the policyholder himself, after a specified number of years if he is then living. If the policyholder dies during the endowment period, payment is made to a beneficiary. Obviously, this type of life insurance policy incorporates the greatest amount of policyholders' saving.

Through policyholders' saving, whole life and endowment insurance provide for a systematic building up of an estate with the assurance that this objective will not be cut short by death. Term insurance does not incorporate a systematic building up of an estate, but does provide assurance that some other method of building up an estate will not be cut short by death. Some persons combine term insurance and systematic direct investment in credit and equity market instruments.

Basic Classes of Life Insurance

Life insurance sales are generally broken down into four broad classes: ordinary life insurance, industrial life insurance, group life insurance, and credit life insurance. Ordinary life insurance includes policies issued in amounts of $1,000 or more with premiums payable on an annual, semi-annual, quarterly, or monthly basis. Nearly three-fifths of all life insurance in force today is ordinary life insurance and approximately 70 per cent of life insurance premiums are paid on ordinary policies. The remainder of life insurance premiums are almost evenly divided between group and industrial. The industrial life classification is also based on size of policy. It includes life insurance issued in small amounts, usually not over $500, with the premiums payable on a weekly or monthly basis. Generally, the premiums are collected at the home by an agent of the company. In response to a demand for policy amounts ranging between $500 and $1,000, life insurance companies have introduced intermediate life insurance, i.e., between industrial and ordinary. Inasmuch as most of the demand for industrial and intermediate life insurance originates in the lower-income groups, and the weekly or monthly collection system is used, companies have established special sales departments to handle the sale and servicing of these policies. Agents who sell industrial and intermediate life insurance are frequently referred to as debit men. However, debit agents are not restricted to the sale of industrial and intermediate life insurance. In some companies, more ordinary life insurance is sold by debit agents than is sold through the company's network of general agencies.

Group life insurance is issued, usually without medical examination, on a group of persons under what is called a master policy. The individual employees, who are members of the group, hold certificates as evidence of their insurance. Many states permit groups numbering as few as ten persons to qualify for this type of protection. At the end of 1959, over one-half of the country's non-agricultural work force was covered by group life insurance. The average amount of group life insurance per insured worker was $3,870.

Closely allied to group life insurance is credit life insurance, which is issued on the lives of borrowers to cover payment of loans in case of death. It is generally used to cover the small loans that are repayable in installments. Therefore, term policies are used, the policies are written through the lenders, and they may be written on either a group or individual policy basis.

At the end of 1959, 81 per cent of credit life insurance was under group plans, and the remainder consisted of individual credit life insurance policies. More than one-half of all consumer credit outstanding is covered by credit life insurance.

Premiums and Reserves

As noted above, insurance may be paid for either in a lump sum or by making a series of payments over a period of time, stretching from a few years to the whole of life. Very few persons are able to pay for their life insurance in one lump sum. To sell a large volume of insurance, companies have devised premium-paying arrangements that permit insureds to pay for their policies over relatively long periods. Through the use of appropriate mathematical techniques, a series of level payments can be made equivalent to an immediate lump-sum payment. The use of level payments has given rise to the concept of "level premium" insurance, which means that the insured's cost of insurance is distributed evenly over the premium-paying period. Mortality experience is not evenly distributed. The older the age, the more likely is death. Therefore, under level premium insurance, the premiums received in the early years total considerably more than the mortality costs during the early years. The premiums received in the latter years, when many of the original participants have passed on, are considerably less than the mortality costs during the latter years. When insureds purchase whole life insurance by paying the full cost at time of issue, the amount collected the first year plus investment income should be adequate to cover the mortality cost over the entire period.

To assure the insurance-buying public that the excess premium payments are retained by the companies until the funds are required to meet the terms of outstanding contracts, state regulations require insurance companies to set up reserves, which are liability accounts. An increase in liabilities must be matched with either an equivalent increase in asset values or a decrease in capital and surplus accounts. Inasmuch as capital and surplus accounts must satisfy certain requirements, the companies are obliged to retain assets to offset the increase in liabilities. At any given time, the required reserves plus the expected future level premium payments should be adequate to meet all future obligations under the then outstanding insurance contracts. Naturally, the retained funds are invested. Since the funds are retained for the benefit of insureds they share in the earnings on these investments. Life insurance companies include expected investment income in determining premiums. In recent years the companies have assumed rates of return ranging between 2½ and 3 per cent.

In summary, life insurance companies consider or assume three basic factors in determining premiums: expected operating expenses, expected mortality cost, and expected investment income. Life insurance policies issued by mutual life insurance companies and participating policies issued by stock life insurance companies contain dividend provisions that allow the insureds to benefit if a company's experience is more favorable than that which was assumed at the time the premium was determined.

Accident and Sickness Insurance (Health Insurance)

The title of this section shows a trend in terminology. Originally, coverages relating to this part of the life insurance companies' operations were referred to as disability insurance, then as accident and sickness insurance, and now as health insurance. The health insurance coverages are a part of life insurance because they relate to the insuring of income. In conjunction with life insurance and annuities, health insurance provides a very comprehensive personal insurance program. Health insurance is also sold by casualty companies and other companies that specialize in writing only disability coverages. Life insurance companies pay out nearly 80 per cent of the benefits paid on health insurance.

Inasmuch as health insurance policy reserves of the life insurance companies are less than $1 billion, this segment of the companies' operation is not very important in consumer saving and investment. However, it should not be overlooked that this form of insurance is important to the consumer. Life insurance companies entered the field by incorporating in life insurance policies income benefits for total and permanent disability and waiver of premium during a period of total disability. Gradually, the coverages were expanded to include benefits to meet the costs of hospital-medical care as well as the loss of income resulting from accidents and illnesses. Coverages are available through both group and individual policies. In 1959, health insurance departments of life insurance companies received more than $3.6 billion premium income and paid out $2.4 billion in benefits. Approximately 80 per cent of the benefits were paid under group contracts.

Annuities

An annuity is a contract that provides an income for a specified period of time, such as a number of years or for life. Life insurance companies are permitted to issue annuities under state insurance laws because issuers assume the risk of mortality. The risk is an actuarial prediction that a certain number of annuitants will survive to specified ages. If the prediction turns out to be incorrect and a substantial number of annuitants live beyond their predicted demise, the issuers will be obligated to make the payments as specified in the annuity contracts. Although the annuity contract is not a life insurance contract, it is a part of the life insurance business because life contingencies are involved.

Annuities may be individually purchased or they may be set up under employer-employee retirement programs. The latter type are referred to as group annuities, under which master contracts are issued to employers for the benefit of employees and certificates evidencing coverages are issued to employees. The concept of "annuities" also includes supplementary agreements, under which the proceeds of life insurance policies are paid out as life income. The extensive use of supplementary agreements in the last two decades is one of the more significant annuity developments. At the end of 1959 there were 5.8 million annuities in force with life insurance companies. Under these annuities, the companies were paying out or guaranteeing to pay out a future annual income of nearly $2.4 billion. A breakdown of annuities in force at the end of 1959 are shown in the tabulation below:

	Number in thousands	Annual income in millions of dollars
Individual annuities	1,197	$ 583
Group annuities	4,342	1,747
Supplementary agreements	407	207
Total	5,946	$2,537

Nearly one-fifth of the annuities were paying out income; nearly two-thirds were fully paid for, but the time had not come to pay out income; and the remainder represented annuities that were not fully paid. At the end of 1959 annuity reserves totaled $20.7 billion.

CLASSIFICATION OF ANNUITIES. An annuity may be used to provide a periodic payment for a specified period of time, such as a number of years, or for life. An annuity contract that provides periodic payments for a specified number of years, regardless of the life or death of the annuitant, is called an annuity certain. An annuity contract that provides periodic payments until the annuitant's death is called a life annuity. It is this latter type of annuity that is unique with life insurance companies. Two or more annuitants may be covered by the same annuity contract. Under a joint annuity, payments continue until the death of the first annuitant. Under a joint and survivorship annuity, periodic payments continue until the death of the last annuitant. The age and sex of an annuitant affect the size of periodic payments.

The circumstances under which an annuity is purchased are important determinants as to method of purchase. An annual payment plan is available to those persons who desire to space out the cost of their annuity contracts. To these people, an annuity is a systematic plan of saving and investing as well as a systematic plan of paying out principal and investment income. An annuity that provides for payments to begin at some future date, such as in a specified number of years or at a specified age, is called a deferred annuity. Obviously, an annuity purchased on an annual-payment basis is a deferred annuity. Annuities are also sold on a single-payment basis for those persons who have accumulated sufficient funds and desire a systematic method of paying out principal and investment income. Under a single-payment annuity the payments may begin immediately, in which case the annuity is referred to as an immediate annuity. Before the date that payments begin, an annuitant can draw down his principal and dispense with the annuity features of the contract unless stated to the contrary in the contract. However, once payments begin and the payments are based solely on life contingency, an annuitant cannot withdraw from the plan.

The question probably arises as to what happens in the event an annuitant dies after having received only a few periodic payments. If the contract is a straight-life annuity, the payments simply cease. Many persons are not satisfied with such a contract, so life insurance companies have designed the refund annuities, which assure an annuitant that payments made by the insurance company will equal at least the total cost of the contract, regardless of the time of the annuitant's death. All other things being equal, the size of a periodic payment is largest under a straight-life annuity.

Two basic types of annuities. Since 1952, there have been in this country two basic types of annuities; the fixed or conventional annuity and the variable annuity. The fixed or conventional annuity contract provides periodic payments in specified and definite fixed-dollar amounts. An issuer of a conventional annuity assumes not only mortality risk, but also the risks that investment income may not be as great as was assumed and that the administrative cost may be more than was assumed in the contract. Generally, life insurance companies adopt conservative assumptions as to mortality, investment income, and expenses so as to minimize risk.

During a period of rising prices, the real purchasing power of periodic payments in fixed-dollar amounts is reduced. To deal with this problem, variable annuity contracts were designed to provide annuities under which the dollar amount of periodic payments would tend to vary with changes in the cost of living. Theoretically, variable annuities should provide reasonable protection to annuitants against future rises in the cost of living. The basic premise underlying the design of variable annuity contracts is derived from historical studies that show a substantial long-term correlation in the movement of average market prices of a selection of common stocks and cost of living indices.

The conventional annuity promises periodic payments in fixed-dollar amounts, and makes no provision for the variation in purchasing power of the fixed-dollar payments. Some conventional annuity contracts are participating contracts. The annuitants may receive slightly higher payments than those specified in the contract. However, the participating feature does not work in reverse. In the event that a company's cost exceeds projected costs, the company assumes the risk and is obligated to make the specified payments. To meet fixed-dollar commitments, the life insurance companies invest funds in accordance with conservative investment standards.

In theory, the variable annuity is designed to provide a periodic income of nearly stable purchasing power produced by variable-dollar payments. The variable annuity introduces two new features into annuity contracts. First, the funds collected from prospective annuitants are to be invested to a much greater degree in equity market instruments, particularly in common stocks. Second, periodic payments to annuitants are to vary with the success of a life insurance company's investment policy. A variable annuity contract does not contain any guarantee of fixed income. Compared with a conventional annuity, the holder of a variable annuity might receive the same, more, or fewer dollars. The investment risks are shifted to the annuitant. It is conceivable that under such a contract an annuitant might receive nothing. In almost all other respects, a variable annuity contract has the same characteristics as a conventional annuity.

The first variable annuity in this country was issued in 1952 through the College Retirement Equities Fund (C.R.E.F.), which is a companion organization to the Teachers Insurance and Annuity Association of America (T.I.A.A.). The T.I.A.A. and C.R.E.F. restrict their insurance operations to college teachers, and both are subject to regulation under the New York Insurance Law. In 1954, the Participating Annuity Life Insurance company began selling variable annuity contracts under the supervision of the Arkansas insurance authority. In 1955, the Variable Annuity Life Insurance Company of America (V.A.L.I.C.) entered the field, and in the following year, the Equity Annuity Life Insurance Company (E.A.L.I.C.) also entered the field. The latter two companies were incorporated under the Life Insurance Act of the District of Columbia and are subject to regulation by the District's Superintendent of Insurance. In 1959, V.A.L.I.C. was also qualified to do business and issue annuity policies in Arkansas, Kentucky, West Virginia, Alabama, and New Mexico; E.A.L.I.C. was qualified in North Dakota. V.A.L.I.C. and E.A.L.I.C. have been able to enter the field because the insurance laws of the District of Columbia permit considerable investment in common stocks, which is an essential ingredient of the variable annuity. Most states' insurance laws severely restrict life insurance company investment in common stocks. In June 1959, New Jersey adopted legislation permitting the sale of variable annuities in the state.

Variable annuity contracts have been and continue to be the focus of much controversy. There is divided opinion as to the merits of such contracts and their regulation. Some states have not accepted the variable annuity contracts as a part of life insurance; they have viewed it more in terms of a security. Some other states have accepted the variable annuity contract as a part of insurance. In 1956, the Securities and Exchange Commission instituted court action to enjoin V.A.L.I.C. and E.A.L.I.C. from offering their variable annuity contracts to the public without registering them under the Securities Act and complying with the Investment Company Act. The United States District Court denied relief and the Court of Appeals affirmed. On March 23, 1959 the United States Supreme Court by a five to four decision reversed the lower courts' decisions. The issue of the variable annuity became subject to the Securities Act of 1933 and the issuers became subject to the Investment Company Act of 1940. (These two acts are discussed in later chapters.) The High Court ruled that the meaning of " insurance " and " annuity " under these two Federal Acts is a federal question, and the court interpreted the variable annuity as being outside the concepts from a federal point of view. The majority opinion stated that " in hard reality the issuer of a variable annuity that has no element of a fixed return assumes no true risk in the insurance sense." The majority of the Court viewed the variable annuity as something closely similar to the securities issued by investment companies. The minority opinion was written by Mr. Justice Harlan, who concluded his remarks in the following manner:

> It is asserted that state regulation, as it existed when the Securities and Investment Company Acts were passed, was inadequate to protect annuitants against the risks inherent in the variable annuity and that therefore such contracts should be considered within the orbit of SEC regulation. The Court is agreed that we should not "freeze" the concept of insurance as it then existed. By the same token we should not proceed on the assumption that the thrust of state regulation is frozen. As the insurance business develops new concepts the States adjust and develop their controls. This is in the tradition of state regulation and federal abstention. If the innovation of federal control is nevertheless to be desired, it is for the Congress, not this Court, to effect.

The immediate reaction of the life insurance companies involved in the sale of the variable annuity and of those vitally interested in entering the field was that dual regulation would not discourage life insurance companies from issuing variable annuity contracts. In 1960, the Securities and Exchange Commission approved prospectuses relating to the sale of variable annuities.

Insured Pension Plans

Insured pension plans involve the application of the basic types of life insurance and annuity contracts to group retirement programs. At the close of 1959, 5.3 million persons in the United States were covered by insured pension plans, which provided for future annual retirement income of approximately $2.7 billion. Reserves behind these insured pension plans amounted to $17.5 billion.

Inasmuch as this is the first mention of pension plans, it is appropriate to trace briefly the development of pension plans. Following this analysis, the major types of insured pension plans will be discussed.

DEVELOPMENT OF PRIVATE PENSION PLANS. Although the first pension plan in this country was started as early as 1875, less than 15 per cent of the labor force was so covered in the early 1930's. During the past three decades the problem of providing resources for retirement has been shifted to a great extent to the government through social security and to employers through group pension plans. In 1960, over 90 per cent of the labor force was covered by either public or private pension plans or a combination of the two.

Social responsibility among employers and their desire to improve employee productivity were basic to the development of pension plans. The adoption of the Old Age and Survivors' Insurance in the middle 1930's encouraged employers to adopt private plans to supplement the benefits offered under the government program. The Wagner Act of 1935 speeded up the labor union movement, and the labor unions, in turn, exerted pressure on management and government to adopt or expand private and public pension plans. Some unions operate their own pension and welfare plans.

Two events during the early 1940's encouraged rapid growth in pension funds. Under Section 165-A of the Internal Revenue Code of 1939, contributions to qualified pension plans became allowable deductions for income tax purposes on the tax returns filed by the creators of trustee pension plans. The income of a trust created under a qualified pension plan was also made exempt from income taxes. During an era of high corporate taxes, tax exemption tends to break down some employer resistance to pension demands. Another contributing factor during the early 1940's was the ceiling on wages, which led to the adoption and expansion of various types of fringe benefits, including pensions. Late in the 1940's, further impetus to the growth of pensions was provided by the ruling that pension and welfare funds were legitimate issues of collective bargaining. Many basic decisions must be made in setting up a group pension plan: (1) eligibility; (2) age for retirement; (3) benefit schedule; (4) contributory or non-contributory; (5) fixed employer contributions or profit sharing; (6) proceeds vested or not vested; (7) funded or not funded; and (8) periodic payments in fixed or variable dollar amounts. Decisions involving (7) and (8) have an important bearing on whether a group pension plan will be insured or noninsured. Under an unfunded plan, retirement benefits are paid out of current income; therefore, such a plan would not be insured. Under a funded plan, costs are anticipated and formal promises are made to meet such costs, and these plans may be insured. Until state insurance laws are amended, pension plans incorporating periodic payments in variable dollar amounts can not be insured.

A breakdown of the existing private and public pension retirement funds is set forth in Table 11-1. The data show that pension retirement funds are about evenly divided between private and public. The noninsured pension retirement funds cover over 16 million persons and account for more than 60 per cent of the total private funds.

TYPES OF INSURED PLANS. An insured pension plan may be set up under either an individual policy plan or a group plan. Under an individual policy plan either life insurance or annuity contracts or a combination of the two may be used. Under some of the individual policy plans a trustee is appointed to perform certain functions: to receive contributions, to apply for and retain policies, and to disburse benefit payments. Under other individual policy plans, trustees are not involved. The former type of plan is sometimes referred to as a formal plan and the latter as an informal plan.

TABLE 11–1
ASSETS OF PRIVATE AND PUBLIC PENSION RETIREMENT FUNDS, END OF 1958
(BILLIONS OF DOLLARS)

	Dollars	Per cent
Total retirement funds, private and public	95.3	100.0
Private		
Insured pension funds	17.5	18.4
Noninsured corporate pension funds	25.3	26.5
Other noninsured funds [1]	1.9	2.0
Total private funds	44.7	46.9
Public		
Railroad retirement	3.7	3.9
Civil Service	9.5	10.0
State and local	17.2	18.0
Old Age and Survivors Insurance	20.1	21.1
Total public funds	50.5	53.0

Note: Details may not add to totals because of rounding.
[1] Includes reserves of nonprofit organizations, multi-employer funds, and union administered plans, as estimated by the Securities and Exchange Commission.
Source: Data derived from the Securities and Exchange Commission Statistical Series, Release No. 1680, May 31, 1960.

Life insurance companies offer four different types of group plans: (1) permanent life insurance with cash values providing funds to finance retirement payments; (2) deferred group annuity, with paid-up units purchased each year, and income payments deferred until retirement; (3) deposit administration, under which a life insurance company accumulates a fund against which the costs of annuities are charged as covered employees reach retirement age; and (4) immediate participation guarantee, under which a life insurance company maintains a fund against which actual investment income is credited and actual expenses are charged. Trust institutions are able to offer considerable flexibility in the management of noninsured pension plans, and plans (3) and (4) were instituted to provide more effective competition. However, life insurance companies still find the competition very rugged because of additional tax obligations and restrictions on investments.

A breakdown of the insured pension plans in force at the end of 1959 are summarized in the following tabulation:

	Number of plans	Number of persons covered
Individual policy pension trusts	17,870	670,000
Group deferred annuity	5,250	2,540,000
Deposit administration	2,530	1,640,000
Other plans	2,780	415,000
Total	28,430	5,265,000

Recalling the fact that annuities are used in the deposit administration plans, the data show that more than 80 per cent of the persons covered by insured pension plans in 1959 were under group annuity contracts, of either the conventional or the deposit administration type. In terms of growth, the deposit administration plan has been the fastest growing insured pension plan.

TABLE 11–2
**OPERATING STATEMENT FOR ALL LEGAL RESERVE LIFE INSURANCE COMPANIES,
1959
(FIGURES IN PERCENTAGES)**

Income	
Premiums	79.7%
Net investment earnings and other income (before Federal income taxes)	20.3
	100.0%
How Used	
Benefit payments and additions to funds for policyholders and beneficiaries:	
Benefit payments in year	50.3%
Additions to policy reserve funds	24.2
Additions to special reserve and surplus funds	3.0
	77.5%
Operating Expenses	
Commissions to agents	7.6%
Home office and other expenses	10.0
	17.6%
Taxes	4.0%
Dividends to stockholders	.9
	100.0%

Excludes direct investment (such as real estate) taxes, but includes Federal income and all other taxes.
Source: *Life Insurance Fact Book*, 1960, Institute of Life Insurance, New York, p. 53.

Financial Pattern of Life Insurance Companies' Operations

Now that nearly all phases of life insurance companies' operations have been considered, attention is turned to the financial pattern of their operations.

The over-all operational pattern of the life insurance companies is well illustrated in the operating statement shown in Table 11-2. The data disclose why life insurance companies are not very much concerned with liquidity. Benefit payments, operating expenses, taxes, and dividends, absorb less than 75 per cent of life insurance companies' income. Furthermore investment in amortized mortgages and bonds with sinking funds provides additional cash inflow.

TABLE 11–3
ASSETS AND LIABILITIES OF LIFE INSURANCE COMPANIES, END OF 1958
(BILLIONS OF DOLLARS)

	Dollars	Per cent
Assets		
Financial Assets:		
Credit and equity market instruments:		
Federal obligations	7.2	6.7
State and local obligations	2.7	2.5
Corporate bonds	44.2	41.1
Corporate stocks	4.1	3.8
Mortgages on 1- to 4-family properties	22.4	20.8
Other mortgages	14.6	13.6
Other loans (almost all policy loans)	4.3	4.0
Cash balances — currency and demand deposits	1.4	1.3
Nonfinancial Assets:		
Real estate	3.4	3.2
Other	3.2	3.0
Total Assets	107.6	100.0
Liabilities		
Insurance policy reserves	64.5	59.9
Annuity reserves	19.0	17.7
Reserves for supplementary agreements	5.1	4.7
Policy dividend accumulations	2.9	2.7
Amounts set aside for policy dividends	1.5	1.4
Other obligations	5.7	5.3
Special surplus funds	1.9	1.8
Unassigned surplus	6.2	5.8
Capital (stock companies only)	.7	.7
Total Liabilities	107.6	100.0

Note: Details may not add to totals because of rounding.
Source: "A Quarterly Presentation of Flow of Funds, Saving and Investment," *Federal Reserve Bulletin,* August 1959; *Life Insurance Fact Book,* 1959.

Aggregate Balance Sheet of Life Insurance Companies

The aggregate balance sheet of life insurance companies (Table 11-3) in conjunction with the operating data sheds considerable light on the investment policy of life insurance companies.

The capital and/or surplus accounts of life insurance companies are relatively small in relation to total assets (8 per cent). One of the factors accounting for the relatively small percentage is the degree of accuracy in predicting mortality costs. Another factor is the importance of the mutual type of operation. Over 70 per cent of life insurance volume is represented either by policies of mutual companies or by participating policies of stock companies. The premiums charged on such policies tend to be more than adequate to cover expected benefit payments and the cost of doing business. All or a part of the excess premiums is generally returned to policyholders in the form of dividends. However, if experience should take a turn for the worse, dividends could be reduced or eliminated. The presence of excess premiums tends to reduce the need for a larger percentage of capital and/or surplus accounts. Last, state insurance laws tend to restrict life insurance investments to credit market instruments, such as bonds and mortgages.

Stability of asset values is very important. If asset values dropped by as much as 10 per cent, the capital and/or surplus accounts would be wiped out and liabilities would exceed assets. The emphasis that must be placed on safety of principal is reflected in the low percentage of assets invested in equity market instruments, such as corporate stock. State insurance laws permitting, some companies have invested as much as 10 per cent of their assets in corporate stocks. As noted earlier, companies incorporated in the District of Columbia are permitted to invest 100 per cent of their assets in corporate stocks. Government and corporate bonds comprise the major portion of life insurance assets. Although bond values fluctuate because of changes in the rate of interest and in the financial condition of the issuers, life insurance asset values are not affected very much. The companies are permitted to carry high-grade bonds on their books at cost if purchased at par and at amortized value if purchased at a discount or premium. Amortized value is cost adjusted for discount or premium over a bond's maturity. By exercising considerable care in the selection of bonds, life insurance companies are able to use amortized values and secure stability of asset values. Mortgages, which account for nearly 35 per cent of assets, also provide stability of asset values.

Investment in the Postwar Period

As in the discussion of investments in previous chapters, the postwar period is broken down into three shorter periods. Considerable variation exists in the investment policies of individual life insurance companies, and the discussion in this section can only reflect the investment policies in an aggregate sense. To understand the investments of life insurance companies in the postwar period, it is important to realize that at the end of the war Federal obligations constituted nearly half of total life insurance assets and the net rate of interest earned on invested funds was down considerably. In response to these conditions, life insurance companies switched out of Federal obliga-

tions into higher-yielding investments, such as corporate bonds and mortgages. It will be recalled that mutual savings banks did not immediately
shift out of Federal obligations into corporate bonds. The difference in
yield, although slight, was more important to life insurance companies than
to mutual savings banks. Also, life insurance companies acquired a major
portion of corporate bonds through direct negotiation rather than through
the purchase of public offered bonds. The yield on direct negotiated bonds
tends to exceed the rate on publicly traded bonds.

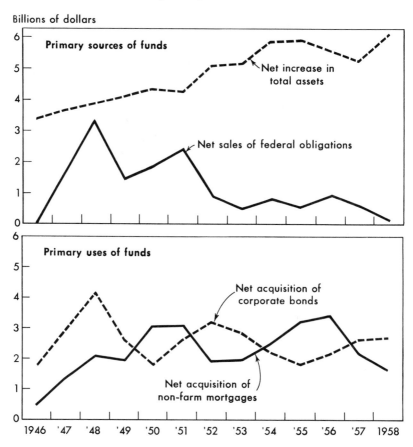

Billions of dollars

**FIGURE 11-1   SELECTED SOURCES AND USES OF FUNDS OF LIFE INSURANCE
COMPANIES, 1946-1958**

Source: Data derived from *Life Insurance Fact Book*, 1959.

Selected sources and uses of funds of life insurance companies for
the postwar period are plotted in Figure 11-1. It should be noted that the
net sale of Federal obligations provided about a third of the 1947 flow and
nearly half of the 1948 flow. The effects of the 1949 recession are noticeable.
The reduced demand of corporations was reflected in lower yields, but at the

same time a housing boom was developing. The net acquisition of corporate bonds fell off rather sharply, but the net acquisition of non-farm mortgages, after a very slight decline, increased sharply. The need to liquidate Federal obligations was not as great, and the volume of liquidation was reduced.

During the years 1950-1953, the pattern of net acquisition and net sales of Federal obligations of corporate bonds was very similar to that of the earlier period. The net acquisition of non-farm mortgages was approximately $3 billion in each of the years 1950 and 1951. During the remainder of the period, net acquisitions continued, but the volume was reduced to the levels of 1948 and 1949. Beginning in 1952, the net sales of Federal obligations fell off sharply. The rise in the interest rate depressed the prices of outstanding bonds that carried lower rates, and the capital losses involved in the sale of these securities discouraged many companies from shifting out of Federal obligations.

TABLE 11–4
NET ACQUISITIONS OF FINANCIAL ASSETS BY LIFE INSURANCE COMPANIES,
1950-1958
(BILLIONS OF DOLLARS)

	1950	1951	1952	1953	1954	1955	1956	1957	1958
Total net acquisitions	3.9	3.9	4.5	4.8	5.0	5.2	5.1	4.8	5.2
Credit and equity market instruments:									
Federal obligations	—1.8	—2.4	—.8	—.4	—.8	—.5	—1.0	—.5	.1
State and local obligations	.1	*	*	.1	.5	.2	.2	.1	.3
Corporate bonds	1.8	2.7	3.1	2.7	2.1	1.7	2.1	2.5	2.6
Corporate stocks	.3	.1	.2	.1	.3	.1	*	*	.1
Mortgages on 1- to 4-family properties	2.4	2.1	1.1	1.4	2.0	2.5	2.5	1.3	1.0
Other mortgages	.8	1.1	.8	.6	.7	1.0	1.1	.9	.8
Other loans	.2	.2	.1	.2	.2	.2	.2	.5	.2
Cash balances	.1	.1	*	.1	*	*	*	*	.1

Note: Details may not add to totals because of rounding.
*Less than $50 million.
Source: "A Quarterly Presentation of Flow of Funds, Savings and Investment," *Federal Reserve Bulletin*, August 1959.

The investment pattern during the years 1954-1958 also reflects the effect of a recession. The lessened corporate demand for funds caused a decline in corporate bond yields, and the life insurance companies tended to shift more investments into the higher-yielding mortgages. Beginning in 1955, corporate bond yields recovered, and life insurance companies began to allocate more funds to corporate bonds. Except for 1958, the liquidation of Federal obligations continued, but at a much lesser volume.

In summary, the postwar investments of life insurance companies reflect the importance of corporate bonds. Life insurance companies tend to look with greatest favor on this segment of the capital market. If the corporate demand for funds is strong, life insurance companies tend to increase the flow of funds into corporate bonds. If the corporate demand for funds is weak, additional funds are invested in mortgages. The status of the corporate bond market determines to a major extent the availability of life insurance funds to non-corporate borrowers. Table 11-4 shows the summary of financial flows of life insurance companies for the years 1950-1958.

Growth

The growth in total assets of life insurance companies is plotted in Figure 11-2. The growth reflects changes in valuation of assets, capital gains or losses

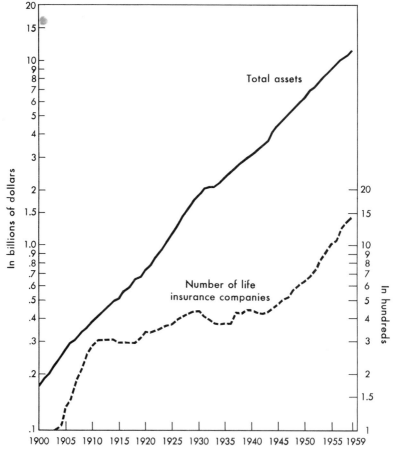

FIGURE 11-2   GROWTH IN TOTAL ASSETS OF LIFE INSURANCE COMPANIES, 1900-1958

Source: *Historical Statistics of the United States, Colonial Times to 1957,* and *Statistical Abstract of the United States, 1960.*

in the acquisition and disposition of assets, a build-up in the capital and/or surplus accounts, and an increase in the volume of operations. The rate of growth is also influenced by composition of the business that is done by life insurance companies, for this influences the structure of the reserves. One kind of business may lead to more reserves than another, and as explained earlier, the creation of reserves tends to retain funds in the companies, thus building up assets.

Compared with the charts presented earlier, the growth in total assets of life insurance companies shows the greater amount of stability. The effects of the Great Depression are noticeable, but the effects are much more moderate than those experienced by almost all other financial institutions. The slope of the curve is similar to that plotted for time deposits in commercial banks. The curve suggests that the rate of increase in total assets of life insurance companies may be slowing down. Whether or not the rate of increase will continue to moderate depends on many unknown factors. First, will the American public continue to experience a gradual rise in the cost of living over the long run? Second, will state insurance laws be modified to permit the sale of the variable annuity, and will individuals be attracted to this new type of contract? Third, will state insurance laws be modified to permit life insurance companies to set up segregated asset accounts for private pension plans? If the first question is answered in the affirmative and the other two in the negative, then there is a strong possibility that the rate of growth may fall off considerably. If all the questions are answered in the affirmative, the growth in the total assets of life insurance companies might be more rapid than at any time in the past. Various combinations of answers are possible. Furthermore, additional innovations may be introduced by life insurance companies. Certainly, life insurance companies will continue for many years to be one of the most important financial institutions.

Government Life Insurance

There are various types of government life insurance programs, most of which were started during either World War I or World War II. Since the Federal government issues the same types of policies as those issued by private companies, it is necessary to make only a few additional comments. First, the net cost of government life insurance is less than that of comparable policies issued by private companies. Second, the individual insured cannot purchase more than a nominal amount ($10,000) of such insurance. Third, consumer savings in Federal government life insurance was $6.2 billion at the end of 1958, which represents an increase of only $200 million since 1950. Four, the reserves are invested in special issues and Federal obligations. Since some of the costs of government life insurance are financed by appropriations, substantial dividends are paid to policyholders, particularly to those holding permanent forms of insurance.

SELF-ADMINISTERED PENSION PLANS

Self-administered pension plans are either self-insured or funded through trust companies. The major concern of this section will be the funded plans administered by trust institutions, which act for corporations as trustees and invest the assets of each fund separately. Some trustees pool the smaller pension funds to achieve greater diversification.

Life insurance companies once provided the major share of the management of pension funds, but in recent years, considerably more assets have been invested in the noninsured plans than in the insured pension funds. As a result of the needs of many employers, trust institutions have been able to attract an increasing share of the pension funds. One of the reasons for this trend is the difference in tax treatment between the trusteed plans and the insured plans. Life insurance companies are required to pay a Federal tax on the earnings on funds deposited under a group annuity or pension trust agreement. Also, some life insurance companies, depending on state insurance laws, are required to pay a tax on all premiums received, including pension business funds. Given the tax structure, taxes become a major consideration. Similar taxes are not imposed on the trust institutions in their administration of pension funds.

Another reason for the difference in the rates of growth of insured and noninsured pension funds is the limitation imposed on the investment of life insurance funds in common stocks. The inclusion of pension funds in collective bargaining contracts and the protracted rise in the cost of living have required additional flexibility in the administration of pension funds. Life insurance companies introduced flexible types of pension administration such as deposit administration and immediate participation, but restrictions on common stock investment continued to prevent the companies from providing as much flexibility as was offered by trust companies. Life insurance companies are required to commingle all assets for the common protection of all policyholders and participants in group plans. Generally, state insurance laws limit common stock investment to a relatively small percentage of assets, say 5 to 10 per cent. Trustees, on the other hand, are not required to commingle assets and they are less restricted in their investments. The legal instrument creating a pension trust may be so drawn that all investment can be made at the discretion of the trustee. Depending on the language of the instrument, the trustee might be able to invest nearly all of the fund in common stocks. Cost considerations and the likelihood that pensions will have to be increased in the near future prompt many employers to decide on trusteed plans.

Assets of Noninsured Pension Funds

The assets of noninsured pension funds reveal an investment policy much different from that of life insurance companies. Legally, and in practice, trustees of noninsured pension funds are able to sacrifice stability of principal in the short run in order to seek higher investment returns over the long run The liabilities of a noninsured pension fund are not formally stated. Therefore, shrinkage in the asset value of a noninsured fund poses less serious consequences for a trustee than it does for a life insurance company. In terms of the two investment factors, safety and profitability, trustees are able to assign more weight to the latter factor. This statement does not imply that trustees invest in any kind of common stock; they are concerned with safety over the long run, but they are able to absorb price fluctuations in the short run. The pension business handled by life insurance companies must show common stock holdings at market value; they are prevented both legally and from a practical point of view from investing very heavily in common stocks. In time, state insurance laws will probably be modified to permit life insurance companies to segregate assets and to consider common stock investment as applying solely to one type of insurance business.

Another factor influencing the investment policy of trustees in the management of pension funds is the large annual net inflow of funds. In this sense, they are very similar to life insurance companies. The total annual benefit payments and expenses of noninsured pension plans absorb only about 20 per cent of the combined annual payments into the funds and investment income earned on the funds. Until the growth of noninsured pension plans slows down, the large net cash inflow will continue. Since 1950, the net annual self-administered pension plan premiums have exceeded $1 billion. Since 1956, the annual net premium has averaged around $2 billion.

The assets of the self-administered plans are shown in Table 11-5. The distribution of assets stands in sharp contrast with that of life insurance companies. About the only similarity is the percentage of assets invested in

TABLE 11–5

**FINANCIAL ASSETS OF SELF-ADMINISTERED PENSION PLANS, END OF 1958
(BILLIONS OF DOLLARS)**

	Dollars	Per cent
Total financial assets	21.3	100.0
Credit and equity market instruments:		
Corporate bonds	11.6	54.5
Corporate stocks [1]	6.7	31.4
Federal obligations	2.1	9.8
Mortgages	.4	1.9
Other loans	.1	.5
Cash balances — currency and demand deposits.........	.4	1.9

Note: Details may not add to totals because of rounding.
[1] Based on original cost (market value, $9.5 billion).
Source: "A Quarterly Presentation of Flow of Funds, Saving and Investment," *Federal Reserve Bulletin*, August 1959.

corporate bonds and Federal obligations. At the end of 1958, noninsured pension funds held 31.4 per cent of their assets in corporate stocks; life insurance companies held only 3.8 per cent. Noninsured pension funds held less than 2 per cent of their assets in mortgages; life insurance companies, nearly 35 per cent. Trustees of some of the larger pension funds have indicated a strong interest in mortgages, but the peculiar nature of mortgage investment has blocked or discouraged them from investing in mortgages. Since 1957, the Federal Housing Administration has permitted lending institutions to sell securities representing an interest in F.H.A. insured mortgages to pension funds. In 1960, a new regulation of the F.H.A. permitted approved mortgagees to sell F.H.A. insured mortgages to individual and institutional investors, if the originators remain responsible for carrying out the terms of the insurance contract. With these changes, a larger share of noninsured pension funds can be expected to flow into mortgages.

Pension funds may invest in the securities of the companies that set up the funds. Actually, there is a high concentration of such investments in only a few funds. A sample survey by the Securities and Exchange Commission in 1956 revealed that less than 8 per cent of the funds owned bonds of the employer company and that 95 per cent of such investments were held by less than 2 per cent of the funds.

Investments in the Postwar Period

The net acquisition of financial assets by self-administered pension funds for each of the years 1950-1958 are shown in Table 11-6. The data show that investment in Federal obligations varied from year to year. In some years, the pension funds acquired Federal obligations; in other years, they liquidated Federal obligations. The funds received from the net sale of Federal

TABLE 11–6
NET ACQUISITION OF FINANCIAL ASSETS BY SELF-ADMINISTERED PENSION PLANS, 1950-1958
(BILLIONS OF DOLLARS)

	1950	1951	1952	1953	1954	1955	1956	1957	1958
Total net acquisition [1]	.8	1.2	1.4	1.7	1.8	1.9	2.1	2.5	2.6
Corporate bonds	.4	.8	1.0	1.0	1.2	.9	1.4	1.6	1.3
Corporate stocks	.2	.3	.4	.5	.6	.7	.8	1.0	1.2
Federal obligations	.2	.1	*	.2	*	.3	—.2	—.2	*
Mortgages on 1- to 4-family properties	*	*	*	*	*	*	.1	.1	.1

*Less than $50 million.
[1] Net annual change in cash balances and other loans is not shown because no change was as great as $50 million.
Source: "A Quarterly Presentation of Flow of Funds, Saving and Investment," *Federal Reserve Bulletin*, August 1959.

obligations were invested primarily in corporate bonds and stocks. The net acquisition of corporate bonds was the major use of funds in each of the years. In 1957 and 1958 the net acquisition of corporate bonds approached $2 billion annually, which represented nearly 25 per cent of the total increase in corporate bonds.

There appears to be no fixed relationship between the net acquisition of corporate stocks and corporate bonds. In 1950, nearly equal amounts of stocks and bonds were acquired. In 1952, the net acquisition of stocks was less than half of the net acquisition of corporate bonds. In 1955, the difference between the two narrowed down to only $200 million. However, during the period 1956-1958 the net acquisition of bonds was nearly twice the net acquisition of corporate stocks. Since 1954, the noninsured pension funds have supplied nearly half of the new funds flowing into corporate stocks. The reductions in fixed-value redeemable claims reflects the liquidation of savings bonds.

Concentration in Management of Pension Funds

A large percentage of total assets held by noninsured pension funds is concentrated in a relatively small number of the funds. For illustration, at the end of 1954 the five largest funds held 34 per cent of all corporate pension fund assets; the ten largest, 42 per cent. Funds of over $100 million comprised less than 2 per cent of the total number of funds, but accounted for almost 60 per cent of total assets; funds under $1 million comprised 40 per cent of the total number, but accounted for only 1 per cent of total assets. When it is realized that the large individual trust institutions manage many funds, even greater concentration exists in the management of pension funds. The investment of funds accumulated in private noninsured pension funds exerts much influence upon the capital markets, in both equity and credit market instruments. The continued growth expected in total assets of noninsured funds poses possible problems as to concentration of financial power among a few large trust institutions.

Growth

The same uncertainties prevail with respect to growth in the self-administered plans as with respect to growth in insured pension plans. It is impossible to predict changes in the state insurance laws, Federal tax laws, and business conditions. The time might come when life insurance companies regain the lead in the management of pension funds. However, if conditions do not change, the noninsured pension plans will probably continue as one of the most rapidly growing financial institutions.

The growth in total assets of self-administered pension funds during the period 1923-1958 is plotted in Figure 11-3. If this rate of growth is compared with those presented in previous charts, it will be observed that it is the most rapid one of all.

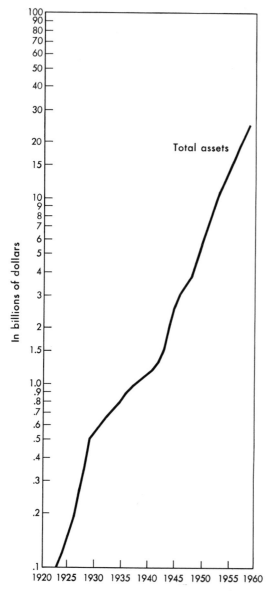

FIGURE 11-3   GROWTH IN TOTAL ASSETS OF CORPORATE PENSION FUNDS — 1923-1959*

*Book value, end of year.
Source: 1920-1944, from Raymond W. Goldsmith, *A Study of Savings in the United States*; 1945-1950, from Roger F. Murray, "Fresh Look at Pension Funds," *Trusts and Estates*, November 1955; 1951-1958, Securities and Exchange Commission.

PUBLIC PENSION AND RETIREMENT PLANS*

Federal Government pension and retirement funds are of relatively recent origin. The Civil Service Retirement System was established in 1920, the Old Age and Survivors' Insurance program in 1935; and railroad pensioners came under the Railroad Retirement System of the Federal Government in 1937. The diversity among the state and local pension and retirement funds precludes our giving any details as to dates of their origin.

Federal Old-Age and Survivors' Insurance Trust Fund

The Secretary of the Treasury, the Chairman of the Social Security Board, and the Secretary of Labor comprise the membership of the Board of Trustees of the Federal Old-Age and Survivors' Trust Fund. The Secretary of the Treasury is designated the managing trustee and is required to invest such portion of the trust fund as is not, in his judgment, required to meet current withdrawals. The investments are restricted to interest-bearing obligations of the United States and obligations guaranteed as to both principal and interest by the United States Government. Through June 30, 1959 the cumulative receipts of the trust fund were $69.4 billion and cumulative expenditures were $47.8 billion. As of June 30, 1959 approximately $17.2 billion were invested in special issues of the U.S. Government and $3.2 billion in public issues of the U.S. Government. Special issues are direct obligations of the Treasury and are issued exclusively to United States Government trust accounts. In view of the long-term nature of the trust fund, the interest rate on these securities is based on the average interest paid on marketable Treasury bonds (by definition having a maturity of five years or more at the time of issue). This arrangement ties the earnings of the fund closely to the market rate of interest, and places the earnings of the fund on a basis comparable to privately administered trust funds.

Since 1935, the social security program has been liberalized many times. Since 1949, for example, benefit payments have been more than doubled to a monthly maximum of $200; the retirement test to determine eligibility has been relaxed; disability benefits have been added to the program; the retirement age for women has been lowered from 65 to 62 years of age; and millions of additional persons have been brought under the social security program. Nearly 11 million persons now draw benefits under the program, and it is estimated that an additional 70 million persons participate in the program. In early 1961, President Kennedy asked Congress to consider the following changes: (1) lower the retirement age for men to 62, (2) increase widow's benefits, and (3) finance medical care for persons over 65 through social security.

*Although the flow-of-funds system of accounts treats social security transactions in connection with old age and survivors' insurance as current rather than investment transactions, the program's scope and relation to retirement make it relevant here.

Civil Service and Disability Fund

The Secretary of the Treasury is authorized to invest from time to time in interest-bearing securities of the United States Government such portions of the Fund as in his judgment may not be immediately required for the payment of annuities, refunds, and so on. The investments are to be made in special issues of Government obligations bearing interest at the rate of 4 per cent. However, the rate of interest paid on special obligations issued to the Fund may be reduced to a lower rate to correspond with prevailing yields in the market for outstanding Government securities. In recent years, most of the special issues have carried a 3 per cent rate.

Total cumulative receipts through June 30, 1959 were $16.0 billion; total cumulative expenditures, $6.8 billion. Total investments as of the same date were about $9.2 billion, of which $8.6 billion were invested in special issues.

Railroad Retirement Account

At the request and direction of the Railroad Retirement Board, the Secretary of the Treasury invests funds that flow into the Railroad Retirement Account. The investments are to be made only in interest-bearing obligations of the United States Government, or in obligations guaranteed as to both principal and interest by the United States. Investments are to bear interest at the rate of three per cent per annum. Although the Secretary is not restricted to special obligations, the minimum 3 per cent rate has required the issuance of special obligations during much of the postwar period.

Total cumulative receipts through June 30, 1959 were $10.8 billion; total cumulative expenditures, $7.1 billion. Total investments as of the same date were $3.7 billion, of which $3.4 billion was invested in special issues.

State and Local Governmental Retirement Funds

At the end of 1958, state and local governmental pension and retirement funds held approximately $15.7 billion in assets. During the period 1954-1958, the annual volume of credits imputed to consumers in connection with savings through state and local government employee retirement funds climbed steadily from $1.1 billion to $1.9 billion.

The investment authority of state and local governmental controllers and fund managers generally permits them to invest funds only in high-grade bonds. The bond portfolio might consist of Federal obligations, state and local obligations, and corporate bonds. Some of the funds are not permitted to invest in corporate bonds, but some are permitted to invest in corporate stocks.

Unless the managers of the state and local governmental funds are under pressure to invest in the securities of their respective state and local governments, a major share of the assets are invested in corporate bonds. During the years 1954-1958, over 50 per cent of the funds' net receipts were invested in corporate bonds. The state and local governmental funds were a dominant factor in the high-grade public utility bond market. Pressure is exerted on the managers of these funds to support state and local borrowing needs, and the pressure is most effective when yields on such securities are attractive. Since 1952, there has been a gradual increase in the net acquisition of state and local obligations, but the amount is less than half the acquisition of corporate bonds. Considering the future financing needs of state and local governments, it is probable that these funds will continue to invest as much as 25 per cent of net receipts in state and local obligations. Throughout the period under review, between $300 and $400 million were invested annually in Federal obligations.

Growth in State and Local Pension and Retirement Funds

In 1958, the net acquisition of financial assets was approximately $1.4 billion, and over the previous ten-year period, the net receipts of the funds increased by about $100 million annually. It is likely that the past rate of growth will continue into the future, so that the size of the funds can be expected to double in approximately seven or eight years. These funds can be expected to provide an important share of the funds that are invested in corporate bonds. It appears that the tax laws may be changed in such a way that state and local obligations will become a more attractive outlet to many savings and thrift institutions. If this happens, the difference in yields between state and local obligations and corporate bonds might become greater. This change would tend to encourage the state and local pension and retirement funds to invest a greater share of funds in corporate bonds. It is also possible that many of the state and local funds will be permitted to invest in corporate stocks.

QUESTIONS

1. Describe the following: term insurance, whole life insurance, endowment insurance, and annuities.

2. Describe three of the four broad classes of life insurance sales.

3. Compare the factors that are considered in determining premiums on life insurance and nonlife insurance.

4. Distinguish between an annuity certain and a life annuity.

5. Distinguish between the fixed or conventional annuity and the variable annuity. What factors underlie the development of the variable annuity? How did the recent United States Supreme Court decision affect variable annuity contracts?

6. Trace the development of private pension plans in the United States.

7. What influence did the noninsured pension plans have on the types of pension plans administered by insurance companies?

8. For the entire life insurance industry, show in percentages income and how it is used. On the basis of your data, discuss the liquidity needs in the operation of life insurance companies.

9. Compare the relationship between capital accounts and total assets for life insurance companies and nonlife insurance companies.

10. Construct a simple aggregate balance sheet for life insurance companies, showing the relative importance of each balance sheet item. Explain the asset composition in terms of the life insurance companies' investment policies.

11. Comment on the past and future growth in total assets of life insurance companies.

12. Comment on the difference in the rate of growth of insured and non-insured pension funds.

13. Compare the asset composition of non-insured pension funds with that of life insurance companies. What accounts for the differences?

14. Comment on the growth of state and local government retirement funds. How are such funds invested?

ADDITIONAL READING

See additional reading listed at end of Chapter 10

Basic college textbooks on life insurance:

Huebner, S. S. *Life Insurance.* (3rd ed.) New York: Appleton-Century-Crofts, Inc., 1959.
———, and Kenneth Black Jr. *Life Insurance.* (5th ed.) New York: Appleton-Century-Crofts, Inc., 1958.
Kedzie, Daniel P. *Consumer Credit Insurance.* Homewood, Ill.: Richard D. Irwin, Inc., 1957.

Group insurance, social insurance pensions, and the investment of life insurance and pension funds:

McGill, Dan M. *Life Insurance.* Homewood, Ill.: Richard D. Irwin, Inc., 1959.
Maclean, Joseph B. *Life Insurance.* (8th ed.) New York: McGraw-Hill Book Co., Inc., 1957.
Magee, John H. *Life Insurance.* (3rd ed.) Homewood, Ill.: Richard D. Irwin, Inc., 1958.
Mehr, Robert I., and Robert W. Osler. *Modern Life Insurance* (Rev. ed.) New York: The Macmillan Co., 1956.
Owen, Henry T. *Fundamentals of Life Insurance.* Englewood Cliffs, N.J.: Prentice-Hall, Inc., 1951.
V Andrews, Victor L. "Interests at Stake in the Investment of Pension Funds," *Monthly Labor Review* (July, 1959), pp. 751-756.

————. "Pension Funds in the Securities Markets," *Harvard Business Review* (Nov.-Dec., 1959), pp. 90-102.

Bankers Trust Company. *A Study of Industrial Retirement Plans.* Issued about every three years; reports on employment retirement programs established or amended since previous study. The 1960 report covers the period, 1956-1959. May be obtained from Bankers Trust, 16 Wall Street, New York 15, N.Y.

Black, Kenneth, Jr. *Group Annuities.* Homewood, Ill.: Richard D. Irwin, Inc., 1955.

Davie, Bruce F. *Investment Practices of Public Employee Retirement Systems.* Research Report to the Federal Reserve Bank of Boston, No. 8. Boston: Federal Reserve Bank of Boston, 1959.

Dearing, Charles L. *Industrial Pensions.* Washington, D.C.: The Brookings Institution, 1954.

Fricke, Cedric. *Variable Annuities: Their Impact on the Investment Market.* Ann Arbor: University of Michigan, Bureau of Business Research, 1960.

Gregg, Davis W. *Group Life Insurance.* (Rev. ed.) Homewood, Ill.: Richard D. Irwin, Inc., 1955.

Hamilton, James A., and D. C. Bronson. *Pensions.* New York: McGraw-Hill Book Co., Inc., 1958.

Harbrecht, Paul D. *Pension Funds and Economic Power.* New York: Twentieth Century Fund, 1959.

Ilse, Louise Wolters. *Group Insurance and Employee Retirement Plans.* Englewood Cliffs, N.J.: Prentice-Hall, Inc., 1953.

McCahan, David (ed.) *Investments of Life Insurance Funds.* The S. S. Huebner Foundation for Insurance Education, Lectures. Philadelphia: University of Philadelphia Press, 1953.

McGill, Dan M. *Fundamentals of Private Pensions.* Homewood, Ill.: Richard D. Irwin, Inc., 1959.

Securities and Exchange Commission. *Corporate Pension Funds, 1959,* Statistical Series Release 1680 (May 31, 1960). Washington, D.C.: The Commission. A similar report is issued each year at about this time.

————. *Survey of Corporate Pension Funds, 1951-1954.* Washington, D.C.: The Commission, 1956.

Snider, H. Wayne. *Life Insurance Investment in Commercial Real Estate.* Homewood, Ill.: Richard D. Irwin, Inc., 1956.

Von Manchenheim, Egon. *Financial Management of Pension Trusts.* National Industrial Conference Board, Studies in Business Policy, No. 66. New York: National Industrial Conference Board, Inc., 1954.

12. Direct flow of consumer saving into securities

IN the previous chapters attention was focused on the flow of consumer saving into fixed-value redeemable claims, consumer saving through life insurance and pension funds, and the reinvestment of these funds by institutions and government agencies. In this chapter attention is shifted to the direct flow of consumer saving into securities. The purchase of investment company shares is logically a part of this subject, but these financial institutions have become so important in their own right that they are discussed separately in the chapter immediately following.

The topics covered in this chapter include: an over-all view of consumer investment in credit and equity market instruments; formulation of an investment policy; structure and operation of financial institutions that provide assistance in the formulation and execution of investment policies; and securities laws. Most of the information presented here applies equally well to institutional investors.

CONSUMER INVESTMENT IN CREDIT AND EQUITY INSTRUMENTS

Before moving on to the discussion of securities, an over-all view of consumer investment in credit and equity market instruments is presented in Table 12-1 to serve as a basic frame of reference. Approximately 90 per cent of consumer investment in credit and equity market instruments is in the form of marketable securities, consisting of Federal obligations, state and local obligations, corporate bonds, and corporate stocks, the latter of which are by far the most important. It is interesting to note that the amount invested in state and local obligations was nearly equal to the combined investment in Federal obligations and corporate bonds, evidencing preference for tax-exempt state and local obligations.

The net acquisition of credit and equity market instruments by consumers during the years 1954-1958 is shown in Table 12-2. The annual flows into these instruments has varied considerably, ranging from $0.4 billion in 1954 to $9.8 billion in 1957. Obviously, individuals shift their preference between market instruments and other forms of financial investment during the business cycle. In prosperity, individuals are more confident and yields on market instruments are relatively more attractive. In recession, the opposite conditions prevail and individuals demonstrate a preference for fixed-value redeemable claims. During the period 1950-1954, individuals reduced their holdings of Federal obligations and corporate bonds, but beginning in 1955 and continuing through 1957, they added sizeable amounts to their holdings of Federal obligations and corporate bonds. Throughout the entire period, individuals invested additional sums each year in corporate stock. The lowest annual net acquisition of corporate stock was in 1954; the highest annual acquisition, in 1956. Like the investment pattern of financial institutions, consumers' financial investment in market instruments is influenced by the structure of yields.

TABLE 12–1
CONSUMER AND NONPROFIT ORGANIZATION INVESTMENT IN CREDIT AND EQUITY MARKET INSTRUMENTS, END OF 1958
(BILLIONS OF DOLLARS)

	Dollars	Per cent
Federal obligations:		
Direct and guaranteed	14.9	3.2
Non-guaranteed	1.6	.3
State and local obligations	25.4	5.4
Corporate and foreign bonds	9.6	2.1
Corporate stocks [1]	386.8	82.7
Mortgages on 1- to 4-family properties	11.3	2.4
Other mortgages	16.6	3.6
Security credit	1.4	.3
Total	467.5	100.0

Note: Details may not add to totals because of rounding.

[1] Corporate stock holdings are valued at estimated market price and hence reflect fluctuations in market prices of stocks held as well as net funds put into stocks.

Source: "A Quarterly Presentation of Flow of Funds, Saving and Investment," Federal Reserve Bulletin, August 1959.

Throughout the entire period, state and local obligations proved to be an attractive outlet for consumer saving: In no year did the net acquisition fall below $1 billion. From 1955 through 1958, the flow of saving into this form of investment averaged about $1.9 billion, which is higher than that of any other instrument. As noted above, their tax-exempt status accounts for much of this flow, and personal trust funds have probably made most of such investments.

TABLE 12–2
NET ACQUISITION OF CREDIT AND EQUITY MARKET INSTRUMENTS BY CONSUMER AND NONPROFIT ORGANIZATION SECTOR, 1954-1958
(BILLIONS OF DOLLARS)

	1954	1955	1956	1957	1958
Total net acquisitions	.4	8.2	7.9	9.8	2.6
Federal obligations	—2.1	2.2	1.2	2.5	—2.9
State and local obligations	1.0	2.1	1.7	2.3	1.5
Corporate and foreign bonds	—.6	1.1	1.2	1.1	.5
Corporate stock	.8	1.4	2.2	1.8	1.7
Mortgages	1.3	1.4	1.6	2.1	1.8

Source: "A Quarterly Presentation of Flow of Funds, Saving and Investment," *Federal Reserve Bulletin,* August 1959.

Although smaller sums were invested in mortgages, there was less fluctuation in this flow than in any of the others. On the average, the annual flow of consumer saving into commercial mortgages was about twice as large as the flow into mortgages on one- to four-family properties.

FORMULATION OF AN INVESTMENT POLICY

The formulation of an investment policy is very important because investors have considerable choice when investing funds directly in securities. Investors must decide what types of securities are most suitable. Should funds be invested in Federal obligations? This category includes all marketable Treasury and Federal agency securities — direct, fully guaranteed, and non-guaranteed. Direct debt refers to Treasury borrowing. Other Federal obligations represent direct borrowing by agencies fom the capital markets, the securities being either fully guaranteed or not guaranteed by the Treasury. Examples of the latter type include securities offered by Banks for Cooperatives, Federal Intermediate Credit Banks, Federal Home Loan Banks, and Federal National Mortgage Association. Obviously, it is one thing to decide to invest in Federal obligations and quite another thing to select the particular type of security.

Should funds be invested in state and local obligations? There is also wide selection in this category. Included are the securities of states, political subdivisions of states, and local housing authorities. Political subdivisions include counties, cities, towns, villages, and boroughs. A subdivision in turn may create school, water, and road districts. The securities may be either backed by the taxing power of the issuer or payable from revenues of specified assets. The variations are of fundamental importance to investors. Care must be exercised in selecting state and local obligations as a form of investment.

Should funds be invested in corporate securities? If so, in stocks, bonds, or a combination of stocks and bonds? The design of the corporate security at the time of its issue determines the contractual or legal relationship between the issuer and the investor. Basically, corporate securities may be classified as either credit or equity instruments. Certificates of stock represent equity or ownership; bonds represent creditorship. All business corporations issue equity instruments, and many also issue credit instruments. Except for a few government corporations, governments are restricted to the issue of credit instruments.

Common stock and preferred stock are the two basic types of corporate stock. The key to understanding the difference between the two is the use of the word "preferred," which represents ownership with certain preferences, such as priority in payment of dividend and in the distribution of funds in the event of liquidation. Many preferred stocks are cumulative, which means that unpaid dividends cumulate and must be paid prior to the payment of dividends on common stock. Generally, limitations accompany preferences. Dividends may be limited to a certain number of dollars regardless of the earnings of the issuer, and the preferred stockholders may have few or no voting rights. Common stock represents ownership without preferences. Given the same issuer, common stock investors assume relatively more risk than the preferred stock and bond investors, and are compensated with voting rights and unlimited income possibilities.

There is also much variety among corporate bonds. The two major classes of bonds are secured and unsecured bonds. The former contain a pledge of security, the purpose of which is to protect the bond investor should the issuer fail to abide by all the covenants or promises included in the bond contract. An investor in an unsecured bond must look to the general credit of the issuer. If an issuer has only unsecured bonds outstanding, then all of the firm's assets may be viewed as providing security to the firm's bondholders. Unsecured bonds are referred to as debentures. Ordinarily, a bond issuer is obligated to pay interest regardless of earnings. In recent years, many corporations have issued income bonds, which pay interest only if earned. Unpaid interest may or may not cumulate. Bonds may be callable and convertible. The call provision is at the option of the issuer, and the conversion right is at the option of the investor. By calling an outstanding convertible issue, the price of which is higher than its call price, an issuer can bring about its conversion. Preferred stock issues may also contain call and conversion provisions.

The many variations among corporate bonds and stocks cloud the distinction between the two major classes, but as long as the provisions of a security establish a creditor type of relationship by promising to pay interest or to repay principal on a specified date, the security is a credit market instrument. Obviously, extreme care must be exercised in the selection of corporate stocks and bonds. Generally, corporate earnings are the most important factor in the selection of corporate securities.

The formulation of an investment policy restricts choice to the investment media that are most suitable. Investors, whether they are institutional or individual, must determine the relative importance of safety, liquidity, and profitability, and select individual securities. Investors differ with respect to need, financial position, and willingness and capacity to assume risks connected with direct investment. Each investor must formulate his own investment policy. Both risk and non-risk factors must be considered in relation to such things as investor's age, family status, financial position as it pertains to assets and income, tax status, and emotions. The analysis should be couched in terms of the future as well as the present.

Risk Factors*

Attention is now directed toward the risk factors that must be considered in the formulation of an investment policy. The more important risk factors or areas of uncertainty are the future financial position of issuers, future investors' attitudes toward securities, future level and structure of interest rates, and future purchasing power of the dollar.

FUTURE FINANCIAL POSITIONS OF ISSUERS. Uncertainty as to the future financial position of an issuer of securities is called " financial risk." In the future an issuer may have labor troubles, severe product and price competition, or some other major difficulty, any one of which might lead to lower profits and even losses, thus exposing the investors in the issuer's securities to loss of income and possible loss of principal. Before assuming financial risk, an investor should determine his capacity to assume it. He should determine his vulnerability to loss of principal and loss of income. He should consider the possibility of being forced to liquidate his investments at a time when the prices of his securities are depressed. Another very important consideration is the investor's ability to select and manage financial risk. After viewing financial risk in these terms, he may decide to adopt which might be called an aggressive investment policy and seek out securities that involve considerable financial risk. If he is confident of his ability to select and manage such investments, he might concentrate his funds on only a few securities. The assumption of higher risks exposes his investments to possible large losses, but these are offset by the possibility of realizing relatively high investment returns. Most individuals who invest directly in securities do not adopt such an aggressive policy; they adopt instead a conservative or defensive policy toward financial risk and select a reasonable number of low financial risk stocks or bonds or a combination of stocks and bonds.

*Many of the ideas expressed here are based on Harry C. Sauvain, *Investment Management*, 2nd Ed. (Englewood Cliffs, N. J.: Prentice-Hall, Inc., 1959). By permission.

FUTURE INVESTORS' ATTITUDES. The term "market instrument" implies determination of price in the market. One of the risks that must be assumed in direct investment is the fluctuation in market prices. The risk is appropriately titled "market risk." Since investors' attitudes toward both the total securities markets and specific securities are influenced by many factors that change rather frequently; investors' attitudes toward securities also change frequently. During the postwar period the Dow-Jones Industrial Average, one of the more widely quoted market averages, has fluctuated somewhat violently. As shown in Figure 12-1, the average has displayed much fluctuation, indicating that investors might incur great financial loss in the event of poor timing in the purchase and sale of securities. Investors must realize

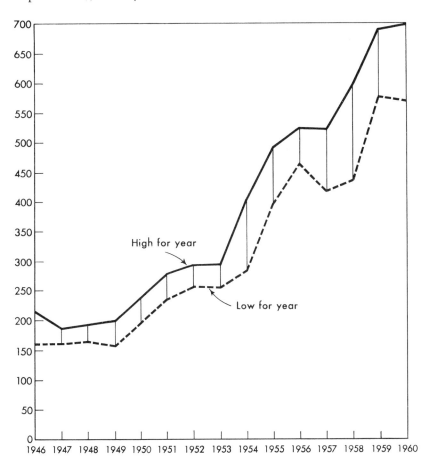

FIGURE 12-1   DOW-JONES INDUSTRIAL AVERAGES, 1946-1960*

*Through October 1960.

Source: *Standard & Poor's Trade and Securities Statistics, Security Price Index Record,* 1960 Edition, and *Current Statistics,* October 1960.

that stock prices fall as well as rise, and adopt policies with respect to the ups and downs in the securities markets. The policy may be one of ignoring price fluctuations, but at least the policy decision is deliberate and is designed to serve some stated purpose. It would be much worse to invest directly in securities without realizing the magnitude of possible fluctuation in market prices. Some investors adopt a policy that involves shifting funds between stocks and bonds. Various formula plans have been devised to cope with and to take advantage of market risk. The basic idea of formula plans is to sell stocks and buy bonds when stock prices are historically high, and to sell bonds and buy stocks when stock prices are historically low.

FUTURE LEVEL AND STRUCTURE OF INTEREST RATES. A change in the level and structure of interest rates affects both the principal value and the flow of income of credit market instruments. The risk is referred to as the interest-rate risk. The 3¼ per cent Treasury bond issued in May, 1953 and callable in 1978 provides a good illustration of interest rate risk. The bond was issued at par (100), and in 1954 its price rose to 111.28, reflecting a decline in the rate of interest. Between 1954 and 1959 the yield on long-term Federal obligations climbed from slightly less than 3 per cent to more than 4 per cent, and the prices on outstanding long-term Federal obligations fell rather sharply. On April 17, 1959 the market price of the 3¼ bond was approximately 89. Conceivably, an investor could have purchased the bond at 111.28 and be forced to liquidate at 89, which would have meant a loss of nearly $223 per bond. To show the effect of maturity it may be noted that during the 1954-1959 period the cyclical swing in average prices of long-term Federal obligations was in a range roughly ten times greater than the corresponding fluctuation in prices of nine- to twelve-month securities.

If it is necessary to turn over credit market instruments during a period of falling interest rates, the total income earned on a given sum also falls off. In some cases investors may turn to other types of investment to offset loss of income. The effect of interest-rate changes on preferred stock is somewhat similar to the effects on credit market instruments, but the effect on common stock is very fuzzy.

Investors who require stability of income and principal are naturally attracted to credit market investments, and must thereby expose themselves to interest-rate risk. The policy as to interest-rate risk will depend on the likelihood of forced sale and the ability or inability to manage the risk. The likelihood of forced sale is a very important consideration because only investors who sell credit market instruments when prices are depressed actually realize loss in principal. Outstanding investments may be held to maturity and redeemed at par.

An investor who has confidence in his ability to manage interest-rate risk may adopt a very aggressive investment policy, which implies prediction of change in both the level and structure of interest rates. In theory, an aggressive investor would tend to hold funds off the market until interest rates were near their maximum and get out of the market when interest rates were at their minimum. He would also concentrate his investment in selected maturities. The prediction of future change in the level and structure of interest rates is very hazardous, so that most investors who must assume interest-rate risk adopt a conservative or defensive policy. They hold a certain amount of funds in liquid reserves at all times and attempt to space maturities of credit instruments so that some investments mature regularly.

FUTURE PURCHASING POWER OF THE DOLLAR. Another risk that has become predominant in the formulation of investment policy is that associated with the possibility of further decline in the purchasing power of the dollar. This risk is referred to as the price level or purchasing power risk. The purchasing power of the dollar in 1960 was only about half what it was during the early 1940's. The investment of funds in credit instruments, whether they are market or redeemable instruments, exposes the investor to loss of purchasing power of both principal and income during a period of rising prices. There is a possibility that the price level may also fall; in this event the purchasing power of the credit instruments would be greater.

An investor who is dependent on investment income for current expenses should adopt a policy that will reduce risk of loss of purchasing power during a period of rising prices. A defensive or conservative policy toward purchasing power risk requires investment in assets that are expected to increase in value and provide additional income in proportion to the probable increase in the price level. Various types of assets might be used in this attempt. In the field of securities investments, common stock is the most suitable investment medium. Historically, there is a long-run relationship between the price level and prices of the higher-grade common stocks. Many investors assume that a higher price level is much more likely than either a lower or stable price level and that the relationship between common stock prices and the price level will continue to hold in the future. Acting on the basis of assumptions, almost all individual investors are attempting to hedge the purchasing power risk by investing in common stocks. If investors believed the price level might fall, high-grade preferred stocks and credit instruments would be preferred.

Non-Risk Factors

Other factors that enter into the determination of an investment policy are taxation, marketability, and legality. *Taxation* refers to the tax status of the individual investor and to tax rates that apply to certain types of financial gain. *Marketability* refers to the time it takes to sell a security at a reasonable price. Considerable variation in marketability exists among securities because all securities are not traded in the same markets nor are all equally attractive to investors. Securities issued by closely held corporations are not easily marketable; securities issued by publicly held corporations and traded on organized securities exchanges are highly marketable. Many securities traded through the over-the-counter markets are also highly marketable. The market structure is described in the following section. As a general rule, individual investors do not require high marketability, but most of the securities they hold are highly marketable. *Legality* refers to the presence of legal restrictions affecting the formulation and execution of an investment policy. Individual investors are not much affected by this factor. However, institutional investors, including trustees, must formulate policies within legal restrictions. Of the three non-risk factors, taxation is probably the only one that is vitally important to the individual who invests directly in securities.

Two aspects of taxation that are important to investors are the treatment accorded capital gains and the tax-exemption status of some securities. Long-term capital gains are taxed at only 25 per cent, even though investors may have incomes that place them in very high income tax brackets. In view of the relatively lower tax rate on long-term capital gains, investors in higher income brackets are attracted to investments that are likely to increase in principal value. They are willing and eager in some cases to sacrifice current investment income that would be taxed at relatively high rates for future capital gains that are likely to be taxed at only 25 per cent. The tax treatment accorded capital losses encourages investors to adjust their portfolios so as to offset losses against gains.

Income earned on state and local obligations is exempt from both the Federal income tax and the income tax of the state in which the securities are issued. Income earned on Federal obligations is exempt from state income taxes. Under present tax laws, a person could invest $1,000,000 in state and local obligations, receive at current yields between $30,000 and $40,000 annual investment income, and not be subject to either state or Federal income taxes. Many persons whose financial and personal circumstances warrant the assumption of considerable financial risk are steered away from providing risk capital because of the relative attractiveness of tax-exempt investments. Although there has been criticism of this loophole in our tax laws, there is little likelihood that these securities will lose their tax-exempt status.

The policy as to taxation will depend on the income status of the individual investor. If tax considerations are important, the major portion of his investible funds might be allocated to state and local obligations and securities that show possible capital appreciation. He would tend to avoid the conservative income-producing corporate stocks and bonds.

All other things being equal, tax exemption, capital gains, legality, and marketability are favorable investment characteristics and to gain them, yields must be sacrificed. If investors disregard these facts, they may invest in securities that do not assure maximum investment returns.

Other Considerations in Formulation of Policy

Successful investment management requires analysis of present and future business conditions and the selection and analysis of industries and companies. Many investment services provide assistance along these lines. To minimize risk for the total investment portfolio, funds should be spread over many unrelated securities. This method is known as diversification and there are various methods and combinations of methods that may be used. Funds may be diversified among securities in different industries, in different parts of the country or the world, and between government and non-government securities. An individual investor should limit his securities to a number that is manageable.

Gaining maximum financial returns on an investment portfolio requires continuous surveillance. Changes in the basic determinants underlying an investment policy may call for considerable change in both the policy and the corresponding investment portfolio. If an investor were no longer dependent on investment income to meet his required expenses, he would be able to switch out of income types of securities into securities that are more likely to appreciate in value. Changes in over-all conditions in the economy and securities markets may also call for changes in the portfolio. Investors might shift funds from bonds into stocks and back into bonds, depending on conditions. Investors might shift investments from certain industries that have become less favorably situated into those which show relatively greater promise. The conditions within a given industry or company may change. Some changes may be favorable; others may be unfavorable. Investors must always be alert to change.

Role of Financial Institutions in Formulation of Policy

A majority of investors, once they realize the problems of investment management, seek out various forms of assistance, and in response to their needs specialized firms have been established and existing financial institutions have added investment services as a part of their total operations. In addition to counseling, which includes both the determination of policy and the selection of individual securities, financial institutions also provide physical safety of securities, mechanical supervision that takes care of maturing bonds and coupons and similar matters, and accounting records.

INVESTMENT COUNSELING FIRMS. Investment counseling firms specialize in providing personal evaluations of investors' over-all financial programs for the purpose of formulating personalized investment policies, planning investors' portfolios, and recommending shifts in portfolio as conditions change. Many of the larger investment counseling firms maintain research departments to appraise economic and industrial trends and to analyze securities of individual companies. In some cases, the investment counselor, who is the individual's personal representative in an investment counseling firm, assumes power of attorney and buys and sells securities for the investor without further authorization. As a general rule, however, these firms serve in a purely advisory capacity.

An investment counseling firm charges a management fee based on the value of the investment portfolio at the beginning of the year, with a minimum fee ranging from as low as $200 to as much as $500. The annual fee is graduated to the size of the fund and may range from 1 per cent on the smaller funds to ¼ of 1 per cent on the larger funds. The size of the minimum fee clearly suggests that these services are not designed to serve small investors. A minimum fee of $200 would absorb the major portion of income earned on a portfolio of, say, $10,000. To meet the needs of small investors, some investment counseling firms sponsor investment companies that reflect the basic investment policy and current research findings of the firms. Through the purchase of these investment company shares, small investors are able to utilize some of the investment counsel services and avoid the payment of large minimum fees charged on personalized accounts.

In addition to serving individuals and investment companies, investment counseling firms also provide investment management services to institutional investors, such as commercial banks, trust companies, insurance companies, noninsured pension plans, and eleemosynary institutions. Investment counseling firms were first established in the early 1920's, and since that time the number of firms has expanded considerably. There are no data available on the assets held or administered by investment counselors.

Persons engaged for compensation in the business of advising others with respect to securities are required under the Investment Advisers Act of 1940 to register as investment advisers. Investment counselors account for most of the registrations. At the end of the fiscal year 1959, there were 1,862 registered investment advisers. Lawyers, accountants, and others who offer advice as an incidental service to their clients and investment advisers who serve only institutional investors or a very limited clientele (15 persons), are not subject to the act. Brokers, dealers, and bankers are regulated under other legislation.

Under the Investment Advisers Act of 1940 it is unlawful for investment advisers to engage in practices that constitute fraud or deceit. In addition to registration, the Act requires the advisers to disclose the nature of their interest in transactions that they may elect for their clients. It prohibits profit-sharing arrangements and the assignment of clients' contracts. The Act does not assure either the competence or the financial responsibility of an investment adviser. The Securities and Exchange Commission, which has the responsibility of enforcing the Act, has requested amendments that would permit more effective enforcement and greater protection to the investing public.*

*Other aspects of securities laws are considered later in this chapter and in Chapter 13.

COMMERCIAL BANKS. Commercial banks make available to investors many types of investment services, including informal discussions with bank officials, custody of portfolios, limited and complete investment management, and trusts. Custodian services include physical care of securities, record-keeping, collection of income, mechanical supervisions, and assistance in the execution of orders. The fee for custodian services is expressed as a percentage of the portfolio's market value with a stated minimum fee of, say, $50. Many commercial banks also provide varying degrees of portfolio management, ranging from periodical review and recommendation to complete management based on power of attorney.

Trust departments of commercial banks and companies that are engaged solely in trust business administer funds under various forms of trustee and fiduciary arrangements. The administration of pension funds was discussed in the previous chapter. Bank-administered personal trust funds dwarf bank-administered pension funds. A recent study revealed that in 1958 bank-administered personal trust funds totaled approximately $80 billion.* The concept of " bank-administered " includes all corporate trustees, whether they are the trust departments of banks or exclusively trust institutions. Attorneys and other non-corporate trustees also administer personal trust funds. Although no data are available as to the size of these funds, it is certain that the total amount is considerably less than $80 billion.

The scope of this study precludes a complete and precise discussion of personal trusts. Suffice it to mention that a trust is an agreement under which a person (called the creator or trustor) transfers ownership of property to another person (either a corporate or individual trustee) for the benefit of a beneficiary or beneficiaries. The beneficiary may be the same person as the creator. Under a trust agreement, a person transfers ownership of property to a trustee who manages the property in the manner directed and pays income to the beneficiary. Personal trusts are those which are created primarily for natural persons. Estate planning and taxes are important considerations underlying the creation and nature of trust agreements. By transferring ownership and management of assets to a trustee, assets are invested only indirectly by the consumer. However, the trust agreement may specify or reflect the wishes of the consumer.

Among the factors that enter into the determination of an investment policy of an individual personal trust are the size and purpose of the trust, age and income needs of the beneficiaries, the probable termination date of the trust, and the law of trust investment. The investment policy may be set forth in the trust instrument creating the trust or it may be the responsibility of the trustee to formulate an appropriate policy. Variations among individual trusts require that specific policies be designed to fit the requirements of the individual trusts.

*Raymond W. Goldsmith and Eli Shapiro, "An Estimate of Bank-Administered Trust Funds," *Journal of Finance*, XIV, No. 1, March 1959, p. 11.

The investment requirements of some of the smaller personal trusts may be sufficiently similar to permit a trust institution to pool some individual trusts into a much larger common trust fund. The major reason for the creation of common trust funds is to hold down the costs involved in administering many small, individual trust accounts. The common trust fund represents collective investment and reinvestment of moneys contributed by a bank in its capacity as trustee, executor, administrator, or guardian. At the close of 1959, there were 373 common trust funds with assets of approximately $2.7 billion. Their investment holdings at market value were distributed as follows: common stock, 53.9 per cent; preferred stock, 29 per cent; domestic corporate bonds, 23.4 per cent; U.S. Government obligations, 7.9 per cent, and other holdings, 6.9 per cent.

The assets of bank-administered trust funds, excluding common trust funds, are presented in Table 12-3. It can be observed that corporate stock accounted for 60.1 per cent of total asets. This is a very high percentage as compared with the asset compositions of the financial institutions studied in previous chapters. It is not surprising that state and local obligations are the next most important asset, accounting for 13.5 per cent of total assets. Federal obligations accounted for about 10 per cent. Like the other financial institutions, the personal trusts held a much larger percentage of assets in Federal obligations during the years immediately following World War II. Although the amount invested in corporate bonds has increased in recent years, the percentage of assets so invested remains very small, reflecting the

TABLE 12–3
ASSETS OF BANK-ADMINISTERED PERSONAL TRUST FUNDS, END OF 1955
(BILLIONS OF DOLLARS)

	$	%
Financial Assets		
Credit and equity market instruments:		
Federal obligations	7.42	9.9
State and local obligations	10.11	13.5
Corporate bonds	3.94	5.3
Corporate stocks	46.00	61.4
Mortgages	1.49	2.0
Fixed-value redeemable claims:		
Cash-demand deposits	3.10	4.1
Non-financial Assets		
Real estate	1.93	2.6
Other	.93	1.2
Total Assets	74.92	100.0

Source: Data derived from Raymond W. Goldsmith and Eli Shapiro, "An Estimate of Bank-Administered Trust Funds," *Journal of Finance*, March 1959, p. 14. Reprinted by permission.

current relative unattractiveness of credit instruments. It is estimated that the net annual acquisition of financial assets by bank-administered personal trust accounts during recent years has averaged slightly more than $1 billion. The authors of the study referred to above suggest two possible reasons for the low rate of net acquisition. First, there is "a continuing decline in the wealth share of the high-income groups to which the personal trust industry has historically always catered." Second "the investment returns on assets held by personal trust funds were at a competitive disadvantage with those handled by the investment counseling industry."*

BROKER-DEALER FIRMS AND INVESTMENT BANKERS. Advice as to formulation and execution of policy is also offered by brokers and investment banking firms. The major functions and operations of these institutions are developed later, so that only their advisory function is developed here. When a prospective investor contacts an account executive (securities salesman) of a reputable broker-dealer firm, the account executive is likely to suggest that the first step is to analyze the person's over-all financial program and to formulate an investment policy suitable to fit the investor's needs. All of this advice is free. Brokerage houses also make library facilities available to investors who wish to pursue independent study. Brokerage houses also provide limited custodian services for their clients at little or no cost to the investor. Some brokerage houses also provide limited investment management, which may or may not be free. Investment bankers also offer free advice to investors as to policy, especially if it is possible to formulate policies and construct portfolios that will include securities in which the investment bankers have an interest.

The free advice from broker-dealer firms and investment bankers may be very good or it may be very superficial and sometimes misleading. The selection of the brokerage firm and the account executive is very important. Investors are cautioned to exercise the same degree of care that they use in selecting professional services in law and medicine. Inasmuch as account executives and investment bankers earn their living by executing orders, there may be a tendency for them to be biased in their advice. Knowledge is probably the best guard against following poor advice.

FINANCIAL PUBLISHERS AND INVESTMENT ADVISORY PUBLICATIONS. There are many financial publishers but only a few will be mentioned in this discussion. Two of the largest are Standard and Poor's Corporation and Moody's Investors Service. Each of these firms supplies a number of services and no attempt is made here to describe all of their services. Some are designed for individual investors; others for institutional investors. Large public libraries subscribe to some of the services. Commercial banks and brokerage firms generally make their copies available to interested investors. These firms also offer

*Ibid., p. 17.

personal investment advisory services, charging a fee comparable to that charged by other financial institutions.

There are a multitude of investment services, some of them very good and others very suspect. The purposes of these services are to assist in the evaluation of the market, individual industries, and the securities of individual companies. As a general rule, the selection of securities is expressed in terms of investment objectives such as income and growth.

Some of the financial services provide portfolio construction in terms of the investor's objective. In most instances, the investment service assumes that the investor is able to select the appropriate investment objective. One of the more widely used investment services asks its prospective customers to indicate his investment objective by selecting one of the following: (1) as good a return as possible with relative stability of principal; (2) long-term capital appreciation — current income return secondary; (3) capital gain and moderate income from medium risk securities; (4) profit is primary aim — willing to accept a high degree of risk. Other required information consists of cash available for investment, government bonds, and other reserve funds.

In summary, the investor should not proceed into direct investment blindly. There are many sources of information and advice that may be used. Realizing that some of the advice may not be the best available, the investor must be on guard against being ill-advised. The best protection is to be as well informed as possible and not shift total responsibility, unless the investor wishes either to establish a trust or to execute a power of attorney to a very reliable investment counselor.

SECURITIES MARKETS*

The term "securities markets" refers to the mechanisms or institutional arrangements through which new securities are initially sold and existing securities are bought and sold. Securities markets provide an essential environment. The creation and maintenance of markets for securities encourages both individual and institutional investors to invest funds in securities. The demand for securities represents a source of funds for business and government. The securities markets add to the over-all fluidity of savings and provide a continuing valuation of securities.

The two basic securities markets are the primary and secondary capital markets. In the primary capital market, new securities are originated and sold. Investment bankers constitute the core of primary capital markets. The investment bankers either singly or as a syndicate may buy from an issuer an entire issue of new securities and, in turn, sell the securities to institutional

*Except where noted, data in this section are taken from Securities and Exchange Commission, 25th Annual Report.

and individual investors. They may also enter into selling agreements under which they agree to exert their best efforts in the sale of new securities. In these instances, the securities are not underwritten, and the bankers receive commissions for their efforts. The number of investment bankers is relatively small; entry into investment banking is difficult. Although the investment banking structure may not be as competitive as many persons would like to have it, the present structure does provide a highly efficient mechanism. The distribution of new securities is accomplished through the over-the-counter market. The resale of securities is executed in the secondary capital market, which is comprised of the over-the-counter market and organized securities exchanges. The over-the-counter market serves both the primary and secondary markets, whereas the organized securities exchanges serve only the secondary market. Broker-dealer firms serve both markets and provide an elaborate nationwide network of securities firms. Many of the larger firms have branches throughout the country.

Not many securities firms engage in all phases of the securities business. Some firms specialize in carrying out the basic investment banking functions; others specialize in the brokerage business. Some firms restrict their operations to certain types of securities. In terms of the number of participants, the secondary market is more competitive than the primary market.

The combined activities of securities firms and organized securities exchanges provide the American economy with an efficient and smoothly functioning system of securities markets. Regulation and supervision require the disclosure of relevant information and the application of reasonably just and equitable principles of trade. The present-day environment instills considerable confidence among investors, thereby inducing them to invest funds into securities.

Broker-Dealer Firms

Individual and institutional investors have contact with the securities markets through broker-dealer firms. When a broker-dealer firm executes an order through the facilities of an organized securities exchange, the firm assumes the position of a broker or agent. The firm attempts to get the most favorable deal for the customer and charges a commission for its services. When a firm executes an order through the over-the-counter markets, the customer has the option of specifying the firm's legal role in the transaction. If the option is not exercised, the firm must reveal its legal role to the customer. The legal role may be that of either broker or dealer. When a firm acts as a dealer or principal, it acts for its own account. The dealer buys directly from customers and sells directly to customers, and attempts to gain by selling securities at prices higher than those at which the securities were acquired.

The diversity among broker-dealer firms makes it difficult to be definitive in describing their structure and operation, so only a few generalizations are set forth here. The number of registered broker-dealer firms and the number of proprietors, partners, and officers, are set forth in Table 12-4. The data indicate that as of June 30, 1959 there were 4,854 registered broker-dealer firms, representing approximately 18,089 persons who were proprietors, partners, or officers of broker-dealer firms. The data show that nearly one-third of the firms have their principal offices in New York City, and that the corporate form is more important than either the sole proprietorship or partnership. The trend is in the direction of incoporation of securities firms. On the same date there were 77,917 individuals doing business directly with the public and registered with the National Association of Securities Dealers as registered representatives.

TABLE 12–4

**BROKERS AND DEALERS REGISTERED UNDER THE SECURITIES ACT OF 1934,[1]
EFFECTIVE REGISTRATION AS OF JUNE 30, 1959**

	New York City	Total
Number of registrants		
Total	1,356	4,854
Sole proprietorship	360	1,762
Partnership	591	1,275
Corporations [4]	405	1,817
Number of proprietors, partners, officers, etc.[2,3]		
Total	6,239	18,089
Sole proprietorship	360	1,762
Partnership	3,699	6,607
Corporations [4]	2,180	9,720

[1] Domestic residents only; excludes 88 outside continental limits of the United States.
[2] Includes directors, officers, trustees, and all other persons occupying similar status or performing similar functions.
[3] Allocations made between New York City and rest of country on the basis of location of principal offices of registrants, not actual location of persons.
[4] Includes all forms of organizations other than sole proprietorship and partnership.
Source: Securities and Exchange Commission, *24th Annual Report*, 1959, p. 241.

The larger firms are departmentalized along functional lines: origination of new securities, distribution of new securities, over-the-counter securities transactions, execution of orders through organized securities exchanges, and research. Smaller firms might restrict their activities to only one or two of these functions. Many of the smaller firms are local in character. The regulation of broker-dealer firms is discussed in the following sections, which concern organized securities exchanges and the over-the-counter markets.

Organized Securities Exchanges

Organized securities exchanges do not buy and sell securities; they provide instead a centralized, regulated, and highly organized market place for securities. Securities exchanges provide a two-way auction market for listed securities. Bidders compete among themselves to buy securities at lowest possible prices; sellers compete among themselves to sell at highest possible prices. A transaction occurs when the buyer bidding the highest price and seller asking the lowest price agree on a price. In a fair and orderly market, the price should reflect the underlying forces of demand and supply for that security.

The purchase and sale of securities is accomplished through members of the exchanges. Memberships are bought and sold, and new members must be approved by the appropriate governing body of an exchange. The record price for a New York Stock Exchange membership was set in February, 1929, when a membership sold for $625,000. Membership is attractive because members are enabled to observe the market firsthand, execute orders for others, and trade in securities for their own account. Members' transactions are executed at relatively low commission rates.

The Securities Exchange Act of 1934 provides, among other things, for the registration and regulation of securities exchanges and registration of securities listed on such exchanges. Section 6 of the Securities Exchange Act states that if it appears to the Securities and Exchange Commission that an exchange applying for registration is so organized as to be able to comply with the provisions of the Act and the Commission's rules thereunder, and that the rules of the exchange are just and adequate to insure fair dealing and to protect investors, the Commission will approve its registration. At the close of 1960, fourteen stock exchanges were registered under the Act as national securities exchanges, and four additional exchanges were exempted from registration. The two largest exchanges, the New York Stock Exchange and the American Stock Exchange, and the most recently approved exchange, the National Stock Exchange, are all located in New York City.

Before a security may be admitted to trading on an exchange, it must be authorized for listing by an exchange and registered with the Commission. To receive authorization of listing, an issuer must apply and qualify for listing; to maintain listing, the issuer must continue to satisfy specified criteria. For example, the New York Stock Exchange applies minimum standards to earning power, number of stockholders, rights of stockholders, and position of the issuer in the industry. A large body of information, including considerable financial data, must be incorporated in a listing application. For instance, an application to the New York Stock Exchange must contain a history of the company and its business, description of the firm's properties, description of its securities, dividend record, officers and their salaries, policies of the firm, and financial statements. The appropriate body within an organized exchange reviews the application and may or may not approve it. The same body may also delist a security.

As of June 30, 1959, a total of 2,236 issuers had 3,808 classes of securities listed and registered on national securities exchanges. Stock issues accounted for 2,631, and bonds accounted for 1,177. Nearly 60 per cent of the issuers and stock issues and 95 per cent of the bond issues were on the New York Stock Exchange. Approximately 90 per cent of all trading on the national exchanges is accomplished through the New York Stock Exchange and the American Stock Exchange.

The membership of the New York Stock Exchange is described in order to illustrate the types of exchange members and their functions. About half of the members are commission brokers, who are sole proprietors, partners, or officers in broker-dealer firms that deal with the public on a commission basis. Commission brokers execute customers' orders that call for the purchase or sale of securities listed on the New York Stock Exchange. These same individuals also function as dealers and buy and sell for their own accounts. Holders of voting stock in member corporate firms and partners in the member non-corporate firms are called allied members and are subject to the same rules and regulations as the members. However, allied members may not do business on the trading floor.

About a quarter of the members are specialists, who specialize in " making a market " for one or more stocks. They are assigned one or more stocks and are expected to maintain insofar as possible a fair and orderly market in these securities. The trading floor of the exchange is very large and it would be difficult for a commission broker to execute orders in many different stocks at the same time. The specialist relieves this problem by accepting from the commission brokers buy and sell orders to be executed at specified prices. If buyers and sellers cannot arrive at a price, a specialist may narrow the spread between the highest bid and lowest asked price by risking his own capital. The specialist receives a commission on orders executed for other brokers and may also profit in trading for his own accounts.

Another group of members, known as floor brokers, also provide assistance to the commission house brokers. Many commission house brokers are not able to execute personally all of their firms' and customers' orders, and so they request the assistance of floor brokers, paying them a commission for their services. Floor brokers may also buy and sell for their own accounts.

A small group of members serve as odd lot dealers. The conventional unit of trading on the New York Stock Exchange is the 100 share unit, which is called the round lot. However, many investors buy and sell securities in less than round lots. The commission brokers execute their customers' odd lot orders through the odd lot dealers, whose primary function is to buy and sell odd lots. These dealers execute the orders at a price slightly different from the last round lot price, e.g., ⅛ of a dollar away from the next round sale if price is under $40; ¼ of a dollar if price is $40 or more. To maintain proper inventories of securities, the odd lot dealers buy and sell round lots for their own accounts. In addition to the income earned on the differential, the odd lot dealers also attempt to make a profit on their inventory management.

Criticism has been leveled at the practice of allowing exchange members to trade for their own accounts. Some critics would like to make the organized securities markets a truly public market. It is alleged that members have " inside " information with respect to short-term price movements and are in a position to take advantage of this information by buying and selling for their own accounts. The rebuttal to this criticism is that trading by members for their own accounts promotes continuity of pricing, which means that securities may be bought and sold quickly and easily with a minimum of price fluctuation at the time of the sale. It is argued that when investment interest is very limited, the intervention of members' trading for their own accounts tends to fill the gap until investment interest is restored. If members believe that investment interest is excessive, they will trade for their own accounts and this trading will, in turn, tend to offset the excessiveness and thus moderate the degree of price change. Although the criticism has not led to the abandonment of members trading for their own accounts, it has led to extensive regulation of securities transactions by both the Securities and Exchange Commission and the exchanges themselves.

REGULATIONS.* The exchanges and their members now operate under a complex set of rules and regulations designed to prevent acts and practices deemed to be fraudulent, deceptive, or manipulative, so as to insure the maintenance of fair and honest markets in securities transactions. Responsibility for exercising control over exchange members and their securities transactions is shared between the exchanges and the Securities and Exchange Commission. Many of the rules and regulations have been established in response to adverse experiences, especially those of the late 1920's.

To throw light on the scope of the present rules and regulations, some of the more important provisions of the Securities Exchange Act of 1934 are cited. The Act provides for: (1) registration and regulation of securities exchanges; (2) registration of securities listed on registered exchanges; (3) submission of financial reports by issuers of registered securities; (4) regulation of proxy solicitations; (5) submission of reports on securities transactions of officers, directors, and principal security holders; and (6) regulation of the use of credit in securities transactions by the Federal Reserve Board.

To provide some insight as to the nature of the rules and regulations imposed by an exchange upon its members, a few illustrations from the New York Stock Exchange are cited. To eliminate secret dealings in securities trading on the floor of the exchange, regulations require that bids and offers

*For a review of the causes, objectives, and principal features of the statutes under which the Commission is charged with responsibilities in the interest of protecting investors and public, see Securities and Exchange Commission, 25th Annual Report, pp. xiii-xxxix.

be called out loud, that the highest bid and lowest offer have precedence, and that all transactions be reported immediately to the public. To promote the financial solvency of member firms, the Exchange requires periodically very complete financial reports. Member firms are subject to unannounced audits by independent public accountants and spot checks of their financial records by Stock Exchange examiners. The Exchange also requires weekly reports on various matters, such as loans by the firms to its members.

Over-the-Counter Market

The over-the-counter securities market consists of all securities markets other than those maintained on organized securities exchanges. It includes the institutional arrangements for the distribution of new securities and the resale or trading in both listed and unlisted securities. The organized securities exchanges account for the bulk of the dollar volume of transactions in common stock issues of nonfinancial corporations, but the bulk of all other forms of securities transactions is executed in the over-the-counter market. Annual over-the-counter transactions in Federal obligations approach $200 billion; $60 billion of state and local obligations are sold and traded in this market; almost all transactions in corporate bonds are effected in the over-the-counter market; and there are some 3,500 domestic corporate issuers that have stocks with 300 or more reported holders that are not listed on any exchange. Many of these issuers are domestic banks and insurance companies. In addition to the 3,500 mentioned above, nearly all issues of those companies that are registered under the Investment Company Act of 1940 are issued and redeemed in the over-the-counter market. A recent study of the over-the-counter market summarized the market in these terms:* there are outstanding 40,000 to 50,000 governmental and corporate issues of securities, each having at least an occasional over-the-counter market; probably less than 20,000 of these issues are traded during a year, and some 3,000 of these issues comprise the active core of the market.

Individual broker-dealer firms create and maintain individual markets in the securities that are traded over-the-counter. Unlike the organized securities exchanges, where all bids and offers are centralized and prices are determined by two-way auction, the over-the-counter market mechanism relies on price determination by negotiation between buyer and seller. Generally, one of the parties in a transaction is a dealer firm that specializes or makes a market in the security that is being traded. A dealer firm makes a market or creates a market by announcing to others, whether they are buyers or sellers, that the dealer firm stands ready either to buy or to sell a security at its own quoted prices. The firm maintains the market by continuing this practice over a period of time. The modern day " counter " is an elaborate

*See Irwin Friend, G. Wright Hoffman, and Willis J. Winn, *The Over-the-Counter Securities Markets*. (New York: McGraw-Hill Book Co., Inc., 1958), p. 5.

system of telephone and private wire communications, which permit orders to be executed in a matter of seconds.

Flexibility and variability are the distinguishing characteristics of the over-the-counter markets. There are few standardized rules, no normal trading units, and considerably less information as to the volume and prices of securities transactions. Diversity among the broker-dealer firms is so great that it is impossible to be very definitive in describing the makeup of the over-the-counter markets. Suffice it to mention that dealer firms tend to specialize in certain securities and these facts are known to investors and other securities firms. (Some firms are known as government bond dealers and municipal bond houses.) When an order is executed, appropriate dealer-houses are contacted for price information.

REGULATION. The major part of the regulations that pertain to the over-the-counter securities markets apply to individual transactions rather than to the over-all markets. Although common-law principles dealing with misrepresentation, manipulation, non-disclosure of facts, and misconduct apply to securities transactions, there is much uncertainty as to their effectiveness in specific cases.

To instill greater confidence among investors, nearly all states have passed legislation aimed at regulating the sale of new securities and activities of brokers and dealers. Kansas is credited with having passed in 1911 the first such legislation. State laws of this nature came to be known as blue-sky laws because of the existence of securities transactions that had no more merit than so much blue sky. There is wide variation among state laws, and generalizations are difficult. It is enough to state that regulation is accomplished primarily through registration as it applies to new securities, brokers, and dealers. The effectiveness of state securities laws depends on the standards applied to registration and the policing of regulations. It is generally agreed that state securities laws have not been very effective in eliminating malpractices in the distribution and resale of securities. Besides lack of uniformity among state laws, none of the states is able to recognize fully the national scope of securities transactions.

Many attempts were made to secure Federal regulation over securities transactions, but it was not until three or four years after the stock market crash in 1929 that pressures became sufficient to overcome resistance to such laws. It is doubtful that the securities acts can be considered part of New Deal legislation; regardless of party, such laws would have been passed in the early 1930's. The only segment of the over-the-counter market which was subject to Federal regulation prior to the 1930's was the stock issues of nationally chartered banks and members banks of the Federal Reserve System. Under the provisions of the Securities Exchange Act of 1934, additional segments of the market came under Federal regulation. By reason of registrations of securities for public sale, issuers, accounting for more than

50 per cent of stock value of those stocks actively traded in the over-the-counter market, have been required to register with the Securities and Exchange Commission and thereby become subject to regulation by the Commission. The Act also provides for the registration and regulation of brokers and dealers doing busines in the over-the-counter market and contains provisions designed to prevent fraudulent, deceptive and manipulative acts and practices in the over-the-counter market. The Act exempts from regulation brokers and dealers whose business is exclusively intrastate or exclusively in exempt securities, such as state and local obligations. The Securities and Exchange Commission may deny or revoke registration to a broker-dealer if the Commission finds such action to be in the public interest and that the applicant or registrant has been guilty of one or more certain types of misconduct. Inexperience in the brokerage business does not prevent registration.

Registration subjects a broker-dealer to certain requirements. Each registered broker-dealer is required to file with the Commission during each calendar year a report of financial condition, which is analyzed to make certain that the registrant is in compliance with set capital requirements. A broker-dealer firm's " aggregate indebtedness " is not to exceed 20 times the firm's net capital. Registered broker-dealers are also subject to inspection, the purpose of which is to obtain compliance with the securities acts and various rules and regulations that are set forth by the Securities and Exchange Commission. Many items are checked, such as financial condition, pricing practices, treatment of customers' funds and securities, disclosures to the customers, and accounting procedures. On June 30, 1959, there were in effect 4,907 registrations of brokers and dealers. During the 1959 fiscal year, the Commission conducted 1,471 inspections which disclosed 2,070 violations, the majority of which related to violations of confirmations and bookkeeping rules. The major shortcomings of these regulations are (1) the inability of the Commission to inspect all registered broker-dealers, and (2) the failure to apply disclosure rules to all securities issued and traded in the over-the-counter market. It should be noted that the principal stock exchanges, some of the states, and the National Associations of Securities Dealers, Inc., also administer inspection programs. Though these other inspection programs cannot serve as a substitute for the Commission's inspections, there is a serious attempt to coordinate the various inspection programs.

By amendment in 1938 (the Maloney Act), the Securities Exchange Act of 1934 provides for the registration with the Commission of national securities associations and establishes standards for such associations. The National Associationof Securities Dealers, Inc., (N.A.S.D.) is the only association registered under the Act. The purpose of the legislation was to encourage the development of a medium for cooperative self-regulation of the over-the-counter market brokers and dealers. Under the Act the rules of such an association must be designed to promote just and equitable principles of trade and to prevent fraudulent and manipulative acts and practices. Such an association acts under the general supervision of the Commission.

The Maloney Act provided incentive to membership by permitting such associations to adopt rules that would place member firms in a more favorable position vis-à-vis nonmember firms. The N.A.S.D. has adopted a rule precluding a member firm from dealing with a nonmember firm, except on the same terms and conditions as the member affords the investing public. Membership is an important determinant of the amount of profit earned in underwriting and over-the-counter trading, because members are permitted to grant price concessions, discounts, and similar allowances to member firms. Loss or denial of membership in the N.A.S.D. imposes a severe economic sanction and tends to make the Association an effective medium for cooperative self-regulation. The disciplinary actions by the Association are subject to review by the Commission on its own motion or on application of the aggrieved person.

PROBLEMS RELATING TO SECONDARY SECURITIES MARKETS

One of the problems concerning the securities markets has to do with the growth and present status of institutional investors as compared with individual investors. The investment needs of institutional investors are different from the needs of many individuals who invest funds directly in securities. The deposit and deposit type of financial institutions tend to invest the major portion of their funds in credit market instruments. The majority of individual investors tend to prefer equity market instruments. As will be pointed out in the chapters dealing with financing business, the issue of credit instruments by business must rest on a firm base of ownership capital. There is a possibility that the flow of newly issued debt securities will be slowed down considerably because of an insufficient base of ownership capital. If institutional investors are not able or willing to absorb additional amounts of ownership capital, a real dilemma may arise. There is also the problem that the present institutional framework of savers and investors will not provide an adequate amount of venture capital to newly established and growing firms. This problem will also be treated in the chapters dealing with financing business.

There is yet another problem that is closely related to the growth of the institutional investor. Even though these investors have become increasingly important, the securities markets have not changed extensively. Questions are raised in some quarters as to the adequacy of the present securities markets in light of the importance of institutional investors.

Specific questions pertain to the limited size of selected markets, the scale of commission rates, and the adequacy of capital of specialists and dealers.

Professional standards among the officers and partners of broker-dealer firms and regulation of their activities are also subject to criticism. Many of the states require little or no experience or knowledge of the securities business of persons seeking registration as brokers and dealers. It was not until mid-1956 that the N.A.S.D. required experience and a satisfactory grade on a written examination, or both, of prospective securities salesmen of member firms. Similar requirements are not imposed on nonmember firms.

Recent abuses in the securities markets have involved the sale of securities, primarily over the telephone, by high-pressure methods ordinarily accompanied by misrepresentation, deception, fraud, and manipulation of prices. The term " boiler room " is used to identify this type of operation. The major problem in this area is that civil injunctions and administrative proceedings are not totally effective in halting such operations, because many of the persons involved have a contemptuous disregard for the law. To be more effective, the Commission has had to resort to criminal prosecutions, which draw very heavily on the limited resources of the Commission. Another approach to this problem is education of the investing public. If the public had relatively complete information on various aspects of the securities markets and acted rationally, self-regulation would correct many of the present abuses and questionable practices. In the absence of such ideal conditions, state and Federal regulation is necessary and on an expanded scale.

In recent years, the Securities and Exchange Commission has submitted numerous proposals to Congress to amend various provisions of the acts administered by the Commission. There is a definite need to strengthen the safeguards and protections afforded the investing public. In time, many of the proposals will probably be adopted by Congress. In the meantime, investors must attempt to exercise greater caution and better judgement in their investment decisions.

QUESTIONS

1. Indicate the magnitude and composition of the consumer and nonprofit organization sector's investment in credit and equity market instruments.

2. Trace the changes in the sector's net acquisition of credit and market instruments during the period 1954-1958.

3. Indicate the breadth of choice that consumers have when investing in credit and equity market instruments. In your answer, list subcategories as well as major categories.

4. What are the more important risk factors that should be considered in the formulation and execution of an investment policy? Discuss two of these factors in some detail.

5. What are the more important non-risk factors that should be considered in the formulation and execution of an investment policy? Discuss two of these factors in some detail.

6. Summarize the role of financial institutions in the formulation and execution of consumers' investment policies.

7. Indicate the magnitude and composition of bank-administered personal trust funds. Explain the asset composition in terms of the trusts' investment policies.

8. Describe briefly the two basic securities markets.

9. Describe briefly the different types of N.Y.S.E. members.

10. Compare a securities transaction in the over-the-counter market with one through an organized exchange.

11. Demonstrate your familiarity with some of the problems relating to secondary securities markets.

ADDITIONAL READING

Almost all of the textbooks on consumer economics and personal finance listed at the end of Chapter 7 and all of the textbooks on corporation finance listed at the end of Chapter 16 treat topics covered in Chapter 12.

Atkinson, Thomas R. *The Pattern of Financial Asset Ownership: Wisconsin Individuals 1949.* N.B.E.R. study. Princeton, N.J.: Princeton University Press, 1956. Relates investment preferences to income, occupation, and city size.

Badger, R. E., and H. G. Guthmann. *Investment Principles and Practices.* (4th ed.) Englewood Cliffs, N.J.: Prentice-Hall, Inc., 1951.

Bellemore, Douglas H. *Investments* (2nd ed.). New York: Simmons-Boardman Publishing Corp., 1960.

Board of Governors of the Federal Reserve System. "Current Data on Security Markets," "Survey of Consumer Finances," and "Survey of Common Trust Funds," *Federal Reserve Bulletin* (see latest 12-month period).

Butters, J. K., et al. *Effects of Taxation: Investment by Individuals.* Boston: Harvard University, Graduate School of Business Administration, 1953.

Choka, Allen D. *An Introduction to Securities Regulation.* Chicago: Twentieth Century Press, Inc., 1958.

Clendenin, J. C. *Introduction to Investments.* (3rd ed.) New York: McGraw-Hill Book Co., Inc., 1960.

Graham, Benjamin. *The Intelligent Investor.* (2nd Rev. ed.) New York: Harper & Bros., 1959.

———, and D. J. Dodd. *Security Analysis.* (3rd ed.) New York: McGraw-Hill Book Co., Inc., 1951.

Grodinsky, Julius. *Investments.* New York: The Ronald Press Co., 1953.

Hayes, Douglas A. *Appraisal and Management of Securities.* New York: The Macmillan Co., 1956.

Investment Counsel Annual. New York: Investment Counsel Association of America. See latest report.

Jordan, David F., and Herbert F. Dougall. *Investments.* (6th ed.) Englewood Cliffs, N.J.: Prentice-Hall, Inc., 1952.

✓ Leffler, George L. *The Stock Market.* (2nd ed.) New York: The Ronald Press Co., 1957.

Livingston, J. A. *The American Stockholder.* Philadelphia: J. B. Lippincott Co., 1958.

✓ Loeser, John C. *The Over-the-Counter Securities Market — What it is and How it Operates.* New York: National Quotation Bureau, Inc., 1940.

✓ Prime, John H. *Investment Analysis.* (3rd ed.) Englewood Cliffs, N.J.: Prentice-Hall, Inc., 1959.

Robbins, Sidney M. *Managing Securities.* Boston: Houghton Mifflin Co., 1954.

Sauvain, Harry. *Investment Management.* (2nd ed.) Englewood Cliffs, N.J.: Prentice-Hall, Inc., 1959.

U.S. Securities and Exchange Commission. *Investment Counsel, Investment Management, Investment Supervisory, and Investment Advisory Services.* Report pursuant to Section 30 of the Public Utility Holding Company Act of 1935. Washington, D.C.: Government Printing Office, 1939.

———. *Annual Report and Statistical Bulletin.* Washington, D.C.: Government Printing Office.

Walter, James E. *The Role of Regional Security Exchanges.* Berkeley: University of California Press, Bureau of Business and Economic Research, 1957.

13: Investment companies

THE basic idea underlying the organization and operation of almost all investment companies is the pooling of the investment funds of many individual and institutional investors by selling investment companies' shares and purchasing other securities for investment. The companies are publicly owned and investments are made for the benefit of shareholders, who share in the net income and profits and losses in proportion to their stock ownership.

Investment company shares represent a form of direct investment in the sense that investors are exposed to both forms of financial risk. Investment companies contend that a given risk situation is minimized by providing a degree of diversification and professional management superior to that which can be attained by the majority of investors. To the extent that investors are familiar with investment companies' policies and make their decisions on the basis of this information, some influence is exerted on ultimate investment of funds that flow into this type of investment outlet. Investors should be familiar with investment policies and make purchases that fit their respective needs. However, it is probably true that many investors neither read nor understand fully the investment policies of companies in which they hold an interest, and in this sense investment companies' shares might be construed as a form of indirect investment.

The protracted rise in security prices, the emphasis on common stocks as an inflation hedge, and intensive selling efforts have led to very rapid growth in both the number of shareholder accounts and the volume of assets held by investment companies. From 1940 to 1960 the number of accounts increased from less than 1 million to more than 4 million, and total investment company assets increased from $1 billion to $20 billion. The accounts of institutional investors represent 4 per cent of the total number of accounts and 10 per cent of the total value of accounts. Eliminating duplication in individuals' accounts, it is estimated that there are at least 2 million individuals holding one or more shares in investment companies. Investment companies experience their more rapid rates of growth when there is a definite upward trend in the general level of securities prices. Favorable tax rulings have also provided some impetus to the growth in this form of financial investment.

CLASSIFICATION OF INVESTMENT COMPANIES

We shall consider three principal classes of investment companies: face-amount certificate companies, unit investment trusts, and management companies. These companies can be further classified on the basis of registration, tax status, capitalization, and portfolio composition. All of these classifications will be treated in this chapter. The small business investment companies are not considered in this chapter, but are treated in Chapter 20, which deals with long-term business financing.

Face-Amount Certificate Companies

A " face-amount certificate " means any certificate, investment contract, or other security that represents an obligation on the part of its issuer to pay a stated or determinable sum or sums at a fixed or determinable date or dates more than 24 months after the date of issuance, in consideration of the payment of periodic installments of a stated or determinable amount; or any security that represents a similar obligation on the part of a face-amount certificate company, the consideration for which is the payment of a single lump sum. The former is known as a face-amount certificate of the installment type; the latter as a fully paid face-amount certificate. Inasmuch as face-amount certificate companies account for only a small part of the investment company industry, no attempt is made here to explain this complicated type of security. Let it suffice to mention that the certificates have loan value and cash surrender provisions. As with life insurance, early surrender of a face-amount certificate involves a considerable loss, because much of the selling and promotional costs are charged against the early years. Face-amount certificate companies are required to maintain at all times minimum certificate reserves, based on minimum reserve payments and rate of investment return.

Unit Investment Trusts

A unit investment trust is organized under a trust indenture, contract of custodianship or agency, or similar contract; it does not have a board of directors; and it issues only redeemable securities, each of which represents an undivided interest in a unit of specified securities. In this type of company, a trustee, or custodian, maintains custody of the assets and the security holder must be notified of all substitutions in the portfolio. The unit investment trust was most popular during the late 1920's and early 1930's, but since that time its importance has declined considerably.

Management Investment Companies

Any investment company not included in either of the above-mentioned classes is considered a management company. Almost all of the investment company industry is comprised of management companies. These companies are also classified on the basis of capitalization and composition of assets. With respect to capitalization, they are divided into open-end and closed-end investment companies. An " open-end company " means a management company that offers for sale or has outstanding any redeemable security of which it is the issuer. The term " open-end " is applicable in the sense that the capitalization of this type of company is undergoing nearly continuous change, and if management has its way, the capitalization increases with the passage of time.* A " closed-end company " is any management investment company other than an open-end management company. In this type of company, the capitalization is fixed.

With respect to composition of assets, management companies are divided into diversified companies and non-diversified companies. Under the provisions of the Investment Company Act of 1940, a " diversified company " is a management company that meets the following requirements: (1) at least 75 per cent of the value of its total assets is represented by cash and cash items, government securities, securities of other investment companies, and other securities; (2) for the purposes of this calculation, other securities are limited for any one issuer to an amount not greater in value than 5 per cent of the value of the investment company's total assets and to not more than 10 per cent of the outstanding voting securities of such issuer. A " non-diversified company " is any management company other than a " diversified company."

Other Classifications

REGISTERED COMPANIES. Investment companies are also classified on the basis of registration. Almost all are required to register with the Securities and Exchange Commission. In order to register, a company must reveal policy with respect to many of its activities, including classification, borrowings, issuance of senior securities, underwriting, investment policy, real estate and commodity transactions, loans, and portfolio turnover. Inasmuch as a non-registered company is severely restricted in its activities under the Investment Company Act of 1940, nearly all investment companies have become registered companies.

REGULATED INVESTMENT COMPANIES. The tax status of an investment company serves as another basis of classification. Under the Internal Revenue Code, an investment company may elect to be taxed as a " regulated investment company " rather than as an ordinary corporation. The term " regu-

*The registration of companies issuing variable annuity contracts introduces another sub-classification, because some of these companies are exempted from certain provisions of the Investment Company Act of 1940. See "Securities and Exchange Commission News Digest," February 25, 1960.

lated" does not refer to securities laws or supervision; it is a technical term that has meaning only in terms of the revenue code. To be taxed as a "regulated investment company," a company must satisfy certain requirements, including the following: (1) it must be a domestic corporation, not a personal holding company; (2) it must be registered as either a management company or a unit investment trust; (3) at least 90 per cent of its gross income for any taxable year must be from dividends, interest, and gains from securities; (4) no more than 30 per cent of its gross income for any taxable year may be derived from sales of securities held for less than three months; (5) it must declare and pay taxable dividends equal to not less than 90 per cent of its net income, exclusive of capital gains, for any taxable year; and (6) at the close of each quarter, at least 50 per cent of the value of its total assets must be composed of financial assets. The net effect of this tax provision is that the shareholders of regulated investment companies are taxed in substantially the same manner as if they were investing directly in the securities held by the investment companies. Almost all such companies qualify as "regulated investment companies" and most of them elect to be taxed as such. The major exceptions include quasi-holding companies and companies primarily interested in special situations. In the latter cases, the assets are concentrated in one or a few securities. A few investment companies elect not to be taxed as regulated investment companies because of technical tax considerations relating to certain types of dividend distributions that can be treated as return of capital rather than as investment income.

PORTFOLIO CLASSIFICATION. Companies may also be classified in terms of portfolio: balanced, diversified, common stock, industry specialized, location specialized, and special situations. A balanced portfolio is comprised of both fixed-income securities and common stocks. It is not necessary that the percentage breakdown between the two types of securities be held constant indefinitely. Common-stock funds might hold a small portion of assets in the form of fixed-income securities, and it is sometimes difficult to draw the line between balanced and common stock funds. Various forms of diversification can be incorporated into both the balanced and the common stock funds. The names of the other types of portfolios are self-explanatory. It is also possible to classify companies in terms of investment objective: long-term growth of capital and income, current income, and tax protection.

ORIGIN AND DEVELOPMENT OF INVESTMENT COMPANIES

Like many of our financial institutions, the basic idea underlying the investment company industry had its origin in England and Scotland. By 1900, the industry was firmly established in these and European countries. However, it was not until the 1890's that this type of financial institution was introduced into the United States, and it was not until the post-World War I period that the investment company industry began to grow. Much of the early growth took place in companies whose purpose was to further American investment abroad. Financial institutions, and particularly banks, were the major class of shareholders.

The protracted rise in stock prices during the 1920's was conducive to very rapid growth in the investment company industry. Approximately 600 companies were formed from 1927 to 1929. The speculative fever that prevailed during much of this period was reflected in the development of the investment company industry. Many of the investment companies operated on the basis of speculative objectives. Some investment companies concentrated their investment in one or a few issues with the expectation of realizing considerable gain in a relatively short time; other companies emphasized market trading.

Many of the investment companies formed in the 1920's adopted high-risk type objectives and manner of operation. When the market break came in the late 1920's, investors in some investment company shares were in a position to suffer great losses. Many investors came into the market late in the upsurge and they expected to " make a killing " in investment company shares. Needless to mention, many of them were sadly disappointed, and it took many years for the investment company idea to get back into the good graces of the investing public in the United States.

In addition to the consequences of a sharp break in the securities markets, the investing public became disturbed by certain abuses. Until the passage of the Investment Company Act of 1940, many companies did not provide adequate, accurate, and explicit information, fairly presented, concerning the character of their securities and the nature of their investment policies. Also, some companies did not spell out their financial responsibilities to investors. Furthermore, securities transactions were not always executed in the interest of all classes of security holders. Instead, some companies were organized, operated, managed, and their portfolios selected in the interest of others, including directors, officers, investment advisers, underwriters, brokers, dealers, special classes of security holders, and other investment companies. Other abuses included the issue of securities containing inequitable or discriminatory provisions, failure to protect preferences and privileges of the holders of outstanding securities, undue concentration of control through pyramiding and other inequitable methods, affiliation with irresponsible persons, application of unsound or misleading accounting procedures, major change in status or character of companies and management without the consent of security holders, excessive borrowing or issue of senior securities, and operation without adequate assets or reserves.

Most of the unit investment trusts were less speculative than the other types of investment companies, and this segment of the industry did experience some growth in the early 1930's. In view of the dynamic nature of our economic system, the severe restrictions on management decision-making within unit investment trusts eventually led to unsatisfactory investment performance, and the fixed trust type of company lost its popularity. The development of investment companies since the early 1930's has been based primarily on the organization and administration of management investment companies that survived the market crash and depression years. The major part of the industry's growth has occurred in both the number and size of open-end companies, particularly those which featured either a balanced or a diversified common stock portfolio.

The passage of the Investment Company Act in 1940 and the upward trend in the level of common stock prices gave rise to a renewed interest and growth in the investment company industry.

ORGANIZATION, ADMINISTRATION OF INVESTMENT COMPANIES

Laws and regulations set forth specific standards relating to an investment company's formation, capital structure, character of affiliated persons, investment contracts, and transactions. The dual system of charter is not a characteristic of the investment company industry. Investment companies are organized under state laws.* As noted previously, securities laws of the individual states vary widely, so that it is impossible in this study to summarize the laws of each state. Let it suffice to mention that investment company shares are subject to state laws pertaining to registration of securities prior to their being offered for sale. Only a few states' laws and regulations deal with organization and administration of investment companies. On the Federal level, investment companies are subject to the Securities Act of 1933, the Securities and Exchange Act of 1934, and the Investment Company Act of 1940, the last of which is the most important.

Some of the provisions of the Investment Company Act of 1940 as they relate to organization and administration of investment companies should be examined. First, no registered investment company, either directly or through an underwriter, can make a public offering of its securities unless the company has a net worth of at least $100,000, and such funds must have come from not more than 25 persons. It will be recalled that nearly all financial institutions that receive funds from investors or depositors, or both, are required to satisfy capital requirements. Second, the capital structure of investment companies must satisfy certain standards. Closed-end companies are permitted to issue securities senior to their common stock issues, but debt issues must have an asset coverage of at least 300 per cent and senior

*Small business investment companies are permitted to secure Federal charters.

stock issues must have an asset coverage of at least 200 per cent. Closely related to this requirement are provisions relating to dividends and voting rights. To avoid excessively complex capital structures, the 1940 Act permits closed-end investment companies to issue only one class of each security representing indebtedness and senior stock. Some of the closed-end companies have more complex structures than that suggested above because they were organized prior to the passage of the Act. Open-end investment companies are not permitted to issue any class of senior security. However, they are permitted to borrow from banks if they maintain asset coverage of at least 300 per cent.

Before noting some of the specific ways in which Federal legislation has affected internal organization and administration of investment companies, some of the basic components comprising organization must be introduced. An investment company may have a board of directors or trustees, an advisory board, an investment advisor, a principal underwriter, and a group of bona-fide officers and employees. Like other corporations, a company's board of directors is elected by vote of the holders of the company's voting securities. The members of an advisory board may be elected or appointed. In either case, an advisory board is composed solely of persons who serve the investment company in no other capacity than as members of the advisory board. The function of the advisory board is to advise as to investments, and it does not have the power to determine that any security or other investments shall be purchased or sold by the investment company. An investment advisor is any other person (other than a bona-fide officer, director, trustee, member of advisory board, or company employee) who, under contract and pursuant to contract, regularly furnishes advice to an investment company with respect to the desirability of investing in, purchasing, or selling securities or other property, or is empowered to determine what securities or other property shall be purchased or sold by the company. The principal underwriter of a company other than a closed-end investment company is one who as principal purchases from or has the right to purchase from an investment company all newly offered securities or acts as the company's agent in the distribution of newly issued securities. The term "principal underwriter" as applied to closed-end companies has the generally accepted meaning introduced in earlier chapters.

To ensure that a part of the structure of investment companies will be filled with persons who have no pecuniary interest in the management, the Investment Company Act of 1940 requires that at least 40 per cent of the members of a board of directors be persons who have no pecuniary interest in a company's management and who are not part of a company's operational staff. In other words, the law requires that not more than 60 per cent of a company's directors shall be officers, employees, or investment advisors of the company, or persons affiliated with an investment advisor of the company. The law also provides that a majority of a company's board shall not be directors who are regular brokers or principal underwriters of the company or who are investment bankers or affiliated persons of either group. The law also restricts the role that bankers may play by providing that a majority of a company's board may not be officers or directors of any one bank. Actually, the exact wording of the provisions in the law has permitted some companies to set up a board with no independent directors, and the S.E.C. is attempting to secure modifications in the wording so as to enforce the idea that there should be a few disinterested directors to act as watchdogs over the conduct of management. The 1940 Act also specified that persons or organizations that have been convicted of any felony or misdemeanor relating to several types of financial transactions are not eligible to serve in any of the capacities indicated above.

The typical management fee is ½ of 1 per cent annually of average assets. Assuming that the average investment return is 5 per cent of total assets, the management fee represents 10 per cent of investment income. In a typical year the ratio of all expenses except income taxes and interest may range from ¼ of 1 per cent to slightly more than 1 per cent, reflecting difference in objective as well as in efficiency of operation.

As noted above, many open-end investment companies use investor advisors and distribute their shares through principal underwriters. For many years, the Securities and Exchange Commission interpreted the Investment Company Act of 1940 as prohibiting the assignment of value of management and underwriting, but this position was later upset by court decisions. During 1959, there was a big surge in public offerings of shares in companies that specialize in the management of investment companies. Some of the investment management companies, such as the Keystone Company of Boston, have made public offerings, making it possible for investors to invest in the management and underwriting functions as well as in the funds themselves. Such offerings have proven particularly attractive to individuals who are involved in the distribution of the open-end investment company shares. Since there is a large element of fixed costs in staffing an investment management company, the future growth in the size and number of funds administered by such a company offers the possibility of substantial financial gain.

OPEN-END INVESTMENT COMPANY SHARES

The capitalization of open-end investment companies is subject to almost continuous change. Most open-end companies continuously offer new shares, and all agree to redeem on demand their outstanding shares. The offering price of an open-end investment share is equal to actual book value plus a loading cost to cover the costs of distribution and promotion. Generally, the actual book value of a company share is determined or calculated twice daily by dividing the current market value of the company's total net assets by the number of its shares outstanding. The redemption price is equal to actual book value. The shares are not traded on organized securities exchanges, and as a general rule are not traded in over-the-counter markets. In recent years, there has been a limited amount of trading in open-end company shares. Some dealers have found it profitable to purchase open-end shares at prices slightly higher than their redemption values, and sell them to others at prices slightly lower than the offering price, including loading.

Distribution of Shares

One of the more common methods of distributing open-end shares is the use of a principal underwriter, who, in turn, utilizes the services of various broker-dealer firms. This method is similar to the use of a general agent in the sale of life insurance. The general agent has a contract with the issuer, and the general agent, in turn, sells through various local agents. Some investment companies distribute their shares through regional offices operated by the principal underwriter. A few companies rely on direct distribution and sell their securities directly to the investing public. Regardless of which method is used, a registered investment company is required to file a registration statement under the terms of the Securities Act of 1933. Advertisements, pamphlets, circulars, form letters, and other sales literature addressed to or intended for distribution to prospective investors must be filed with the Securities and Exchange Commission. As a result of various types of abuses relating to these matters, the Commission has set forth standards of policy indicating selected types of sales literature that will be construed as materially misleading, and selected formats to which approved tables and charts should conform. The Commission also has rules pertaining to prices and loading charges. Rules also regulate the switching of investments among investment company shares. Similar laws relate to switching of life insurance policies.

Systematic Accumulation Plans

During a given period, say a year, the net capital changes in an open-end investment company represent the difference between the sales and repurchases of its own shares. In each of the years 1941-1958, there was a net increase in the capital of these companies. In most years, sales exceeded repurchases by three or four times, but in a few years, the sales were only slightly higher than repurchases. With the exception of 1947 and 1953, each year's sales were greater than those of the previous year. The annual volume of repurchases has also shown a definite upward trend, but in only eight of the years was the annual volume greater than in the previous year. The volume of sales and repurchases and the difference between the two are determined primarily by the level of national income and the state of the securities markets.

Various types of investment services are connected with most open-end investment company shares. A majority of the companies sponsor systematic accumulation plans under which investors can make systematic purchases or automatic reinvestment of dividends. The aim of such plans is to promote or accelerate the accumulation of savings through investment company shares. A shareholder account can be classified as either a regular or an accumulation account. A regular account is one in which the shareholder makes a lump sum investment and does not indicate a desire to make additional investments periodically. Obviously, the regular shareholder can purchase additional shares at any time. An accumulation account is one in which the shareholder indicates a desire to make additional investments in a company's shares at periodic intervals, such as monthly or quarterly. Many shareholders have their distribution payments automatically reinvested.

PREPAID CHARGE PLAN. Two basic types of systematic accumulation plans are available to investment company shareholders. One is a contractual type, under which the investor formally agrees to make regular periodic investments for a specified period, and the other is a voluntary type in which the investor does not specify either the total time period or the ultimate amount of investment. The Investment Company Act of 1940 refers to the contractual type of plan as a period plan certificate. In the literature, the contractual type of plan is referred to as a prepaid charge plan, because the loading deductions are made in the first year or two. The Act sets a maximum sales load and limits the amount of the first year's payments that can be deducted for sales load. Generally, life insurance can be purchased to provide for completion of the plan in the event of death and disability. Actually, this type of plan incorporates many features similar to those found in the life insurance industry. The shareholder receives payment notices; he can draw on accumulations and repay later without additional loading charge. It is also possible to provide for the transfer of the plan to beneficiaries upon the death of the shareholder. A shareholder is free to discontinue and liquidate the plan at any time, but if he does so in the early years of a plan, the loading represents a sizeable portion of total payments made by shareholders.

LEVEL CHARGE PLAN. The other systematic accumulation plan is less formal. The shareholder fills out an application, giving the following information: amount of initial purchase, amount and timing of probable periodic investment, and disposition of distribution payments. Since the loading charge is paid each time a periodic payment is made, this type of plan is referred to as a level charge plan. Almost all the investment companies offering level charge plans specify minima for the first subsequent purchases. As noted above, the shareholder need not specify either the duration of the plan or the actual amounts that will be invested. The only requirements are that the amount of the payment be at or above a specified minimum and that the payment be made within a given period. Early liquidation of a level charge plan is not as costly to the shareholder as is the premature liquidation of the prepaid charge plan.

At the end of 1958, open-end companies held 3,630,096 shareholder accounts.* On the same date, there were 878,147 accumulation plans and an estimated 469,000 dividend reinvestment plans in force, the latter of which include only those in which a shareholder is reinvesting all distribution received through a formal automatic plan of reinvestment and is not investing new money at regular intervals. The number and asset value of both types of plans increased nearly four times in the period 1954-1958. It might be noted that the majority of shareholders investing under accumulation plans incorporate the automatic reinvestment of distributions.

Distributions to shareholders are composed of two types: net investment income and net realized capital gain. For the years 1955-1958, the total distributions have been almost evenly divided between the two. In 1955 and 1956, distributions in the form of net realized capital gains were slightly greater, and in 1957 and 1958, the net investment distributions exceeded the distributions from net realized capital gains.

Regular Withdrawal Plans

Various types of withdrawal plans are also offered by open-end investment companies. One type enables an investor to receive a specified, level amount at regular intervals. To avoid reduction of principal, the specified amount must not exceed expected investment income, although it is possible to incorporate reduction of principal to achieve stability in the amount of periodic withdrawal. Another type of plan provides for a gradual and complete liquidation of a shareholder's account over a specified number of years. The amount received each year will vary with future changes in the net asset value of the share and the amount of distribution paid on each share. In a sense the plan is closely similar to the variable annuity discussed earlier, except that the investment company is not permitted to use life contingency. The payout period is specified and is not connected with the shareholder's age. Generally, a shareholder must hold a fairly large account to be able to arrange a withdrawal plan, and a special fee may be charged to cover the added administrative costs.

INFLUENCE ON SECURITIES MARKETS

As noted earlier in this chapter, most investment companies invest a large portion of their assets in capital stock. At the end of 1959, the estimated holdings of New York Stock Exchange listed stocks of open-end and closed-

---

*All data in this paragraph and the next one are drawn from National Association of Investment Companies, *Investment Companies, A Statistical Summary, 1940-1958* (New York).

end investment companies were respectively $12.8 and $5.2 billion. These holdings accounted for approximately 5.8 per cent of the market value of all N.Y.S.E. listed stocks.* To the extent that shareholders in open-end and closed-end investment companies consist of individuals and institutions that would not otherwise have invested in equities, the investment companies are responsible for attracting a greater portion of the flow of savings into the equity segment of the securities markets.

To provide a general idea as to the influence of investment company trading activities on the N.Y.S.E., it may be noted that the open-end investment company purchases of portfolio securities in 1958 were slightly greater than $3 billion, and their sales of portfolio securities were slightly less than $2 billion. Since about 70 per cent of the total assets of open-end companies are invested in common and preferred stocks listed on the New York Stock Exchange, it might be assumed that 70 per cent of the trading in securities by investment companies involved N.Y.S.E. listed stocks. On the basis of these assumptions, investment company purchases of portfolio securities accounted for approximately 6.4 per cent of the total trading volume on the N.Y.S.E. Considering that sales and redemptions of investment company shares were respectively $1,620 million and $511 million in the same year, it is estimated that approximately half of the company purchases of portfolio securities represented the investment of new money and the other half represented the turnover of existing portfolio securities. It would appear that the market trading of open-end investment companies is not a major influence on the organized securities markets.

Before leaving the topic of investment companies, we shall make a few observations on the influence of redemption of open-end investment company shares. The motivation underlying purchases of open-end shares is probably one of the more important factors to consider in appraising the likelihood of excess liquidations. If most of the investment in open-end company shares represents long-term investment to meet long-term investment objectives, large-scale redemptions would not be very likely. However, if a large portion of such investment were designed to take advantage of cyclical movements in the prices of securities, large-scale redemptions would be more likely. Past experience tends to support the former assumption. Furthermore, the company holdings of cash (4 to 5 per cent of total assets) and the inflow of cash from continuous sales of new shares tend to dampen the effect of redemptions. During the 1941-1958 period, sales exceeded redemptions in each year, and during the 1954-1958 period, sales exceeded redemptions in each month. Recent experience suggests that redemption of open-end investment company shares does not pose a serious problem.

A related question is whether or not investors react in one way when they are shareholders in investment companies and in a different way when

*New York Stock Exchange Fact Book, 1960.

they invest directly in the types of securities held by investment companies. No data are available to answer the question. If liquidation of portfolio were more likely when funds were channelled through investment companies, the companies would probably not attempt to liquidate the same securities. Their portfolios are well diversified and are made up of nearly 3,000 securities. Only to the extent that a large number of investment companies held a common group of securities would it be possible for liquidation to be concentrated among a few issues. In this case, the price declines might be larger than they would otherwise be.

FUTURE GROWTH OF INVESTMENT COMPANIES

The future growth of investment companies will depend primarily on the future level and trend of prices in the markets for securities, goods, and services. If the purchasing power of the dollar declines and common stock prices continue to offset this decline, many investors will continue to rely on this investment medium and additional investors will be attracted to this form of financial investment. However, investment companies will be competing with two new forms of financial investment: variable annuities and small investor participation in real estate investment trusts. The sales force in the insurance industry is just as aggressive as that now pushing investment company shares, and if the majority of agents and brokers qualify to sell the variable annuity contracts, the sales force behind this new form of financial investment will outnumber that of the investment companies. A real estate investment trust is very similar to an investment company, except that the real estate investment trusts pool their funds in various forms of real estate. In 1960 real estate investment trusts were given essentially the same tax treatment as that afforded regulated investment companies, thereby making this form of investment more attractive to the small investor. Within a few years, state and Federal laws will probably be liberalized to permit real estate investment trusts to incorporate and function in a manner very similar to the way in which investment companies now function. In summary, there is a large untapped market for investment company shares, but there is also a threat of greater competition from other investment media.

QUESTIONS

1. What basic idea underlies the organization and operation of an investment company?
2. Differentiate between face-amount certificate companies, unit investment trusts, and management companies.

3. Differentiate between the two major types of management companies.

4. What is a registered investment company? What is a regulated company?

5. Classify investment companies on the basis of portfolio.

6. Trace the origin and development of investment companies, placing special emphasis on their growth since 1940.

7. Demonstrate your familiarity with the Federal regulations relating to the investment company industry.

8. What is an investment management company?

9. Differentiate between two systematic accumulation plans.

10. What influence does the investment company industry have on the securities markets?

ADDITIONAL READING

The textbooks on consumer economics and personal finance listed at the end of Chapter 7 and the textbooks on investments listed at the end of Chapter 12 deal with the subject of investment companies.

Bullock, Hugh. *The Story of Investment Companies.* New York: Columbia University Press, 1959.

Cam, Gilbert A. *A Survey of the Literature on Investment Companies, 1864-1957.* New York: The New York Public Library, 1958.

National Association of Investment Companies. Publishes numerous pamphlets on investment companies, including an annual *Statistical Summary.* (61 Broadway, New York 6, N.Y.)

U.S. Securities and Exchange Commission, *Investment Trusts and Investment Companies,* a report in five parts, 1939-1942; a report on commingled or common trust funds administered by banks and trust companies, 1939; a report on companies issuing face amount installment certificates, 1939; a report on companies sponsoring installment investment plans, 1940; a report on fixed and semifixed investment trusts, 1940; a report on investment trusts in Great Britain, 1939; and an index digest, compiled and edited by Adelaide R. Hasse, 1946; Washington, D.C.: Government Printing Office.

Weissman, Rudolph. *The Investment Company and the Investor.* New York: Harper & Bros., 1951.

Wiesenberger, Arthur. *Investment Companies.* (See latest edition.) New York: Arthur Wiesenberger & Co.

14: One- to four-family mortgages

U P to this stage of our study, the consumer and nonprofit organization sector has been studied in terms of a supplier of funds to the savings institutions and insurance sectors and as an investor in credit and equity market instruments. This sector also borrows funds from financial institutions. At the end of 1958, the sector's liabilities totaled $171.4 billion, nearly all of which was in the form of credit market instruments. Of this amount, over $111 billion was in the form of mortgages on one- to four-family properties, and over $45 billion was related to financing goods and services for personal consumption and to refinancing of debt originally incurred for consumption purposes. Logically, a broad definition of consumer credit would include one- to four-family mortgages, but by tradition this type of credit is omitted. However, loans to finance modernization and improvement of owner-occupied houses are considered consumer credit in the Federal Reserve's compilation of consumer credit statistics. The omission of real estate mortgage credit means that consumer credit transactions, as currently defined, are of short- and intermediate-term maturities. Real estate mortgage credit is long-term at the time the credit is extended. The sector's other liabilities include security credit, loans on insurance policies, and nonprofit organization bank loans and trade payables.

In this chapter we shall focus our attention on the one- to four-family mortgages and the role that financial institutions play in the mortgage market. The major topics covered include credit principles, Federal incentives to home ownership and home financing, demand for and supply of mortgage credit, and recent changes in the one- to four-family mortgage market.

DOLLAR IMPORTANCE OF REAL ESTATE MORTGAGE CREDIT

At the end of 1958, the total real estate mortgage debt outstanding in the United States was $171.2 billion, which was nearly five times greater than the amount outstanding at the end of World War II. This type of debt accounted for over 16 per cent of the total credit and equity market instruments outstanding at the end of 1958, and mortgages on one- to four-family properties accounted for approximately 70 per cent of total mortgages. The importance of mortgage financing in relation to the total financial markets is shown clearly in the following tabulation (amounts in billions of dollars):

	1954	1955	1956	1957	1958
Net increase in credit and equity market instruments	$28.4	$43.8	$30.6	$36.7	$45.2
1- to 4-family mortgages	9.6	12.6	10.8	8.6	10.4
Other mortgages	2.9	3.6	3.8	3.5	4.2

The postwar peak in mortgage financing was reached in 1955, when the number of non-farm home mortgage recordings of $20,000 or less exceeded 3.9 million and their total value exceeded $28 billion.

The ultimate source of funds available for real estate loans is consumer saving. As noted in earlier chapters, the major portion of consumer saving flows into the savings institutions and insurance sectors, and mortgages are an important investment of these institutions. Of the total amount of mortgages on one- to four-family properties outstanding at the end of 1958, the savings institutions sector held $59.3 billion; the insurance sector held $22.9 billion; the commercial bank sector held $17.5 billion; the Federal Government sector held $4.7 billion; and the consumer and nonprofit organization sector held $11.3 billion. The remainder, amounting to about $2.3 billion, was held by the other sectors.

Since 1900, the mortgage holdings of financial institutions have risen rapidly. The rise has resulted primarily from four factors: (1) the legal restrictions on mortgage lending by financial institutions have been liberalized; (2) financial institutions have been receiving an increasing share of consumer saving; (3) the nature of mortgage debt is ideally suited to many of the savings and insurance institutions; and (4) the technical advances in transportation and communication extended the effective geographical areas within which some of the larger financial institutions may operate.

CREDIT PRINCIPLES

The funds constituting real estate credit are for the most part obtained by borrowers as long-term loans through the various financial institutions. Because these are long-term loans there is a need for security to back up the funds advanced, and this security takes the form of the real estate mortgage. Analysis of the value of the property and a predetermination of the legal position of the creditor (lender) in the event of debtor default are vitally important to the lending institution. Many of the principles discussed in this section also apply to multi-family and commercial mortgages.

Appraisal of Value

In making any long-term residential mortgage loan, the supplier of funds proceeds to determine the value of the security for the purpose of the loan. In the case of a home mortgage, the analysis of the security is done on the basis of an appraisal of the property, or an estimate of the property value for the purpose of the loan. The lender wants an appraisal that will stand up through the years so that it can be relied on to assure a " sound " loan. The need for an appraisal becomes more apparent when we recognize that loans are often made up to 95 per cent of the value of residential property. Depending on the nature and location of the property, an appraiser will take one of three or a combination of three different approaches to an appraisal to arrive at a figure that becomes his estimate of property value; namely, the market approach, the cost approach, and the income approach. The latter approach involves determination and capitalization of expected future income, and is used chiefly for rental property.

Predetermination of Lender's Legal Position

Before a supplier of mortgage funds can safely lend money with a particular parcel of real property as security for the loan, the status of the title to the property must be determined. Does the seller have clear title to the property? Are there any prior liens against the property?

Answers to these questions are provided either by having an attorney prepare and examine the abstract of the seller's title, or by having a title insurance policy placed on the property. The abstract of title is the history of the title. It contains, among other things, a listing of the previous owners of the property; a record of other mortgages that have been placed on the property and whether or not they were paid; whether or not any judgments exist against the seller's property; whether or not other types of liens exist against the property; and too many other items to be included here. If a title insurance policy is to be obtained, the insuring company prepares an abstract of title, and on the basis of its determination that there are no " clouds " on the title, issues a policy insuring the title.

Credit Documents

In borrowing funds to finance the purchase of real estate or the construction of a house, the borrower generally gives the lender a personal promissory note, promising to repay the loan, and a pledge of the property to serve as security. In conjunction with the note any of the following three instruments is given by the debtor to prove that the property is the security for the loan: (1) mortgage; (2) trust deed in the nature of a mortgage; and (3) installment land contract. The specific type of instrument used in a transaction depends on state law.

THE REAL PROPERTY MORTGAGE. A mortgage is the creation of an interest in property as security for the payment of a debt or the fulfillment of an obligation. There are two principal theories of mortgages used in the United States, the title theory and the lien theory.

Under the title theory, upon making the mortgage, the mortgagor (the borrower) passes title to the property, the subject of the mortgage, to the mortgagee, subject to a condition subsequent. The principal condition subsequent is payment of the debt. Upon fulfillment of the condition, title to the property divests (reverts to) the mortgagor. However, during the period of the mortgage, the mortgagor is generally entitled to remain in possession of the property even though technically he has passed title to his mortgagee.

The majority of the states use the lien theory of mortgages. Under this concept, title remains with the mortgagor, and the mortgage that is placed on the property is a charge on the title. The charge or lien gives the mortgagee the right to foreclose on the mortgage in the event that the mortgagor defaults in payment or breaches any of the other convenants (promises) of the mortgage.*

THE TRUST DEED IN THE NATURE OF A MORTGAGE. Nine states use a trust deed in the nature of a mortgage. This deed of trust is used in place of the ordinary real property mortgage as outlined above. Where the deed of trust is used, the borrower executes the deed of trust whereby he conveys the property to a third party known as the trustee, who receives from the transaction sufficient title to carry out the provisions of the trust indenture. This trustee holds title for the benefit of the owner of the note, which is also executed at the time of the transaction by the borrower. If the borrower defaults, the property is disposed of according to the terms of the trust agreement after proper legal proceedings. Although this instrument has the same effect as a mortgage, the period necessary for the completion of the legal proceedings is considerably less than the time consumed in foreclosure proceedings on a real property mortgage. With the time element in mind some states that have adopted the deed of trust have done so in order to induce financial institutions, and particularly life insurance companies, from outside the state to lend their funds within the state.

INSTALLMENT LAND CONTRACT. An installment land contract is an agreement between a buyer and a seller to give possession and occupancy of premises to

---

*For a more complete discussion of property rights and property ownership see: Maurice A. Unger, *Real Estate: Principles and Practices*, 2nd ed., Parts 2 and 3. (Cincinnati: South-Western Publishing Company, 1959).

a buyer upon the payment of a stated sum, and to deliver later a deed to the buyer after he has paid the balance in full. The contract may also provide that after a specified number of payments are made, the seller will take back an ordinary mortgage or the buyer will attempt to refinance the balance through a mortgage given by one of the financial institutions.

During the time the contract remains in force, title remains with the seller, although the deed and the contract are generally deposited with a third party known as an escrow agent. In the event of default on the part of the buyer, most states require that the seller have recourse to formal proceedings similar to a mortgage foreclosure.

The Typical Conventional Mortgage Loan

A conventional mortgage is one that is not F.H.A. insured or V.A. guaranteed. (F.H.A.-insured and V.A.-guaranteed mortgages are discussed in the following section.) The down payment made by a purchaser under the terms of the conventional mortgage can range from 20 per cent to 33⅓ per cent of the value placed upon the property by the lending institution. Commercial banks and mutual savings banks require the larger down payments, whereas the savings and loan associations may lend up to 80 per cent of the valuation of property.

When an individual seeks to obtain a loan on a one- to four-family property, he may be required to submit in his loan application a personal balance sheet, detailing his assets, liabilities, and net worth. After he does so, the lending institution appraises the property, has the title examined, prepares the mortgage instrument, examines the deed (the instrument by means of which title is transferred), and makes the loan.

The terms of a typical conventional mortgage require that the loan be amortized: that is, part of the principal together with interest is repaid monthly. Principal is gradually reduced over the term of the mortgage. This type of mortgage was introduced in the early development of savings and loan associations.

The widespread adoption of the amortized mortgage grew out of the experiences that investors had with standing or straight mortgages during the Great Depression. A standing mortgage is one on which the interest is paid periodically and the principal becomes due and payable at the end of the mortgage term. It is believed that the amortized mortgage will work less hardship on both lenders and borrowers in the event of another depression.

FEDERAL INCENTIVES TO HOME OWNERSHIP AND FINANCING

Before discussing the demand for and supply of mortgage funds, we must develop further our idea of the framework within which mortgage funds flow. General economic conditions became so bad during the Great Depression that both mortgagors and mortgagees sought various forms of temporary Federal assistance. Some of the Federal programs developed during this period were later abandoned, but others were expanded and made permanent. Federal incentives to home ownership and financing were further expanded in the mid-1940's with the passage of the G. I. Bill, which provided, among other things, a guarantee program on real estate loans made to eligible veterans. Recent legislation has continued this program beyond the original cut-off date and provided for similar types of loans to Korean War veterans. Our discussion of Federal incentives follows a chronological pattern.

Federal Home Loan Bank System

With the creation of the Federal Reserve System in 1913, the possibility of establishing a comparable reserve system for home financing institutions was given much deliberation. Finally the financial crisis, beginning in 1929 and continuing for some years, prompted action, and in 1932 the Federal Home Loan Bank System was created.

The Federal Home Loan Bank System was intended to provide a reservoir of reserve credit that would be available for institutions holding mortgage loans on residential property. In short, it was created to give " greater flexibility and expansion of lending powers to member building and loan associations (savings and loan associations or cooperative banks as they are sometimes called), mutual savings banks, insurance companies, and similar private thrift and home-financing institutions."*

The system is designed to serve its members (the institutions enumerated above) in much the same way as the Federal Reserve System serves the commercial banks. It permits them to expand their lending power by the use of their present resources as collateral. Thus, it places an additional large volume of credit at the disposal of private home-financing institutions so that they can make a larger number of mortgage loans to home owners on reasonable terms and can also meet more readily the cash requirements of their investors. However, the system cannot create funds as do the Federal Reserve banks.

Originally, the law provided that each member of a Home Loan bank must purchase stock equivalent to 1 per cent of the unpaid principal of home loans held in its portfolio, or $2,500, whichever was the greater. Later, the 1 per cent of home loans was interpreted as a minimum and members began purchasing more stock. In addition, some members bought additional amounts of stock to increase their borrowing capacity because their capacity to borrow was limited to twelve times the amount of stock owned by them.

*Federal Home Loan Bank Board, *Third Annual Report* (Washington, D.C., 1936), p. 5.

In June, 1950 Congress amended the Home Loan Bank Act by requiring that within one year after the enactment of the amendment each member would acquire and maintain stockholdings of not less than 2 per cent of its home mortgage loans. Since July 2, 1951 all stock of all Home Loan banks has been owned by member institutions. The Home Loan banks have become a quasi-public financial institution.

In addition to the capital of the Home Loan banks, another source of funds is consolidated debentures. Consolidated debentures are sold on the open market by the Home Loan Bank Board as funds are needed. The funds are then distributed among the various regional banks on the basis of their probable loan demands.

A member may secure advances from the regional Home Loan bank if the funds are to be used for a legitimate purpose. If withdrawals increase rapidly, the member may call upon the Home Loan bank for an advance. If the institution sees an opportunity to make mortgages in excess of its immediately available funds, it may also secure an advance. Generally, advances of any member are limited to twelve times the amount of the bank's stock owned by the borrowing member and to 50 per cent of the unpaid balance of the home loans held in its portfolio. However, these limitations may be varied so as to lead to either ease or tightness, the direction depending on economic conditions and the available supply of mortgage funds.

Table 14-1 shows recent Federal Home Loan bank lending figures. In recent years, short-term advances outstanding have been about one and one-half times larger than long-term advances outstanding. Short-term advances include secured or unsecured loans maturing in one year or less; the long-

TABLE 14–1
FEDERAL HOME LOAN BANK LENDING, 1950-1958
(MILLIONS OF DOLLARS)

Year	Advances	Repayments	Total	Advances outstanding (end of period) Short-term	Long-term
1950	675	292	816	568	248
1951	423	433	806	597	209
1952	586	528	864	634	230
1953	728	640	952	637	314
1954	734	818	867	572	296
1955	1,251	702	1,417	943	474
1956	745	934	1,228	820	408
1957	1,116	1,079	1,265	887	378
1958	1,364	1,330	1,298	892	407

Source: "Savings and Home Financing Source Book," Federal Home Loan Bank Board, Washington, D. C., 1959, p. 9.

term advances represent secured loans having maturities of more than one year but not more than ten years. The long-term advances are amortized quarterly. During a year of tightness in the mortgage markets, Federal Home Loan bank lending may channel as much as one billion dollars into mortgages through its member financial institutions.

Home Owners Loan Corporation

For the relief of mortgagors and to assist lending institutions, Congress created in 1933 the Home Owners Loan Corporation (now liquidated). The H.O.L.C. was empowered to make direct loans to mortgagors about to lose their homes. These loans were for a fifteen-year period at an interest of 5 per cent and provided for their amortization on a monthly basis. By June, 1936, the H.O.L.C. financed more than a million homes and disbursed nearly $3 million for defaulted mortgages.

Federal Housing Administration

In 1934, Congress passed the National Housing Act, establishing the Federal Housing Administration, whose major task was to get private funds flowing back into mortgages. The time had come to shift emphasis from relief to recovery. To stimulate private lending, the F.H.A. provided mortgage insurance whereby private lending institutions could make insured first mortgage loans on one- to four-family dwellings. Mortgage insurance consists of an agreement between the F.H.A. and the lending institutions, whereby the F.H.A. will issue debentures to the lender for the unpaid balance of any insured mortgage, after the lender forecloses on the mortgage or receives a deed in lieu of foreclosure and transfers title to the F.H.A. The debentures are unsecured debt instruments, guaranteed by the Federal government, and paying an interest rate not exceeding 3 per cent. It is not necessary to concern ourselves with the details of foreclosure and the allocation of foreclosure costs. The F.H.A. has several types of mortgage programs, but we are concerned only with Title II, Section 203, which refers to privately owned homes.

The terms of a F.H.A. insured mortgage were devised to attract both borrowers and lenders. Borrowers were attracted by the low down payments and the longer maturities. Lenders were attracted by the reduction of risk provided by insurance and by the fact that individuals should have an easier time repaying an amortized loan based on a long maturity. Under this phase of the F.H.A. programs, the government does not provide the funds; instead, they are supplied by private financial institutions. Furthermore, the actual terms of a mortgage loan are mutually agreed upon by the borrower and the lender, although the terms are subject to certain standards or limits.

To be eligible for insurance, a mortgage loan must meet or satisfy certain standards: it must be fully amortized; maturity must not be in excess of a certain number of years; and the interest rate must be no higher than a specified maximum. The cost of insurance is ½ of 1 percent and is paid by the borrower. Housing officials and Congress change the standards from time to time, and so, instead of specifying any one set of standards, a brief summary of government actions taken over a period of years to affect the flow of funds into mortgages will be presented following a description of other government agencies and programs.

Beginning in July, 1960, the Federal Housing Administration permitted for the first time F.H.A. approved mortgagees to sell F.H.A. insured mortgages to individual and institutional investors. The approved mortgagees remain responsible to the F.H.A. for carrying out the terms of the insurance contract, and they service the mortgages for the investors. Mortgage bankers will have a broader market in which to place new mortgages, and F.H.A. approved mortgagees will have a broader market in which to sell old mortgages in order to raise additional funds for new mortgage investment. The success of this new program will depend on the public's awareness, the relative attractiveness of the net yield on such investments, and the attitude of those institutions that are in a position to sell mortgages. The immediate reaction was mixed.* Officers of mutual savings banks and savings and loan associations questioned the suitability of such an investment for individuals and doubted whether this new ruling would actually lead to more financial investment in mortgages. They expressed the fear that the program might lead to a transfer of saving from the institutions to mortgages in the institutions' portfolios. Although the F.H.A.-insured mortgages are high quality in terms of financial risk, there is the possibility of incurring legal expenses in the event of default. Furthermore, mortgages are one of the less liquid forms of financial investment. Mortgage bankers are less critical of the new ruling. Mortgages as an investment for individuals will be considered further in a later section to this chapter.

There is a possibility that the F.H.A. will also offer an insurance plan to stimulate the flow of funds into conventional mortgages. It will be recalled that many financial institutions will not lend more than 60 per cent of the value of a home on a conventional mortgage. This limit requires that the borrower make a sizeable down payment. If a lender were insured against loss of the top 20 per cent of the unpaid balance of each risk he assumed, the lender would be able to loan as much as 80 per cent of the home value, thereby reducing by one-half the amount of the down payment. An insurance program for conventional mortgages would stimulate the flow of funds into mortgages, and at the same time reduce some of the " unsound " financing relating to the family dwelling. Obviously, this innovation will require an act of Congress.

*Wall Street Journal, August 17, 1960.

The Veterans' Administration (V.A.)

The Servicemen's Readjustment Act of 1944 made provision for the guarantee by the Veterans' Administration of first and second mortgage loans made by private lenders to veterans for the purchase of homes. Originally, the V.A. could guarantee 50 per cent of the value up to $4,000. Under Section 505a of the original act, a V.A.-guaranteed second mortgage could be combined with an F.H.A.-insured first mortgage so that a veteran could finance a $20,000 home without a down payment. The combined F.H.A.-V.A. loan was eliminated, effective October 20, 1950.

At present, it is only possible to obtain a guarantee of 60 per cent of the value of the property, as determined by a V.A. appraiser, to a maximum of $7,500. It is also possible to obtain a direct loan from the V.A. to a maximum of $10,000 in the event that the veteran's application for a loan is rejected by two private lending institutions.

Although the original act only provided a guarantee for loans to veterans of World War II, the act was amended to provide guarantees for veterans who were on active service between June 27, 1950 and January 31, 1955, provided the veteran had served at least 90 days or received a discharge sooner because of a disability. The V.A.-guaranteed loans to veterans of World War II were supposed to end July 25, 1958, but were later extended to July 25, 1962. For Korean veterans, the termination date is January 31, 1965. Of the nearly fifteen million veterans eligible for these loans, only about two million have used the V.A. guarantee in buying a home.

Like F.H.A. loans, there are certain standards that a mortgage loan must satisfy if it is to qualify for the V.A. guarantee, and these standards have been changed from time to time. The changes will be noted in our summary of government actions, which will follow. Changes in the maximum interest rate on V.A. loans have caused great controversy. Generally, there has been a lag in interest rate changes. Lenders believe that rates have not been adjusted upward sufficiently. Naturally, veterans would prefer lower rates to higher rates. Originally, the maximum interest rate was set at 4 per cent; in late 1960, the effective maximum interest rate was 5¼ per cent.

Housing and Home Finance Agency

In 1947, under the President's Reorganization Plan No. 3 of that year, the first peacetime housing agency (H.H.F.A.) was created " with the responsibility of coordinating the principal housing programs and functions of government, and of providing a focal point for cooperative effort by government and private enterprise in solving housing problems."* In 1956, legislation removed the Home Loan Bank Board from the direct supervision of the H.H.F.A. In late 1960, the following agencies were under direct supervision of the Office of the Administrator: Public Housing Administra-

*First Annual Report, Housing and Home Finance Agency, 1947.

tion, Federal Savings and Loan Insurance Corporation, Federal Housing Administration, Urban Renewal Administration, and Federal National Mortgage Association. The powers of the Federal National Mortgage Association will probably be expanded and its operations placed under the control of a three-man governing body appointed by the President. The revamped Association would probably operate along the lines of a central mortgage bank, providing a secondary market for conventional mortgages as well as for Federally underwritten mortgages.

Federal National Mortgage Association

The Housing Act of 1938 provided for the establishment of the Federal National Mortgage Association. " Fannie Mae," as it is called, was financed with goverment funds and authorized to buy and sell F.H.A.-insured mortgages on new residential structures. In 1948, it was given authority to buy and sell V.A.-guaranteed mortgages. The purpose of this function was to fill a gap in the home financing system by providing a secondary market in which approved mortgagees could sell mortgages.

Until the late 1940's, the V.A. loans at 4 per cent and the F.H.A.'s at 4½ per cent were attractive investments. Faced with the alternative of Federal obligations at 2.15 per cent and the 4 and 4½ per cent Federally underwritten mortgage loans, the loans were attractive, because the cost of servicing such loans and risk premium required a differential yield of only 1½ per cent. The mortgage loans provided a realizable net yield ranging from 2½ to 3 per cent, whereas the net yield on Federal obligations was only 2.15 per cent. Funds were attracted to home mortgages. However, with a rise in the level of interest rates, the attractiveness of F.H.A. and V.A. mortgages declined. Fannie Mae purchased these mortgages from approved mortgagees to supplement the flow of funds from the private sector. At times the activity of Fannie Mae was on such a large scale that it became a primary supplier of funds instead of providing a secondary market facility.

In the course of time, Fannie Mae came under attack. It had become a primary supplier of funds. It was a wholly owned government corporation that obtained funds directly from the Treasury instead of from the market. The critics asked that Fannie Mae be made a truly secondary mortgage facility and be privately owned. Under the provision of the Housing Act of 1954, Fannie Mae was rechartered and reorganized to undertake three separate and distinct functions: (1) to continue to provide a secondary market for Federally underwritten residential mortgages; (2) to furnish special assistance for the financing of mortgages originating under Federal housing programs; and (3) to liquidate the mortgages it acquired under the old charter. The terms under which Fannie Mae bought and sold mortgages in the secondary market were to reflect current market conditions. To make Fannie Mae privately owned, sellers of mortgages were required to subscribe for common stock of the F.N.M.A. in an amount equal to a certain percentage of the unpaid principal of the mortgages sold. The specific percentage depends on the state of the market, but it cannot be less than 1 per cent nor more than 3 per cent.

Before commenting on the secondary market operations of F.N.M.A., we shall examine briefly discounts on Federally underwritten mortgages. Rates on conventional mortgage loans rise and fall with other interest rates, but rates on Federally underwritten mortgages are less flexible. In fact, there have been serious lags in rate adjustments during the postwar period. If long-term interest rates rise, and nominal rates on F.H.A.-insured and V.A.-guaranteed mortgages remain fixed, Federally underwritten mortgages become unattractive to investors. To make them attractive, their prices must fall or the rates must be increased. For instance, assume that a borrower signs a mortgage note of $10,000, agreeing to pay a stated or nominal rate of 4½ per cent. Assume the rate is not attractive to lenders or investors, and they will advance funds only on the condition that the amount advanced is less than the face of the note. Assume the lender proposes to advance only $9,000. In this instance, the lender is requiring a lower price, i.e., a discount of $1,000 from the regular price. A discount of this amount on a 25-year, 4½ per cent amortized loan raises the effective yield to 5.56 per cent. Discount has to be absorbed by the other parties, including contractors, suppliers, and mortgagors. Extreme discounts are unattractive to all parties.

In recent years, F.N.M.A. has been performing a market stabilizing service in the discount market. Eligible mortgages have been purchased at prices varying according to geographical areas and market conditions. The actual terms are set in accordance with continuing price surveys that reflect average market prices.

To conduct its secondary market operations, F.N.M.A. draws on four sources of funds: (1) preferred stock issued to the Treasury; (2) common stock issued to those who sell mortgages to the F.N.M.A.; (3) open market borrowing in the form of debentures; and (4) direct borrowing from the Treasury. As of June 30, 1959, the importance of these sources was: preferred stock, $134 million; common stock, $43 million; debentures, $1.1 billion; and notes payable to the Treasury, $42 million. In carrying out this phase of its operations in 1959, Fannie Mae acquired mortgages amounting to $735 million. At the close of the year, the total holdings were approximately $2 billion.

With respect to the second function of F.N.M.A., which is to furnish special assistance for the financing of mortgages originating under Federal housing programs,* F.N.M.A. has increased its portfolio considerably in recent years. During the calendar year 1959, it acquired $1.2 billion of mortgages through these operations, and total holdings at the close of the

*Refers to urban renewal multi-family housing, cooperative housing, armed services housing, and low- and moderate-priced housing.

year were approximately $1.6 billion. Almost all of these purchases were financed by direct borrowing from the Treasury.

With respect to the management and liquidation functions, the activities of F.N.M.A. have been restricted primarily to servicing its mortgage portfolio and conducting two exchanges of mortgages for government bonds. Mortgage holdings under this phase of its operations amounted to $2 billion at the end of 1959. To finance these mortgages, funds are obtained by direct borrowing from the Treasury and from the sale of obligations to private investors. On June 30, 1959, these sources of funds provided respectively $1.1 billion and $800 million.

The combined purchase and sale operations and mortgage holdings for the period 1950-1959 are summarized in Table 14-2. The operations and holdings in 1959 were at an all-time high.

TABLE 14–2
FEDERAL NATIONAL MORTGAGE ASSOCIATION ACTIVITY, 1950-1959
(MILLIONS OF DOLLARS)

End of Year	Mortgage Holdings			Mortgage Transactions	
	Total	FHA-insured	V.A.-Guaranteed	Purchases	Sales
1950	1,347	169	1,177	1,044	496
1951	1,850	204	1,646	677	111
1952	2,242	320	1,922	538	56
1953	2,462	621	1,841	542	214
1954	2,434	802	1,632	614	513
1955	2,615	901	1,714	411	61
1956	3,047	978	2,069	609	15
1957	4,012	1,237	2,737	1,046	3
1958	3,938	1,484	2,417	623	482
1959	5,582	2,517	3,025	1,922	4

Source: Housing and Home Finance Agency.

A new method of liquidating mortgage holdings was introduced by the Treasury and F.N.M.A. in late 1959. The holders of nonmarketable investment series bonds* were offered the right to exchange these bonds for a like amount of 4 per cent V.A. mortgages. Holders included commercial banks, mutual savings banks, and life insurance companies, all of whom are investors in residential mortgages. Those bond holders who had satisfactory facilities to manage mortgages or planned to use approved mortgage services were invited to submit competitive bids for the V.A. mortgages. Since the bond yield was

*These bonds were first issued in April, 1951 and again in June, 1952. The bonds yield 2.75 per cent and do not mature until 1980. Though the bonds cannot be sold in the market, they can be traded to the Treasury for 1½ per cent 5-year Treasury notes. Neither the yield nor the exchange provision has been attractive in recent years.

only 2.75 per cent, the average exchange price of the accepted offers would be at a premium. The Treasury and F.N.M.A. received nearly $191 million for $188 million of mortgages. Upon completion of the exchange, the F.N.M.A. transferred the bonds to the Treasury for retirement.* The success of the first exchange offer in December, 1959, prompted the officials to offer a similar exchange in early 1960. It was less successful than the first; the average exchange price was $101.28 on each $100 of outstanding mortgages compared with $102.03 in 1959, and the total amount exchanged fell $70 million short of the $200 million goal.

DEMAND FOR MORTGAGE FUNDS

The major components of the total demand for mortgage funds can be stated in terms of the basic types of mortgages: (1) mortgages on one- to four-family properties; (2) commercial and multi-family mortgages; and (3) farm mortgages. Almost all the mortgages on the one- to four-family properties represent obligations of consumers. The other types of mortgages represent obligations of economic units in the business sectors. At the end of 1958, corporate nonfinancial businesses owed $29.0 billion of mortgage debt; non-corporate nonfinancial businesses owed $18.8 billion; and farm businesses owed $11.2 billion. In recent years, the annual net increase in home mortgage debt has averaged about three times the annual net increase in other mortgages. With the exception of savings and loan associations, the major types of mortgage lenders supply funds to all segments of the mortgage market. In this section only the demand for home mortgage credit will be discussed in detail.

Determinants of Demand for Home Mortgage Funds

The demand for home mortgage funds is tied to the demand for one- to four-family properties, and the demand curve for one- to four-family properties is a function of many determinants: income (past, current and expected), tastes, liquid assets, credit terms, family formation and composition, migration, and price substitutes. There are definite relationships between general business conditions and the demand for family properties. The decision to purchase family property and the calculation of the amount to be expended are both related to the expected size of the family income during the period of investment.

Since the cost of family property is high in relation to the immediately

*The Treasury treats the retirement of these bonds as cash receipts from F.N.M.A., and the Treasury offsets the cash receipts against an equal amount of F.N.M.A. spending. In the absence of the exchange of bonds for mortgages, the expenditures of F.N.M.A. would be financed by additional borrowing from the Treasury, which in turn would require an increase in Treasury obligations. The use of the exchange was one means of holding down the net increase in the Federal debt in 1959 and 1960.

available funds of most purchasers, real estate terms are very important in the determination of effective demand for home ownership and mortgage loans. Other things being equal, low down payments, lower interest rates, and long maturities increase the demand for mortgage funds. On the assumption that a large number of marginal buyers will enter the market as prices, credit terms, or other recurring costs become more favorable, Congress and housing officials attempt to influence the level of housing construction by varying these factors. The closing section of this chapter summarizes some of the measures used in recent years to affect the demand for and the supply of mortgage funds.

In general, higher-income groups pay a larger monthly sum for housing than do lower income groups, but it is a lower percentage of their total income. Low-income groups spend between 25 and 30 per cent of their income for housing; higher-income groups, between 15 and 20 per cent. Therefore, credit terms are very important to the low-income groups, and when credit terms become favorable or when expectations as to future income brighten, many of the low-income families are attracted into the market.

Approximately 90 per cent of all married couples maintain their own households. An increase in the rate of family formation tends to increase the demand for home mortgage loans.

In the final analysis, it can be said that all these factors combined and variables within these factors are among the more basic determinants of the demand for home mortgage funds.

As home ownership becomes more common throughout almost all income groups, and as advantage is taken of the general availability of mortgage credit, it is not surprising to find that the proportion of mortgaged homes among the owner-occupied dwellings is increasing. In 1900, only 34.0 per cent of the occupied dwelling units in non-farm areas were owner-occupied; at the end of 1958, 60 per cent of such units were owner-occupied. During the same period, a nearly identical change took place in the percentage of owner-occupied dwellings on which there was a mortgage. The Surveys of Consumer Finance reveal that between 80 to 85 per cent of all homes purchased in recent years have involved mortgage financing.

Flow-of-funds data show that 94.3 per cent of the one- to four-family mortgages outstanding at the end of 1958 represented liabilities of the consumer and nonprofit organization sector. The importance of this form of liability to the sector is reflected in the fact that such mortgages accounted for 64.9 per cent of the sector's liabilities at the end of 1958. Relatively small amounts of such mortgages represent liabilities of corporate and non-corporate nonfinancial business sectors. The relative importance of the business sectors' holdings of one- to four-family mortgages depends primarily on the state of the housing market and mortgage market.

SUPPLY OF ONE- TO FOUR-FAMILY MORTGAGE FUNDS

The supply of one- to four-family mortgage funds is analyzed in terms of annual net flows during the period 1954-1958, and the amount outstanding at the end of 1958. (See Tables 14-3 and 14-4.) Before analyzing the data two additional financial institutions must be discussed to complete the institutional framework; one of these is the mortgage company and the other is mortgage warehousing.

Mortgage Companies

"The modern mortgage company is a closely held, private corporation, with a comparatively small capital investment relative to its volume of business, subject to a minimum degree of Federal or state supervision, whose principal activity is originating and servicing mortgage loans for institutional investors."* Mortgage companies are highly specialized financial institutions that operate generally as servicing media or agents for others, instead of operating as principals for their own accounts. Mortgage companies have facilitated the use of short-term and intermediate-term commercial bank credit in mortgage operations and have provided a bridge between primary and secondary mortgage markets.

The advent of Federal programs in housing was the major stimulant to the growth of mortgage companies. The introduction of Federal mortgage insurance and guaranty programs and the consequent adoption of more standardized procedures in mortgage lending broke down the historic geographic barriers to mortgage investment by institutional leaders, such as life insurance companies and mutual savings banks. In fact, to satisfy their needs, life insurance companies and some mutual savings banks had to turn to a national market to acquire a reasonable number of mortgages. Mortgage companies assumed the task of acquiring mortgage investments for life insurance companies, mutual savings banks, and other savings and insurance institutions. Had the life insurance companies established branch offices to handle all of their mortgage lending, the mortgage companies would not be nearly as important.

The introduction and widespread use of the amortized mortgage also created a need for servicing organizations. Mortgagors prefer to make their periodic payments through a local collection office, and the mortgagees prefer to have someone on the local scene to follow up on delinquent payments and to observe periodically the condition of the property. Mortgage companies perform these functions. In fact, they service many more mortgages than they originate. For example, at the end of 1955 mortgage companies were servicing close to a quarter of the total one- to four-family

*Saul B. Klaman, "Mortgage Companies in the Postwar Mortgage Market," *Journal of Finance*, May 1957, p. 57.

mortgage debt and about half of all F.H.A. and V.A. loans. Of the mortgage loans held by life insurance companies and mutual savings banks, about two-thirds are serviced by mortgage companies.

There are probably slightly less than 1,000 mortgage companies; their total assets approach $2 billion. During the postwar housing boom, the number of companies doubled and assets increased tenfold. Mortgage companies use funds principally for closing mortgage transactions and for carrying mortgages temporarily in inventory. At their peak, mortgage loans may account for as much as three-fourths of total assets. It is not surprising, therefore, that notes payable to banks are their major source of funds. These notes may account for as much as two-thirds of total liabilities and net worth. The nature of the borrowing is short- and intermediate-term, and almost all of these funds are borrowed from commercial banks. Earnings consist principally of a finder's fee and a servicing fee. The servicing fee tends to average ½ of 1 per cent of the declining balance of the mortgage.

Mortgage Warehousing

The mortgage warehousing procedure is an excellent institutional arrangement with which to demonstrate the complex interrelationships among financial institutions, the corresponding complex flow of funds from saver to investor, and one of the functions performed by mortgage companies.

In one of the major types of mortgage warehousing arrangements, four parties are involved: a builder, a mortgage company, an institutional investor, and a commercial bank. The builder, desiring to build, say, a development consisting of a large number of homes, approaches a mortgage company to arrange financing for the project. Since the mortgage company usually acts as an agent for institutional lenders, the company contacts, say, a life insurance company, which may or may not have sufficient funds on hand to finance the project. Although the life insurance company may not have funds available at present, they will be available in the future, either from premiums, "pay-backs" on existing mortgages, or maturing investments. To tell the mortgage banker that funds will be available in 1963 for a project proposed in 1961 is unsatisfactory to both the builder and mortgage banker. Instead, the insurance company can commit part of its 1963 funds to this project. This is called a forward commitment; the life insurance company obligates itself to acquire specified mortgage loans from the mortgage company (originator) within two years. With this commitment, the mortgage banker contacts a large commercial bank interested in making a sound intermediate-term loan on the strength of the commitment by the insurance company to take over the mortgage in the future.

A note, signed both by the mortgage company and the builder, and a mortgage on the land are given to the commercial bank, which, in turn, makes funds available. The builder goes on with his construction and sells the buildings. The mortgages placed on these individual properties are for all practical purposes held by the commercial bank until the insurance company is prepared to go through with its previous commitment. In the illustration, the insurance company " takes-out " the mortgages held by the commercial bank during the two-year period.

In summary, funds flow from the commercial bank via the mortgage company to the builder in the first instance. Prior to the agreed take-out date, funds are transferred from the life insurance company to the commercial bank in return for mortgage instruments given to the commercial bank a few years before. Long-term funds eventually replace the intermediate-term bank credit. Mortgage warehousing is most widespread during a period of credit stringency.

It can readily be recognized that this practice might prove inflationary under certain conditions. When it is felt that inflationary pressures are resulting from such practices, the Federal Reserve Board tends to exert pressure on commercial banks to reexamine their mortgage warehousing practices.

Annual Flows and Holdings of Mortgages

For many years financial institutions have been the predominant suppliers of mortgage funds. Their share of mortgage holdings increased from about 50 per cent at the turn of the century to nearly 85 per cent at the end of 1958. The combined mortgage holdings of saving and loan associations, life insurance companies, mutual savings banks, and commercial banks account for about 85 per cent of the total mortgages on one- to four-family properties and about 60 per cent of other mortgages. The annual net flow of mortgage credit supplied by these financial institutions depends on their anuual net increase in total assets and the amounts allocated to mortgages. Only savings and loan associations are specialized home financing institutions.

Mortgages provide an attractive investment outlet for these institutions. The actual amounts invested in mortgages depend partly on the relative attractiveness of mortgage yields. The yield or rate of return on an investment is determined by the interaction of demand and supply for that investment. The gross yield on mortgages depends on the interaction of the supply of mortgage funds and demand for mortgage credit. The net yield depends on the quality of the mortgage and efficiency in handling the mortgage loan. As noted in earlier chapters, the over-all stability and growth in the assets of these institutions permit the investment of funds in long-term credit instruments. Also, it is not necessary that all of their assets be highly marketable. Mortgages possess relatively unfavorable investment characteristics, such as long maturity and illiquidity, but the holders of such investments are compensated by relatively high yields. Therefore, financial institutions are able to acquire a relatively high yield on mortgage investments. The fact that mortgages can account for a large percentage of an institution's assets means that a financial institution can specialize in mortgage lending and thereby earn a very respectable rate of return.

New savings plus the pay-off on existing amortized mortgages constitute the major potential sources of real estate credit. With the exception of the savings and loan associations, which are strictly mortgage lending institutions, the flow of funds into savings and thrift institutions does not ensure that the funds will flow into mortgages. There are alternative investment opportunities, and the financial institutions exercise discretion over the investment of new funds. The availability of mortgage money is irrevocably tied to the relative attractiveness of the net financial return on mortgages, and this factor varies from time to time.

The flow-of-funds data in Tables 14-3 and 14-4 show respectively the annual net flows into mortgages on one- to four-family properties for the period 1954-1958, and the amount of such mortgages outstanding at the end of 1958. The flow data reveal that the annual flows have ranged between $8.6 billion and $12.6 billion, and have averaged approximately $10.4 billion. The largest annual flow occurred during 1955, at the postwar peak in housing demand; the smallest annual flow occurred during 1957, a year of recession. A strong upturn in housing got underway in late 1957 and

TABLE 14–3
ANNUAL FLOWS INTO MORTGAGES ON ONE- TO FOUR-FAMILY PROPERTIES, 1954-1958
(BILLIONS OF DOLLARS)

Sector	1954 $	1954 %	1955 $	1955 %	1956 $	1956 %	1957 $	1957 %	1958 $	1958 %
Net issues (all sectors)	9.6	100.0	12.6	100.0	10.8	100.0	8.6	100.0	10.4	100.0
Consumer and nonprofit.	9.0	93.8	12.3	97.6	11.1	102.8	8.7	101.2	10.0	96.2
Other	.6	6.2	.3	2.4	—.3	(2.8)	—.1	(1.2)	.4	3.8
Net acquisitions (all sectors)	9.6	100.0	12.6	100.0	10.8	100.0	8.6	100.0	10.4	100.0
Savings and loan ass'ns and credit unions	4.0	41.7	5.0	39.7	4.1	38.0	4.2	48.8	5.3	51.0
Life insurance companies.	2.0	20.8	2.5	19.8	2.4	22.2	1.3	15.1	1.1	10.6
Commercial banks	1.3	13.5	1.7	13.5	1.2	11.1	.1	1.2	1.3	12.5
Mutual savings banks	1.6	16.7	2.1	16.7	1.9	17.6	1.2	14.0	1.6	15.4
Consumer and nonprofit organizations	.4	4.2	.4	3.2	.4	3.7	1.0	11.6	.6	5.8
Finance, n.e.c. [1]	.2	2.1	.5	4.0	—.1	(.9)	—.3	(3.5)	.5	4.8
State and local government	.1	1.0	*	*	.1	.9	.1	1.2	.1	1.0
Federal Government	—.1	(1.0)	.2	1.6	.7	6.5	1.1	12.8	*	*

*Less than $50 million.

Note: Details may not add to totals because of rounding.

[1] Mainly mortgage company holdings.

Source: "A Quarterly Presentation of Flow of Funds, Saving and Investment," *Federal Reserve Bulletin*, August 1959; subsector data provided by the Flow of Funds Division, Board of Governors of the Federal Reserve System.

continued through most of 1959. As noted earlier, the mortgages on one- to four-family properties accounted for 69 per cent of all mortgages outstanding at the end of 1958, and the annual flow into home mortgages has been about three times greater than the annual flow into other types of mortgages. If this flow pattern continues, it can be expected that the importance of home mortgages will increase from 69 per cent to 75 per cent of all mortgages outstanding.

TABLE 14–4

MORTGAGES ON ONE- TO FOUR-FAMILY PROPERTIES OUTSTANDING, END OF 1958
(BILLIONS OF DOLLARS)

	Dollars	Per cent	Mortgages as a percentage of issuers' liabilities and/or investors' financial assets
Issuers (all sectors)	118.0	100.0	
Consumer and nonprofit	111.3	94.3	64.9
Corporate nonfinancial business.	1.5	1.3	.8
Non-corporate nonfinancial business	5.1	4.3	11.2
Investors (all sectors)	118.0	100.0	
Savings and loan ass'ns and credit unions	43.6	36.9	75.3
Life insurance companies	22.5	19.1	22.3
Commercial banks	17.5	14.8	7.3
Mutual savings banks	15.7	13.3	41.9
Consumer and nonprofit organizations	11.3	9.6	1.3
Finance, n.e.c.[1]	1.5	1.3	
State and local government	.9	.8	1.9
Federal Government	4.7	4.0	11.5
Self-administered pension plans..	.4	.3	1.9

Note: Details may not add to totals because of rounding.
[1] Mainly mortgage company holdings.
Source: "A Quarterly Presentation of Flow of Funds, Saving and Investment," *Federal Reserve Bulletin*, August 1959.

Attention is now focused on each of the major classes of investors in home mortgages.

SAVINGS AND LOAN ASSOCIATIONS. The savings and loan associations are the single most important holder of home mortgages. They have supplied the major portion of the annual flow into such mortgages. Although the tables show combined data for savings and loan associations and credit unions, virtually all of the mortgage holdings are those of savings and loan associations. The data show that the associations held about a third of all such mortgages outstanding, and their mortgage holdings accounted for nearly three-fourths of their assets. The savings and loan associations supplied as much as 50 per cent of the total flow in 1958, and in no year did the associations supply less than 38 per cent of the total flow.

The importance of the savings and loan associations is not surprising. They are specialized home financing institutions. Such investments enable the associations to pay relatively attractive dividends on outstanding shares, which, in turn, attracts additional consumer saving. Through the combination of aggressive advertising and attractive dividends, the savings and loan associations have been able to attract a sizeable portion of consumer saving.

During the period immediately following World War II, their mortgage investment portfolio was financed from new savings, liquidation of Federal obligations, and borrowings from the Federal Home Loan Bank. Since 1950, the flow of net saving has provided almost all of the new funds employed in their mortgage investment.

LIFE INSURANCE COMPANIES. In terms of the amount of home mortgages held at the end of 1958, life insurance companies would be ranked as the second most important investor in home mortgages. However, in terms of recent annual flows, the mutual savings banks have supplied more funds to this market than have life insurance companies. Therefore, in ranking the importance of investors, it is important to distinguish between present holdings and recent annual flows. The data show that at the end of 1958 the life insurance companies held $22.5 billion of home mortgages, and such investments accounted for 23 per cent of their total assets. In terms of flow data, the life insurance companies have supplied between 10.6 per cent and 22.3 per cent of the annual flows into home mortgages during the period 1954-1958. The yield on corporate bonds has trended upward, and the life insurance companies have allocated a smaller share of new savings into home mortgages. During much of the postwar period, the life insurance companies raised a substantial amount of funds from the liquidation of Federal obligations, and some of these funds went into mortgages. In recent years, this source of funds has no longer been available.

COMMERCIAL BANKS. Commercial banks are an important source of funds for all types of mortgages. However, the data show that commercial banks in some years allocate relatively small amounts to home mortgages, and in other years allocate sizeable amounts to mortgages. For example, in 1957 commercial banks allocated only about $100 million to home mortgages, but in both the preceding and following years, the commercial banks allocated respectively $1.2 billion and $1.3 billion. The degree of fluctuation in annual flow is greater for commercial banks than for any other private institutional investor.

In terms of the amount of home mortgages held at the end of 1958, commercial banks ranked third with holdings of $14.8 billion. It is interesting to note that such investments accounted for only 7.3 per cent of the commercial banks' total assets. Except for 1957, the commercial banks' share of annual flows was nearly identical to the banks' share of outstanding home mortgages. Commercial banks supply funds to all segments of the money and capital markets, and mortgage investments must compete with many other possible uses of funds. The allocation of commercial banks' funds into mortgages depends on the total demand for bank credit and the relative attractiveness of other uses of funds. Also, since many commercial banks are viewed as community banks, they are under some pressure to supply funds to home mortgages even though the yields may not be relatively attractive. The flow of bank funds into other mortgages does not vary nearly as much as the flow into home mortgages.

MUTUAL SAVINGS BANKS. During World War II, the major portion of mutual savings bank funds flowed into Federal obligations. During the postwar period, their investment policy was redirected toward mortgage investment. In recent years, the mutual savings bank annual flows into mortgage on one- to four-family properties have been second in importance to those of the savings and loan associations. At the end of 1958, the mutual savings banks held 13.3 per cent of all home mortgages, and such investments accounted for 41.9 per cent of their assets.

CONSUMER AND NONPROFIT ORGANIZATION SECTOR. In relation to the consumer and nonprofit organization sector's total holdings of financial assets, the sector's holdings of home mortgages are relatively unimportant. Nevertheless, this sector held nearly 10 per cent of the one- to four-family mortgages outstanding at the end of 1958. The annual flows into such mortgages have not been uniform. Except for 1957, the sector's share of annual flows was considerably less than the sector's share of all mortgages outstanding. The data indicate that the consumer and nonprofit organization sector is becoming a less important supplier of home mortgage funds. Now that individuals may invest in government-insured home mortgages, the trend may be reversed.

MORTGAGE COMPANIES. Although mortgage companies are not shown separately in the Tables, the sector called "finance, n.e.c." consists mainly of mortgage company holdings. As indicated earlier, mortgage companies are not important suppliers of funds. In some years, the companies actually reduced their holdings of mortgages. At the end of 1958, the mortgage holdings of mortgage companies represented slightly more than 1 per cent of the home mortgages outstanding. Considering the size of mortgage companies, mortgages represent a sizeable proportion of the total assets of mortgage companies.

GOVERNMENT SECTORS. The state and local government sector is not an important supplier of mortgage funds. During the period under review, the sector supplied about $100 million annually to such mortgages. As for the Federal government sector, its mortgage financing was discussed in the early part of the chapter.

Ownership of Government-Underwritten Mortgage Debt

Since the inauguration of the F.H.A.-insured and the V.A.-guaranteed mortgages, a major portion of the total mortgage debt outstanding on non-farm one- to four-family properties has become government-underwritten. Table 14-5 shows the percentage distribution of mortgage debt on non-farm homes, by types of mortgage during the period 1950-1958. It should be noted that in 1945, government-underwritten debt accounted for only 23 per cent of the total. Since 1950, the relative importance of government-underwritten debt has undergone very little change. The lag in interest rate adjustments on government-underwritten mortgages resulted in a lower rate of growth of these mortgages. However, taking the entire period since 1945, the government-underwritten mortgages have increased more rapidly than conventional mortgages.

TABLE 14-5
PERCENTAGE DISTRIBUTION OF MORTGAGE DEBT ON NON-FARM HOMES, BY TYPE OF MORTGAGE, 1950-1958

| End of year | Total [1] | Government-underwritten | | Conventional |
		F.H.A.-insured	V.A.-guaranteed	
1950	45.2	19.0	22.8	58.2
1951	51.7	18.8	25.5	55.7
1952	58.5	18.5	24.9	56.6
1953	66.1	18.1	24.3	57.6
1954	75.7	16.9	25.5	57.6
1955	88.2	16.2	27.9	55.9
1956	99.0	15.7	28.7	55.6
1957	107.6	15.3	28.5	56.2
1958	118.0	16.7	25.8	57.5

[1] In billions of dollars.
Source: *Federal Reserve Bulletin.*

The government-underwritten mortgages are not equally attractive to the major institutional lenders. Table 14-6 shows the amount and percentage distribution of residential mortgage loans held by financial institutions at the end of 1958. It is interesting to note that the relative importance of the F.H.A.-insured and V.A.-guaranteed loans also varies among institutional holders. Savings and loan associations restrict most of their lending to conventional loans. The reason for this limitation is that these institutions have been established principally for handling this type of mortgage loan. Furthermore, savings and loan associations offer a higher loan-to-value ratio than do the other three types of financial institutions shown in the table. For example, savings and loan associations may loan up to 80 per cent of the value of the property, whereas other institutional lenders restrict loans to an amount no higher than 75 per cent of value, and in practice these financial institutions may insist on down payments as high as 50 per cent. Therefore, a major portion of conventional loans will be attracted to the highest bidder, which in this case is the savings and loan association.

TABLE 14–6
TYPES OF RESIDENTIAL MORTGAGE LOANS HELD BY FINANCIAL INSTITUTIONS,
END OF 1958
(MILLIONS OF DOLLARS)

Type of Holder	F.H.A.-insured	V.A.-guaranteed	Conventional	Total
Savings and loan associations	$2,210 (4.8%)	$7,093 (15.6%)	$36,296 (79.6%)	$45,599 (100.0%)
Mutual savings banks	$5,501 (26.3%)	$8,360 (39.9%)	$7,074 (33.8%)	$20,936 (100.0%)
Life insurance companies	$7,449 (33.2%)	$7,455 (33.2%)	$7,546 (33.6%)	$22,450 (100.0%)
Commercial banks	$5,205 (28.8%)	$3,355 (18.6%)	$9,495 (52.6%)	$18,055 (100.0%)
Federal National Mortgage Ass'n....	$1,483 (38.0%)	$2,418 (62.0%)	None	$3,901 (100.0%)

Source: *Federal Reserve Bulletin*, July 1959.

Mutual savings banks show more balance among the three classes of mortgage debt than do savings and loan associations. At the end of 1958, two-thirds of the mutual savings banks' residential mortgage loans were government-underwritten, reflecting the importance of this type of residential loan when investing funds in other states. The allocation of bank funds between F.H.A.-insured and V.A.-guaranteed mortgages is about the same as the ratio of outstanding F.H.A.-insured to outstanding V.A.-guaranteed mortgage loans.

At the end of 1958, the life insurance companies held the largest dollar amount of outstanding government-underwritten mortgage debt. It is interesting to note that life insurance company residential mortgage loans were evenly divided among the three types of mortgages. However, it must be realized that all individual life insurance companies are not equally attracted to government-underwritten mortgages. Some companies, as a matter of policy, concentrate most of their mortgage lending in conventional loans because of higher yields. Other life insurance companies are willing to sacrifice yield for the greater security offered by the government-underwritten mortgages. In the aggregate, life insurance companies are a major supplier of government-underwritten mortgage loans.

Commercial banks are the least specialized mortgage lenders of the five financial institutions shown in Table 14-6. The pattern of their residential mortgage loans is different from that of the others. The commercial banks have about equal amounts invested in government-underwritten mortgages and in conventional loans. Considering that at the end of 1958 the total amount of V.A.-guaranteed loans outstanding was over 50 per cent greater than the amount of F.H.A.-insured loans outstanding, the data show that commercial banks have a definite preference for the F.H.A.-insured mortgages. The allocation of the commercial banks' funds between V.A.-guaranteed and F.H.A.-insured mortgages is about the same as the allocation of the mutual savings bank funds between F.H.A.-insured and V.A.- guaranteed mortgages. In other words, the ratios are about the same, but the numerator and the denominator are inverted. The commercial bank holdings of residential mortgage loans reflect the more attractive yields on F.H.A.-insured mortgages and the liquidation of some of their V.A.-guaranteed loans to meet other credit demands.

About two-thirds of the Federal National Mortgage Association's mortgage holdings are in V.A.-guaranteed mortgages and the other third are in F.H.A.-insured mortgages, reflecting the relative unattractiveness of the former type of mortgage to private lenders.

RESIDENTIAL MORTGAGE MARKET CHANGES 1953-1957

This concluding section will illustrate the use of government measures to affect the demand for and the supply of mortgage credit. It should be recalled that the demand for and the supply of one- to four-family mortgage credit have been stimulated by public policies in the postwar period. There has been created a large, marginal group in this market. The actions of prospective home buyers who have weak asset positions and relatively low and uncertain incomes and the reception they receive from lenders can be affected by government measures. Deliberate action was undertaken during 1953 and 1954 to stimulate the flow of funds into mortgages. Following the recession of 1953 and 1954, the national problem became one of inflation, and restrictive measures were undertaken to curb inflationary pressures. Although over-all economic activity continued at a very high level during most of 1956 and 1957, there was a mild decline in residential building, with the result that measures similar to those taken in 1953-1954 were initiated in 1957 and continued on into 1958.

Steps to Improve the 1953 and 1954 Housing Situation

1. April, 1953: Maturities on F.H.A.-insured loans were extended from 20 to 25 years; on V.A.-guaranteed loans, 25 to 30 years. Down payment of 4 per cent for V.A.-guaranteed loans removed.

2. May, 1953: Maximum interest rates on F.H.A.-insured and V.A.-guaranteed loans were raised from 4¼ to 4½ per cent, and from 4 to 4½ per cent respectively, to make them more effective in a period of rising interest rates.

3. July, 1953: F.N.M.A. initiated a $500 million one-for-one program under which it issued advance commitments to lenders to purchase F.H.A.-insured and V.A.-guaranteed mortgages for an amount equal to such mortgages bought by lenders from F.N.M.A.

4. February, 1954: To discourage purchases of mortgages from F.N.M.A., F.N.M.A. raised its sales price on 4 and 4½ per cent mortgages by two points in order to funnel private money into new government-underwritten home loans bearing the 4½ per cent interest rate.

5. August 2, 1954: Presidential approval of the Housing Act of 1954. This act liberalized terms of government-underwritten mortgages. For example: under this Act the maximum F.H.A.-insured mortgage amounts on two-family dwellings were increased from $16,000 to $20,-000. The maximum loan-value ratios on new homes were also increased. Prior to the Act, the maximum loan-to-value ratio on new homes was 95 per cent of the first $7,000 of value plus 70 per cent of the excess up to a maximum mortgage of $9,450, and 80 per cent of value where higher mortgage amounts on existing properties were involved. The new terms allowed mortgages equal to 95 per cent of the first $9,000 of appraised value plus 75 per cent of additional value for proposed construction, and to 90 per cent of the first $9,000 plus 75 per cent of remaining value for existing construction. Even further liberalization was allowed to persons on active duty in the Armed Forces.

6. August, 1954: The Housing Act of 1954 authorized completely new programs, such as liberal insured home financing for urban rental housing, initiation of the secondary market purchase operation by the F.N.M.A. to provide a better geographical distribution of private mortgage funds, and the establishment of the Voluntary Home Mortgage Credit Program, which assisted in obtaining government-underwritten home loans from private sources for remote areas and small communities and minority housing.

Steps in 1955 to Tighten up Terms on Home Mortgage Loans

1. April, 1955: The F.H.A. and V.A. required that closing costs for any home purchase financed with an F.H.A.-insured or V.A.-guaranteed loan be paid in cash. Prior to this date, the regulations permitted payment of closing costs out of loan proceeds.

2. July, 1955: F.N.M.A. ceased operation of its one-for-one program.

3. July, 1955: F.H.A. and V.A. issued regulations requiring an additional 2 per cent down payment and limiting loan maturities to 25 years, instead of the statutory maximum of 30 years. (To January, 1956 the F.H.A. and V.A. restored the maximum of 30 years.)

4. July, 1955: F.N.M.A. decreased the prices at which it would sell mortgages from its liquidating and management portfolio, thus seeking to attract more private mortgage investment funds to the purchase of existing mortgages owned by the government.

Steps Taken in 1957 to Liberalize Terms

1. August, 1957: F.H.A. rescinded the additional 2 per cent down payment requiremment, which had been imposed in July, 1955.

2. August, 1957: Under the Housing Act of 1957, the F.H.A. authorized lower down payments for home purchasers. Instead of the previous maximum loan-to-value ratio equal to 95 per cent of the first $9,000 of value plus 75 per cent of the value in excess of $9,000, the loan-to-value ratio was set at 97 per cent of the first $10,000, 85 per cent of the next $6,000, and 70 per cent of the value over $16,000.

3. August, 1957: The maximum interest rate on F.H.A.-insured mortgages was increased from 5 per cent to 5¼ per cent. Earlier, in December, 1956, the rate was increased from 4½ to 5 per cent. In both instances, the rate was increased to make mortgages more attractive investment, or at least to reinstate its previous relative positions.

4. December, 1957: The President made available $127 million of funds to be used by F.N.M.A. to purchase mortgages under special-assistance housing programs.

5. January and February, 1958: F.N.M.A. increased its purchase prices and reduced its purchase and marketing face.

6. April, 1958: Under the Housing Act of 1958, down payments were reduced, the rate on the V.A.-guaranteed loans was raised to 4¾ per cent from the previous 4½ per cent. In addition, the F.N.M.A. was permitted to purchase government-underwritten mortgages up to a limit of $13,500 at their full value.

A similar exhibit could be built up to illustrate the steps taken in the period 1958 through 1960.

One of the problems encountered in administering a policy designed to attract mortgage credit is the possibility of conflict with other policy-making agencies, such as the Treasury and the Federal Reserve. Another problem is the extent to which government-sponsored programs supplant private mortgage credit instead of stimulating the flow of private mortgage credit. The private financial institutions look with favor upon F.N.M.A. as long as its operations are strictly secondary. However, when its operations are keyed to supporting or pegging artificially low interest rates on home mortgage loans, its activities begin to supplant the private flow of credit. It becomes a primary financing operation. In a sense the Federal agency becomes the primary lender and the private financial institutions perform the more limited role of an intermediary. Rather than rely on direct government lending and the support of artificially low interest rates, or both, the rates on government-underwritten mortgages should be more sensitive to changes in the capital markets. Under this scheme, general monetary policy would play a more important and effective role in regulating the total flow of funds.

QUESTIONS

1. Cite a few figures illustrating the importance of real estate mortgage credit.

2. Set forth the basic credit principles underlying real estate mortgage credit.

3. Distinguish between a standing mortgage and an amortized mortgage. Which is more common in today's mortgage market?

4. What is the purpose of the Federal Home Loan Bank System, and how does it operate?

5. How did the Federal Housing Act stimulate private lending in the 1930's? Did the practice carry over into the postwar period?

6. What incentives to home ownership and financing are included in the Servicemen's Readjustment Act of 1944 (G. I. Bill)?

7. What is the purpose of the Federal National Mortgage Association and how does it operate?

8. What are the basic determinants of the demand for one- to four-family mortgages?

9. Describe the operation of a modern mortgage company.

10. Describe mortgage warehousing. Are there any dangers inherent in mortgage warehousing?

11. Indicate the relative importance of the following investor classes in the one- to four-family mortgage market: government sectors, commercial banking, consumer and nonprofit organization sector, mutual savings bank subsector, savings and loan associations and credit unions subsector, life insurance subsector, and mortgage companies.

12. Are the government-underwritten mortgages equally attractive to each of the investor classes listed in Question 11?

ADDITIONAL READING

Behrens, Carl F. *Commercial Bank Activities in Urban Mortgage Financing.* N.B.E.R. publication. Princeton, N.J.: Princeton University Press, 1952.

Bryant, Willis R. *Mortgage Lending.* New York: McGraw-Hill Book Co., Inc., 1956.

Case, Frederick E. *Modern Real Estate Practices.* Boston: Allyn & Bacon, Inc., 1956.

Colean, Miles L. *The Impact of Government on Real Estate Finance in the United States.* N.B.E.R. study. New York: National Bureau of Economic Research, 1950.

Fisher, E. M. *A Study of Housing Programs and Policies.* Washington, D.C.: U.S. Housing and Home Finance Agency, 1960.

———, and Robert Fisher. *Urban Real Estate.* New York: Holt, Rinehart, and Winston, Inc., 1959.

———, and Chester Rapkin. *The Mutual Mortgage Insurance Fund: A Study of the Adequacy of its Reserves and Resources.* Institute for Urban Land Use and Housing Studies publication. New York: Columbia University Press, 1956.

Grebler, Leo, David M. Blank, and Louis Winnick. *Capital Formation in Residential Real Estate: Trends and Prospects.* N.B.E.R. publication. Princeton, N.J.: Princeton University Press, 1956. Measurement and description of data from about 1890 to 1950.

Hoagland, Henry E. *Real Estate Finance.* Homewood, Ill.: Richard D. Irwin, Inc., 1954.

Holmes, Lawrence G. (ed.). *The Real Estate Handbook.* Englewood Cliffs, N.J.: Prentice-Hall, Inc., 1948. Section VII deals with financing.

Husband, Wm. H., and F. R. Anderson. *Real Estate.* (3rd ed.) Homewood, Ill.: Richard D. Irwin, Inc., 1960.

Klaman, S. B. *The Postwar Rise of Mortgage Companies.* Occasional Paper No. 60. New York: National Bureau of Economic Research, 1959.

Martin, Preston. *Real Estate Principles and Practices.* New York: The Macmillan Co., 1957.

Morton, J. E. *Urban Mortgage Lending — Comparative Markets and Experience.* N.B.E.R. publication. Princeton, N.J.: Princeton University Press, 1956.

McMichael, Stanley L., and Paul T. O'Keefe. *How to Finance Real Estate.* (2nd ed.) Englewood Cliffs, N.J.: Prentice-Hall, Inc., 1953.

North, Nelson L., and Alfred A. Ring. *Real Estate Principles and Practices.* (5th ed.) Englewood Cliffs, N.J.: Prentice-Hall, Inc., 1960.

Pease, Robert H. (ed.), and Homer V. Cherrington. *Mortgage Banking.* New York: McGraw-Hill Book Co., Inc., 1953.

Ratcliff, R. V., D. B. Rathbun, and J. Honnold. *Residential Finance.* New York: John Wiley & Sons, 1957.

Saulnier, R. J. *Urban Mortgage Lending by Life Insurance Companies.* N.B.E.R. Study. Princeton, N.J.: Princeton University Press, 1950.

———, Harold G. Halcrow, and Neil H. Jacoby. *Federal Lending and Loan Insurance.* N.B.E.R. study. Princeton, N.J.: Princeton University Press, 1958. Reviews and analyzes government credit-granting on housing and related activities in all sectors since 1917; describes in detail how the various credit programs developed, the services offered, and lending experience.

U.S. Federal Home Loan Bank Board. *Federal Home Loan Bank System, 1932-1952.* Washington, D.C.: Federal Home Loan Bank Board, 1952.

———. *Savings and Home Financing Source Book.* Washington, D.C.: Federal Home Loan Bank Board. Issued annually.

U.S. Housing and Home Finance Agency. *Annual Report, Housing Statistics.* Issued monthly; see latest reports.

U.S. Senate Subcommittee on Housing of the Committee on Banking and Currency. *Study of Mortgage Credit* (Does the decade 1961-1970 pose problems in private housing and mortgage markets which require Federal legislation by 1960?). Washington, D.C.: Government Printing Office, 1958.

Unger, Maurice A. *Real Estate.* (2nd ed.) Cincinnati: South-Western Publishing Co., 1959.

Weimer, Arthur, and Homer Hoyt. *Principles of Real Estate.* (4th ed.) New York: Ronald Press Co., 1960.

15: Consumer credit

WE now turn to consumer credit, which covers credit that is extended to consumers exclusive of real estate mortgage credit. To define the term in a more positive manner, consumer credit includes the financing of goods and services for personal consumption and the refinancing of debts originally incurred for such purposes. It also includes loans to finance maintenance and improvement of owner-occupied houses. The term "credit" includes an advance of goods as well as an advance of funds to purchase goods and services. The term "consumption" may be defined as the process of using up goods and services as an end in itself rather than as a stage in the productive process.

The nature of consumer credit is the first topic we shall cover. This subject is followed by an examination of reasons for the use of such credit. With this background information, we shall focus our discussion on consumer credit markets: including rates and terms, suppliers of consumer credit, and types of consumer credit markets. After we note the growth of consumer credit, we shall deal with the relationship between consumer credit and economic instability and the pros and cons of consumer credit regulation.

NATURE OF CONSUMER CREDIT

The definitions cited above are used by the Federal Reserve System in its statistical consumer credit series. The basic objective of the System's series is to represent as completely as possible the short- and intermediate-term indebtedness of individuals in their role as consumers. Data are shown as to type of credit and ultimate source of credit. A cursory review of the System's definitions of basic concepts and method of classification will serve as an effective means of gaining an understanding of the nature and role of consumer credit in today's economy.

Classification of Consumer Credit

The Federal Reserve System classifies consumer credit transactions by type of credit and type of holder. Consumer credit transactions are broadly classified as either installment or non-installment credit. Installment credit includes credit that is scheduled to be repaid in two or more installments. The sub-classifications of installment credit include automobile paper, other consumer goods paper, repair and modernization loans, and personal loans. The sub-classifications of non-installment credit are single-payment loans, charge accounts, and service credit. Charge accounts that permit scheduled repayment on a periodic basis, such as revolving accounts under which customers pay their monthly bills in equal periodic payments and budget accounts, are considered a form of installment credit.

Consumer credit is classified under two major types of holders, financial institutions and retail outlets, and each of these is further subdivided into five classes. Financial institutions are subdivided into commercial banks, sales finance companies, credit unions, consumer finance companies, and others. Retail outlets are subdivided into department store sales, furniture stores, household appliance stores, automobile dealers, and others.

All loans held by financial institutions, whether made directly or purchased from retail outlets, are classified by the institution holding the credit. Only credit extended and retained by retail outlets is attributed to retail outlets. This system of classification represents a departure from the one used a few years ago. The Federal Reserve System formerly classified consumer credit transactions as either sale or loan credit, which meant that all credit originated by retail stores, whether retained on the books of the store or sold to a financial institution, was classified as sale credit. Only loans made directly to the borrower by financial institutions were classified as loan credit. In terms of economic analysis, the new system of classification is much more useful.

To clarify the meaning of the various types of consumer credit, definitions used by the Federal Reserve System are set forth below:*

> "Automobile paper" and "other consumer goods paper" represent credit extended for the purpose of purchasing automobiles and other consumer goods and secured by the items purchased.
> "Repair and modernization" include both F.H.A.-insured and non-insured loans made to finance maintenance and improvement of owner-occupied dwelling units. These loans are used to finance the purchase and installation of equipment such as furnaces, hot water heaters, storm windows, and kitchen equipment, as well as major alterations and additions.
> "Personal loans" include all installment loans not covered in the previous categories made by financial institutions to individuals for consumer purposes. Most of these loans are for such purposes as consolidation of consumer debts, payment of medical, educational, or travel expenses, and payment of personal taxes and insurance premiums. Some personal loans are used for the purchase of consumer goods but they are not included under "automobile paper" or "other consumer goods paper" unless they are secured by the goods purchases.

*From "Revision of Consumer Credit Statistics," *Federal Reserve Bulletin*, April 1953, pp. 6-7.

"Single-payment loans" are loans made to individuals for consumer purposes and scheduled to be repaid in one payment. Most of the amount outstanding in this area is held by commercial banks. Small amounts are held by pawnbrokers, mutual savings banks, and savings and loan associations. While some credit of this type is used for the purchase of consumer goods, most is for meeting short-term needs such as the payment of personal taxes or life insurance premiums.

"Charge accounts" are the outstanding balances owed to retail dealers for purchases made by individuals for consumer purposes.

"Service credit" is the amounts owed by individuals to professional practitioners and service establishments. The largest component of this type of credit is the amount owed by consumers to doctors, hospitals, and other medical practitioners. Amounts owed to public utilities, after deduction of deposits and prepayments, are another substantial component of service credit. The remainder represents amounts owed for a variety of personal services such as cleaning and dyeing, education, and recreation.

Application of the Definitions

Compiling consumer credit statistics is a difficult task. Modifications must be introduced to provide for various traditional and institutional factors that prevent the available data from conforming exactly to the definitions cited above. Diligent care must be exercised in the selection of benchmarks to be used in deriving estimates of consumer credit. Only the modifications are of immediate concern in this chapter.

Some durable goods such as trucks and farm equipment are used primarily for business purposes and the credit extended for the purchase of these goods is not considered consumer credit. However, some individuals use credit-financed automobiles for both consumer and business purposes. In the absence of reliable guides, these transactions are considered consumer credit.

Just as activities of farm households are difficult to segregate as to consumption and production, loans to farmers are also difficult to classify. In the absence of reliable guides to the approximate distribution of farm loans between consumption and production, these transactions are excluded from consumer credit statistics.

Non-farm households that are involved in the operation of businesses present a similar problem concerning loans on life insurance policies. Policy loans can be used as a source of business funds as well as a source of consumer funds. Inasmuch as the total number of policy loans is relatively large and available data do not provide a breakdown as to purpose, the loans are excluded from consumer credit statistics.

Another problem concerns loans to individuals for consumption purposes that are secured by deposit and deposit types of accounts. In a sense, such borrowers are using their own funds. Inasmuch as many consumer credit loans are secured, loans of this nature are simply viewed as one form of secured loans and are included in consumer credit statistics.

Credit is also extended to consumers for consumer purposes through media other than regular business channels, such as loans extended by one individual to another and loans extended by a business to its employees. In the absence of data, we have no choice but to exclude these loans from consumer credit statistics.

As a result of practical difficulties associated with collection and compilation of consumer credit data, the final figures should be viewed as reasonable approximations. The net effect of the modifications is an understatement of certain components of consumer credit. The data are certainly valuable, and they do provide much insight into the structure and operation of consumer credit markets.

REASONS FOR CONSUMER CREDIT

Consumer credit offers many advantages. (1) It promotes greater efficiency and convenience in carrying on many types of consumer transactions. (2) It facilitates the purchase of relatively high-priced consumer goods and services. (3) It provides a means by which individuals are enabled to ease emergency financial strains. (4) It enables consumers to accelerate their purchases of many goods and services. They are able to enjoy the services provided by durable goods while paying for them. The alternative would be to build up cash prior to the purchase of the goods. The prospects of higher total sales and greater profits encourage retailers to sell on credit. The net effect on sales and profits depends on the policies and practices relating to credit extension and credit collection. Credit sales require that sellers build up their investments in accounts receivable and incur bad-debt expense. Some retail outlets offer credit terms to meet the pressure of competition. Financial institutions supply funds to finance consumer transactions because consumer credit is profitable business for them. Growth and fluctuations in consumer credit are considered later in this chapter.

Convenience is probably the major reason for much "service credit." It is difficult to imagine the degree of inconvenience that would be experienced by households and businesses if utility services were done on a cash basis. Today, electricity, water, gas, and telephone service are paid for on a monthly or a bi-monthly basis. Convenience is also an important factor in the use of "charge accounts" at retail outlets. When a person makes frequent purchases from the same retail outlet, it is more convenient for him to make a monthly lump sum payment than it is to pay cash on each purchase. Furthermore, goods may be ordered over the telephone or through the mail and need not be paid for at time of delivery. In recent years service credit and charge accounts have been extended to many types of consumer transactions, and especially to those relating to travel.

Humanitarianism is an important consideration in explaining the service credit owed by individuals to professional practitioners and hospitals. A request for full cash payment prior to treatment or care would subject medical practitioners and hospital officials to considerable criticism. Widespread use of accident and sickness insurance and Blue Cross-Blue Shield plans has eased the problem to some degree, by collecting funds from those covered under the plans and using the funds to pay medical practitioners and hospitals the expenses relating to treatment or care of insured members. These programs reduce the uncertainty of possible financial loss by the insureds and at the same time provide a method of payment. However, many persons are not covered and some who are covered are not fully indemnified. Many can only pay medical bills by stretching out the payments over a period of a year or longer. The payment schedule may be arranged between the patient and the medical practitioner, or the patient may arrange a loan through a financial institution and pay off the original bill.

The existence of the major portion of consumer credit is explained by the relatively high cost of many durable goods. The prices of many durable goods and services are high in relation to the consumers' holdings of immediately available liquid assets. Only a few persons could afford to purchase the early automobiles because the terms of sale were cash. Yet the automobile appealed to many consumers. Their preferences were not effective in the market because they were not backed up by purchasing power. To increase sales, either dealers had to advance cars to consumers in exchange for promises to pay or consumers had to obtain funds prior to purchase. Dealers were not able to advance the cars because manufacturers required cash. Either the dealers or the consumers had to obtain financing from financial institutions. The need was filled by the establishment of specialized credit institutions and by the extension of credit to dealers and consumers by existing financial institutions.

Some "personal loans" are made with the purpose of consolidating already existing consumer debts. If an individual commits himself to repayment schedules that are beyond his ability to pay, he can consolidate all the separate debts into one debt that will have a more realistic repayment schedule. The individual uses the newly borrowed cash to pay off the other creditors.

Consumer credit transactions provide the means of financing a large portion of the flow of goods and services into final consumption, and also create a multitude of disciplined savings programs. The repayment of consumer indebtedness requires that some income be diverted from current consumption. However, as some consumers reduce indebtedness, others increase it. The net change in consumer indebtedness is determined by the difference between the flow of total credit extensions and the flow of total repayments.

CONSUMER CREDIT TERMS AND FINANCE CHARGES

The phrase "credit terms" refers to the down payment and the length of maturity. "Finance charges" refers either to the difference between the "time price" and "cash price" of goods bought on credit or to the difference between the amount of a loan a consumer receives and the amount he must pay back. Among the factors influencing both credit terms and finance charges are: the purpose of the credit, the consumer's credit worthiness, the collateral, the method of financing, and the laws. Generally, goods purchased on credit can and do serve as collateral. If a purchase is not involved, the consumer might still use consumer durable goods as collateral.

Credit terms and finance charges will also depend on the consumer's choice of retailers and financial institutions. Alternative methods of financing the purchase of goods include: (1) the retailer holds the finance paper: (2) the retailer discounts the finance paper at a lending institution; and (3) the consumer borrows directly from a financial institution. As a general rule, consumers obtain lower finance charges by borrowing directly from financial institutions, but at the same time these institutions may be more selective and more strict in setting the credit terms.

There are more laws applying to finance charges than to credit terms. Common law and state statutes limit finance charges on non-installment cash loans; nearly all states regulate finance charges on installment cash loans; many states regulate finance charges on installment sale credit. Even where maximum rates are not in effect, certain rates become associated with different types of consumer credit. Credit terms are more varied than finance charge terms. Financial institutions and retailers vary credit terms to affect sales or loan volume. Lower down payments or longer maturities result in lower monthly payments, which to many consumers is the vital factor.

Down Payments

In financing durable consumer goods, the down payment is a consideration important to both the consumer and the supplier of credit. To the consumer the down payment is important because of its influence on the required amount of cash at time of purchase and on the size of the monthly repayments. To the supplier of credit, the down payment is important because of its influence on sale or loan volume and the degree of risk. Losses are more commonly associated with low down payments than with high down payments. Buyers who have little or no equity in consumer durable goods are more likely to be indifferent to delinquency and repossession. Abuse of the goods or price changes may also result in extensive loss if there is little or no down payment required.

The down payment required in a specific transaction depends on over-all economic and credit conditions, the nature of the collateral, the method of financing, and the characteristics of the individual consumer. True down payments are probably on the order of 25 to 30 per cent for new cars and mobile homes, and 10 to 15 per cent on appliances.

The practices of packing prices or allowing unrealistic trade-in allowances on certain types of durable goods make it very difficult for consumers to ascertain true down payments. Automobile dealers and appliance dealers tend to pack factory-suggested prices in order to grant impressive discounts or trade-in allowances. Beginning in late 1958, a determined effort was made to eliminate this practice in the sale of automobiles. If the balance owed is related to the price after packing, the down payment may appear very large, but if the balance owed is related to a realistic sale price, the down payment may appear very small. For instance, assume that a realistic price of $2,500 is packed by as much as $500. If the seller of the product allows the consumer a trade-in allowance of $1,000, the balance owed is $2,000. With the packing included, the down payment appears to be one-third. If there were no price packing, and if the seller allowed a trade-in allowance of $500, the net price to the consumer could still be $2,000, but the down payment would be only one-fifth.

Even in the absence of price packing, the down payment can be misleading. If a seller allows an unusually large trade-in allowance, the balance owed in relation to selling price may appear reasonable in comparison with normal credit terms, but if the overstated value of the traded-in good were subtracted from the selling price, the down payment might appear inadequate. This example can be carried one step further to illustrate the point. Assume that the price of $2,500 represents a non-packed price. If the traded-in good were overvalued by $400, the down payment would be less than 5 per cent of the selling price. In this instance, the dealer is sacrificing his profit for a sale. If the $2,500 selling price is realistic, the down payment can be considered as 20 per cent. However, the person still purchased the good with less than a 5 per cent down payment.

To offset the risk associated with low down payment loans, suppliers of funds tend to include relatively high finance charges. As a general rule, suppliers of consumer credit who advertise very low down payment loans limit such loans to persons who possess excellent credit ratings. These individuals neither need nor ask for minimum down payments. In other words, the advertisements are used to attract customers; they do not represent the typical terms of consumer credit transactions.

Maturities

There is a trend toward longer maturities on consumer credit loans as there is on real estate mortgage credit. In recent years, maturities on loans to finance automobiles and other consumer durable goods have ranged between 36 and 48 months. There is a limit to the lengthening of maturities because of the risk to the lender. In theory, the value of the good that serves as security should have a market value in excess of the unpaid portion of the loan. The size of the down payment is used to compensate for the length of maturity. Therefore, when maturities are stretched out, down payments are increased. Generally, consumers who can meet the larger down payments do not desire the very long maturities. It appears that maturities have approached their maximum.

Finance Charges

The same principles that apply to finance charges on consumer credit loans also apply to other types of loans. Finance charges are expected to cover the cost of funds, expenses relating to the loan decision, and risk. The finance charges on a specific consumer credit transaction depend on the method of financing, the consumer's choice as to supplier of credit, and the consumer's credit standing.

Knowledge, which is one of the necessary characteristics of a highly competitive market, is sorely lacking among consumers when it comes to a knowledge of or understanding of finance charges on consumer credit transactions. Some of the practices adopted by financial institutions and retailers do not help to clear up the muddle. The 86th Congress gave serious consideration to a bill requiring the disclosure of finance charges in connection with the extension of credit.* The bill would have required that creditors furnish each person to whom credit is extended, prior to the consummation of a transaction, a clear statement in writing setting forth, to the extent applicable and in accordance with rules and regulations prescribed by the Board, the following information: (1) the cash price or delivered price of the property or service to be acquired; (2) the amounts, if any, to be credited as down payment or trade-in; (3) the difference between the amounts set forth under clauses (1) and (2); (4) the charges, individually itemized, which are paid or to be paid by such person in connection with the transaction but which are not incident to the extension of credit; (5) the total amount to be financed; (6) the finance charge expressed in terms of dollars and cents; and (7) the percentage relationship that the finance charge bears to the total amount to be financed, expressed as a simple annual rate.

Much of the bargaining is done on a non-price basis. Although there is not much competition among lenders in the determination of finance charges, " shopping around " by a marginal group of informed consumers tends to promote comparable rates on comparable loans.

Finance charges on many types of consumer credit transactions are

*U.S. Senate Subcommittee of the Committee on Banking and Currency, *Consumer Credit Labeling Bill*, Hearings on S. 2755, a bill to assist in the promotion of economic stabilization by requiring the disclosure of finance charges in connection with extensions of credit. 86th Cong., 2nd sess. (Washington, D.C.: Government Printing Office, 1960).

very complex. Charges may cover insurance and other fees as well as the cost of credit. Furthermore, installment loans may be calculated in various ways, none of which states the cost in terms of the effective or true annual interest rate. The three basic methods of calculating finance charges are the add-on, the discount, and the interest on the unpaid balance.

Under the add-on method the monthly payment is based on the original amount of credit plus the finance charge. Under the discount method, the monthly payment is based on the original amount of credit minus the finance charge. Assume that an individual borrowed $100, to be repaid in twelve monthly installment payments. Under the add-on method the borrower receives $100, signs a note for $106, and promises to make twelve monthly installment payments of, say, $8.33. Under the discount method the borrower receives only $94, signs a note for $100, and promises to make approximately the same monthly repayments. The add-on method is commonly used in financing durable goods. The discount method is used in repair and modernization loans. Either method may be used in personal loans.

The third method, which consists of interest on the unpaid balance, represents the amount of interest due on the balance outstanding since the previous payment. Since the unpaid balance declines from one month to the next, the interest cost declines throughout the period of the loan. However, the repayment schedule is still stated in terms of an equal monthly repayment. A declining portion of each monthly payment is toward interest, and an increasing portion of each monthly payment is toward reduction of principal. This is the method used by consumer finance companies and credit unions, and it is closely similar to home mortgage loans.

To permit accurate comparison of finance charges on installment credit loans, the finance charges must be stated in terms of annual interest rates. If the finance charges are stated in terms of a certain per cent per month on the unpaid balance, it is only necessary to multiply the rate by 12 to state it in terms of an annual rate. Two per cent per month on the unpaid balance is equivalent to 24 per cent per year.

Computation of an effective annual interest rate under the other two methods is more difficult. The interest cost is computed in terms of the original or initial amount of credit, but the average amount of credit outstanding over the entire period of the loan is only about half the initial amount of credit because of the monthly repayment or reduction of principal. Therefore, the effective annual interest rate is about twice the nominal rate. In the examples used to illustrate the add-on discount methods, the nominal rate against the initial credit was 6 per cent, but the effective annual rate of interest was approximately 11 per cent.

Various methods may be used to calculate the effective annual rate on installment credit. Only one of the more simple and approximate methods is introduced in this chapter. The basic formula and one example are cited below:

i = rate of charge expressed as an annual interest rate
m = number of payments in one year
n = number of payments necessary to discharge debt
D = finance charge expressed in dollars
P = principal or cash advanced

Formula for the constant-ratio method: $i = \dfrac{2\,m\,D}{P\,(n+1)}$

Borrower receives $100, signs a note for $106, and makes a monthly payment of $8.83 per month for 12 months.

$$i = \frac{2 \times 12 \times 6}{100 \times (12) + 1)}$$

$$i = \quad 11 \text{ per cent}$$

In addition to interest, lenders or retailers may include charges related to both life and property insurance. The nominal interest may be applied against the total amount of credit, including the credit used to cover these other costs.

Many installment contracts are sold by dealers to financial institutions. Generally, finance charges are shared between them. In many retail lines, the dealer's share in finance charges is an important part of his total income, and is figured into both the prices of goods and trade-in allowances. In the absence of this income, prices might be slightly higher and trade-in allowances slightly lower. The dealer's choice as to the ultimate holder of the paper is affected not only by the size of the share, but also by the form of purchase agreement, allied financing services, and other related services. Typically, the dealer's share of the finance charges ranges between one-fifth and one-third of the total finance charge.

In recent years, new-car dealers have charged add-on rates of 5 to 7 per cent, and used car dealers have charged rates as high as 12 per cent. Typical add-on rates on mobile homes are similar to those charged on automobiles. Rates on appliances run slightly higher, ranging from 6 to 10 per cent. Federal Housing Administration repair and modernization loans on discount loans and maximum rates are specified. Generally, finance charges on loans obtained directly from a financial institution, and particularly from a commercial bank, are lower than charges on loans obtained from a dealer.

Consumer finance companies and credit unions generally state their finance charges on personal loans in terms of a certain per cent per month on the unpaid balance. The actual rates tend to vary with the size of the loan. State small loans laws specify maximum rates. Most of the states have set 3 per cent per month on the unpaid principal as the maximum rate. Stated in terms of annual rate, this charge is 36 per cent. Commercial banks generally charge 6 per cent per annum on a discount basis for personal loans.

Although finance charges on consumer credit loans appear to be high, suppliers of credit must be able to charge rates that will cover cost of funds, administrative costs, and risks. If the law did not permit rates as high as, say, 36 per cent per year, many individuals would be denied credit, and many of them would undoubtedly turn to illegal sources and pay much higher rates. " When it became apparent that neither law nor love was going to meet the needs of small borrowers, efforts were made to permit rates high enough for operations of legitimate lenders."*

PRINCIPAL HOLDERS OF CONSUMER CREDIT

TABLE 15–1
CONSUMER CREDIT OUTSTANDING, END OF 1958
(BILLIONS OF DOLLARS)

Assets	Dollars	Per cent
Installment credit	33.9	75.2
Corporate business	3.9	8.6
Non-farm non-corporate business	1.2	2.7
Commercial banking	12.7	28.2
Savings institutions [1]	3.0	6.7
Finance companies	13.1	29.0
Non-installment credit	11.2	24.8
Corporate business	3.6	8.0
Non-farm non-corporate business	3.9	8.6
Commercial banking	3.1	6.9
Savings institutions	.5	1.1
Total Assets	45.1	100.0
Liabilities		
Installment credit	33.9	75.2
Automobile	14.1	31.3
Other	19.8	43.9
Non-installment credit	11.2	24.8
Total Liabilities [2]	45.1	100.0

Note: Details may not add to totals because of rounding.
[1] Mainly credit unions.
[2] Owed by consumer sector.
Source: *Federal Reserve Bulletin*, April 1959, p. 422.

The holding pattern of consumer credit outstanding at the end of 1958 is shown in Table 15-1. The data show that commercial banks and finance

*Tyran Smith and Robert W. Johnson, "Operating Characteristics of Consumer Credit Institutions," U.S. Federal Reserve System, *Consumer Installment Credit*, Part I, Vol. I, p. 63.

companies are the major holders of consumer credit, accounting respectively for 35 per cent and 29 per cent. The corporate and non-corporate business sectors supply a substantial portion of consumer credit in conjunction with their sales of goods and services, but most of the credit, and particularly installment credit, is sold to commercial banks and finance companies. Approximately $2.7 million of all the holdings of savings institutions are accounted for by credit unions. The remainder that is outstanding is spread thinly among the various savings institutions.

Since commercial banks and credit unions have been discussed in previous chapters, only a few additional comments on their operations are necessary. The subject of consumer credit introduces for the first time finance companies, which are specialized consumer credit institutions. The major part of this section is devoted to finance companies.

Finance Companies*

Although there is much diversity of activities among finance companies, it is possible to classify them according to the composition of their consumer receivables. The two major classifications are sales finance companies and personal finance companies. Sales finance companies are engaged primarily in the purchase of dealers' time-sales contracts arising out of the sale of goods and services to consumers. Personal finance companies are engaged principally in making personal loans.

The differences among personal finance companies with respect to the laws under which they operate provide a basis for further breakdown. Companies that specialize in making loans under effective state small loan laws are referred to as consumer finance companies. The remaining personal finance companies are referred to by the Federal Reserve System as " other personal finance companies." The survey of finance companies included the following types of enterprises in the category " other personal finance companies":† (1) companies operating in states that do not have small loan laws or have inoperative ones, (2) companies operating under industrial loan or other cash lending laws, (3) employer loan funds, and (4) remedial, fraternal, or church loan groups. The Russell Sage Foundation undertook in 1909 the study of remedial loan problems and promoted the passage of state laws that legalized small loan business and allowed regulated companies to charge higher rates than those allowed under the general usury statutes. In the absence of legislation or adequate regulation, loan sharks and others tend to charge consumers exorbitant rates. The laws specify maxima for both the size of loans and rates charged.

The phrase " engaged principally in " was used in describing the major types of finance companies because of their diversity in activities. Some

---

*This section of the chapter is based mainly on "Survey of Finance Companies, Mid-1955," *Federal Reserve Bulletin*, April 1957.

†*Ibid.*, p. 593.

finance companies, and particularly the larger ones, engage in many types of consumer lending as well as in business financing. Prior to the introduction of the automobile and other consumer durable goods, specialized financial institutions were organized to finance short-term business needs through short-term loans secured by trade accounts receivable and through the purchase of trade paper. It was natural for many of these same financial institutions to adapt their operations to finance the flow of goods from retailers or dealers to consumers. Consequently, in addition to serving manufacturers, wholesalers, jobbers, and distributors, the financial institutions began to serve retailers and dealers. In time, the purchase of dealers' time-sales contracts arising out of the sale of automobiles and other consumer durable goods became their primary financing service, and the sales finance company became firmly entrenched as a new kind of financing institution in the American economy.* Many sales finance companies continue to make business loans to dealers. All three types of finance companies make some loans under state small loan laws. In 1955, the Federal Reserve survey estimated that sales finance companies accounted for 12 per cent of these loans and other personal finance companies for 3 per cent.

A diversified company may operate under either a single corporate organization or the holding company device. In the latter instance, subsidiary companies specialize in particular types of consumer credit and business loans. Most finance companies concentrate on a particular type of consumer credit. Many specialize in buying automobile paper; some specialize in buying other consumer goods paper; and some specialize in making personal loans to consumers.

TABLE 15–2
TYPES OF FINANCE COMPANIES, JUNE 30, 1955

Item	Sales finance	Personal finance Consumer finance	Others
Number of companies	2,620	3,180	2,200
Number of offices	5,970	8,830	3,640
Outstanding consumer loans (in millions)	$ 7,317	$2,398	$ 748
Total assets (in millions)	10,077	2,891	1,419

Note: Estimates for all companies based on the survey of sales and personal finance companies as of June 30, 1955.

Source: "Survey of Finance Companies, Mid-1955," *Federal Reserve Bulletin*, April 1957.

An over-all view of finance companies is provided in Table 15-2,

*Clyde William Phelps, *The Role of the Sales Finance Companies in the American Economy*, Studies in Consumer Credit, No. 1, Commercial Credit Company.

which shows the number of companies and offices and the volume of credit for each type of company. The data for 1955 show that there were at that time about 8,000 finance companies with about 18,440 offices. In terms of the number of companies and offices, the personal finance group was the largest, but in terms of the volume of loans, the sales finance group was by far the largest.

Although the number of finance companies is rather large, there is much concentration in this segment of our financial system. This fact is highlighted by the data contained in Table 15-3. To illustrate the degree of concentration: ½ of 1 per cent of all sales finance companies (13 companies, according to the data in Table 15-2) had over 50 offices each and accounted for

TABLE 15–3
NUMBER OF FINANCE COMPANIES AND AMOUNT OF CONSUMER LOANS,
BY NUMBER OF OFFICES, JUNE 30, 1955*

Number of offices	Number of companies		
	Sales finance companies	Consumer finance companies	Other personal finance companies
1	89.5	85.4	91.8
2 to 5	7.2	10.0	6.0
6 to 10	1.8	2.1	1.1
11 to 50	1.0	2.0	0.9
Over 50	0.5	0.5	0.2
Total	100.0	100.0	100.0
	Amount of consumer loans outstanding		
1	13.3	16.7	55.9
2 to 5	4.6	7.3	10.9
6 to 10	6.1	4.5	7.6
11 to 50	7.0	16.2	6.8
Over 50	69.0	55.3	18.8
Total	100.0	100.0	100.0

*Percentage distribution within type-of-company groups.
Source: "Survey of Finance Companies, Mid-1955," *Federal Reserve Bulletin*, April 1957.

nearly 70 per cent of consumer loans held by sales finance companies in 1955. Among consumer finance companies, the degree of concentration was not quite as great; it was the lowest among "other personal finance companies."

ASSETS OF FINANCE COMPANIES. It can be observed in Table 15-4 that only about 77 per cent of the loans made by sales finance companies are consumer loans. The non-consumer loans of sales finance companies, which represent wholesale financing of inventory and other business loans, are considered in the chapters of this book that deal with the business sector.

TABLE 15–4
MAJOR TYPES OF ASSETS OF FINANCE COMPANIES, JUNE 30, 1955*

Type of asset	Sales finance companies	Consumer finance companies	Other personal finance companies
Loans:			
Consumer	92.6	83.0	52.7
Non-consumer	20.9	3.4	7.6
Total loans (gross)	93.5	86.4	60.3
Less: Reserves	—7.9	—5.1	—3.9
Total loans (net)	85.6	81.3	56.4
Investments	5.7	7.3	29.8
Cash and bank balances	6.6	8.0	8.4
Other assets	2.1	3.4	5.4
Total assets	100.0	100.0	100.0

*Percentage distribution within type-of-company groups.
Source: "Survey of Finance Companies, Mid-1955," *Federal Reserve Bulletin*, April 1957.

Almost all the loans made by consumer finance companies are consumer loans. The variety of enterprises included in the category "other personal finance companies" is reflected in the data. Although the majority of their loans are consumer loans, a relatively large percentage of assets represents investments. These other personal finance companies specialize in consumer loans, but not to the extent that the other two types of finance companies do.

The nature of consumer loans outstanding at finance companies in 1955 is shown by the data in Table 15-5. The importance of automobile paper to sales finance companies and of personal loans to personal finance companies is plainly evident.

LIABILITIES (SOURCES OF FUNDS) OF FINANCE COMPANIES. The manner in which a finance company finances its operations depends on management's attitude toward debt, the age and location of the company and its offices, general type of business, and size.

Like most other financial institutions, finance companies secure the major portion of their funds by borrowing. As pointed out earlier, a high ratio of low-cost debt permits a greater volume of operations per dollar of owners' capital investment. If the margin of profit exceeds the rate of interest being paid on borrowed funds, the rate of return on owners' capital investment is magnified. In a recent study of 78 sales finance companies, the net yield on total resources was only 1.5 per cent in 1955, but the rate of return on average net worth in the same year was 13.5 per cent, which compares favorably with the rate of return for all manufacturing companies. Consumer finance companies earn a higher rate of return on total assets than sales finance companies do, but have about the same rate of return on average net worth.*

TABLE 15-5
TYPES OF CONSUMER LOANS OUTSTANDING AT FINANCE COMPANIES, JUNE 30, 1955*

Type of loan	Sales finance companies	Consumer finance companies	Other personal finance companies
Automobile paper	81.7	6.2	6.4
Other consumer goods paper	12.3	11.3	7.4
Repair and modernization loans	0.3	0.1	1.4
Personal loans	5.7	82.4	84.8
All types	100.0	100.0	100.0

*Percentage distribution within type-of-company groups.
Source: "Survey of Finance Companies, Mid-1955," *Federal Reserve Bulletin*, April 1957.

The data in Table 15-6 show that nearly 85 per cent of the funds employed by sales finance companies are raised through short- and long-term debt. Consumer finance companies and other personal finance companies also rely very heavily on debt as a source of funds. Inasmuch as some of the firms included in the category "other personal finance companies" raise funds by issuing share certificates, the percentage of debt as a source of funds is lowest for this category. Through the combination of short-term notes payable to banks and the direct placement of commercial paper, sales finance companies raise nearly half of their funds through short-term debt. The large percentage of short-term debt reflects the fact that the volume of consumer loans held by sales finance companies tends to fluctuate more violently than do the loans of other finance companies. The smaller sales finance companies and other finance companies do not issue their promissory notes directly to investors; instead they go through commercial paper dealers.

Although debt is an important source of funds for all types of finance

*Board of Governors of the Federal Reserve System, *Consumer Installment Credit*, Part I, Vol. II, Supplement, p. 8.

companies, it must be realized that some of the debt consists of subordinated debentures, which are subordinated to other debt. Some persons consider the subordinated debentures as part of the capital base. Also, many of the companies are relatively large and firmly entrenched in consumer credit, which is a permanent institution in itself. For all three types of finance companies, the ratio of debt to capital is directly related to company size. It was stated in the "Survey of Finance Companies" that "ability and willingness of certain consumer lenders to borrow more in relation to their capital than others appear to be both an effect and a cause of their larger size."*

TABLE 15–6
MAJOR TYPES OF LIABILITIES OF FINANCE COMPANIES, JUNE 30, 1955*

Type, of liability	Sales finance companies	Consumer finance companies	Other personal finance companies
Short-term notes payable to banks	25.0	24.4	14.4
Commercial paper and other short-term debt	23.0	10.2	20.8
Total short-term debt	48.0	34.6	35.2
Long-term notes payable to banks	2.3	3.4	1.9
Other long-term debt (excluding subordinated debentures)	22.0	20.9	4.8
Subordinated debentures	7.5	6.7	3.0
Total long-term debt	31.8	31.0	9.7
Total debt	79.8	65.6	44.0
Other liabilities	5.3	4.8	11.3
Capital and surplus	14.9	29.6	43.8
Total liabilities	100.0	100.0	100.0

*Percentage distribution within type-of-company groups.
Source: "Survey of Finance Companies, Mid-1955," *Federal Reserve Bulletin*, April 1957.

The scope of our study precludes going into the detailed characteristics of finance company borrowing, but it should be mentioned that finance companies must compete with non-financial corporations in the money and capital markets. Their short-term bank loans are generally unsecured, have a maturity of less than a year, and carry a lower rate than the average for all business borrowers. Large sales finance companies sell their short-term paper directly to investors, including many non-bank investors. Other finance companies sell their short-term paper through commercial paper dealers. The issue of open-market paper by finance companies is considered in greater

*Ibid., p. 398.

detail in Chapter 18. Approximately two-thirds of the dollar volume of long-term debt securities is placed directly with investors and the remainder is offered in the form of public issues.

One of the major problems currently affecting the growth and development of sales finance companies is the extent to which manufacturers have set up their own subsidiaries to finance the distribution and sale of their goods. Many of the company-affiliated finance companies offer relatively more attractive terms to both consumers and dealers than the independent finance companies do.

Commercial Banks

Commercial banks entered the field of consumer installment credit financing in the 1920's, but it was not until the mid-1930's that many banks were actually participating in such financing. The success of specialized consumer financing institutions in terms of both profit-and-loss ratios and large excess reserves prompted many banks to set up personal loan departments. During the late 1930's there was a marked expansion in the role of commercial banks in consumer credit.

The role of commercial banks in consumer credit is both direct and indirect. Its direct role is reflected in the volume of consumer loans held by commercial banks. At the end of 1958, commercial banks held 38 per cent of total installment credit and 28 per cent of total non-installment credit. The percentages of holdings of financial institutions alone for the same date were 44 per cent and 85 per cent respectively. The indirect role of commercial banks was noted in the previous section, where we pointed out that short- and long-term notes payable to commercial banks provided about 27 per cent of the total funds employed by sales finance and consumer finance companies. Commercial banks provide additional funds to finance companies by the purchase of commercial paper and debt securities. Probably about 50 per cent of all consumer installment credit is financed directly or indirectly by commercial banks.

Commercial banks hold all types of installment credit. At the end of 1958, their holdings by type of credit were as follows: automobile credit, 48 per cent; other consumer goods paper, 18 per cent; repair and modernization loans, 13 per cent; and personal loans, 21 per cent. About two-thirds of the automobile paper holdings was purchased from dealers; the remainder represented direct automobile loans. Although data are not available, it is probable that a considerable part of the other consumer goods paper was also purchased from dealers.

When we realize that at the end of 1958 the total assets of commercial banks exceeded $230 billion and their total loans exceeded $97 billion, it is not surprising that those banks, as a group, were supplying a major portion of consumer credit. Commercial bank consumer loans represented only 16 per cent of their total loans. Many commercial banks do relatively little consumer lending. From a survey of member banks,* it was discovered that "consumer installment loans accounted for less than one-tenth of total loans outstanding at 37 out of every 100 banks, and as much as one-third at less than nine out of every 100 banks. About 5 per cent of member banks had one-third or more of their total loans in the form of consumer installment loans both in mid-1953 and at the end of 1955. The consumer installment loans of these banks represented 10 per cent of all such loans held by commercial banks. The data tend to show that relatively few commercial banks can be considered specialized consumer lending institutions; the personal loan department is simply one of their many operating departments.

The salient financial characteristics of the commercial banks holding one-third or more of their total loans in the form of consumer installment loans are summarized as follows:† (1) Total capital accounts, as a percentage of total resources, are about the same as for other banks (8 per cent). (2) Making no distinction with respect to the size of the bank, their time deposits account for a slightly larger percentage of total resources. However, the larger banks (those with deposits of more than $100 million) have a greater proportion of time deposits and average rate of interest paid on time deposits than other member banks of the same size. These facts suggest that some of the larger banks are more aggressive in soliciting both funds and consumer loans. (3) Total loans form a larger percentage of total assets for the group of banks tending to specialize in consumer loans. (4) There is a direct relationship between net return on loans and the proportion of consumer installment loans held, which carries over into the rate of return on capital accounts.

Credit Unions

Credit unions have been described in Chapter 9, so that only a few additional comments are necessary. It should be realized that credit unions make loans only to credit union members, and the enabling state and Federal laws specify the types of loans, credit terms, and finance charges. As a general rule, the main finance charge is 1 per cent per month on the unpaid balance, which is equivalent to an annual rate of 12 per cent. Actually, the relatively low operating costs of some credit unions enable them to charge a rate as low as ½ of 1 per cent per month on the unpaid balance.

At the end of 1958, credit unions held $2,664 million of installment paper, which represented about 8 per cent of total installment credit and 9 per cent of that held by financial institutions. The percentage breakdown of installment credit held by credit unions, by type of credit, for September 30

---

*Board of Governors of the Federal Reserve System, *Consumer Installment Credit,* Part I, Vol. II, Supplement 1, pp. 32-34.

†*Ibid.,* pp. 33-34.

of that same year was: automobile paper, 33 per cent; other consumer goods paper, 8.7 per cent; repair and modernization loans, 4.4 per cent; and personal loans, 54 per cent.

Other Financial Institutions

The Federal Reserve Board data on consumer credit include an "other" financial institutions category, which is comprised of estimates for (1) mutual savings banks, (2) savings and loan associations, and a single estimate for (3) a miscellaneous group of lenders that includes (a) companies operating under industrial loan or other cash lending laws, (b) personal finance companies operating in states that do not have small loan laws or have inoperative laws, (c) employee loan groups other than credit unions, and (d) remedial, fraternal, or church loan groups. It will be recalled that in the previous section the miscellaneous group is sometimes referred to as "other personal finance companies."

An estimated breakdown at the end of 1957 by type of institution gave these figures: mutual savings banks, 5 per cent; savings and loan associations, 25 per cent; and miscellaneous lenders, 70 per cent. An estimated breakdown by type of credit held by all lenders in this category is as follows: automobile credit, 1 per cent; other consumer goods paper, 4 per cent; repair and modernization loans, 25 per cent; and personal loans, 70 per cent. Considering the nature of the lenders included in the category, the type of credit held is nearly what one would expect.

CONSUMER INSTALLMENT CREDIT MARKETS

The structure of the consumer credit market is very complex because it includes a series of consumer credit markets and a variety of consumer credit institutions. There is a market for installment credit and a market for non-installment credit. Within each of these markets, the structure is further subdivided. Some financial institutions extend nearly all forms of consumer credit, whereas others tend to restrict their credit extensions to one or two types of consumer credit. Some are specialized consumer credit institutions and others are not; some operate on a national level, some on a regional level, and others on a local level. Some receive the major portion of their funds from individuals in the form of deposit accounts and accounts of the deposit type; still others finance their activities through loans from commercial banks and other sources. The terms and rates on consumer credit transactions vary with the type of credit and the type of institution extending credit.

In the early part of this chapter the type of credit, credit terms, and finance charges were examined. In the previous section we reviewed the principal holders of consumer credit. In this section we shall summarize much of the consumer installment data previously presented in terms of the individual consumer credit markets. The data reflect the markets for the entire country. It must be realized that from the individual consumer's point of view, the consumer credit markets are restricted to a local geographical area. Also, a large amount of the consumer paper is originated by the dealers, who then sell the paper to the institutions. Since the major types of holders of consumer credit operate throughout the United States, the aggregate figures are probably representative of many local markets.

TABLE 15–7
CONSUMER INSTALMENT CREDIT MARKETS — AMOUNTS OUTSTANDING
BY MAJOR PARTS: SEPT. 30, 1950, SEPT. 30, 1958, SEPT. 30, 1959
(MILLIONS OF DOLLARS)

Holder and Type of Credit	9/30/50	9/30/58	9/30/59
Total Consumer Instalment Credit			
Commercial banks	$ 5,819	$12,607	$14,664
Sales finance companies	3,825	8,891	9,949
Consumer finance companies	1,192	3,280	3,542
Credit unions	585	2,591	3,093
Other financial institutions	396	1,389	1,706
Total financial institutions	11,817	28,758	32,954
Retailers	2,635	4,321	5,008
Total	14,452	33,079	37,962
Retail Automobile Credit			
Commercial banks	2,519	6,146	7,246
Sales finance companies	3,034	6,601	7,328
Consumer finance companies	112	123	125
Credit unions	154	850	1,030
Other financial institutions	86	179	155
Total financial institutions	5,905	13,899	15,884
Retailers	286	433	586
Total	6,191	14,332	16,470
Other Consumer Goods Credit			
Commercial banks	1,429	2,274	2,494
Sales finance companies	576	1,551	1,761
Consumer finance companies	104	325	400
Credit unions	36	225	253
Other financial institutions	52	49	60
Total financial institutions	2,197	4,424	4,968
Department stores (incl. mail order)	687	1,393	1,907
Furniture stores	777	1,110	1,078
Household appliance stores	260	344	288
Other retailers	625	1,041	1,149
Total retailers	2,349	3,888	4,422
Total	4,546	8,312	9,390

Repair and Modernization Credit			
Commercial banks	816	1,583	1,882
Sales finance companies	65	20	30
Credit unions	29	115	170
Other financial institutions	86	389	531
Total	996	2,107	2,613
Personal Loans			
Commercial banks	1,055	2,604	3,042
Sales finance companies	150	719	830
Consumer finance companies	970	2,832	3,017
Credit unions	366	1,400	1,640
Other financial institutions	178	773	960
Total	$2,719	$8,328	$9,489

Source: *Federal Reserve Bulletin*, October 1951, October 1956, November 1959.
Credit union outstandings, by major parts, from "Report on Credit Unions," Reports, Inc., R. Modley, Editor, Kent, Connecticut.
Consumer finance company outstandings, by major parts, from Board of Governors of the Federal Reserve System, Release G.22, dated December 3, 1958, December 3, 1959.
Note: Table prepared by Ernst A. Dauer. Reprinted by permission.

The major consumer installment credit markets are shown in Tables 15-7 and 15-8. Since the figures are self-explanatory, we shall make only a few general comments. Commercial banks and sales finance companies are the major holders of installment credit, accounting respectively for 38.6 per cent and 26.2 per cent. In terms of the share of the market, the most significant changes between 1950 and 1959 have been the decline in the retailers' share and an increase in the importance of credit unions.

The combined holdings of commercial banks and sales finance companies accounted for nearly 85 per cent of the market in automobile paper. In this segment of the market, the growth of credit unions has been at the expense of the sales finance companies and consumer finance companies.

As to holdings of other consumer goods paper, the market is almost evenly divided between financial institutions and retailers. Between 1950 and 1959 the relative importance of commercial banks declined, but the decline was more than offset by the increase in the share of the market by other financial institutions.

The structure of the market for repair and modernization loans changed considerably during the 1950's. Both commercial banks and sales finance companies lost a sizeable share of the market to credit unions and other financial institutions. Much of this represents the fast rate of growth of credit unions and savings and loan associations.

In the personal loan market, the major portion of the loans was made by consumer finance companies and commercial banks, but neither type of institution was able to maintain its share of the market during the 1950's. Like the market for repair and modernization loans, credit unions and other

345

financial institutions have captured a bigger share of the market for personal loans.

TABLE 15–8
CONSUMER INSTALMENT CREDIT MARKETS
BY MAJOR PARTS: SEPT. 30, 1950, SEPT. 30, 1958, SEPT. 30, 1959
PERCENTAGES HELD BY MAJOR CONSUMER CREDIT INSTITUTIONS

Holder and Type of Credit	9/30/50	9/30/58	9/30/59
Total Consumer Instalment Credit			
Commercial banks	40.3%	38.1%	38.6%
Sales finance companies	26.5	26.9	26.2
Consumer finance companies	8.2	9.9	9.3
Credit unions	4.1	7.8	8.2
Other financial institutions	2.7	4.2	4.5
Total financial institutions	81.8	86.9	86.8
Retailers	18.2	13.1	13.2
Total	100.0%	100.0%	100.0%
Retail Automobile Credit			
Commercial banks	40.7%	42.9%	44.0%
Sales finance companies	49.0	46.1	44.5
Consumer finance companies	1.8	.9	.8
Credit unions	2.5	5.9	6.2
Other financial institutions	1.4	1.2	.9
Total financial institutions	95.4	97.0	96.4
Retailers	4.6	3.0	3.6
Total	100.0%	100.0%	100.0%
Other Consumer Goods Credit			
Commercial banks	31.4%	27.3%	26.6%
Sales finance companies	12.7	18.7	18.7
Consumer finance companies	2.3	3.9	4.3
Credit unions	.8	2.7	2.7
Other financial institutions	1.1	.6	.6
Total financial institutions	48.3	53.2	52.9
Department stores (incl. mail order)	15.1	16.8	20.3
Furniture stores	17.1	13.4	11.5
Household appliance stores	5.7	4.1	3.1
Other retailers	13.8	12.5	12.2
Total retailers	51.7	46.8	47.1
Total	100.0%	100.0%	100.0%
Repair and Modernization Credit			
Commercial banks	81.9%	75.1%	72.0%
Sales finance companies	6.5	.9	1.2
Credit unions	2.9	5.5	6.5
Other financial institutions	8.7	18.5	20.3
Total	100.0%	100.0%	100.0%

Personal Loans			
Commercial banks	38.8%	31.3%	32.1%
Sales finance companies	5.5	8.6	8.7
Consumer finance companies	35.7	34.0	31.8
Credit unions	13.5	16.8	17.3
Other financial institutions	6.5	9.3	10.1
Total	100.0%	100.0%	100.0%

Source: *Federal Reserve Bulletin*, October 1951, October 1956, November 1959.
Credit union outstandings, by major parts, from "Report on Credit Unions," Reports, Inc., R. Modley, Editor, Kent, Connecticut.
Consumer finance company outstandings, by major parts, from Board of Governors of the Federal Reserve System, Release G.22, dated December 3, 1958, December 3, 1959.
Note: Table prepared by Ernst A. Dauer. Reprinted by permission.

GROWTH OF CONSUMER INSTALLMENT CREDIT

During the early 1920's, consumer installment credit exceeded $1 billion for the first time, and since then the average yearly rate of growth has been about 10 per cent. As shown in Figure 15-1, the rate of growth has not been constant. The effects of the Great Depression and World War II are clearly evident. The rate of change during both the declines and the catching-up periods was greater than the over-all rate of change for the entire period. During the 1920-1929 period, the growth rate was about 15 per cent; during the 1936-1941 period, the rate was about 11 per cent; and during the 1947-1957 period, it was about 19 per cent.

The mass production of durable consumer goods required mass markets, and mass markets for relatively high-priced goods required credit for the masses. Many of the changes noted above have come about because experience with consumers has been favorable from the start. The use of consumer credit has become more acceptable and practicable with the passage of time.

Among the many factors underlying growth in consumer installment credit are the higher level of economic activity, greater variety in the types of goods and services sold on credit, more liberal credit terms, more efficient and widespread consumer credit markets, continued breakdown of negative attitudes toward consumer debt, suburbanization, increased home ownership, and an improvement in the asset and income position of consumers. Throughout the period of growth there was much interaction between consumer credit and many of these factors; all of them stimulated the use of consumer credit, the growing success of which, in turn, stimulated further change in the factors.

Limited space precludes extensive commentary here on each of the factors underlying the growth of consumer installment credit. A higher level of economic activity is accompanied by a higher level of consumer expenditures, and it is only natural that consumer credit should increase. However, the growth of consumer credit has been faster than that of national

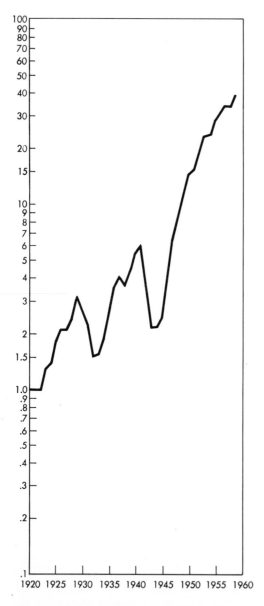

FIGURE 15-1   CONSUMER INSTALMENT CREDIT, 1920-1959

Source: Board of Governors of the Federal Reserve System, "Historical Supplement to Federal Reserve Chart Book on Financial and Business Statistics," September 1960.

product and also faster than the increase in consumer expenditures. One of the reasons for this growth is that a greater portion of consumer goods and services are now being sold on credit. More liberal credit terms, including longer maturities and lower down payments, result in a larger amount of consumer credit per dollar of consumer expenditure. The amount of automobile paper credit would only be about half as great as it is today if the credit terms and standards of the 1920's were still in force. It should be realized that more liberal credit terms result in an increase of finance charges per dollar of consumer expenditure. Most of the other factors have been discussed in other parts of our study.

CONSUMER CREDIT AND ECONOMIC STABILITY

The nature of consumer installment credit suggests that it might be one of the more important factors underlying economic instability. A rapid expansion in consumer installment credit extensions might be a partial cause of an upturn in general business conditions, or it might be a cause of inflationary pressures during a period of high-level production and employment. A rapid contraction might help to bring on a downturn in general business conditions, or it might also offset what would otherwise have been disturbing factors.

A major paper prepared by the Board of Governors of the Federal Reserve System made the following general observations on the relationship between consumer installment credit and economic instability:*

> (1) *A Prime Factor in Business Fluctuations.* Consumer installment credit has often been a factor in changes in the level of business activity, but it has not been the principal cause of such changes. Although consumer credit has been associated with economic fluctuations, other factors have been of greater importance. This was clearly evident in 1929-33, 1937-38, 1949, and the downturn in 1953.
>
> Possible exceptions may be the recovery starting in late 1954 and the boom of 1955. Even in these periods, the influence of consumer installment credit probably was equalled or exceeded by other credit-financed expenditures, such as for business plant and equipment and for residential construction; but these expenditures — especially those of business — may have represented, in part, secondary responses to a rapid expansion of installment credit. In cases when changes in expenditures for durable consumer goods played a major role in the change in business activity, installment credit can be regarded as an important contributory factor.
>
> (2) *A Leading and Amplifying Force.* Although not the principal factor in any cycle, consumer installment credit has been both a leading and an amplifying force in economic fluctuations. In an impressive number of times, credit extended appears to have moved ahead of

*Ibid., Part I, Vol. I, pp. 232-234.

other economic changes — to have led at turning points. Time leads appear to have been longer in recoveries than in downturns . . . the lead record remains impressive even when allowance for growth is made.

As an amplifying factor, consumer installment credit has been rather similar to other forms of credit in that its movements have conformed to the general business cycle. The secondary and stimulating effects of credit extensions come more during booms; the secondary and retarding effects of repayments have often hung over into periods of recession. This amplifying effect is probably of greater relative importance in the modest turns in business activity.

(3) *A Greater Influence in Booms Than in Recessions.* The major influence of installment credit has been to add fuel to booms; it has less often been an aggravating factor during recessions. A number of periods illustrate the expansive role of installment credit: pre-1929, 1934-37, 1946-50, 1952-53, and 1955. In each of these periods, installment credit buying contributed to a rate of sales of consumer durable goods that could not be sustained.

In expansion periods, easier terms in the form of longer maturities and lower down payments have been an important stimulus. An easing of terms was a specified characteristic in 4 of 5 periods mentioned above. In periods of contraction, terms have been tightened less frequently and less than they were eased in preceding expansion periods.

Installment credit has added to the over-all credit demands during the major business booms. This has contributed to an expansion of bank credit and has intensified inflationary pressure. Forced liquidation of installment debt represented a substantial economic influence only in the 1929-32 downturn.

(4) *A Growing Influence in Credit Market Fluctuations.* Consumer installment credit has grown in influence as a factor in the credit market and in credit market fluctuations . . . the statistical record of consumer installment credit seems to put it among the less stable kinds of credit.

The influence of consumer installment credit on the amount of savings is indirect and uncertain . . . this institution tends to make the fluctuations of saving cycle-aggravating rather than countercyclical.

(5) *An Increasingly Important Influence.* If the rapid installment credit growth continues, its potential contribution to the expanding side of the cycle will also increase. If the growth trend slows down, cyclical decreases in installment credit, when they occur, will likely exert more of an easing influence on credit markets and wider influence on economic activity than in most earlier cycles. Although in upswings installment credit expansion will continue to be a stimulative influence on activity generally, the degree of stimulation is likely to be less than during preceding periods of vigorous credit growth.

REGULATION OF CONSUMER CREDIT

The regulation of consumer credit may be accomplished through general monetary and credit measures, selective credit measures, or a combination of the two. Selective regulation consists of specifying minimum down payments and maximum permissible maturities on both sale and loan credit transactions involving consumer expenditure. There have been three distinct periods during which consumer credit was regulated through selective credit measures: (1) September 1, 1941 through November 1, 1947; (2) September 20, 1948 through June 30, 1949; and (3) September 18, 1951 through May 7, 1952. Regulations were imposed during World War II to channel a maximum of goods and services into military uses and to restrain inflationary pressures. Even before the outbreak of fighting in Korea, inflationary pressures were mounting, and the consumers' reactions to the possibility of a full wartime economy prompted many of them to accelerate their buying plans. The objective of the regulation was to assure that easy consumer credit terms would not add to the inflationary pressures. During both of these periods, direct controls were also imposed on various segments of the economy. Selective controls were imposed in 1948 because of the inflationary pressures prevailing at the time. General monetary and credit measures were not operative then because of the policy of supporting the market for Federal obligations. We shall consider now whether or not consumer credit regulations should be a continuing tool of monetary policy, even during peacetime.

In the previous section we pointed out the relationship between consumer installment credit and economic instability. In other parts of this chapter we have discussed the degree to which non-monetary financial institutions and non-financial enterprise are involved in consumer credit. One of the basic issues is the degree of response of consumer credit markets to general monetary and credit measures. This topic was dealt with in a Federal Reserve study that presented the following conclusion:*

> . . . the evidence indicates that the influences of developments in the general credit market, including the effects of general credit and monetary policy, reach in some degree the consumer installment credit area. This response is most marked at the "wholesale" level and is evidenced by changes in prices, terms, and willingness with which funds are made available to borrowing-lending intermediaries as well as in changes in the availability of bank funds to their consumer credit departments. At the retail level, concrete evidence of response in the quantity and terms of credit as a direct result of a change in general credit conditions is difficult to document apart from an apparent tendency for retail interest charges to rise, for standards of credit-worthiness to stiffen, and for downpayment-maturity requirements at least to hold the line as credit tightness becomes fairly severe, and for consumer lenders to cut back on their new business promotion efforts. . . . Unavoidably an important question must remain unanswered. That question is whether the response of the consumer installment credit area as a whole to changes in credit conditions, and in particular to general monetary restraint, is sufficient either in degree or in timing to facilitate a national economic policy directed toward sustained high and rising levels of activity without inflation.

*Ibid., p. 285.

The many arguments both for and against peacetime regulation of consumer credit are summarized under three headings: (1) general principles; (2) interpretation of the evidence of the effects of installment credit on instability; and (3) practicality.* The reader is encouraged to draw his or her own conclusions.

General Principles

PRO. Economic instability is costly in terms of human and other resources. The effects of general credit and monetary measures are too limited. It is possible to moderate instability related to consumer installment credit by means of selective controls. Also, regulation of consumer credit may permit productive investment without inflation of prices.

CON. Selective consumer credit measures interfere with economic freedom and distort the allocation of resources through competitive markets. Regulation may also deter economic growth. Furthermore, it may be argued that selective credit regulation is not a proper function of monetary management. It is estimated that over 200,000 enterprises are involved in consumer credit, and a large proportion of them are not even financial institutions.

Effects of Installment Credit on Instability

PRO. In the absence of regulation, installment credit lenders suffer an undue risk exposure, which, in turn, poses a potential danger to the general stability of our financial system. It is also alleged that lenders need regulation for their own protection against unsound competition.

CON. It is argued that installment credit is both sound and self-regulating, and is responsive to general credit and monetary measures if these measures are not frustrated by other considerations. It is also alleged that consumer credit is relatively unimportant in the over-all credit structure.

Practicality

PRO. Proponents agree that there are administrative and enforcement problems under normal peacetime conditions; nevertheless, the problems are manageable. It is also alleged that standby authority by itself, without application, would be an inhibiting force to ill-advised consumer credit management.

CON. The opposition arguments are the expected ones. The regulations place an undue burden on business; in addition, the administrative and enforcement problems are too formidable for peacetime conditions.

*Ibid., Chapter 16.

QUESTIONS

1. What is meant by " consumer credit "? Classify consumer credit by type of credit and type of holder.

2. Indicate some of the difficulties in compiling statistics to fit the general definition of consumer credit.

3. What functions are served by consumer credit?

4. Distinguish between " credit terms " and " finance charges." What are some of the factors influencing credit terms?

5. What is meant by " price pack "? How does it influence credit terms?

6. Describe briefly the methods of calculating finance charges.

7. Describe briefly the holding pattern of consumer credit outstanding.

8. Compare sales finance companies and personal finance companies in terms of the following: composition of credit receivables, laws under which each operates, origin and development, and sources of funds.

9. " The role of commercial banks in consumer credit is both direct and indirect." Explain.

10. Why is the structure of the consumer credit market so complex?

11. What has been the rate of growth in consumer credit since 1920? What are some of the factors underlying this growth?

12. What is the relationship between consumer installment credit and economic instability?

13. Summarize the arguments for and against the regulation of consumer credit. What is your position?

ADDITIONAL READING

The personal finance and consumer economics texts listed at the end of Chapter 7 treat all of the topics covered in Chapter 15; the money and banking texts listed at the end of Chapter 4 treat the regulatory aspects of consumer credit.

American Finance Conference. *Fact Book and Special Bulletins.* The *Fact Book* is published annually. *Special Bulletins* on the sales financing industry are published throughout the year. *Special Bulletin 65,* published in 1956, presents a bibliography of reference materials on consumer installment credit.

Board of Governors of the Federal Reserve System. *Consumer Instalment Credit.* Six books, Parts I-IV. I — *Growth and Report* (Vols. I-II); II — *Conference on Regulation* (Vols. I, II); III — *Views on Regulation;* and IV — *Financing New Car Purchases.* Washington, D.C.: Government Printing Office, 1957. The six books give the results of an intensive study of consumer instalment credit, undertaken by the Board on request of the Council of Economic Advisers by Direction of the

President.

———— "Survey of Consumer Finances." An annual survey, the results of which are published in various issues of the *Federal Reserve Bulletin*. See latest 12-month period. Consumer credit data are published regularly in the *Federal Reserve Bulletin*.

National Bureau of Economic Research. See Studies in Consumer Instalment Financing, 1-10.

National Foundation for Consumer Credit. A source of current consumer credit statistics. Address is 1627 K Street, N.W., Washington, D.C.

Phelps, Clyde Wm. *The Role of the Sales Finance Companies in the American Economy*. Studies in Consumer Credit, No. 1. Baltimore: Commercial Credit Company, 1952.

————. *Installment Sales Financing: Its Services to the Dealer*. Studies in Consumer Credit, No. 2, 1953.

————. *Financing the Instalment Purchases of the American Family*. Studies in Consumer Credit, No. 3, 1954.

————. *Using Instalment Credit*. Studies in Consumer Credit, No. 4, 1955.

Proceedings of the National Consumer Credit Conference. The eleventh annual conference was held in 1959. The *Proceedings* contain many excellent papers on various aspects of consumer credit.

U.S. Senate Subcommittee on Banking and Currency. *Consumer Credit Labeling Bill*. Hearings on S. 2755, a bill to assist in the promotion of economic stabilization by requiring the disclosure of finance charges in connection with extensions of credit. 86th Cong., 2nd sess. Washington, D.C.: Government Printing Office, 1960. This set of hearings contains many excellent statements on the subject of consumer credit by representatives of institutions involved in consumer credit, Federal Reserve officials, members of Congress, and professors.

part 4: Nonfinancial business sectors

I N the flow-of-funds system of accounts, a private business transactor or firm is classified as either a financial or a nonfinancial business firm. It is so termed because it is one of the purposes of the system of accounts to reveal the flow of funds into and out of financial institutions; that is, to reveal the functional role of those institutions in our modern economy. As pointed out in Chapters 2 and 3, there are also important differences between financial and nonfinancial firms and among financial firms. There are four financial institution sectors: commercial banking, savings institutions, insurance, and finance not elsewhere classified; and there are three nonfinancial business sectors: farm, non-corporate, and corporate.

The assignment of nonfinancial firms into three separate business sectors reflects the fact that financial requirements and the means of meeting them are different for all types of nonfinancial business firms. In the flow-of-funds system of accounts it is recognized that there are many differences between non-farm and farm business firms, and between non-farm corporate and non-farm non-corporate business firms. The unique nature of farming and the development of an elaborate system of public and semi-public sources of farm credit are among the reasons for setting up a farm sector. Similar reasons explain the division of non-farm business firms into the corporate and non-corporate sectors. Some equity and credit market instruments, such as corporate stocks and bonds, can only be issued by corporations. The market for corporate securities is very different from the capital markets available to unincorporated firms. Consumers may go to the same financial institutions for both short- and long-term credit, but businesses must generally seek out different institutions for short- and long-term credit. The long-term credit market is limited primarily to incorporated firms. In practice, unincorporated firms find that long-term credit is either unobtainable or very difficult to obtain.

The corporate business sector is comprised of all private, nonfinancial, non-agricultural corporations. Almost all of our financial institutions, including those of the mutual type, are incorporated, but since their major activity is of a financial nature, they are excluded from the sector. Also excluded are certain financial activities of nonfinancial corporations, such as pension, welfare, and profit-sharing plans. It will be recalled that these activities were discussed in the chapters dealing with pensions and insurance. The incorporated nonprofit organizations are also excluded; these were considered in conjunction with consumers. It should also be pointed out that in the flow-of-funds system of accounts the closed-end investment companies are included in the corporate business sector because of the difficulty of distinguishing between these and holding companies that are clearly a part of the nonfinancial non-corporate business sector.

The non-corporate business sector consists of all private, nonfinancial, non-agricultural unincorporated business firms. As noted earlier, consumer activities of business proprietors are part of the consumer and nonprofit organization sector. The lessorship activities of individuals are considered part of the non-corporate sector, as are the nonprofit organizations that serve business, e.g., trade associations.

The farm sector covers all farm operating enterprises, including corporate farms as well as the farm activities of non-farm landlords of farm property and farm credit cooperatives. The inclusion of the latter type of transactor is one of the few exceptions to the segregation of financial institutions. The farm marketing, purchasing, and utility cooperatives are considered part of the non-farm, non-corporate nonfinancial business sector. As remarked earlier, the non-farm business activities of farm families and most of their consumer activities (other than housing) are excluded from the farm sector.

In Part 3 we dealt primarily with the flow of funds into financial institutions. Part 4 deals primarily with the flow of funds from financial institutions to the three nonfinancial business sectors. The structure and financial positions of the three business sectors are reviewed, their need for outside funds is established, and the flow of funds to the sectors is analyzed. Within this framework the facilitating roles of various financial institutions are also examined.

16: Structure
and financial position
of corporate and
non-corporate business
sectors

W E shall now examine the over-all perspective of the corporate and non-corporate, non-farm business sectors. The business population, including financial firms, will be examined in terms of legal form of organization, number of firms, and size of firms. In the last part of the chapter, we shall deal with the financial positions of the non-farm, nonfinanical business sectors.

LEGAL FORM OF ORGANIZATION*

The legal form of organization is the basis upon which the flow-of-funds system of accounts divides non-farm business enterprises into two sectors: non-corporate and corporate. The non-corporate sector consists almost entirely of sole proprietorships and partnerships; the corporate sector consists of corporations, business trusts, and joint-stock companies; the latter two are quite similar to the corporate form of organization. Only about 2 or 3 per cent of the firms included in the corporate sector are either business trusts or joint-stock companies.

Division of the non-farm business enterprises into two sectors permits a more meaningful analysis of the flow of funds to business, because the credit and market instruments of corporations are the primary investment media of many savings and thrift institutions. Furthermore, the securities

*Almost all the data contained in this section are drawn from Betty C. Churchill, "Business Population by Legal Form of Organization," Survey of Current Business, April 1955, pp. 14-20.

industry has developed in response to the need for facilitating the issue, distribution, and trading in credit and equity market instruments of corporations.

Inasmuch as the legal form of organization will have been studied in basic economics and accounting courses, we shall examine only a few characteristics of the different legal forms of organization. The unique characteristic of the corporation is that it is a legal entity. That is, the corporation is legally separate and distinct from those who own it. Almost everyone thinks of a business unit as being separate from its owners, but only the corporation is so considered in a legal sense. The corporation has the legal status of a person, although it is a fictitious person. Neither a sole proprietorship nor a partnership is a legal entity; the owner(s) and the firm are one. Such firms are legally recognized as either natural persons or groups of natural persons.

Each legal form of organization has both advantages and disadvantages when it is compared with other legal organizations. It is not our purpose to explain all the factors that a person or group of persons should consider in deciding on the legal form of organization. It is sufficient to mention that if a business firm must raise a relatively large amount of capital, it must draw on numerous sources of funds, and to do so, it must be able to issue various types of credit and equity market instruments. Therefore, it must adopt the corporate form of organization. Generally, a successful corporation can operate perpetually, even though its ownership may change daily. Large corporate firms that are capable of operating indefinitely are able to turn over their debt instruments instead of retiring or reducing their debt obligations. Also, investors holding an ownership interest in a corporation have limited liability with respect to the debts of the business. The liability of owners is restricted to the amounts invested. In owner-managed corporations, lenders may require that promissory notes represent obligations of both the firms and the owner(s). In these instances, limited liability is not a vital consideration.

If a business firm is not required to raise a relatively large amount of capital, then there is real choice in most instances as to legal form of organization. Generally, the non-corporate form of organization offers the relative advantages of ease of formation, minimum regulation, and possible tax advantages. If most of the income earned by a business is to be paid out to its owners, the corporate form may prove undesirable because of double taxation. The corporate income is subject to the corporate income tax and the dividend income, after allowance for nominal credits, is taxed as personal income. However, if the owners were not dependent on income from the business and there were legitimate uses for funds retained in the business, then the corporate form would probably be the more desirable. The tax factor is so important that if the decision were to turn on this factor, elaborate assumptions and calculations would be necessary in each instance. Non-corporate firms secure most of their long-term and permanent funds from owners' savings and from loans secured by mortgages on family and business property.

If we consider the number of private non-agricultural enterprises, the sole proprietorship is the most prevalent legal form of organization. In 1947, individually owned businesses comprised nearly 70 per cent of all firms, excluding those classified as farms and those performing professional services. In terms of major industry classifications, the sole proprietorship is most important in the service industry and least important in mining and manufacturing. Obviously, both partnerships and corporations are well outnumbered by sole proprietorships. In 1947, partnerships accounted for 17 per cent of all firms, and corporations accounted for 11 per cent. The remaining 2 per cent was accounted for by mutual firms, estates, trusts, receiverships, and corporations organized under special state laws.

Although the origin of the corporate form of organization can be traced back to the Romans if we use historical analogies, the corporate form as it exists in our modern economy rests largely upon a body of legislation formulated during the 19th century. The passage of general corporate laws, under which a group of qualified persons can form a corporation by the proper filing of legal documents and the payment of required fees, prompted extremely rapid growth in the number of corporations during the 19th century. From 1900 to 1940, the rate of growth was about the same as that for the total business population. During the postwar period, the growth in the number of corporations has been slightly greater than the growth in the other forms of organization, and in 1959 corporations accounted for nearly 13 per cent of all non-farm business firms, excluding those engaged in professional services.

From the standpoint of employment and origination of national income, the corporate form is clearly predominant, since approximately 75 per cent of private non-agricultural national income and employment, outside the professions, originates in firms that are incorporated. In industries that require large-scale operations or heavy capital investment, almost all of the employment and income originate in corporations. It is generally agreed that the modern corporation is one of the most important social and economic institutions.

NUMBER OF NON-FARM BUSINESS FIRMS *

Excluding the activities classified in agriculture and the professional services, there were 4,589,000 non-farm business firms in operation at the beginning of 1959. In compiling business population statistics, the Department of

*Almost all the data contained in this section are drawn from Betty C. Churchill, "Rise in Business Population," Survey of Current Business, May 1959, pp. 15-19, 26.

Commerce does not consider a self-employed person a business firm unless that person has either at least one paid employee or an established place of business. The firms included in compiling commerce data account for approximately 85 per cent of the income originating in the private economy and about the same percentage of all non-governmental wage-earning and salaried workers.

In the long run, the rate of growth in the number of business firms has exceeded the growth in population, but in recent years the rates of growth of the two have been about the same. For example, there were 21 firms for each 1,000 persons in 1900, and in 1948 the number had risen to approximately 27 per 1,000 persons. Since 1948, the number has remained relatively constant. The growth in the number of firms reflects the underlying growth of total output and aggregate demand. During both the Great Depression and World War II, the ratio of firms to population declined.

The number of business firms by major industry groups is shown in Table 16-1. By far the greatest number of firms are involved in retail trade, which accounted for 42.6 per cent of all firms in operation in January, 1959. The service industries ranked second, accounting for 19.0 per cent. Finance,

TABLE 16–1
NUMBERS OF FIRMS IN OPERATION JANUARY 1, 1959 BY INDUSTRY GROUPS*
(NUMBERS IN THOUSANDS)

Industry groups	Number	Per cent of total
All industries	4,589.2	100.0
Mining and quarrying	42.0	.9
Contract construction	475.9	10.4
Manufacturing	331.0	7.2
Transportation, communication, and other public utilities	211.8	4.6
Wholesale trade	317.0	7.1
Retail trade	1,956.3	42.6
Finance, insurance, and real estate	403.3	8.8
Service industries	851.9	19.0

*Business population statistics relate to the entire private economy of the United States, excluding activities classified in agriculture and the professional services. Data for Alaska and Hawaii not included in table.

Note: Details may not add to totals because of rounding.

Source: *Survey of Current Business*, May 1959.

insurance, and real estate firms numbered over 400,000, and accounted for 8.8 per cent of all firms.

During each year there is a turnover in business concerns. New firms are established and some existing firms are either discontinued or transferred to other businesses. In the long run, there is a small net annual gain in the number of firms. Between 1950 and 1958, it averaged 60,000. The year 1958 serves to illustrate the nature of business turnover. During that year, 411,000 firms were newly established, 356,000 firms discontinued operations, and 372,000 going concerns were sold, reorganized, or otherwise acquired by new owners. Of the firms that discontinued operations, about half were liquidated in order to prevent or minimize a loss. Slightly fewer than 5 per cent of the firms that discontinued business operations resulted in a known loss to creditors. No attempt will be made at this point to develop the connection between the financial system and the number and turnover of business firms. It is sufficient to mention that inadequate or inappropriate financing has been and will probably continue to be an important factor in business failures. However, it must also be realized that over 400,000 new firms are established annually, proving that the present financial system is not holding down unduly the formation and operation of new firms.

SIZE OF BUSINESS FIRMS*

Various criteria may be used to classify the size of business firms, including number of employees, total assets, fixed investment, sales, and net income. The analysis in this section is based mainly on the number of employees.

The size characteristics of the business population in terms of employee-size classes are shown in Table 16-2. The patterns shown in this table probably resemble closely those existing in the early 1960's, because the relative distribution of firms and their employment by size of firm tend to change slowly. In 1956, the top 1 per cent of business firms, consisting of those which employed 100 or more, furnished 60.1 per cent of all paid employment; the top 5 per cent of the firms accounted for 76.4 per cent of all paid employment. Firms with less than four employees accounted for nearly 75 per cent of all firms, but only 6.5 per cent of all paid employment. As an illustration of differences among industries, it may be noted that retail trade firms with less than four employees accounted for 79 per cent of all such firms, but only 14.7 per cent of all paid employment in retail trade. The figures for firms in the service industries were nearly the same. In manufacturing, firms of this size accounted for 43 per cent of all manufacturing firms, but only 0.9 per cent of all paid employment in manufacturing.

The relationship between the size of firms and legal form of organization is clearly revealed in Figure 16-1. At the lower end of the employee-size classes, the sole proprietorship firm accounts for about 80 per cent of the firms, but as the employee-size classes get larger, the corporate form of organization becomes predominant. Less than 4 per cent of the firms with 100 or more employees are sole proprietorships. The chart shows that firm size has only a moderate effect upon the use of the partnership form of organization. However, in the financial segment of the economy, there

*Almost all the data contained in this section are drawn from Betty C. Churchill, "Size of Business Firms," *Survey of Current Business*, September 1959, pp. 14-20.

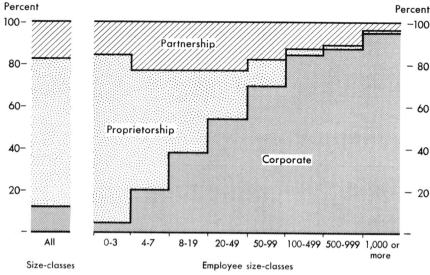

FIGURE 16-1   **DISTRIBUTION OF FIRMS BY LEGAL FORM OF ORGANIZATION FOR EACH EMPLOYEE-SIZE CLASS, 1947***

Source: *Survey of Current Business*, May 1955, p. 17.

has recently occurred a shift from the partnership to the corporate form, especially among the larger broker-dealer firms.

TABLE 16–2
NUMBER FIRMS AND PAID EMPLOYMENT BY EMPLOYEE-SIZE CLASSES, 1956*

Employee-size class	Number of firms as a percentage of total number of firms	Percentage of all paid employment in mid-March, 1956
All size classes	100.0%	100.0%
0 – 3	75.3	6.5
4 – 7	11.6	6.6
8 – 19	8.1	10.5
20 – 49	3.1	10.1
50 – 99	1.0	7.4
100 – 499	.7	15.2
500 – 999	.1	5.6
1,000 or more	.1	38.1

Note: Firms in the business population as here defined provide employment to about 85 per cent of all non-governmental wage-earning and salaried workers. Early in 1956, 40.7 million employees were associated with 4.4 million firms.
Source: *Survey of Current Business*, September 1959.

It is interesting to note that in 1947, four out of five firms with 100 or more employees were corporations, but that more than 90 per cent of all corporations were firms of smaller size. More than one-fourth of the corporations had fewer than four employees, and nearly 75 per cent had fewer than 20 employees.

Meaning of "Small Business"

A subject closely related to the topic of size of business firms is the meaning of " small business." In the past decade " small business " has become one of the most widely used classifications in the study of financing business. Nevertheless, it has remained an elusive concept, because of the extreme variations among different kinds of small business. The differences in financial needs between a small manufacturing firm and a small retail outlet are much greater than the differences between a small and a large manufacturing firm. In spite of the difficulties, various criteria have been used in the attempt to identify small business, including employee-size classes, total assets, volume of sales, and net income. If small business is defined to include all firms with fewer than 100 employees, approximately 99 per cent of all firms fall within the classification. If the cut-off point is 500 employees, the percentage becomes 99.7. Obviously, such cut-off points are not very meaningful.

The problem of defining small business was well stated in a background study prepared for a congressional committee: " No generally accepted definition of small business exists, and it is quite obvious that the same criteria cannot be used in different segments of the economy. Whatever set of criteria may be chosen, the resulting numbers are to a certain degree arbitrary: the resulting delineation of the universe is neither sharp nor unequivocal."* There is no simple criterion for determining where small business begins and ends. When help to small business is set up as a goal of public policy, it is questionable whether or not help should be extended to all small firms. The owners of some small firms are no more than agents for larger firms. Some small firms are set up to provide only supplementary income to their owners. In contrast, many of the small manufacturing firms want to grow and exploit new processes or new products. Should a firm, just because it is small, be entitled to special considerations? Should only certain types of small businesses be so treated? It is much easier to raise these questions than it is to answer them.

An excellent statement on the problem of relating the meaning of small business to public policy is set forth in Mr. Garvy's study:†

"... public policy based on economic considerations cannot be equally concerned with all businesses that are small, nor should it be interested

---

*George Garvey, "Observations Based on the Background Studies," in U.S. Committees on Banking and Currency, and the Select Committees on Small Business," *Financing Small Business,* Report by the Federal Reserve System, Parts 1 and 2, 85th Cong., 2nd sess. (Washington, D.C.: Government Printing Office, 1958), p. 1. Hereafter referred to as *Financing Small Business.*

†*Ibid.,* p. 3.

in promoting any concern merely because it is small. Some criteria are needed to identify the types of small concerns that are making a real contribution to the maintenance of competition and to economic vitality and growth, and to sort out any which may have little economic basis for special consideration, or which may even involve a clear uneconomic allocation of human, physical, and financial resources. This is one of the most difficult aspects of any public program of financial assistance, and clearly argues for an experimental approach until more experience is gained. In addition there may be social reasons for supporting and promoting certain types of small concerns that are not economically competitive (for example, businesses suitable for handicapped people), and whose support may even make possible a net economic gain over time."

It is appropriate at this point to recognize the size standards that are used in determining eligibility for financial assistance from the Small Business Administration, which is the Federal Government's primary lending agency to small business. A manufacturing firm is considered small if it employs 250 or fewer persons, including employees of affiliates; it is considered large if it employs more than 1,000 persons. If a firm has more than 250 but less than 1,000 employees, its size classification depends upon the type of manufacturing activity. Non-manufacturing firms are classified according to annual sales or receipts. For example, a wholesale firm is considered small if its annual sales are less than $5 million; a retail or service firm is considered small if its annual sales or receipts are less than $1 million.

In the 1957 Federal Reserve business loan surveys, total assets were used as the criterion for classifying borrowers as " small," " medium," or " large " in each industry. For example, a " small business " in metals and metal products was identified as one with total assets under $5 million; a " small business " in construction was defined as one with total assets under $50,000. The size classes were designed so as to include a significant number of firms in each classification.

Before considering the aggregate financial position of non-farm business firms, it is appropriate to comment on the extent to which financial institutions have hindered or encouraged the formation and growth of individual firms. The degree of risk involved in the formation and operation of new firms has prevented many of our private, high-leverage financial institutions from providing optimum financial assistance.* The financial system has lagged in its development of institutions to finance the growth and development of small firms, which, from a production point of view, have the potential of becoming more efficient and competitive if permitted a more rapid rate of growth. In other words, our system has not provided an optimum rate of risk capital formation in this segment of the economy. The problem has been serious enough to warrant a limited amount of government

---

*"High leverage" is the term applied to a financial institution whose capital accounts are very small in relation to its total assets.

intervention in the form of government loans and guarantees to "small business." At the same time, our financial system has promoted and facilitated the growth of large business firms. Generally, large corporations have raised a large amount of outside capital, issued various types of credit and equity market instruments fitted to the needs of savings and insurance institutions, and utilized underwriting and distribution services provided by the investment banking industry. Furthermore, many mergers and consolidations have been conceived by and carried out by investment bankers. In summary, the financial system has been more helpful to the large business enterprises than it has to the development of small- and medium-sized business enterprises.

FINANCIAL POSITION OF NON-FARM BUSINESS SECTORS

The financial position of the non-farm business sectors is reviewed in two types of financial statements: a statement of financial assets and liabilities, and a statement of sources and uses of funds. The former statement shows financial position at a given time and reflects the cumulative effects of all previous financing; the latter type of statement shows the changes in the balance sheet between two dates, and reflects the uses to which funds were put and the manner in which they were raised.

Although the basic ideas underlying these statements were presented in Chapters 2 and 3, it may still be valuable to review these statements. The assets of business represent the uses of or the investment of funds; the liabilities and stockholders' equity represent the sources of funds or methods of financing. By comparing balance sheets between two dates, it is possible to summarize the changes in assets, liabilities, and stockholders' equity by means of a statement of sources and uses of funds. Such a statement does not provide an indication of the total cash or funds flow; instead it portrays only shifts among various assets and liabilities and the expansion or contraction in the total funds employed. It does not portray the continuous flow of funds from cash into non-cash assets and back into cash. An increase in an asset represents a use of funds; an increase in a liability or stockholders' equity represents a source of funds. A decrease in an asset is a source of funds, and a decrease in a liability or stockholders' equity is a use of funds.

Sources of funds are classified under two headings, internal and external. Internal sources, or those within a business, consist of net savings and capital consumption. Net savings is equal to profits minus inventory valuation adjustment, profits tax payments, and net dividend payments. Inventory valuation adjustment reflects the fact that profits are affected by changes in the prices of materials included in inventory, and the adjustment is made to exclude inventory gains and losses relating to the pricing of inventory. Capital consumption consists of charges of depreciation, amortization, and accidental damage. If capital consumption were not charged against revenue, the final profit figure would be that much larger. Although capital consumption charges refer to specific assets, no cash is actually paid out. Management may decide to allocate the funds retained through capital consumption in any of a number of ways. Obviously, if a firm is to maintain modern plant and equipment, funds will have to be allocated eventually to capital replacement. External sources, or those outside the individual business firm, are broken down on the basis of maturity: short- and intermediate-term and long-term.

Uses of funds are classified under two headings, capital expenditures and net acquisition of financial assets. Capital expenditures consist of private business purchases of plant and equipment (including business purchases of residential construction), and net changes in private business inventories. The latter refers to change in physical volume of inventory valued at average prices. Capital expenditures represent business investment in tangible assets. The net acquisition of financial assets represents business investment in financial assets. In the long run, the business sectors must increase their holdings of financial and tangible assets. Generally, an increase in sales requires that additional funds be tied up or invested in cash balances, near-money assets, receivables, and inventory. Also, as United States businesses expand their operations abroad, direct investments in foreign branches and holdings of foreign cash are increased.

Corporate Business Sector

FINANCIAL ASSETS AND LIABILITIES. The financial assets and liabilities of the corporate nonfinancial business sector at the end of 1958 are shown in Table 16-3. The data show that the sector had $75 billion of funds tied up in trade credit, and this item accounted for slightly more than 45 per cent of the sector's total holdings of financial assets. However, it should be noted that the major portion of trade credit represented interbusiness lending. If the sector's trade debt was offset against its trade credit, net use of funds relating to trade credit would amount to only $22.7 billion. The importance of liquidity is reflected in the sector's holdings of $33.7 billion of currency and demand deposits, $18.4 billion of Federal obligations, and $1.6 billion of time deposits. Other holdings of financial assets included consumer credit, other loans, foreign currency and deposits, and direct investment abroad.

As a guide to the relative importance of liabilities, it should be noted that at the end of 1954,* the total stockholders' equity (net worth) of all nonfinancial corporations was 52.8 per cent, and for corporations with assets under $250,000, net worth accounted for 48.2 per cent of total liabilities and

*United States Internal Revenue Service, *Statistics of Income, 1954,* Part II, Corporation Tax Returns.

net worth. The data suggest that credit transactions provide about 50 per cent of the funds employed in the corporate business sector. Most of the credit transactions involve credit market instruments, particularly corporate bonds, mortgages, and bank loans not elsewhere classified.

TABLE 16–3
FINANCIAL ASSETS AND LIABILITIES OF CORPORATE NONFINANCIAL
BUSINESS SECTOR, END OF 1958
(BILLIONS OF DOLLARS)

	Dollars	Per cent
Financial Assets		
Financial Assets	164.7	100.0
Credit market instruments	27.6	16.8
Federal obligations	18.4	11.2
Consumer credit	7.5	4.6
Other loans	1.7	1.0
Trade credit	75.0	45.5
Miscellaneous financial assets [1]	26.7	16.2
Fixed-value redeemable claims:		
Time deposits	1.6	1.0
Cash balances — currency and demand deposits	33.7	20.5
Liabilities		
Liabilities	179.0	100.0
Credit market instruments	121.7	68.0
Corporate bonds	69.2	38.7
Mortgages on 1- to 4-family properties [2]	1.5	.8
Other mortgages	27.5	15.4
Bank loans, n.e.c.	19.8	11.1
Other loans	3.7	2.1
Trade debt	52.3	29.2
Miscellaneous financial liabilities	5.0	2.8

Note: Details may not add to totals because of rounding.
[1] Foreign currency and deposits and direct investment abroad.
[2] Construction loans.
Source: "A Quarterly Presentation of Flow of Funds, Saving and Investment," *Federal Reserve Bulletin*, August 1959, p. 1058.

SOURCES AND USES OF FUNDS. The sources and uses of funds of the corporate nonfinancial business sector for the period 1955-1958 are shown in Table 16-4. Internal sources accounted for two-thirds of the total, with capital consumption about three times as important as net savings (retained earnings). In the table, Federal obligations are shown as a source of funds. Normally, Federal obligations represent a use of funds, but over this four-year period, the business sector reduced its holdings of Federal obligations by $700 million. As for external sources, the long-term and permanent sources provided more than twice the amount of funds obtained from short- and intermediate-term sources, the latter of which include credit transactions having a maturity up to ten years. Within the category "long-term and permanent," credit transactions, in the form of net new issues of corporate bonds and mortgages, were twice as important as net new issues of corporate stocks. However, it should be noted that net savings is also a form of equity

TABLE 16–4
SOURCES AND USES OF FUNDS OF THE CORPORATE NONFINANCIAL
BUSINESS SECTOR, 1955-1958
(BILLIONS OF DOLLARS)

Sources of Funds	Dollars	Per cent
Internal Sources	105.3	66.6
Net savings [1]	26.3	16.6
Capital consumption	79.0	49.9
External Sources	52.9	33.4
Federal obligations [2]	.7	.4
Short and intermediate-term	16.4	10.4
Bank loans, n.e.c.	3.4	2.2
Other loans	.9	.6
Trade debt	12.1	7.6
Long-term and permanent	35.8	22.6
Corporate stocks	9.0	5.7
Corporate bonds	18.7	11.8
Mortgages	8.1	5.1
Total Sources	158.2	100.0
Uses of Funds		
Capital expenditures	117.4	74.2
Fixed investment	111.3	70.4
Plant and equipment	106.8	67.5
Other	4.6	2.9
Changes in inventory [3]	6.2	3.9
Net acquisition of financial assets	31.2	19.7
Currency and demand deposits	2.7	1.7
Credit market instruments	1.1	.7
Consumer credit	1.3	.8
Other loans (finance paper)	.5	.3
Trade credit	21.1	13.3
Other financial assets [4]	6.0	3.8
Total Uses	149.3	94.4
Statistical discrepancy	8.9	5.6

Note: Details may not add to totals because of rounding.

[1] Net savings equals profits, after inventory valuation, minus net profits, tax payments, and net dividend payments. In 1958, the dollar figures (in billions) for these items were: profits, $31.0; net profits tax payments, $18.8; net dividend payments, $9.5.

[2] Normally, Federal obligations represent a use of funds, but over this four-year period there was a net liquidation; hence, it appears as a source of funds.

[3] After inventory valuation adjustment.

[4] Direct investment in foreign branches and holdings of foreign cash.

Source: Data derived from "A Quarterly Presentation of Flow of Funds, Saving and Investment," *Federal Reserve Bulletin*, August 1959.

financing, and the combined total of net savings and net new issues of corporate stock for the four-year period was $8.5 billion greater than the total of corporate bonds and mortgages.

Short- and intermediate-term sources of funds provided slightly more than 10 per cent of the additional funds employed by corporate nonfinancial business firms during the period 1955-1958. If trade credit were offset against trade debt, bank loans, n.e.c. would represent the major source of short-term and intermediate-term funds.

Capital expenditures by corporate nonfinancial business firms accounted for nearly three-fourths of total uses of funds, of which plant and equipment were the major item. The additional fixed investment of $111.3 billion exceeded capital consumption by $32.3 billion, reflecting higher costs of replacement and net expansion in the stock of capital goods. During the four-year period, an additional $6.2 billion was invested in inventory. During shorter periods of time, such as quarterly or annually, inventories might be reduced and might thus be a source of funds (negative use of funds). For example, in 1958 inventories were reduced by $4.8 billion, but over a longer period, such as the four-year period under review in this section, an increase in inventories can be expected. However, if boom conditions prevailed at the beginning of the period and recession conditions at the end, the data would probably show a reduction in inventories although four or five years had passed. The use of the four-year period also covers up large annual changes in the amounts invested in Federal obligations. In 1955, the sector increased its holdings of Federal obligations by $4.4 billion; in 1956 and 1957, the sector drew down its holdings of Federal obligations, $4.3 billion in 1956 and $1.5 billion in 1957; in 1958, the sector acquired $0.7 billion of Federal obligations. The changes reflect the changing liquidity needs of the corporate business sector in relation to over-all business conditions and the availability of credit.

Financial Position of Non-corporate Business Sector

FINANCIAL ASSETS AND LIABILITIES. The financial assets and liabilities of the non-corporate non-financial business sector at the end of 1958 are shown in Table 16-5. Compared with the corporate sector, it should be noted that the amount and distribution of the non-corporate sector's assets differ widely. At the end of 1958, the non-corporate sector's financial assets totaled only $25.6 billion, whereas the corporate sector's holdings were $164.7 billion. The difference in magnitudes reflects the dominant role of the corporation in the American economy. Cash balances, expressed as a percentage of the sector's financial assets, are much more important in the non-corporate sector. For example, in 1958 the non-corporate sector's cash balances accounted for 51.2 per cent of the sector's financial assets; the corresponding percentage in the corporate sector was 20.5 per cent. The reason for this difference consists of two factors. One, corporate business uses Federal obligations as well as

TABLE 16–5
FINANCIAL ASSETS AND LIABILITIES OF THE NON-CORPORATE, NONFINANCIAL
BUSINESS SECTOR, END OF 1958
(BILLIONS OF DOLLARS)

	Dollars	Per cent
Financial Assets		
Financial assets	25.6	100.0
Consumer credit	5.1	19.9
Trade credit	7.3	28.5
Cash balances — currency and demand deposits......	13.1	51.2
Liabilities		
Liabilities	52.7	100.0
Credit market instruments	42.1	79.9
Mortgages on 1- to 4-family properties [1]	5.1	9.7
Multi-family and commercial mortgages	13.7	26.0
Bank loans, n.e.c.	16.9	32.1
Other loans [2]	6.3	12.0
Trade debt	10.6	20.1

Note: Details may not add to totals because of rounding.
[1] Construction loans.
[2] Mainly loans from finance companies and from the Federal Government.
Source: "A Quarterly Presentation of Flow of Funds, Saving and Investment," *Federal Reserve Bulletin*, August 1959.

cash balances to satisfy its need for liquidity. If Federal obligations were combined with cash balances, the difference between the two percentages would be reduced by 11.2 per cent. Two, there is a much larger number of independent business units in the non-corporate sector, so that there is less economy in the use of cash balances to carry on a given volume of business activity. The large-scale business unit allows economy in the use of cash balances as well as in the use of physical materials. Only 28.5 per cent of the non-corporate sector's financial assets were tied up in the form of trade credit, compared with 45.5 per cent in the corporate sector. The difference between the sectors reflects the small amount of interbusiness lending among firms in the non-corporate business sector and the net flow of trade credit from the larger (corporations) to the smaller (non-corporate) firms.

The liabilities of the non-corporate sector are approximately twice as great as its financial assets, whereas the corporate sector's liabilities were not much greater than financial assets. Unlimited liability of the owners of non-corporate firms provides an explanation for part of the difference between the two sectors. Part of the consumer sector's financial assets serve as a backstop to the financial assets in the non-corporate sector. Instead of holding Federal obligations to back up cash balances, many non-corporate firms may look to personal assets. Also, part of the difference might be accounted for by the inability of many non-corporate firms to attain a satisfactory degree of liquidity. For example, if the long-term liabilities were removed from the table, the ratio of financial assets to liabilities would still be less than one to one.

Since the non-corporate firms cannot utilize as many different sources of funds as corporate firms can, the importance of each type of liability differs between the two sectors. Mortgages accounted for 35.7 per cent of total liabilities in the non-corporate sector and 16.2 per cent in the corporate sector. It might also be noted that mortgages on one- to four-family properties accounted for nearly a third of total liabilities secured by mortgages. In the corporate sector, bonds as well as mortgages were used to secure long-term credit. Probably less than 20 per cent of the non-corporate sector's liabilities represent long-term credit, compared with over 50 per cent in the corporate sector. At the end of 1958, bank loans, n.e.c. was the sector's largest single source of borrowed funds. It is interesting to note that the volume of bank loans, n.e.c. owed by the corporate sector was only $3 billion greater than the amount owed by the non-corporate sector, showing the importance of commercial banks to non-corporate firms. The relative importance of other loans to the non-corporate sector stems from their need for loans from finance companies and government agencies. Many of the larger, corporate firms do not resort to finance companies, and many are not eligible for government loans. The excess of trade debt over trade credit indicates that the sector is a net user of trade credit.

SOURCES AND USES OF FUNDS. The sources and uses of funds of the non-corporate nonfinancial sector for the period 1955-1958 are shown in Table 16-6. Before we comment on the sources of funds, we must offer a definition of the term "proprietors' net disinvestment." In the four-year period, the sector's capital consumption allowances and increase in liabilities exceeded its investment expenditures. Rather than record this difference as a negative source of funds, we record it as a use of funds and refer to it as "proprietors' net disinvestment." Internal sources of funds are not quite as important in the non-corporate sector as they are in the corporate sector. The small size of the individual non-corporate firms probably accounts for this fact. A study of sources of funds in the corporate sector reveals that large corporations derived approximately 63 per cent of their financing from internal sources during the period 1946-1955. Excluding the 300 largest corporations from the data, internal sources provided only 55 per cent of total sources. The data indicate a direct relationship between firm size and the relative importance of internal sources of funds.* The data in Table 16-6 show that the major portion of short- and intermediate-term funds was provided by bank loans, n.e.c. and trade debt.

*V. L. Andrews, Seymour Friedland, and Eli Shapiro, "Who Finances Small Business?" *Financing Small Business*, p. 22.

TABLE 16–6
SOURCES AND USES OF FUNDS OF THE NON-CORPORATE, NONFINANCIAL
BUSINESS SECTOR, 1955-1958
(BILLIONS OF DOLLARS)

	Dollars	Per cent
Sources of Funds		
Internal sources	30.6	61.9
Capital consumption	30.6	61.9
External sources	18.7	37.8
Short and intermediate term	14.7	29.8
Bank loans, n.e.c.	8.3	16.8
Other loans	1.8	3.6
Trade debt	4.6	9.3
Long-term and permanent	4.0	8.1
Mortgages	4.0	8.1
Total Sources	49.3	99.8
Statistical discrepancy	0.1	0.2
Uses of Funds		
Capital expenditures	39.8	80.6
Plant and equipment	39.1	79.1
Change in inventories	.8	1.6
Net acquisition of financial assets	3.2	6.5
Currency and demand deposits	2.2	4.4
Consumer credit	.9	1.8
Proprietors' net disinvestment [1]	6.4	13.0
Total Uses	49.4	100.0

Note: Details may not add to totals because of rounding.

[1] In the four-year period under consideration, capital consumption allowances and increase in liabilities exceeded investment expenditures; therefore "proprietors' net disinvestment" is shown as a use of funds.

Source: Data derived from "A Quarterly Presentation of Flow of Funds, Saving and Investment," *Federal Reserve Bulletin*, August 1959.

As for uses of funds, the non-corporate sector employed a greater percentage of its funds in financing capital expenditures than did the corporate sector. The major difference between the two sectors during the four-year period was the rather large disinvestment of proprietors compared with the sizeable increase in net new issues of common stock.

QUESTIONS

1. Why is a distinction drawn between corporate and non-corporate non-farm businesses in the flow-of-funds system of accounts?

2. Explain the unique characteristics of the corporate form of organization.

3. If a business firm must have a large amount of capital, it must adopt the corporate form of organization. Explain.

4. Under what conditions would it be unwise for a firm to adopt the corporate form of organization?

5. Approximately how many non-farm business firms were in operation in 1959? What proportion of this number were corporations? Is it the best measure or guide to the importance of corporations? Explain.

6. What is meant by " business turnover "?

7. The concept of " small business " is very elusive. Explain.

8. How has our financial system facilitated the growth of large business?

9. What is meant by a " statement of sources and uses of funds "? Illustrate the major internal and external sources of funds.

10. Indicate the two most important financial assets and liabilities of the corporate and non-corporate nonfinancial business sectors.

11. How important are internal sources of funds in the corporate and non-corporate nonfinancial business sectors?

ADDITIONAL READING

All of the references cited below are applicable to Chapters 16 through 20.

Bradley, Joseph E. *Fundamentals of Corporation Finance.* (Rev. ed.) New York: Holt, Rinehart, & Winston, Inc., 1958.

Dewing, Arthur Stone. *The Financial Policy of Corporations,* Vols. I, II. (5th ed.) New York: The Ronald Press Co., 1953.

Donaldson, Elvin F. *Corporate Finance.* New York: The Ronald Press Co., 1957.

Gerstenberg, Charles W. *Financial Organization and Management of Business.* (4th rev. ed.) Englewood Cliffs, N.J.: Prentice-Hall, Inc., 1959.

Guthman, H. G., and H. E. Dougall. *Corporate Financial Policy.* (3rd ed.) Englewood Cliffs, N.J.: Prentice-Hall, Inc., 1955.

Howard, B. B., and M. Upton. *Introduction to Business Finance.* New York: McGraw-Hill Book Co., Inc., 1953.

Hunt, Pearson, C. M. Williams, and G. Donaldson. *Basic Business Finance.* Homewood, Ill.: Richard D. Irwin, Inc., 1958.

Husband, Wm. H., and James C. Dockeray. *Modern Corporation Finance.* (4th ed.) Homewood, Ill.: Richard D. Irwin, Inc., 1957.

Johnson, R. B. *Financial Management.* Boston: Allyn & Bacon, Inc., 1959.

Jome, Hiram L. *Corporation Finance.* New York: Holt, Rinehart, & Winston, Inc., 1948.

Kent, Raymond P. *Corporate Financial Management.* Homewood, Ill.: Richard D. Irwin, Inc., 1960.

Mason, Edward S. (ed.). *The Corporation in Modern Society.* Cambridge, Mass.: Harvard University Press, 1959.

Meyer, John R., and Edwin Kuh. *The Investment Decision: An Empirical Study.* Cambridge, Mass.: Harvard University Press, 1957.

National Bureau of Economic Research. *Studies in Business Financing,* 1-10. Selected studies are cited at the end of the next three chapters.

Osborn, Richard C. *Corporation Finance.* New York: Harper & Bros., 1959.

Prather, Charles L. *Financing Business Firms*. Homewood, Ill.: Richard D. Irwin, Inc., 1955.

Taylor, W. Bayard. *Financial Policies of Business Enterprise*. (2nd ed.) New York: Appleton-Century-Crofts, Inc., 1956.

Welfing, W. *Financing Business Enterprise*. New York: American Institute of Banking, 1960.

17: Short- and intermediate-term financing, I

IN this chapter and the next, we shall examine short- and intermediate-term financing of the non-farm business sector. The basic outline for these two chapters is based on flow-of-funds transaction categories: trade credit, bank loans, n.e.c., and other loans. Under the heading "bank loans, n.e.c.," we shall discuss commercial and industrial loans that are negotiated between the commercial banks and non-farm businesses. Under the heading "other loans," commercial and finance company open-market paper, commercial financing and factoring, and loans made by state development credit corporations and Federal non-farm lending agencies are considered. All of these financial transactions involve either specialized financing techniques or specialized financial institutions.

TRADE CREDIT

The unique characteristic of trade credit is that it is both a source and a use of funds in the business sectors. The subject could be subtitled "inter-business lending," because almost all outstanding trade credit represents financing that occurs directly between nonfinancial firms. As shown in Table 17-1, nearly all of the trade credit outstanding at the end of 1958 was being extended by firms in the corporate business sector, and over three-fourths of the trade debt was owned by corporate firms. The Federal government was supplying a small amount of trade credit through prepayments and advances to firms working on government contracts; the insurance sector was supplying a limited amount of trade credit through its holdings of receivables owed by agents.

Normally, firms engaged in the intermediate stages of production extend more trade credit than they receive because goods gain in value as they move through the many stages of production. The trade credit data for

TABLE 17–1
TRADE CREDIT OUTSTANDING, END OF 1958
(BILLIONS OF DOLLARS)

Sector	Dollars	Per cent	Trade credit as a percentage of financial assets and trade debt as a percentage of liabilities
Trade credit	85.6	100.0	
Corporate business	75.0	87.6	45.5
Non-farm non-corporate business [1]	7.3	8.5	28.5
Federal Government [2]	1.7	2.0	4.2
Insurance [3]	1.6	1.9	1.1
Trade debt	71.6	100.0	
Corporate business	52.3	73.0	29.2
Non-farm non-corporate business	10.6	14.8	20.2
Farm business	2.1	2.9	11.0
Federal Government [4]	2.8	3.9	1.1
State and local government	2.0	2.8	2.6
Nonprofit organizations	1.8	2.5	

Note: Details may not add to totals because of rounding.
[1] Financial assets and liabilities, without netting receivables against payables.
[2] Prepayments and advances to corporations.
[3] Receivables from agents.
[4] Payables to corporations.
Source: Data derived from "A Quarterly Presentation of Flow of Funds, Saving and Investment," *Federal Reserve Bulletin*, August 1959.

the corporate sector are influenced in an important way by the large corporations and by the extensive use of the corporate form of organization in the intermediate stages of production. As shown in Table 17-1, the corporate business sector at the end of 1958 had $75 billion of trade credit outstanding and owed over $52 billion of trade debt. The firms engaged in the distribution of consumer goods receive much more trade credit than they extend. At this stage, the offsetting transaction is the extension of consumer credit. In fact, the growth in consumer credit has been one of the factors giving rise to the growth in trade credit. Since the points of final distribution consist mainly of small unincorporated firms, the trade debt of the noncorporate business sector exceeds its trade credit.

The data for manufacturing corporations provide some indication of the relationship between size of firm and reliance on trade credit as a source of funds. At the end of 1958, trade payables comprised nearly 18.3 per cent of total liabilities and net worth of manufacturing corporations with assets under $1 million, whereas the comparable figure for all corporations was only 7.8 per cent.* The smaller corporations tend to receive more trade credit than they extend, whereas the opposite relationship prevails among the larger corporations. If receivables were netted against payables, the remainder would probably represent the extension of trade credit to small business.†

The aggregate data shown in Table 17-2 cover up the obscure differences in the relative importance of trade credit among different industries. A few examples will emphasize some of the more extreme differences that existed at the end of 1958:** trade payables of manufacturers of apparel and related finished products were equal to 21.6 per cent of the firms' total liabilities and net worth; the comparable percentage for manufacturers of basic chemicals was only 6.0 per cent.

Reasons for Trade Credit

The reasons underlying trade credit are examined from three points of view: creditor, debtor, and the over-all economy. The decision-making of trade creditors is reviewed in greater detail in a later section dealing with the extention of trade credit.

CREDITOR'S POINT OF VIEW. A firm is able to attract more business by offering to sell goods on credit. If sales volume can be increased with little or no change in physical plant, the unit cost of production will probably be lowered through the spreading of fixed costs over a larger number of units. With no change in price, the per unit and total profit of the firm will be increased.

Theoretically, a credit and collection department should attempt to assign trade debtors to groups based on expected degree of risk, and then extend trade credit to the point at which the expected losses of the marginal group of trade debtors equal the expected gross margin on sales to that group of accounts. If credit extension were stopped short of this point, the firm would not be achieving maximum profits. The same idea can be stated in slightly different terminology. The expected collections from a group of credit accounts, after discounting for risk, should exceed the costs involved in making the sales. So long as some excess remains, the firm should allow further expansion in credit sales until the excess disappears at the margin. A firm may want to go beyond this point at times to maintain production or sales outlets. In summary, trade creditors expect to realize credit losses, but the additional profits are more than adequate to offset these losses.

*Federal Trade Commission and Securities and Exchange Commission, *Quarterly Financial Report for Manufacturing Corporations, First Quarter 1959.*

†"Trade Credit: A Factor in the Rationing of Capital," *Monthly Review of the Kansas City Federal Reserve Bank,* June 1957, pp. 7, 8.

**Quarterly Financial Report.*

DEBTOR'S POINT OF VIEW. Many firms make extensive use of trade debt because they are are unable to secure adequate financing from private lenders. If bank credit is not available or if it has been used to the maximum, few if any additional sources of loan credit might be available. Commercial banks are unable to assume either the costs or the risk commensurate with much of the credit that is granted in the form of trade credit. The seller can assume both because trade credit is primarily a stimulant to sales at a margin of profit well in excess of the margin at which banks operate. The buyer-seller relationship is about the only basis upon which many firms can seek additional credit.

Many firms would not be able to maintain adequate inventories in the absence of trade debt. A recent study of the relationship between trade debt and inventories drew the following tentative conclusions:*

"It is clear, from our interviews and the fragments of data obtained, that a substantial part of the inventories carried by small business may be financed by the use of ordinary accounts receivable credit (trade credit). In a few cases small businesses obtain enough credit from their suppliers to provide them with other working capital as well as to carry their inventories, and in the majority of cases they probably obtain a minimum of one-half of their inventory finance requirements. Furthermore, it is clear that small businesses with well-established relations with their suppliers can slow up their payments if they encounter temporary adversity, or if credit from other sources diminishes, without fearing that the supplier will cut off the flow of merchandise to them. They may also, of course, request extended credit terms on current orders. The fact that future datings of bills for seasonal and special promotions are becoming more widespread indicates that the volume of inventories financed by suppliers is increasing."

The volume of a firm's minimum inventory is just as permanent as plant and equipment and should be financed with long-term or permanent sources of funds if at all possible. To the extent that trade credit permits firms to maintain larger inventories than would otherwise be possible, there are fewer bottlenecks in the processes of production and distribution.

OVER-ALL POINT OF VIEW. Trade credit permits the flow of goods to precede the flow of financial payments. It is inconceivable that the current volume of economic transactions could be accomplished without the use of trade credit. Certainly, the stock of money would be inadequate in its absence.

Trade credit tends to reallocate the capital obtained by the larger corporate firms to the small corporations and unincorporated firms, thereby shifting the demand for loan credit to firms that are relatively more capable of obtaining loan credit. To quote from a recent article, ". . . a firm which is barred from direct access to particular capital markets because of high costs can be financed indirectly by these same capital markets at lower rates because

*Robert S. Einzig, "Credit from Large to Small Business," *Financing Small Business,* p. 489.

of the interposition of a selling firm with a better credit rating."*

Although trade credit represents short-term financing, it turns over continuously, thereby requiring firms that extend trade credit to tie up a portion of their funds permanently in trade receivables. One of the basic principles of business financing is that the long-term and permanent needs or uses of funds should be financed by long-term or permanent sources of funds. Accordingly, a substantial portion of trade credit is financed ultimately in the capital markets. The monthly or seasonal variations in trade credit are generally financed with short-term loan credit from commercial banks and finance companies. Accounts receivable financing, which is discussed in the latter part of this chapter, developed in response to the need to finance trade receivables.

Trade Credit Terms

Trade creditors have much larger gross operating margins and much larger net worths in relation to total assets than do financial firms. As a result, they are able to apply lower standards than financial institutions can in making trade credit decisions. In a recent survey of trade credit extended by large business to small business, it was found that " all respondents indicated that open-book credit is extended to their customers, irrespective of the size of the order, with only few exceptions. In some cases a minimum weight or dollar amount per order or delivery is required, but the amount is so low that most small business would qualify."† Some firms may be more strict than others in policies and practices relating to the extension and collection of trade credit. Nevertheless, in the development of trade credit, particular credit terms become institutionalized, and the pressure of competition tends to force firms within a given line of activity to extend similar credit terms.

An initial request for trade credit is screened by the seller (trade creditor) to determine whether or not the customer is credit-worthy. Generally, the screening process consists of applying credit standards relating to financial position and past payment experience. In response to the need for specific information, general and specialized credit rating services have developed on both a regional and a nationwide basis. At the local level, credit interchange bureaus collect data on payment practices of trade debtors. Other sources of information include commercial banks and direct personal contact with the buyer (trade debtor). Continuation of trade credit to a customer depends almost entirely on the debtor's payment experience. Generally, trade creditors establish maxima on trade credit accounts, and in the event that a buyer requests credit beyond his credit limit, the seller may deny additional credit.

*V. L. Andrews, Seymour Friedland, and Eli Shapiro, "Who Finances Small Business?" *Financing Small Business*, p. 26.

†Robert S. Einzig, "Credit From Large to Small Business," *Financing Small Business*, p. 484.

Normally, trade credit terms allow trade debtors the option of earning cash discounts by reducing credits promptly. For example, if credit terms are stated 2/10, net 30, the trade debtor is permitted to deduct 2 per cent from the stated amount if payment is made within ten days. However, the trade debtor is not required to take the cash discount, and may delay payment for 30 days. Failure to exercise the option to take the discount may prove to be a very expensive source of short-term credit. Continuing the example cited above, assume the trade debtor failed to take advantage of the cash discount in order to delay payment for the additional 20 days. Expressed in terms of an annual rate of interest, the opportunity cost of the 20 days' credit would be 36 per cent. The calculation is very simple: 360 days divided by 20 days times 2 per cent equals 36 per cent. Technically, the rate would be slightly higher because it is a discount type of credit in the sense that the goods would have been fully paid for had the debtor paid an amount equal to 98 per cent of the stated amount.

Considering the diversity in credit terms among the many different industries and stages of production, it is very difficult to generalize. Maturities may range from 10 to 120 days, but the typical maturity is 30 days. The discount period generally runs from 10 to 15 days; in some credit transactions, the discount period refers to the date of the month following shipment of goods. Discounts may range from less than 1 per cent to as much as 10 per cent, but the typical discount is 2 per cent. Long maturities and large discounts are used in industries that are highly seasonal, such as manufacturers of electric fans, fuel oil, and fertilizers. Deferred billings or seasonal datings may provide credit for periods ranging from three to six months. Trade creditors in these and other industries are motivated to offer such terms in order to achieve more stable production and to minimize storage costs.

Other Forms of Interbusiness Lending

Other forms of interbusiness lending include direct cash loans between suppliers and customers, provisions of equipment and supplies, and equipment financing. The provision of equipment and supplies is a form of financing in the sense that customers' funds are not tied up in equipment and supplies, but are available for other uses. If equipment and supplies were not furnished, it would be necessary to secure funds to finance the acquisition and installation of equipment. Equipment financing may involve either an installment sale agreement or a lease. Installment sale paper may be handled in any of three different ways: (1) the supplier may hold the paper until maturity; (2) the supplier may sell the paper to a financial institution, and particularly to a commercial finance company; and (3) the supplier may set up a subsidiary as a specialized financial institution to handle the credit sales of the firm. Commercial finance companies are discussed in the latter part of this chapter.

Annual Flows Into Trade Credit

The annual flows into trade credit during the period 1950-1958 are shown in Table 17-2. The data show a definite upward trend in the volume of trade credit. Among the more important factors underlying the postwar growth in trade credit were a shift from sellers' markets to buyers' markets, greater use of consumer credit, and a change in the structure of the retail segment of the economy. Forward integration has led to larger retail outlets and more aggressive merchandising. The number and variety of goods have required larger and more varied inventories, much of which has been financed by trade credit.

TABLE 17–2
ANNUAL FLOWS INTO TRADE CREDIT, 1950-1958
(BILLIONS OF DOLLARS)

Sector	1950	1951	1952	1953	1954	1955	1956	1957	1958
Net change in trade credit......	11.1	4.5	5.2	—.6	4.5	10.3	7.2	2.6	2.0
Corporate nonfinancial business	9.7	3.5	3.3	—.7	3.8	10.2	6.2	2.2	2.6
Non-corporate nonfinancial business	1.0	*	.8	.1	.4	.1	.8	.3	—.1
Federal Government [1]	.4	.9	1.0	—.1	.2	—.1	.1	—.1	—.6
Insurance [2]	*	.1	.1	.1	.1	.1	.1	.2	.1
Net change in trade debt	8.5	4.8	3.7	.1	3.1	9.1	4.4	2.8	2.8
Corporate business	7.4	2.0	1.4	—.1	2.1	10.6	4.8	—1.8	—1.5
Non-corporate nonfinancial business	—.4	.8	1.8	.4	.5	—1.6	—1.0	4.3	4.0
Farm business	.2	.4	.1	—.2	*	*	*	*	*
Federal Government [3]	1.1	1.6	.1	—.2	—.2	—.1	.3	.2	*
State and local government...	.1	*	.1	.1	.2	.1	.1	*	.2
Nonprofit organizations	.1	—	.2	.1	.1	.1	.2	.1	.1

*Less than $50 million.
Note: Details may not add to totals because of rounding.
[1] Prepayments and advances to corporations.
[2] Receivables from agents.
[3] Payable to corporations.
Source: Data derived from "A Quarterly Presentation of Flow of Funds, Saving and Investment," *Federal Reserve Bulletin*, August 1959.

Year-to-year changes in the annual volume of trade credit are related to the level and composition of inventories and the degree of credit tightness. The volume of trade credit may be expected to increase as inventories are increased. Annual flows into trade credit have been largest in the boom years (1950, 1955, and 1956) and least in the recession years (1953-1954 and 1957-1958). Corporate business added $9.7 billion to its holdings of trade receivables in 1950, but in 1953, a year in which recession set in, it decreased its holdings of trade credit by $700 million. Quarterly data show that trade credit increases as inventories are restocked. The forward shifting in inventory tends to place the inventory in firms that rely rather heavily on trade credit. Also, during periods of credit tightness, many firms, particularly small and medium-sized firms, resort to trade debt to offset reduction in the availability of other forms of short-term financing. A recent study of quarterly flows into trade credit for manufacturers indicated that trade credit possessed "fluidity that could not be explained by the increase in the volume of sales, shifts in demand, or the growth of corporate installment credit."* The findings tend to support the conclusion that "credit restrictions played a part in the expansion of trade credit during the period 1954 to 1956."† One of the more important implications of these findings is that credit availability to small and medium-sized business should not be judged solely on the basis of direct availability of bank credit and capital funds. A credit policy that imposes severe credit restrictions on large business firms as a means of facilitating or rationing the flow of credit to small and medium-sized firms might be unsuccessful, for it might lead to a reduction in the flow of trade credit from the larger to the smaller firms and thus nullify or offset any changes in the flow of loan credit to small and medium-sized business firms.

BANK LOANS, N.E.C.

In this section we shall review the loan function of commercial banking as it relates to financing the short- and intermediate-term needs of non-farm, non-financial business firms. Since the structure of the commercial banking system and the basic organization of an individual commercial bank were examined in Chapter 6, we shall restrict our inquiry here to policies, standards, and practices relating to commercial and industrial loans. In conventional market terms, we shall cover the principal lenders in the customers' market. The other sources of short- and intermediate-term credit will be examined in the following chapter. In flow-of-funds terminology, the latter sources of funds are recorded in the transaction category "other loans, n.e.c."

A business firm that requires loan credit for a period of less than five years tends to initiate its loan request with a local commercial bank because that is the financial institution most familiar to the firm. A commercial bank or banking office is probably located in the immediate area, and it is very likely that the firm has had some contact with the bank through its deposit balance and business activities. A local bank or banking office is often thought of as a community-serving financial institution. Furthermore, it is generally known that if the firm can satisfy a commercial bank's loan standards, the cost of the loan credit will probably be lower than the cost of some alternative loan arrangement.

*"Trade Credit: A Factor in the Rationing of Capital," Monthly Review of the Kansas City Federal Reserve Bank, June 1957, p. 8.
†Ibid., p. 8.

Factors Influencing Commercial Bank Loan Policies

Commercial bank loan policies reflect many basic factors. First, a bank is able to earn a certain minimum rate of return by investing in risk-free Federal obligations. Since the costs of administering a bank's portfolio of Federal obligations is very small, net yield is nearly equivalent to gross yield. Second, usury laws or custom place a ceiling of 6 or 7 per cent on the rate that banks charge on business loans. The implication of these first two considerations is that the spread in the yields on Federal obligations and business loans is only about 2 or 3 per cent, whereas there is much difference between Federal obligations and business loans in terms of degree of risk and administrative costs. Third, a commercial bank's net current earnings before income taxes probably amount to less than 1½ per cent of total assets, which means that excessive losses on business loans could easily wipe out all the bank's net current earnings. A commercial bank is a profit-making institution, and the owners expect to receive dividends on their ownership equity. Fourth, the capital accounts of a commercial bank are less than 10 per cent of total assets, so that excessive losses on business loans could not only wipe out net current earnings but could also reduce capital accounts below the minimum required level, and force the bank into liquidation. The significance of all these considerations is simply that, after allowing for the costs incurred in investigating and making decisions on business loan requests, a bank is able to net only slightly more than it might have earned on Federal obligations. In the process, the bank subjects itself to possible loan losses that could exceed its net income and force it into liquidation. To maintain a respectable rate of return on total capital accounts, a bank must avoid making too many of the high-risk type of business loans.

A bank's policy toward loans is also influenced by its desire to gain or maintain the minimum deposit balances of business firms. The term "minimum" implies that a business attempts to maintain its deposits at or above a certain level at all times, and from the point of view of the depositary bank, the minimum deposit balance can be viewed as a primary deposit. It will be recalled that primary deposits constitute a commercial bank's major source of funds. Obviously, a bank's decision on a loan request has an important bearing on the ultimate location of the firm's minimum deposit balance. Loans are a form of competition for deposit balances. Also, when a bank makes a loan, it generally requires the borrowing customer to maintain during the loan period a compensating deposit balance equal to 15 to 20 per cent of the loan. In effect, this requirement raises the cost of the loan to the borrower. For example, if a bank required that the borrower maintain a 20 per cent compensating balance against a 6 per cent, a one-year loan, the effective cost of the money actually used would be 7.5 per cent. The ability of commercial banks to enforce the compensating balance requirement is directly related to the degree of credit tightness.

Loan Procedure

Business firms tend to establish contacts with commercial banks prior to the time at which they might need loan funds in order to facilitate eventual loan requests. The character and reputation of a firm's management are very important considerations in a bank's appraisal of a loan request. A loan request may come either directly from the prospective borrower or through a correspondent bank acting on behalf of one of its customers.

In making a loan, the bank's first task is to gather information about the business and its management. Much of it, including financial statements, is supplied by the borrower in a loan application and a personal interview with the bank's loan officer. Other sources of information include credit rating services, credit exchange bureaus, correspondent banks, and the firm's major suppliers and customers. The second step is to arrange the qualitative and quantitive data in a form that permits meaningful analysis. The third step is to analyze the data in terms of established loan standards or criteria. The reputation of the prospective borrower is determined. Past financial statements and business practices are analyzed to determine the capabilities of the firm's management. If the request originates with a newly established firm, the content and presentation of the loan request provide considerable insight into the potential capabilities of management. The purpose of the loan, maturity, method of repayment, and timing of repayment are clearly established. If the bank determines that the loan could not be repaid for many years, the request would probably be denied and the borrower would be informed that some source of funds other than bank credit should be sought. The method of repayment is determined by analyzing the firm's projected cash flows. Generally, if a bank loan has to run beyond a year, a periodic method of repayment will be arranged.

Recalling some of the basic factors influencing a bank's loan policy, it is reasonable for a bank to attempt to assure itself that the " cushion " in the loan is large enough to offset possible adverse developments. In other words, the maturity and repayment schedules are not based on the borrower's most optimistic outlook. In some loans, especially those granted to large business firms, a bank may consider that the cushion is adequate to support a general creditor status, but in the majority of loans, and especially those granted to small business firms, a bank may not consider that the cushion is adequate to support a general creditor status, and so it requests the borrower to pledge specific assets as additional security for the loan.

The scope of this text does not permit an examination of the many factors that enter into the determination of the specific security, the specific legal document that should be used to prove the bank's secured position, and the size of margin or spread between the size of the loan and the stated value of the asset(s) pledged as security (loan margin). It is sufficient to mention that accounts receivable, inventory, life insurance policies, machinery and equipment, and land and buildings are frequently used as security. The legal document giving evidence of the secured position of the lender and the loan margin vary with the nature and quality of the security. The final terms depend on negotiation between the bank and the borrower.

Structure and Characteristics of Bank Loans*

The structure and characteristics of bank loans outstanding at the time of the October, 1957 survey reflected the economic and financial conditions that prevailed in the preceding months and years. Nearly half of the dollar loan volume outstanding in October had been made before July, and over one-third of the loans had a maturity of one year or more. The period 1955-1957 was one of prosperity, featured by record high business investment expenditures and a strong business demand for funds. During most of the period, monetary authorities imposed restraint, and the liquidity positions of both banks and business firms were under pressure. Given this economic background, the 1957 survey data are used to illustrate the structure and characterictics of bank loans. Although the loan classifications used in the survey are not identical to bank loans, n.e.c., the data are very useful in that they illustrate the nature of commercial bank lending.

SIZE OF BORROWER. The majority of business loans outstanding at member banks had been made to small business firms, but the majority of the dollar volume was to large business firms. For example, 39.4 per cent of the total number of loans were made to businesses with assets of less than $50,000, but these same loans accounted for only 3.6 per cent of the total dollar amount of business loans. The corresponding figures for loans to businesses with total assets of less than $250,000 were 78 per cent of the number of loans and 16.5 per cent of the amount of loans. The basic relationship noted in the opening statement is even more pronounced for loans to businesses with total assets of $100 million or more. This size of borrower owed only ½ of 1 per cent of the total number of loans, but owed 21.7 per cent of the total amount of loans.

LOAN MATURITY. Originally, commercial banks served only the short-term, self-liquidating needs of agriculture, commerce, and industry. Loan maturities were of only a few months, and the uses to which the funds were put were expected to generate the means of repayment. Loans of this nature could be analyzed rather accurately, making it possible for commercial banks to minimize the risk in their loan portfolios. Commercial banks departed

*The data presented in this section are based on a survey of business loans at member banks as of October 16, 1957. The survey was conducted by the Board of Governors of the Federal Reserve System, in cooperation with the Federal Reserve banks, as part of a broad inquiry into small business financing. The results of the survey are published in *Financing Small Business*, Part II, Vol. I.

from this traditional type of lending and entered into many loan agreements with maturities of longer than one year. The reasons underlying this shift are fairly clear. First, many short-term loans were renewed year after year, and the writing of loans with original maturities longer than one year simply recognized existing practice. Second, the loanable funds of the commercial banks exceeded the demand for short-term loans, and rather than place the excess funds in investments, it was more profitable to adopt new loan practices. Furthermore, the relaxed standards on the types of assets that could be discounted or pledged at the Federal Reserve banks improved the banks' liquidity position and permitted them to make a larger number of intermediate and long-term loans.

Term loans and revolving credit arrangements have become widespread among commercial banks. The major distinguishing characteristics of a term loan are its maturity and the method of repayment. A term loan has a maturity of at least one year and is generally repayable in the form of periodic or serial repayments. The loan is negotiated directly between the bank and borrower, and it is evidenced by a formal loan agreement incorporating various restrictive provisions designed to maintain an adequate cushion throughout the loan period. The loans may or may not be secured. Revolving credit loans are loans secured by working capital assets, under which the lender agrees to lend for a period longer than a year an amount equal to a stated percentage of the firm's accounts receivable or inventory.

The survey data indicated that short-term loans represented about 62 per cent of both the amount and number of business loans of member banks. In fact, the short-term loans were predominant in the business loan portfolios of member banks for groups of borrowers of all sizes. The remainder of the business loans represented term loans in terms of maturity classification. Between 1955 and 1957, the ratio of term loans to total loans at all member banks rose from 34 to 38 per cent. Term loan data were related to size of borrower. It was found that the smallest size group (assets under $50,000) increased its term loans most between 1955 and 1957, the percentage of term loans rising from 39 to 46 per cent of the total loans. The expansion of term loans during the 1955-1957 period reflect the intermediate and long-term needs related to capital expenditures and the increased use of trade credit to finance short-term needs. The willingness of the banks to enter into additional term loans can be explained by examining the term loan characteristics: security, restrictive provisions, periodic repayments, and slightly higher interest rates.

IMPORTANCE OF SECURITY. Most loans to small businesses, and particularly term loans, were secured by collateral, endorsed, or guaranteed by someone other than the borrower, whereas most loans to larger businesses were unsecured. In dollar amounts, business loans were almost evenly divided between secured and unsecured loans. In numbers of loans, two-thirds were secured. There is a very close relationship between size of borrower and percentages of secured loans. For businesses with total assets of less than $50,000, 68 per cent of the loans were secured and these accounted for over 78 per cent of the amount of loans outstanding to this size of borrower. For businesses with assets of $100 million or more, only about 35 per cent of the number of loans were secured and these accounted for only 17.5 per cent of the amount of loans outstanding to this size of borrower. On the average, the secured loans to small businesses were larger than unsecured loans to small businesses. The opposite prevailed among the large-sized borrowers.

INTEREST RATES. Rates tend to vary inversely with the size of loan, and for loans of a given size, small businesses generally pay higher interest rates than do large businesses. In 1957, the interest rates on member bank loans to business by size of borrower ranged from 6.5 per cent on loans to businesses with total assets less than $50,000, down to 4.4 per cent on loans to businesses with total assets over $100 million. Interest rates were also related to loan maturity, with the highest effective rates being paid on loans with maturities ranging from one to five years. For example, businesses with total assets of less than $50,000 were paying, on the average, an effective rate of 8.7 per cent on one- to five-year loans and an effective rate of 4.7 per cent on loans of over five years. The explanation for this variation is that many of one- to five-year loans are installment loans with the nominal rate assessed against the original amount of the loan. It will be recalled that, in the discussion of consumer credit, the effective rate on loans of the installment type is approximately twice the nominal rate, if the installment payments are of equal amounts.

Bank Loans, n.e.c., Outstanding

Bank loans, n.e.c., outstanding at the end of 1958 are shown in Table 17-3. Loans in this category accounted for 52.3 per cent of total bank loans and 25.1 per cent of the banks' total financial assets. Approximately 70 per cent of the loans in this category represented liabilities of the corporate and non-corporate, nonfinancial sectors. When we realize that finance companies use bank loans to finance their financial transactions with nonfinancial firms, the nonfinancial business sectors were probably receiving directly and indirectly more than 80 per cent of bank loans, n.e.c. The farm business sector owed 8 per cent of the total amount of such loans outstanding.

The importance of bank loans, n.e.c. to various sectors is shown in the third column of figures in Table 17-3 which shows bank loans, n.e.c. as a percentage of sector liabilities. The figures show that these loans are most important to the non-corporate, nonfinancial business sector, accounting for nearly one-third of that sector's liabilities at the end of 1958. Although the

TABLE 17–3
BANK LOANS, N. E. C. OUTSTANDING, END OF 1958
(BILLIONS OF DOLLARS)

	Dollars	Per cent	Bank loans, n.e.c. as a percentage of bank assets and of sectors' liabilities [1]
Assets			
Total bank loan assets	100.0	100.0	
less: 1- to 4-family mortgages	17.5	17.5	
Other mortgages	7.7	7.7	
Consumer credit	15.8	15.8	
Security loans	4.7	4.7	
C.C.C. guaranteed loans	.8	.8	
Open market paper	1.2	1.2	
equals: Bank loans, n.e.c.	52.3	52.3	25.1
Liabilities (by sector)			
Total bank loan liabilities	52.3	100.0	7.5
Non-corporate nonfinancial business...	16.9	32.3	32.1
Finance, n.e.c.	6.0	11.5	25.5
Farm business	4.2	8.0	22.2
Corporate nonfinancial business	19.8	37.8	11.1
Rest-of-the-world	2.6	5.0	5.0
Consumer and nonprofit	2.0	3.8	1.2
Other	.8	1.6	

Note: Details may not add to totals because of rounding.

[1] In computing percentages, trade receivables were not offset against trade payables.

Source: Data derived from "A Quarterly Presentation of Flow of Funds, Saving and Investment," *Federal Reserve Bulletin*, August 1959.

finance, n.e.c. and farm business sector do not owe a very large proportion of such loans, this form of borrowing does provide from one-fifth to one-fourth of their total borrowed funds. In dollar amounts of such loans, the corporate, nonfinancial business sector was the most important, but in the relative importance of such loans in each sector's liabilities, the sector ranks fourth. Only 11.1 per cent of that sector's liabilities were in the form of bank loans, n.e.c. at the end of 1958.

Annual Flows into Bank Loans, n.e.c.

The annual flows into bank loans, n.e.c. for the period 1950-1958 are summarized in Table 17-4. The top half of the table shows the relative importance of the flows from the point of view of the commercial banks, and the bottom half of the table shows the allocation of bank loans, n.e.c. among various sectors. In each of the years, total bank loans increased, but the relative importance of bank loans, n.e.c. fluctuated from year to year. In 1953, the commercial banks reduced the volume of such loans by $900 million, and in all other years, increased such loans. In 1951, the banks allocated 56.3 per cent of net increase in bank loans to this category of loans. On the average the banks allocated about half of the net increases in bank loans to loans classified under the heading bank loans n.e.c. A complete explanation for the variability in the allocation of bank loans requires a thorough review of the supply of and demand for bank funds and the level and structure of yields. It is sufficient to mention at this point that bank loans, n.e.c. are assigned a high priority in the use of bank funds. If there is a strong demand for bank loans, n.e.c. and funds are available, banks will make a large volume of such loans. However, when the level of rates becomes high, and there are opportunities to acquire high-yield intermediate and long-term loans and investments, the commercial banks tend to pick up additional amounts of such loans and investments, thus reducing the amount of funds available for " other loans, n.e.c." Also, if funds are scarce, the commercial banks attempt to allocate part of their funds to all segments of the financial markets. If there is a strong demand for consumer credit, the relatively attractive yields on such loans are bound to attract bank funds.

TABLE 17–4
ANNUAL FLOWS INTO BANK LOANS, N. E. C., 1950-1958
(BILLIONS OF DOLLARS)

	1950	1951	1952	1953	1954	1955	1956	1957	1958
Total bank loans [1]	53.0	58.6	65.1	68.6	71.6	83.6	91.7	95.4	100.0
Bank loans, n.e.c.	28.2	33.0	35.3	34.4	34.6	42.6	48.5	50.9	52.3
Bank loans, n.e.c. as a percentage of total bank loans	53.2	56.3	54.2	50.1	48.3	51.0	52.9	53.4	52.3
Net changes in liabilities	6.1	4.8	2.2	—.8	.1	7.9	5.8	2.3	1.4
Corporate nonfinancial business	2.1	4.5	2.4	—.3	—1.2	1.9	3.6	.2	—2.2
Non-corporate nonfinancial business	2.3	—.3	—.9	.1	.7	2.1	2.2	1.2	2.8
Farm business	.5	.6	.1	—.4	.1	.4	*	.3	.6
Finance, n.e.c. [2]	.9	—.1	.7	—.1	.1	2.6	—.4	—.1	—.7
Nonprofit organizations	.3	*	—.1	*	.1	.5	.1	.3	.4
Rest-of-the-world	*	.1	*	—.1	.3	.4	.3	.4	.5

*Less than $50 million.
Note: Details may not add to totals because of rounding.
[1] Total bank loans include real estate loans, consumer credit, security credit, commercial paper, finance company paper, and banker's acceptances, as well as bank loans, n.e.c.
[2] Finance companies only.
Source: "A Quarterly Presentation of Flow of Funds, Saving and Investment," *Federal Reserve Bulletin*, August 1959.

During such periods the percentage of total bank loans that fit into the category, bank loans, n.e.c. will probably fall off.

The bottom half of Table 17-4 shows the annual flows into bank loans, n.e.c. from the point of view of the debtors. The allocation of such loans between the corporate and non-corporate, nonfinancial business sectors was not uniform during the period under review. In 1951 and 1952, the amount of such loans owed by the non-corporate sector declined $1.2 billion, whereas the corporate sector's liabilities increased $6.9 billion; in 1953 and 1954, just the opposite occurred; the corporate sector's liabilities declined $1.4 billion and the non-corporate sector's liabilities increased $800 million. In 1955, nearly equal amounts were allocated to each sector; in 1956, the corporate sector's liabilities increased $1.4 billion more than the non-corporate sector's liabilities; in 1957, the reverse was true, and in 1958 the pattern was similar to that of 1953 and 1954. The data suggest that during periods of credit ease, non-corporate business firms are able to secure bank loans that were not available in the previous period, and corporate firms are able to reduce bank loans built up in the previous period. Corporate firms obtain the funds from inventory reduction and debt funding, the latter of which is the conversion of short- and intermediate-term debt into long-term debt. As noted in the previous chapter, the small-sized firms tend to feel the effects of credit tightness in the availability of bank loans. However, it should not be forgotten that trade credit tends to offset some of the strain. The variability in the net change in liabilities owed by the finance, n.e.c. sector reflects the changing volume of consumer credit and the availability of long-term funds at attractive long-term rates.

Aggregate data cover up many differences among banks and bankers. Many factors influence the loan decision-making of a particular bank's management: size of bank, nature of deposit liabilities, investment opportunities, and the persons involved in the decision. Loan decisions of a particular bank should be reviewed in the light of the bank's existing loans and investments. If a bank has fully extended itself in business loans, it would have to turn down a disproportionately large number of loan requests. However, if the bank has only a small amount of its assets in the form of business loans, it is in a position to accept a disproportionately large number of loan requests. Also, the response of the banking system to loan requests from the non-farm, nonfinancial business sectors during a particular period must be viewed in terms of the banks' financial position at the beginning of the period.

QUESTIONS

1. In what sense is trade credit " interbusiness lending "? Mention two or three other forms of " interbusiness lending." What types of firms extend more trade credit than they receive?

2. What are the reasons for the existence of trade credit?

3. In what sense is a major portion of trade credit financed ultimately in the capital markets?

4. How is it possible for nonfinancial firms to impose lower standards in making trade credit decisions than financial institutions impose in making loan decisions?

5. Interpret the following trade credit terms: 2/10, net 30. If this trade credit were used for the maximum period of time, express its cost in terms of an annual rate of interest.

6. What factors underlie the year-to-year fluctuations in trade credit? What factors underlie the long-term growth in trade credit?

7. What basic factors influence commercial banks' loan *policies*?

8. Outline the procedures that a commercial bank follows in making a short-term loan to a non-farm business firm.

9. With respect to business loans at member banks, comment briefly on the following: (a) relationship between size of borrowers and number of loans; (b) relationship between size of borrowers and dollar amount of loans; (c) relative importance of short-term loans; (d) relative importance of secured loans; and (e) relationship between size of borrowers and secured loans.

10. Commercial banks have departed from "traditional banking" and entered into many other forms of lending. Explain.

11. What are the major distinguishing characteristics of a term loan? What are the major distinguishing characteristics of a "revolving credit loan"?

12. Indicate the importance of "bank loans, n.e.c." in relation to other types of bank loans. What sectors rely most heavily on this source of funds?

13. Explain why the allocation of bank loans, n.e.c. between the corporate and non-corporate business sectors is not uniform from year to year.

ADDITIONAL READING

See list of money and banking texts at end of Chapter 4, books dealing with bank management listed at end of Chapter 6, and the corporation finance texts listed at end of Chapter 16 for description of the loan function of commercial banks.

Jacoby, Neil H., and Raymond J. Saulnier. *Term Lending to Business*. N.B.E.R. study. Princeton, N.J.: Princeton University Press, 1942.
———. *Financing Inventory on Field Warehouse Receipts*. N.B.E.R. study. Princeton, N.J.: Princeton University Press, 1944.
———. *Business Finance and Banking*. N.B.E.R. study. Princeton, N.J.: Princeton University Press, 1947.
Saulnier, Raymond J., and Neil H. Jacoby. *Accounts Receivable Financing*. N.B.E.R. study. Princeton, N.J.: Princeton University Press, 1943.
———. *Financing Equipment for Commercial and Industrial Enterprises*. N.B.E.R. study. Princeton, N.J.: Princeton University Press, 1944.
U.S. Committees on Banking and Currency, and the Select Committees on Small Business, United States Congress. *Financing Small Business*, Parts

I and II. Report by the Federal Reserve System, 85th Cong., 2nd sess. Washington, D.C.: Government Printing Office, 1958. See table of contents for reading relating to trade credit and bank loans.

18: Short- and intermediate-term financing, II

I N the previous chapter, the major sources of short- and intermediate-term credit were considered. We now turn to the less important sources, including commercial and finance company open-market paper and loans made by commercial finance companies, factors, agencies of the Federal government, and state development credit corporations. The role of the commercial paper dealer is considered in the discussion of commercial open-market paper. Although the dollar amount of funds from all of these sources is small in relation to the volume of trade credit and bank loans, n.e.c., they are very important to many thousands of firms, both large and small.

COMMERCIAL AND FINANCE COMPANY OPEN-MARKET PAPER

Open-market paper consists primarily of single-name, unsecured promissory notes of business firms and finance companies that are placed on a discount basis with banks and other investors. A very small portion of open-market paper consists of guaranteed promissory notes and notes that are secured by collateral. Promissory notes constituting open-market paper are usually written in denominations of 5, 10, 25, 50, 100, 250, and 500 dollars. In order to get wide distribution of the notes, the borrower (maker of the notes) might execute notes in many denominations and maturities. The maturities of open-market paper range from one to nine months, with most of the notes concentrated within the four- to six-month maturities. No rate is specified on the promissory notes; instead, the notes are sold at a discount. Appreciation in their value from the discount price to par provides the return to the investor. The paper may be placed either indirectly or directly. To place paper indirectly, the notes are sold first to commercial paper dealers, who resell the paper as quickly as possible to banks and non-bank investors, including trust departments of commercial banks, pension funds, mutual funds, and nonfinancial companies. When paper is placed directly, commercial paper dealers are not involved. Generally, only a few of the larger finance companies place their paper directly with investors. Nonfinancial business firms almost always utilize the services of commercial paper dealers in placing their paper.

In May, 1958, commercial paper outstanding reached what was then an historic peak of $3,709 million; $2,763 million was issued directly by nine finance companies, and the remainder ($981 million) was dealer-sold paper. During 1959, the amount of commercial paper outstanding continued near this level. In 1960, the spread between the bank prime rate and the rates on commercial paper widened, and the amount of commercial and finance company paper outstanding approached $4.5 billion.

It is important to distinguish between a bank's purchase of commercial and finance company open-market paper and a bank's short-term loans to its customers, because the transactions occur in two different types of markets. The former type of transaction takes place in the commercial paper market; the latter, in the customers' loan market. In the commercial paper market the relationship between a bank and the firms whose open-market paper the bank holds is indirect and impersonal, especially if the paper was acquired through dealers. In the customers' loan market the relationship between a bank and its borrowing customers is direct and personal. The credit standards that a bank applies to the maker of open-market paper are more strict than those applied to its own customers. Also, a bank is much more likely to renew a customer's loan than it is to reinvest in open-market paper of the same maker.

Origin and Development of the Market

Although the origin of the market for open-market paper can be traced back more than 150 years, its basic structure was not firmly established until after the panic of 1907. The most significant recent change in the market's structure is the growing importance of directly placed paper. Prior to World War I, all commercial paper was placed through dealers, but shortly after that war, the General Motors Acceptance Corporation, a finance company subsidiary of General Motors, began to place its paper directly with investors. Gradually, the practice was adopted by other large finance companies, such as the Commercial Credit Company and the C.I.T. Financial Corporation. To illustrate the degree of change in the structure of the market, it should be noted that in the 1920's nearly 80 per cent of all commercial paper was placed through dealers, and the remainder was placed directly. In the late 1950's the figures were about reversed.

A relatively small number of firms borrow on the basis of commercial paper. During the mid-1920's, almost 3,000 firms obtained funds through open-market paper, but the number fell off sharply with the onset of the Great Depression, and the number of borrowers has since remained well under 1,000. During the period 1950-1958, the number of commercial paper borrowers each year varied from 335-449.* In 1958, there were 376 borrowing firms and the following lines of business were represented: finance, 111; manufacturers, 167; wholesalers, 47; retailers, 43; and others, 8. Among manufacturers, textile and metal products accounted for over two-fifths of the total. One of the recent trends is the increasing importance of consumer finance companies in both segments of the market. The major reasons for the relatively small number of firms currently using this means of financing are the strict credit standards, the introduction of alternative short-term sources of funds for business, and the unavailability of the market to small business. It is rare that a firm with a net worth of less than $1 million can qualify for " open-market " paper. The importance of size is demonstrated in the tabulation below, which shows commercial paper borrowers by net worth groups for the year 1958:†

Net worth group	Number	Percentage
$ 500,000- 1,000,000	6	1.6%
1,000,001- 2,500,000	55	14.7
2,500,001- 5,000,000	76	20.2
5,000,001-25,000,000	130	34.5
over $25,000,000	109	29.0
	376	100.0%

On the dealer side of the market, at the end of 1958, there were seven dealers in the market; three of them handled commercial paper only, and the others were more diversified and participated in other types of brokerage transactions, including securities. As for the legal form of organization, two of the dealer firms were incorporated.**

Commercial Paper Dealers

Commercial paper dealers purchase paper at a discount, charging a commission equivalent to an annual rate of ¼ of 1 per cent per year, and resell the paper as quickly as possible to banks and other investors. Most of the paper is sold on the basis of time options, ranging from 10 to 14 days, to allow the investor time to investigate the paper. If the investor deems the credit standing of the commercial paper borrower as unsatisfactory, the paper may be returned to the dealer. Specialized mercantile concerns provide appraisal assistance to investors.

*"The Commercial Paper Market," January 1959, p. 2, from Current Industry Comment, The National Credit Office Consulting Service, New York.
†Ibid., p. 3.
**Data provided by the National Credit Office.

The dealers handle large transactions, achieving nationwide distribution through branch offices and correspondent relationships. Most of the paper is placed with small and medium-sized banks.

To achieve and maintain a rapid turnover of their capital, the dealers must be able to sell the open-market paper very soon after purchase. Therefore, dealers appraise the quality of commercial paper borrowers in terms of very strict credit standards; for that reason, only a relatively small number of firms borrow on the basis of commercial paper. Generally, a dealer does not purchase a firm's paper unless the following conditions are satisfied: (1) the firm has a net worth of at least $1 million and preferably as much as $5 million; (2) the firm's credit record is excellent; (3) it is clearly evident that the firm will be able to meet its new obligations; and (4) the firm is widely and favorably known. The fact that no losses were suffered by commercial paper holders from 1937 through 1960 attests to the application of high credit standards. From the point of view of the commercial paper borrowers, the need to supply credit information to prospective investors as well as to commercial paper dealers constitutes one of the strongest disadvantages to this means of financing.

Discounts on Indirectly Placed Paper

Discounts on open-market commercial paper depend on the paper's maturity and the status of the money market. The money market is defined as the " active market for money and close substitutes which financial institutions and others rely upon to provide the liquidity need in the usual course of their operations."* The yields on money market instruments are very sensitive to changes in demand and supply, and it is only natural that discounts on commercial paper are subject to rapid rate fluctuations. For example, the rate charged on prime commercial paper with four to six months maturity in July, 1958 was 1½ per cent and within one year the rate climbed to over 4 per cent. In January, 1960, the rate exceeded 5 per cent; at the close of the year the rate had fallen below 3 per cent. The level and structure of money market rates are examined fully in chapter 24. Generally, the discount rate on open-market commercial paper is lower than the rate charged in the customers' loan market and higher than the discount on directly placed finance company paper. Since the rates charged in the customers' loan market are rather sticky, the spread between these rates and discounts on commercial paper is not uniform. During a period of monetary ease, money market rates are depressed and the spread between the rates is quite large; during a period of credit restraint, the money market rates are relatively high and there is little or no spread between the rates. Firms that use open-market paper because of the cost savings tend to enter the market during a period of monetary ease and to leave the market during a period of monetary restraint.

*Robert V. Roosa, *Federal Reserve Operations in the Money and Government Securities Markets*, Federal Bank of New York, 1956, p. 11.

During the period 1950-1958, the number of commercial paper borrowers reached its peak of 449 in 1954, a period of recession and low money market rates. Since dealers purchase paper outright, they assume the risk of being unable to place the paper at a rate of discount that will assure their commissions. If discounts rise before dealers are able to resell the paper, the prices received by the dealers are lower than the prices the dealers paid. Depending on the degree of change in money market rates, the dealers' losses may exceed their commissions. However, when rates move in the opposite direction, the dealers' profits may exceed their commissions.

Directly Placed Finance Company Paper

In the 1950's, nine finance companies were placing commercial paper directly with investors. The characteristics of this paper are nearly identical to those of the paper placed through dealers. The major difference is that the borrowing firms can tailor the paper to fit the needs of specific investors. Notes are offered to mature on any day specified by the purchasers (investors), with minimum maturity at 30 days and maximum maturity at 270 days. Normally, there is a differential of ⅛ of 1 per cent among the maturity classes, and the over-all level of the rate structure is about ¼ of 1 per cent below that of dealer-sold paper. For each maturity, the paper of each of the nine finance companies generally carries the same rate of discount, and rate change is accomplished through price leadership.

During the postwar period, considerable growth has occurred in the dollar volume of directly placed paper. Among the factors accounting for this growth have been an increase in the amount of receivables held by the larger finance companies, the relatively low cost of this means of financing, an increase in the demand for such paper by non-bank investors, and the effective limits on the amount of funds that larger finance companies have been able to borrow from commercial banks. The latter two factors probably require explanation.

At various times, financial and nonfinancial firms hold surplus or excess funds that can or should be invested in near-money assets for periods of less than a year. Commercial paper of the leading finance companies is of very high quality and satisfies fully the liquidity needs of the firms. Although the financial return on directly placed paper is not very high, it is higher than that obtainable on some other forms of near-money assets. Furthermore, the paper can be designed to fit the specific liquidity needs of the investors. Non-bank investors purchase about 80 per cent of all directly placed paper, and the larger corporate nonfinancial business firms constitute the most important investor class. Other non-bank investors include endowment funds, pension funds, mutual funds, and insurance companies.

The finance companies have financed part of their additional holdings of receivables through short-term debt, consisting of notes payable to banks and commercial paper. Much of the increase in short-term debt has been in the form of directly placed commercial paper because the finance companies have not been able to expand their bank credit lines in proportion to the increase in their short-term financing needs, much of which has occurred during periods of credit restraint. In addition to the reduction in credit availability, many of the large banks from whom the large finance companies borrow have not been able to expand credit lines to finance companies because of regulations limiting total obligations to one borrower. It will be recalled that a bank is not permitted to lend more than 10 per cent of the bank's capital and surplus to any one borrower, unless the type of borrower falls into one of the exceptions to the general rule. Finance companies are not one of the exceptions. Under normal operating conditions, the policy of the finance companies is to maintain a 50 per cent rate of borrowing against bank credit lines so as to maintain unused credit lines equal to one-half of the directly placed paper outstanding. This is one of the factors accounting for the high quality of directly placed paper. Assuming the policy noted above, the limit on the expansion of bank borrowing can be brought into focus by the following computation.* At the end of 1953, the average amount of outstanding short-term indebtedness of the three largest sales finance companies was $650 million. To have credit lines totaling this amount, it would have been necessary to utilize the full lending capacity to individual borrowers of the 400 largest member banks. Then, assuming a 10 per cent increase in the demand for bank credit lines, it would have been necessary to utilize the full lending capacity to individual borrowers of the next 400 largest banks.

The sales finance companies have probably approached the ideal or optimum distribution among the various sources of funds. To increase further the proportion of funds raised through the direct placement of paper would involve additional risk in the sense that the non-bank demand for the paper may not hold up in the future. If sales finance companies were to increase the amount of directly placed paper at the expense of bank credit lines, bank relations might become strained. Also, the quality of the paper would decline because of a lower margin of safety in terms of unused credit lines. If further expansion is required at a time when bank credit lines cannot be increased, then the sales finance companies will probably be obligated to rely on the capital markets to a greater extent than in the past.

Advantages of Open Market Paper

BORROWERS' POINT OF VIEW. Borrowers are able to secure funds when their short-term financing needs exceed the legal loan limits of their respective

*"Directly Placed Finance Company Paper," *Federal Reserve Bulletin*, December 1954, p. 4.

customer banks. The cost is relatively low because the discount (plus commission if sold through dealers) is lower than the prime bank loan rate. Although no compensating bank balance is involved, the investors assume that the borrowers have unused bank credit lines equal to 50 per cent of the amount of outstanding paper. The nationwide distribution of the borrowing firms' paper enhances the reputation of the firms among financial institutions and improves the market climate for their issues of long-term credit and market instruments.

There are also some disadvantages. The borrowers are subject to numerous credit investigation inquiries. Unlike bank loans, commercial and finance company open-market paper cannot be renegotiated, prepaid, or extended. Furthermore, a borrower's position in the customers' loan market may be strained if the firm goes in and out of open market in response to rate fluctuations.

INVESTORS' POINT OF VIEW. Both non-bank and bank investors are able to put their excess funds to work by contacting either a commercial paper dealer or one of the sales offices of a large sales finance company. The range of maturities allows the investors to fit the paper to their needs. From the banks' point of view, the yield on open-market paper is lower than that earned on bank loans, but banks are able to achieve greater diversification by purchasing the paper, and the paper is eligible for discount at Federal Reserve Banks.

There are also some disadvantages, especially to bank investors. The yield is not as favorable as that on bank loans. Also, it must be determined whether or not the cost of credit investigation exceeds the differential between the yield on Treasury bills and open-market paper. Also, the market for the resale of open-market paper is not as reliable as the resale market for some other money market instruments, such as Treasury bills.

FACTORING AND COMMERCIAL FINANCE COMPANIES

Basically, there are two major classes of finance companies: specialized consumer financing institutions and specialized business financing institutions.

The distinctions between the two major classes are not clear-cut. Some sales finance companies are actively engaged in commercial financing and factoring; some commercial finance companies are engaged in factoring; and some factoring companies are engaged in commercial financing. Normally, the name of a finance company does not reveal whether it is a personal finance company, sales finance company, commercial finance company, or factoring company. Most finance companies tend to concentrate or specialize in one or two types of specialized financing, and it is on this basis that the companies can be classified.

Sales finance and personal finance companies were considered in Chapter 15, which dealt with consumer credit. The finance companies' use of open-market paper as a source of funds was discussed in the previous section. Attention is now centered on the role of commercial finance and factoring companies in the financing of business firms.

Factoring companies and commercial finance companies serve mainly the short- and intermediate-term needs of small businesses in manufacturing and wholesale trade. At the end of 1956, the outstanding credit supplied by commercial finance companies and factors was probably less than $2 billion, and the number of their clients was probably less than 20,000.* Recently, there have been increases in both the number of such borrowers and the amount of such borrowing, and further increases can be expected.

Factoring Companies (Factors)

A factoring company is a non-bank financial institution specializing in the purchase of accounts receivable without recourse against the sellers and with notification of debtors. "Without recourse" means that a factoring company assumes the risk of credit losses; "with notification" means that the factoring company informs the trade debtors that the sellers' trade receivables have been sold or assigned to the factoring company. Although there are many financial institutions engaged in factoring, there are only "a score of established, well-known factoring companies in the United States, and they are concentrated mainly in New York City."† Some of the companies are independent, and others are subsidiaries or divisions of large finance companies.

ORIGIN AND DEVELOPMENT. The origin of the modern-day factoring company can be found in the methods used in selling British manufactured goods in the American colonies. The commission merchants performed both the selling and the credit and collection functions for the foreign manufacturers. Gradually, American manufacturers, particularly those in textiles, supplanted some of the foreign manufacturers. Inasmuch as the commission merchants were already specialists in handling the selling and the credit and collection functions relating to textiles, American mills continued the practice that was started by the foreign manufacturers. In time, the selling function was assumed by the manufacturers, but the financial functions were left in the hands of commission merchants. The net effect of these shifts in function was that commission merchant firms became financial institutions.

Factoring companies confined their services to the basic lines of the textile industry until the 1920's, when they began to branch out into related

*Francis R. Pawley, "Survey of Commercial Finance Companies and Factors," *Financing Small Business*, Part II, Vol. II, Chapter 4, p. 449.

†Clyde William Phelps, *The Role of Factoring in Modern Business Finance*, Studies in Commercial Finance, No. 1, Commercial Credit Company, 1956, p. 13.

lines. Currently, factoring is being used to some extent in almost all lines of business at both the manufacturing and the wholesale level, but textile and related lines continue to obtain more factor credit than do other manufacturing lines. The annual volume of factoring is probably around $4 billion.

Factoring companies also provide other services, including inventory and equipment financing, unsecured loans, and advisory service. However, the non-factoring forms of financing and the advisory services are restricted to firms that are having their accounts receivable factored.

TERMS AND CONDITIONS OF FACTORING AGREEMENTS. The relationship between the finance company and the firm that is having its accounts receivable factored is evidenced by a formal agreement, which sets forth the terms and conditions. Although factoring is considered a short-term source of funds, the agreement may cover a much longer period, as, for instance, when the factor assumes the client's credit and collection functions.

Credit and collection involve three basic tasks: granting or extending credit, maintaining records or accounts receivable bookkeeping, and collecting accounts. In most factoring agreements, the factors assume all of these tasks, and agree to remit cash to the firms ten days after the average due date of the firms' accounts receivables. The factors charge a flat commission for performing these tasks. The commission is expressed as a percentage of the face value of the receivables.* A survey of factors revealed that " the medium typical flat commission rate charged in late 1957 on the face amount of receivables purchased was one and one-half per cent. The average typical factoring charge, weighted by receivables outstanding, for five of the larger factors was 1.4 per cent in late 1957. The factoring charge tends to be larger for clients with smaller cash volume with a given size of invoice, because of the higher unit costs of handling small volume."† The commission has nothing to do with lending; instead, it represents payment to the factoring companies for their handling of the credit and collection tasks.

A factoring agreement may also set forth terms under which a factor will advance cash against outstanding accounts receivable. Professor Clyde Phelps has estimated that " a substantial proportion (from 15 to 40 per cent) of the typical factor's volume is done with clients who, by preference or by agreement with the factor, do not withdraw funds prior to the average due date of the receivables they sell the factor."** For many years, 6 per cent was the traditional rate charged by the factor for advancing cash against receivables. On the basis of the 1957 survey referred to above, " about half of the

---

*For a list of the variables that enter into the determination of the rate, see Phelps, op. cit., pp. 52-64.

†Francis R. Pawley, "Survey of Commercial Finance Companies and Factors," *Financing Small Business*, p. 462.

**Phelps, op. cit., p. 35.

old line factors reported that in late 1957 they were still charging the traditional 6 per cent interest rate on cash advanced. The others had raised the interest charge to 7.0 or 7.2 per cent following the increase in the prime bank rate in August 1957. The weighted average typical rate in late 1957 was 6.7 per cent."* In 1959, further pressure was exerted on the policy of holding the line at 6 per cent, with the result that nearly all factoring companies in late 1959 were charging an annual interest rate higher than 6 per cent. The reasons given for increasing the rate were the increase in the " prime " rate from 4.5 per cent to 5.0 per cent at commercial banks, and higher operating costs. When it is realized that factoring companies borrow heavily from commercial banks, and that borrowers are required to maintain compensating balances equal to 20 per cent of their loans, a prime rate of 5 per cent works out to an effective rate of 6.67 per cent. If the higher rates are expected to prevail for some time, factoring companies cannot be expected to borrow at 6.67 per cent and lend at 6 per cent.

Commercial Finance Companies

A commercial finance company is a non-bank financial institution specializing in accounts receivable financing, or the purchase of firms' accounts receivables with recourse and without notification to debtors or the advance of funds secured by accounts receivables. "With recourse" means that a finance company does not assume the risk of credit losses; "without notification" means the trade debtors are not informed that their debts to the firm have been sold or assigned to a finance company. "Nonnotification financing" developed in response to the attitude that the payment of debts to a third party was a signal of financial weakness, a final step short of liquidation. Therefore, when accounts receivable financing was introduced as a regular type of financing outside the textile industry, secrecy was considered to be a vital element. There has been a gradual breakdown in this attitude. In fact, some state laws now require that accounts receivable financing be made public information.

The procedure involved in accounts receivable financing has been summarized concisely by Professor Clyde Phelps:†

> The business firm passes its own credits, makes shipments on its usual terms, and handles its own collections. As it makes shipments, it sends copies of the invoices it wishes to finance, with evidence of shipment or delivery, to the financing institution. The latter immediately sends its check to the firm for the amount of the agreed-upon advance. As the firm receives checks from debtors in payment of invoices financed, it endorses them "Pay to any Bank or Bankers," and forwards them to the financing institution. By arrangement with its banks, this institution deposits the checks without its name appearing as an endorser —

*Pawley, op. cit., p. 462.

†Clyde W. Phelps, Accounts Receivable Financing as a Method of Business Finance, Studies in Commercial Financing, No. 2, Commercial Credit Company, 1957, p. 17.

so that the debtors are not made aware that it has handled the checks or has made advances against the receivables of the firms. The funds advanced against these receivables are thus automatically repaid as the firm's customers pay the invoices financed. Hence, there are no maturities to meet. Moreover, each day as checks of trade debtors are received by the financing institution from the firm being financed, this institution sends its check to the firm, remitting the difference between the amounts advanced and the amounts the firm's customers have paid on the invoices advanced.

Essentially, this is a revolving credit type of arrangement. The funds that are supplied have a maturity as short as the underlying receivables, but to the extent that there is a constant turnover of receivables, there is a constant flow of short-term funds. The finance company supplies funds for as long as the basic agreement remains in effect and the firm receives advances on its accounts receivable.

Commercial finance companies also provide time-sales financing of equipment and accommodation financing, the latter of which includes loans on inventory, equipment, and real estate. Almost all of the financing is on a secured basis. As with factoring companies, supplementary financing is available only to firms receiving accounts receivable financing.

ORIGIN AND DEVELOPMENT. The development of the commercial finance industry may be accounted for by the large number of business firms, and particularly of smaller firms, that could not obtain adequate financing from commercial banks. By introducing and specializing in new lending techniques and by increasing the finance charges, commercial finance companies were able to provide financing to these firms. The basic idea underlying accounts receivable financing is an offshoot of factoring. The commercial finance companies concentrated their efforts on the financing aspects of accounts receivable financing. Such loans had been made by commercial banks, but not as a regular method of financing. Gradually, the methods of commercial finance companies became widely known and respected, and many commercial banks began to develop accounts receivable financing. However, by the time commercial banks entered the field on a large scale, the commercial finance companies were firmly established in our financial system. Today, commercial banks and commercial finance companies compete against each other for accounts receivable financing, and in some cases participate jointly in providing such financing. As a general rule, the credit standards imposed by commercial banks are more strict than those imposed by finance companies.

Unlike the situation in the field of factoring, no one industry or product is dominant in accounts receivable financing of commercial finance companies. However, the clients are either manufacturers or wholesalers. The practice has not developed in those industries that have their own financing practices or in those industries in which such short-term financing involves undue risk. An example of the former is the farm equipment industry, in which the manufacturers provide the financing; an example of the latter is dress manufacturing, in which changing fashions introduce considerable risk.

There are probably four to five thousand commercial finance companies, but the field is dominated by a relatively small number. The annual volume of accounts receivable financing is probably $5 billion, and the amount outstanding at any given time probably averages about one-tenth of the total annual volume of receivables or sales invoices that are assigned or purchased.

ACCOUNTS RECEIVABLE FINANCING AGREEMENTS. The relationship between a finance company and its client is evidenced by a formal agreement that may run for a period of years. In our description of accounts receivable financing, it was pointed out that the checks sent by commercial finance companies to business firms are based upon an agreed-upon advance, or the ratio of credit actually advanced to the face amount of receivables that are sold or advanced. The scope of this text does not permit discussion of the factors that determine the ratio. It is sufficient to mention that the advance will be stated in the agreement. In a survey of 29 companies, 16 reported 80 per cent as the typical advance. For all 29 companies, the typical advance ranged from 65-85 per cent.*

The finance charge for accounts receivable financing tends to be high because of the costs and risks that are assumed by the lender: cost of borrowed money, expense of investigation, continuing costs of handling and policing the accounts receivables, and risks that the agreed-upon advance may be excessive and that accounts may be falsified. The finance charge is expressed as a fraction of 1 per cent and it is applied against the average daily face value of the accounts outstanding during the month. To compare costs of alternative methods of financing, a more meaningful measure of the finance charge is the effective interest rate per annum on the amount of cash advanced. On the basis of the survey referred to above, " the typical reported charge for this finance late in 1957 ranged from 8 to 24 per cent. . . . The median typical rate in late 1957 was 14 per cent, and median highest rate was 16 per cent . . . the arithmetic mean of typical rates weighted by the amount of receivables outstanding was 12.4 per cent in late 1957."†

SELECTED FINANCIAL DATA OF FINANCE COMPANIES. The sources of funds of commercial finance companies and sales finance companies are closely similar. As shown in Table 18-1, the major differences in the sources of funds between these two types of finance companies are in the relative importance of unsubordinated long-term debt and the amount due customers. The

*Pawley, *op. cit.*, p. 458.
†*Ibid.*, p. 461.

TABLE 18–1
SELECTED BALANCE SHEET AND INCOME STATEMENT DATA OF COMMERCIAL FINANCE AND SALES FINANCE COMPANIES, 1957

Item	Commercial Finance Companies [1]	Sales Finance Companies [2]
Ratio (per cent) to total resources, Dec. 31		
Commercial receivables (before reserves)	87.5	8.9
Short-term notes payable	39.8	41.9
Unsubordinated long-term debt	17.9	27.9
Subordinate long-term debt	6.8	9.2
Due customers	17.1	3.8
Capital and surplus	14.7	12.9
Ratio of net income to:		
Capital funds	12.2*	15.0
Total Resources	1.7	1.9

[1] Based on the financial data of seven commercial finance companies, consisting of one large and six medium-sized or small.
[2] Based on the financial data of three large sales finance companies whose commercial financing and factors subsidiaries and divisions account for a significant amount of such financing.
[3] Ratios for commercial finance companies based on only five companies.
Source: Francis R. Pawley, "Survey of Commercial Finance Companies and Factors," in U. S. Committees on Banking and Currency and the Select Committees on Small Business, *Financing Small Business*, Report by the Federal Reserve System, Parts 1 and 2, 85th Cong., 2nd sess., Washington, D. C.: Government Printing Office, 1958, p. 469.

item "due customers" represents the difference between the agreed-upon advance in relation to the face value of the receivables. The ratio of net income to total resources and capital funds is slightly higher for sales finance companies. The degree of specialization of each type of finance company is shown by the ratio of commercial receivables to total resources. Almost 90 per cent of the assets of commercial finance companies were in this form, whereas less than 10 per cent of sales finance company assets were in the form of commercial receivables.

SHORT- AND INTERMEDIATE-TERM FINANCING BY GOVERNMENT

The effects of the Great Depression, the need to achieve high production goals during World War II, and the continuing problems relating to financing small business have prompted Congress to introduce various types of programs designed to provide financial assistance to private business firms. In some instances, special agencies have been created, such as the existing Small Business Administration and the now-defunct Reconstruction Finance Corporation, and in other instances the financial programs have been administered by already established agencies, such as the Federal Reserve Banks and the Veterans Administration.

Our primary purpose in this section is to present the general characteristics of the Federal Government's loan programs, to survey the scope and magnitude of business loans and loan guarantees of Federal agencies, and to examine the structure and operation of the Small Business Administration.*

Characteristics of Federal Loan Programs

THREE BASIC TYPES OF FINANCIAL ASSISTANCE. Basically, there have been and are three basic types of financial assistance: direct loans, participation loans, and loan guarantees. The nature of a direct loan is self-evident — the funds are advanced directly by a government agency. A participation loan is a loan agreement under which the government agency agrees to participate in a loan with a private lender. The participation may be either immediate, in which case the government agency advances its agreed-upon proportion at

---

*A complete listing of lending and loan guarantee programs of Federal agencies in effect in fiscal year 1960 follows; it is based on the finding reported in U.S. Joint Economic Committee, Subsidy and Subsidylike Programs of the U.S. Government (materials prepared for the Joint Economic Committee and printed for its use), 86th Cong., 2nd sess., Washington, D. C.: Government Printing Office, 1960.

Direct loan programs:
  Housing and Home Finance Agency:
    Federal National Mortgage Association: purchases Government-insured mortgages, and is currently self-supporting.
    Urban Renewal Administration: loans to local public agencies for slum clearance and urban renewal projects, and is currently self-supporting.
    Community Facilities Administration: construction loans to colleges and universities, and is currently self-supporting.
    Public Housing Administration: loans to local authorities for construction of low-rent public housing, and is currently self-supporting.
  Veterans' Administration: direct housing loans in rural areas and small towns, and is currently self-supporting.
  Department of Agriculture:
    Rural Electrification Administration: loans, chiefly to cooperatives, to provide electric power and telephone service to farms.
    Farmers Home Administration: loans to farmers to "strengthen the family-type farm and encourage better farming methods."
    Commodity Credit Corporation: loans to farmers with commodities as collateral.
  Department of Commerce: Maritime Administration: direct loans for vessel construction; no new commitments made since 1956.
  Department of Health, Education, and Welfare: Office of Education: loans funds for student financial aid, construction, and acquisition of teaching equipment.
  Department of State:
    International Cooperation Administration: loans under Agricultural Trade Development and Assistance Act to promote multilateral trade and economic development.
    Development Loan Fund: loans to governments of underdeveloped nations or organizations and persons therein.
  Export-Import Bank: principal foreign-lending agency of the government; loans to finance exports and imports and to promote economic development in lesser developed countries, and is currently self-supporting.
  Small Business Administration:
    Business loans to small business, disaster loans to small business.

the time the loan is made, or it may be deferred, in which case the full amount of the loan is advanced by a private lender with the provision that the lender has the option of transferring at any time an agreed-upon proportion of the loan to a government agency. A loan guarantee is a loan agreement under which a government agency agrees to guarantee either all or an agreed-upon portion of a loan made by a private lender. Except for V.A. guarantees, the guarantee may be made effective at the lender's option; on V.A.-guaranteed loans, the guarantee does not come into play until the borrower defaults. In practice, there is little difference between a deferred participation and a loan guarantee, and the terms are used interchangeably. Sometimes "loan commitment" is used to refer to a loan agreement under which a government agency agrees to underwrite all or a portion of a loan. Two other terms closely related to those already mentioned are "loan authorization" and "loan disbursement." The former term refers to the principal sum that is specified in the loan agreement; the latter term refers to the actual amount of funds advanced or disbursed to the borrower.

Purchases of debentures of and loans to small business investment companies.

Loans to state and local development companies.

Expansion of defense production: The Treasury Department (for domestic loans) and the Export-Import Bank (for foreign loans) have authority to make direct loans for expansion of industrial capacity, development of technological process or production of essential materials. No new commitments made in 1959 or expected in 1960 or 1961.

Loan guarantee and insurance programs:

(Several of the programs listed below do not now involve losses to the Federal Government. Insurance and loan guarantees involve Federal commitments which could result in losses to the Government at some future time. These programs are in the nature of subsidies in the sense of providing insurance or loan guarantee services not available or available only at higher cost from private enterprise.)

Housing and Home Finance Agency:

  Federal Housing Administration: insures wide range of real estate loans, and is currently self-supporting.

Veterans' Administration: housing, business, and farm loans to veterans guaranteed.

Farmers Home Administration: insures farm ownership and soil and water conservation loans.

Commodity Credit Corporation: private loans on commodities guaranteed.

Maritime Administration: guarantees private construction loans and mortgages on most types of passenger and cargo-carrying vessels.

Civil Aeronautics Board: guarantees loans for aircraft purchases by local air services and other small airlines.

Interstate Commerce Commission: guarantees loans to railroads for certain purposes under Transportation Act of 1958.

Defense Production Act(sec. 301): authorizes guarantees by various agencies on loans to defense contractors and subcontractors.

Development Loan Fund: guarantees loans to governments of underdeveloped nations, their organizations and citizens.

Small Business Administration: guarantees loans to small business.

See the most recent *Annual Report of the Secretary of the Treasury* for details on each of these agencies and programs; see the most recent *Federal Reserve Bulletin* for information on assets and liabilities of Federal business-type activities, classified by purpose of loans and agencies.

To avoid competition with private lenders, enabling legislation has specified that government credit will be extended only if it cannot be obtained from private financing institutions on reasonable terms. In practice, more than 50 per cent of the government loans have been participation loans, which represent cooperative credit rather than competing credit.

CLOSING. Generally it takes more time to close a loan transaction with a government agency that it does with a private lender, because of the nature of the risk and the nature of government programs. Although involved procedures and lengthy negotiations may lead to sound loans, the total process probably discourages many prospective borrowers from applying for government credit. Most of the Federal Government's loan programs have denied at least half of the applications for credit, indicating the application of credit standards and deliberate avoidance of outright subsidies to businesses that are likely to fail.

SECURITY. Almost all business loans and loan guarantees of Federal agencies have been secured loans. The statutes have not required that all loans be secured; instead, they have specified that there should be assurance of repayment. Considering the nature of the loans made by government agencies and possible scrutiny by Congressional committees, administrators have equated reasonable assurance with collateral, which is objective and measurable.

INTEREST. As a general rule, interest rates are specified in the statutes. Administrators have not had the discretion of imposing rate differentials based on location, loan size, risk, and maturity. Also, changes in rates have been infrequent. During a period of tight money and rising interest rates, the demand for direct loans from government agencies tends to rise, because private lenders tend to reject a larger number of marginal lenders and to avoid participation loans that carry relatively low rates of interest. Considering the nature of many of the borrowers of government credit, it is probably true that many firms, especially small, newly established ones, have received government credit at bargain rates, in relation to the rates that would have been charged by private lenders on identical loans. It is also true that very few of the small loans granted to business firms by government and private lenders provide income adequate to cover costs of investigation and administration. Private lenders have been able to make a profit on their total loan portfolios by offsetting losses against income earned on larger loans. Most government loan programs have not been financially self-sustaining.

MATURITY. The statutes relating to most government loan programs permit loan maturities of up to ten years. In practice, the maturities have been slightly in excess of five years. Clearly, the government lending programs have provided primarily intermediate-term credit. The government loan programs have undoubtedly been an important factor in the development of the term loan among private lenders.

MANAGERIAL ASSISTANCE. Many of the government lending programs have incorporated managerial assistance and made it available to past, present, and prospective lenders. Although private lenders also supply managerial assistance, it appears that managerial services are more deliberate and more thorough in the case of government programs. Perhaps this characteristic explains in part why the programs have not been self-sustaining.

RECIPIENTS OF FINANCIAL ASSISTANCE. Manufacturing firms have received the major proportion of business loans and loan guarantees, in spite of the fact that manufacturing firms represent less than 10 per cent of all firms. The disproportionate flow of government-sponsored financial assistance to manufacturing firms can be explained by the much greater need that these firms have for intermediate-term financing. Although private lenders do make intermediate-term loans, they turn down a disproportionately large number of such requests on the ground that the loans are either too large or run for too long a period. If a participation loan can be arranged, private lenders are more likely to go along with such requests. Also, manufacturing firms are in a much better position to offer security for intermediate-term loans than are other firms, such as those in retail and service lines.

Federal Agencies

The business loans and loan guarantees of Federal agencies for the period 1934-1957 are summarized in Table 18-2. Each of the agencies or programs is discussed briefly. It should be noted that government agencies have participated in a very small proportion of all business loans. When we realize that there are over 4,000,000 firms and that many of these are marginal borrowers, the total number of loans shown in Table 18-2 does not seem very large.

RECONSTRUCTION AND FINANCE CORPORATION. The Reconstruction and Finance Corporation (R.F.C.) was initially created to provide financial assistance to financial institutions and railroads, but in 1934 its scope of operations was expanded to provide financing to all types and sizes of non-financial businesses. Its activities were originally limited to providing assistance to firms that could not obtain private credit on reasonable terms. During the period 1934-1941, the R.F.C. made over 10,500 loans and authorized $765 million of loans. During the war, the scope of operations of the R.F.C. was expanded considerably. The R.F.C. made loans and bought securities of businesses engaged in national defense operations. Special assistance was provided to small business. In 1945, the R.F.C. lending

TABLE 18–2

BUSINESS LOANS AND LOAN GUARANTIES OF FEDERAL AGENCIES, 1934-1957,
BY PERIODS AND BY AGENCY
(MILLIONS OF DOLLARS)

Agency, program, or type of lending	Program established (year)	Authorizations of direct loans, participations or commitments, and insured or guaranteed loans					
		1934-41		1942-53		1954-57	
		Number	Amount	Number	Amount	Number	Amount
By agency or program							
Reconstruction Finance Corporation	1934	10,527	765	51,288[1]	4,848[1]	....	....
Federal Reserve banks	1934	3,202	280	563	535	21	36
Smaller War Plants Corporation	1942	....	....	4,775[1]	480[1]	....	....
Regulation V loans	1942[2]	....	....	9,965	12,702	206	530
Veterans' Administration	1944	....	....	210,986	566	20,221	72
Small Business Administration	1953	....	....	....	....	8,597	398
Fisheries loan program (Department of the Interior)	....	....	....	....	....	174	5
By type of lending							
Direct loans	....	9,520[3]	638[3]	30,253	3,254	2,839	120
Immediate participations[4]	....	692	36	3,606	191	3,535	178
Deferred participations[4]	....	1,614	145	22,204	1,883[5]	2,397	104
Loan guaranties[6]	....	....	....	220,951	13,268	20,427	602
Unclassified[7]	....	1,903	220	563	535	21	36

[1] RFC loan program terminated Sept. 28, 1953; SWPC program terminated in January 1946.

[2] 1st program inaugurated in 1942; 2nd in 1950.

[3] Figures for Federal Reserve banks are for 1934-40. Classified data not available for 1941.

[4] A precise classification of RFC participation loans is not available. Figures for the 2 types of participations for this agency are estimates based on information indicating that deferred participation loans accounted for 70 per cent of the number and 30 per cent of the amount of all participation loans in 1934-41, and for 85 per cent of the number and 90 per cent of the amount in 1942-53. See R. J. Saulnier, Harold G. Halcrow, and Neil H. Jacoby, *Federal Lending and Loan Insurance* (Princeton University Press, 1958), pp. 482-486.

[5] Includes $172,000,000 as SWPC share of deferred participations.

Data on bank share of participations not available (see Comptroller General of the United States, Report on Audit of Smaller War Plants Corporation, 80th Cong., 2nd sess., H. Doc. 549 (1948), pp. 2 and 14).

[6] Includes VA-insured as well as guaranteed loans.

[7] Figures are for the 13b program of the Federal Reserve banks, except that direct loans under that program in the 1934-40 period have been classified (see note 3).

Source: Carl T. Arlt, "Government Loan Programs for Small Business," in U. S. Committees on Banking and Currency and the Select Committees on Small Business, *Financing Small Business*, Report by the Federal Reserve System, Parts 1 and 2, 85th Cong., 2nd Sess., Washington, D. C.: Government Printing Office, 1958, p. 255.

operations were further modified by the establishment of the so-called Blanket Participation Agreement program, under which the R.F.C. automatically guaranteed bank loans to business up to 75 per cent of loan authorizations, providing the loans conformed to the standards set forth in the program. Over 11,000 loans, representing approximately $525 million in loan authorizations, were made under this program in the subsequent 22 months. This phase of R.F.C. lending came under severe attack, and Congress modified it by limiting the size of individual loan authorizations and restricting loan approval procedures. During the period January, 1948 through March, 1950, nearly $1 billion of loans were authorized. The Korean War shifted the emphasis back to defense-related activities. The R.F.C. charter was renewed several times, but in 1954 it was allowed to lapse.

FEDERAL RESERVE BANKS. In 1934, Federal Reserve banks were authorized to provide financial assistance to firms that could not obtain needed financing from usual sources at reasonable terms. The assistance was in the form of loan commitments, participation loans, and direct loans. It was not expected that the assistance would be granted except under exceptional conditions. As shown in Table 18-2, the Federal Reserve banks made 3,202 loans during the period 1934-1941. Since 1941, and especially in recent years, very few loans have been made through the Federal Reserve banks.

SMALLER WAR PLANTS CORPORATION. In 1942, the Smaller War Plants Corporation was created to provide both direct and participation loans to small firms, defined in the enabling legislation as those employing less than 500 people. From 1942 to its termination in 1946, this government corporation authorized 4,775 loans, aggregating $480 million.

REGULATION V LOANS. There have been two Regulation V loan programs, one during World War II and the other during the Korean emergency. Defense agencies guaranteed the loans, and the Federal Reserve Banks administered the program. As shown in Table 18-2, the number of loans authorized under Regulation V exceeds the total authorizations under all other programs. However, this program has not been very active in recent years.

VETERANS ADMINISTRATION. The Veterans Administration has been authorized to guarantee and/or insure loans to veterans, when the purpose of the loan is to establish or expand a business. Depending on the nature of the security, the maximum guarantee ranges from $2,000 to $4,000. Financial institutions that qualify as supervised lenders generally elect the insurance option, which insures the lender against loss up to 15 per cent of the aggregate amount of eligible loans made, making it possible for a lender that makes a large volume of V.A. loans to have full protection against individual losses as long as aggregate losses do not exceed 15 per cent of that loan portfolio. The greatest number of business loans and loan guarantees of Federal agencies has been made under the V.A. program. However, because of the small amount of each loan, the total amount loaned under the V.A. program has been lower than that of other programs.

Small Business Administration

A Republican slogan in the 1952 Presidential campaign was " Clean up the mess in Washington," and one of the agencies frequently mentioned as in need of cleaning up was the R.F.C., which had been involved in a number of scandals. In September, 1953, Congress terminated the R.F.C., but it also created a successor agency in the form of the Small Business Administration. In fact, the S.B.A. made its first loan one month prior to the termination of R.F.C. The initial entry of the government into this role came during World War I; it was stepped up during the Great Depression and World War II; by 1953, the role of the Federal government had expanded so much that Congress created a new agency during a period of peace and prosperity. Initially, S.B.A. was given only temporary status and was required to operate under much more severe limits than its predecessor, the R.F.C. However, with the passage of time the restrictions were relaxed. In 1958, the S.B.A. was given permanent status and its annual lending exceeded the average annual lending of the R.F.C.

Since 1953, the Small Business Administration has been the major government lending program. In this section we shall examine the S.B.A.'s functions, lending authority, lending policy, and lending terms. The fisheries loan program, which is administered jointly by the Department of Interior and the S.B.A., is designed to provide financial assistance to fishermen. The scope of this section will not permit more than a mere mention of the program.

FUNCTIONS OF THE S.B.A. In setting up the S.B.A., Congress assigned to this new agency the following responsibilities: (1) to help small business gain access to adequate capital and credit; (2) to help small business obtain a fair share of government procurement; (3) to help small business obtain competent management, technical, and production counsel; and (4) to make disaster loans to persons whose homes or businesses have been damaged by storms, floods, and other disasters, and to small business concerns that have suffered substantial economic injury because of excessive rainfall or draught conditions in their areas. In 1958, Congress established in the S.B.A. a Small Business Investment Division to administer the Small Business Investment Act of 1958, which is designed to make equity capital and long-term credit more readily available for small-business concerns. This part of the program is discussed in Chapter 20.

LENDING AUTHORITY. The S.B.A. is authorized to provide financial assistance to small businesses that are unable to obtain needed financing from private lending sources on reasonable terms. However, the financial assistance must be in the public interest and there must be reasonable assurance of repayment. Government lending programs, including the program administered by the S.B.A., have been severely criticized on the ground that an economic criterion is forsworn in that the firm must have failed to get assistance from private sources. This is not a valid criticism, because the economic criterion is not forsworn; the same analytical techniques are used, except that the standards against which the firm is compared are lowered. It might be recalled that finance companies make loans to firms that have been turned down by commercial banks and other private lenders; the finance companies have not thereby forsworn an economic criterion. Also, it should be noted that a lending agency as large as the S.B.A. can make many more loans to small business than can any other single lender. The law of large numbers tends to reduce the risk.

Loans are not authorized to finance certain types of business activity, and the maximum loan to any one borrower or S.B.A. share of a loan may not exceed $250,000; the maximum maturity is set at 10 years. Congress has established the maximum lending authority for business and disaster loans, thereby setting a limit on the total amount of outstanding loans and commitments. The funds that are disbursed by the S.B.A. are appropriated by Congress, and S.B.A. pays a rate of interest on the funds equivalent to the average interest rate on Treasury borrowing. The total volume of loans can be much greater than the total authorization or appropriation because of the revolving nature of the funds. Whenever the total outstanding loans have approached an established limit, Congress has increased the authorization and appropriated additional funds. The program has much political appeal.

LENDING POLICY. Assuming that an applicant is eligible for S.B.A. assistance, the S.B.A. makes a direct loan only if a participation loan is not possible. The policy reflects the mutual advantages of participation loans. The borrower establishes and maintains a working relationship with a private lender. With the S.B.A.'s participation, it is usually possible for private lenders to make larger and longer maturity loans than if the S.B.A. were not participating. Participation loans offer many advantages to the S.B.A. The administration of the loan is shifted to a private lender; there is less drain on the revolving loan funds; and there is a strong possibility that the entire loan may be transferred to the private lender if the loan works out better than the lender envisioned. During a period of rising interest rates, private lenders tend to shy away from participation loans. To counter this trend, the S. B. A. in 1958 reduced by one-half the participation fees charged private lenders on deferred participation loans, and introduced service fees for banks that service immediate participation loans. On the average, approximately

60 per cent of the business loans approved by the S.B.A. have been participation loans, and the immediate participation loans have been more important than deferred participation loans.

Although the law does not require that all loans be secured, it has been the policy of the S.B.A. to require that loans be secured by adequate collateral. In 1956, a Limited Loan Participation Program was introduced to cover the loans under which applicants are not able to pledge as much tangible collateral as is required for regular business loans. Under this program, the S.B.A. joins with a bank in a loan up to a maximum of $15,000 or 75 per cent of the loan, whichever is the smaller. The maturity of these loans is limited to five years. During 1958 most of the loans under this program were made to retailers, wholesalers, and service establishments, for which the program was chiefly designed. In these loans, major emphasis is placed on earnings, management, and credit record.

Interest rates are specified in the law, introducing an element of inflexibility. All direct loans are made at 6 per cent, and the participation loans are made at the rate arranged between the private lender and the borrower, but in no case can the rate exceed 6 per cent.

Most of the loans have a maturity ranging from five to ten years. The S.B.A. has been a strong advocate of term loans.

SUMMARY OF OPERATIONS.* From the beginning of the S.B.A.'s business lending operations through the close of 1959, the S.B.A. has approved 18,271 business loans for $856.3 million. During the same period, the cumulative ratio of approvables to applications acted on has been about 54 per cent. Loans to manufacturing firms accounted for 32 per cent of the total number of loans and 46 per cent of the dollar amount. Loans to non-manufacturing industries accounted for the remainder. The actual and estimated losses as of December 31, 1959 represented only 1.1 per cent of S.B.A.'s share of loans disbursed. However, the financial results cannot be effectively measured until the longer maturity loans come due.

STATE DEVELOPMENT CREDIT CORPORATIONS

Since the major portion of credit extended by state development credit corporations has an original maturity of less than ten years, it is appropriate to examine the subject in this chapter. The title of this type of institution is both revealing and misleading. "Development" is probably the best descriptive term that can be used, since these institutions extend credit for the purpose of developing a state's economy. However, "state" may be misleading because the institutions are neither owned nor administered by the

*Data from 13th Semiannual Report of the Small Business Administration.

government. Instead, they are privately owned and administered by a board of directors elected by these who supply funds. " State " refers merely to the location of the stockholders and borrowers.

In addition to state development credit corporations, there are literally thousands of local development corporations or associations, which provide financial and counseling assistance for the purpose of developing the local economy. Because of the absence of reliable aggregate data, they are not covered in this text. It is enough to mention that many of these local institutions have done a remarkable job at the local level. There are also a few state credit authorities, which are public agencies using public funds in development work. Generally, state credit authorities lend money to and purchase securities from the state development credit corporation and local credit corporations. This type of public agency should not be confused with the privately owned state development credit corporations.

Origin and Development

The basic reasons for the origin and development of state development credit corporations are very similar to those that gave rise to Federal loan programs. Individual private lenders realized that they were having to turn down loan requests of many firms that failed to meet the institutions' credit standards, but they also realized that if the loans could have been made, many might have turned out to be sound and the firms' successes would have contributed to the economic development of their respective communities and states. Beginning in 1934 and continuing through 1958, Federal programs have been set up to plug this gap in our financial system. The state development credit corporations represent the combined efforts of private lenders to accomplish the same objective. By pooling funds of individual private lenders through the facilities of these corporations each private lender, in effect, loans a small amount to each of many high-risk borrowers. By spreading an individual lender's funds over a greater number of borrowers, the risk to that lender is less than if the funds were loaned out to only a small number of borrowers within a given community. Furthermore, additional funds are allocated in the higher-risk type of business loans in the sense that the private lender continues to make individual loans.

The first state development credit corporation was established in Maine in 1949, and by 1958, 14 states had passed legislation authorizing such corporations. An equal number showed strong interest. The Federal Reserve Bank of Boston reports frequently on the status of these corporations in the New England area, and these reports serve as the major frame of reference for this section of the chapter. It has already been observed that operating patterns of these institutions in other states are similar to those followed in the New England states.

Development credit corporations have both stockholders and members; the former group consists of individuals and nonfinancial institutions, and the latter consists of financial institutions, including commercial banks, savings banks, insurance companies, and others. The charters under which the credit corporations operate permit the payment of dividends, but the very low net income and the need to build up reserves and capital accounts have not permitted the declaration of dividends. In fact, dividends are not likely to appear for many years. Undoubtedly, most stockholders in the state development credit corporations consider themselves donors rather than investors. The major source of funds is supplied by the member financial institutions, which individually pledge a line of credit stated in terms of a percentage of the member's total capital accounts. Therefore, the loan pool is comprised of funds received from the sale of stock and from calls made against the various lines of credit.

Directors are elected by both stockholders and members, with the latter group generally electing two-thirds of the total number of directors. As in other corporations, the directors elect the officers. Member financial institutions provide much assistance to the relatively small staffs that administer development credit corporations. Credit investigations and counseling may be provided at little or no cost to the development credit corporations.

Lending Policy

The development credit corporations consider a loan request only if it has been rejected by a conventional private lender; in fact, many of the requests represent referrals by member institutions and the Small Business Administration. A loan request is intensively reviewed, and after a somewhat time-consuming process, it is either approved or rejected. The fact that the loan request was initially refused by a private lender in the competitive market does not preclude the application of credit standards by the development credit corporations. Instead, the conventional set of standards is relaxed, especially with regard to earnings ability, capital, and collateral. Up to 1960, the development credit corporations had turned down over half of the total formal loan applications.

Assuming that a loan request is approved, it is likely that the borrower will be a manufacturing corporation, and that the loan will be secured, intermediate-term, and on a participation basis. Based on outstanding loans of the New England development credit corporations on September 30, 1957, 95 per cent of the dollar amount was secured, and nearly all of the residual represented loans in which the borrower had agreed not to pledge any asset for other loans. The data also suggest that the development credit corporations rely much more heavily on second mortgages than do conventional lenders and that they loan more in relation to market value of collateral. On the same date, less than 10 per cent of the number and amount of loans had maturities of less than five years; the majority were within the range of five to ten years.

There is great variation in policy with regard to interest rates. Originally, the flat 6 per cent rate was common, but the more recent practice is to set the rate 2 or 3 per cent above the prime bank rate. The Rhode Island development credit corporation has a flexible rate structure with 12 per cent as the ceiling. As noted in the discussion of bank loans and loans from finance companies, rates as high as 10 per cent are not uncommon on high-risk loans made by private lenders. The policy with regard to cost of funds also varies among credit corporations. Generally, it is related to Federal Reserve discount rates. In relation to other private lending institutions, development credit corporations secure and disburse funds at low rates.

Volume of Lending

A recent study of the New England credit corporations summarized the volume of lending in these terms:*

> [It] has not been large in absolute terms. On December 31, 1957, outstanding loans of the five New England corporations totalled $8.7 million. While it must be emphasized that these loans are primarily to manufacturers, the total amount is small when compared to the $414 million small business loans to commercial and industrial firms by first district member banks as of October 16, 1957. . . . Thus credit corporation loans in the region are equivalent to only about two per cent of small-business loans of commercial banks and the ratio would be smaller if all sources of small-business credit were taken into account. While contribution to small-business financing of this magnitude seems small, it may be a quite important amount at the credit margin. Moreover, lending activities of the credit corporations are expanding rapidly — total loans outstanding rose by almost one-fourth in 1957, although potential growth is limited if funds continue to be sought on the present basis. Outstanding business loans of the Small Business Administration in New England outside Vermont were even somewhat smaller — $8.1 million as of June 30, 1957 — than those of the five credit corporations.

QUESTIONS

1. Describe open-market paper.

2. Distinguish between a bank's purchase of open-market paper and its short-term loans to customers.

3. Describe the market for open-market paper, placing special emphasis on the reasons for the relatively small number of borrowers and dealers.

*Paul S. Anderson, "State Development Credit Corporations," *Financing Small Business*, p. 349.

4. What is the relationship between the size of discount on open-market paper and the prime bank rate charged in the customers' loan market?

5. Explain the growth in the dollar value of directly placed finance company paper.

6. What are the advantages and disadvantages of open-market paper from both the borrowers' and investors' point of view?

7. Define factoring. Trace its origin and development.

8. Compare the factor's commission for assuming the credit and collection functions with the factor's rate for advancing cash against receivables.

9. Distinguish between factoring and accounts receivable financing.

10. Trace the origin and development of accounts receivable financing.

11. Illustrate how to compute the cost of accounts receivable financing that is handled through a finance company.

12. List and describe the three basic types of financial assistance provided under the auspices of the Federal Government.

13. With respect to the Federal Government's loan programs, comment briefly on competition with private lenders, closing, security, interest rates, and maturity.

14. What are state development credit corporations? Trace their origin and development.

15. Compare the lending policies of the Small Business Administration and the state development credit corporations.

ADDITIONAL READING

See list of additional reading and references to other chapters at the end of Chapter 17.

Greef, Albert O. *The Commercial Paper House in the United States.* Cambridge, Mass.: Harvard University Press, 1938.

Phelps, Clyde Wm. *The Role of Factoring in Modern Business Finance.* Studies in Commercial Financing, No. 1. Baltimore: Commercial Credit Company, 1956.

————. *Accounts Receivable Financing as a Method of Business Finance.* Studies in Commercial Financing, No. 2. Baltimore: Commercial Credit Company, 1957.

Saulnier, Raymond J., Harold G. Halcrow, and Neil H. Jacoby. *Federal Lending and Loan Insurance.* N.B.E.R. study. Princeton, N.J.: Princeton University Press, 1958.

Small Business Administration. *Semiannual Report.* Washington, D.C.: Small Business Administration. See latest report.

U.S. House of Representatives. Select Committee on Small Business. *Problems of Small-Business Financing.* A report of the Committee, 85th Cong., 2nd sess. Washington, D.C.: Government Printing Office, 1958.

————. *Problems of Small-Business Financing.* Hearings on H. Res. 56, a resolution creating a select committee to conduct a study and investigation of the problems of small business, held during November, 1957, 85th Cong., 1st sess. Washington, D.C.: Government Printing Office, 1957.

———. *Final Report* pursuant to H. Res. 56.

U.S. House of Representatives Subcommittee No. 1 of the Select Committee on Small Business. *Organization and Operation of the Small Business Administration.* Hearings, Parts I, II, 86th Cong., 1st sess. Washington, D.C.: Government Printing Office, 1959. Also, Report, 86th Cong., 2nd sess. Washington, D.C.: Government Printing Office, 1960.

U.S. House of Representatives Subcommittee No. 2 of the Select Committee on Small Business. *Definition of "Small Business" Within Meaning of Small Business Act of 1953, As Amended.* Hearings, 85th Cong., 2nd sess. Washington, D.C.: Government Printing Office, 1959.

U.S. Senate Select Committee on Small Business. *Briefing on the Investment Act.* Briefing session on the Small Business Investment Act of 1958, sponsored by the American Management Association, New York, December 1-2, 1958, and printed for use of Committee. 85th Cong., 2nd sess. Washington, D.C.: Government Printing Office, 1959.

U.S. Senate Subcommittee of the Committee on Banking and Currency. *Credit Needs of Small Business.* Hearings, Parts I, II, 85th Cong., 2nd sess. Washington, D.C.: Government Printing Office, 1958.

———. *Financing Small Business.* Hearings, 85th Cong., 2nd sess. Washington, D.C.: Government Printing Office, 1958.

19: Long-term and permanent financing, I

IT was pointed out in Chapter 16 that long-term and permanent, external sources of funds supplied $35.8 billion or approximately 22.6 per cent of the corporate nonfinancial business sector's total funds during the period 1955-1958. Net new issues of corporate stock supplied $9.0 billion or 5.7 per cent; net new issues of corporate bonds supplied $18.7 billion or 11.8 per cent; and mortgages supplied $8.1 billion or 5.1 per cent. During the same period, the non-corporate, nonfinancial business sector acquired $4 billion or 8.1 per cent of its funds from external sources, all of which was in the form of mortgage credit.

As we noted in earlier chapters, there are many uses to which consumer saving may be put: durable consumer goods, family residential property, direct investment in unincorporated business, fixed-value redeemable claims, non-corporate credit market instruments, and corporate market instruments. Financial institutions also have considerable investment choice. In the light of these facts, business firms must offer market instruments that are attractive in relation to the alternative financial and nonfinancial investment opportunities.

Since there is much variety among investment policies of individual and institutional investors, business firms must offer a variety of market instruments. To secure funds in the long-term capital market, they must decide on what segment of the market to tap, issue market instruments that will fit the needs of investors, and include provisions and terms that will be relatively attractive.

The long-term market instruments that are used by business firms have already been described. It will be recalled that there are two main categories of corporate securities: capital stock and bonds. Capital stock represents an ownership or equity interest; a bond represents a debtor-creditor relationship. Various types of securities are included in each category. Common and preferred stocks are the two basic classes of capital stock; secured and unsecured (debentures) are the two basic classes of corporate bonds. Securities can be further classified by type, method of participation in earnings, and method of retirement or repayment. Obviously, there is a fair amount of "product differentiation" in corporate securities. Mortgages consist of debt that is secured by property, which in this case includes multi-family and commercial property. In this type of credit transaction, the debtor gives the creditor a promissory note and a legal instrument specifying certain property as security for the note. Although the type of legal instrument or document used in a specific transaction depends on state law, all such loans are considered mortgage loans. The use of mortgage debt by nonfinancial firms is understated to the extent that mortgages on one- to four-family residential property is also used as a source of business funds.

In this chapter, we shall draw heavily on the previous discussion of individual and institutional investment policies, and shall integrate background information that is relevant in terms of the market for corporate stock, the market for corporate bonds, and the market for commercial and multi-family mortgages. The amounts outstanding and the annual flows into these markets are analyzed from the point of view of major sectors. In the following chapter, attention will be focused on investment banking, regulation of public offerings, competitive bidding, direct placement, and small business investment companies.

MARKET FOR CORPORATE STOCK

The market for corporate stock is fairly well portrayed by a pair of tables based on flow-of-funds data. Table 19-1 shows by major sectors the ownership pattern of corporate stock and the relative importance of corporate stock in the sectors' total holdings of financial assets. Table 19-2 shows the level and composition of annual flows into corporate stock for the years 1954-1958. By comparing the percentages in Tables 19-1 and 19-2, it is possible to determine some of the recent trends in the market for corporate stock. At the end of 1958, the consumer and nonprofit organization sector held 91 per cent of the corporate stock outstanding, but during the period 1954-1958 this sector's share of net purchases was approximately 40 per cent, and in no year did it exceed 60 per cent. The relative importance of this sector in the market for corporate stock is gradually declining, and the non-bank financial institutions' share of the market is increasing. The insurance sector supplied between 27.5 per cent and 42.3 per cent of the annual net purchases during the period 1954-1958. These percentages are much higher than the sector's share of corporate stock outstanding. A similar relationship prevailed in the finance, n.e.c. sector. Between 1949 and 1958, the dollar amount of institutional investors' holdings of N.Y.S.E.-listed stock increased from $9.5 billion to $44.1 billion, and their share of the market value of all N.Y.S.E.-listed stock increased from 12.4 per cent to 16.0 per cent. At the close of 1959, their holdings totaled $51 billion and their share was 16.6 per cent.* The data illustrate the growing importance of the institutional investors in the market for corporate stock. This development has several implications. First, the institutional investors tend to purchase corporate stock for the long pull, which means that a greater share of corporate stock is being "locked up," thus reducing the potential volume of trading in corporate stock. Second, the institutional investors tend to purchase stock more regularly than do individuals, thereby providing greater buoyancy in the market for corporate stock. Third, the institutional investors are able to exercise greater influence on corporate management than can individual investors. The institutional investors are probably more concerned with management because of long-run interests, and they are

TABLE 19–1

CORPORATE STOCK OUTSTANDING, END OF 1958*

(BILLIONS OF DOLLARS)

Sector	Dollars	Per cent	Corporate stock as a percentage of total financial assets
Consumer and nonprofit organizations	386.8	91.0	44.6
Non-bank financial	32.1	7.6	11.1
Insurance	19.4	4.6	12.9
Finance, n.e.c. [1]	11.8	2.8	27.4
Savings institutions	0.9	.2	0.9
Rest-of-the-world	6.0	1.4	12.2
Total	425.0	100.0	

*Market value; excludes stock held by nonfinancial corporations, holding companies, and closed-end companies.

[1] Open-end investment companies.

Source: "A Quarterly Presentation of Flow of Funds, Saving and Investment," *Federal Reserve Bulletin*, August 1959.

able to communicate more effectively with corporate management. Institutional investors are able to make elaborate studies of companies in which they hold stock, and corporate management recognizes the fact that they may be able to offer sound advice. There is a remote possibility that these investors may in the future exert an undue amount of control over corporate management. Considering the degree of concentration among institutional investors, the control over corporate capital would also be concentrated.

Given this over-all background, we shall now focus our attention on the supply of and the demand for corporate stock, the latter of which is examined from the point of view of the sectors that invest a significant amount in corporate stock.

*New York Stock Exchange Fact Book, 1960, p. 29.

Net Issues of Corporate Stock

There are no reliable estimates as to the amount of corporate stock outstanding by issuers, but there are estimates of recent annual flows of corporate stock by issuers. The data in Table 19-2 show that net annual issues of nonfinancial corporate business firms have accounted for approximately 60 per cent of total net issues of corporate stock. The net new issues of open-end investment companies account for almost all of the net issues of non-bank financial institutions. The major portion of net issues shown under the category "other" represents the issues of commercial banks. The data show that financial institutions must compete in a capital market dominated by nonfinancial corporate firms.

TABLE 19–2
ANNUAL FLOWS INTO CORPORATE STOCK, 1954-1958
(BILLIONS OF DOLLARS)

Sector	1954		1955		1956		1957		1958	
	$	%	$	%	$	%	$	%	$	%
Net Issues	2.6	100.0	3.0	100.0	3.8	100.0	4.0	100.0	4.2	100.0
Corporate nonfinancial business	1.6	61.5	2.0	66.7	2.3	60.5	2.4	60.0	2.3	54.8
Non-bank financial [1]	.5	19.2	.9	30.0	1.1	28.9	1.2	30.0	1.6	38.1
Other [2]	.5	19.2	.1	3.3	.4	10.5	.4	10.0	.3	7.1
Net Purchases	2.6	100.0	3.0	100.0	3.8	100.0	4.0	100.0	4.2	100.0
Consumer and nonprofit ..	.8	30.8	1.4	46.7	2.2	57.9	1.8	45.0	1.7	40.5
Nonbank financial	1.7	65.4	1.5	50.0	1.3	34.2	2.0	50.0	2.5	59.5
Insurance	1.1	42.3	.9	30.0	1.0	26.3	1.1	27.5	1.4	33.3
Finance, n.e.c.	.6	23.1	.5	16.7	.3	7.9	.9	22.5	1.0	23.8
Savings institutions	*	*	.1	3.3	*	*	*	*	.1	2.4
Other (rest-of-the-world)..	.1	3.8	.1	3.3	.3	7.9	.2	5.0	*	*

*Less than $50 million.
[1] Open-end investment companies account for almost all of net issues; insurance institutions and open-end investment companies account for almost all of net purchases.
[2] Commercial banks account for the major portion of net issues; the rest-of-the-world sector accounts for almost all of net purchases.
Source: "A Quarterly Presentation of Flow of Funds, Saving and Investment," *Federal Reserve Bulletin*, August 1959.

The annual volume of net new issues of corporate stock is determined by the need of financial and nonfinancial firms to obtain external long-term or permanent funds, and by the popularity of open-end investment companies. Corporations attempt to attain an optmium or ideal capital structure; that is, an ideal distribution among capital stock, surplus, and bonds, and as the need for long-term capital increases there will be additional issues of corporate stock. During certain periods, the state of the securities market prompts corporate officials to delay or accelerate their offerings of stock.

For example, when a company's stock is selling at an exceptionally high price, then is the time to issue stock.

Consumer and Nonprofit Organization Sector

At the end of 1958, the consumer and nonprofit organization sector held 91 per cent of the total market value of corporate stock outstanding, and this type of financial asset accounted for about 45 per cent of the sector's total holdings of financial assets. The importance of this sector's holdings is accounted for by two facts: (1) the sector holds more financial assets than any other sector, and (2) individuals and trustees can and do adopt investment policies that permit a relatively high percentage of financial assets to be invested in corporate stock. It is estimated that nonprofit organizations held at the end of 1958 over $11 billion of corporate stock, and these holdings accounted for about 50 per cent of their total assets.

During the 1954-1958 period, this sector's net purchases accounted for a much smaller percentage of total net purchases than its share of total holdings. This relationship does not mean that corporate stock has become less attractive to economic units in this sector; it means instead that economic units in other sectors have been stepping up their net purchases at a more rapid rate. The 1959 Census of Shareholders conducted by the N.Y.S.E. revealed that nearly 12,500,000 individuals owned shares in publicly held corporations in early 1959, an increase of six million since 1952. In early 1959, approximately 1,500,000 individuals owned shares in privately held companies, which are defined as corporations with fewer than 300 shareholders or whose shares are not available for purchase by the general public.

The net annual flow data show that the sector's net purchases are influenced by business conditions and market conditions. For example, the sector's net purchases in 1954 accounted for only 30.8 per cent of total net purchases, but in 1956 and 1957 net purchases were respectively 46.7 per cent and 57.9 per cent. In 1958, a year of recession, the sector's net purchases dropped to a low of 40.5 per cent. There was a very sharp reduction in the sector's net purchases in the third quarter of 1957, at which time the 1957-1958 recession became evident. In the second quarter of 1958, during which the upturn became evident, there was a sharp upturn in the sector's net purchases. During the 1957-1958 recession, there was a fairly close relationship between public attitude toward corporate stock and toward business conditions.

When we realize that there are literally thousands of personal trusts and nonprofit organizations and millions of individual investors in corporate stock, we see that there must be an elaborate sales and distribution organization to reach this large and diverse group of investors. It is not practical for individual corporate issuers to maintain their own distribution and sales organizations to handle infrequent public offerings. It is much more economical and efficient to use the services of the investment banking industry to achieve public distribution of new stock offerings.

425

Non-bank Financial Sectors

Although the non-bank financial sectors held less than 8 per cent of corporate stock outstanding at the end of 1958, the sectors' net purchases of corporate stock during the period 1954-1958 accounted for more than half of total net purchases. Obviously, the ownership pattern of corporate stock is undergoing change; a greater portion of the corporate stock is being purchased and held by institutional investors. As noted earlier, the growing importance of non-bank financial institutions in the market for corporate stock represents one of the most important developments in the postwar market for corporate stock.

INSURANCE SECTOR. The insurance sector is comprised of three major classes of investors: nonlife insurance companies, self-administered trust funds, and life insurance companies. The combined corporate stock holdings of these three types of investors totaled nearly $20 billion at the end of 1958. The corporate stock investments of the first two classes are closely similar; at the end of 1958, each had invested approximately 30 per cent of its assets in corporate stock. As previously mentioned, the nonlife insurance companies are able to invest a large percentage of their assets in corporate stock because their capital accounts are equal to about 35 per cent of their assets. The trustees of self-administered trust funds are able to sacrifice liquidity and stability of principal, at least in the short run, because their liabilities are not formally stated and most funds have a sizeable net annual cash inflow. In 1956, each of these two sectors held about the same amount of corporate stock, but since that time the corporate stock holdings of self-administered trust funds have increased. At the end of 1958, the market value of the corporate stock holdings of self-administered trust funds and nonlife insurance companies were respectively $9.5 billion and $5.8 billion.

Only a small percentage of the life insurance subsector's assets is invested in corporate stock, but because of the size of the sector, its holdings are significant. Prior to 1951, laws in many states either prohibited or severely restricted life insurance companies' investment in common stocks. Since that time New York and many other states have relaxed restrictions on such investments. New York now allows common stock holdings up to 5 per cent of assets or half of surplus, whichever is less. The latter limit is the one that applies to most New York companies. State laws also specify investment criteria for common stock investments. Some companies hold as much as 16 per cent of their assets in common stock, whereas some other companies do not hold any common stock.

During the 1954-1958 period, the life insurance subsector's annual purchases of corporate stock ranged between $100 and $300 million. Compared with the other insurance subsectors, this subsector's purchases have been less stable, indicating that life insurance companies are not committed to corporate stock investment as much as other subsectors. However, future developments in the life insurance industry may bring about an increase and greater stability in the volume of net purchases of corporate stock by life insurance companies. More and more companies have been adopting an investment policy that includes investing in corporate stock. The sale of variable annuity contracts is underway. State laws may be changed to improve the competitive position of life insurance companies in the management of pension and retirement funds.

FINANCE, N.E.C. The corporate stock holdings of the finance, n.e.c. sector represent primarily those of open-end investment companies. At the close of 1958, the companies held nearly $12 billion of corporate stock. As we remarked in the chapter dealing with investment companies, the common-stock funds have been extremely attractive during the postwar period. Assuming prosperity and a strong market, the net new capital issues of open-end investment companies should continue to increase. There may develop more intensive competition between life insurance companies and investment companies, but, regardless of the outcome, the funds will be invested primarily in corporate stock.

SAVINGS INSTITUTIONS. At the end of 1958, the savings institutions sector held $900 million of corporate stock, representing only 0.2 per cent of all corporate stock outstanding. However, in 1955 and 1958 the sector's annual net purchases reached $100 million. The relationship between the sector's holdings of corporate stock and the total market value of corporate stock is approximately 1:425, but the relationship between the sector's net purchases of corporate stock and total net purchases of corporate stock has been as low as 1:40. These figures show part of the growing importance of institutional investors.

The financial institutions that comprise this sector are legally prevented from investing a very large percentage of their assets in corporate stock, and in states that have permitted such investments, the institutions have moved very slowly in this direction. However, it can be expected that additional states will liberalize investment laws and that investment officers of savings institutions will become more accustomed to this form of investment. This sector is not a major purchaser of corporate stock in the existing market for such stock, but the trend is significant.

Other Sectors

At the end of 1958, other sectors held only $6 billion of corporate stock. These holdings have been built up over a period of years, for the largest net annual purchase of corporate stock by the other sectors was $300 million in 1956. In many years, the sectors' net annual purchases have been less than $50 million. The major portion of these holdings represent those of investors in the rest-of-the-world sector. When major trading countries eliminate or moderate exchange restrictions on securities transactions, this sector will probably become a more important purchaser of corporate stock in the United States. A small part of the holdings are those of the state and local government retirement funds. In the future, this sector could become an important investor in corporate stock. Many states have passed enabling legislation that permits partial investment in corporate stock. This legislation represents a sharp break from the past, and it will take time for the trustees of state and local retirement funds to adjust themselves to the new freedom. Undoubtedly, the trustees will move very slowly into corporate stocks.

MARKET FOR CORPORATE BONDS

The discussion of the market for corporate bonds is couched in a framework similar to that used in the previous section; the market is examined in terms

TABLE 19–3
CORPORATE AND FOREIGN BONDS OUTSTANDING, END OF 1958
(BILLIONS OF DOLLARS)

Sector	Dollars	Per cent	Bonds as a percentage of issuers' liabilities and of investors' financial assets
Issuers (all sectors)	81.4	100.0	
Corporate business	69.2	85.0	38.6
Finance, n.e.c. [1]	7.2	8.8	30.6
Rest-of-the-world [2]	5.0	6.1	9.6
Investors (all sectors)	81.4	100.0	
Non-bank financial	63.3	77.8	21.9
Life insurance companies	44.2	54.3	43.8
Self-administered pension plans	11.6	14.2	54.5
Savings institutions [3]	3.8	4.7	4.0
Nonlife insurance companies..	2.6	3.2	9.2
Finance, n.e.c. [4]	1.1	1.4	2.6
Consumer and nonprofit organizations	9.6	11.8	1.1
State and local government.....	6.7	8.2	14.2
Commercial banking	1.3	1.6	.5
Rest-of-the-world	.5	.6	1.0

[1] Finance companies.
[2] Includes United States net purchases of issues by World Bank and International Monetary Fund.
[3] Mutual savings banks account for almost all of the sector's holdings.
[4] Investment companies, security brokers, and dealers.

Source: "A Quarterly Presentation of Flow of Funds, Saving and Investment," *Federal Reserve Bulletin*, August 1959.

TABLE 19–4
ANNUAL FLOWS INTO CORPORATE AND FOREIGN BONDS, 1954-1958
(BILLIONS OF DOLLARS)

Sector	1954 $	1954 %	1955 $	1955 %	1956 $	1956 %	1957 $	1957 %	1958 $	1958 %
Net Issues (all sectors).....	3.7	100.0	4.0	100.0	5.0	100.0	7.5	100.0	6.9	100.0
Corporate nonfinancial business	3.5	94.6	2.8	70.0	3.7	74.0	6.3	84.0	5.9	85.5
Non-bank financial (finance companies)	.3	8.1	1.4	35.0	1.1	22.0	.7	9.3	.1	1.4
Other (rest-of-the-world)..—.1	—.1	(2.7)	—.2	(5.0)	.2	4.0	.5	6.7	.9	13.0
Net Acquisitions (all sectors)	3.7	100.0	4.0	100.0	5.0	100.0	7.5	100.0	6.9	100.0
Non-bank financial	3.8	102.7	2.4	60.0	3.6	72.0	5.1	68.0	4.7	68.1
Life insurance companies	2.1	56.8	1.5	37.5	2.2	44.0	2.4	32.0	2.6	37.7
Self-administered pension plans	1.2	32.4	.9	22.5	1.4	28.0	1.6	21.3	1.3	18.8
Other non-bank financial	.5	13.5	*	*	*	*	1.1	14.7	.8	11.6
Consumer and nonprofit organizations	—.6	(16.2)	1.1	27.5	1.2	24.0	1.1	14.7	.5	7.2
State and local government	.7	18.9	.5	12.5	.5	10.0	1.1	14.7	1.6	23.2
Other	—.2	(5.4)	*	*	—.3	(6.0)	.2	2.7	.1	1.4

*Note: Details may not add to totals because of rounding.
Source: "A Quarterly Presentation of Flow of Funds, Saving and Investment," *Federal Reserve Bulletin*, August 1959.

of amounts outstanding and annual flows. At the end of 1958, outstanding credit market instruments totalled $538 billion, of which $81.4 billion were corporate and foreign bonds. Obviously, the market for corporate bonds is only part of a much larger long-term credit market. Also, the ownership pattern of corporate bonds differs widely from that of corporate stock. Institutional investors hold more than 90 per cent of corporate bonds outstanding. It will be recalled that this same group of investors holds less than 10 per cent of corporate stock outstanding. Almost all of the data referred to in this section are contained in Tables 19-3 and 19-4, which show respectively ownership pattern of corporate and foreign bonds outstanding and annual flows into corporate and foreign bonds. Inasmuch as foreign bonds total only $5 billion, no attempt has been made to remove them from the data.

Issuers of Corporate Bonds

Generally investors in corporate bonds can shift funds from one type of credit market instrument to another. Therefore, the corporate demand for long-term creditor funds must compete with Federal, state, and local governmental bond issues and demand for additional mortgage credit. Also, most of the investors in corporate bonds can shift part of their investment funds between the market for corporate stock and the markets for credit market instruments. Obviously, corporations must design their bond issues to fit the needs of the market and price their offerings competitively. The relatively low level of interest rates and the relatively high level of corporate income taxes have motivated firms to rely rather heavily on bonds as a source of long-term funds. As shown in Table 19-3, bonds comprise more than 30 per cent of the liabilities of corporate nonfinancial businesses and finance companies.

At the end of 1958, corporate nonfinancial business firms and corporate financial firms respectively had $69.2 billion and $7.2 billion of corporate bonds outstanding, and domestic holdings of foreign bonds amounted to $5 billion. As shown in Table 19-3 there was a steady rise in the volume of net issues of corporate and foreign bonds during the period 1954-1958. The relative importance of each sector's net issues is about the same as the percentages shown in Table 19-3, indicating the absence of any significant shift in the composition of the supply of corporate bonds outstanding. The shifts between the private and public markets are considered in the following chapter. The net issues of finance companies show the greatest degree of year-to-year variation, which reflects the year-to-year variations in the level and composition of consumer credit and in the state of the money and capital markets.

Non-bank Financial Sectors

The data in Table 19-3 show that at the end of 1958 the non-bank financial sectors held 77.8 per cent of corporate and foreign bonds outstanding, with most of these holdings accounted for by the life insurance companies and self-administered pension plans. Savings institutions and nonlife insurance companies each held less than 5 per cent of the total amounts outstanding. The holdings of investment companies, security brokers, and security dealers barely exceeded $1 billion. The data in Table 19-4 show that the non-bank financial sectors' annual net purchases between 1954 and 1958 provided a major portion of total net purchases. In 1954, the net purchases of these sectors actually exceeded the net purchase for the total economy. Not only did these sectors supply nearly all of the new funds that flowed into the corporate bond market, the sectors also acquired corporate bonds from the consumer and nonprofit organization sector.

LIFE INSURANCE COMPANIES. The life insurance companies held the largest percentages of corporate and foreign bonds outstanding and have been the largest net purchasers of such bonds during the postwar period. High-grade corporate bonds provide a reasonable degree of safety of principal and a reasonable assurance of adequate and stable income, both of which are important to life insurance companies. Life insurance companies have acquired nearly all of their bonds through direct placements; that is, they have acquired bonds directly from the issuers rather than from investment bankers. We shall defer the discussion of direct placement to the next chapter. During the postwar period the life insurance companies increased their share of the total corporate and foreign bonds outstanding. Other investors allocated more of their new funds into mortgages and corporate stocks, leaving more of the corporate bond market available to life insurance companies.

SELF-ADMINISTERED PENSION PLANS. Self-administered pension plans are important in the corporate bond market as well as in the market for corporate stock. In fact, the plans have invested rather heavily in corporate bonds to offset the risk inherent in their holdings of corporate stock. Also it must be remembered that during much of the postwar period, the assets of the plans were not invested in mortgages. As long as the pension plans avoided mortgages, there was very little choice among credit market instruments.

Although the self-administered pension plans' dollar holdings of corporate and foreign bonds are considerably less than those of life insurance companies, such investments constitute a larger share of the plans' assets than of life insurance company assets. It is the large volume of life insurance company assets that makes that subsector so dominant in the corporate bond market. During the 1954-1958 period, the self-administered pension plans' net purchases of corporate and foreign bonds accounted for over 20 per cent of total net purchases. The plans' net purchases ranged from $900 million in 1955 to $1.6 billion in 1957. The data clearly show that the self-administered pension plans can be counted upon as a major purchaser of corporate bonds, especially in the future, because many of the plans have now caught up on their purchases of corporate stock.

OTHER NON-BANK FINANCIAL SECTORS. At the end of 1958, the savings institutions sector's holdings of corporate and foreign bonds totalled $3.7 billion, represented 4.7 per cent of the total outstanding, and accounted for only 4 per cent of the sector's financial assets. Most of the sector's holdings of corporate bonds represent those of mutual savings banks. At the close of 1958, such holdings represented approximately 10 per cent of the banks' assets. Mutual savings banks constitute a marginal purchaser of corporate bonds. During some of the postwar years, mutual savings bonds reduced their holdings of corporate bonds, whereas in 1957 they increased their holdings by nearly $600 million. The level of annual net purchases of corporate bonds is influenced primarily by the availability of mortgages and the relative attractiveness of the corporate bond yields. In general, it can be stated that the savings institutions are not an important corporate bond investor, but the savings institutions are important at the margin.

At the end of 1958, nonlife insurance companies held $3.2 billion of corporate and foreign bonds, which represented 3.9 per cent of the total outstanding and accounted for only 8.8 per cent of their financial assets. The figures do not differ widely from those of the savings institutions. Corporate bonds are not particularly attractive to nonlife insurance companies because of tax and liquidity considerations. The interest income earned on stock companies' corporate bond holdings is taxed at 52 per cent, the corporate income tax rate. Other forms of income receive a more favorable tax treatment. Also, corporate bonds are not as liquid as Federal obligations, and the difference in yield does not offset the sacrifice of liquidity, an important consideration in the formulation of the companies' investment policies. On the average, the nonlife insurance companies' net annual purchase of corporate bonds do not exceed $100 million.

As for the finance, n.e.c. sector, corporate bond investment is not very important. At the end of 1958, this sector held only $1.1 billion of corporate and foreign bonds. As pointed out in the chapter dealing with open-end investment companies, the companies tend to invest the major portion of their funds in corporate stock.

The data in Table 19-4 show that in some years net aggregate purchases of the savings institutions sector, nonlife insurance companies, and the finance, n.e.c. sector were less than $50 million, whereas in other years, their net aggregate purchases approached or exceeded $1 billion. During 1957 and 1958, their net aggregate purchases accounted for respectively 14.7 per cent and 11.6 per cent of total net purchases. Their increased importance in the corporate bond market in 1957 probably reflects the decrease in the availability of mortgages. It is very doubtful that their net aggregate purchases in the future will continue to exceed 10 per cent of all net purchases.

Consumer and Nonprofit Organization Sector

At the end of 1958, the consumer and nonprofit organization sector held $9.6 billion of corporate and foreign bonds. These holdings represented 11.8 per cent of all corporate and foreign bonds outstanding, and accounted for only 1.1 per cent of the sector's financial assets. The sector's net purchases ranged from a negative $600 million in 1954 to $1.2 billion in 1956. In 1955 and 1956 this sector's net purchases accounted for nearly one-fourth of all net purchases. Undoubtedly, the high level of stock prices that prevailed during the period 1955-1958 prompted the trustees of many personal trust accounts to invest a larger portion of the trusts' assets in corporate bonds. As long as stock prices and corporate bond yields remain relatively high, the consumer and nonprofit organization sector will probably continue to purchase a larger than normal amount of corporate bonds.

State and Local Government Sector

At the end of 1958, the state and local government sector held $6.7 billion of corporate and foreign bonds, and such investments accounted for 14.2

per cent of the sector's financial assets. The increased importance of this sector in the market for corporate bonds is one of the more significant postwar developments in the corporate bond market. During the period 1954-1958 more than one-fourth of the sector's net acquisition of financial assets was in the form of corporate bonds, thereby increasing the relative importance of corporate bonds in the sector's holdings of financial assets from about 8 per cent in 1954 to over 14 per cent in 1958. In 1945, corporate bonds accounted for less than 3 per cent of the sector's financial assets. In recent years, the relative importance of the sector's net purchases of corporate bonds has exceeded the relative importance of its holdings of corporate bonds, which is another indication of the growing importance of this sector in the market for corporate bonds. For example, in 1958 the sector's net purchases accounted for 23.2 per cent of all net purchases of corporate bonds. Whether or not this sector will continue to be a major part of the market for corporate bonds will depend upon the degree to which such funds are shifted into corporate stock and upon the pressure to invest in state and local obligations.

Other Sectors

Neither the commercial banking sector nor the rest-of-the-world sector is an important holder of corporate bonds. At the end of 1958, the combined holdings of these two sectors were only $1.8 billion. The commercial banking sector's holdings of corporate bonds at the end of World War II were $2.2 billion, and since that time there has been a gradual downward trend, reaching a postwar low of $1.3 billion in 1956. Instead of investing in corporate bonds, the commercial banks have liquidated some of their holdings to support additional loans. The rest-of-the-world sector has not been attracted to the corporate bond market because of exchange restrictions and relatively unattractive yields.

MARKET FOR MULTI-FAMILY AND COMMERCIAL MORTGAGES

The market for multi-family and commercial mortgages is summarized in Tables 19-5 and 19-6. Approximately two-thirds of the mortgages outstanding at the end of 1958 were obligations of corporate nonfinancial business firms and almost all of the remainder consisted of non-corporate nonfinancia. business firms' obligations. The data also make it apparent that the mortgages as a percentage of liabilities are higher for the non-corporate firms than for the corporate firms. With respect to issuers the pattern of annual flows in 1954, 1955, 1956, and 1958 departed very slightly from the percentage breakdown of mortgages outstanding. The only exception was 1957, when the corporate firms' net additional borrowing through mortgages fell off by about $200 million, whereas the mortgage borrowing of non-corporate firms increased by about $100 million. The reduction in size of the net annual flow simply reflected the over-all reduction that occurred in the sector's net annual increase in liabilities.

The effective demand for mortgage credit increased during the 1954-1958 period, reflecting the growth in the construction of multi-family housing units, industrial plants, and commercial buildings. The composition of the demand for mortgage credit did not change during that period.

In contrast to the market for corporate stock, the market for multi-family and commercial mortgages is a negotiated market; that is, the issuer

TABLE 19–5
MULTI-FAMILY AND COMMERCIAL MORTGAGES OUTSTANDING, END OF 1958
(BILLIONS OF DOLLARS)

Sector	Dollars	Per cent	Mortgages as a percentage of sector's financial assets or liabilities
Issuers (all sectors)	42.0	100.0	
Corporate nonfinancial business...	27.5	65.5	16.7
Non-corp. nonfin. business	13.7	32.6	30.2
Consumer and nonprofit [1]	.9	2.1	.5
Investors (all sectors)	42.0	100.0	
Consumer and nonprofit	12.1	28.8	1.4
Federal Government	.3	.7	.7
State and local government.......	.6	1.4	1.3
Commercial banking	6.2	14.8	2.6
Mutual savings banks	7.5	17.9	20.0
Savings and loan associations	2.4	5.7	4.4
Finance, n.e.c.	.2	.5	.5
Insurance [2]	12.7	30.2	

Note: Details may not add to totals because of rounding.
[1] Nonprofit organizations entirely.
[2] All but $800 million held by life insurance companies; mortgages as a percentage of life insurance company total financial assets.
Source: "A Quarterly Presentation of Flow of Funds, Saving and Investment," *Federal Reserve Bulletin*, August 1959.

and the investor come in direct contact with each other. Of course, this contact may be accomplished through a mortgage company or banker. A relatively small number of these mortgages are Federally underwritten, so that investors must exercise considerable care in such investments. Also multi-family and commercial mortgage lending requires expert staffs. The determination of value of multi-family apartment buildings, commercial property, and industrial property requires considerable knowledge and the application

TABLE 19–6
ANNUAL FLOWS INTO MULTI-FAMILY AND COMMERCIAL MORTGAGES, 1954-1958
(BILLIONS OF DOLLARS)

Sector	1954		1955		1956		1957		1958	
	$	%	$	%	$	%	$	%	$	%
Issuers (all sectors)	2.1	100.0	2.9	100.0	2.7	100.0	2.6	100.0	3.2	100.0
Corporate nonfin. business..	1.4	66.7	1.9	65.5	1.8	66.7	1.6	61.5	2.2	68.8
Non-corp. nonfin. business...	.6	28.6	.9	31.0	.8	29.6	.9	34.6	1.0	31.2
Nonprofit organizations	.1	4.8	.1	3.4	.1	3.7	.1	3.8	*	*
Investors (all sectors)[1]	2.1	100.0	2.9	100.0	2.7	100.0	2.6	100.0	3.2	100.0
Consumer and nonprofit org..	.7	33.3	.8	27.6	.9	33.3	.9	34.6	.8	25.0
State and local government..	.1	4.8	*	*	.1	3.7	.1	3.8	.1	3.1
Commercial banking[2]	.2	9.5	.5	17.2	.2	7.4	.2	7.7	.7	21.9
Mutual savings banks	.4	19.0	.4	13.8	.3	11.1	.3	11.5	.5	15.6
Savings and loan associations.	.2	9.5	.3	10.3	.3	11.1	.3	11.5	.4	12.5
Insurance	.5	23.8	.9	31.0	.9	33.3	.8	30.8	.7	21.9
Life insurance companies..	.5	23.8	.8	27.6	.9	33.3	.8	30.8	.7	21.9
Other insurance companies	*	*	.1	3.4	*	*	*	*	*	*

*Less than $50 million.
Note: Details may not add to totals because of rounding.
[1] Includes small amounts for finance, n.e.c. not shown separately.
[2] Flow data adjusted downward by changes in amount of farm mortgage debt held by all operating banks.
Sources: "A Quarterly Presentation of Flow of Funds, Saving and Investment," *Federal Reserve Bulletin*, August 1959; *Agricultural Financial Review*, U. S. Department of Agriculture Vol. 20, April 1958.

of complete appraisal procedures. The significance of the complexity is that the smaller financial institutions are not adequately staffed to handle such loans.

The supply of mortgage credit is summarized in the bottom half of each table. There are four major types of investors: consumers, commercial banks, mutual savings banks, and life insurance companies. At the end of 1958, these four investor groups held over 90 per cent of all multi-family and commercial mortgages outstanding. In contrast to the market for mortgages on one- to four-family properties, none of these investors can be considered as specializing in multi-family and commercial mortgages. Except for mutual savings banks and life insurance companies, which respectively hold 20 per cent and 8.4 per cent of their assets in multi-family and commercial mortgages, such investments account for less than 5 per cent of the investors' total assets. Although investors in these mortgages are not specialized mortgage lenders, their net annual acquisitions of mortgages are relatively stable. During the period 1955-1958, only the net acquisitions of commercial banks showed very much variation. The variation in the commercial banks' annual flows is explained by the relationship of its mortgage holdings with its total assets. Commercial banks are not committed to this type of investment, and in the face of strong competing demands for bank credit, the banks tend to reduce their annual flows into mortgages and divert the funds into higher-yielding short- and intermediate-term loans and investments. The annual flow data did not show any significant shifts in the market for multi-family and commercial mortgages. Each of the major investor groups supplied about the same percentage of annual flows as its percentage of total holdings.

Consumer and Nonprofit Organization Sector

At the end of 1958, the consumer and nonprofit organization sector held $12.1 billion of multi-family and commercial mortgages, and these holdings accounted for 28.8 per cent of total mortgages outstanding. Although this sector is almost the most important source of funds to this market, such investments accounted for only 1.4 per cent of the sector's total financial assets. The use of the amortized mortgage and the yield obtainable on such investments have been attractive to individuals. A relatively large number of individuals invest the major portion of their funds in such mortgages. In relation to high-grade corporate stocks and bonds, such investments involve more financial risk to investors, but evidently many investors believe that the higher yields offset the additional risk.

Insurance Sector

As noted in the tables, nearly all the multi-family and commercial mortgages held by the insurance sector are in the portfolios of life insurance companies. At the end of 1958, life insurance companies held nearly $12 billion of multi-family and commercial mortgages, and these holdings accounted for 30.2 per cent of the total mortgages outstanding. Compared with the other investors, the life insurance companies have invested a relatively large percentage of their assets in such mortgages. These investments are closely similar to some of their bond investments. The life insurance companies are attracted to such investments because of their safety, yield, and amortization schedules.

Mutual Savings Banks

As noted above, mutual savings banks have a higher percentage of their assets invested in multi-family and commercial mortgages than any other type of investor. At the end of 1958, the mutual savings banks held $7.5 billion of such mortgages, and their holdings accounted for nearly 18 per cent of the total amounts outstanding. Many of the larger mutual savings banks have well-staffed mortgage departments that are capable of negotiating commercial and multi-family mortgages as well as mortgages on one- to four-family properties. The banks' funds are attracted by the higher yields that are obtainable on such mortgages.

Commercial Banks

The commercial banks are a marginal supplier of funds to the market for multi-family and commercial mortgages. When money is tight, commercial banks tend to turn down the long-term loans, and restrict more of their loans to short- and intermediate-term maturities. However, that there are many situations in which such loans are appropriate is made clear by the fact that the commercial banks held $6.2 billion of such mortgages at the end of 1958. If commercial banks continue to expand their intermediate- and long-term loans they will probably assume a more important role in the market for multi-family and commercial mortgages.

QUESTIONS

1. Set forth the ownership pattern of corporate stock.

2. Explain the growing importance of institutional investors in the market for corporate stock. What are the implications?

3. Explain the ownership pattern of corporate bonds.

4. During the postwar period, and particularly since 1953, what major shifts have occurred in the market for corporate bonds?

5. Compare the ownership pattern of multi-family and commercial mortgages with that of corporate bonds, and explain the differences.

6. Compare the ownership pattern of multi-family and commercial mortgages with that of one- to four-family mortgages, and explain the differences.

ADDITIONAL READING

See list of additional reading at end of Chapter 14 for information on the market for multi-family and commercial mortgages; see list of reading at end of Chapters 16-18 for information on the markets for corporate stock and bonds.

Hickman, W. Braddock. *The Volume of Corporate Bond Financing Since 1900.* N.B.E.R. Study. Princeton, N.J.: Princeton University Press, 1952.

New York Stock Exchange. *Fact Book and Annual Report.* See latest editions.

Smith, D. T. *Effects of Taxation — Corporate Financial Policy.* Boston: Harvard Business School, Division of Research, 1952.

U.S. Senate Subcommittee on Banking and Currency Committee. *Stock Market Study, Regulation of Unlisted Securities.* Hearings on S. 2054, 84th Cong., 1st sess. Washington, D.C.: Government Printing Office, 1955.

U.S. Senate Committee on Banking and Currency. *Stock Market Study.* Report together with individual views and minority views of Committee, 84th Cong., 1st sess. Washington, D.C.: Government Printing Office, 1955.

————. *Factors Affecting Stock Market.* Staff Report, 84th Cong., 1st sess. Washington, D.C.: Government Printing Office, 1955.

20: Long-term and permanent financing, II

THE market for corporate securities is comprised of several major investor groups and literally thousands of investors within each of these groups. Issuing corporations cannot personally contact all prospective investors, for the issuers have neither the organization nor the manpower to accomplish this herculean task. Individual demands for corporate securities must be pooled or assembled; they must be funnelled into specific offerings of corporate issues. Until recently, this function was performed primarily by the investment banking industry. Investment banking firms assisted in the origination of issues and assumed responsibility for the sale and distribution of newly offered securities. Beginning in the early 1940's and continuing up to the present, the issues of many of our public utilities and railroads have been subject to competitive bidding, which reduces the role of investment banks in the origination of issues. In the non-regulated industries, competitive bidding is neither required nor practiced. Very large companies that have nationwide reputation and make frequent offerings could probably circumvent the investment banking industry and conduct sale and distribution of their own securities. At the opposite pole, investment bankers may refuse to underwrite new issues of small companies. Either there is no market or the issuer presumes that the costs connected with such an issue are excessive.

The growth in savings and investment institutions has brought about considerable change in the assembly function. Their growth has led to fewer, but larger pools of capital. Where the individual institutional pools of capital are not very large, investment bankers carry on additional pooling or assembling of funds, but many of the larger savings and insurance institutions now pool such large amounts of capital that corporations are able to tap them directly. Various terms are used to identify this practice: "private placement," "direct placement" and "private offering." About the only role left for the investment bankers in direct placements is to serve in an agency capacity; that is, turning up either prospective direct placements for the institutional investors or direct sources of funds for prospective borrowers.

In this chapter we shall consider the topics noted above: investment banking, regulation of publicly offered securities, competitive bidding, direct placement, and small business development companies. The last-mentioned represent an innovation introduced in 1958 to foster the flow of private investment funds to small business.

INVESTMENT BANKING

In a broad sense, the total structure of the investment banking industry includes broker-dealer firms, commercial banks and investment banking firms that deal primarily in underwriting the distribution of public corporate offerings. Commercial banks are mentioned because they are important underwriters of state and local and Federal agency obligations. There are about 300 firms that regularly accept corporate underwriting commitments, and in addition about 400 firms that participate less frequently in public corporate offerings. It is interesting to note that over 700 firms participated in underwriting the Ford Motor Company public offering in 1954.

We quote here a good summary description of the firms that comprise the investment banking industry as it relates to underwriting.*

> [The] firms, which may be either partnerships or corporations, range in size from very small organizations with limited capital and restricted distribution capacity to nationwide firms with large capital and many distribution outlets. Even among the larger underwriting firms, there are considerable differences: some are almost exclusively "wholesale" underwriters, which distribute issues primarily to investment dealers and institutions; other firms supplement their underwriting facilities with large distributing organizations which sell securities to all types of investors, particularly individuals.
>
> There are less than fifty firms which manage *major* security offerings; half of these manage most of the major issues. It is from these fifty firms that most medium-sized and larger firms select one or more managers to handle their security issues. Most of the major firms have their headquarters in New York City, but a few of the largest have Chicago or San Francisco headquarters. In any case, underwriting groups usually include firms from several sections of the country, often with emphasis on firms in the issuing company's area of operation. In addition, the assistance of hundreds of investment dealers outside the underwriting group is available for nationwide distribution of the issue.
>
> No two investment banking firms operate in exactly the same way, but it is customary to divide the organization into three major departments — a buying department, a syndicate department, and a sales department. The principal functions of a buying department are to originate underwriting business, to conduct investigations of prospective clients, to perform the preliminary work involved in preparing issues for the market, to deal with institutional investors in private sales of new issues, and to maintain contacts with corporate clients. A syndicate

*George L. Leness, Gillette K. Martin, Roger T. Gilmartin, *New Money for Business* (New York: McGraw-Hill Book Co., Inc., 1956), pp. 16-17.

department deals primarily with other investment banking firms: its function is to organize groups of underwriters to handle issues which the firm is managing, and to discuss with other firms participation in their underwriting accounts. A sales department, as the name indicates, performs the function of distributing publicly offered issues of securities to all types of investors.

To staff the three major departments, an important banking firm must employ a relatively large number of highly qualified, experienced persons. In order to underwrite large corporate offerings, the firm must have a large equity base and ready access to much larger amounts of short-term funds to carry inventories of underwritten but unsold securities. These personnel and capital requirements are probably the major reasons why there are less than 50 firms that manage major security offerings.

Functions

Most of the publicly offered issues of industrial and financial firms are negotiated underwritings, under which all the details of the issue are worked out or negotiated between the issuer and the underwriter(s). Public utilities and railroads, both of which are highly regulated, do not engage in negotiated underwriting. Instead, their issues are awarded to the underwriter or underwriting syndicate that submits the most favorable sealed bid. In other words investment bankers participate in competitive bidding to underwrite the public offerings of public utilities and railroads. Some functions described in this section are not applicable to public offerings under competitive bidding.

ORIGINATING A SECURITIES OFFERING. Since it seldom issues securities the individual corporation must secure expert advice on the form, timing, and method of issue. The initial contact between a corporation and a prospective issuer may be initiated by either party. It is possible for a prospective issuer to contact many investment banking firms, but when serious negotiations are actually underway, additional "shopping around" for a better deal is not an accepted practice. If a corporation has sought the advice and services of an investment banking firm in the past, and if the relationship was mutually satisfactory, it is likely that the corporation will contact the same firm in future financing. In fact, after a public offering, the investment banking firm that underwrote the issue may be represented on the corporation's board of directors.

The decision as to form of security depends upon both internal and external factors. The issuing corporation is probably striving to attain an optimum or ideal distribution among bonds, preferred stocks, common stocks, and surplus. However, securities must be sold in the markets, and it may be necessary for the issuer to deviate from what it deems ideal. Also, if a corporation is to minimize the costs of long-term and permanent capital, the form and timing of a public offering must be adjusted to fit the state of the markets. For example, a corporation may desire to issue additional bonds, but the market for corporate bonds may not be suitable at the time funds must be raised, so it is possible that the corporation will have to defer the bond offering and issue stock instead.

A proposed public offering must be saleable; that is, its provisions must be tailored to fit the needs of the investor classes that are to be solicited, and the terms must be attractive in relation to other investment opportunities. The setting of an offering price on a stock offering and the interest rate and maturity on a bond offering are crucial decisions in determining the success or failure of a corporate offering. However, the terms and provisions should not be overly attractive to investors, since, in the long run, investment banking firms must satisfy both the corporate clients and the investors.

The provisions and terms of a corporate issue depend on whether the issue is a private or a public offering. If it is the former, an investment banking firm is able to determine directly what potential investors expect of forthcoming issues and can advise the issuer accordingly. The firm must base its advice on public offerings, however, on its "feel" of the market, which is based on experience and current contacts with prospective investors.

The originating function culminates either in the form of an underwriting contract or in a distribution agreement drawn up between the issuer and an investment banking firm or syndicate. The relationship between the syndicate manager and the other investment banking firms is embodied in a legal contract known as the agreement among underwriters.

UNDERWRITING A PUBLIC OFFERING. To underwrite a public offering, an investment banking firm, acting either singly or on behalf of a syndicate, agrees to purchase an entire issue of securities. Such an agreement transfers the ultimate distribution of the securities from the issuer to the underwriters. It assures the issuer of receiving a designated amount of long-term or permanent capital or both. In a syndicate, the obligations of the underwriters are "several and joint," that is, each member of the syndicate agrees to purchase a specified amount or percentage of the issue and each is responsible for only that specified portion.

Investment banking firms assume the risk of distribution because they believe issues can be sold readily at prices slightly higher than those paid the issuers. If prices fall sharply just after an issue has been underwritten and put on the market, the underwriters must either sell the securities at prices below the price paid or hold them off the market until prices recover. Either action can be serious for the underwriters. If the securities are sold for less than the underwriter's price, the equity base of the undewriters may be impaired. If the securities are held off the market for an extended period, capital is tied up and the firms may be unable to participate in new underwritings until inventories are worked down. Turnover and avoidance of underwriting losses are necessary if an investment banking firm is to realize a reasonable rate of return on invested capital.

The nature of an underwriter's commitment depends on whether it is a straight public offering or a subscription of rights offering to stockholders. In a straight public offering, an underwriter agrees to purchase on a fixed date at a fixed price either an entire issue or a specified portion of an issue. In a rights offering to stockholders, the underwriter agrees to purchase all of a specified portion of securities that are not subscribed for by stockholders during the subscription period. Some corporations are legally bound to offer equity securities to existing stockholders before offering them to non-stockholders. This arrangement is referred to as the pre-emptive right of stockholders. Other corporations use rights offering to minimize commissions and to improve stockholder relations.

BEST-EFFORT DISTRIBUTION AGREEMENT. Under a best-effort distribution agreement, an investment banking firm or syndicate undertakes the distribution function, but does not underwrite the issue. The firm or syndicate merely agrees to use its best efforts in the distribution and sale of the public offering. Unsold securities are returned to the corporate issuer at the end of the contract period. Obviously, the corporate issuer assumes the risk that the required amount of capital may not be raised. The investment banking firm or syndicate receives a commission for handling the selling function. Corporate firms that enter into such agreements are at opposite poles. At one extreme are companies whose securities are so appealing to the investors that there is little chance that a public offering, assuming terms and conditions are appropriate, would be unsuccessful. At the other extreme are companies whose securities are so difficult to sell that either the investment banking firms refuse to act as underwriters or the issuers believe that the full cost of underwriting is excessive.

DISTRIBUTION OF A PUBLIC OFFERING. The distribution of newly issued securities is accomplished in the primary segment of the over-the-counter market. Large investment banking firms maintain elaborate and efficient sales organizations capable of placing securities with many different investor classes. During the waiting period between the date of registration and the date of public sale, the market is alerted and investment bankers receive indications of interest from broker-dealer firms, individuals, and institutional investors. Assuming that the basic decisions relating to form, timing, method of issue, and price are correct, the entire issue might be sold within a few hours on the first day it is offered. If investment bankers did not believe this success possible, they would hesitate to assume the risk. In practice, mistakes are made and sudden breaks in the market do occur, and in instances the issue may remain unsold for a much longer period.

To assist in the retail distribution of public offerings, underwriters form selling groups, consisting of the investment banking firms that are members of the purchase syndicate plus other investment banking firms. By bringing in additional firms, the underwriters are able to get a wider and more rapid distribution of offerings. The entire operation is administered by a syndicate manager, who may carry out market stabilization measures during the offering period.

OTHER FUNCTIONS. Investment banking firms underwrite and distribute large blocks of outstanding securities in the over-the-counter market, and these transactions are referred to as secondary distributions. Investment bankers perform a wide variety of advisory services for firms whose securities they have underwritten. In addition, they serve in an agency capacity in a large number of private or direct placements; they participate in the sale of companies and exchange offers; and they handle invitations for the tender of securities. As noted earlier, investment bankers serve on the boards of many corporations.

TABLE 20-1
REPRESENTATIVE UNDERWRITING COMMISSIONS

	Industrial companies
Debt securities	
Mortgage bonds	*
Debentures	.75 – 1.50%
Convertible debentures [1]	
Straight offering	1.00 – 1.75
On "rights"	1.00 – 1.25
Preferred stocks	
Non-convertible	2.25 – 3.00
Convertible	
Straight offering	2.00 – 4.00
On "rights"	1.60 – 3.50 [2]
Common stocks	
Straight offering	4.00 – 8.00
On "rights"	1.00 – 4.00 [2]

*Insufficient offerings to establish a pattern.

[1] Includes subordinated debentures.

[2] Minimum underwriting fee payable; additional charges in some cases, based upon amount of unsubscribed stock.

Source: George J. Leness, Gillette K. Martin, and Roger T. Gilmartin, *New Money for Business*, McGraw-Hill Book Co., Inc., 1956, p. 116.

Underwriters' Commissions

An underwriter's commission is the gross spread or difference between an agreed public offering price and the price paid to the issuing corporation. The commission is meant to cover expenses and to compensate the underwriter for the assumption of risk. The expenses include legal fees, advertising, selling costs, and the syndicate manager's fee. The commission, expressed as a percentage of the offering price, depends upon many factors, including size of issue, type and nature of security, nature and history of both the industry and corporate issuer, type and length of agreement, market conditions, and price.* In order to provide some idea as to representative underwriting commissions, the approximate range of commissions for better-grade issues, based upon 1955 public offerings, are shown in Table 20-1. Aggregate data are influenced primarily by the type and nature of security and the nature of the agreement. The commissions are lowest for bonds and highest for common stocks; the commissions on straight offerings are lower than commissions on subscription or rights offerings.

REGULATION OF SECURITIES PUBLICLY OFFERED †

State and Federal regulations pertaining to exchanges, over-the-counter markets, bankers and dealers, advisers, and investment companies have already been investigated. We shall now consider Federal regulations pertaining to publicly offered securities. We shall make no attempt to summarize the various state laws and regulations; it is sufficient to mention that a majority of the states require that securities must be registered before they can be offered for sale within those states. In some states, mere notification of sale satisfies the requirement; in others, information is requested and reviewed prior to qualification and registration of a public offering. Since the passage of the Securities Act of 1933, most of the states have accepted Federal registration as compliance with state registration requirements.

Prior to 1933, there existed only a minimum of Federal regulation over public offerings. The Mail Fraud Act of 1909 forbade the use of the mails to defraud and provided for the punishment of fraudulent acts, but it did not prevent fraud from taking place. Some control was exercised over the flow of corporate capital by the Secretary of the Treasury during World War I with the intent of correlating security offerings. Under the terms of the Transportation Act of 1920, the Interstate Commerce Com-

Ibid., pp. 109-111.

† Some aspects of regulation were considered in earlier chapters. It may be recalled that the foreword to the *25th Annual Report of the Securities and Exchange Commission* reviews the development of securities regulation.

mission was given the power to regulate the issue of the new securities by railroads. Beginning in 1933 with passage of the Securities Act, many Federal acts have been designed to regulate various aspects of securities transactions.

Securities Act of 1933

"The Securities Act of 1933 is designed to provide disclosure to investors of material facts concerning securities publicly offered for sale by use of the mails or instrumentalities of interstate commerce, and to prevent misrepresentation, deceit, or other fraudulent practices in the sale of securities."* The basic philosophy underlying the Act is that the facts about a company and its securities should be available to prospective investors, and in the event that an investor is deceived by misrepresentation or concealment, an effective remedy is available for use against the responsible parties. The Act is often referred to as the "truth in securities Act."

Extensive Federal regulation of the flow of corporate capital is a delicate balancing operation. In order to encourage and maintain a flow of capital into publicly offered securities, it is imperative that investors have confidence in both issuers and underwriters. Experience, especially that gained in the 1920's, has demonstrated that moral principles alone cannot be relied upon to regulate securities transactions. For many years, the receipt and use of funds by banks and insurance companies had been regulated. The time came in 1933 to apply effective legal controls and standards to the direct flow of savings into securities. In order to encourage and maintain a flow of publicly offered securities, issuers and underwriters must not be discouraged or blocked by unduly burdensome regulations. The initial response of many issuers and underwriters to Federal regulation was based on this criticism. Initial compliance with registration and the necessity for disclosing information to the public for the first time were difficult for both issuers and underwriters, but with the passage of time resistance and criticism subsided. The large annual flow of new public offerings in recent years is good evidence that regulations have not posed major obstacles to the flow of corporate capital.

Regulations pertaining to the public offerings of smaller corporations are less restrictive than those applied to large public offerings; nevertheless, the regulations probably pose a much greater obstacle in this segment of the corporate capital market. However, the protection afforded the investing public probably offsets the negative effects on capital flow.

REGISTRATION STATEMENT AND PROSPECTUS. Disclosure is assured by requiring that an issuer of publicly offered securities file with the Securities and Exchange Commission a registration statement and related prospectus, both

*25th Annual Report of the Securities and Exchange Commission, 1959, p. 26.

of which are lengthy legal documents containing significant information about the issuer and the offering.

> In general the registration statement of an issuer other than a foreign government must set forth such matters as the names of persons who participate in the direction, management, or control of the issuer's business; their security holdings and remuneration and the options or bonus and profit-sharing privileges allotted to them; the character and size of the business enterprise, its capital structure, past history and earnings and financial statements certified by independent accountants; underwriters' commissions; payments to promoters made within two years or intended to be made; acquisitions of property not in the ordinary course of business, and the interest of directors, officers, and principal stockholders therein; pending or threatened legal proceedings; and the purpose to which the proceeds of the offering are to be applied. . . . The prospectus constitutes a part of the registration statement and presents the more important of the required disclosures.*

The documents are available for public inspection as soon as they are filed. Generally, only underwriters and institutional investors request or receive personal copies of registration statements. However, a copy of the prospectus must be supplied every investor who purchases or indicates an interest in purchasing the security at or before the time of its public offering. Although many investors do not read the prospectus, it is read by many security analysts and they in turn advise investors. After the close of the public offering, the security may be bought and sold in regular trading without the use of the prospectus.

False and misleading statements or omission of material facts from the registration statement may serve as the basis of civil liability suits; if the violation is wilful, the guilty parties are subject to criminal liability. Obviously, the registration must be prepared with a great deal of care. Underwriters, legal firms, directors, accountants, engineers, and other professional persons are involved in the preparation of a registration statement and in the event of legal suit, any or all may be sued. After much time and effort, the registration statement is submitted to the issuer's board of directors for approval, and it is then filed with the Commission.

The Commission's staff examines each registration statement for compliance with the standards of accurate and full disclosure and usually notifies the registrant by an informal letter of comment, sometimes called a "deficiency letter," of any material respects in which it appears that the statement fails to conform to standards. Generally, the registrant makes the suggested changes in the form of an amendment. If conditions warrant, the Commission may either initiate an investigation leading to a stop-order proceeding or institute the proceedings immediately. A public offering cannot lawfully be made until the registration statement is amended. The legislative goal with respect to the time period from filing date to effective

*Ibid., p. 27.

date is 20 days. The average time in 1959 was 28 days.* When the registration becomes effective, the securities may be issued. It must be emphasized that when the Commission allows a registration to become effective it does not mean that the Commission either approves or advises the purchases of the securities. The Commission's objective is to determine to the best of its ability and without guarantee whether or not the disclosure is accurate and adequate. The Act requires inclusion of the following statement in bold type on the cover page of each prospectus:

> THESE SECURITIES HAVE NOT BEEN APPROVED OR DISAPPROVED BY THE SECURITIES AND EXCHANGE COMMISSION NOR HAS THE COMMISSION PASSED UPON THE ACCURACY OR ADEQUACY OF THIS PROSPECTUS. ANY REPRESENTATION TO THE CONTRARY IS A CRIMINAL OFFENSE.

During the waiting period, the underwriters are permitted to disseminate advertisements and a preliminary prospectus with the understanding that this material must contain legends calling attention to the fact that a registration statement has been filed, and cautioning the prospective investor that offers or sales may not be made until there has been compliance with state and Federal requirements. An offering is made only by the prospectus.

It was reported in the 25th Annual Report of the Securities and Exchange Commission that during the 1959 fiscal year, 1,226 registration statements were filed for offerings of securities aggregating approximately $16.6 billion. Up to June 30, 1959, a cumulative total of 15,930 registration statements had been filed under the Act by 7,397 different issuers covering proposed offerings of securities aggregating almost $151 billion.

Exemptions from Registration

New issues of public authorities, banks, carriers whose issues are subject to the Interstate Commerce Act, intrastate issues, and private offerings are the more important exemptions from registration. The Commission is empowered to exempt any class of securities from registration if it finds that the enforcement of the registration provisions of the Act with respect to such securities is not necessary in the public interest and for the protection of investors because of the small amount involved or the limited character of the public offering. It was pointed out in the previous section that the preparation and filing of a registration statement is both a time-consuming and an expensive process, and its strict application to all issues would stifle the raising of capital by small corporations.

The Commission exempts certain offerings not in excess of $300,000

---

*In early 1961, a Government-sponsored study of the Securities and Exchange Commission reported that the Commission is losing ground in its efforts to regulate the securities industry. The delay in processing registration statements was singled out as the "most serious" problem. It was reported that only about 10 per cent of all registration statements were processed in 20 days, and in 34 per cent of the cases, processing required more than 51 days. See *Wall Street Journal*, January 17, 1961, p. 5.

in any one year if the issuer and the underwriters comply with Regulation A. Other less important exemptions are permitted under other specified regulations, but we shall discuss only Regulation A here. To comply with Regulation A, the issuer must file in the appropriate regional S.E.C. office proper notification and must supply basic information about the company, financial exhibits, and the offering circular. An offering circular is supposed to contain basic information about the issuer and security and is to be delivered to each prospective purchaser at or before the time any offer is made. If the offering is not to exceed $50,000 and the company has an earnings history, no offering circular is required. The S.E.C. regional office examines the exhibits and offering circular to determine whether or not the exemption is available and the required disclosures have been made. Just as with the examination of the registration statement, the notification must be filed at least 10 days prior to the date that an offer is to commence, and during the waiting period letters may be sent requesting amendments. If necessary, the S.E.C. may deny or suspend the exemption. The anti-fraud provisions of the Act apply to persons offering securities under exemption.

Underwriters are used in the majority of offerings under Regulation A. During the 1959 fiscal year, underwriters were used in 318 of the 854 Regulation A offerings, and of those underwritten, commercial underwriters participated in 251. When commercial underwriters are not used, commissions are paid to officers, directors, or other persons not regularly engaged in the securities business. These persons are likely to approach friends and relatives who are in a position to invest funds in the business. It is questionable whether a firm's management is making the best use of its human resources when it asks members of the management to sell securities.

Trust Indenture Act of 1939

In addition to meeting the requirements of the Securities Act of 1933, certain types of credit market instruments publicly offered for sale must be issued under an indenture that meets the requirements of the 1939 Act and that has been duly qualified with the S.E.C.

> Indentures to be qualified are required to include specified provisions which provide means by which the rights of holders of securities issued under such indentures may be protected and enforced. These provisions relate to designated standards of eligibility and qualification of the corporate trustee to provide reasonable financial responsibility and to minimize conflicting interests.*

The Act exempts offerings of $250,000 or less made during 12 consecutive months, when the debt security is not issued under an indenture. Also exempted are offerings of $1 million or less in 36 consecutive months when they are issued under an indenture limiting the total securities outstanding to $1 million or less.

*Ibid., p. 156.

COMPETITIVE BIDDING

In competitive bidding, an underwriter cannot enter into an underwriting contract with an issuer unless the underwriter has submitted the most favorable bid from the issuer's point of view. The major difference between negotiated underwriting and competitive bidding underwriting is that the final selection of an underwriter is delayed until the registration statement becomes effective for bidding purposes. Under competitive bidding it is possible for an issuer to utilize the advisory services of an underwriter prior to this date, but this action does not guarantee that the contract will be awarded to that underwriter. Generally, an offering becomes effective on the same day the issue is awarded, and assuming that the announced price is attractive to investors, an issue may be "out the window" in a matter of hours. If the announced terms are not attractive to investors, the offering price will have to be reduced. In this case the firm or syndicate members may incur loss instead of gain on the transaction.

Competitive bidding is required of electric utility companies that come under the jurisdiction of either the Public Utility Holding Company Act or Federal Power Act. The rule of competitive bidding was introduced under the former Act in 1941, and under the latter Act in 1948. The Interstate Commerce Commission has required competitive bidding for railroad securities since 1944. Exemptions from competitive bidding are granted by each of the regulatory commissions. The majority of electric utilities are regulated by the respective state commissions and, therefore, they do not come under the jurisdiction of either the Public Utility Holding Company Act or the Federal Power Act. Competitive bidding is not required by all the state commissions. The commissions that do require it do not apply the requirements to all types of securities. The basic reason for applying competitive bidding to public utilities and railroads is that there is a high degree of uniformity among individual companies, and the market should serve as a reliable guide to underwriters.

The stated goal of competitive bidding is to assure the availability to issuers of public offerings underwritten at commissions lower than they would be if the underwritings were arranged through negotiation. Attainment of the goal is much more likely in the issue of credit market instruments than it is in the issue of equity market instruments. Also, the status of the markets has an important bearing on the degree to which the goal of competitive bidding is realized. In a rising market it is likely that the net proceeds received by an issuer will be higher under competitive bidding than under negotiation, but in a falling market, the opposite is likely to occur. Although investment bankers express great dissatisfaction with competitive bidding, the practice has been accepted by the investment banking industry. It is unlikely that the laws will be modified to permit negotiated underwriting for public utilities and railroads.

DIRECT PLACEMENT

Direct placement is a procedure or method of selling new corporate issues under which the corporate issuer and one or a few investors deal directly with one another. It is a negotiated offering in which the securities are sold or placed directly with the investors. The requirements of competitive bidding preclude direct placement of the debt issues of many railroads and public utilities. Although many direct placements involve long-term notes instead of bonds, many of the issues are nearly identical to publicly offered issues. Relatively small amounts of preferred stock and common stock are privately placed. An investment banking firm may or may not be involved in direct placement negotiations; however, in no instance does an investment banking firm underwrite a direct placement.

Direct placement has led to the development of two markets for corporate capital, the public market and the private market. The Securities and Exchange Commission, acting under section 4(1) of the Securities Act of 1933, exempts "transactions by an issuer not involving any public offering." Such transactions are given these names: "private transaction," "private offering," "private placement," and "direct placement." However, the term "direct placement" has become the most popular of the four because it is descriptve and avoids the connotations associated with "private."

Among the factors that determine whether a particular transaction is a "public" or "private" offering are the number and class of investors to whom the securities are offered, the number and class of investors in the final transaction, the relationship between the issuer and the offerees, the size of the offering, and the number of security units included in the offering.* The presence of so many factors makes it difficult to draw a line between the two types of offering. Generally, if an offering transaction involves less than 25 offerees and each purchaser or investor provides a written representation that the securities are taken for investment and not for the purpose of distribution, it would probably be considered a private offering. Basically, the correctness of a decision turns on the question as to whether a small number of offerees need the protection afforded by registration. Certainly, large institutional investors do not need this protection.

Inasmuch as a private offering must be restricted to a small number of offerees, it follows that it must be offered to potential investors having large amounts to invest, for otherwise the issuer would not be able to raise a large amount of funds. Accordingly, almost all private offerings are directly placed or sold to institutional investors because they are able to purchase and hold for long maturities large blocks of a single offering. Since most of the direct placements are negotiated with life insurance com-

---

*Statement of Hon. Edward N. Gadsby, Chairman of the Securities and Exchange Commission, "Briefing on the Investment Act," (Washington, D.C.: U.S. Government Printing Office, 1959), pp. 22-24.

panies and trust institutions, most of the issues are credit market instruments. The importance of debt issues in private placements is clearly stated in Table 20-2, which shows a summary of corporate securities publicly offered and privately placed in each year from 1934 through June, 1959. The debt issues consist of debentures, mortgage bonds, convertible mortgage bonds, convertible debentures, subordinated debentures, and long-term notes. The long-term notes are closely similar to debentures. The data show that in no year did private placements of equity issues exceed $200 million; in all but five of the years, private placements of equity issues were less than $100 million. Annual private placements of debt issues exceeded $3.3 billion in each year since 1951. In the first half of 1959, 50 per cent of the debt issues was privately placed.

Direct placements closely resemble term loans. In fact, in some direct placements, both commercial banks and life insurance companies are involved. The commercial banks take the shorter maturities and the life insurance companies take the longer ones. In direct placements the lender(s) and the borrower negotiate directly with one another, and the final financing terms and provisions depend on the relative bargaining strength of the parties involved. The restrictive provisions that are worked out in a private offering are similar to those included in commercial banks term loan agreements. Furthermore, both types of transactions generally require installment repayments. In private offerings, these provisions are referred to as sinking fund provisions. The advantages and disadvantages of direct placements from both an issuer's and an investor's point of view and the reasons for the growth in the amount of direct placements are much like those cited in the discussion of term loans. The major differences between the two are maturity and the legal instrument used to evidence the transaction.

Advantages

Direct placement offers many advantages to both institutional investors and issuers. Direct placement is attractive to institutional investors because it permits them to invest in large blocks of securities with provisions that are tailor-made to fit their investment requirements. For example, one study revealed that direct placements accounted for nearly 88 per cent of the dollar amount of the industrial and miscellaneous bonds acquired by 18 large life insurance companies during the four-year period 1946-1949.* The rate of investment return tends to be slightly higher on privately offered securities, and since the life insurance companies are under pressure to increase the net rate of return on invested assets, they have actively sought private placements.

From the issuers' point of view, direct placements are less time-consuming and more simple than comparable public offerings. In the case of

*E. Raymond Corey, *Direct Placement of Corporate Securities* (Boston: Harvard University, Graduate School of Business Administration, Division of Research, 1951), p. 7.

TABLE 20–2
A SUMMARY OF CORPORATE SECURITIES PUBLICLY OFFERED AND PRIVATELY PLACED IN EACH YEAR FROM 1934 THROUGH JUNE 1959
(MILLIONS OF DOLLARS)

Calendar year	Total			Public offerings			Private placements			Private placements as percent of total	
	All issues	Debt issues	Equity issues	All issues	Debt issues	Equity issues	All issues	Debt issues	Equity issues	All issues	Debt issues
1934	397	372	25	305	280	25	92	92	0	23.2	24.7
1935	2,332	2,225	108	1,945	1,840	106	387	385	2	16.6	17.3
1936	4,572	4,029	543	4,199	3,660	539	373	369	4	8.2	9.2
1937	2,309	1,618	691	1,979	1,291	688	330	327	3	14.3	20.2
1938	2,155	2,044	111	1,463	1,353	110	692	691	1	32.1	33.8
1939	2,164	1,979	185	1,458	1,276	181	706	703	4	32.6	35.5
1940	2,677	2,386	291	1,912	1,628	284	765	758	7	28.6	31.8
1941	2,667	2,389	277	1,854	1,578	276	813	811	2	30.5	33.9
1942	1,062	917	146	642	506	136	420	411	9	39.5	44.8
1943	1,170	990	180	798	621	178	372	369	3	31.8	37.3
1944	3,202	2,670	532	2,415	1,892	524	787	778	9	24.6	29.1
1945	6,011	4,855	1,155	4,989	3,851	1,138	1,022	1,004	18	17.0	20.7
1946	6,900	4,882	2,018	4,983	3,019	1,963	1,917	1,863	54	27.8	38.2
1947	6,577	5,036	1,541	4,342	2,889	1,452	2,235	2,147	88	34.0	42.6
1948	7,078	5,973	1,106	3,991	2,965	1,028	3,087	3,008	79	43.6	50.4
1949	6,052	4,890	1,161	3,550	2,437	1,112	2,502	2,453	49	41.3	50.2
1950	6,362	4,920	1,442	3,681	2,360	1,321	2,680	2,560	120	42.1	52.0
1951	7,741	5,691	2,050	4,326	2,364	1,962	3,415	3,326	88	44.1	58.4
1952	9,534	7,601	1,933	5,533	3,645	1,888	4,002	3,957	45	42.0	52.1
1953	8,898	7,083	1,815	5,580	3,856	1,725	3,318	3,228	90	37.3	45.6
1954	9,516	7,488	2,029	5,848	4,003	1,844	3,668	3,484	184	38.5	46.5
1955	10,240	7,420	2,820	6,763	4,119	2,644	3,477	3,301	176	34.0	44.5
1956	10,939	8,002	2,937	7,053	4,225	2,827	3,886	3,777	109	35.5	47.2
1957	12,884	9,957	2,927	8,959	6,118	2,841	3,925	3,839	86	30.5	38.6
1958	11,558	9,653	1,906	8,068	6,332	1,736	3,490	3,320	170	30.2	34.4
1959 (January-June)	4,978	3,518	1,460	3,160	1,746	1,413	1,818	1,772	47	36.5	50.4

direct placement, negotiation may be started and completed within one week, particularly if the issuer and institutional investor(s) have negotiated direct placements previously. Conversely, two to three months may pass from the day a decision is made to negotiate a public offering to the day it is formally offered to the public. In a direct placement, the same basic facts that would have to be incorporated in a registration statement may be presented to the offerees in a much more direct and less time-consuming manner. Since financial management and other corporate officials have to devote considerable time to the preparation of documents that accompany public offerings, the simple procedures involved in direct placement appeal to them.

COSTS. The costs involved in offering securities can be broken down into three major components: (1) compensation to investors; (2) compensation to underwriters, agents, or finders; and (3) other expenses. From the point of view of the common stockholders, an issuer should elect the least costly methods of financing, given the capacity to assume risks. During the period 1934-1958, the combination of record-low interest rates and record-high corporate income tax rates made debt issues a relatively low-cost method of financing. Since direct placements are mainly debt issues, the development of direct placement has been advantageous to outstanding common stockholders. With respect to compensation of underwriters, agents, or finders, direct placement offers additional cost savings. Direct placements are not underwritten, so that there is no underwriting commission. In about half of the direct placements, agents' or finders' fees are paid to investment banking firms, but the fees are much lower than underwriting commissions because the firms perform a limited role in comparison with that of underwriting. The size of the fees is related to the size of the issues. In 1951, 1953, and 1955 the median agents' or finders' fees on issues of less than $300,000 represented 1.9 per cent of gross proceeds; on issues of $20 million and over, the median fee was only 0.2 per cent of gross proceeds.*

"Other expenses" include legal and accounting fees and other out-of-pocket expenses related to preparation and execution of an offering. In order to compare the costs of direct placement with the costs of a public offering, these expenses should be broken down into three categories: (1) those entirely attributable to Securities and Exchange Commission regulations; (2) those attributable only in part to regulation; and (3) those unrelated to regulation. In a direct placement, the costs in the first category are eliminated and those in the second category are reduced. Costs in the third category are involved in both direct placements and public offerings. In 1951, 1953, and 1955, "other expenses" averaged about 0.4 per cent of gross proceeds; in small issues, "other expenses" absorbed as much as 1.5

*Richard C. Pickering, "Security Financing of Small Business," *Financing Small Business*, p. 302. These fees are much lower than the representative commissions shown in Table 20-2.

per cent of gross proceeds.* It is estimated that "other expenses" are reduced by as much as one-half when the issuer uses direct placement.†

The following quotation effectively summarizes the discussion of costs**

> The cost of placing debt securities privately with large financial institutions is considerably less than the cost of floating a debt issue of similar size in the public market, but more so for small than for large issues. This is true for both compensation to investment bankers and other expenses. Lack of adequate data on compensation to investors and other indenture terms for both public offerings and private placements makes it impossible to ascertain the extent to which lower initial flotation costs for private placements are offset by higher interest rates or more restrictive terms.

Disadvantages

From the investors' point of view, there are two disadvantages connected with direct placements. Probably the most important is that there is little or no opportunity to "market test" a direct placement issue. A public issue may have a rating, and the reaction of investors can be observed. However, in a direct placement, an institutional investor cannot verify his own judgment by looking to the market. Of course, if a relatively large number of institutional investors are involved in the same direct placement, the individual investor can look around and discover what others think about the issue. Another often-stated disadvantage is that of limited marketability. It is argued that since direct placements are not "market tested," it is more difficult to liquidate such an issue in the market. This statement is probably true to some extent. If the issue had been acquired in a public offering, there might be an established market for it, and prospective purchasers of the resold securities would have access to a registration statement and prospectus. However, in practice limited marketability does not pose a serious disadvantage because of the small likelihood that institutional investors would ever be forced to liquidate. After all, institutional investors, and particularly life insurance companies, have a net cash inflow in addition to the periodic repayments received on outstanding loans and investments.

From the issuers' point of view, private placement has some disadvantages. Probably the greatest is that institutional investors tend to require that issuers incorporate more restrictive provisions in the loan agreements or indentures than would be necessary in public offerings. Generally, repayment schedules and call provisions are more stringent, and additional debt obligations cannot be issued without permission. Issuers cannot repurchase directly placed securities. However, they may be permitted to accelerate repayments. Furthermore, issuers in the private market are de-

*Ibid., pp. 303-304.
† Leness, Martin, and Gilmartin, op. cit., p. 96.
**Pickering, op. cit., p. 305.

prived of the publicity associated with public offerings. The only publicity that direct placements receive is a capsule comment in financial newspapers. Obviously, each issuer must weigh advantages against disadvantages. The relatively large volume of direct placements indicates that the disadvantages of this market are more than offset by its advantages.

Competition

In the development of direct placement, it has become an established practice for some of the larger financial intermediaries to form direct placement groups, similar to the purchase syndicates that are formed by investment bankers. The major difference is that the investment banking groups purchase for resale, whereas the savings and insurance groups purchase for investment. As noted earlier, direct placement has led to the development of two distinct markets for long-term corporate capital. There is a limited degree of competition within the direct placement market, and between the public and private markets. It has been suggested by one student of direct placement that one way to promote greater competition would be to redefine public offering so as to broaden the private markets, thereby creating a larger supply of corporate securities in the private market. This step would make it possible for the smaller institutional investors to assume a more active role in the market, and to break down the tendency of the larger institutional investors to restrict such acquisitions.*

SMALL BUSINESS INVESTMENT COMPANIES

During the past 25 years numerous studies have pointed out the difficulties that small business has in obtaining long-term credit and equity capital. Neither of the established long-term capital markets is well suited to fit the needs of small business. Investment bankers underwrite a relatively small volume of issues of small business, and for those which are underwritten, the commissions are made very high to offset the risks inherent in such offerings. Also, compliance with registration requirements tends to discourage some businesses from making public offerings. The data pertaining to new corporate debt issues during 1951, 1953, and 1955 show that only about 20 per cent of the registered public offerings involved issues of less than $5 million and issuers with assets of less than $20 million. The data for registered public offerings of equity issues were slightly more favorable from the point of view of small business; about 20 per cent of the issues were less than $1 million, and about 24 per cent of the issuers had assets of less than $5 million.†

Life insurance companies have not acquired very large holdings of

*Corey, op. cit., pp. 150-151.
† Pickering, op. cit., p. 286.

privately offered issues of small business. A special survey of life insurance companies accounting for more than three-fourths of the assets held by all life insurance companies revealed that in 1956 less than 6 per cent of the number and 1 per cent of the amount of their authorized business and industrial bond investments went to businesses having assets under $2 million. For issuers or borrowers with assets of less than $5 million the corresponding figures were 15.5 per cent and 5 per cent.* Various reasons may be cited to explain these relatively small holdings. First, a substantial amount of money and time is involved in determining the financial position of an issuer and the merits of the issuer's securities. Since life insurance companies tend to place a ceiling of 6 or 7 per cent on direct placements, the yield may not cover costs. Second, the Committee on Valuation of Securities of the National Association of Insurance Commissioners may rule that an issue of a small business cannot be carried at amortized value on the grounds that the earnings record and the financial position of the issuer are not adequate. Generally, life insurance companies minimize their investments in assets that cannot be carried at amortized values. Third, a great deal of risk is involved in the issues of small business. Considering the need for safety of principal, losses must be minimized.

Some small business enterprises offer a promising growth potential, but are prevented from realizing it because their financing needs in the longer term debt and equity capital areas are not being met by the existing structure of financial institutions. Throughout the postwar period, Congressional committees and private groups presented various proposals to plug this gap in our financial system, but it was not until 1958 that a definite proposal was prepared and made into law. The following statement of policy is set forth in Section 102 of the Small Business Investment Act of 1958: "It is declared to be the policy of the Congress and the purpose of this Act to improve and stimulate the national economy in general and the small-business segment thereof in particular by establishing a program to stimulate and supplement the flow of private equity capital and long-term loan funds which small-business concerns need for the sound financing of their business operations and for their growth, expansion, and modernization, and which are not available in adequate supply: Provided, however, that this policy shall be carried out in such manner as to insure the maximum participation of private financing sources." The term "small-business concern" has the same meaning in this Act as it has in the Small Business Act. Essentially, S.B.I.C.'s are restricted to financing companies with annual sales of less than $5 million and earnings of less than $150,000.

Congress encouraged the formation and development of small business investment companies by providing financial assistance in the form of equity capital and loans to investment companies, favorable tax treatment for the companies as well as for the investors, and exemptions from certain

*Saul B. Klaman, "Life Insurance Companies," *Financing Small Business*, p. 515.

456

regulations pertaining to securities. Actual operation of the program started in March 1959, and within the first year, 80 companies had been licensed and nearly $15 million in long-term financing had been provided to 240 small firms in 60 different types of business. With the passage of time and the adoption of major amendments in 1960, there has been a marked acceleration in the number of proposals for licenses and the volume of financing. As of September 1960, the cumulative proposals, including licensees, have increased to nearly 250, with planned and actual initial capital of $200 million. The majority of the capital is coming from investment companies that raise or plan to raise major sums through public stock offerings.*

In this section we shall set out a description of the basic organization of small business investment companies and their financing of small business.

Organization of Small Business Investment Companies

The Small Business Investment Act provides for a system of dual charter. However, unlike the dual charter in other areas of the financial system, a Federal charter will not be granted unless the proposed company demonstrates that it cannot be chartered under the laws of a given state and at the same time operate in accordance with the purposes of the Act. After June 30, 1961 all companies are to be chartered under state law. It is assumed that state laws can be changed to conform to the Act within the specified two-year period. All companies, regardless of source of charter, are required to obtain licenses from the S.B.A. in order to operate under the Act.

The approval of the establishment of an investment company and its proposed articles of incorporation are not automatic. Approval is at the discretion of the S.B.A. Among the factors considered are economic need for the company in the area to be served, character of the proposed management, number of companies already organized, and the expected volume of operations. The same set of standards are used in the issuance of licenses. The Act also provides for the conversion of state-chartered investment companies and state development companies into small business investment companies.

To form such a company, there must be ten or more incorporators and the firm must have a minimum paid-in capital and surplus of $300,000. To facilitate the formation of investment companies, the S.B.A. is authorized to purchase a company's subordinated debentures in an amount equal to not more than $150,000, and the debentures can be considered part of the required minimum paid-in capital and surplus. Therefore, only $150,000 of private capital is required to form a company. However, a company with

*The Reporter, a pamphlet published by the Small Business Administration Investment Division, Vol. 1, No. 4, September 1960, p. 1.

the minimum amount of capital will have difficulty covering the cost of investigating and closing loans, unless it is tied in with an existing financial institution, such as a commercial bank or life insurance company. It may be necessary to increase the minimum capital requirement to reach a company size that will be profitable for an independent operation.

The Act makes the shares of stock of small business investment companies eligible for purchase by commercial banks up to 1 per cent of a bank's capital and surplus. This provision makes it possible for banks to invest in common stock, and also allows them to get back into the field of investment banking in a very limited fashion. As of June 1960, 13 companies were wholly owned by banks, and 18 were partly owned by banks or bank holding companies. Many of these companies were of the minimum capital type. The banks are able to operate the companies at a very low cost and at the same time maintain a foothold in one of the newer segments of the financial system.

Small business investment companies have the right to borrow and to issue various types of securities. After a company has loaned out or invested its initial $300,000 capital, it is permitted to borrow additional amounts from the S.B.A. and other sources in order to build up its capital to ten times its initial investment. The ratio of debt to equity cannot exceed four to one. There is no limit on the issue of stock.

The favorable tax treatment accorded investors in these companies and the companies themselves has helped considerably to promote their development. Let it suffice to mention that investors are permitted to charge off fully capital losses on S.B.I.C. stock against ordinary taxable income, whereas only limited deductions are permitted on other forms of financial investment. The companies are permitted the same treatment with respect to their capital losses. The companies are permitted to charge a 15 per cent rate of interest on their loans. Many investors expect Congress to allow the companies to charge income and set up sizeable tax-free loan reserves. As the public becomes more aware of the preferential tax treatment, the stock of the large, publicly-held companies will be sought by more investors.

Financing Small Businesses

Small business investment companies may finance small businesses in many different ways: (1) long-term loans without equity interests, (2) unsecured convertible debentures, (3) secured convertible debentures, (4) debt securities having detachable or non-detachable stock purchase warrants or options, and (5) stock of any class, with or without warrants, options or conversion privileges, of the businesses being financed. Under S.B.A. regulations, equity securities are defined as debt securities that carry conversion privileges, detachable or non-detachable stock purchase warrants or options, as well as capital stock of any class. Prior to the amendments in 1960, equity financing was possible only through convertible debentures. The greater flexibility in equity financing "should result in a greater flow of private financing to small business . . . the new law should enhance the ability of the S.B.I.C.'s to borrow money from private sources against their portfolios of small business securities; for the S.B.I.C.'s now will be able to create types of securities that may meet the eligibility requirements of trust funds, endowment funds, pension funds, and insurance companies. The end result should be a higher degree of liquidity for the securities of small business concerns."* Convertible securities and stock options will make it easier for companies to transfer or sell seasoned investments to other investors and thereby enable the companies to realize capital gains and to raise additional funds for financing small businesses.

The Act authorizes the companies to make long-term, direct and participation loans to unincorporated and incorporated small business concerns. The original maturity of the loans should be at least 5 years but not more than 20 years. Loans may be renewed or extended for an additional 10-year period. Borrowing firms may be required to consolidate their outstanding obligations and agree not to incur additional indebtedness without approval of the lender. Bonds issued to small business investment companies by small businesses in return for equity financing must have a maturity of at least 5 years. They are callable on three months' notice and subject to the conversion privileges. Loans and bonds may be amortized during the first 5 years, but amortization may not be greater than 5-year straight line, or the equivalent. Small business investment companies must determine that the firms they are financing are in fact "small businesses," and file with the S.B.A. information establishing this fact.

The Act originally required that a small business obtaining financing from a small business investment company purchase stock in the investment company in an amount equal to a stated per cent of the capital obtained. The purpose to be served was to build up the investment of private funds and reduce or eliminate the use of Federal funds. Such a requirement might have led to the dilution of ownership and gradual development of a mutual type of ownership. From the point of view of the firm being financed, the purchase of stock has the same effect as a discount against the loan. Under the amendments to the Act, such reinvestment is at the option of the borrower, who has the privilege of purchasing stock up to 5 per cent of the amount of financing obtained. The change in the law pleased both the investment companies and the small businesses being financed.

The act also promotes diversification in a small business investment company's loans and investment by limiting a company's holdings of a single firm's obligations and securities to not more than a stated percentage of the investment company's combined capital and surplus. The scope of

*Ibid., p. 1.

this discussion does not permit examination of the many other regulations affecting the financing operations of small business investment companies.

Outlook

Congress has created conditions that are favorable to the development of private small business investment companies. It was not the purpose of the Act to set up companies that would merely serve as intermediaries in the dispersal of Federal funds. The major portion of the funds to date have come from the private sector. Much of the growth will depend on the development of the large, publicly-held small business investment companies. However, these companies do not allocate their funds to the very small firms; instead they allocate their funds to companies that are on the border line between being small businesses and medium-sized businesses. By concentrating their efforts on the large loans, the companies are more profitable and their portfolios are more liquid. There is very little prospect of capital gains in a transaction with a very small firm. Instead, the prospect of capital gains rests with the firms that are on the brink of having their stock traded actively in the over-the-counter market or listed on a national exchange. Also, the overhead is much less when funds are spread out over a few small businesses. The larger investment companies will probably operate on a nationwide basis and restrict their operations to loans or investments of $100,000 or more. Although this type of financing is not helping the very small firms, it is helping firms that might otherwise be absorbed by larger firms through mergers and the purchase of assets. The program should contribute to more competition.

It is very doubtful if the program is plugging the gap in our financial system as it pertains to financing the long-term and equity needs of the very small business firms. To do so, it may be necessary to introduce some form of discounting that will make the loans and investments of the minimum capital small business investment companies and the small loans and investments of the large, publicly-held small business investment companies as liquid as the larger loans and investments of the publicly-held companies. In other words, it may be necessary for a Federal agency to become a primary supplier of long-term funds to very small businesses. To the extent that the S.B.A. is necessary to assist directly in financing small businesses, it is also necessary that the S.B.A. or some other Federal agency assist directly in long-term financing of small businesses.

Many years of experience will be necessary to measure the impact of this innovation in our financial system. Many changes in rules have been introduced to widen the operating scope of S.B.I.C.'s and to provide additional incentive for financing small business. Further changes in rules can be expected. If the program does not have positive results, it can be expected that Congress will pass additional amendments. One thing is certain, a move has been made to eliminate this gap in our financial system.

QUESTIONS

1. Describe briefly the structure of the investment banking industry.

2. Explain how the growth of institutional investors has affected the structure and operation of the investment banking industry.

3. Describe briefly the major functions that are performed by the investment banking industry.

4. Distinguish between a straight public offering and a rights offering.

5. Explain why regulation of public offerings of securities is a delicate balancing operation.

6. Explain in some detail how the Securities Act of 1933 protects investors in corporate stocks and bonds.

7. Should competitive bidding be required for publicly offered securities of all large corporations?

8. How important are direct placements?

9. From the investor's point of view, what are the advantages and disadvantages of direct placement?

10. From the issuer's point of view, what are the advantages and disadvantages of direct placement?

11. What prompted the passage of the Small Business Investment Company Act of 1958?

12. Describe briefly the structure and operation of a typical small-business development company.

13. How do they differ from the credit development corporations discussed in Chapter 18?

ADDITIONAL READING

See list of corporation finance texts at end of Chapter 16, investment texts at the end of Chapter 12, and publications of the United States Government at the end of Chapters 18 and 19.

"Contemporary Problems in Securities Legislation," *Virginia Law Review*, October 1959. Entire volume devoted to subject.

Corey, Raymond E. *Direct Placement of Corporate Securities*. Boston: Harvard University, Graduate School of Business Administration, Division of Research, 1951.

Leness, George L., Gillette K. Martin, and Roger T. Gilmartin. *New Money for Business*. New York: McGraw-Hill Book Co., Inc., 1956.

"Symposium on the Securities and Exchange Commission," *George Washington Law Review*, October 1959. Entire volume devoted to subject.

U.S. District Court, New York (Southern District). *Corrected Opinion of U.S. Circuit Judge Harold R. Medina in the case of the U.S., Plaintiff, v. Morgan Stanley & Co. et al., Defendants.* Filed February 4, 1954.

U.S. Securities and Exchange Commission. *Annual Report.* Washington, D.C.: Government Printing Office. See latest report.

U.S. Senate Subcommittee of the Committee on Banking and Currency. *SEC Legislation.* Hearings, 86th Cong., 1st sess. Washington, D.C.: Government Printing Office, 1959. This set of hearings contains copies of the Securities Act of 1933, Securities Exchange Act of 1934, Trust Indenture Act of 1939, Investment Company Act of 1940, and the Investment Advisers Act of 1940, proposed amendments to the Acts, explanation and related memoranda on amendments to the Acts, and staff memorandum on amendments.

21: Financing the farm business sector

I N the early 1800's the functions of the farm included growing, processing, storing, and merchandising. Farming was not considered to be a commercial undertaking, and many of the farms were subsistance units. With the application of technology and specialization, farming gradually achieved a commercial status, and the functions of the farm were reduced essentially to the single function of growing crops and livestock. The functions of processing, storing, and merchandising were transferred in large measure to the non-farm business sectors, resulting in considerable interdependence between farm and non-farm sectors. These interrelated functions have given rise to the term "agribusiness," which refers to the "sum total of all operations involved in the manufacture and distribution of farm supplies; production operations on the farm; and the storage, processing, and distribution of farm commodities and items made from them."* Agribusiness encompasses the functions that the term "agriculture" denoted in the early 1800's.

The magnitude and composition of agribusiness are suggested by the following 1954 data.† Total assets of agribusiness were approximately $220 billion. The agribusiness labor force of 24,000,000 accounted for approximately 37 per cent of the civilian labor force. The farm component of agribusiness accounted for about one-third of the workers and three-fourths of the assets in agribusiness. The 1954 output in agribusiness totaled $75 billion. To illustrate the degree of change in the structure of agribusiness, it may be noted that the farm portion of agribusiness output in 1910 was 54 per cent; in 1954 it was only 17 per cent.

To emphasize some of the recent changes in the farm sector, we compare 1957 census data with 1940 census data. The number of farms declined 27 per cent; farm population declined 29 per cent; the number of farm workers declined 50 per cent; the inventory value of machinery increased 600 per cent; the dollar input of fertilizer increased 400 per cent;

*John H. Davis and Ray A. Goldberg, A Concept of Agribusiness (Boston: Harvard Business School, Division of Research, 1957), p. 2.
† Ibid.

investment per farm increased 500 per cent; investment per farm worker increased 550 per cent; and the value of farm output increased 50 per cent. The financial implications of these changes are that present-day commercial farming requires relatively large fixed investments in land and machinery and considerable financing during the growing season. For example, the investment per farm worker for corn-belt grain farms approaches $60,000. In some segments of farming there is a trend toward contract farming, under which non-farm business enterprises — many of them part of the agribusiness structure — finance the total farm operations.

The operation of fewer but larger agricultural units and the use of improved seeds, feeds, and breeding stock, more and better fertilizers, insecticides, herbicides, and other agricultural chemicals, and the application of modern farm machinery have enabled a much smaller number of farm workers to produce a much larger farm output. Research and the dissemination of research findings to individual farmers have been basic to all of these developments. The technological revolution in farming has facilitated the shifting of farm workers from the farm sector in the non-farm business sectors, including industries that comprise the other components of agribusiness. Farm income data suggest that additional shifting is likely. Approximately 60 per cent of the farm families are classified as low-income families. The data show that many farm families have a sub-standard level of living, and it is unlikely that many of these farm families could become efficient and profitable farm operators. A large portion of these farm families could make a much greater contribution to total production by shifting to the non-farm business sectors.

Farming in the United States continues to be primarily a family enterprise, and it is difficult to segregate the business activities of farming from the consumer activities of farm families. If consumer activities of farm families could be segregated from aggregate consumer activities, it would be possible to analyze farms in terms of their total activities. Since this analysis is not possible, we shall focus our attention primarily on the business activities of farm enterprises.

The flow-of-funds system of accounts defines the farm business sector so as to cover all farm operating activities in the United States. Specifically, the sector "includes unincorporated farm enterprises, corporate farms, and, on a consolidated basis, farm credit cooperatives (national farm loan associations and production credit associations) and the farm activities of nonfarm landlords of farm property. The sector excludes farm marketing, purchasing, and utility cooperatives and the non-farm business activities of farm families, all of which are in the non-farm business sectors. It also excludes most of the consumer transactions, other than housing of farmers."*

*"A Quarterly Presentation of Flow of Funds, Saving and Investment," *Federal Reserve Bulletin*, August 1959, pp. 846-847.

FINANCIAL POSITION OF FARM OPERATING ENTERPRISES

Balance Sheet of Agriculture*

The balance sheet of agriculture provides a convenient first step in portraying the aggregate financial position of farm operating enterprises. The comparative balance sheet of agriculture in the United States, as of January 1, 1940, 1958, and 1959 is shown in Table 21-1. On January 1, 1959 farm assets were $203 billion. Liabilities were slightly more than $23 billion, and the proprietors' equities were nearly $167 billion. The increase in farm land values has been the major factor underlying the growth in total asset value and proprietors' equities. For example, it is interesting to note that agricultural real estate, valued at 1940 prices, increased less than $5 billion between 1940 and 1959. Machinery and motor vehicles valued at 1940 prices increased by nearly the same amount. The data in Table 21-1 show a greater rate of increase in physical assets than in liabilities during the 1940-1960 period.

Financial Assets and Liabilities

The financial assets shown in Table 21-1 are not restricted to farm operations. It can be assumed that United States savings bonds, part of deposits and currency, and a portion of the investment in cooperatives represent consumer investments of farm families. The flow-of-funds data shown in Table 21-2 reflect only the business activities of farms. The data indicate that the financial assets of the farm sector consist almost entirely of currency and deposits. Farm enterprises extend neither trade nor consumer credit. The ratio of financial assets to liabilities is much lower for the farm sector than for either of the other two business sectors. However, farmers can and do draw on financial assets (of farm families) to back up or lend support to their farm operations.

The liabilities shown in Tables 21-1 and 21-2 reflect the nature and extent of the farm sector's borrowing. The need for farm credit is influenced by the length of the production period for crops and livestock, the level of farm income, expectation as to future farm prices and farm income, capital investment opportunities in farm operating enterprises, and the borrowing capacity of farmers.†

The farm sector relies heavily on mortgages and bank loans, n.e.c. At the end of 1958, mortgages and bank loans, n.e.c. provided respectively

---

*The balance sheet of agriculture is based on annual reports on the financial condition of agriculture, issued by the United States Department of Agriculture. The data referred to in this section are taken from the "The Balance Sheet of Agriculture 1959," *Federal Reserve Bulletin,* July 1959, pp. 724-732.

† Lawrence E. Kreider, "A Look at Farm Credit Experience," *Monthly Review of the Federal Reserve Bank of St. Louis,* December 1955. The article provides an excellent review of farm credit since 1919.

TABLE 21-1
COMPARATIVE BALANCE SHEET OF AGRICULTURE, UNITED STATES,
JANUARY 1, 1940, 1958, AND 1959
(BILLIONS OF DOLLARS)

	1940	1958	1959	Net increase[1] (Per cent) 1940-59	1958-59
Assets					
Physical assets:					
Real estate	33.6	116.3	125.1	271.9	7.6
Non-real-estate:					
Livestock	5.1	14.1[2]	18.1	252.8	28.7
Machinery and motor vehicles..	3.1	17.4[2]	18.4	501.6	6.0
Crops stored on and off farms[3]	2.7	7.6	9.4	250.8	22.8
Household furnishings and					
equipment[4]	4.3	12.8	13.1	206.7	2.7
Financial assets:					
Deposits and currency	3.2	9.5[2]	10.0	207.7	5.1
U. S. savings bonds	.2	5.1	5.2	1,992.1	1.8
Investment in cooperatives......	.8	3.6[2]	3.8	360.7	6.3
Total[5]	53.0	186.4	203.1	282.5	9.0
Claims					
Liabilities:					
Real estate debt	6.6	10.5	11.3	71.0	7.2
Non-real-estate debt to:					
Commodity Credit					
Corporation[6]	.4	1.2	2.5	459.1	102.9
Other reporting institutions[7]...	1.5	5.0	5.8	283.3	15.4
Nonreporting creditors[8]	1.5	3.5	3.7	146.7	5.7
Total liabilities[5]	10.0	20.2	23.3	131.4	14.8
Proprietors' equities	43.0	166.2	179.8	317.7	8.3
Total[5]	53.0	186.4	203.1	282.5	9.0

[1] Computed from unrounded data.

[2] Revised.

[3] Includes all crops held on farms for whatever purpose and crops held off farms as security for Commodity Credit Corporation loans. The latter on Jan. 1, 1959, totaled $1,877 million.

[4] Estimated valuation for 1940, plus purchases minus depreciation since then.

[5] Total of rounded data.

[6] Although these are nonrecourse loans, they are included as liabilities because borrowers must either repay in cash or deliver the commodities on which the loans were based. The values of the underlying commodities are included among the assets; hence the loans must be included as liabilities to avoid overstating the amount of proprietors' equities.

[7] Loans of all operating banks, the production credit associations, and the Farmers Home Administration, and discounts of the Federal intermediate credit banks for agricultural credit corporations and livestock loan companies.

[8] Loans and credits extended by dealers, merchants, finance companies, individuals and others. Estimates based on fragmentary data.

Source: *Federal Reserve Bulletin*, July 1959, p. 725.

TABLE 21-2
FINANCIAL ASSETS AND LIABILITIES OF THE FARM BUSINESS SECTOR, END OF 1958
(BILLIONS OF DOLLARS)

	Dollars	Per cent
Financial assets		
Financial assets	6.3	100.0
Currency and demand deposits	6.2	98.4
Federal obligations [1]	.1	1.6
Liabilities		
Liabilities	18.9	100.0
Credit market instruments	16.9	89.4
Mortgages	11.2	59.2
Bank loans, n.e.c.	4.2	22.2
Other loans	1.6	8.5
Trade debt	2.1	11.1

Memorandum: C.C.C. direct and guaranteed loans not
included above 2.4
Note: Details may not add to totals because of rounding.
[1] Held by production credit associations.
Source: "A Quarterly Presentation of Flow of Funds, Saving, and Investment," *Federal Reserve Bulletin*, August 1959.

60 per cent and 22 per cent of total farm credit. Loans from Federally sponsored credit agencies and C.C.C. guaranteed loans provided less than 10 per cent of borrowed funds. Trade debt provided slightly more than 11 per cent of total credit.

Sources and Uses of Funds

A sources and uses of funds statement (Table 21-3) provides additional insight into the financing of the farm sector. The basic format of the statement is similar to those shown in Chapter 16.* As the non-corporate nonfinancial business sector's statement of sources and uses of funds does, the farm business sector's statement shows proprietors' net investment as a use of funds. During the 1955-1958 period, the net investment expenditures of farm enterprses were lower than depreciation of farm assets and the increase in farm liabilities. In the previous four-year period, there was a net inflow of equity funds.

Internal sources provided more than three-fourths of the total sources of funds, or about the same proportion as those reported for the other two business sectors. Long-term mortgage credit was the major external source of funds, providing 14.5 per cent during 1955-1958 period.

*C.C.C. nonrecourse price-support loans, both direct loans and guaranteed loans held by banks, are treated as sales to the C.C.C. rather than as a form of secured borrowing.

TABLE 21–3
SOURCES AND USES OF FUNDS OF THE FARM BUSINESS SECTOR, 1955-1958
(BILLIONS OF DOLLARS)

	Dollars	Per cent
Sources of funds		
Internal sources	15.3	76.5
Capital consumption	15.3	76.5
External sources	4.7	23.5
Short- and intermediate-term	1.8	9.0
Bank loans, n.e.c.	1.3	6.5
Other loans	.5	2.5
Long-term and permanent	2.9	14.5
Mortgages	2.9	14.5
Total Sources	20.0	100.0
Uses of funds		
Capital expenditures	18.2	91.0
Construction and equipment	16.6	83.0
Changes in inventory	1.8	9.0
Net acquisition of financial assets	1.7	8.5
Proprietors' net disinvestment [1]	1.7	8.5
Total Uses	19.9	99.5
Statistical discrepancy	0.1	0.5

Note: Details may not add to totals because of rounding.
[1] Normally a source of funds, but over this four-year period there was a decrease in proprietors' net investment; hence, it is shown as "proprietors' net disinvestment" and, therefore, a use of funds.
Source: "A Quarterly Presentation of Flow of Funds, Saving and Investment," *Federal Reserve Bulletin*, August 1959.

Bank loans, n.e.c. were the most important short- and intermediate-term source of credit. Other loans, which represent mainly Federal Government loans, provided only $500 million of additional funds to the farm business sector during the four-year period.

The uses of funds during the 1955-1958 period were almost entirely accounted for by construction and equipment expenditures and changes in inventories. As noted above, there was a small amount of proprietors' net disinvestment during the period.

PRIVATE SOURCES OF FARM CREDIT

For our purposes in this chapter, the description of the sources of farm credit is broken down into two areas: private sources and public and semi-public sources. Private sources include commercial banks, life insurance companies, individuals, and non-farm business firms. Public and semi-

TABLE 21–4
NON-REAL ESTATE LOANS TO FARMERS, JANUARY 1, 1949 AND 1959 [1]
(MILLIONS OF DOLLARS)

	Jan. 1, 1949		Jan. 1, 1959	
	$	%	$	%
All operating banks	1,946	71.8	4,161	72.2
Production credit association	367	13.5	1,115	19.3
Federal intermediate credit banks	56	2.1	84	1.5
Farmers Home Administration:				
Operating loans	249	9.2	340	5.9
Emergency loans	3	.1	60	1.0
Emergency crop and feed loans	90	3.3	6	.1
Total	2,710	100.0	5,765	100.0

Note: Details may not add to totals because of rounding.
[1] Excludes loans guaranteed by C.C.C.
[2] Loans to and discounts for livestock loan companies and agricultural credit corporations.
Source: *Agricultural Finance Review*, U. S. Department of Agriculture, Washington, D. C., July 1959, Vol. 21, pp. 134, 135.

TABLE 21–5
FARM MORTGAGES OUTSTANDING, END OF 1958
(BILLIONS OF DOLLARS)

Sector	Dollars	Per cent	Mortgages as a percentage of sector's total financial assets or liabilities
Issuer: Farm business	11.2	100.0	59.2
Investors (all sectors)	11.2	100.0	
Consumer and nonprofit	4.5	40.2	.5
Federal Government	2.4	21.4	5.9
Commercial banking	1.5	13.4	.6
Mutual savings banks	.1	.9	.3
Insurance	2.7	24.1	1.7

Note: Details may not add to totals because of rounding.
Source: "A Quarterly Presentation of Funds, Saving and Investment," *Federal Reserve Bulletin*, August 1959.

public sources consist primarily of Federally sponsored credit services, many of which are now owned by the farmers, who are member-borrowers.

To provide an over-all perspective as to the sources of farm credit, data pertaining to non-real estate loans to farmers and the ownership pattern of farm mortgages outstanding are presented respectively in Tables

21-4 and 21-5. The data show that private sources predominate in both markets. At the beginning of 1959, commercial banks were providing approximately 72 per cent of non-real estate loans to farmers, which was nearly identical to their share of the market in 1949. The remainder of non-real estate loans to farmers were being obtained from public and semi-public sources, including production credit associations, Federal intermediate credit banks, and the Farmers Home Administration. These sources of credit are described later in this chapter. The comparison of 1949 and 1959 data show that nearly all the changes in the composition of the sources of non-real estate loans to farmers took place among the public and semi-public sources; that is, the growth in the production credit associations has been at the expense of the Farmers Home Administration, not of the commercial banks.

Private sources predominate to an even greater extent in the market for farm mortgages, accounting for 78.6 per cent of farm mortgages outstanding at the end of 1958. The holdings of the Federal Government represent those of national farm loan associations, Federal land banks, and the Farmers Home Administration. The data show that individuals, commercial banks, and insurance companies are the three major private sources of farm mortgage credit. The insurance company holdings represent mainly those of life insurance companies.

Commercial Banks

The commercial banks supply more than 25 per cent of the total credit received by the farm sector. Commercial banks extend all forms of farm credit, and in mid-1956 nearly half of the operating farms in this country had loans outstanding at insured commercial banks. Commercial banks probably provide as much as three-fourths of the institutional farm credit used to finance the short- and intermediate-term needs of agriculture, and about one-sixth of the credit used to finance farm real estate purchases.

In extending farm credit, commercial banks encounter problems much like those the banks encounter in making loans to small non-farm business firms. Generally, farmers and small businessmen lack the necessary training and experience to carry out short- and long-range financial planning. They usually seek credit only as it is needed. Their financing tends to be on a piecemeal basis. Frequently, they have outstanding obligations payable to two or three different creditors. Under these circumstances lenders must analyze borrowers' total financial positions and arrange loans that fit realistically their debt repayment abilities. In a specific loan, a lender must determine the borrower's character and ability, the financial progress and position of the farm enterprise, the purpose of the loan, the repayment capacity of the borrower, and possible collateral. Finally, lenders must disburse counsel as well as funds.

Many of the small commercial banks in the farm areas are not adequately staffed to handle a large volume of farm loans, and many of the larger commercial banks in the cities do not have direct contact with farm borrowers. However, in recent years, there have been definite improvements. Some of the smaller commercial banks have acquired well-trained staffs, and some of the larger city banks have set up agricultural departments to service the needs of correspondent banks dealing in farm loans. Commercial banks stepped up their lending to farm operating enterprises during the postwar period. Between 1947 and 1956, the number of bank farm loans increased 45 per cent, and the average size of the outstanding farm loans increased 60 per cent. The figures are even more impressive when it is realized that during this period the number of farms declined by about 20 per cent.

Terms of Bank Farm Loans

A recent national survey of agricultural loans outstanding in insured commercial banks provides much data on this subject.* For the survey, farm loans were classified by purpose under five categories: current expense, intermediate-term investments, farm real estate purchase, repayment of debt, and other, or not ascertained. The composition and importance of each category are shown in Table 21-6. The discussion of terms of bank farm loans is based entirely on survey findings.

Short maturities and demand notes are frequently used in farm loans even though the purposes of the loans might suggest that longer maturities would be more realistic or appropriate. It is interesting to note in Table 21-7 that the percentage of farm loans written with demand notes was about the same for all types of farm loans. Approximately 28 per cent of the demand loans outstanding on June 30, 1956 had been made or last renewed more than one year before that date. Of the farm loans outstanding at the time of the survey, 35 per cent had been renewed one or more times, and about 70 per cent of the renewals were made according to plan.

The widespread use of demand notes and short maturities can probably be explained by the uncertainties associated with farming and farm loans. When farmers have a very good year, banks can expect full payment of the farm loans. However, there is a definite trend toward more intermediate-term farm loans. In 1955, the Board of Governors of the Federal Reserve System made it known "that no Federal law or regulation prevents commercial banks from extending credit for agricultural purposes on an intermediate-term basis, and such loans are not to be considered undesirable as a class.† Currently many commercial banks and other farm lenders

*See *Farm Loans at Commercial Banks.* A series of articles reporting the findings of the Agricultural Loan Survey made as of June 30, 1956 by the Federal Reserve System, issued by the Board of Governors of the Federal Reserve System, Washington, D. C.

† Letter from Board of Governors of the Federal Reserve System to the Presidents of the Federal Reserve Banks, dated October 4, 1955.

TABLE 21-6
PURPOSE OF FARM LOANS OUTSTANDING AT BANKS, JUNE 30, 1956

Purpose of loan	Number of notes		Amount of loans		Average size of note
	In thousands	Percentage distribution	In millions of dollars	Percentage distribution	
All purposes	3,528	100.0	5,050	100.0	$1,431
Current expenses — total	1,697	48.1	1,903	37.7	1,121
Feeder livestock operations.........	134	3.8	497	9.8	3,717
Current operating and living expenses	1,564	44.3	1,406	27.8	899
Intermediate-term investments — total..	1,325	37.6	1,685	33.4	1,271
Other livestock	234	6.6	447	8.9	1,911
Machinery, etc.	723	20.5	781	15.5	1,081
Consumer durable goods	215	6.1	138	2.7	641
Improvement of land and buildings..	153	4.3	319	6.3	2,076
Farm real estate purchase............	216	6.1	883	17.5	4,086
Repayment of debt	152	4.3	346	6.9	2,274
Other, or not ascertained............	137	3.9	233	4.6	1,699

Note: Details may not add to totals because of rounding.
Source: *Federal Reserve Bulletin*, November 1956, p. 1167.

extend credit for periods longer than a year. Many of the intermediate-term loans provide for installment repayment.

Almost 70 per cent of the legal contracts underlying commercial bank farm loans specified repayment in a single payment, and the remainder specified repayment by installment. The most frequent use of installment repayment was in the intermediate-term investment loans and in loans used to purchase farm land. The widespread use of the renewal device allows many single-payment loans to be reduced by irregular installment repayments. Only the portions that cannot be paid in the current year are renewed for the next period.

More than 70 per cent of the commercial bank farm loans were secured, and the most common forms of security were chattel mortgages and conditional sales contracts. The data in Table 21-8 show that farm mortgages were used to secure 16 per cent of loans for intermediate-term investment and 47 per cent of the loans for repayment of debt. Obviously, the nature of the underlying security does not necessarily reveal the purpose of the loan. The survey data show an inverse relationship between net worth and frequency of secured and endorsed loans. A similar relationship also prevails in non-farm business loans.

Interest rates on farm loans tend to be higher than rates on non-farm business loans. In mid-1956 the average interest rate on farm loans not secured by farm real estate mortgages was 6.4 per cent, and the rate

TABLE 21-7

MATURITY OF FARM LOANS FOR SPECIFIED PURPOSES, JUNE 30, 1956

(LOANS OUTSTANDING AT INSURED COMMERCIAL BANKS)

Original maturity	All pur- poses	Cur- rent ex- penses	Inter- mediate term invest- ments	Pur- chase of farm real estate	Repay- ment of debt	Other, or not ascer- tained
			Percentage distribution within groups			
All maturities	100	100	100	100	100	100
Demand	8	7	8	8	8	10
1 month	1	1	2	1	1	3
3 months	9	14	7	2	5	14
6 months	27	42	22	8	18	26
9 months	10	16	7	2	7	9
1 year	16	15	19	10	20	14
15 months	1	*	2	*	*	1
18 months	2	1	5	*	1	1
2 years	6	1	13	3	4	2
3 years	3	*	5	4	7	4
4-5 years	6	1	4	18	10	5
6-10 years	8	*	4	30	16	8
Over 10 years	3	*	1	12	2	3

*Less than $0.5 million or 0.5 per cent.

1 Loans are classified under the nearest maturity listed; for example, 5-month and 7-month loans are included with 6-month loans.

Note: Details may not add to totals because of rounding.

Source: Federal Reserve Bulletin, November 1956, p. 1171.

ranged from 7.4 per cent on small loans to 5.3 per cent on larger loans. The average interest rate on farm loans secured by real estate mortgages was 1 per cent lower; by size of loan, the range was nearly the same as that indicated above.

Life Insurance Companies

In dollar amounts of mortgages held, the life insurance companies are the most important institutional source of farm mortgage credit; in numbers of mortgages held, they are the second most important. The life insurance companies tend to invest their funds in the larger-sized farm mortgages. As noted earlier, the commercial banks and the Federal government (national farm loan associations) are the other major institutional investors. These lenders tend to avoid the very large farm mortgage loans. However, all three actively compete for the medium-sized loans.

TABLE 21–8
SECURITY FOR FARM LOANS FOR SPECIFIED PURPOSES, JUNE 30, 1956
(LOANS OUTSTANDING AT INSURED COMMERCIAL BANKS)

Purpose of loan	Total loans	Unsecured	Endorsed	Chattel mortgage	Farm real estate mortgage [1]	Other
				Secured by:		
	Percentage distribution within groups					
All purposes	100	22	5	43	27	2
Current expenses, total	100	35	5	52	5	3
Feeder livestock operation ...	100	30	3	63	2	2
Current operating and living expenses	100	37	6	48	6	3
Intermediate-term investments, total	100	16	7	58	16	2
Other livestock	100	23	6	63	5	3
Machinery, etc.	100	12	9	73	6	1
Consumer durable goods....	100	9	8	78	4	1
Improvement of land and buildings	100	22	4	9	63	3
Farm real estate purchase......	100	6	1	4	88	1
Repayment of debt...........	100	11	4	35	47	3
Other, or not ascertained......	100	30	6	27	31	6

Note: Details may not add to totals because of rounding.
[1] Includes loans insured or guaranteed by U. S. Government.
Source: Federal Reserve Bulletin, November 1956, p. 1169.

The institutional structure within which life insurance companies invest in farm mortgages is similar to that involving non-farm mortgages. The loans are made through branch offices, farm mortgage loan companies, local loan agents, and local banks. Generally, life insurance companies enter into purchase agreements under which they agree to purchase the farm mortgages that meet previously agreed-upon standards. The companies' sales forces also provide leads to possible mortgage loans. Inasmuch as life insurance companies are not specialized farm mortgage lending institutions, the flow of life insurance funds into farm mortgages is directly affected by the yields obtainable on alternative investment outlets, particularly of corporate bonds. The unsteady flow of funds from private institutions was a major factor underlying the establishment of Federally sponsored farm credit agencies. Of course, another important factor leading up to the introduction of a Federal program was the attitude of private investors toward the small-sized, low quality farm mortgage loan.

Terms of life insurance farm mortgage loans.* The terms of life insurance farm mortgage loans outstanding on June 30, 1956 were revealed by a survey in conjunction with that done for commercial banks. During 1956, life insurance companies held 211,000 farm mortgage loans. The average size of the farm mortgage loans of the life insurance companies included in the survey was $10,800. To illustrate the importance of the large size loans, we note that during the period January 1, 1955 to June 30, 1956, 15 per cent of the insurance company loans were for $25,000 or more. Life insurance companies prefer to invest their funds in large single amounts, and this practice carries over to farm mortgages. They solicit the large mortgages, and, like private placements in the corporate sector, the life insurance companies may offer attractive terms to very large farm borrowers to acquire the mortgages. For the life insurance companies that supplied information as to purpose of loan, the data show that 35 per cent of the amount loaned was for real estate purchases; 45 per cent for refinancing debts; and the remainder for improvements and other purposes. The distribution of farm-mortgage-loan commitments was similar in 1958 and 1959.†

The survey data revealed that loans made by 17 life insurance companies from January 1, 1955 to June 30, 1956 had an average stated maturity of 19 years, and that almost 90 per cent of the loans had a maturity of 20 years or less. The same companies reported that only 4 per cent of the loans outstanding on June 30, 1956 were for 26 or more years.

Compared with rates charged by other lenders, the farm mortgage interest rates on loans of life insurance companies are on the low side. It was estimated that in 1957 the average rate on loans held by life insurance companies was 4.6 per cent. The averages for other lenders were as follows: Federal land banks, 4.1 per cent; banks, 5.4 per cent; individuals, 4.8 per cent; and miscellaneous lenders, 5.1 per cent.** In the latter part of 1958, interest rates began to rise, and they continued to rise through 1959. On July 1, 1959 insurance companies' minimum rate on farm mortgages was 5.5 per cent. Other mortgage lenders also increased their minimum rates.‡ The lower rate charged on insurance company loans tends to reflect the relative importance of higher-quality and larger-sized farm mortgages in the loan portfolios of life insurance companies. Interest rates on farm mortgage loans made by life insurance companies averaged 5.9 per cent in the fourth quarter of 1959 and 6.1 per cent in the first quarter of 1960. By the end of 1959 all land banks were charging 6 per cent, the statutory limit.

*Data in this section are based on: Russell W. Bierman and Betty A. Case, "Farm-Mortgage Loans of the Federal Land Banks and of Life Insurance Companies, 1950-1957," *Agricultural Finance Review*, Vol. 20, April 1958.
†*Agricultural Research Service*, 43-112, November 1959, p. 6.
**Agricultural Finance Review*, Vol. 20, U.S. Department of Agriculture, April 1958, p. 100.
‡ *Federal Reserve Bulletin*, July 1959, p. 730.

PUBLIC AND SEMIPUBLIC SOURCES OF FARM CREDIT

*Development of Public Sources of Farm Credit**

Interest in improving the farm credit services prompted Congress to appoint in 1912 a commission to go to Europe to study European farm credit institutions and to develop recommendations for the improvement of our domestic agricultural credit facilities. The commission was favorably impressed with the European cooperative agricultural lending agencies and declared that similar credit facilities should be established in the United States. The commission believed that the differences relating to long-term and short-term agricultural financing warranted separate institutions, and since it was agreed that the greatest gap in our financial system was in the area of long-term credit, Congress established in 1917 the Federal land banks, a cooperative credit system designed to provide a permanent and dependable source of farm mortgage credit. The system is described later in this chapter.

In the following year, 1918, the Federal Government initiated a very limited program of direct short-term farm loans to finance the purchase of seed and similar operating expenses in specific disaster areas. When the flow of short-term farm credit was seriously interrupted by the widespread commercial bank failures that occurred in the early 1930's, the direct loan program was expanded on a nationwide basis. During each of the years in the early 1930's, nearly $60 million was loaned under this program.

In response to the collapse of agricultural prices in 1921 and the near panic conditions that followed in the agricultural credit markets, Congress authorized the then-existing War Finance Corporation to initiate a loan program designed to "unfreeze" sound loan assets in lenders' farm loan portfolios. Nearly $300 million was loaned out under this program. Although the loans were not made directly to farmers, the program did enlarge the flow of credit to the farm sector because lenders were able to convert agricultural and livestock paper into loanable funds. On the basis of favorable experience with this loan program, a Congressional commission on agricultural credit recommended the creation of a permanent credit system to discount loans. In 1923, Congress established a system of intermediate credit banks to rediscount agricultural loans for commercial banks, livestock loan companies, and agricultural credit corporations.† The newly

---

*The introductory material in this section is based on the monograph by C. R. Arnold, "Production Credit System, Farm Credit Administration," Washington, D. C., 1958.

† Cattle loan companies developed during the first two decades of this century to provide financial assistance to the expanding cattle industry. Essentially, the cattle loan companies served as middlemen between the financial centers and the livestock industry. The companies introduced a degree of standardization in cattle paper and made short-term loans on livestock security. The paper was sold to banks or discounted through the system of intermediate credit banks. The cattle loan companies suffered a major blow with the

established system of intermediate credit banks did not have much effect on the flow of short-term farm credit, because private lenders did not use the discount facilities to a very great extent. The enabling legislation specified that the lenders' loans to farmers could not exceed the discount rate by more than a specified percentage. Although the allowable spread was increased at various times during the 1920's, it remained relatively unattractive to the majority of private lenders.

Under the auspices of the Reconstruction Finance Corporation, there were established in the early 1930's 12 regional agricultural credit corporations. The purpose and method of operation of this new system of farm credit institution were very similar to those of the loan program that operated under the War Finance Corporation. The purpose of the institutions was to make sound agricultural loans and to assist commercial banks by exchanging cash for loans that appeared to be ultimately sound and collectible. Funds to support this program were secured directly from the Treasury. This was a short-lived program, and the system of agricultural credit corporations was placed in liquidation in 1934.

In March, 1933 President Roosevelt established by executive order the Farm Credit Administration, which consolidated into one agency the functions of Federal organizations that were primarily involved in agricultural credit. Future Federally sponsored farm credit institutions also came under the Farm Credit Administration, hereafter refered to as F.C.A. For six years, the F.C.A. operated as an independent agency, and then was placed under the Department of Agriculture. In 1953, the F.C.A. was reestablished as an independent agency in the executive branch of the government, and it has continued in this status ever since.

In June, 1933 Congress created the framework under which local production credit associations and banks for cooperatives were to be established. Production credit associations were designed to increase the flow of short-term credit to the farm sector, and banks for cooperatives were designed to provide loan credit to farm cooperatives. Both of these credit services are a part of the present system, and their operations are under the jurisdiction of the F.C.A. The credit services are described later in this chapter.

Other farm credit institutions were established, but most of them

---

collapse of livestock prices in the early 1920's, and very few are still in operation. The agricultural credit corporations are also organized and incorporated under state laws. However, to be eligible to discount loans with the intermediate credit banks, the agricultural credit corporations must satisfy certain specifications as to capital and operations. These corporations are sponsored by commercial banks, cooperative marketing associations, and individual investors. Many of the agricultural credit corporations never attained adequate capital positions, and fared badly during the periods of falling farm prices. Today, relatively few agricultural credit corporations are in operation. It should be noted that there is a similarity between these agricultural credit corporations and the newly formed small business investment companies.

have been either discontinued or merged with other organizations. In this chapter, we shall concentrate primarily on the credit services offered under the F.C.A. Before discussing these credit services, three other government agencies or programs are described briefly. These are the Commodity Credit Corporation, the Farmers Home Administration, and the Rural Electrification Administration.

Commodity Credit Corporation

The Commodity Credit Corporation, hereafter referred to as C.C.C., was organized in 1933 to engage in the purchase and sale of farm commodities and to make non-recourse price-support loans, the latter of which may be either direct loans or guaranteed loans held by banks. The over-all purpose of the program was and is the support of prices of certain farm commodities and the provision of more orderly marketing. As an illustration of a non-recourse price-support loan, assume that a farmer has complied with various regulations, such as planting restrictions and the like, and is eligible for such a loan. The loan may be made directly with the C.C.C. or with a commercial bank, and the stored farm commodity serves as security for the loan. The loan value of the commodity is based on a certain percentage of parity, a value determined by the relationship between the prices of goods that farmers purchase and the prices of goods that they produce. The prevailing market price of the commodity at the time of the loan may be higher or lower than the loan value. Obviously, a large loan volume can be expected when loan values are above current market prices, and a small volume when they are below current market prices. The loan that the farmer received may or may not be repaid; the option or decision rests with the farmer, and this decision depends on the movement of the commodity's market price in relation to the loan value. If the market price is less than the loan value at the end of the loan period, the farmer would be expected to default on the loan, and the title to the pledged commodity would pass to the C.C.C. The net effect of such a loan is that the farmer receives the stipulated floor or support price of this crop.

The C.C.C. non-recourse price-support loans are of such a nature that they may be treated either as borrowing or as sale transactions. Both the direct loans and the guaranteed loans held by banks are a unique form of borrowing in the sense that borrowers have the option of not paying interest on the loans and not repaying the loans in cash. When treated as sales transactions, they are also unique, because sellers have the option of repurchasing the goods at a minimum penalty rate. The manner in which the C.C.C. non-recourse price-support loans are treated does not affect the farm sector's total saving and investment, but it does affect the composition of the farm sector's investment. National income and flow-of-funds accounts treat these loans as sales. The commodities that serve as security for the loans are not assumed to be part of the sector's investment, so that the sector's tangible investment is that much smaller, but, since the loans are not really treated as loans, the sector's liabilities are also that much smaller. Therefore, the sector's total investment is unchanged. As for the government sector, both direct and guaranteed loans are recorded as debts of the Federal Government sector. Since national income and flow-of-funds accounts do not incorporate a separate account for tangible investment, the commodities that serve as security for these loans are not considered part of government investment, and, therefore, the goods do not enter into the total of national investment. If, in practice, the loans are not repaid in cash and the stored crops are taken over by C.C.C., the above accounting treatment merely accelerates the proper recording of a sales transaction.

The C.C.C. finances its operations by borrowing from the Treasury. As of June 30, 1959 the borrowing authority of the C.C.C. was $14.5 billion and its outstanding obligations to the Treasury were nearly $13 billion. As of July 31, 1960 the investment of C.C.C. in the price-support program was $8.6 billion, consisting of loans outstanding of $1.4 billion and $7.2 billion of inventories at cost. Approximately $250 million of the loans were financed by private lending agencies.

Farmers Home Administration

The Farmers Home Administration was established in 1946 by the merger of two existing programs, one of which was the Farm Security Administration and the other the emergency crop and food loan division of the F.C.A. The Farmers Home Administration makes direct loans and also operates an insured loan program. The basic principle underlying the direct and insured loans of the Farmers Home Administration is that borrowers are not eligible for such loans unless they can prove that they have been unable to obtain needed credit from local lenders. The majority of the loans are used to develop and strengthen the family type of farm. Also, loans are made for the operation and development of farms whose operators are employed part-time in industry. The purposes of the direct and insured loans cover a wide range: to finance equipment and livestock; to finance farm and home operating costs; to finance the development and expansion of farms; to refinance existing debts; to finance soil conservation; to finance the construction and repair of farm houses and other essential farm buildings; and to assist in emergencies of flood, drought, and similar causes.

To provide a general idea of the scope of the Farmers Home Administration's loan program, it should be noted that during a year approximately 200,000 farmers, including those who have not completely repaid advances obtained in previous years, use the Administration's credit services, and the Administration makes over 100,000 loans. As of June 30, 1959 the following loans were outstanding: loans to cooperative associations, $9.9 million; crop, livestock, and commodity loans, $4.8 million; farm mortgage loans, $406 million; and other loans, $409 million. As of the same date, the Farmers Home Administration's total borrowing authority under its programs was $662 million.

Rural Electrification Administration

The Rural Electrification Administration was created in 1935 to provide funds to finance the construction and operation of electric facilities in rural areas. In the late 1940's the R.E.A.'s authority was expanded to include the improvement and expansion of rural telephone service. As of June 30, 1959 the R.E.A. had nearly $3.6 billion of loans outstanding to cooperative associations.

Farm Credit Administration*

Under the terms of the Farm Credit Act of 1953, Congress re-established the Farm Credit Administration as an independent agency in the executive branch of the government. A 13-member Federal Farm Credit Board was set up to direct, supervise, and control the F.C.A. A Governor, who is appointed by the Board, is responsible for the execution of F.C.A. policy. The declaration of policy in the Farm Credit Act of 1953 provided for borrower participation in the F.C.A. policy making. Accordingly, 12 of the Board's members have been appointed by the President from a list of nominees submitted by the lending institutions. Since individual farmers have a voice in the management of these institutions, they have a voice in the selection of the nominees. The thirteenth member of the Board is designated by the Secretary of Agriculture.

CREDIT SERVICES. There are three major divisions or credit services within the F.C.A.: the land bank service, the short-term credit service, and the cooperative bank service. The term "service" refers to administration. The land bank service supervises the 12 Federal land banks and the numerous Federal land bank associations.† The Federal land banks make long-term farm mortgage loans, and the associations are local cooperatives through which member-borrowers obtain such loans. The land bank service establishes standards for farm appraisals, conducts appraisals of farms offered as security for loans, and assists in planning the issuance and marketing of the land banks' consolidated farm loan bonds.

The short-term credit service supervises the 12 Federal intermediate credit banks and the numerous production credit associations. The Federal intermediate credit banks extend credit to production credit associations and other financing institutions that make short-term agricultural

---

*All data in this section of chapter based on *26th Annual Report of the Farm Credit Administration and the Work of the Cooperative Farm Credit System, 1958-1959* (Washington, D.C.: Government Printing Office, 1960).

† Name changed from "national farm loan associations" to "Federal land bank associations," effective December 31, 1959, by the Farm Credit Act of 1959.

loans. The cooperative bank service supervises the 12 district banks for cooperatives and the central bank for cooperatives. As noted above, the purpose of this service is to make loans to farmers' cooperative associations. The declaration of policy in the Farm Credit Act of 1953 pointed toward eventual member-borrower ownership of local associations and district banks. In line with this policy, the Farm Credit Acts of recent years have provided for the retirement in a systematic manner of the government capital in the banks for cooperatives and Federal intermediate credit banks. Eventually, each of the institutions will be wholly owned by its member-borrowers. The Federal land banks became wholly owned by member-borrowers in June, 1947.

The land bank service and the short-term credit service have direct contact with individual borrowers through their respective local cooperative credit associations. As noted above in the discussion of the development of public sources of farm credit, national farm loan associations were introduced in 1917 and production credit associations in 1933. For many years, the intermediate credit banks served only private financial institutions, but in 1933 it was decided that the production credit associations were necessary in order to obtain maximum use of the facilities provided by the intermediate credit banks.

The local cooperative credit associations can be formed by ten or more farmers who apply for and receive loans. In the case of a proposed national farm loan association, the loans must aggregate at least $20,000. Each association is a separately Federally chartered organization of member-borrowers operating under its own by-laws, and administered and supervised by the appropriate credit service. On June 30, 1959 there were 854 national farm loan associations, operating from 787 main offices and 204 branch offices. All of these associations were fully member-owned. On the same date, there were 495 production credit associations, and 454 of them were fully member-owned. Like the trend in the private sector of our financial system, mergers have taken place among the cooperative credit associations, and many of the associations have established branch offices.

Borrowers are required to own, at the time the loans are made, capital stock of their respective associations in an amount equal to 5 per cent of the amounts borrowed. The associations, in turn, are required to hold stock of their respective credit service banks in an amount equal to 5 per cent of the loans made through the associations. The stock requirements have the effect of making the associations member-owned. The member-borrowers (stockholders) of each association elect a board of directors, and the board, in turn, appoints officers and loan committee members.

In arranging a loan through a national farm loan association, the application is investigated by the loan committee, and if the committee makes a favorable report, the association forwards the loan application and loan committee report to the federal land bank for final approval. In the case of a production credit association, the loan committee is permitted to make loans under prescribed rules and regulations. However, if a borrower should request a loan in an amount in excess of 15 per cent of a production credit association's capital and surplus, the loan application would have to be approved by the Federal intermediate credit bank.

LAND BANK LOANS. Land bank loans are made for general agricultural purposes and for other requirements of the mortgagors. The purposes are so broad as to include the financing of the living expenses of a loan applicant engaged in farming. The loans are secured by first mortgages on farm land within the bank's farm credit district. Loans cannot exceed 65 per cent of the normal value of the farm mortgaged, the value of which is determined by appraisal. It should be noted that the land banks' appraisals tend to be more conservative than those of private lenders. The loans are amortized, and the principal cannot be extinguished in less than five years nor can it be outstanding for more than 40 years. Advance payments on principal are permitted. The rate of interest on a land bank loan is equal to the interest rate on the land bank's most recent issue of farm loan bonds plus 1 per cent to cover administrative costs and profits. In no case can the rate exceed 6 per cent. The amount of loans to any one borrower cannot exceed $200,000, and loans to any one borrower in excess of $100,000 must be approved by the F.C.A. Preference is given to loans of $10,000 and under, but loans of less than $100 are not made. In a locality in which a Federal land bank association either is not available or is not likely to be formed, the F.C.A. has the power to authorize the district Federal land bank to make the loan through an approved agent. Otherwise, all loan requests filter through local Federal land bank associations.

On June 30, 1959 the total assets of the twelve Federal land banks were approximately $2.4 billion. During the previous 12-month period, their mortgage loan account increased $273 million. Unlike most of the private lending institutions, the land banks have a relatively low ratio of borrowed funds to net worth. At the close of the 1959 fiscal year the ratio was 4.8 to 1.

PRODUCTION CREDIT ASSOCIATIONS' LOANS. Production credit associations make short- and intermediate-term loans to finance all types of farm operations. Most of the loans are secured, with the security consisting of a first lien on crops, livestock, and equipment. Most of the loans have a maturity of less than one year, but partial renewals are anticipated in many loans. Beginning in 1954, some of the production credit associations experimented with loans having maturities of up to three years. The intermediate-term maturities were restricted to loans in which the funds were to be used for capital and semi-capital purposes. Favorable experience with these loans led to loans with maturities of up to five years. On June 30, 1959 about

12 per cent of the total amount of production credit associations' loans had maturities in excess of one year. The cost of production credit associations' loans is minimized by the use of budgeted loans, under which borrowers are able to arrange for annual credit needs and borrow funds only when needed, repaying immediately when funds are available.

During fiscal year 1959, production credit associations made loans totaling $2.4 billion, and their loans outstanding on June 30, 1959 totaled $1.5 billion. These figures represented 25 per cent increase over the previous year's figures. Farmers and ranchers with loans outstanding on June 30, 1959 numbered 283,000. During the calendar year 1958, the average total cost of money to the borrowers, including loan services fees, was 6.72 per cent on an annual basis. Considering the nature of the loan and the fact that the associations collect interest at the time a loan is paid, this rate appears very reasonable.

FEDERAL INTERMEDIATE CREDIT BANKS' LOANS. During the fiscal year 1959 the intermediate credit banks extended $3.2 billion of credit, and nearly 93 per cent of the total was extended to production credit associations. On June 30, 1959 approximately $1.5 billion of loans and discounts were outstanding. Like trends in other services, the 1959 figures represented all-time highs in loan and discount activity and amount of outstanding loans. The interest and discount rate charged by the intermediate credit banks was based primarily on the cost of money in the market. During much of the fiscal year 1959 the rate was 4 per cent or more. At the close of fiscal 1959 the rate of borrowed funds to net worth was approximately 9 to 1.

COOPERATIVE BANK LOANS. The system of banks for cooperatives represents only one of the many ways in which the Federal Government encourages the formation and growth of farmers' marketing and purchasing cooperatives. Eligible farmers' cooperatives include those which provide one or more of the following functions: process, prepare for market, handle, or market farm products; purchase, test, grade, process, distribute or furnish farm supplies; and furnish farm business services. The banks for cooperatives make the following types of loans to cooperatives: short-term loans secured by commodities held in storage, working capital loans, and long-term capital or facility loans. Maturities may run for as long as 20 years.

During the fiscal year 1959 the banks for cooperatives extended $637 million of credit to 2,378 cooperatives. On June 30, 1959, $526 million in loans were outstanding to 2,689 cooperatives. Like trends in other services, 1959 was a year of record high activity. The growth in these banks parallels the growth of cooperatives served by the banks. Over its first 25-year period of operation, more than 5,700 cooperatives have borrowed a grand total of $8.9 billion.

SOURCES OF FUNDS. The Federal land banks obtain the funds that farmers borrow through the Federal land bank associations principally from sales to the investing public of consolidated Federal farm loan bonds. These bonds are the joint and several obligations of the 12 land banks. The bonds are not guaranteed either as to principal or interest by the Federal Government. During the fiscal year 1959, the land banks entered the investment market five times with a total of seven issues aggregating nearly $880 million. The maturities ranged from one to nine years. A Federal land bank is also permitted to borrow from commercial banks, other land banks, intermediate credit banks, and cooperative bank on an interim basis. The proceeds from the sale of consolidated Federal farm loan bonds are used to redeem maturing bonds and to repay interim borrowings. At the end of June, 1959 approximately $1.9 billion of Federal farm loan bonds were outstanding.

The funds used by the Federal intermediate credit banks to discount farmers' notes presented by production credit associations and selected private lenders and to cover direct loans to associations are raised principally through the issue of consolidated trust debentures, with the collateral consisting of loans and discounts of the credit banks, Federal obligations, and cash. Like the Federal farm loan bonds, the debentures are joint and several obligations and are not guaranteed as to principal or interest by the Federal Government. In fiscal 1959, there were 27 issues aggregating nearly $1.9 billion. The maturities ranged from three to nine months and averaged nearly nine months. Compared with the consolidated Federal farm loan bond issues, the consolidated trust debentures are issued more frequently and have shorter maturities. It is the policy of the intermediate credit banks to coordinate the maturities of their debentures with the maturities of their loans and discounts. The intermediate credit banks have interim borrowing privileges similar to those of the Federal land banks. At the end of June, 1959 approximately $1,456 million of consolidated trust debentures were outstanding.

The banks for cooperatives also raise the major portion of their funds by the sale of consolidated collateral trust debentures to investors. During the fiscal year 1959, there were five issues, aggregating about $464 million. The maturities ranged from six to ten months. At the end of June, 1959 the banks had outstanding nearly $284.5 million of unmatured consolidaetd debentures.

The issues of the three credit services are priced competitively, and are attractive to an investor seeking low-risk, short-maturity bond investments.

Outlook

At the time of their inception, the Federally sponsored farm credit institutions were Federally owned and operated and were financed primarily by Treasury funds. Now, after the passage of many years, the local associations and district banks are almost wholly owned and operated by member-borrowers, and the institutions obtain almost all of their funds in the capital markets at competitive rates. There is vigorous competition among individual lenders, institutional lenders (such as commercial banks and life insurance companies), and the credit services that operate under the supervision of the F.C.A. In the past, institutional lenders complained that the competition provided by the credit services was unfair. However, now that the credit services are mutually owned and managed by member-borrowers and they secure their funds in the capital markets at competitive rates, the use of the adjective "unfair" would seem to be less appropriate. The Federally sponsored credit institutions are firmly established, and in the future they will probably increase their share of the farm credit markets.

QUESTIONS

1. What is meant by the term "agribusiness"?
2. Compare the financial assets and liabilities of the farm business sector with the financial assets and liabilities of the other business sectors.
3. Compare the sources and uses of funds of the farm business sector with the sources and uses of funds of the other business sectors.
4. What is the relative importance of private financial institutions in the extension of non-real estate loans to farmers? What private financial institutions are in this market?
5. What is the relative importance of private financial institutions in the extension of mortgage credit to farmers? What private financial institutions are in this market?
6. Compared with loans to non-farm business firms, what are some of the unique characteristics of loans to farmers?
7. What prompted the development of public and semipublic sources of farm credit?
8. Should C.C.C. non-recourse price-support loans be treated as sale transactions or loan transactions? Explain.
9. List and describe briefly the three major credit services within the F.C.A.
10. With respect to the credit services, trace the flow of funds from the capital market to the individual farmer.

ADDITIONAL READING

Almost all of the money and banking texts listed at the end of Chapter 4 contain one or more chapters on topics covered in Chapter 21.

Arnold, C. R. *Production Credit System.* 1933-1958 "Farmers Build Their Own Production Credit System — Organization and First 25 Years." Washington, D.C.: Farm Credit Administration, 1958.

Bierman, Russell W. "Farm Investments of Life Insurance Companies — 1958," ARS 43-84, October 1958, Agricultural Research Service, U.S. Department of Agriculture.

Board of Governors of the Federal Reserve System. *Farm Loans at Commercial Banks.* A series of articles reporting the findings of the Agricultural Loan Survey made as of June 30, 1956 by the Federal Reserve System. Reprinted from *Federal Reserve Bulletin*, Nov. 1956, Jan., Feb. and March 1957, and issued in pamphlet form. Washington, D.C.: Board of Governors of the Federal Reserve System, 1957.

Davis, J. H., and R. A. Goldberg. *A Concept of Agribusiness.* Boston: Harvard Business School, Division of Research, 1957.

Duggan, I. W., and R. V. Battles. *Financing the Farm Business.* New York: John Wiley & Sons, Inc., 1950.

Horton, Donald C. *Patterns of Farm Financial Structure: A Cross-Section View of Economic and Physical Determination.* N.B.E.R. study. Princeton, N.J.: Princeton University Press, 1957. Physical and economic factors related to ways in which farms are financed.

Mitchell, R. I. *American Agriculture — Its Structure and Place in the Economy.* Prepared for the Social Science Research Council in cooperation with the U.S.D.A., Agriculture Research Service, and U.S. Department of Commerce, Bureau of the Census. New York: John Wiley & Sons, 1955.

Murray, W. C. *Agricultural Finance.* (Rev. ed.) Ames, Iowa: Iowa State College Press, 1947.

Tostlebe, Alvin S. *Capital in Agriculture: Its Formation and Financing Since 1870.* N.B.E.R. study. Princeton, N.J.: Princeton University Press, 1957.

U.S. Department of Agriculture, Agricultural Research Service. This publication is a contribution of the Agricultural Finance Research Branch, Farm Economics Research Division, Agricultural Research Service. Issued annually, and contains lead articles, reports on various aspects of agricultural finance, book reviews, report on research projects, list of available publications and reports related to agricultural finance, and statistical appendix. Washington, D.C.: Government Printing Office. See latest report.

———. *Farm-Mortgage Loans of the Federal Land Banks.* Prepared in the Farm Economic Research Division, Agricultural Research Service. Washington, D.C.: USDA, 1958.

U.S. Department of Agriculture, Agricultural Research Service. Periodically the Department publishes surveys of the farm-mortgage lending experience of life insurance companies, the Federal land banks, and the Farmers Home Administration. See ARS 43-112 of November, 1959 and more recent ARS bulletins.

U.S. Farm Credit Administration. *Annual Report, Bulletin,* and *Circular.*

part 5: Government sectors

IN the flow-of-funds system of accounts the government or public sector of the economy is broken down into two sectors, the Federal Government sector and the state and local government sector. The Federal government sector, as described in this system of accounts:

> . . . covers, with certain exceptions, all departments and branches of the Government, including trust funds, deposit fund accounts, the Postal Savings System, Government corporations and credit agencies, and other Federal enterprise funds, whether wholly or partly owned by the Government. It includes two Government-sponsored institutions — the Federal land banks and Federal home loan banks — that became wholly privately owned when the Treasury capital investment in them was retired. The following instrumentalities of the Government are not included in this sector: (1) the Exchange Stabilization Funds, the Federal Reserve System, and certain monetary accounts, all of which are in the commercial banking sector, and (2) the District of Columbia, which is included in the sector for State and local governments. The sector account is consolidated; transactions between components of the sector are not shown.*

Many of the financial transactions and activities of the Federal Government sector as defined above have been considered in previous chapters, e.g., charter and regulation of financial institutions, effect of taxes on financial and nonfinancial transactions, establishment and operation of government-sponsored financial institutions, operation of government insurance and retirement programs, the Postal Savings System, and the United States savings bond program. In this part of our study, the following aspects of financing the Federal Government sector are considered: management of the Treasury's cash balance, nature and characteristics of Federal obligations; ownership pattern of Federal obligations; and annual flows into the market for Federal obligations. The term "Federal obligations" covers all marketable Treasury and Federal agency securities — direct, fully guaranteed, and non-guaranteed — net of holdings by agencies and funds that are part of the Federal Government sector. The holdings of the more important

---

* "A Quarterly Presentation of Flow of Funds, Savings and Investment," *Federal Reserve Bulletin*, August 1959, p. 847.

agencies and funds were considered in the chapters dealing with insurance. The state and local government sector, as defined in the flow-of-funds system of accounts:*

> "comprises all political subdivisions in the United States, including the government of the District of Columbia. It includes all departments, trust and sinking funds, corporations and enterprises (such as state liquor monopolies and municipally owned utilities), and authorities (such as toll road and port authorities) of such governmental units. The sector account is a combined statement of consolidated accounts for individual governmental units. The latter consolidations are not complete, however, with respect to debt and interest transactions between governmental units and their own trust and sinking funds. The securities of a government held by trust or sinking funds of that government are included in both the assets and liabilities of the sector account.

In this part of our study, we shall concentrate on the nature and characteristics, the ownership pattern, and the annual flows into the market of state and local obligations.

The use of deficit financing and Federal debt management to attain national goals are not discussed here. Instead, these topics will be considered in Part 7 in conjunction with monetary and credit policy, because monetary policy, debt management, and fiscal policy are interrelated. Furthermore, all of these policies should be directed toward a common set of national goals. In Part 5 we establish the framework within which monetary authorities implement monetary and credit measures and Treasury officials manage the debt. The scope of our study precludes examination of the structure of Federal, state, and local governments' receipts and expenditures.

*Ibid.

22: Financing federal, state, and local governments

THE size of government budgets and debt and the use of fiscal policy and debt management to influence the level and composition of national output make the study of the government sectors very important. As an illustration of the magnitude of Federal fiscal operations, we should note that during the calendar year 1958 the Federal Government's total cash receipts from the public totaled $81,728 million and its total cash payments to the public totaled $89,014 million. The excess of payments to the public had to be financed through net Federal cash borrowing. At the end of 1958, the gross public debt and guaranteed issues of the United States Government totaled $282.9 billion. The corresponding figures for 1959 were slightly higher. Since the purpose of this study is to focus attention on financial institutions and the annual flows into financial assets, we shall restrict our inquiry with respect to the Federal Government sector to the management of the Treasury's cash balance and the market for Federal obligations.

The magnitude of state and local fiscal operations is made plain by these figures: during the calendar year 1958, the state and local government sector's tax receipts totaled $30.9 billion; its net purchases of goods and services totaled $34.4 billion; and its net increase in liabilities amounted to $7.5 billion. Concerning the net increase in liabilities, $5.7 billion was in the form of state and local obligations; $1.5 billion represented consumer saving through retirement funds; and the other liabilities represented trade debt and loans from the Federal government. Like those of the Federal Government sector, the corresponding figures for 1959 were slightly higher.

At the end of 1958, the gross state and local government debt totaled $57.2 billion. We shall examine here primarily the market for state and local obligations. The most unique characteristic of this market is the tax-exempt status of state and local obligations. In view of the fact that the Federal government loses more in revenue than the state and local governments gain in the form of lower interest costs, the tax status of these securities may be changed in the not-too-distant future.

MANAGEMENT OF TREASURY'S CASH BALANCES

Like other economic units, the Treasury must maintain working cash balances, consisting of checking accounts and currency. There is uncertainty as to timing of the Treasury's cash flows, as well as non-coincidence in those cash flows. The Federal Government's revenues and its receipt of proceeds from the sale of securities are not uniform from day to day. Many taxes are paid on a quarterly basis and almost all taxpayers delay payments until final due dates. United States savings bonds are available for sale continuously, and Treasury bills are issued on a weekly basis, but other Federal obligations are issued irregularly. The Federal Government does not have complete control over the timing of its cash payments. The dates of delivery of goods to the government and thus the dates of payment for them are also uncertain. Holders of some types of government obligations have the option of redeeming the securities for cash. Obviously, the Treasury must have working cash balances.

The Treasury's balances differ from those of state and local governmental units and private economic units in one important respect. The Treasury's active cash balances are in the form of deposit accounts at Federal Reserve banks and their branches. Nearly all Treasury disbursements come out of the deposit balances held in Federal Reserve banks.

In the absence of special arrangements relating to the management of the Treasury's cash balances, the level of its balances held in Federal Reserve banks might vary by a large amount, which would, in turn, cause corresponding changes in the level of commercial bank reserve balances. Treasury cash receipts represent checks drawn on commercial banks, and in the process of check clearing, the reserve balances of drawee banks are debited and the Treasury's balances at Federal Reserve banks are credited. Treasury cash payments have, of course, the opposite effect. In the absence of any type of offsetting transaction, an excess of Treasury cash receipts over Treasury cash payments would cause the Treasury's balances at Federal Reserve banks to rise and commercial bank reserve balances to fall. Arbitrary changes in commercial bank reserve balances could have serious consequences on the state of the money market, which might in turn affect adversely the flow of goods and services.

To minimize possible adverse effects of the Treasury's cash flows upon commercial banks' reserve balances, the Treasury uses tax and loan accounts, which represent its accounts held on deposit at commercial banks rather than at Federal Reserve banks. The basic idea underlying tax and loan accounts is to channel the major portion of the Treasury's cash receipts into these accounts and make transfers from the accounts to the Federal Reserve banks to coincide with the flow of the Treasury's cash payments. By using such accounts, it is possible to avoid a temporary excess inflow of cash, which would reduce commercial bank reserve balances. The deposits remain in the commercial banks; however, the ownership of the deposits is transferred to the Federal Government, and a build-up in these accounts is a prelude to a future withdrawal. When the funds are needed to cover cash payments, the Treasury shifts funds from tax and loan accounts to Federal Reserve banks. In banking terminology, the Treasury makes calls on commercial banks. However, the Treasury makes cash payments to the public at the same time, so that the effect of the Treasury's operations on commercial bank reserves is minimized. A similar mechanism was used during World Wars I and II. However, the present tax and loan accounts encompass a much larger portion of the Treasury's cash flows than the mechanisms that were used during the two wars.

The magnitude of the Treasury's cash flows, the diversity in payments and receipts, and the unpredictable characteristics of the cash flows make it impossible to predict Treasury cash flows perfectly. However, a sufficient amount of cash receipts flows through the tax and loan accounts and the estimates of cash flows are close enough to actual cash flows to permit reasonable regulation of the impact of Treasury operations on the money market and commercial banks' reserves.

Slightly more than 11,000 commercial banks are designated as special depositaries; they are divided into two groups based on size of their tax and loan accounts. Group A includes banks whose tax and loan account balances are $150,000 or less, and Group B includes banks with balances of over $150,000. The X balances, which relate to quarterly income and profits taxes, are not included in determining the cut-off point between Groups A and B.

The tax and loan accounts are not used in handling government expenditures, for almost all expenditures involving checks are paid out of the Treasury's balances with Federal Reserve banks, and those not involving checks are handled by crediting commercial banks' accounts at Federal Reserve banks. Nearly all governmental operating expenditures are made by checks and a major portion of expenditures relating to debt management, such as payments for the redemption of bearer securities and interest coupons, are made by crediting the appropriate commercial banks' reserve accounts held in Federal Reserve banks. The effects of both types of transactions are identical. Treasury balances with Federal Reserve banks are reduced, and member bank reserve balances are increased. About the only significant difference between the two types of payments is that commercial banks realize a more rapid collection of funds when payment is made in the form of a credit to reserve balances.

Tax and loan accounts are used mostly in handling the Treasury's receipts. A large portion of the proceeds from the sale of securities and government revenues are credited to tax and loan accounts. Furthermore, banks designated as special depositaries are frequently permitted to pay for

United States Government obligations purchased by them for their own account, or for the account of their customers who enter subscriptions through them, by crediting the Treasury's accounts. During fiscal 1959, approximately $23 billion was credited to tax and loan accounts as a result of Treasury issues. Taxes eligible for credit consist mostly of those deposited by taxpayers in the depositary banks. They include the following: withheld income taxes, almost all social security taxes, railroad retirement taxes, and a number of excise taxes. The procedure is very simple: the taxpayer makes a deposit in his local bank and receives a validated deposit receipt from the depositary bank and forwards the receipt and his tax return to the Director of Internal Revenue. Income-tax payments made by checks of $10,000 or more and drawn on special depositary banks can be credited to the tax and loan accounts in those banks if the Treasury so authorizes. The authorization is usually made during quarterly periods of heavy tax payments. The procedure is more complex than that described above: the relevant checks are separated by tax authorities and deposited in Federal Reserve banks, and these banks, in turn, prepare special tax letters and certificates indicating the amount of checks eligible for credit in tax and loan accounts and forward them to the depositary banks for executing, after which the certificates are returned to the Federal Reserve banks. This procedure makes it known to the Treasury, to Federal Reserve banks, and to depositary banks that the checks have been credited to tax and loan accounts.

The accumulation of funds in tax and loan accounts from quarterly tax checks is known as an "X" balance. During fiscal 1959, about $29 billion of withheld and excise taxes and about $6 billion of income-tax payments made by checks were credited to tax and loan accounts. The total credits for that fiscal year from proceeds from sales of securities and government revenues approached $60 billion. It is neither necessary nor practical to channel all the Treasury's receipts through tax and loan accounts.

Since a major portion of the Treasury's receipts flows into tax and loan accounts, the direct flow of receipts into the Treasury's balances with Federal Reserve banks is less than the Treasury's normal cash outflow. Therefore, more-or-less continuous transfers of funds are made from tax and loan accounts to Federal Reserve banks. By estimating as carefully as possible the probable cash outflows and probable direct cash inflow, transfers from tax and loan accounts can be managed so as to minimize possible adverse effects on bank reserves.

Calls on or transfers from tax and loan accounts are usually announced on Mondays and Thursdays. Generally, the calls require that funds be transferred into the Treasury's accounts at Federal Reserve banks on the fourth or fifth day following the date of such calls, thereby allowing the depositaries adequate time to make necessary adjustments in reserve balances. Calls on B depositaries and on X balances are usually made twice weekly, and calls on A balances are usually made monthly. If conditions warrant, the Treasury can depart from these established practices. Generally, the calls on the "A" accounts approximate 50 per cent of the balance, while the calls on "B" accounts fluctuate from week to week, with the percentage usually below 25 per cent.

If the goal of the Treasury is to maintain the level of its working balances at Federal Reserve banks, then the calls or withdrawals can be made to equal the estimated net cash outflow from Treasury's balances. If the goal is to work down the size of the Treasury's balances with Federal Reserve banks, then the amount of the calls can be made less than estimated net cash outflow. If the goal is to increase the level of such balances, then the amount of the calls can be made to exceed estimated net cash outflow.

The Treasury's balances with Federal Reserve banks average around $500 million, and credits to tax and loan accounts average around $4 billion. In fiscal 1959, the highest tax and loan balance was $8,055 million and the lowest was $912 million. Since the Treasury's estimates of cash flows may miss the mark widely, it is necessary to hold sizeable working cash balances to avoid frequent shifting of funds among Federal Reserve banks and direct borrowing from those banks. Tax and loan accounts must be maintained at a reasonable level to make such accounts attractive to depositary banks.

MARKET FOR FEDERAL OBLIGATIONS

For the purpose of this study, "Federal obligations" are marketable Treasury and Federal agency securities, including both the direct obligations of the Treasury and the fully guaranteed and non-guaranteed obligations of Federal agencies, and the non-marketable investment bonds that are convertible into marketable securities. The non-guaranteed obligations of Federal agencies consist of bonds, notes, and debentures of the banks for cooperatives, Federal land banks, Federal intermediate credit banks, Federal home loan banks, and the Federal National Mortgage Association. The term "Federal obligations" excludes two important components of the public debt of the United States Government: (1) special issues held by Federal Government agencies and funds, and (2) United States savings bonds. These two components of the public debt were considered in earlier chapters.

The Public Debt of the United States

The level and composition of the public debt at the end of 1959 was a legacy of the Great Depression of the 1930's, the methods used to finance World War II, and the use of deficit financing in the postwar period to promote full employment and national security. In 1929, the gross public debt and guaranteed issues of the United States Government totaled approximately $16 billion; by 1940, the volume of debt had increased to almost $51 billion; at the end of World War II the debt totaled nearly $279 million. During 1946 the level of debt was reduced by nearly $20 billion, by liquidation of the Treasury's excess cash balances. Although the level of the debt has varied from year to year since 1946, there has been a definite upward trend. In the fiscal year 1960 the United States Government debt approached $292 billion, which was very close to the prevailing debt ceiling of $293 billion.

The debt structure has also undergone considerable change. In 1929, the interest-bearing public debt of the United States Government was in the form of marketable public issues, except for $600 million of special issues. Since 1929, the volume of special issues held by United States Government investment accounts has increased considerably, reaching a peak of $46.8 billion in 1957. At the end of 1959, about $45 billion of special issues was outstanding. Although non-marketable public issues were not issued until the mid-1930's, over $66 billion of the debt was in the form of non-marketable, public issues in 1951. Since that time, the volume of such issues has declined, and as of the end of September, 1959, non-marketable public issues totaled $50.6 billion. Almost all of the non-marketable debt is in the form of savings bonds. The major portion of the public debt is in the form of marketable public issues, consisting almost entirely of Treasury bills, certificates of indebtedness, notes, and bonds.

By resorting to a variety of debt instruments that differ in eligibility, marketability, redeemability, maturity, and interest rates, the Treasury has been able to tap all segments of the money and capital markets. Therefore, the ownership of the public debt is distributed among all sectors of the economy. In some instances, the investment in public debt issues represents a major part of an investor's holdings of financial assets. The widespread ownership of the Federal debt has made debt management and open-market operation much more important than it was in the past.

Assuming that the economy will not experience another failure of private investment comparable to that of the 1930's and the cold war does not turn into a fighting war, it is likely that the public debt of the United States Government will remain at approximately its present level for many years. The debt is a relatively permanent fixture of our financial system. If either of the assumptions turns out to be incorrect, then the level of the debt might increase by many billions of dollars.

Changes in the level of the debt or changes in the ownership and structure of a relatively stable volume of Federal debt can exert important financial and economic effects. The Federal Government can enter directly into the market for goods and services and finance its spending with borrowed funds. Debt management can bring about changes in both the stock and circulation of money, which, in turn, can exert important influences on the level and structure of interest rates and the level of effective demand for goods and services. All these measures are analyzed in conjunction with monetary policy in the concluding chapters.

Direct Federal Obligations

Direct Federal obligations consist of bills, certificates, notes, marketable bonds, and convertible bonds. Bills and certificates are short-term obligations maturing within one year or less; notes are intermediate-term obligations and their maturities range from one to five years from the time they are issued. Legally, bonds may be issued for any maturity, but in practice their use is restricted to the longer maturities, ranging from five to forty years. The Treasury is not obligated by statute to maintain any fixed relationship among the various types of securities. However, to meet both the Treasury's needs for funds and the investors' needs for various maturities, all types of issues are used. The tabulation below shows the level and composition of direct Federal obligations outstanding as of the end of September, 1959 (amounts in billions of dollars):

Bills	$ 37.1	19.5%
Certificates of indebtedness	20.3	10.7
Notes	40.8	21.4
Bonds	84.8	44.5
Convertible bonds	7.5	3.9
	$190.5	100.0%

The maturity pattern of the outstanding direct Federal obligations is much shorter than the above breakdown suggests, because with the passage of time the maturity of outstanding bonds lessens. The tabulation below shows the maturity pattern as of the end of July, 1959. Convertible bonds are not included in the data. (Amounts in billions of dollars.)

Within 1 year	$ 78.0	42.7%
1 to 5 years	56.8	31.0
5 to 10 years	18.5	10.1
Over 10 years	29.7	16.2
	$183.0	100.0%

One of the long-run goals of debt management is to issue additional bonds and thus lengthen the maturity pattern of the debt. In practice, the Treasury has found it very difficult to issue long-term marketable bonds. During periods of prosperity, the Treasury has held off issuing long-term bonds because such issues might have upset unduly the total capital market. If the Treasury receipts had exceeded payments, and if it had reduced the level of the Federal debt during such periods, then it could have issued some long-term bonds. However, in practice the Treasury has had either a very small surplus or a deficit during such periods. Until the budget picture improves, the Treasury will find it very difficult to achieve its long-run goal of lengthening the maturity of the debt.

DISCOUNT SECURITIES. Treasury bills, both the weekly series and the tax anticipation series, are the only type of marketable security that is ordinarily issued on a discount basis. No interest rate is specified, so that the yield depends on the amount of discount and length of maturity. Bills are offered on a competitive bid basis, although nominal non-competitive bids ($200,000 or less) are accepted at either a stated price or an average price of accepted competitive bids. Bid prices are expressed in terms of discounts based on 100. Legally, the Treasury has discretion to offer all types of marketable securities on a competitive basis, but this method of sale has only been extended to a few intermediate-term issues.

FIXED-RATE SECURITIES. As of the end of 1959, all outstanding certificates, notes, and bonds were fixed-rate securities, the coupon depending on the level and structure of security yield rates at time of issue. On certificates, the coupons are paid at maturity; on other fixed-rate securities, the coupons are paid semiannually. The coupon rates on Federal obligations are generally expressed in fractions, with eighths being the smallest division. The division is made much smaller for corporate bonds and state and local obligations; furthermore, these securities are not necessarily priced at par at the time of issue. In other words, newly issued corporate and municipal issues are priced very close to prevailing market conditions. Beginning in June, 1958 the Treasury attempted to follow this practice by pricing some of its new issues at a premium or discount in order to fit the issue as closely as possible into the prevailing market conditions. An example of one such offering was a bond issue in February, 1959. This bond carried a 4 per cent coupon rate and its maturity was in 1980. It was priced at $99 per $100 of par value, so that the return to the investor was 4.07 per cent per year on the life of the bond. The bonds outstanding that were issued during the war, a period of low interest rates, carry 2½ per cent coupons. Since the war, long-term interest rates have risen, and some of the more recent bond issues have carried coupon rates of 3, 3½, and 4 per cent. Under the provisions of a World War I loan act, there is a limit of 4½ per cent on the coupon rate for Treasury bonds. Considerable pressure was exerted by the Administration in 1959 and 1960 to have the law changed so that the Treasury could issue bonds at higher coupons but Congress would not authorize the change. There is no statutory limit on the rate that may be paid on bills, certificates, and notes. At the close of 1960, the highest coupon rate was 5 per cent on notes issued in October, 1959. In this particular debt issue, the Treasury competed directly with savings institutions. In addition to attracting new savings, individual investors withdrew funds from demand deposits, time deposits, savings and loan and credit union shares, and savings bonds.

TYPE OF OWNERSHIP. Almost all of the direct Federal obligations are bearer types of securities. Bills, certificates, and notes are issued only in this form. The form in which Treasury bonds are issued depends on the choice of the original subscriber. After the bonds are issued and outstanding, investors continue to have the right to specify the form of ownership. Inasmuch as investors tend to prefer the bearer form and there is some delay involved in transferring the ownership of registered securities, this form of security tends to trade in the market at prices slightly below those of bearer forms of securities. On registered securities, the Treasury sends checks to the owners. On bearer securities, the coupons must be presented.

METHOD OF PURCHASE. Subscriptions to new issues of Federal obligations are handled through Federal Reserve banks and branches. As noted in the previous section, proceeds from the sale of new issues may be credited to tax and loan accounts. As a result, depositaries do not have to pay cash immediately into Treasury accounts at Federal Reserve banks. Subscriptions that do not go through depositary banks must be accompanied by a specified deposit. Of course, commercial bank customers who place subscriptions through commercial banks are required to submit a specified deposit to commercial banks with their subscriptions. When the allotments are announced, either full payment is made to Federal Reserve banks or tax and loan accounts are credited for the full amount. When the proceeds from the sale of new securities are credited to tax and loan accounts and there is a passage of time before the funds are shifted to Treasury's balances at Federal Reserve banks, commercial banks at the time of allotments need only transfer to Federal Reserve banks the additional required legal reserves. Therefore, it is possible for commercial banks to realize relatively attractive yields considering that funds equal to only 15 to 20 per cent of the face value of securities is being tied up. Of course, after the calls are made on tax and loan accounts, the banks are tying up an amount of funds equal to the face value of the securities.

To make new long-term issues more attractive to investors, the Treasury has, on occasion, permitted completion of payment over an extended period, say, three months. For example, in the 4 per cent, 1980 bond issue, the Treasury permitted the savings type of investors to pay one-fourth of purchase price upon issuance, with an additional 25 per cent payment in cash over the next three months.

ADVANCE REFUNDING. In September, 1960 the Treasury introduced advance refunding as a means of lengthening the maturity of the debt. The basic idea of advance refunding is to allow holders of outstanding issues an opportunity to swap their present holdings for new bonds. This approach to the problem of lengthening the maturity of the debt minimizes the diversion of new long-term investment funds from the private sector to the public sector. Advance refunding appeals to investors who acquired their present holdings when the level of interest rates was low and who do not want to sell their present holdings at a capital loss. In other words, it appeals to investors who are "locked in" with a low coupon bond. By offering a higher coupon bond in exchange, existing holders can be encouraged to swap their present holdings for longer term bonds. In the September advance refunding the Treasury offered long-term 3½ per cent bonds for 2½ per cent World War II bonds. The terms of the advance refunding were as follows: (1) outstanding 2½ per cent bonds scheduled to mature June 15, 1967 and callable after 1962 for 20-year 3½ bond maturing November 15, 1980; (2) outstanding 2½ per cent bonds scheduled to mature December 15, 1968 and callable after 1963 for 30-year 3½ per cent bond maturing February 15, 1990; and (3) outstanding 2½ per cent bond scheduled to mature on June 15 and on December 15, 1969 and both callable after 1964 for 38-year 3½ bond maturing November 15, 1998. No limit was placed on the 20-year bond exchange, but limits were placed on the 30- and 38-year bonds. The September advance refunding was a success. Non-Government holders of $3.4 billion of the 2½ per cent bonds accepted the exchange offers; Government investment accounts exchanged nearly $600 million of their holdings. The exchanges lengthened the average maturity of the marketable debt from 50 months to about 57 months, and the exchanges were accomplished with little or no disturbance to the market.

TAXABILITY. Almost all of the securities that comprise the present Federal debt are fully taxable and are subject to all Federal income taxes. Prior to 1941, government securities were partially tax exempt; holdings up to $5,000 were exempt from the normal and surtax rates applicable to income. Holdings over $5,000 were exempt from the normal tax. Tax exemption did not apply to estate and inheritance taxes. With the passage of time, almost all tax-exempt issues have been retired. Federal obligations are subject to state inheritance, estate, gift, or other excise taxes, but they are exempt from all other taxations imposed on principal or interest by state and local tax authorities.

MARKETABILITY. All the direct Federal obligations are not fully marketable. In 1951, the Treasury issued in exchange for outstanding marketable bonds an investment series bond that was neither redeemable nor negotiable. However, the bond was convertible into five-year marketable notes yielding 1.5 per cent. Approximately $13.6 billion of these bonds were issued in 1951. An attempt to issue the same type of bond in the following year was unsuccessful. Institutional investors constituted the major segment of the market for this type of security. The unsuccessful offering in 1952 suggested that this type of holder would not invest additional funds in this form of security unless the initial yield or the conversion privilege were made much more attractive. As noted in the discussion of the Federal National Mortgage Association, some of these bonds have been exchanged for higher-yielding mortgages.

During World War II, the Treasury restricted the market for long-term bonds to non-bank investors. Long-term bond issues during most of 1942 and 1943 were ineligible for purchase by commercial banks until after a lapse of ten years from date of issue, at which time the bonds would have a remaining maturity of around ten years. Beginning in 1944, commercial banks were permitted to purchase newly issued long-term bonds, with purchase quotas related to banks' savings deposits. Beginning in 1952, many of the previously issued long-term bonds became eligible for bank purchase, and in 1962 all outstanding long-term bonds will be eligible for bank purchase.

CALLABILITY. One of the characteristics of our peacetime economy is changing interest rates, and the Treasury, as well as non-government issuers of securities, is concerned with the cost of financing its obligations. Therefore, almost all long-term bonds are sold with an optional redemption or call date. Beginning with the call date and any subsequent interest payment date, the Treasury has the right to redeem bonds upon four months' notice. The redemption or call dates are set two to five years ahead of stated maturities.

In July, 1957 the Treasury employed a rather unique form of "call" provision, by making two issues redeemable at the option of the investors. The issue could either be redeemed at par after its maturity was half gone or, at the investors' discretion, be held for the full period. One issue had a maturity of four years and the other a maturity of five years. In a period of rising interest rates, the inclusion of such an option makes the issue attractive to investors. In both issues an investor must give the Treasury advance notice three months prior to date of redemption.

ACCEPTABILITY FOR TAX PAYMENTS. A unique characteristic of some Federal obligations is that they can be used for direct payment of various types of taxes. Tax anticipation bills are acceptable at or near maturity for the direct payment of Federal income and profits taxes. The Treasury may also designate certificates and notes as acceptable. Many of the long-term bonds are acceptable before maturity at par and accrued interest for the payment of Federal estate taxes. The offering circular relating to a particular debt issue specifies whether the issued securities are acceptable in payment of taxes.

Ownership Pattern and Annual Flows Into Federal Obligations

The ownership pattern of Federal obligations outstanding at the end of 1958 and the annual flows into Federal obligations for the period 1950-1958, are shown respectively in Tables 22.1 and 22.2. Table 22.1 shows the importance of each sector's holdings of Federal obligations in relation to its holdings of financial assets and the total amount of Federal obligation

TABLE 22–1
FEDERAL OBLIGATIONS OUTSTANDING, END OF 1958
(BILLIONS OF DOLLARS)

Sector	Dollars	Per cent	Federal obligations as a percentage of total financial assets
Total Federal obligations [1]	185.7	100.0	——
Short-term direct [2]	71.9	38.7	——
Other direct and guaranteed	108.0	58.2	——
Non-guaranteed [3]	5.8	3.1	——
Investors (all sectors) [1]	185.7	100.0	——
Consumer and nonprofit org.	16.4	8.8	1.9
Direct and guaranteed	14.9		
Non-guaranteed	1.6		
Corporate business	18.4	9.9	11.2
State and local government	17.8	9.6	37.8
Direct and guaranteed	17.4		
Non-guaranteed	.4		
Commercial banking and monetary authorities	95.0	51.2	39.8
Commercial banks	68.6	36.9	32.9
Short-term direct	16.6		
Other direct and guaranteed .	49.7		
Non-guaranteed	2.2		
Monetary authorities	26.4	14.2	49.3
Short-term direct	21.0		
Other direct	5.4		
Savings institutions	12.0	6.5	12.6
Mutual savings banks	7.6	4.1	20.3
Savings and loan ass'ns and credit unions	4.4	2.4	7.6
Insurance	16.1	8.7	10.7
Life insurance	7.2	3.9	7.1
Self-administered pension plans .	2.1	1.1	9.9
Other insurance	6.7	3.6	23.8
Finance, n.e.c.	3.1	1.7	7.2
Rest-of-the-world	6.8	3.7	13.9

[1] "Federal obligations" covers all marketable Treasury and Federal agency (including Federal land bank and Federal home loan bank) securities, net of holdings by agencies and funds that are part of the Federal Government sector. The category includes some non-marketable securities, such as savings bonds held by others than consumers, investment series bonds, depositary bonds, and matured debt. It also includes accrued interest on outstanding Treasury bills and on savings bonds not held by consumers.

[2] Covers direct marketable Treasury debt maturing within one year.

[3] Mainly securities issued by F.N.M.A., Federal land banks, Federal home loan banks, Federal intermediate credit banks, and banks for cooperatives.

Source: "A Quarterly Presentation of Flow of Funds, Saving and Investment," *Federal Reserve Bulletin*, August 1959.

outstanding. The annual flow data indicate the year-to-year variation in each sector's holdings of Federal obligations.

At the end of 1958, the commercial banking and monetary sector held 51.2 per cent of outstanding Federal obligations. The consumer and non-profit organization sector, the corporate business sector, the state and local government sector, and the insurance sector each held between 8 and 10 per cent of Federal obligations outstanding. Since each of these sectors holds different amounts of financial assets, the relative importance of Federal obligations in each sector's holdings of financial assets was not as uniform. It is significant that in five sectors or subsectors, Federal obligations accounted for more than 20 per cent of financial assets. The widespread

TABLE 22-2

ANNUAL FLOWS INTO FEDERAL OBLIGATIONS, 1950-1958*

(BILLIONS OF DOLLARS)

Sector	1950	1951	1952	1953	1954	1955	1956	1957	1958
Net change in Fed. oblig.[1]..	−.2	.5	4.4	5.2	1.5	1.0	−5.1	1.4	9.0
Short-term direct[2]	2.7	−11.0	7.0	16.5	−11.8	−7.1	7.4	5.5	−1.2
Other direct and									
guaranteed .·.........	−3.3	11.3	−2.6	−11.3	13.3	6.6	−13.0	−6.2	10.7
Non-guaranteed[3]	.4	.3	−.1	*	*	1.5	.6	2.1	−.5
Net acquisitions (liquidations):[1]									
Consumer and nonprofit..	−.5	−.8	−.2	.1	−2.1	2.2	1.1	2.5	−2.9
Direct and guaranteed..	−.5	−.9	−.2	.1	−2.1	1.7	.8	1.8	−2.5
Non-guaranteed	*	.1	*	*	*	.6	.3	.7	−.3
Corporate business	2.9	1.1	−.8	1.6	−2.4	4.2	−4.3	−1.5	.7
State and local government	.7	1.1	1.6	1.6	1.7	.8	1.1	1.0	.3
Commercial banking and									
monetary	2.7	2.4	2.6	1.2	4.6	−7.1	−3.1	−.6	10.0
Commercial banks									
Short-term direct ...	−4.3	−6.4	3.4	9.0	−10.7	−8.5	4.8	1.9	.9
Other direct and guar.	−.7	5.9	−1.6	.9	6.2	1.1	−7.8	−2.2	6.8
Non-guaranteed	.4	−.1	−.1	−.2	*	.5	−.2	.5	.1
Monetary authorities ..	1.9	3.0	.9	1.2	−1.0	−.1	.2	−.7	2.2
Savings institutions	−.6	−.9	−.1	−.1	−.4	.2	.1	.4	.3
Direct and guaranteed..	−.5	−.9	−.3	−.1	−.3	*	*	*	.3
Non-guaranteed	*	*	.1	.1	−.1	.2	.1	.4	−.1
Mutual savings banks	−.6	−1.0	−.4	−.2	−.5	−.2	−.4	−.3	−.3
Savings and loan ass'ns									
. and credit unions..	*	.1	.2	.1	.1	.4	.6	.6	.6
Insurance	−1.2	−2.2	−.3	.1	−.6	−.3	−1.5	−.9	.2
Life insurance companies	−1.8	−2.4	−.8	−.4	−.8	−.5	−1.0	−.5	.1
Self-admin. pension plans	.2	.1	*	.2	*	.3	−.2	−.2	*
Other insurance									
companies	.4	.2	.4	.3	.2	−.1	−.3	−.2	.1
Finance, n.e.c.	−.1	−.3	.6	−.1	.5	−.4	.3	.2	.5
Rest-of-the-world	1.2	−.1	1.0	.5	.2	1.1	.8	.2	*

*Footnotes correspond to the footnotes appearing in Table 22-1.

Source: "A Quarterly Presentation of Flow of Funds, Saving and Investment," *Federal Reserve Bulletin*, August 1959.

ownership of Federal obligations and the relative importance of such holdings in the portfolios of major investor groups make open-market operations of the monetary authorities one of the more important monetary measures.

An examination of annual flows during this period reveals that only the state and local government sector supplied additional funds during each of the years. The savings and loan associations and credit unions subsector and the rest-of-the-world sector supplied additional funds to the market for Federal obligations during all but one of the years. The other sectors supplied funds in some years and withdrew funds in others. During the period 1950-1955, there was a gradual increase in the supply of Federal obligations, rising from $168 billion at the beginning of 1950 to $180.4 billion at the end of 1955. During 1956, the supply of Federal obligations was reduced by approximately $5 million. During 1957 and 1958, the supply was increased by approximately $10.5 billion. The composition of Federal obligations also varied during each of these years, reflecting primarily the frequent refunding of outstanding obligations. Quarterly data would reveal even greater variations in both the level and composition of Federal obligations. Throughout most of this period, the Treasury had to refund outstanding Federal obligations and issue additional Federal obligations in the face of strong competing demands for funds at all maturities. Attention is now focused on the role of each of the major sectors in the market for Federal obligations.

Consumer and nonprofit organization sector. At the end of 1958, the consumer and nonprofit organization sector held $16.4 billion of Federal obligations, which accounted for 8.8 per cent of Federal obligations outstanding, and 1.9 per cent of the sector's total holdings of financial assets. In some years, this sector was a net supplier of funds to the market and, in other years, it withdrew funds from the market. The sector's net acquisitions in 1955, 1956, and 1957 were in response to an improvement in the yields on Federal obligations. In 1959, a year of even higher yields, this sector supplied additional funds to the market. Over the entire period 1950-1958, the sector withdrew $600 million more than it supplied. However, this sector was a major supplier of funds to the market for non-guaranteed Federal obligations. The higher yields that were obtainable on the non-guaranteed securities attracted funds in every year but 1958. Many of the consumer and nonprofit organization units are not as concerned with marketability as are institutional investors, so that the "thinness" of the markets for the non-guaranteed Federal obligations was not too unfavorable an investment characteristic. The data tend to suggest that this sector is sensitive to yields on Federal obligations. This theory was substantiated by the public's response to 5 per cent Treasury notes that were offered in the fall of 1959.

Corporate business sector. At the end of 1958, the corporate business sector held $18.4 billion of Federal obligations, which accounted for 9.9 per cent of Federal obligations outstanding. This type of investment represented 11.2 per cent of this sector's financial assets. Almost all of this sector's holdings are concentrated in the direct and guaranteed issues, most of which are short- and intermediate-term.

This sector's investment in Federal obligations is directly related to the management of cash balances, particularly those of large corporations. Temporary excess funds arising from non-cash expenses, retained earnings, and the proceeds of newly issued corporate securities are invested for short periods in Federal obligations, because this type of financial asset involves little or no risk and is highly liquid. Furthermore, such investments provide additional income. The yields obtainable on Federal obligations have been higher than those obtainable on time deposits in commercial banks, with the result that many corporations have become important short-term investors in Federal obligations at the expense of time deposits in commercial banks. As some corporations withdraw funds from the market, other corporations supply funds to the market. In some years, more funds are withdrawn than are supplied, and the opposite is true of other years. The forces underlying the management of the corporate business sector's financial assets tend to require that corporations hold about 15 per cent of such assets in the form of Federal obligations. Specifically, the forces probably include the need to provide adequate liquidity and an attempt to fund a portion of tax liabilities. In 1945, Federal obligations accounted for about 29 per cent of the sector's financial assets, reflecting high tax liabilities and the restrictions on capital outlays. During the period 1947-1953, the proportion of financial assets held in the form of Federal obligations ranged from 16 to 18 per cent. Beginning in 1953, the relative importance of Federal obligations in the financial assets of the corporate business sector began to decline, falling to 11.1 per cent in 1958. It is expected that corporations will build up their holdings to around 15 per cent of financial assets.

This sector's annual flows into Federal obligations is highly volatile. During the period 1950-1958, this sector withdrew funds from the market in four of the years, and supplied additional funds to the market in the other years. In 1955, the sector supplied $4.4 billion, and in the following year, it withdrew $4.3 billion. The acquisitions in 1955 reflected the temporary increase in liquidity during the early stage of recovery. In 1956, the execution of planned capital outlays was financed partially by withdrawing funds from the market for Federal obligations. Also, the credit restraint in 1956 prompted many corporations to liquidate additional Federal obligations instead of borrowing funds at the level of rates that prevailed in that year. In other words, the corporate sector's large holdings of Federal obligations can be worked down if conditions require such action. The data also suggest that the sector tends to supply funds to the market during a period of inventory liquidation and during the early stage of expansion in over-all business activity, and tends to withdraw funds from the market during a period of inventory accumulation and during the middle stage of expansion in over-all business activity. Quarterly data show these relationships more clearly than annual flow data. For example, the corporate sector acquired Federal obligations during the last two quarters of both 1957 and 1958. The 1957 period was one of inventory liquidation, and in 1958 came the early stage of economic recovery. Unless the Federal Government is able to reduce the level of debt during periods in which the corporate business sector tends to withdraw funds from the market for Federal obligations, the Treasury's refundings must include obligations that are relatively attractive to other sectors. Otherwise, the commercial banking sector will have to supply funds to the market during these periods, and such a shift in ownership of debt can be inflationary. The problem of managing shifts in debt ownership is considered in Chapter 26, which deals specifically with debt management policies.

STATE AND LOCAL GOVERNMENT SECTOR. At the end of 1958, the state and local government sector held $17.8 billion of Federal obligations, which accounted for 9.6 per cent of Federal obligations outstanding, and 37.8 per cent of the sector's financial assets. This sector's holdings of Federal obligations represent primarily the investments of state and local retirement and pension funds. The importance of Federal obligations in the portfolios of these funds reflects conservatism as well as legal restrictions. Another source of demand is the investment of temporary excess cash balances held by state and local governmental authorities.

This sector was a major net supplier of funds to the market during each of the years. Between 1950 and 1958, it acquired an additional $9.3 billion of Federal obligations, and thereby more than doubled its holdings. The rate of growth in state and local retirement funds is gradually slowing down, and some of the funds are exercising more discretion in the investment of new funds. To the extent that the trustees of these funds become more yield-conscious, some of the funds that used to flow into Federal obligations might be channelled into corporate securities. Also, these funds may be pressured into investing a greater percentage of their funds in state and local obligations.

COMMERCIAL BANKING AND MONETARY SECTOR. At the end of 1958, the commercial banking and monetary sector held $95 billion of Federal obligations, and such holdings accounted for 51.2 per cent of Federal obligations outstanding. The commercial banks' holdings accounted for 32.9 per cent of their financial assets; the monetary authorities' holdings accounted for 49.3 per cent of their financial assets. As in the corporate business sector, there is a minimal demand for Federal obligations by commercial banks and

Federal Reserve Banks. The commercial banks' minimum demand is determined by the banks' need, first for liquidity and second, to offset their higher-risk type of financial assets with the "non-risk" Federal obligations. The term "non-risk" refers to the certainty that the Federal government will pay interest and repay principal. Obviously, Federal obligations are subject to interest-rate risk. The monetary authorities' minimum demand is determined by the need to hold a ready inventory of securities that can be used in conducting open-market operations. The annual flows in and out of Federal obligations reflect the influence of many variables, including change in size of the debt, structure of yields, the demand for bank loans, the offering policy of the Treasury, and monetary and credit policy. During the 1950-1958 period, the commercial banks withdrew funds from, and the monetary authorities supplied funds to, the market. As noted earlier in this study, the acquisition of Federal obligations by monetary authorities results in an equal increase in bank reserves. The effect on the money supply depends on whether the securities were held by banks or non-bank investors.

The commercial banks' holdings of Federal obligations are part of their secondary reserve accounts as well as part of their investment accounts. Safety, liquidity, and yield are among the more important determinants underlying the composition of the banks' secondary reserves. "Yield" in this case refers to the attainment of maximum yield, assuming that the asset also provides adequate safety and liquidity. The price fluctuations of the long-term obligations preclude their use as secondary reserves; therefore, the securities held as secondary reserves must have short- and intermediate-term maturities. Yield becomes the dominant consideration in the investment accounts. Since commercial banks in their published statements of condition do not break down their Federal obligations in these terms, we must examine the maturity pattern of their holdings of Federal obligations to determine the relative importance of these two factors.

The maturity pattern of the banks' portfolios of Federal obligations is revealed only partially in Table 22.1, which shows that 24 per cent of the banks' holdings were short-term, direct obligations; that is, direct marketable issues maturing within one year. To provide additional insight into the maturity pattern of the banks' holdings, the tabulation below presents a breakdown of the bank-held marketable debt at the end of 1958 in terms of four maturity classes:

Total	100.0 per cent
Within 1 year	24.4 per cent
1-5 years	50.4 per cent
5-10 years	17.7 per cent
Over 10 years	7.5 per cent

The data show that nearly three-fourths of the bank-held Federal obligations were scheduled to mature within five years, suggesting that about three-fourths of the banks' holdings represented secondary reserves. Data as to maturity of non-guaranteed Federal obligations were not available, but most of these holdings were probably short-term and were held as secondary reserves.

The commercial banks' annual flows into Federal obligations were nearly as volatile as those of the corporate business sector. For example, in 1954, a recession year, the commercial banks acquired an additional $5.6 billion of Federal obligations, but in the following year the banks reduced their holdings by $6.5 billion. The Federal obligations were replaced by loans to the business and consumer sectors. The data in Table 22.2 show that banks acquired intermediate-term obligations in 1954, reflecting the Treasury's attempt to lengthen maturities. In 1955, the banks' liquidations of Federal obligations were concentrated entirely in short-term obligations. In 1958 the banks acquired nearly $7 billion of intermediate-term obligations.

The banks' annual flows tend to coincide with changes in business conditions. During a period of recession, banks tend to add to their holdings of Federal obligations, and during a period of prosperity, they tend to reduce them. During the last two quarters of 1957 and the first two quarters of 1958, the commercial banks acquired $9.3 billion of Federal obligations. Banks' free reserves increase during a recession because the demand for loans falls off and because monetary authorities take measures to increase bank reserves. Banks are profit-motivated and attempt to achieve maximum earning assets, so that the released funds are not held in the form of excess reserves at Federal Reserve banks; instead, they are invested. Since banks expect the demand for loans to increase in the near future, the released funds are invested in highly liquid financial assets, e.g., short- and intermediate-term Federal obligations. When the upturn in business conditions develops and the demand for loans increases, inflationary pressures are likely to develop. As a result, credit and monetary measures are directed toward credit restraint. Commercial banks adjust to these conditions by withdrawing funds from the market for Federal obligations. If the supply of Federal obligations is not increased, the banks might be able to shift Federal obligations to the marginal investor groups, such as the state and local retirement funds and nonlife insurance companies. If the supply of Federal obligations is increased, then such shifts become more difficult, and monetary authorities may have to acquire Federal obligations by open-market operations. Although the banks might realize capital losses on the liquidation of intermediate-term obligations because of a rise in interest rates, they believe that the higher returns obtainable on new loans and investments will offset these losses. The shift in ownership from banks to non-bank investors does not increase the reserves of commercial banks, but it does lead to excess reserves, which, in turn, can support new loans.

The monetary authorities' holdings of Federal obligations and their annual flows into and out of the market for Federal obligations are directly related to monetary and credit measures and to the need to maintain orderly conditions in the market for Federal obligations. Monetary authorities buy and sell Federal obligations to influence reserves of commercial banks, either to offset other transactions or to bring about net change in the commercial banks' reserve positions. It should be noted that the acquisition of Federal obligations by the monetary authorities does not necessarily indicate monetary ease. For example, Federal obligations might be purchased during a period of credit restraint to offset other transactions, such as a net gold outflow. The present level of holdings represents an equal creation in commercial banks' reserves.

The maturity pattern of the monetary authorities' portfolio of Federal obligations is revealed only partially in Table 22.1, which shows that 80 per cent of the authorities' holdings were due to mature within one year from that date. Such a maturity pattern reflects the offering policy of the Treasury and the nature of open-market operations in recent years, both of which were restricted almost entirely to short- and intermediate-term maturities. The arguments for and against such policies are developed in Part 7. To provide additional insight into the maturity pattern of the Federal Reserve banks' holdings, the tabulation presented below gives a breakdown at the end of 1958 in terms of four maturity classes:

Total	100.0 per cent
Within 1 year	79.7 per cent
1-5 years	14.7 per cent
5-10 years	.8 per cent
Over 10 years	4.8 per cent

If the open-market policy of dealing only in the short end of the market were modified, and the monetary authorities decided to conduct open-market operations in all maturity classes, it would first be necessary to change the maturity pattern of the portfolio, unless the policy were limited to buying Federal obligations. To accomplish a change in the composition of the portfolio, it would be necessary to sell to the market short- and intermediate-term obligations, and to acquire long-term obligations. As long as monetary authorities attempt to maintain orderly conditions in the market for Federal obligations, the size and composition of their portfolios depend to some extent on investment decisions in other sectors.

SAVINGS INSTITUTIONS SECTOR. At the end of 1958, the savings institutions sector held $12 billion of Federal obligations, which accounted for 6.5 per cent of Federal obligations outstanding. Mutual savings banks' holdings totaled $7.6 billion and these holdings accounted for 20.3 per cent of the banks' total financial assets. The combined holdings of the savings and loan associations and credit unions totaled $4.4 billion, and these holdings accounted for 7.6 per cent of the subsector's financial assets. These facts by themselves are very misleading as to the relative importance of each of these subsectors in the market for Federal obligations. The mutual savings banks withdrew funds from the market in each of the years, 1950-1958, whereas the other savings institutions subsector supplied funds to the market in each of those years.

The savings institutions' investments in Federal obligations are influenced by their total financial assets, alternative investment outlets, the structure of yields on market instruments, and the need for liquidity. During the 1950-1958 period the mutual savings banks withdrew funds from the market for Federal obligations and shifted these funds into mortgages and corporate securities, both of which provided higher yields than Federal obligations did. Evidently, the mutual savings banks' holdings of Federal obligations in 1950 were more than adequate to their need for liquidity. It is unlikely that the mutual savings banks will allow their holdings of Federal obligations to fall much below 20 per cent of their financial assets, so that their withdrawal of funds from the market may be coming to an end.

The maturity pattern of the mutual savings banks' holdings of direct Federal obligations at the end of 1958 is shown in the following tabulation:

Total	100.0 per cent
Within 1 year	5.0 per cent
1 to 5 years	20.3 per cent
5 to 10 years	15.8 per cent
Over 10 years	59.0 per cent

The data above show that mutual savings banks hold mostly long-term Federal obligations. Since the prices of long-term marketable obligations fluctuate within fairly wide limits with changes in the level of interest rates, mutual savings banks are deterred from liquidating long-term Federal obligations during a period of credit restraint. The maturity pattern suggests that Federal obligations are held for the purpose of offsetting risk in other assets rather than to provide liquidity. To encourage the banks to reacquire Federal obligations, the Treasury would have to offer long-term bonds carrying high-interest rate coupons.

The net acquisitions of Federal obligations by savings and loan associations and credit unions reflected primarily the need to provide adequate liquidity. The associations' share of accounts has been growing at the rate of $5 billion dollars annually, so that it has been necessary for these institutions to acquire additional Federal obligations in order to maintain adequate liquidity and to moderate the degree of risk in their mortgage portfolios. This subsector will probably continue to be one of the more important marginal suppliers of funds to the market for Federal obligations.

INSURANCE SECTOR. At the end of 1958, the insurance sector held $16.1 billion of Federal obligations, which accounted for 8.7 per cent of Federal obligations outstanding and 10.7 per cent of the sector's financial assets. Life insurance companies held slightly more Federal obligations than did nonlife insurance companies, but in relation to total financial assets, Federal obligations were much more important in the portfolios of nonlife insurance companies. Nearly one-fourth of the nonlife insurance companies' assets were invested in Federal obligations; approximately 7 per cent of life insurance companies' assets were invested in Federal obligations.

The patterns of the insurance subsectors' annual flows into Federal obligations for the 1950-1958 period are similar to those of the savings institutions subsectors. Life insurance companies withdrew funds from the market in every year except 1958. The forces underlying this investment behavior were almost identical to those cited for mutual savings banks. The life insurance companies' minimum demand for Federal obligations is determined by the need to offset the risk in their other financial assets. Their holdings of Federal obligations exceeded minimum demand, and there were plentiful alternative credit market instruments available at sufficiently higher yields. Therefore, life insurance companies shifted funds out of the market for Federal obligations, and into the markets for mortgages and corporate securities. To attract life insurance companies' funds back into the market for Federal obligations, one of two things must occur. Either the supply of alternative credit market instruments must become inadequate, or the Treasury must offer new long-term securities at such attractive yields that life insurance companies cannot pass up the investment opportunity.

Three factors suggest that the liquidation of Federal obligations by life insurance companies has probably come to an end. First, Federal obligations, expressed as a percentage of their financial assets, have reached a record low. Second, offerings of the Treasury may be more attractively priced. Third, there was a net annual flow of life insurance companies' funds into Federal obligations during 1959.

The nonlife insurance companies' annual flows into Federal obligations can be compared with the annual flows of the savings and loan associations and credit unions. As noted in the chapters dealing with insurance, the nonlife companies are much more concerned with liquidity than are the life insurance companies. As the nonlife companies' assets increased, it was necessary to acquire additional Federal obligations to satisfy the need for a given state of liquidity. During the period 1945-1954, the nonlife companies added to their holdings of Federal obligations. However, the rate of acquisition was much lower than the rate of increase in total assets, so that the percentage of nonlife insurance companies' assets held in the form of Federal obligations declined, falling from approximately 40 per cent in 1945 to 32 per cent in 1954. In 1955, 1956, and 1957 the nonlife companies reduced their holdings of Federal obligations slightly, and in

1958, they reentered the market as a net supplier of funds. It is likely that the present percentage of assets in Federal obligations is nearly optimum, and if it is, it can be expected that the companies will be a net supplier of funds to the market for Federal obligations in the future. To be more specific, the annual flows into Federal obligations from the nonlife insurance companies should average about 25 per cent of their increase in financial assets.

REST-OF-THE-WORLD SECTOR. At the end of 1958, the rest-of-the-world sector held $6.8 billion of Federal obligations, and such holdings accounted for 13.9 per cent of the sector's financial assets. This sector's holdings represent the temporary investment of foreign funds. Liquidity is the vital consideration in the investment of such funds, and the specific allocation of these funds depends primarily on the structure of yields. In recent years, the short- and intermediate-term Federal obligations have been relatively attractive to this sector. With expansion in world trade and further increase in this sector's total dollar holdings, it can be expected that it will not only maintain its demand for Federal obligations, but will also probably increase its holdings. This sector is likely to continue to be a net supplier of funds to the market for Federal obligations. However, if foreigners were to believe that the purchasing power of the dollar was about to depreciate rapidly, they would reduce their holdings of Federal obligations and would not reenter the market until confidence in the dollar was restored. Under such conditions, domestic investors would also attempt to liquidate their holdings of Federal obligations. Stability in ownership of Federal obligations is directly related to confidence in the dollar.

Outlook

Review of the portfolios of major sectors and the annual flows into Federal obligations suggests that the ownership pattern of Federal obligations may be stabilizing. If the total volume of Federal obligations is reasonably constant, and if the refundings are tailored to fit the investment needs of the various sectors and are priced to compete with outstanding credit market instruments, it should be possible to maintain within rather narrow limits the present ownership pattern. Since some of the sectors are consistent net suppliers of funds to the market for Federal obligations, limited shifts in debt ownership may occur without requiring the commercial banking and monetary sector to acquire additional Federal obligations. However, if it becomes necessary to increase substantially the volume of Federal obligations within a relatively short period, either the commercial banking and monetary sector must acquire additional Federal obligations, or the Treasury must attempt to place additional Federal obligations in the portfolios of other investor groups at the cost of creating a less stable ownership pattern of Federal obligations.

Government Securities Dealers

The widespread ownership of Federal obligations, their importance in the portfolios of nearly all institutional investors, and the investors' need to shift into and out of Federal obligations emphasize the importance of the market mechanism for Federal obligations. Although a small volume of trading in Federal obligations occurs through the facilities of the New York Stock Exchange, the major volume of trading is accomplished in the over-the-counter market. As in the over-the-counter market for corporate securities, dealers or specialists stand ready to "make markets" in all maturities of Federal obligations. Almost all of the trading is done by telephone and wire.

Dealers in Federal obligations consist of both commercial banks and non-bank dealers. Testimony before the Joint Economic Committee in 1959 identified 17 government securities dealers who were making markets on a continuing basis, that is, they were buying and selling Federal obligations at prices quoted over the telephone.* Although many commercial banks buy and sell Federal obligations, only 5 banks are considered dealers in Federal obligations. The other banks rely on one or more of the bank and non-bank dealers for quotations and inventory adjustments. Two of the bank dealers have headquarters in Chicago, and the other three have headquarters in New York City. All of the bank dealers are connected with other financial centers through branch offices. Most of the trading in Federal obligations takes place in New York.

A recent study of the dealer market for Federal obligations summarized the nature of the dealer firms in a very succinct manner.† Aside from their transactions in the government securities market, there are few similarities among the dealers. Four of the non-bank dealers are partnerships. Two of the firms are leading underwriters of new corporate issues, and two others participate in many offerings. Two are members of the New York Stock Exchange; at least two are active in the acceptance market. Several are dealers in municipal, agency, and International Bank bonds, and some underwrite the initial distribution of such issues.

The economic function of the dealers is to provide the mechanism that brings together all potential buyers and sellers at a given time, thereby establishing prices that come closest to satisfying all buyers and sellers. The narrow spreads between bid and offer quotations indicate that the dealers are performing this function efficiently. The dealers risk their own capital in trading at quoted prices. They are in constant contact with potential buyers and sellers. At times, the dealers borrow securities from investors to cover short positions, and at other times borrow considerable funds to

*U. S. Joint Economic Committee, *Employment, Growth, and Price Levels*, Hearings, Part 6B, 86th Cong., 1st sess. (Washington, D. C.: Government Printing Office, 1959), p. 1508.

† U. S. Economic Committee, *A Study of the Dealer Market for Federal Government Securities*, prepared for the Committee, 86th Cong., 1st sess. (Washington, D. C.: Government Printing Office, 1960), p. 2.

cover larger-than-normal inventories. Considering the nature of their inventory, dealers are able to borrow relatively large amounts in relation to their capital accounts. However, the spread between their borrowing costs and the yields on obligations held in inventory is narrow, and at times is costly to the dealers. The distinguishing elements in the dealers' unique role are as follows: "first, the *specialization* in detailed knowledge of the Government securities market, the factors affecting the market, and the holdings and interests of various customers across the country; second, the *stake* of each dealer, trading for his own position; and third, the *competition* among dealers, seeking customers and quick to take advantage of any mistake in judgment revealed by another dealer."* It is generally agreed that the dealer organization has provided a market of considerable scope and diversity for Federal obligations.

As we noted in the earlier part of this chapter, Treasury bills are issued on a discount basis and are sold at sealed-bid auctions. Generally, dealers in Federal obligations bid for sizeable portions of such issues, and distribute the issues to investors as demand develops. The underwriting role of the dealers in Federal obligations can best be emphasized by noting that both the Treasury and the Federal Reserve confine all of their market transactions for the purchase and sale of outstanding Federal obligations to dealer firms. Previous examples citing open-market purchases from commercial banks and non-bank investors were over-simplified for the purpose of discussion. Actually, such transactions are executed through the dealer mechanism. It should be noted that this dealer mechanism is inextricably linked with the money market and the underwriting and distribution of all other securities. The money market is the mechanism through which the dealers secure funds to finance their positions in securities. Almost all dealers in Federal obligations also deal in markets for state and local and World Bank obligations and bankers' acceptances. Some of the non-bank dealers are actively engaged in trading in corporate securities in both the organized securities and the over-the-counter markets. Some of them also underwrite or participate in underwriting syndicates relating to non-guaranteed Federal obligations, state and local obligations, corporate bonds, and corporate stock.

MARKET FOR STATE AND LOCAL OBLIGATIONS†

State and local obligations offer investors many favorable investment characteristics. The income earned on such obligations is exempt from Federal

*Robert V. Roosa, "Federal Reserve Operations in the Money and Government Securities Markets," Federal Reserve Bank of New York, p. 36.
† See Roland I. Robinson, *Postwar Market for State and Local Government Securities*, N.B.E.R. study (Princeton, N. J.: Princeton University Press, 1960).

corporate and personal income taxes, making this form of investment very attractive to investors in higher tax brackets, including financial institutions that are taxed at the corporate rate of 52 per cent. The majority of such obligations provide considerable safety of principal and certainty of income. The use of serial maturities by state and local governmental units provides investors an opportunity to select maturities that are most appropriate to their needs. The major unfavorable investment characteristic of many state and local obligations is the "thinness" of their markets, which means that these obligations may not be as marketable or liquid as Federal obligations and many corporate bonds.

Demand for Funds

The operating costs of state and local government have risen as a result of inflation, an increasing scale of operations, and assumption of new and expanded responsibilities. Rapid population expansion and its increasing concentration in urban and suburban areas have required that state and local governments provide additional facilities relating to education, highways and other modes of transportation, public health and housing, sanitation, and police and fire protection. Revenues have not been adequate to finance capital outlays as well as higher general expenditures, so that state and local governments have borrowed heavily during the postwar period. State and local government debt increased considerably, rising steadily from a level of $13.6 billion in 1946 to nearly $60 billion in 1958. At the end of 1958, local debt accounted for 72.5 per cent of total state and local debt. As shown in Table 22-4 the annual increase in state and local debt in recent years has climbed from around $3 billion and $4 billion to nearly $6 billion. The basic forces underlying the growth in state and local debt continue unabated, and further expansion in such debt may be expected over the next several years.

There is great variety in state and local obligations because of the diversity among issuers and the nature of contracts. Local obligations are issued by counties, cities, townships, school districts, and special districts. The relative importance of these issuers at the end of fiscal 1957 is shown in the following tabulation:*

Local Debt by Type of Issuing Unit	
County	9.4 per cent
City	48.3
Township	2.8
School district	23.7
Special district	15.8

State obligations are issued by state authorities as well as by state govern-

*Tax Foundation Inc., *Facts and Figures on Government Finance*, 10th ed., 1958-1959, p. 221.

ments. Authorities include port authorities, turnpike authorities, specialized building corporations and many others.

The nature of state and local debt contracts range from obligations on which the payment of interest and principal are backed by the unlimited power of issuers to levy taxes on obligations on which the payment of interest and principal are dependent upon the collection of specific revenues. The first type of obligation is referred to as a general or full-faith and credit obligation. Obligations that are payable solely from pledged specific sources are referred to as limited or non-guaranteed obligations. They may also be referred to as revenue bonds. The state gross long-term debt is about evenly divided between full-faith and credit bonds and non-guaranteed bonds. The local gross long-term debt is heavily weighted in favor of the full-faith and credit bonds. At the end of fiscal 1957, approximately 70 per cent of local gross long-term debt was in the form of full-faith and credit bonds, and the remainder was in the form of non-guaranteed obligations. During the postwar period, the percentage of debt in the form of non-guaranteed obligations has been increasing. In 1946, only 15.4 per cent of state gross long-term debt was in the form of non-guaranteed obligations, but at the end of 1957, the total had climbed to 52 per cent. Comparable data are not available for local debt before 1952. At the end of 1952, 20.7 per cent of local gross long-term debt was non-guaranteed, but at the end of 1957, the amount had climbed to 29.2 per cent. State and local agencies and authorities rely heavily on non-guaranteed bonds to finance a major part of capital outlays on water, electricity, gas, sewage disposal, public markets, transportation, public housing, and non-instructional buildings (dormitories and student unions) at state-supported institutions of higher learning. The functions indicate clearly why the bonds are often referred to as revenue bonds.

The state gross long-term debt as of the end of fiscal 1957 is summarized by function in the tabulation below:*

Total	100.0 per cent
Highways	54.2
State toll facilities	37.5
Other	16.7
Education	13.1
State institutions of higher learning	5.2
Other	7.9
Veterans' bonuses	8.9
Natural resources	3.5
Hospitals	1.2
All other [1]	19.0

[1] Includes public welfare, public safety, non-highway transportation, housing community redevelopment and miscellaneous and unallocable gross long-term debt.

A similar breakdown is not available for local debt.

*Ibid., p. 202.

Ownership Pattern and Annual Flows

The ownership pattern of state and local obligations outstanding at the end of 1958 and the annual flows into such obligations for the 1954-1958 period are shown respectively in Tables 22-3 and 22-4. The data show that almost all of the state and local obligations outstanding at the end of 1958 were held by four classes of investors: consumers, commercial banks, insurance companies, and state and local retirement and pension funds. In terms of the investors' holdings of financial assets, state and local obligations were most important in the portfolios of nonlife insurance companies and state and local government retirement and pension funds. Compared with the market for Federal obligations, investors in state and local obligations do not supply funds to the market in one year, and withdraw funds in the next year. Instead, the investors supply funds year after year. During the period 1954-1958, consumers added $8.6 billion of state and local obligations to their portfolios; commercial banks, $4.7 billion; life insurance companies, $1.3 billion; nonlife insurance companies, $3.5 billion; and state and local retirement and pension funds, $2.2 billion. The pattern of annual flows does not depart drastically from the ownership pattern shown in Table 22-2. However, it is obvious that the institutional investors are becoming an increasingly important part of the market for state and local obligations.

CONSUMERS. The use of the term "consumer" is deliberate, because the tax-exempt state and local obligations are not attractive investments to the non-taxed, nonprofit organizations. At the end of 1958, the consumer sector held $24.5 billion of state and local obligations, or 43.4 per cent of the total obligations outstanding. Such investments accounted for only 2.9 per cent of the consumer and nonprofit organization sector's financial assets. During the 1954-1958 period, consumers were the major supplier of funds to the market for state and local obligations, in three of the years, supplying more than half of the total annual flows into state and local obligations. It should also be noted that the consumers did not supply a steady flow of funds into the market. The irregularity probably reflects the uneven movements in the structure of yields. As long as marginal tax rates imposed on personal income remain at their present high levels, consumers can be counted upon in the future to supply a major portion of the total annual flows into these obligations.

COMMERCIAL BANKS. Commercial banks are the second most important class of investors in state and local obligations, and by far the most important institutional investor. At the end of 1958, the banks held $16.5 billion of these obligations, or 28.2 per cent of the total amount outstanding and 6.9 per cent of the banks' financial assets. Since the banks are taxed at 52 per cent, tax considerations account for these large holdings. Many of the higher-quality state and local obligations compare very favorably

515

TABLE 22–3
STATE AND LOCAL OBLIGATIONS OUTSTANDING, END OF 1958
(BILLIONS OF DOLLARS)

Sector	Dollars	Per cent	State and local obligations as a percentage of total financial assets
Total outstanding: [1]	$ 58.5	100.0	——
State			
Local			
Investors (all sectors)			
Consumer	25.4	43.4	2.9
Commercial banks	16.5	28.2	6.9
Mutual savings banks	.7	1.2	1.9
Insurance	9.1	15.6	6.0
Life	2.7	4.6	2.7
Nonlife	6.4	10.9	22.7
Finance, n.e.c.	.3	.5	——
State and local gov't agencies...	6.5	11.1	13.8

Note: Details may not add to totals because of rounding.
[1] Includes state and local obligations held by state and local government agencies.
Source: "A Quarterly Presentation of Flow of Funds, Saving and Investment," *Federal Reserve Bulletin*, August 1959.

TABLE 22–4
ANNUAL FLOWS INTO STATE AND LOCAL OBLIGATIONS, 1954-1958
(BILLIONS OF DOLLARS)

Sector	1954 $	1954 %	1955 $	1955 %	1956 $	1956 %	1957 $	1957 %	1958 $	1958 %
Net issues [1]	4.4	100.0	3.5	100.0	3.3	100.0	4.9	100.0	5.7	100.0
State										
Local										
Net acquisitions	4.4	100.0	3.5	100.0	3.3	100.0	4.9	100.0	5.7	100.0
Consumer	1.0	22.7	2.1	60.0	1.9	51.5	2.3	46.9	1.5	26.3
Commercial banks	1.8	40.9	.1	2.8	.2	6.1	1.0	20.4	2.6	45.6
Mutual savings banks ...	.2	4.5	*	*	*	*	*	*	*	*
Insurance	1.3	29.5	.9	25.7	1.0	30.3	.8	16.3	1.0	17.5
Life	.5	11.4	.2	5.7	.2	6.1	.1	2.0	.3	5.3
Nonlife [2]	.7	15.9	.7	20.0	.7	21.2	.7	14.3	.7	12.3
Finance, n.e.c. [3]	—.1	(2.9)	*	*	—.2	(6.1)	.2	4.1	*	*
State and local gov't.....	.2	4.5	.4	11.4	.5	15.2	.5	10.2	.5	8.8

*Less than $50 million.
Note: Details may not add to totals because of rounding.
[1] Includes state and local obligations held by state and local government agencies.
[2] Mainly fire and casualty companies.
[3] Mainly brokers and dealers.
Source: "A Quarterly Presentation of Flow of Funds, Saving and Investment," *Federal Reserve Bulletin*, August 1959.

with after-tax yields on corporate bonds and Federal obligations, and it is to the banks' advantage to invest in such obligations. The banks' pattern of annual flows into the market for state and local obligations is more volatile than that of the other classes of investors. In 1954 and 1958, the banks supplied more than 40 per cent of total annual flows, but in 1956, the banks supplied only 6 per cent of the total annual flow. It will be recalled that 1954 and 1958 were recession years, and that 1956 and 1957 were years of economic boom. It will also be recalled that banks reduced their holdings of Federal obligations by $9.7 billion during 1955 and 1956. Obviously, the demand for business loans has priority over state and local obligations, as well as over Federal obligations, but to a lesser degree. The banks did not liquidate state and local obligations; instead they merely stopped acquiring such obligations. Commercial banks enter the market in periods of easy money and withdraw from the market in periods of tight money. The reverse is true for individuals.

INSURANCE COMPANIES. At the end of 1958, the combined holdings of state and local obligations by the life and nonlife insurance companies amounted to $9.1 billion, or 15.6 per cent of state and local obligations outstanding. The data show that the holdings of the nonlife insurance companies were much more important than those of life insurance companies, although the latter held more than four times the amount of financial assets. At the end of 1958, less than 3 per cent of life insurance company financial assets were invested in state and local obligations, whereas more than 22 per cent of nonlife insurance company assets were so invested.

The difference in amount of holdings of life and nonlife insurance companies is explained primarily by the difference in tax treatment. Most of the nonlife insurance companies pay the regular 52 per cent corporate tax rate on bond interest income. Up to 1959, life insurance companies paid the regular 52 per cent corporate tax rate, but only on 15 per cent of their investment income. Therefore, the effective tax rate on bond interest income earned by life insurance companies was only 7.8 per cent. However, in 1959 Congress passed a bill increasing the 1958 Federal income tax payments of life insurance companies by about 60 per cent. According to the new formula under which they are taxed, life insurance companies pay the regular 52 per cent corporate tax rate on some 21 to 22 per cent of their investment income. The higher effective tax rate will probably result in larger annual flows of life insurance company investible funds into the market for state and local obligations.

Both life insurance companies and nonlife insurance companies were steady suppliers of funds to the market for state and local obligations. The data show that nonlife insurance companies supplied $700 million in each of the years, and, in relation to total annual flows, these companies supplied more than their share of the total amount outstanding. The life insurance company annual flows were not as uniform, ranging from $500 million in 1954 to only $100 million in 1957. During 1957, life insurance companies were able to invest funds in corporate securities at more than 5 per cent, so that companies tended to shift funds to the market for corporate securities. Now that life insurance companies are taxed at a higher rate, the annual flows into state and local obligations will probably be more constant.

STATE AND LOCAL GOVERNMENT. The holdings of state and local obligations by the state and local government sector represent the investments of state and local retirement and pension funds. The flow of such funds into these obligations cannot be explained by tax considerations because the retirement and pension funds are not subject to Federal income tax. Legal restrictions and political considerations or pressures explain the steady flow of funds from this sector into state and local obligations. The annual flow data show a slight upward trend. If interest rates continue to be high, the pressures will become greater on retirement and pension funds, forcing them to increase the size of their annual flows into state and local obligations.

OTHER SECTORS. Among the other sectors, the corporate business sector is probably the most important supplier of funds to the market for state and local obligations. If the markets for such obligations were more active, and if a larger proportion of such obligations were of short maturity, the corporate business sector would probably be a major investor in the market. At the end of fiscal 1957, only $216 million of state gross short-term debt was outstanding, and only $1,982 million of local gross short-term debt was outstanding. Data for the last few years do not show any trend toward a greater proportion of short-term debt. In fact, in terms of percentages, short-term state and local debt has declined in importance. However, it is possible that in the future some of the larger issuers may issue more short-term debt to attract more funds from the corporate business sector.

Unless savings institutions are required to pay higher corporate income taxes, these institutions will probably continue to be relatively unimportant in the market for state and local obligations. The data show that savings institutions held only $700 million of such obligations at the end of 1958.

Underwriting and Dealing in State and Local Government Obligations

The description of investment banking in Chapter 19 must be modified to fit the market for state and local obligations. Prior to the Banking Act of 1933 (Glass-Steagall Act), a large number of commercial banks and their securities affiliates were active in the underwriting and distribution of both corporate and government obligations. The Banking Act of 1933 prohibited commercial banks from underwriting and dealing in corporate securities, but it did not prohibit them from performing investment banking functions relating to direct obligations of the United States Government and the general obligations of any state or political subdivision thereof. The significance of this difference in regulation is that the investment banking industry includes commercial banks as well as specialized investment banking firms. The majority of underwriting is accomplished at a cost of less than 1½ per cent. Some investment banking firms and commercial banks specialize in state and local obligations. Many of the larger commercial banks act as underwriters and distributors of state, municipal, and public housing agency bonds and notes. The commercial banks participate with the non-commercial investment banking firms in underwriting and distributing state and local obligations. Also, commercial banks serve as dealers in and distributors of non-guaranteed Federal obligations and securities of the International Bank for Reconstruction and Development.

The facts collected in Robinson's study of the secondary market in state and local obligations indicated that the liquidation of an appreciable volume of these obligations may require considerable time as well as some price concession. Compared with the markets for other types of securities, the frequency and range of price movements in state and local obligations are greater.

Outlook

As noted in earlier discussion, the basic forces underlying the growth in the volume of state and local obligations will continue to operate for many years. However, there is uncertainty as to the future flow of funds into this market. The future value of tax-exemption is uncertain. With the passage of time more and more funds are being channeled through institutions that are not concerned with tax-exempt securities. More and more ways are being developed to minimize Federal tax payments. These forces have narrowed the spread between yields on tax-exempt securities and yields on full taxable securities. Although the change in the yield structure may attract more funds into tax-exempt securities, it may also lead to a change in the tax status of state and local obligations. In recent years the issuers of these obligations have gained a smaller advantage in terms of lower interest costs than the Federal government has lost in tax revenue. Although politics may block any immediate change in their tax-exempt status, the economics of the market warrants that serious consideration be given to its elimination. It can be argued that the Federal government could provide a subsidy to the issuers of state and local obligations, and finance this outlay with increased revenue. Another uncertain factor is marketability. If the investors' preference for marketability increases, and secondary market facilities for trading in state and local obligations does not provide additional marketability, some investors will reduce their acquisitions of state and local obligations. In summary, it is very difficult to be very precise on the future outlook of the market for state and local obligations.

QUESTIONS

1. Describe the present system of managing the Treasury's cash balances. Why is such management necessary?
2. Define "Federal obligations" as the term is used in the flow-of-funds accounts.
3. Summarize briefly the changes in level and composition of the public debt of the United States Government since 1929.
4. Describe briefly the major characteristics of direct Federal obligations.
5. Set forth the ownership pattern of Federal obligations.
6. Discuss the corporate business sector's investment in Federal obligations as it relates to present ownership and annual flows.
7. Discuss commercial bank investment in Federal obligations as it relates to present ownership and annual flows.
8. Discuss the insurance sector's investment in Federal obligations as it relates to present ownership and annual flows.
9. What factors suggest that the ownership pattern of Federal obligations may be stabilizing? What factors might lead to greater instability in ownership?
10. Describe briefly the specialized dealer market in Federal obligations. What are its strong and weak points?
11. Illustrate the variety in state and local obligations, making certain to define carefully the major classifications of state and local obligations.
12. Compare the ownership pattern of Federal obligations with that of state and local obligations, and explain the differences.
13. Describe briefly the structure of the investment banking industry as it relates to state and local obligations.

ADDITIONAL READING

Abbott, C. C. *The Federal Debt — Structure and Impact.* New York: Twentieth Century Fund, 1953.

Buchanan, James M. *The Public Finances.* Homewood, Ill.: Richard D. Irwin, Inc., 1960.

———. *Public Principles of Public Debt.* Homewood, Ill.: Richard D. Irwin, Inc., 1958.

Colm, G., assisted by H. O. Nicol. *Essays in Public Finance and Fiscal Policy.* New York: Oxford University Press, 1955.

Due, John F. *Government Finance* (Rev. ed.). Homewood, Ill.: Richard D. Irwin, Inc., 1959.

Fabricant, Soloman. *The Trend of Government Activity in the United States Since 1900.* N.B.E.R. Study. Princeton, N. J.: Princeton University Press, 1952.

Groves, Harold M. *Financing Government*. (5th ed.) New York: Holt, Rinehart, & Winston, Inc., 1958.

Kimmel, Lewis H. *Federal Budget and Fiscal Policy*. Washington, D.C.: Brookings Institution, 1959. Emphasizes change in American attitude toward government taxing, spending, and borrowing.

Lindholm, Richard W. *Public Finance and Fiscal Policy*. New York: Pitman Publishing Co., 1950.

————, ed. *Public Finance*. The Committee on Public Finance. New York: Pitman Publishing Co., 1959.

Mortstein, Marx F. *The Organization of Financial Functions in the Federal Government, USA*. Washington, D.C.: Government Printing Office, 1959.

Murphy, Henry C. *National Debt in War and Transition*. New York: McGraw-Hill Book Co., Inc., 1950.

National Tax Foundation. *Facts and Figures on Government Finance*. See latest edition, tenth edition covered period, 1958-1959. New York: Tax Foundation, Inc.

Poole, K. E. *Public Finance and Economic Welfare*. New York: Holt, Rinehart, & Winston, Inc., 1956.

Robinson, Roland I. *Postwar Market for State and Local Government Securities*. N.B.E.R. Study. Princeton, N. J.: Princeton University Press, 1960.

U.S. House of Representatives Committee on Ways and Means. *Public Debt Ceiling and Interest Rate Ceiling on Bonds*. 86th Cong., 1st sess. Washington, D.C.: Government Printing Office, 1959.

U.S. Joint Economic Committee. *Employment, Growth, and Price Levels, Part 6A, The Government's Management of Its Monetary, Fiscal, and Debt Operations*. Hearings, 86th Cong., 1st sess. Washington, D.C.: Government Printing Office, 1959.

————. *A Study of the Dealer Market for Federal Government Securities*, Materials prepared for the use of the Committee. 86th Cong., 2nd sess. Washington, D.C.: Government Printing Office, 1960.

U.S. Secretary of the Treasury. *Annual Report on the State of the Finances*. Washington, D.C.: Government Printing Office. See latest report. In addition to considerable data on all phases of Federal finances, the reports contain messages, letters, and statements of highly placed Treasury officials.

U.S. Treasury Department. *Treasury-Federal Reserve Study of the Government Security Market*, Parts 1-3. Washington, D.C.: Government Printing Office, 1959.

part 6:
Rest-of-the-world sector

N the flow-of-funds system of accounts, the rest-of-the-world sector "comprises the residents and governments of countries outside the United States and its territories and possessions. It includes international organizations (such as the International Monetary Fund, the International Bank for Reconstruction and Development, and the United Nations) and employees of these organizations who are not citizens of the United States. The sector account is consolidated; it records only transactions of the rest of the world with the United States and not transactions within the rest-of-the-world sector, that is, within and among other countries.*

Financial transactions are behind the flow of goods and services among countries. The financing of exports is one of the more important factors influencing the growth and development of export markets, especially when many exporting countries are competing in the same markets. For example, if United States exporters are attempting to sell industrial machinery on two-year installment contracts and exporters in certain other countries are offering comparable machinery at comparable prices on five-year installment contracts, the attractiveness of the five-year credit terms might be the deciding factor. If the situation were reversed, and it was a sellers' market, importers would have to bid aggressively for the scarce goods, and the problem of financing would be shifted to the importers. Those importers unable to arrange financing would simply be out of the market. Commercial banks are the most important financial institutions in financing the movement of goods in international trade as well as in domestic trade. Many countries have established public agencies to provide short- and intermediate-term financing to exporters and to importers who purchase goods in those countries. The United States has the Export-Import Bank, which makes loans to finance rest-of-the-world purchases from the United States.

Long-term or permanent investment in foreign countries is accomplished by the purchase of credit and equity market instruments and

* "A Quarterly Presentation of Flow of Funds, Saving and Investment," *Federal Reserve Bulletin*, August 1959, p. 848.

through direct investment abroad. These financial transactions are carried out in the capital and foreign exchange markets, and underlying these transactions is the actual flow of goods and services among countries. Direct investment abroad represents the increase in asset value of foreign companies or branches that are controlled by domestic firms. The increase in asset value may arise through foreign-retained earnings as well as through the international movement of capital. American firms and individuals have promoted considerable foreign investment by the purchase of foreign securities and by direct investment, and the United States government has sponsored various loan and assistance programs. In recent years, Congress has established the Development Loan Fund and the Inter-American Development Bank to promote a larger flow of funds into foreign investment.

To supplement financial organizations that are provided by individual countries, there have been developed during the postwar period four international financial organizations: The International Monetary Fund, the International Bank for Reconstruction and Developmet, the International Finance Corporation, and the International Development Association.

Our purpose in Part 6 is to examine the functions of domestic and international financial institutions as they relate to the flow of goods, services, and capital between the United States and the rest-of-the-world sector.

23: Financing international trade and investment

BECAUSE of the length of our introduction to Part 6, only a few additional comments will be made before we consider specific topics. In order to establish the importance of trade and investment and the financial relationships between the United States and the rest of the world, three topics are considered: the basis of international trade, the significance of trade to the United States, and the financial statements of the rest-of-the-world sector. The body of the chapter deals with three major subjects: the New York foreign exchange market, the financing of exports and imports, and the development and operation of international financial organizations.

BASIS OF INTERNATIONAL TRADE AND INVESTMENT

The basic economic principles underlying the flow of goods, services, and capital between countries are similar to those governing the flow of goods, services, and capital within a single country. Take our own country as an example. The Midwest farm belt has a natural advantage in the production of certain food products, and it is to the advantage of this region to specialize in the production of these goods and to exchange surplus production for other goods and services. Conceivably, the New England region could clear additional land and, by using the most modern methods of farm production, produce food products in ample supply to feed the population concentrated in New England. However, the economic cost would be high in relation to the cost incurred in producing the same products in the Midwest farm belt. Instead of attempting to be self-sufficient, the New England region can realize a higher level of production and income by concentrating on the economic pursuits of which it is more capable, considering the supply of natural and human resources, climate, and potential markets. For many years, New England accounted for the major portion of textiles and shoes produced in the United States, and exchanged the surplus production of these goods for food and other products through the market mechanism. Using the same line of reasoning, it is conceivable that coffee could be produced in the United States, but the cost would be excessive in comparison with the costs incurred in Brazil and other coffee-producing countries, to say nothing of possible loss in quality of the product. The natural coffee-producing countries can produce large amounts of coffee in excess of their own needs and can use the proceeds earned from coffee exports to finance the importation of other goods and services.

Even if a country or a region within a country were capable of producing all goods and services more efficiently than all other countries or regions within that country, specialization and trade would still be advantageous. To use a simple analogy, assume that a high-powered business executive is a genius and is capable of performing all tasks within his firm more efficiently than all other employees. Realizing that it takes time to make good decisions, he would have to sacrifice time from decision making to perform other tasks, such as typing his own letters. Since there is an extreme scarcity of people capable of good decision making, the high-powered executive would make the greatest contribution to the firm by restricting his activities to decision making and by allowing other employees to do the typing and other tasks. In economic terms, he has an absolute advantage in all tasks, but he has the greatest comparative advantage in his ability to make decisions. The same type of reasoning, but in a much more complicated form, can be used to support the proposition that countries or regions should specialize in the production of those goods and services for which they have the greatest comparative advantage and should exchange surpluses for other goods and services. Specialization and international trade promote a higher level of output for the world economy and make the economic systems of the participating countries highly interdependent.

If countries are to be willing to specialize or to concentrate in the production of certain goods and services, they must be reasonably confident that foreign markets for these goods and services can be established and maintained over the foreseeable future. Otherwise, those countries would not be able to earn enough foreign exchange to finance the importation of vital goods and services that are not produced in their respective domestic economies. It is a fact that all countries impose various types of barriers to foreign trade to protect new industries, declining industries, and domestic wage and price structures, and to provide a degree of self-sufficiency in the event of war and loss of imports. Fortunately, the barriers are not so great as to make impossible a large volume of world trade and a reasonable flow of public and private capital between various countries. Also, the current trend appears to be reduction rather than expansion in trade barriers.

The flow of private capital to and from the United States is affected by interest rates and economic and political considerations. A low level of interest rates in the United States prompts many Americans to shift short-term funds to capital markets in the rest-of-the-world sector that provide short-term investment outlets at higher yields. Foreign commercial banks, corporations, and individuals holding liquid dollar assets would also be prompted to shift funds out of the domestic capital and money markets to foreign markets. In fact, Americans and foreigners might borrow funds in the United States and shift those funds into foreign markets. Although the risks associated with long-term investments — either through securities or through direct ownership of foreign companies — are normally greater than those associated with domestic investment, many American commercial banks, corporations, and individuals believe that lower material and labor costs and more favorable tax treatment are sufficient to offset the assumption of additional risks. The flow of public or government loans and grants is prompted by our concern with military security and the development of the so-called underdeveloped nations.

SIGNIFICANCE OF TRADE TO THE UNITED STATES*

International trade is important to the United States' economy. During the period 1954-1958, the rest-of-the-world purchases of goods and services from the United States ranged between $17.6 billion and $26.3 billion. (See Table 23-1.) In each of the years 1956, 1957, and 1958, this sector's purchases exceeded $22 billion. Although these purchases represent only 6 per cent of our gross national product, the loss of these foreign sales would affect domestic production and income by much more than 6 per cent. In recent years the sales of goods and services by the rest-of-the-world sector to the United States have been slightly less than the sector's purchases of goods and services from the United States. That sector's net purchases of goods and services ranged from $1.5 billion to $5.3 billion during the 1954-1958 period. Its largest net purchases occurred in 1957, the year of the Suez crisis.

Many of the imported goods are critical components in our productive process and our military program, and if their supply were cut off, a sizeable contraction and shifts in production would be necessary. As an example of the importance of certain raw material imports, we note that in 1957 the following relationships prevailed between domestic production and imports: iron ore, 75 per cent to 25 per cent; lead, 38 per cent to 62 per cent; bauxite, 21 per cent to 79 per cent; cobalt, 16 per cent to 84 per cent; manganese, 15 per cent to 85 per cent; chromite, 7 per cent to 93 per

*See Edward M. Bernstein, "International Effects of U.S. Economic Policy," Study Paper No. 16 in U.S. Joint Economic Committee, Study of Employment, Growth, and Price Levels, 86th Cong., 2nd sess. (Washington, D.C.: Government Printing Office, 1960).

cent; nickel, 6 per cent to 94 per cent; and tin, all of which was imported. When we realize the importance of all these raw materials in the total production of goods and services, and particularly in the production of military hardware, the importance of trade is self-evident.

The rest-of-the-world sector's purchases of goods and services from the United States are closely related to our purchases of goods and services from that sector, because our purchases create the supply of dollar exchange that is used by that sector to finance its purchases from the United States. During the late 1940's the United States had a very large export surplus, which was financed by loans and grants from the Federal Government to the rest-of-the-world sector, the flow of private capital from the United States to the rest-of-the-world sector, and foreign sales of gold to the United States. All of these measures made additional dollar exchange available to the rest-of-the-world sector. As a result of monetary adjustments in almost all of the trading nations and the Korean hostilities, the pattern of trade changed in the early 1950's and our large export surplus became smaller. The outflow of private capital and government grants and loans continued, with the result that the rest-of-the-world sector was able to build up its gold and dollar holdings. The trade pattern has changed to such an extent that our export surplus has proved inadequate. The resultant build-up in foreigners' liquid assets and drain on our gold supply has been a major news item ever since 1958.

The modern trading nations are competing vigorously with United States manufacturers. Furthermore, some of these nations continue to discriminate against imports from the United States. As an offset to the change in the trade pattern, the capital outflow began to fall off slightly in 1958 and 1959, and much pressure was exerted on the more highly developed nations in the rest-of-the-world sector to assume greater responsibility in financing their military establishments and the economic development of the so-called underdeveloped countries.

In summary, the financing of international trade and investment is important to the United States. Our productive process is dependent on vital raw material imports and on the rest-of-the-world market. In 1959, our trade position commanded attention because the combined balance-of-payments deficit was $3,980 million. This deficit was matched by net purchases of United States gold ($1,076 million) and short-term financial assets ($2,904 million) by foreigners. The balance-of-payments deficit continued to persist in 1960, but an increase in United States exports will probably reduce the future size of the deficit.

REST-OF-THE-WORLD SECTOR STATEMENTS

The rest-of-the-world sector's statement of sources and uses of funds and of financial assets and liabilities are shown respectively in Tables 23-1 and 23-2. The data serve to summarize some of the points already covered, and to emphasize the financial relationships between the United States and the rest of the world. In Table 23-1, it may be seen that the sector's net purchases of goods and services during the period 1954-1958, were more than offset by net unilateral receipts in 1954, 1955, and 1958. The sector had a current surplus of $100 million in 1958. The note appended to the table shows that during this period the sector received annually approximately $3 billion of unilateral transfers in kind, consisting of grants in the form

TABLE 23–1
SOURCES AND USES OF FUNDS OF THE REST-OF-THE-WORLD SECTOR, 1954-1958,
END OF 1958
(BILLIONS OF DOLLARS)

	1954	1955	1956	1957	1958
Net purchases of goods and services	1.5	1.6	3.4	5.3	1.8
Purchases of goods and services [1]	17.6	19.5	23.2	26.3	22.8
Sales of goods and services	16.1	17.9	19.8	20.9	21.0
Net unilateral receipts [1]	2.0	2.1	1.9	1.9	1.9
Current surplus	.4	.4	—1.5	—3.5	.1
Net financial investment	.3	*	—2.1	—4.2	—.4
Net acquisition of financial assets	1.8	1.5	1.5	—.1	3.5
Gold	.3	.1	—.3	—.8	2.3
U. S. currency and demand deposits....	.1	*	.2	.2	*
Time deposits	.6	—.1	—.1	*	.9
Federal obligations	.2	1.1	.8	.2	*
Other credit market instruments [2]	.3	—.1	.5	.4	—.1
Miscellaneous financial assets [3]	.2	.7	.4	—.1	.3
Net increase in liabilities	1.5	1.5	3.6	4.1	3.8
Securities	.2	*	.4	.5	1.2
Loans [4]	.2	.4	.6	.9	1.1
Miscellaneous [5]	1.1	1.2	2.6	2.8	1.4
Discrepancy [6]	.2	.4	.6	.7	.4
Memo: Unilateral transfers in kind [7].......	3.5	2.8	3.0	2.9	2.9

*Less than $50 million.
[1] Excludes unilateral transfers in kind, which are shown in memo.
[2] Corporate securities, security credit, and commercial paper.
[3] Direct investments, unidentified assets, I.M.F. holdings of special United States notes, and miscellaneous deposits.
[4] Security credit, bank loans, n.e.c., and other loans (mainly from the United States Government).
[5] Direct investments, foreign currency and deposits held by United States domestic sectors, and other liabilities.
[6] "Errors and omissions" in United States balance-of-payments statement.
[7] Grants in the form of goods and services by United States Government and private individuals and institutions.

Source: "A Quarterly Presentation of Flow of Funds, Saving and Investment," *Federal Reserve Bulletin,* August 1959.

of goods and services by the United States Government and private individuals and institutions.

In theory, the sector's net financial investment should equal its current surplus, but because of errors and omissions in the United States balance-of-payments, there was a statistical discrepancy in each of the years. The data show that the sector's net acquisitions of financial assets in 1958 totaled $3.5 billion and its net increase in liabilities in 1958 was $3.8 billion, resulting in net financial disinvestment of $400 million. The sector's net acquisitions of financial assets were concentrated in three types of assets: gold, time deposits, and miscellaneous deposits, the latter consisting of direct investments, unidentified assets, International Monetary Fund holdings of special United States notes, and other liabilities. Its net increase in liabilities involved securities, loans, direct investments, foreign currency and deposits held by United States domestic sectors, and other liabilities.

In Table 23-2, it may be seen that at the end of 1958 the rest-of-the-world sector held $49 billion of financial assets and its total liabiliteis vis-à-vis the United States domestic sectors were $52.3 billion. The financial asset "gold" represents the holdings of international institutions and foreign central banks and governments, excluding the U. S. S. R. The gold constitutes the monetary reserves of the rest-of-the-world sector. The present stock of gold reflects the net foreign gold output plus net U. S. S. R. gold exports, less consumption and net increase in private holdings as well as gold transactions with the United States. However, it should be noted that the gold flows shown in Table 23-1 reflect only transactions with the United States. The $4.7 billion in United States currency and demand deposits represent the working cash balances of foreign commercial banks, corporations, individuals, central banks, and international financial institutions. During the period 1945-1958, the sector's year-end holdings of United States currency and demand deposits were not more than $4.8 billion nor less than $4.2 billion. The sector's holdings of time deposits, Federal obligations, and commercial paper represent interest-earning liquid-dollar assets. The level and composition of the sector's holdings of such assets depends on the characteristics of yields in the United States vis-à-vis the characteristics of yields in other major trading nations. Quarterly data on sources and uses of funds show that the rest-of-the-world sector acquired $1.1 billion of Federal obligations in the last two quarters of 1958, reflecting the relative attractiveness of the higher yields on Federal obligations. The data in Table 23-2 show that the sector held $6 billion of corporate stock and a much lesser amount of corporate bonds. The sector's direct investment in the United States at the end of 1958 was slightly less than $8.5 billion. Excluding direct investments and corporate stock, the holdings of liquid-dollar assets of the rest-of-the-world sector exceeded $15 billion. As noted earlier, it is possible for private foreign holdings to be transferred

TABLE 23-2
ASSETS AND LIABILITIES OF THE REST-OF-THE-WORLD SECTOR, END OF 1958
(BILLIONS OF DOLLARS)

	Dollars	*Per cent*
Total financial assets [1]	49.0	100.0
Gold [2]	19.3	39.4
U. S. currency and demand deposits	4.7	9.6
Deposits of foreign banks	1.9	3.9
Other deposits and currency	2.8	5.7
Time deposits	2.5	5.1
Credit and equity market instruments	14.0	28.6
Federal obligations	6.8	13.9
Corporate stock [3]	6.0	12.2
Other [4]	1.2	2.4
Miscellaneous [5]	8.5	17.3
Total liabilities [6]	52.3	100.0
Credit and equity market instruments [7]	20.0	38.2
Bonds [3]	5.0	9.6
Bank loans, n.e.c.	2.6	5.0
Other loans [8]	12.2	23.3
Miscellaneous	32.3	61.8
U. S. subscription to I.M.F. and I.B.R.D.	3.4	6.5
Other [9]	28.9	55.3

Note: Details may not add to totals because of rounding.

[1] Excludes amounts for unidentified assets (in miscellaneous category) for which estimates of amounts outstanding are unavailable.

[2] Holdings of international institutions and foreign control banks and governments, excluding U. S. S. R.

[3] At estimated market value.

[4] Commercial paper, corporate bonds, and security credit.

[5] Mainly direct investments in U. S., deposits with U. S. agencies of foreign banks, and notes of I.M.F.

[6] Excludes amounts for corporate stock and unidentified liabilities (in miscellaneous category) for which estimates of amounts outstanding are not available.

[7] Includes security credit not shown separately.

[8] Predominantly U. S. Government loans.

[9] U. S. direct investment abroad and holdings of foreign currency.

Source: "A Quarterly Presentation of Flow of Funds, Saving and Investment," *Federal Reserve Bulletin*, August 1959.

to foreign central banks, and it is possible for the foreign central banks to purchase gold from the United States Treasury. Since these liquid-dollar assets represent working balances and are needed to support the present volume of world trade and investment, it is most unlikely that such large transfers will occur. Probably less than 15 per cent of foreign short-term dollar balances in the United States are subject to interest-rate arbitrage. However, if foreigners lost confidence in the strength of the dollar, such transfers and gold purchases would occur. It is important that the United

States maintain reasonable stability in the purchasing power of the dollar. The argument that the United States should return to the gold standard in order to pose a continuing threat to ill-advised fiscal policy is rather shallow when it is realized that foreign central banks already pose a sufficient threat.

Approximately 80 per cent of the sector's liabilities are concentrated in United States Government loans, United States direct investment abroad, and holdings of foreign currency. United States domestic sectors hold $5 billion of foreign bonds. The United States commercial banks had $2.6 billion in loans outstanding to economic units in this sector. The other major liability item represented the United States subscription to the International Monetary Fund and the International Bank for Reconstruction and Development. In the latter part of this chapter, we shall take note of the increases in these subscriptions.

FOREIGN EXCHANGE MARKETS*

Money has been introduced into the economic systems of nearly all countries, and financial institutions have developed within those systems to facilitate both financial and nonfinancial transactions, including the settlement of claims. Inasmuch as all countries have neither adopted a common monetary unit nor defined identically their respective monetary units, the financial aspects of international financial and nonfinancial transactions are more complex than those of domestic transactions. Also, nearly all countries exercise complex controls over the buying and selling of foreign exchange. The term "foreign exchange" refers to short-term monetary claims on foreigners or on foreign banks, expressed in terms of foreign currency.

In response to the needs of importers, exporters, investors, and tourists, complex and efficient foreign exchange markets have developed to bring together the buyers and sellers of foreign exchange. Many American firms and individuals receive foreign exchange in payment for goods, services, and financial assets sold abroad, and many American firms and individuals must secure foreign exchange to pay for those items acquired abroad, and to make remittances to foreign countries. The proportion of payments to and from an individual foreign country that is made in foreign exchange depends upon the relative importance of the country, the strength of its currency, customs relating to particular transactions, nature and extent of exchange controls, and the relative stage of development of the country's financial system.

*Much of the material presented in this section is based on: "The New York Foreign Exchange Market, I, II," *Monthly Review of Credit and Business Conditions*, Federal Reserve Bank of New York, November and December, 1957. Much of the same information is also available in a monograph: Alan R. Holmes, *The New York Foreign Exchange Market*, Federal Reserve Bank of New York, March 1959.

Americans receiving foreign exchange desire to convert their holdings into dollars, and Americans having to make payments or remittances in foreign exchange must convert dollars into foreign exchange. The price of a foreign country's monetary unit expressed in terms of United States dollars is referred to as the foreign rate of exchange for that country's money. Foreign exchange rates are the various prices at which dollars can be exchanged or converted into foreign money, and foreign money can be converted into dollars. The determinants of the level and structure of foreign exchange rates will be examined following a description of. the structure and operation of the New York foreign exchange market. Of course, if all payments to and receipts from the rest-of-the-world sector were carried out solely in dollars, a foreign exchange market would not be needed in the United States, but such markets would be needed in the rest of the world. However, it is a fact that many American firms and individuals are involved in one way or another with some form of foreign exchange activity, and the New York foreign exchange market is a vital part of our financial system.

The major function of foreign exchange markets is to facilitate the conversion or exchange of one country's money into the moneys of other countries. Since the conversion or exchange function is essentially a banking function, commercial banks are the major financial institutions in foreign exchange markets. Commercial banks maintain inventory positions in foreign exchange, and the ultimate users of foreign exchange generally deal directly with the banks. As a result of the banks' dealings with commercial customers, inventories may get out of line, and banks adjust their inventories by trading with each other and with foreign banks. Generally, foreign exchange brokers bring together buyers and sellers in the inter-bank segment of the foreign exchange markets. Central banks and government-sponsored stabilization and exchange control agencies also participate in foreign exchange markets of some countries.

Organization of the New York Foreign Exchange Market

American firms and individuals who are the ultimate users and suppliers of foreign exchange in the New York market contact commercial banks when dealing in foreign exchange. Although many banks handle foreign exchange transactions for their customers, practically all such transactions are channeled through a relatively small number of large banks because only the larger banks in the major trading areas can afford to staff capable foreign exchange departments and to maintain the necessary number and volume of deposit accounts in foreign countries. Approximately 23 New York commercial banks maintain deposits abroad to facilitate foreign exchange transactions, and probably fewer than half of these banks account for the bulk of the foreign exchange business of American firms and individuals. Other financial institutions that are involved and located in the New York foreign exchange market include agencies of foreign banks and specialized foreign exchange dealers. The latter group deal primarily in foreign bank notes rather than in deposits held abroad. There are only eight foreign exchange brokers involved in the New York inter-bank market in foreign exchange.

There are other financial institutions involved in the market, but they are not located in New York City. New York banks are in almost constant contact with foreign banks, and extensive trading is carried on between them, with the initiative for such trading originating from either group. Foreign central banks and exchange authorities also execute transactions in the market. The domestic and foreign networks of financial institutions are connected by the most modern means of communication, including direct telephone and teletype connections.

Trading in a particular foreign exchange in the New York market reflects the supply of, and the demand for, that exchange by Americans as well as the relationships between the dollar and that foreign exchange in the other exchange markets throughout the world. Given freedom of movement of short-term capital among the many foreign exchange markets, arbitrage operations tend to eliminate differentials among markets. An arbitrage operation is essentially that of buying foreign exchange in one market and selling it in another market at a slight price differential. The transactions themselves tend to bring price relationships back into line.

Instruments of the Foreign Exchange Market

As noted above, foreign exchange consists of short-term monetary claims on foreign banks or foreigners expressed in terms of foreign currencies. Specifically, foreign exchange consists of deposits held in banks abroad and various types of foreign bills of exchange, including commercial and bankers' bills and acceptances. Under the provisions of the Negotiable Instruments Act, which was patterned after the Bills of Exchange Act in England, and was adopted by all states, a bill of exchange is defined as "an unconditional order in writing addressed by one person to another, signed by the person giving it, requiring the person to whom it is addressed to pay on demand or at a fixed or determinable future time a sum certain in money to order or to bearer." A credit instrument that conforms to this definition is a negotiable instrument and passes from one person to another very much like money.

Commercial bills are used in both domestic and international trade. In the latter, a commercial bill arises when an exporter draws a bill or draft directly on the importer for the amount of the export, naming himself as the payee. A bill of lading, invoice, shipping and insurance papers, and other legal documents would be attached to the draft. To get possession of the bill of lading and thereby take possession of the imported goods, the importer would have to pay the amount specified if it were a sight draft or accept it if it were a time draft. To accept, the importer would indicate on the face of the bill that it was accepted and payable at a designated bank; he would also sign his name and date the acceptance. The accepted draft would then be returned to the drawer, who might either hold the accepted draft until maturity or discount it in the market. In practice, commercial banks handle such transactions for both buyers and sellers. Part of the supply of foreign exchange in the New York foreign exchange market consists of such bills of exchange drawn by Americans and expressed in terms of foreign currencies. It is possible for foreigners to make payments by checks drawn in their own currencies. In this case the payees would convert the checks into American dollars and the American banks would thereby build up credits in their foreign bank accounts.

A banker's bill or acceptance is similar to a commercial bill or acceptance in form; the major difference is that the banker's bill of exchange is drawn on and accepted by a bank. Since exporters prefer the credit of a bank over that of an importer, the volume of bankers' bills exceeds that of commercial bills. The procedure that would be followed in using a banker's acceptance is as follows: An exporter or seller would draw a draft on the basis of a letter of credit drawn up between the buyer and the buyer's bank. This letter of credit would be forwarded to the seller. Assuming that the draft was drawn in accordance with the terms set forth in the letter of credit, the drawee bank would pay the amount specified if it was a sight draft, or accept it if it was a time draft. The drawee or accepting bank would receive a fee for issuing the letter of credit. Generally, the bank would expect to pay the drafts with funds provided by the buyer. In practice, none of the above forms of foreign exchange accounts for a very large portion of the total supply of foreign exchange in New York markets because most bills of exchange drawn in connection with our imports and exports are expressed in dollars rather than in foreign currencies. However, these dollar bills of exchange are of great importance in foreign exchange markets abroad and comprise part of the total supply and demand for dollars in those markets.

The greatest volume of transactions in foreign exchange involves cable and mail transfers of bank balances held abroad. American banks hold deposit accounts in commercial banks abroad, and the foreign banks hold deposit accounts in American banks. A transfer by an American bank is accomplished by sending an order to a commercial bank abroad, directing that bank to debit the account of the party who sold the foreign exchange to the American bank, and to credit the account of the party who purchased the exchange. For example, assume that an American exporting firm had built up its account in a London bank beyond what was required, and it decided to transfer some of its excess deposit balances abroad to its depositary banks in the United States. To accomplish this transfer, the export firm would offer for sale in the New York foreign exchange market a cable sterling transfer. Assume that the buyer of the pound sterling exchange is a New York bank. To complete the transaction the American export firm will send a cable transfer to its London bank, ordering that bank to debit the firm's account and to credit the New York bank's account. The net effects of such a transaction are a change in ownership of the London deposit balance, and an increase in the firm's deposit balance in its depositary banks in the United States. The cable transfer could have been made at the time goods were originally sold in London by ordering the London importers to make payment to the London account of the New York bank. By building up its account, the New York bank would now be in a position to sell pound sterling exchange to American importers.

Assume that a United States importer needs to build up his account in a London bank. He would enter the market on the demand side of sterling balances, and would pay an equivalent amount of dollars to the New York bank that sold the pound sterling exchange. This bank would direct its London correspondent bank to create a sterling balance to the credit of the importer, and to debit its own deposit account held abroad in London. The importer could avoid going through a foreign bank by purchasing a draft on the New York bank's London balance, and mailing the draft directly to the London exporter, who would simply cash the draft in a London bank.

The examples cited above illustrate only a few of the many possible ways in which American banks could build up or replenish deposit balances with foreign banks. We shall do no more than mention other methods. First, the American bank could have purchased foreign balances owned by other American banks. Second, the American banks, in the aggregate, could replenish their balances abroad by selling dollar exchange to foreign banks. The foreign banks might need to build up their inventories of dollar exchange during the same period that American banks need to build up their deposits abroad. Three, American banks could also replenish balances abroad by purchasing foreign bills of exchange, travelers' checks, dividend warrants, bond coupons, and other financial instruments.

The foreign exchange trading rooms of the New York banks constitute the nerve center or core of the New York foreign exchange market. Inasmuch as the banks operate on both the supply and demand side of the market, the banks tend to serve as a clearing house where liabilities to foreigners are offset against claims on foreigners. The operations of a bank trader are well summarized in the following statement:*

> Each bank trader is confronted by a constant flow of offers of, and bids for, foreign exchange not only from commercial interests, but also from other banks through the interbank market, and by cable from foreign banks. As he sells exchange he must buy in order to make delivery, and as he buys he must sell in order not to accumulate balances. And

*Monthly Review of the Federal Reserve Bank of New York, November 1957, p. 152.

through it all the exchange rate (the price of the commodity in which he deals) is being pushed first one way, then the other, by the changing balance of all the forces that make up supply and demand in the market. The manner in which the foreign exchange traders try to steer a straight course through these constantly changing tides provides a large part of the fascination of the market for its participants and much of its mystery for the layman.

Exchange Rates

Exchange rates are prices of foreign currencies, and are similar to the prices of other commodities. They are subject to market fluctuations as demand and supply conditions change. The establishment of exchange rates between countries having unqualified gold standards was discussed in Chapter 4. Although very few of the major trading countries presently maintain gold standards under which money is convertible freely into gold at fixed prices and gold flows are not restricted, almost all major trading countries have officially declared a parity relationship to either the United States dollar or to gold. Unless the parity relationship is related realistically to basic economic factors such as relative incomes, prices, and interest rates, it cannot be maintained in the absence of exchange controls and regulation over foreign trade and investment. Even under these conditions, an unrealistic parity relationship cannot be maintained indefinitely. Fluctuations in exchange rates reflect relative shifts in the demand for and the supply of exchange, resulting from actual and expected developments relating to seasonal, temporary, and purely random factors. For example, if a country's exports were concentrated within a period of a few months, its currency would probably be traded at a premium during the export season and at a discount during the other months. Political instability is a good example of a possible temporary factor. A condition of political instability causes severe shifts in the flow of capital investments. The flow of new investment capital into the country falls off, and holders of financial assets in that country attempt to shift funds to other countries. Unusually large transactions and accidental bunching of foreign exchange transactions are representative of what is meant by purely random factors.

The degree of fluctuation in exchange rates depends on the strength of the factors noted above, their assessment by traders in foreign exchange, the nature and degree of exchange controls, action by exchange stabilization agencies and central banks, and possible assistance from the International Monetary Fund. Many of the member countries of the International Monetary Fund agree to maintain their exchange rates within 1 per cent either side of their officially declared parity values. The establishment and operation of the Fund are considered in a later section of this chapter.

Role of Monetary Authorities

As noted above, member countries of the International Monetary Fund have agreed to maintain their exchange rates within 1 per cent either side of their official exchange rates. If all countries maintained interconvertibility of their respective monetary units and gold, monetary authorities (central banks) would not have to play an active role in their respective foreign exchange markets in order to maintain stability of exchange rates. Assuming that the exchange rates were realistic and gold reserves were adequate, gold flows would keep the exchange rates within 1 per cent either side of official exchange rates. However, very few countries maintain interconvertibility of their respective monetary units and gold, so that the monetary authorities of many countries must intervene in their respective foreign exchange markets to maintain stability of exchange rates. Since the United States is one of the few countries that does maintain interconvertibility, neither the Federal Reserve nor the Treasury has to intervene in the New York foreign exchange market to influence exchange rates. Therefore, the New York market is strictly a free market. The Federal Reserve Bank of New York restricts its buying and selling of foreign exchange to the execution of orders for the Treasury, other government agencies that must use foreign exchange in their operations, and foreign central bank correspondents. Execution of these orders and continuous contact with the trading banks enable the monetary authorities to observe the operation of some of the basic forces underlying the relationship between the United States and the rest of the world.

Foreign Exchange Quotations

Examples of typical foreign exchange rate quotations are shown in the following tabulation:*

Selling Prices for Bank Transfers in the United States for Payment Abroad,
As Quoted at 4 P.M., January 20, 1961
(in dollars)

Canada (Dollar)	1.00	45-64
England (Pound)	2.8074	
30-day futures	2.8054	
90-day futures	2.8010	
France (Franc)	.2041	

Prices for Foreign Banknotes, as Quoted at 4 P.M. on January 20, 1961
(in dollars)

	Buying	Selling
England (Pound)	2.78	2.83
France (Franc)	.2000	.2030

Banks do not charge a commission on their sales of foreign exchange; instead, they operate on the basis of a small spread between buying and selling rates. For example, the spread in the Canadian dollars and pound sterling exchange

*Wall Street Journal, January 23, 1961, p. 16.

is only a fraction of a cent. The spread in the buying and selling of bank notes is considerably greater. The quotations in the above tabulation show both spot and forward (or futures) rates for the English pound. The spot rates shown above refer to cable transfers. A forward or futures exchange transaction involves delivery after the passage of time, e.g., either 30 or 90 days in the above example. The futures rate fixes the price at which a futures transaction can be executed; the actual payment for the exchange is not made until the exchange is actually delivered. In the above example, the English pound 30-day and 90-day futures are quoted at slight discounts. At other times, futures may be quoted at slight premiums. The factors influencing the relationship between spot and forward exchange are very complex, and no attempt will be made in this study to explain the structure of the spot and forward exchange shown above.*

Forward exchange performs the same functions as do futures contracts in commodities. Exporters and importers are able to know today the dollar value of their respective future foreign exchange receipts and payments. The uncertainties of the foreign exchange market quotations are minimized. As in futures trading in commodities, speculators also operate in the forward foreign exchange market; however, they are probably much less important in this market than they are in most of the organized commodity markets.

FINANCING IMPORTS AND EXPORTS

Financial burden and risk are greater in international trade than in domestic trade. Some shipments of goods stretch over long periods, and it is difficult to make credit investigations. Assuming that parties dealing with each other in international transactions have confidence in one another, the execution of such transactions might be similar to that of domestic transactions, except for the complications relating to foreign exchange and possible trade controls. Various forms of financing are used with imports, exports, shipments of goods, and storage of goods. Some transactions are financed by the extension of trade credit, including conditional sales contracts. Loans are also widely used. Commercial banks extend loans to both exporters and importers, and enter into acceptance agreements with importers and exporters. Financing is also provided by the discounting of documentary bills. Almost all commercial and bankers' bills relating to international trade are "documentary," meaning that various types of documents such as bill of lading, invoice, shipping, and insurance papers are attached to the bills. Since the attached documents carry title to the goods, such documentary bills or drafts may be used as security for loans or may be discounted

*For a discussion of the relationship of the spot and forward rates, see Holmes, op. cit., Chapter 9.

in foreign exchange markets. The Export-Import Bank and privately sponsored foreign financing corporations also finance United States exports.

Commercial Banks

Commercial banks are ideally situated to provide export and import financing because most of the financing is concentrated in short- and intermediate-term maturities and banks are directly involved in a multitude of foreign banking services. Commercial banks are a major source of information on the credit standing of foreign buyers and sellers. Generally, exporters work through commercial banks to collect foreign drafts, and importers rely on commercial banks to verify transactions prior to making partial or full payment for imports. As noted above, commercial banks purchase and sell spot and futures foreign exchange, and sell foreign bank drafts to facilitate direct payment to foreign countries. Commercial banks are directly involved in bankers' bills and acceptances. The use of bankers' acceptance financing in the United States is discussed below.

UNITED STATES BANKING ORGANIZATIONS ABROAD. United States banks conduct foreign business services through correspondents, branches, and subsidiary institutions; the latter comprised of "foreign banking" and "foreign financing" corporations. These corporations operate under either state or Federal charters. Most banks do not carry on a sufficient volume of foreign business to justify the establishment of either branches or subsidiaries, and these banks rely on domestic and foreign correspondents. The largest banks, which account for most of the foreign commercial banking business in the United States, operate foreign branches or subsidiaries. By setting up subsidiary institutions, the banks are able to conduct separately their foreign activities. In fact, the subsidiaries may not engage either directly or indirectly in domestic United States business. The establishment of these subsidiaries enables banking and non-banking interests to participate jointly in various transactions relating to foreign trade and investment.

Regulations restrict the operations of both "foreign banking" and "foreign financing" corporations. A foreign banking corporation "may conduct deposit business, accept drafts or bills of exchange, and make loans related to foreign business. Subject to specific permission of the Board of Governors of the Federal Reserve System, it may also invest in stock of other corporations engaged in foreign banking activities. Such a banking corporation is not permitted to issue, underwrite, sell, or distribute securities, or to issue its own obligations except promissory notes due within one year and evidence borrowing from banks."* In contrast, a foreign financing corporation "is not authorized to receive deposit accounts or to accept drafts or bills of exchange, but may finance itself by the issuance of deben-

*"United States Banking Organization Abroad," *Federal Reserve Bulletin*, December 1956, p. 1285.

tures, bonds, and other such obligations, and, upon application to the Board, may obtain general advance permission to make certain kinds of investment in other foreign corporations not engaged in banking business."*

BANKERS' ACCEPTANCE FINANCING. The largest part of international trade is financed through the issuance of bank letters of credit. All of these letters of credit do not result in the creation of bankers' acceptances, because many call for sight rather than time drafts. Bankers' acceptances also arise from acceptance agreements between banks and their customers. Under such agreements, the banks agree to accept drafts drawn by American importers as well as by American exporters. Some of the bankers' acceptances are referred to as "dollar exchange" bills. They are created when United States banks permit foreign banks to draw on them dollar drafts. Generally, foreign banks use the dollar exchange so obtained to finance importers in their respective countries. Bankers' acceptances may have 180-day maturities, but most mature within a period of 90 days or less.

At the end of 1958, there were $1,194 million of acceptances outstanding. The financial uses of these acceptances are shown in the following tabulation:†

To finance foreign trade		72 per cent
Exports	29 per cent	
Imports	21	
Foreign storage, or shipment	22	
To finance domestic trade		21
Domestic storage	19	
Domestic shipments	2	
Dollar Exchange bills		7

The bulk of United States bankers' acceptances are generated by a relatively small number of banks in the major American cities. On the basis of a survey of acceptances outstanding at the end of 1954, it was revealed that nearly two-thirds of such acceptances were created by 10 banks; seven-eighths were created by 25 banks; and the total number of banks accepting time bills of exchange did not exceed 100.** Of the acceptances outstanding on December 31, 1958, nearly 71 per cent were created by New York City banks and nearly 15 per cent were created by banks in San Francisco.‡ Our attention in this section will be concentrated on bankers' acceptances used to finance foreign trade.

The tabulation above shows that most bankers' acceptances out-

*Ibid., p. 1285.
†Carl E. Madden, "The Money Side of the Street," Federal Reserve Bank of New York, September 1959, p. 65.
**"Bankers' Acceptances Financing in the United States," Federal Reserve Bulletin, May 1955, p. 485.
‡Madden, op. cit., p. 66.

standing at the end of 1958 were being used to finance exports. The bankers' acceptances used to finance American exports are created in two different ways. First, American banks issue letters of credit on behalf of foreign importers and in favor of American exporters. Such letters of credit are usually arranged by foreign banks having correspondent relationships and lines of credit with American banks. The importers agree to put the banks in funds to cover the accepted drafts at maturity. Exporters, after arranging properly for the shipments covered by the letters of credit, draw time drafts on the banks that issued the letters of credit, attach appropriate legal documents, and request their respective depositary banks to forward the drafts and attached documents to the issuing American banks for acceptance. The acceptance of these drafts by the issuing American banks creates dollar bankers' acceptances. The accepted drafts are returned to the exporters, and upon receipt, the dollar bankers' acceptances are either discounted in the market or held to maturity. Since the drafts are documentary, they may be discounted prior to acceptance. The net effects of such transactions are that the exporters receive immediate payments, importers delay payments until the bills mature, and banks realize income in the form of commissions or fees without having to loan funds. The other way in which acceptances are created to finance exports is much more simple. Exporters enter into acceptance agreements with American banks, under which the exporters are permitted to draw time bank drafts based on export transactions. The accepted drafts are discounted in the market. The foreign importers are not directly involved with the accepting American banks. The exporters expect to pay the accepting American banks upon maturity of the acceptances out of funds received from the foreign importers.

The bankers' acceptances that are used to finance American imports are also created in two different ways. In the first, American importers go to American banks and request that letters of credit be issued in favor of foreign exporters to cover specific imports. Naturally, the importers agree to put the banks in funds to cover the accepted drafts at maturity. The American banks notify their branches or correspondents that such letters of credit have been issued, and they, in turn, notify the exporters. The procedure is then the same as that outlined above. Shipments are made; drafts are drawn; the drafts, with documents attached, are discounted at the exporters' depositary banks; and these banks send the drafts and attached documents to their American branches or correspondents for presentation to the American banks that issued the letters of credit. The accepting banks retain the shipping documents and notify the importers to call for the documents. Generally, the importers are required to execute legal documents leaving title to the goods in the names of the banks until importers pay the banks. The second way in which acceptances are created to finance imports involves acceptance agreements. American importers draw time drafts on American banks.

Upon acceptance, the bankers' acceptances are discounted in the market, and the proceeds are used to pay sight drafts drawn by foreign exporters. Proceeds from the sales of imported goods are used to pay the banks at maturity of the acceptances. It is not necessary to review here the manner in which bankers' acceptances are created to finance foreign storage and shipments, because the mechanics are nearly the same as those outlined above. The creation of "dollar-exchange" bills was described above. The major relative disadvantages of bankers' acceptance financing are the amount of paper work and the lack of flexibility.

The costs involved in bankers' acceptance financing consist of the fees or commissions charged by the banks that issue the letters of credit and the rate of discount of bankers' acceptances. The typical fee is 1.5 per cent per year, and the rate of discount depends on money market conditions.

MARKET FOR BANKERS' ACCEPTANCES. The market for bankers' acceptances is concentrated in New York City, and New York banks hold approximately 70 per cent of acceptances outstanding. A few non-banking firms act as dealers in acceptances in conjunction with dealings in other money market instruments. The dealers act as intermediaries between buyers and sellers, and their activities have led to the development of an open market in acceptances. Bankers' acceptances are highly liquid and involve little or no risk, because the accepting banks consist of large, financially strong institutions. There is no record of a holder of a United States banker's acceptance having suffered a loss on his investment. In the event that an accepting bank was not too well known, the quality of its bankers' acceptances could be improved by having them endorsed by other banks. In this instance, the acceptances would become three-name paper, that is, each acceptance would carry the names of the drawer, the accepting bank, and the endorsement of another bank. Some countries restrict bank investment in bankers' acceptances to three-name paper, so that some acceptances are deliberately resold to make them three-name paper.

Foreign central banks and commercial banks are important buyers of bankers' acceptances, because such paper offers safety, liquidity, and favorable tax treatment. Without going into tax laws and tax treaties, we shall mention that acceptances do have some tax advantages over other liquid dollar assets, such as Treasury bills. Furthermore, bankers' acceptances are every common in foreign countries, and the resultant familiarity also explains the preferences of foreign central banks and commercial banks.

ROLE OF MONETARY AUTHORITIES. The Federal Reserve Bank of New York, acting on behalf of the Federal Reserve System, can and does purchase bankers' acceptances "to carry out credit policy and to stimulate greater interest in and wider participation in the acceptance market."*

*Madden, op. cit., p. 71.

During the period 1923-1934, the System's purchases were rather substantial. During the next 20 years, the System confined its activity to merely posting buying rates and purchasing acceptances offered at the posted rates on the initiative of sellers. Very few purchases were made. In 1955, the Federal Reserve shifted to active participation in bankers' acceptances by going into the market and buying acceptances. However, such purchases have been in limited amounts.

Export-Import Bank

To enhance the competitive position of United States exporters, both public and private specialized financial institutions have been established to meet competition from other exporting countries where similar credit is usually available through government channels. In 1934, Congress established the Export-Import Bank (hereafter referred to as Eximbank), which has carried on a variety of international financing chores. The main function is to provide a stimulus to exports through loans and U.S. export guarantees. Like most other Federally sponsored financing agencies, the Eximbank does not extend credit unless it is shown that private credit is not available, and where credit is extended, the Eximbank prefers that it be in the form of guaranteed or participation loans.

Various types of financing activities are carried on by the Eximbank to stimulate U.S. export trade. It makes economic development project loans to private enterprises abroad or to foreign government entities. At the request of American exporters, it extends credit to finance foreign sales of capital equipment. The Eximbank enters into commitments under which exporters are able to enter into negotiations, knowing that Eximbank financing will be available if neither the exporter nor the importer is able to finance the transaction with private capital. The Eximbank provides a system of export guarantees covering political risk in short-term transactions where credits are not in excess of 180 days. In this latter type of program, coverage is provided for all types of U.S. products, both consumer goods and producer goods.

In exporter credit financing, the Eximbank will finance without recourse up to 68 per cent of the contract price of the sale. The foreign buyer or importer must make a 20 per cent down payment on the purchase. If Eximbank financing is at the maximum, the exporter need carry only 12 per cent of the amount of the sale. In the medium-term credit field (180 days to five years) Eximbank participation depends solely upon the credit judgments of U.S. commercial banks if either of the following sets of conditions prevails: (1) a commercial bank is prepared to finance, for its own account and without recourse on the exporter, the first three or four semiannual installments of a three- to five-year credit; or (2) the exporter and a commercial bank participate in each of the installments, the exporter to the extent of 15 per cent of the invoice value and the commercial bank to the extent of 10 per cent of the invoice value for its own account and without recourse on the exporter. In either situation, the foreign buyer must have paid at least 20 per cent of the invoice value by the time of delivery.

Under the export guarantee program, private capital provides the financing and insurance with respect to the normal commercial risks, and the Eximbank provides guarantees covering noncommercial or political risks. Among the noncommercial risks are the following: (1) inconvertibility or nontransferability of foreign currencies, (2) imposition of laws or regulations beyond the control of exporter and buyer which prevent delivery of goods, (3) cancellation of an import license, (4) war, hostilities, rebellion, and civil commotion, and (5) expropriation of goods by foreign authorities. The program provides coverage up to 90 per cent of the losses incurred. The Eximbank has authorized U.S. commercial banks having foreign departments which finance export business and U.S. insurance companies which offer export credit insurance to act as agents for the Eximbank in the issuance of export guarantees.

Compared with the export financing of commercial banks and other private financial institutions, the Eximbank assumes more risk and makes loans of longer maturities. In many instances Eximbank participation or issuance of guarantees reduces risks sufficiently to attract private capital into financing that would otherwise be deemed too risky. The Eximbank also sells seasoned loan obligations from its portfolio to private investors.

The Eximbank finances its operations with interest on its loans, fees from its guarantees, repayments of outstanding loans, sales of seasoned loans to private investors, and the issue of obligations to the Treasury. The Eximbank pays annual dividends of $22.5 million on the $1 billion of capital stock held by the Treasury, and it pays interest at current rates on its borrowing from the Treasury. During its first 25 years of operations, the Eximbank authorized 1,645 credits in 69 countries totaling $10.2 billion. Active credits on June 30, 1959 totaled $6.8 billion, against which $1.3 billion had not yet been disbursed.

INTERNATIONAL FINANCIAL INSTITUTIONS

During the late 1920's and early 1930's, world-wide depression and deflation undermined the internatoinal flow of investment capital and the system of international payments. Countries acted independently to promote economic recovery and to maintain international reserves. Currency devaluation, exchange controls, high tariff rates, import quotas, and bilateral trade agreements were widely adopted. The adoption of such measures by one country increased the difficulties of other countries, and these countries, in turn, adopted retaliatory or competitive measures. The net result was a sharp reduction in the total volume of international trade and investment.

Some attempts were made in the 1930's to promote international monetary cooperation, but only a few countries participated and the agencies lacked essential ingredients such as binding commitments, machinery for continuous consultation, and a common pool of funds to enable countries to withstand short-run strains on their monetary reserves. Realizing that the problems of international trade and investment would be even greater after World War II, many of the leading countries, including the United States, Great Britain, and Canada, submitted proposals for the establishment of an international stabilization fund.

At the Monetary and Financial Conference at Bretton Woods, New Hampshire in the summer of 1944, the groundwork was laid for the eventual establishment in 1946 of the International Monetary Fund (hereafter referred to as the Fund), and the International Bank for Reconstruction and Development (hereafter referred to as the World Bank). The Fund's operations center around currency stabilization objectives. The World Bank's operations initially centered around reconstruction loans, but in recent years it has concentrated on loans to finance large development projects, such as transportation systems, power projects, steel mills, and the like. In the last few years additional international financial institutions have been established, and more are under serious study. Brief comments on some of these follow, and then we shall turn our attention to the Fund and the World Bank.

International Finance Corporation

The International Finance Corporation (hereafter referred to as the I.F.C.) was organized in 1956 and operates under the same Board of Directors as that of the World Bank. However, its operations differ greatly from those of the World Bank. World Bank loans must carry government guarantees. The I.F.C. deals exclusively with private business, and it does not require that borrowing firms' respective governments guarantee the loans. Also, its authorized capital is much smaller than that of the World Bank; $100 million compared with the $20 billion for the World Bank.

The I.F.C. restricts its investments to the underdeveloped areas and it invests in private enterprises that are predominantly industrial. The basic objective of the I.F.C. is to aid economic development by stimulating the flow of private investment capital and by promoting the growth of private management. The forms of investment that the I.F.C. enters into are summarized in the following statement:*

> Under its charter IFC cannot invest in capital stock or shares. However, its investments are not conventional fixed-interest loans; they combine certain features of both debt and equity, thus containing elements of venture capital. They are longer term loans carrying interest and some right to share in the profits and growth of the business. Such

*International Finance Corporation, *Third Annual Report*, 1958-1969.

shares may take the form of a right to some additional income related to earnings, or an option to subscribe to share capital, and frequently a combination of the two. Conversion and option rights cannot be exercised by the IFC, but they can be sold to private investors. IFC does not have a standard rate of interest — the rate is only one feature of the investment terms. All the terms of investment are matters for negotiation to suit the circumstances of each case. In its investments IFC considers earning power and a balanced capital structure more important than a lien or mortgage on assets. Where justified, IFC is prepared to make its investments junior to other creditors, as to maturity or security.

The quotation above makes it clear why I.F.C. considers itself an investing rather than a lending institution.

Both the World Bank and the I.F.C. extend only "bankable" loans; that is, the loans do not carry particularly "easy" terms. Both of these institutions encourage the participation of private investors and lenders, and are prepared to sell seasoned loans to them. During the year ended June 30, 1959 the I.F.C. entered into 13 commitments for projects located in 10 countries, totaling $10,400,000. This addition brought its total commitments to 22 projects, totaling $19,800,000.

International Development Association

In 1958, informal negotiations got under way for the establishment of the International Development Association, and in October, 1959 the member nations of the World Bank and the Fund approved the establishment of this lending organization. Its capital was set at $1 billion; member countries' quotas were set in the same proportion as subscriptions in the World Bank. The I.D.A. began operations on November 8, 1960 with a membership of 22 countries.

The purpose of this new lending organization is to spur economic development in some of the so-called poorer countries and in countries whose foreign indebtedness prevents them from receiving additional loans on "hard" terms. In other words, the basic loan policy of the International Development Association is to lend funds on easier terms than those required by private lenders, the World Bank, and the International Finance Corporation. The Development Association's loans will carry low interest rates, long maturities, and will allow repayment in local currencies. It is likely that the policies and operations of this lending agency will be more controversial than the policies and operations of either the World Bank or the International Finance Corporation.

United States Development Loan Fund

In response to strong pressures for more foreign loans and less foreign aid, the United States Development Loan Fund was established in 1957 and was made an independent corporation by the Mutual Security Act of 1958. Its purpose is the provision of capital for productive economic growth; that is, the promotion of economic development. The Development Loan Fund will not be capitalized on a long-term basis until experience with this form of lending justifies such capitalization. The Mutual Security Act of 1959 authorized $700 million beginning in fiscal 1960 and $1,100 million in fiscal 1961.

The Development Loan Fund was designed to supplement but not compete with other free world sources of financing. Lenders, such as the Export-Import Bank, the World Bank, and the International Finance Corporation generally require repayment in the form of foreign exchange, and repayments must be completed within 10, 15, or 20 years. Many of the less-developed nations cannot earn the foreign exchange necessary to make such repayments, so that they are unable to secure needed development loans from these lenders. The United States Development Loan Fund was designed to fill this gap in the system of international lending organizations. The Development Loan Fund has considerable flexibility in setting its terms, and it does not have to accept repayment in foreign exchange.

The operational procedures of the Development Loan Fund were well summarized by its managing director in a statement before the Committee on Foreign Affairs, House of Representatives:*

> The Development Loan Fund makes loans only for specific, sound projects. Loans are made only on the basis of firm commitments by the borrower to repay and upon a finding that there are reasonable prospects for repayments. To make such determinations we act as follows: (1) The potential borrower submits an application describing the nature and location of the project for which a loan is sought, the purposes of the proposed loan, the items to be financed, the total cost of the activity, the relationship of the project to the development of the country, the amount of the loan request, and a description of efforts to obtain financing from other sources. (2) The Development Loan Fund staff examines the project to determine its eligibility for Development Loan Fund financing, taking into account such criteria as the contributon of the proposed actvity to the growth of the borrower's country, the economic and technical soundness of the activity, the availability of other sources of finance, and its possible adverse effect upon the economy of the United States. (3) If the proposal passes the preliminary review, which includes checking to determine whether financing is available from private sources, the Export-Import Bank, and World Bank, or the IFC, a decision is made to subject it to intensive review and evaluation. (4) Intensive review and evaluation entails detailed study of a project's economic aspects and technical details. Views of experts in other agencies of the United States Government are sought. Comments are sought from our missions overseas. Usually the applicant is required to submit more detailed data. (5) Upon completion of intensive evaluation, the Development Loan Fund staff submits a memorandum to the Board of Directors recommending approval, supported by appropriate justification and documentation.

*U.S. House Committee on Foreign Affairs, *Mutual Security Act of 1959*, Hearings, 86th Cong., 1st sess. (Washington, D.C.: Government Printing Office, 1959), Part I, pp. 179-180.

If approved, the decision is incorporated in a formal resolution adopted by the Board, and is submitted for advice of the National Advisory Council on International Monetary and Financial Problems; following the Council's action, a letter of advice is sent to the applicant informing him of approval of his application and the terms and conditions on which it is proposed to extend a loan. A loan agreement is tailored to the project and is negotiated with the borrower. The Development Loan Fund is also involved in the implementation of such loans. Although the procedures that the Development Loan Fund goes through in making a loan are nearly identical to those used by other lenders, the loans are not considered "bankable" loans; instead they are "soft" loans. The major question is whether or not the local currencies will have much use to the United States. If the local currencies cannot be used to make purchases, then there is no great difference between a "soft" loan and a grant.

The cumulative total commitments of the Development Loan Fund to September 15, 1959 were as follows:*

Number of loans		Dollar amount of loans	Number and location of borrowers
18	....	$ 65,790,000	12 Latin American countries
9	....	30,140,000	7 countries in Africa
7	....	77,100,000	3 European countries
18	....	166,200,000	7 countries in Near East
24	....	310,000,000	3 countries in South Asia
25	plus 1 guarantee		
	....	166,276,000	7 Far Eastern countries
		$833,656,000	

The principal borrowing countries have been India and Pakistan. As of September 15, 1959 India had received eight loans totaling $195,000,000 and Pakistan has received 13 loans totaling $111,550,000. Loans have been made for roads, power generation and transmission, port facilities, railways, telecommunications, irrigation, and industrial plants. Also, the lending resources of development banks in some of these countries have received funds, enabling the banks to make more foreign exchange available for investment by small entrepreneurs in those countries. The Development Loan Fund joins with other lenders, such as the Export-Import Bank, the International Bank for Reconstruction and Development, and the governments of other free-world countries, in specific loan transactions. Considering the magnitude of the problem relating to the development of the so-called underdeveloped countries, this government corporation could become one of the giants.

Inter-American Development Bank

The charter of the Inter-American Development Bank (I.B.D.) was signed by representatives of the American Republics in early 1959, and by the close of the year more than the necessary number of countries had ratified its constitution and authorized capital subscriptions. The Board of Governors of the I.D.B. held its first meeting in early 1960, and during the year various member nations paid their initial installments of subscribed capital. The I.D.B. officially began to accept applications for long-term credits in late 1960. The review of events indicate the amount of time involved in the formation of a new international financial institution.

The objectives of the I.D.B. are as follows:* (1) to enlist the full cooperation of the Latin American countries in a joint and mutual enterprise in which all will share in the financial costs and in responsibility for its success; (2) to concentrate exclusively on the economic problems of the members of the Organization of American States, so that it will be in a position to adapt its policies to provide maximum assistance to the needs of the area; (3) to mobilize and channel foreign private investment funds for use in financing economic development; (4) to stimulate the investment of Latin America's own resources in the economic development of the area; (5) to supplement private capital and existing public lending institutions in providing financing to meet the large capital needs of the area; and (6) to provide technical assistance for the preparation of sound and broad programs of economic growth.

The capital of I.D.B. was set at $1 billion, with the United States providing $450 million. Although most of the loans will be in dollars, some may also be made, and repayable, in local currencies. Similar institutions have been proposed for other regions, such as the Middle-East.

International Monetary Fund

The basic economic principle underlying the Fund is that economic well-being of all countries is affected by each country's trade and exchange policies. Therefore, with respect to foreign exchange terms and the settlement of international payments, as much responsibility as possible has been shifted to the Fund to achieve fair standards and to provide a common pool against which countries can draw in times of financial strain. Compared with previous attempts at international monetary cooperation, the Fund was given considerable powers as well as resources.

PURPOSES. The purposes of the Fund, as stated in the Articles of Agreement, are as follows:

> To promote international monetary cooperation through a permanent institution which provides the machinery for consultation and collaboration on international monetary problems.
> To facilitate the expansion and balanced growth of international

*As reported in *International Financial News Survey*, International Monetary Fund, Vol. XII, No. 34, March 4, 1960, p. 269.

trade, and to contribute thereby to the promotion and maintenance of high levels of employment and real income and to the development of the productive resources of all members as primary objectives of economic policy.

To promote exchange stability, to maintain orderly exchange arrangements among members, and to avoid competitive exchange depreciation.

To assist in the establishment of a multilateral system of payments in respect of current transactions between members and in the elimination of foreign exchange restrictions which hamper the growth of world trade.

To give confidence to members by making the Fund's resources available to them under adequate safeguards, thus providing them with opportunity to correct maladjustments in their balance of payments without resorting to measures destructive of national or international prosperity.

In accordance with the above, to shorten the duration and lessen the degree of disequilibrium in the international balances of payments of members.

After we have examined the structure of the Fund, its operations will be analyzed in terms of the purposes listed above.

ORGANIZATION. Nearly all the major non-communist countries are members of the Fund. In late 1960, total membership exceeded 70. The powers of the Fund are vested in a Board of Governors, which delegates most of its powers to an Executive Board. The Board of Governors is comprised of one Governor and one alternate appointed by each member country, and it meets annually. The Executive Board is comprised of sixteen Executive Directors, five of whom are appointed respectively by the United States, the United Kingdom, China, France, and India. The other eleven members are elected by the other member countries. A member country has 250 votes on the basis of membership, plus an additional vote for each share of the Fund's stock. Therefore, the voting power of a member country is related to the size of its quota. As of April 30, 1960 the United States had 25.98 per cent of the total voting power. Many of the member countries have less than 1 per cent of the total voting power.

The reserves of the Fund have been built up by quota payments of member countries. Twenty-five per cent of a country's quota is payable in dollars or gold, and the rest is payable in the country's own currency. However, a country is not required to invest more than 10 per cent of its gold or dollar reserves in the Fund, so that some countries pay more than 75 per cent of their quotas in their own currencies. As of April 30, 1959 the countries' quotas totaled $9,228 million. The United States' quota was $2,750 million. The next few largest quotas were as follows: United Kingdom, $1,300 million; China, $550 million; France, $525 million; and India, $400 million. At the thirteenth annual meeting (October, 1958) of the Board of Governors of the Fund, a resolution was referred to the Executive

Directors, directing them to consider the question of enlarging the resources of the Fund by increases in quotas. This action was prompted by the current high volume of world trade and the extent to which the Fund's resources were being used. The Executive Directors recommended a general increase of 50 per cent in members' quotas; higher proportional increases in the quotas of seventeen countries in view of their relative economic growth in the postwar period, e.g., Canada, Germany, and Japan; and that an opportunity be given some of the countries with small quotas to increase their quotas up to stated amounts beyond the general increase of 50 per cent. The Board of Governors approved these recommendations in early 1959, and it then remained for each member to complete necessary formal procedures and to make required payments to the Fund. The increases became effective later in the year when members having not less than 75 per cent of the total of quotas consented to the increases. As a result of these actions, the Fund's total resources are being increased from about $9 billion to $15 billion. The aggregate of Fund quotas on April 30, 1960 exceeded $14 billion.

OPERATIONS OF THE FUND. The over-all operations of the I.M.F. provide ample evidence that it has promoted international monetary cooperation. There has been more consultation between the Fund and individual member countries than was originally planned. At the time the Fund's Articles of Agreement were drawn up, it was assumed that member countries would be able to remove exchange restrictions within five years after the establishment of the Fund. The Articles indicated that member countries that continued exchange restrictions beyond that time would be required to consult annually with the Fund. In practice, very few countries were able to eliminate exchange restrictions, so that many consultations have taken place during the postwar period. These consultations cover a review of a country's economic conditions, its fiscal and credit policies, and its exchange restrictions. In addition, the Fund provides technical assistance to member countries and provides a training program for member countries' technicians.

In view of the many complex problems that faced almost all countries at the end of World War II, the Fund has been able to promote a reasonable degree of exchange stability and to provide orderly adjustments in exchange arrangements. Almost all member countries have established par values for their currencies in terms of gold or United States dollars and have not allowed the maximum and minimum spot rates of foreign exchange to deviate from parity by more than 1 per cent. Although the Fund neither opposes nor proposes par value changes, it does examine the need for such changes and attempts to insure fairness among member countries. Almost all of the adjustments of exchange rates in the postwar period have taken place under the auspices of the Fund.

In early 1961, an important milestone was reached in attaining a multilateral system of payments. Belgium, France, Germany, Ireland, Italy, Luxembourg, the Netherlands, Peru, Sweden, and the United Kingdom accepted the obligations of convertibility for their currencies. Under the terms of their acceptance, these countries agree to avoid restrictions on current payments, multiple exchange rates, and discriminatory currency practices. To resort to one or more of these practices, these countries agree to consult with the Fund and obtain its approval. With this notable development in the Fund's operations, almost all currencies that are currently used to finance international trade are convertible.

The Fund's resources serve as a common reserve against which member countries, acting through their treasuries, central banks, or other appointed fiscal agencies, can draw out needed currencies or secure standby agreements under terms and conditions set forth by the Executive Directors. Under a standby agreement, the Fund assures a member country that a specified amount of currency will be available during a specified period. As a general rule, such assistance is restricted to helping a member country meet a deficit in its international payments on current accounts, which include payments relating to trade, services, normal short-term banking and credit facilities, interest on loans, net income from other investments, moderate amortization of loans, and depreciation of direct investments. Since the Fund's resources constitute a revolving fund, currencies acquired from the Fund should be repaid within three years, with an outside limit of five years. A rising scale of interest charges is imposed to encourage early repayment.

The maximum financial assistance that a country can obtain from the Fund is equal to its quota, and as a general rule the annual flow of financial assistance is restricted to 25 per cent of a country's quota. The Fund gives almost automatic approval to requests for drawings not exceeding 25 per cent of a country's quota. However, the policy is more strict with respect to drawings above this amount. For the next 25 per cent, a drawing country is required to show that it is making a reasonable effort to solve its payments difficulties. For drawings beyond 50 per cent of a country's quota, the Fund must be shown that the drawings are in support of a program that is likely to ensure stability at realistic rates of exchange. Such a program usually involves domestic policy, especially with respect to anti-inflationary fiscal, credit, and monetary measures.

Most of the drawings from the Fund have been concentrated in four currencies — United States dollar, pound sterling, Belgian franc, and the German mark — with the largest volume of drawings in United States dollars. The acceptance of the obligations of convertibility by additional member countries now encourages the use of a larger number of currencies.

The Fund can be repaid in either of two ways. First, the drawing country can repurchase its currency from the Fund or the Fund can sell the drawing country's currency to another member. In either case payment is made in gold or convertible currency. To illustrate, assume that the Fund sold dollars to the United Kingdom and received sterling. The drawing can be reduced either by the repurchase of sterling from the Fund by the United Kingdom with gold and convertible currency or by the sale of sterling to some other member country. In either case, the Fund's holdings of sterling will be reduced and its holdings of gold and convertible currencies will be increased.

The drawings are used to even out the seasonal effects of a country's pattern of trade, to assist countries in carrying out stabilization programs, and to provide emergency financial assistance during a period such as that of the Suez crisis. In many instances drawings from the Fund parallel other forms of financial assistance. Argentina's standby of $75 million, which was arranged in December, 1958 in support of a program that included exchange, fiscal, and credit reforms, illustrates this plan well. At the same time, Argentina made these arrangements: (1) an exchange agreement for $50 million with the United States Treasury; (2) balance of payment loans of $78.5 million from the Export-Import Bank and United States commercial banks; and (3) development loans of $125 million from the Export-Import Bank and the United States Development Loan Fund. As of April 30, 1960, the cumulative purchases by members totaled $3,443 million, and cumulative repurchases by members totaled $2,179 million. Total standby arrangements in force on that date totaled $291 million. During the period 1948-1960, 40 countries made use of the Fund's resources, and 3 countries concluded standby arrangements without making purchases.

The operations of the Fund have facilitated the expansion and balanced growth of international trade and have reduced the degree of disequilibrium in the international balances of payments of members. Its organization and operations have created a sound foundation for the eventual establishment of a multilateral system of payments. It is a serious error in logic to appraise the operation of the Fund only in terms of the volume of drawings from it. Actually, the more success the Fund and its members have in achieving their basic purposes, the less the members will need to draw from the Fund. The Fund has not and does not intend to supplant the international finance functions of private commercial banks; instead, its role is to supplement the existing private facilities and establish conditions under which private banks can operate more efficiently and securely.

It is doubtful if the I.M.F. provides a long-run solution to the problem of international liquidity. One of the more widely discussed proposals is that of Professor Robert Triffin of Yale University.* He has proposed that the International Monetary Fund be transformed into an international central bank. The member countries would be asked to renounce the use of

*See statement of Robert Triffin before the Joint Economic Committee on October

national currencies as international reserves and accept in their place deposits in an international central bank. These deposits would be fully as useable as gold itself, and the new bank would have the power to create reserves in the form of deposits. In other words, he proposes a system of international money and credit creation. These future developments in the international sphere would be very much like the past developments in our domestic monetary system. However, it must be recalled that many obstacles had to be overcome before it was possible to establish the Federal Reserve System. Furthermore, there are many people who believe that the Federal Reserve has been made too independent in the formation and application of financial policy. Undoubtedly, the same obstacles must be overcome at the international level. Member countries would become subject to international financial policies of the new bank, and the new bank would have the power to create reserves. Many people would fear that such a bank would have an inflationary bias. However, in the absence of change, there is a deflationary bias in the world economy.

Another proposal is to maintain the present structure of the International Monetary Fund, and rely on periodic increases in quotas.* The major drawback of this proposal is suggested in the above discussion of the recent increase in quotas. It was a long-drawn-out process. Furthermore, it is doubtful if this procedure will balance the Fund's supply of national currencies with the demand for national currencies. Another proposal is to give the Fund power to issue debentures in those countries whose national currencies are being drawn most heavily by countries borrowing from the Fund.† The major drawback of these proposals is that each represents only a temporary solution to a long-range problem. It will be interesting to watch developments in this area of international cooperation. In the author's opinion, Professor Triffin's proposal is the ultimate and most logical solution to the problem of international illiquidity.

International Bank for Reconstruction and Development

There are many similarities between the International Monetary Fund and the International Bank for Reconstruction and Development. Both organizations were founded at the Economic Conference at Bretton Woods, New Hampshire. Both the World Bank and the Fund are international cooperative organizations and are associated with the United Nations, each

---

*Bernstein, op. cit., pp. 84-86.
  † Ibid.

28, 1959, U.S. Joint Economic Committee, Employment, Growth, and Price Levels, Hearings, 86th Cong., 1st sess. (Washington, D.C.: Government Printing Office, 1959), pp. 2905-2954. Robert Triffin, Gold and the Dollar Crisis (New Haven: Yale University Press, 1960).

having the status of a specialized agency. Both organizations have a common membership, consisting of over 70 member countries. Each member country subscribes to the World Bank's and the Fund's capital stock in accordance with its economic strength, as measured by national income and international trade. Their basic structure is also similar. Each member country nominates a Governor to the Board of Governors, and the Board delegates many of its powers to the Bank's Executive Directors, five of whom represent the five largest stockholders. The voting power of each Director is directly related to the amount of stock held by the country or countries he represents. As in the Fund, the United States is the largest stockholder and has the largest voting power. On June 30, 1960, the United States had 30.34 per cent of the total voting power.

Both the World Bank and the Fund attempt to promote balanced growth of international trade and equilibrium in balances of payments. Although the Fund is primarily concerned with short-run adjustments, heavy drawings from the Fund must be supported by soundly conceived long-range plans. The Bank is primarily concerned with long-range developments. The difference in emphasis with respect to short-run and long-run plans is clearly illustrated in the statements of purposes of the Fund and of the World Bank. By referring to employment and real income, the Fund's statement of purposes emphasizes the promotion and maintenance of high levels of employment and real income, whereas the World Bank's statement of purposes emphasizes better productivity, standards of living, and conditions of labor. Although the World Bank deals primarily in long-term financial transactions and the Fund deals in short- and intermediate-term financial transactions, their operations are linked very closely with each other. The World Bank must concern itself directly with a borrowing member's foreign exchange stiuation, because the Bank's loans are made and must be repaid in currencies other than those of the borrowing countries. Under conditions of nonconvertibility, the World Bank must make a very detailed study of a country's balance of payments to determine whether or not it has the ability to earn a balance of payments surplus in the currency that is lent. Once the Fund is successful in promoting international monetary cooperation and fully convertible currencies, the World Bank need consider only the total balance of payments of the borrowing country. Since long-term investment may be one of the necessary ingredients in a country's over-all program to attain equilibrium in its balance of payments, the loans of the World Bank may be used to diminish some of the Fund's problems.

Both the Fund and the World Bank are guided by the same fundamental principle — they both strive to supplement rather than supplant private capital. Only when private capital is unavailable on reasonable terms does the World Bank lend funds and most of its loanable funds consist of private capital secured by its own securities issues.

When the World Bank was set up, its authorized capital was set at $10 billion. The member countries were asked to pay in only 20 per cent of their subscriptions; 2 per cent in gold or dollars, and the remainder in local currencies. The remainder was subject to call if required to meet the World Bank's obligations. At the Bank's annual meeting in 1958, the Board of Governors passed a resolution requesting the Executive Directors to consider the question of raising the capital subscription. The Executive Directors reported favorably to the Governors in late 1958, recommending that the authorized capital be increased from $10 billion to $21 billion, that member countries be invited to double their capital subscriptions, and that 17 of the member countries be invited to more than double their subscriptions. It will be recalled that a parallel proposal to increase quotas in the Fund had also been approved by the Governors of the Fund. In September, 1959 the recommendations were formally approved, and the required minimum amount of new subscriptions to make the change effective was received. It is expected that none of the additional subscriptions will require cash payment of the Bank; instead, the entire amount of the additional subscriptions will be left subject to call. The purpose of the doubling in capital was to provide support for future bond issues of the World Bank. The large amounts subject to call serve as a large guarantee fund to back up the Bank's borrowing operations. At the end of June, 1960, the subscribed capital of the Bank was $19,308 million. The most important component of the uncalled subscriptions is that of the United States, which totaled $5,715 million on June 30, 1960. The World Bank's outstanding bonds are in a sense guaranteed by the United States.

Purposes. In the introductory material we have suggested some of the purposes of the World Bank. The title of the Bank makes it clear that it was set up to assist in the reconstruction and development of member countries. Actually, only its four loans in 1947 were reconstruction loans; the loans made since that year have been development loans. In 1948, the United States adopted the Marshall Plan, allowing the Bank to shift its attention to development loans outside of Western Europe. In some of its loans, the World Bank participates with United States aid and loan programs.

Reconstruction and development were to be achieved by facilitating the investment of capital that would lead to an increase in the output of goods and services. In practice, almost all uses of funds are productive to some extent, and one of the guiding principles in the operation of the loan program is to allocate the funds to development projects that are more useful and urgent. This practice requires a fairly complete investment program for the borrowing country, and the Bank has provided considerable assistance in the form of general survey missions.

Another stated purpose is "to promote private foreign investment by means of guarantees of participations in loans and other investments made by private investors; and when private capital is not available on reasonable terms, to supplement private investment by providing, on suitable conditions, finances for productive purposes out of its own capital, funds raised by it, and its other resources." In practice, the World Bank uses guarantees very seldom, but it does sell some of its loans to private investors and guarantees payment in case of default. The Bank also sells some of its loans to private investors without guarantees. Most of the Bank's financial transactions have been loans financed out of funds raised by the World Bank in private capital markets. The World Bank is performing a function similar to that proposed for the Small Business Investment Companies in the United States. It issues its own obligations and relends funds to others. This function is well stated in the Bank's *Tenth Annual Report:* "It was never to have been the purpose of the Bank, however, simply to deploy government funds; it was the purpose of the Bank to encourage the international investment of capital from other sources. The authors of the charter had believed that one of the new institution's chief means of performing its function would be to attach its guarantee to bond issues offered to private investors by its member countries. But when the Bank concluded that it would have to become an active lender itself, it had to decide also that it would become an active issuer in the capital market."

POLICY AND OPERATIONS. The leading policy of the World Bank can be summarized by the following criteria: (1) the borrower must be unable to obtain needed capital on reasonable terms without the intervention of the Bank; (2) the borrowing country must be able to repay the loan; (3) the World Bank loan, in conjunction with other loans, must promote the more useful and urgent projects; and (4) the project or projects must be well planned and the borrowing country must be equipped technically, financially, and administratively to carry out the project. The interest rate charged on such loans is based on the Bank's own borrowing cost plus a 1 per cent annual commission charge, of which the latter is allocated to a special reserve. The Bank does not distinguish between borrowers in regard to the rate of interest charged.

The general procedure that is followed by the World Bank in making a loan to a member country or firm within a member country is similar to the procedure followed by private lenders, except that the World Bank is dealing with much larger loans and it has to be more thorough. The Bank determines the financial position of the prospective borrowing country and makes a general appraisal of the merits and priority of the country's proposed project or program. If the Bank is favorably impressed up to this point it then makes a very detailed study of the project, and if the proposed loan continues to look favorable, the Bank and country begin serious negotiations. The World Bank normally finances only the foreign costs of the imported goods and services that enter directly into the proposed development project. It is expected that the country will be able to finance the costs of goods and services that can be secured within its own borders. While the development project is underway, the Bank usually requires that competition prevail in obtaining the foreign goods and services and that detailed progress reports be submitted periodically. Furthermore, the World Bank sends teams into the field to observe all phases of the development program. It is not difficult to understand why World Bank loans are referred to as "bankable" loans.

The tabulation below summarizes the loan activity of the World Bank from the day it started operations to June 30, 1960:*

Original principal amount of loans signed		$5,180,637,893
Deduct:		
Cancellations, terminations and refundings	$112,732,164	
Principal repayments to the Bank	337,914,825	
Loans sold or agreed to be sold	804,192,557	
Loans not yet effective	242,600,000	1,497,439,546
		$3,683,198,347
Deduct: Exchange adjustments		19,492,427
Effective loans held by Bank		$3,663,705,920

The volume of new loans in recent fiscal years has exceeded $650 million. The loans have financed and are financing projects in more than 50 countries. Bank loans classified by purpose and area are shown in Table 23-3. The data show that the majority of loans relate to the development of electric power and transportation and that Asia and the Middle East have received a third of the development loans. Over 150 commercial banks, insurance companies, and other private and public financial institutions have participated in World Bank loans without guarantees. The Bank charges 6 per cent on most of its loans, and for a brief period during 1960 capital market conditions forced the Bank to raise the rate from 6 per cent to 6¼ per cent. Subsequent conditions in capital markets made it possible for the Bank to lower the rate to 6 per cent. The World Bank is a profitable operation, and accumulated net earnings and commissions provide a significant portion of its funds.

The World Bank has five sources of funds: paid-in capital subscriptions, earnings, commissions, the issue of obligations in the capital markets, and participations and sales from the Bank's portfolio. At the end of June, 1960 these sources were providing the following amounts: paid-in capital, $1,600 million; reserves accumulated from net earnings, $341.5 million; special reserves to which are credited receipts from the commission of 1 per

*International Bank for Reconstruction and Development, *Fifteenth Annual Report, 1959-1960*. All data in the remaining part of chapter are from this same source.

cent charged on the outstanding balances of all loans, $165 million; and funded debt, $2,073 million. During the fiscal year 1960 participations and sales from the Bank's portfolio were equal to more than 44 per cent of the Bank's cash disbursements. Not only do the sales provide a source of funds, they also promote private investment in development financing. It should

TABLE 23-3
BANK LOANS CLASSIFIED BY PURPOSE AND AREA, JUNE 30, 1960
(MILLIONS OF DOLLARS)

Purpose	Total	Africa	Asia and Middle East	Australia	Europe	Western Hemisphere
Grand Total	5,067.9	771.9	1,568.8	317.7	1,356.5	1,053.0
Development Loans: Total	4,571.1	771.9	1,568.8	317.7	859.7	1,053.0
Electric power Generation and distribution	1,604.9	178.0	441.3	29.3	333.0	623.3
Transportation	1,526.2	418.2	617.0	132.3	68.4	290.3
Railroads	778.6	263.2	348.9	37.3	2.3	126.9
Roads	388.4	87.8	112.0	50.9	—	137.7
Shipping	12.0	—	—	—	12.0	—
Ports and waterways	226.3	17.2	136.5	—	46.9	25.7
Airlines and airports	56.9	—	5.6	44.1	7.2	—
Pipelines	64.0	50.0	14.0	—	—	—
Communications Telephones, telegraph, radio	23.9	1.5	—	—	.2	22.2
Agriculture and forestry	375.7	31.2	84.7	103.4	87.8	68.6
Farm mechanization	119.8	—	—	89.4	2.0	28.4
Irrigation and flood control	187.0	15.5	69.9	6.0	73.3	22.3
Land clearance; land and farm improvement	41.1	13.7	13.8	6.0	2.1	5.5
Crop processing and storage	7.0	1.0	—	—	4.2	1.8
Livestock improvement	12.6	1.0	1.0	—	—	10.6
Forestry	8.2	—	—	2.0	6.2	—
Industry	835.4	103.0	350.8	52.7	280.3	48.6
Iron and steel	338.1	—	302.0	13.4	22.7	—
Pulp and paper	113.7	—	4.2	1.1	88.4	20.0
Fertilizer and other chemicals	57.0	—	—	.3	56.7	—
Other industries	94.0	—	5.2	23.7	58.8	6.3
Mining	149.0	101.0	—	14.2	12.0	21.8
Development banks	83.6	2.0	39.4	—	41.7	.5
General development	205.0	40.0	75.0	—	90.0	—
Reconstruction Loans: Total	496.8	—	—	—	496.8	—

Source: International Bank for Reconstruction and Development, *Fifteenth Annual Report, 1959-1960.*

be recalled that the Bank is designed to supplement and encourage the flow of private capital, not to supplant it.

During the postwar period the market for the Bank's obligations has steadily expanded. More than half of the Bank's obligations are held outside the United States, and two-thirds of new borrowing during the fiscal year 1960 was done outside of the United States. The Bank relies on private placement as well as upon public offerings. As an illustration of the breadth of the market, a $100 million issue in August, 1959 was privately placed with 63 institutional investors in 35 different countries.

QUESTIONS

1. "Financial transactions underly the flow of goods and services among countries." Explain and illustrate.

2. Why are the financial aspects of international financial and nonfinancial transactions more complex than those of domestic transactions?

3. What is the basis of international trade and investment?

4. How significant is international trade to the United States?

5. Set forth the level and structure of the rest-of-the world sector's holding's of financial assets?

6. How do international trade and investment affect the gold stock of the United States Government?

7. Why did a foreign exchange market develop in this country? Why in New York City?

8. Describe briefly the organization of the New York foreign exchange market.

9. What are the instruments of the New York foreign exchange market?

10. Describe and illustrate the ways in which American banks can build up or replenish their deposit balances with foreign banks.

11. Define foreign exchange rates. How are fluctuations in rates minimized?

12. What are "documentary" bills?

13. Illustrate the use of bankers' acceptances in financing imports and exports.

14. Describe the market for bankers' acceptances and indicate the role of the monetary authorities.

15. Describe the role of the Export-Import Bank.

16. What prompted the development of international monetary organizations?

17. Compare the International Monetary Fund and the International Bank for Reconstruction and Development with respect to the following: organization, capital, purposes, successes, failures.

18. Identify and discuss briefly other international monetary organizations.

ADDITIONAL READING

Boskey, Shirley. *Problems and Practices of Development Banks.* Baltimore: John Hopkins Press, 1959.

Ellis, Howard S., and Lloyd A. Metzler (selection committee). *Readings in the Theory of International Trade.* Homewood, Ill.: Richard O. Irwin, Inc., 1959.

Ellsworth, P. T. *The International Economy.* (Rev. ed.) New York: The Macmillan Co., 1958.

Gordon, Wendell C. *International Trade.* New York: Alfred A. Knopf, Inc., 1958.

Harrod, Roy F. *International Economics.* (3rd ed., rev.) Chicago: University of Chicago Press, 1958.

Henning, Charles N. *International Finance.* New York: Harper & Bros., 1958.

Holmes, Alan R. *The New York Foreign Exchange Market.* New York: Federal Reserve Bank of New York, 1959.

International Monetary Fund. *Annual Report, Summary Proceedings, Annual Meeting,* and *International Finacial News Survey* (weekly). See latest publications.

International Finance Corporation. *Annual Report.* See latest report.

Kindleberger, Charles P. *International Economics.* (Rev. ed.) Homewood, Ill.: Richard D. Irwin, Inc., 1958.

Krause, Walter. *The International Economy.* New York: John Wiley & Sons, Inc., 1955.

Loftus, H. L. *The International Monetary Fund, 1946-1950.* A Selected bibliography. Washington, D.C.: International Monetary Fund, 1951.

Morgenstern, Oskar. *International Financial Transactions and Business Cycles.* N.B.E.R. Study. Princeton, N.J.: Princeton University Press, 1959.

Pratt, Edward E. *Modern International Commerce.* Boston: Allyn & Bacon, Inc., 1956.

Peck, H. Austin. *International Economics.* New York: Thomas Y. Crowell Co., 1957.

Schelling, Thomas C. *International Economics.* Boston: Allyn & Bacon, Inc., 1958.

Shaterian, Wm. S. *Export-Import Banking — The Documents and Financial Operations of Foreign Trade.* New York: The Ronald Press Co., 1956.

Tarshis, Lorie. *Introduction to International Trade and Finance.* New York: John Wiley & Sons, Inc., 1955.

Towle, Lawrence. *International Trade and Commercial Policy.* (2nd ed.) New York: Harper & Bros., 1956.

U.S. House of Representatives Committee on Foreign Affairs. *International Lending Agencies.* Staff memorandum, 86th Cong., 1st sess. Washington, D.C.: Government Printing Office, 1959.

World Bank. *Annual Report.* Washington, D.C.: International Bank for Reconstruction and Development. See latest report.

part **7**: **F**inancial
markets, national
economic objectives, and
financial policies

FINANCIAL institutions provide a variety of outlets for consumer saving and allocate funds to users through a variety of financial markets. The institutions and markets have developed in response to growing needs for balancing changing volumes and forms of saving on the supply side with changing volumes and forms of investment opportunities on the demand side. The structure and operation of these institutions and markets affect the rate of economic growth, the rate of employment, and the general level of prices.

The reliance of financial institutions on personal current saving as their major source of funds, and the share of financial institutions in financing consumers, firms, and the governmental units make financial institutions and financial markets very sensitive to the state of economic conditions. The level of national output, the volume and composition of current saving, and the demand for outside financing are interrelated. Inasmuch as financial institutions and financial markets exert important influences upon the markets for goods and services, financial policies may be used to assist in the achievement of national economic objectives.

The matching up of the supply of and the demand for loanable funds takes place within a complicated system of financial markets, and the level and structure of interest rates and equity yields reflect the underlying supply and demand relationships and expectations. Changes in the level and structure of interest rates affect decisions of ultimate suppliers and users of funds, as well as the decisions of the financial intermediaries. The frequency and magnitude of changes in the level and structure of interest rates reflect the degree of sensitivity in our system of financial markets.

Government financial policies are directly related to financial markets and national economic objectives. For the purpose of this study, financial policies of government are monetary and debt management policies. The

563

Federal Reserve has primary responsibility for monetary policy, and the Treasury has primary responsibility for debt management. Fiscal policy, which refers to changes in and relationships between the level and composition of taxes and expenditures, is a subject in itself, and is not considered here. It is enough to mention that fiscal policy is a vital part of an over-all program to achieve our national economic objectives, and monetary and debt management policies must be employed in coordination with fiscal policy. Inappropriate fiscal policy imposes a heavy burden on monetary and debt management policies.

Monetary authorities have some responsibility for the status of financial markets, and particularly for the market for Federal obligations. The financial markets constitute the main channel through which government financial polices are carried out; the effects of these measures permeate the entire economy through the financial and nonfinancial markets.

A basic question and one that cannot be answered on the basis of available knowledge is whether or not our financial system has been as innovating, efficient, and responsive as it should have been in promoting our national economic objectives. Obviously, there have been lags in the origin and development of some of our financial institutions and markets. Many of the changing needs in the past have had to be met by the formation of new types of institutions. Laws have had to be changed to enable existing institutions to respond more fully to the changing needs of our economy. Operating with an established framework of laws and customs, financial institutions have developed patterns of operation that tend to present barriers to further innovation. It must be recognized that institutions and markets result from social invention, and it is almost axiomatic that their development must be evolutionary. It must be recognized that one of the major obstacles to more rapid development of the so-called underdeveloped countries is the absence of organized and efficient financial institutions and markets. A basic question in our system is whether or not our existing financial system is adequate to meet the changing needs of our economy. It is enough to mention that public officials and leaders in our financial system must be alert to changing needs and promote needed innovations.

In Chapter 24 we shall describe the structure and operation of the financial markets and shall explain the level and structure of interest rates, including the maturity structure of those rates. In Chapter 25 we shall establish the existence and nature of three of the more important national economic objectives. In Chapter 26 we shall describe the structure of policy-formulating agencies and the impact of monetary and debt management measures upon financial markets. The influence of these measures upon the achievement of our national economic objectives is examined in the concluding chapter. Also, the question of whether or not non-bank financial institutions should be subject directly to monetary and debt management measures is examined in Chapter 27.

24: Financial markets

LMOST all the individual components of the total system of financial markets have been examined in previous chapters. At this stage of our study, the individual market components are aggregated into two financial markets, the national money market and the investment or capital market. The money market is the mechanism through which the supply of and the demand for short-term funds interact. It is comprised of many individual market components, including the markets for Federal funds, short-term Federal obligations, bankers' acceptances, and commercial paper. The common characteristic of money market instruments is that each is highly liquid. The investment market is comprised of credit and equity market instruments not included in the money market.

There is extensive interaction between the money market and the capital market. The capital market relies on the money market for liquidity and accommodation loans. Many financial and nonfinancial firms and governmental units deal in both markets. Almost all financial institutions are capable of shifting funds within and between the money and capital markets. Much of the shifting is influenced by the level and structure of interest rates and expectations as to the future of those rates.

In this chapter the stage is set for a close examination of interrelationships between the financial markets, national economic objectives, and financial policies.

THE MONEY MARKET

The term "money market" has been used to denote any one of the following types of markets: the total system of financial markets, the market for short-term credit instruments; and the market for specific types of credit market instruments. Inasmuch as the influence of financial policies is of major concern in Part 7, the definition adopted for the purpose of this study should be one that is meaningful in terms of government financial policies.

Persons directly involved in the formulation and implementation of financial polices have defined the money market, and their definitions provide considerable insight into the selection process. Dr. Robert V. Roosa of the Federal Reserve Bank of New York has defined the money market as the "active market for money and close money substitutes which financial institutions and others rely upon to provide the liquidity needed in the usual course of their operations."* Mr. Harold V. Roelse, another officer at the Federal Reserve Bank of New York, has defined the money market as "the central national market in New York City where temporary surplus funds of various types of organizations (including secondary reserves of the banks) go to find income-producing employment without sacrifice of liquidity, and where short-term needs for funds are satisfied, usually at interest rates that are advantageous to the borrower. It is a place where final adjustments between the supply of funds and the demand for funds are made for the country as a whole, after much regional clearing has been effected." † Either of these definitions may be considered appropriate.

Since the money market serves to balance out the distribution of bank reserves and to provide liquidity needed by both financial and nonfinancial firms, it serves as an ideal point of initial impact for government financial measures. Inasmuch as the money market is interrelated with all other financial markets, the measures permeate the entire system of financial markets. However, it should be recognized that is is possible to adopt financial measures that influence the investment market directly. One of the points of disagreement between monetary officials and their critics concerns this very question. With few exceptions, monetary and debt management measures have been restricted to those which influence directly only the money market.

The market money operates mostly through financial dealers and bankers who are in constant contact with each other and with major suppliers and users of short-term funds through direct-wire switch-boxes, telephone, and teletype. The market is impersonal as compared with the highly personal customers' loan market.

We must now turn our attention to the instruments and institutions that comprise the money market.

Money Market Instruments

The instruments of the money market consist of the active margin of bank reserves and that part of all outstanding credit market instruments which can be readily liquidated to meet the need for money. Inasmuch as the market is dynamic, the specific instruments that are actively traded in the money market tend to change with the passage of time. Whether or not a specific credit market instrument is a money market instrument depends primarily upon the attitudes of those who hold that particular asset and the willing-

*"Federal Reserve Operations in the Money and Government Securities Markets," Federal Reserve Bank of New York, 1956, p. 11.

† "The Money Market," Money Market Essays, Federal Reserve Bank of New York, March 1952, p. 1.

ness of banks and financial dealers to make a market in the instrument.* Demand deposits of most individuals and firms are not considered part of the stock in trade of the money market because these assets are already in the form of "absolute liquidity." However, the excess cash balances of large nonfinancial firms and governmental units are part of the stock in trade of the money market because these assets provide a source of demand for other money market instruments. Fixed-value redeemable claims are excluded from the stock in trade of the money market because the holders of such assets do not rely directly on the money market for conversion of these assets into money. Instead, they look directly to the issuers of these liabilities, including the United States Government.

Since it is clear that the composition of the stock of money market instruments and the arrangements for issuing, trading, and holding of money market instruments are subject to continuous change, the discussion in this chapter should be considered tentative. In a rather short period, one or two money market instruments may decline in importance and new ones may be added. In recent years, Federal funds and short-term Federal obligations have been the most important money market instruments.

CLEARING HOUSE FUNDS. Almost all money market transactions are settled in terms of either clearing house funds or Federal funds. Clearing house funds are checks drawn on New York banks and cleared through the New York Clearing House Association for collection. As noted in Chapter 6, a certain amount of time is required to clear checks, and checks drawn on New York banks and deposited by recipients in New York banks, will pass through the New York Clearing House Association for collection on the following business day. Therefore, the recipients of such checks must delay drawing checks against their new deposits in New York banks for at least one day after deposit. This one-day period involves an element of "opportunity cost." If the deposit were immediately available for drawing checks, the funds could be invested immediately and could earn an additional day's interest. The delay resulting from clearing involves a loss of interest, and the higher the level of money market interest rates, the greater is the "opportunity cost." When dealing in amounts in excess of $100 million, a day's interest may be as great as $1,000.

FEDERAL FUNDS. Federal funds are the same as "immediately available Federal Reserve funds." In contrast to checks drawn on clearing house banks, checks drawn on balances held in Federal Reserve banks may be presented for immediate payment; that is, the checks are collectible at Reserve banks in funds immediately available at those banks. The use of Fed-

*To illustrate, in February 1961 several large banks encouraged corporate time deposits, and securities dealers indicated that they would make a market in time certificates (*Wall Street Journal*, February 27, p. 7).

eral funds to settle money market transactions eliminates the delay and loss of interest.

Member banks, the United States Treasury, foreign official banks, and disbursing officers of the Federal Reserve System are able to draw checks on Federal Reserve banks, and all Federal funds arise from such drawings. The Federal Reserve System provides wire transfer facilities through which banks may wire Federal funds to other banks for their own use or for the use of their customers. In a wire transfer, the sending bank's reserve account is reduced, and the receiving bank's reserve account is increased. Most of the Federal funds originate in the transfers of deposit balances between member banks.

The market for Federal funds is one of the most important components of the money market. Commercial banks utilize the Federal funds market to adjust reserve positions. Banks with reserve balances in excess of their needs lend reserve balances to banks with deficient reserve balances. Such transactions provide an investment outlet to the lending banks and eliminate the need for borrowing banks to arrange loans at their respective Federal Reserve banks.

There is a brokerage function to be performed in the Federal funds market, and broker-dealer houses have entered the market both as intermediaries and as principals, collecting information with respect to the supply of and demand for Federal funds, buying and selling Federal funds on narrow spreads, and accommodating small buy and sell orders for Federal funds. These functions are performed by some of the larger New York City banks as well as by non-bank brokers.

Most of the trading or swapping in Federal funds is done by about 150 large banks in the money centers throughout the country. Many of the larger commercial banks confine their trading in Federal funds to their respective correspondent banks. When there is a net source or net need within a given correspondent system, the large bank in the financial center may seek the assistance of a broker in Federal funds. Even if the large bank did not utilize the brokerage service, it would rely on the list and asked prices that are quoted by a broker. For many years, there has been only one non-bank broker for the transfer of Federal funds.

The brokerage function is performed as an accommodation without charge, on the assumption that the banks utilizing the Federal funds brokerage services will give the same firm a reasonable amount of the banks' securities brokerage business. The commission on the additional securities transactions is supposed to offset the cost of the Federal funds services. Some banks prefer to have their securities brokerage business conducted by broker-dealer firms not active in the market for Federal funds, and these banks generally pay a small commission for Federal funds brokerage services.

The daily volume of trading in Federal funds averages around $1 billion. The rates charged for Federal funds change in response to the day-to-day change in the supply of and demand for Federal funds. Since reserve-shy banks may borrow from Federal Reserve banks instead of borrowing Federal funds from other banks, the Federal Reserve discount rate tends to be a ceiling on the level of rates charged for Federal funds. The minimum rate may fall as low as ⅛ of 1 percent.

In summary, the Federal funds market provides the mechanism through which banks may adjust reserve positions. The market is a vital part of the mechanism through which newly created reserves are allocated or shifted into the regional money centers. In other words, the impact of general monetary controls may not be uniform, and the Federal funds market corrects for improper initial allocation of new reserves. Banks with idle funds are encouraged to invest the temporarily idle funds in the Federal funds market. The Federal funds market furnishes funds for a large share of the payments in money market transactions.

SHORT-TERM FEDERAL OBLIGATIONS. Short-term Federal obligations consist of Treasury bills, special "tax anticipation bills," certificates of indebtedness, non-guaranteed obligations of governmental agencies, and other Federal obligations scheduled to mature within one year. In 1959, the Treasury extended bill maturities from three months to six months, and then to twelve months. In 1960, the Treasury had outstanding thirteen issues of three-month bills, thirteen issues of six-month bills, and four issues of one-year bills. The Treasury bills are placed on a periodic rollover basis. Three-month and six-month bills mature weekly and are replaced by new bill offerings. The one-year bills mature once each quarter, in January, April, July, and October. They may or may not be rolled over. The "tax anticipation" bills are tailored to attract corporate funds that are being accumulated to make payment of corporate income taxes and to enable the Treasury to meet seasonal gaps between tax receipts and expenditures. The use of bills has overshadowed the use of certificates of indebtedness. Non-guaranteed obligations having an original maturity of one year or less enjoy a fairly active and broad trading market, comprised of banks, non-bank financial institutions, and nonfinancial firms.

As noted in previous chapters, short-term Federal obligations are attractive to both financial and nonfinancial firms. Considering the nature of the issuer and the shortness of maturity, there is very little risk of loss from either financial risk or interest-rate risk. The investment of funds in short-term Federal obligations provides investment income with little loss of liquidity. Investors are able to sell relatively large amounts of short-term Federal obligations at little or no loss for immediately available funds.

Dealers make markets in short-term Federal obligations. The prices or yields reflect the supply of and demand for such obligations and the market is closely related to the market for Federal funds and other money market instruments. The outstanding volume of short-term Federal obliga-

569

tions reflects the level and composition of debt financing of the United States Government and its agencies. The supply of short-term Federal obligations reflects resale of outstanding issues as well as the weekly turnover of maturing bills. Inasmuch as the demand for and supply of such short-term Federal obligations depend upon the demand for and supply of temporarily available money, the market for short-term Federal obligations is one of the most important components of the money market.

COLLATERAL LOANS AND REPURCHASE AGREEMENTS OF GOVERNMENT SECURITIES DEALERS. Almost all trading in Federal obligations takes place in the over-the-counter market, which is comprised of a relatively small number of non-bank dealer firms (twelve in 1960) and five dealer banks. Most of the dealer firms and banks also make markets in other types of credit instruments, and especially in money market instruments. To finance their inventory positions, the dealer firms and dealer banks must negotiate collateral loans and repurchase agreements with holders of temporary liquid balances.

Each day after the New York money market banks establish their own preliminary reserve positions and determine their supplies of excess funds or shortages of funds, the banks announce or post interest rates on loans to brokers and dealers, secured by Federal obligations. Although the banks rarely call such loans, they do post higher interest rates when money market conditions tighten and thereby discourage the continuation or expansion of collateral loans to brokers and dealers. When the posted interest rates in New York money market banks are higher than the yields that out-of-town suppliers of money are willing to accept, dealers in Federal obligations are motivated to seek out and tap these pools of liquidity that are scattered throughout the country.

The collateral loans obtained from out-of-town sources are different from those secured from the New York money market banks. In the latter instance, the rates are posted, and the loans are made at those rates. The collateral loans involving out-of-town sources are negotiated.

It should be recognized that brokers and dealers are also able to arrange loans secured by collateral other than Federal obligations at slightly higher rates.

Under repurchase agreements, the dealers sell Federal obligations to the holders of temporary idle balances, and agree at the same time to buy back the securities at specified future dates, ranging from one to a few days, at specified future prices equal to the sales price plus interest. From the point of view of the dealers, repurchase agreements are a form of borrowing money; from the point of view of the grantors of repurchase agreements, the transactions are a form of short-term investment. Some of the transactions are left open as to maturity. This type of deal is referred to as a "buy back." Both collateral loans and repurchase agreements are settled in

Federal funds. The management of the open market account at the Federal Reserve Bank of New York also enters into repurchase agreements with the established dealers in Federal obligation. The timing and magnitude of these repurchase agreements is decided in accordance with the instructions of the Open Market Committee.

OTHER MONEY MARKET INSTRUMENTS. The other money market instruments include bankers' acceptances, commercial and finance company open-market paper, and discounts from Federal Reserve banks. The nature of these instruments and the corresponding market structure and operation were discussed in previous chapters. At this stage of our study, it is necessary only to set forth the circumstances that prompt member banks to borrow from Federal Reserve banks.

Commercial banks manage their primary and secondary reserves on the basis of predicted money flows. Obviously, the banks cannot predict with perfect accuracy the weekly and seasonal flows, and banks must always be prepared to adjust in response to inaccurate predictions. A bank's response to miscalculation in the net change in its reserve balances depends upon the expected duration of the need for additional reserves, the state of its secondary reserve account, and its over-all policy. If an individual bank decides not to liquidate some of its secondary reserve account to cover a deficiency in its reserve account, it may borrow from many sources, including the district Federal Reserve bank. The discussion above indicates that Federal funds may be used to tide the bank over a short period of strain. In this section, our attention is focused on borrowing from Federal Reserve banks.

Borrowing from Federal Reserve banks is not an automatic right of the member banks.

> The Board of Governors of the Federal Reserve System has established regulations, under authority of the Federal Reserve Act, which outline the general circumstances under which a member bank may properly borrow. Discount administration is intended to assist member banks temporarily in need of reserves, but to do so without impairing the ability of the Federal Reserve System to discharge its principal responsibility, the regulation of the supply of money and credit. The criteria for appropriate borrowing apply uniformly and objectively to all member banks; they do not attempt to make distinctions, for example, between the needs of very active banks in fast-growing communities and those of less active banks located in communities that are not growing so rapidly. Nor are the criteria changed from one month to the next or over the various phases of the business cycle.*

The Federal Reserve banks influence the amount of bank borrowing through discount administration at the Reserve banks and through changes in Fed-

*Monthly Review of the Federal Reserve Bank of New York, September 1959, pp. 138-139.

eral Reserve discount rates. Continuous borrowing by an individual bank is not appropriate under any circumstance and even temporary borrowing may be unavailable to some banks. The discount privilege is designed to cover the unexpected net loss in reserves until other adjustments can be worked out. "So long as the member bank is making every reasonable effort to operate its business with its own resources, arrangements for temporary accommodation at the discount window can always be worked out. It is only when the borrowing bank relies upon the discount window of the Federal Reserve Bank as a continuing source of funds for its own operation that it is necessary for the Reserve to discourage its use."*

Institutions of the Money Market

The major volume of clearing of funds is effected in regional financial centers, and the final adjustments between the supply of funds and demand for funds for the country as a whole are effected in the New York money market. The money market institutions actually operate in three financial markets: the New York customers' loan market, the nationwide customers' loan market, and the money market proper. In contrast to the customers' loan markets, the money market proper is open and impersonal. The major institutions involved in the money market proper are the large money market banks and government securities dealers. Other institutions involved in the money market include stock brokerage firms, investment banking firms, home offices of large financial and nonfinancial firms, the New York Clearing House, organized securities exchanges, organized commodity trading markets, and the Federal Reserve Bank of New York, the latter of which executes transactions on behalf of the Federal Open Market Committee, the Treasury, and foreign official banks. Since the large banks and dealers and brokers seek funds outside New York City, many other financial and nonfinancial firms and state and local governmental agencies are in and out of the market. Inasmuch as these groups have already been described, it is not necessary to expand on the subject at this point.

Before considering the level and structure of money market rates in detail, the broad components of the supply of and demand for money market funds should be noted. Money market funds are supplied by Federal Reserve banks, commercial banks, nonfinancial firms, insurance companies, and foreign central banks. Money market funds are demanded by Federal Reserve banks, commercial banks, the Federal Government, nonfinancial corporations, and finance companies. It is obvious that many of these participants are both suppliers and users of money market funds. The Federal Reserve banks operate on both sides of the market in carrying out policy. Commercial banks also operate on both sides of the market because of the diversity among individual commercial banks. The reserve funds of commercial banks may be adequate in terms of the aggregate reserve position

*Ibid., p. 142

of the banking system, but the reserves may not be distributed properly among the member banks. As a result, it is not uncommon for some banks to supply funds in the money market at the same time as other banks are demanding funds in the money market. The market for Federal funds is established to deal with this very situation. Nonfinancial firms may supply funds to the market during periods of excess liquidity and demand funds from the money market when liquidity is under pressure. Finance companies are generally net demanders of money market funds. The role of the Federal Government depends upon the volume and composition of Federal borrowing.

Level and Structure of Money Market Rates

Before we consider the level and structure of money market rates, a brief discussion of the theory of interest is appropriate. We turn first to the Swedish approach, as represented by Bertil Ohlin, and then to a brief summary of the Keynesian theory.

Bertil Ohlin states that the "rate of interest cannot . . . be determined by the condition that it equalizes the supply of and the demand for savings. . . . Nor can one say that the rate of interest equalizes planned savings and planned investment."* Instead, Ohlin defines the rate of interest as the price of credit. This approach gives the banking system a predominant role in the determination of the interest rate level. Ohlin introduces an ex-ante causal analysis to explain how the rates of interest are actually determined.

> What governs the demand and supply of credit? . . . The willingness of certain individuals during a given period to increase their holdings of various claims and other kinds of assets minus the willingness of others to reduce their corresponding holdings gives the supply curves for the different kinds of new credit during the period. Naturally, the quantities each individual is willing to supply depend on the interest rates. In other words, the plans are in the nature of alternative purchase and sales plans. Similarly, the total supply of new claims minus the reduction in the outstanding volume of old ones gives the demand — also a function of the rate of interest —for the different kinds of credit during the period. The prices fixed on the market for these different claims — and thereby the rates of interest — are governed by this supply and demand in the usual way.†

Lord Keynes approached the question from a slightly different angle. He held that the "rate of interest is the reward for parting with liquidity for ,a specified period. . . . It is the "price" which equilibriates the desire to hold wealth in the form of cash with the available quantity of cash."** In

* "Some Notes on the Stockholm Theory of Savings and Investment," *Economic Journal*, XLII, June 1937, p. 221.
†*Ibid.*, pp. 224-25.
**John Maynard Keynes, *The General Theory of Employment, Interest and Money* (New York: Harcourt, Brace & Co., 1935), p. 167.

this framework, the quantity of money in conjunction with liquidity preference determines the actual rate of interest in given circumstances. Keynes recognized uncertainty as to the future of the rates of interest as a necessary condition for the phenomenon of interest. He stressed uncertainty as the basis for the complex of rates of interest for varying maturities. As noted in earlier chapters, Keynes summarized liquidity preference in terms of the transaction, precautionary, and speculative motives, and he considered the speculative motive as the most important in the determination of the structure of rates. Actually, these two theories are merely alternative explanations, and it may be shown that they are consistent with each other.

Although money market instruments possess the common characteristic of liquidity, they do not possess identical investment characteristics. They differ with respect to risk, maturity, tax status, legal status, and marketability. A few examples are cited here to illustrate the influence of these factors in the determination of the rate structure. Federal funds and Federal obligations involve no financial risk; bankers' acceptances involve only a slight degree of risk; and commercial paper involves only a slightly greater degree of risk. Although none of these instruments involves very much risk, the difference is great enough to account for a slight differential in rates.

The maturities of money market instruments range from one day to one year. Transactions involving Federal funds, repurchase agreements, and discounts may involve only one or a few days, whereas other types of money market instruments may involve maturities of up to one year. Generally, the interest rate is lower on the shorter maturities.

With respect to tax status, it should be noted that bankers' acceptances have a tax advantage over some of the other money market instrumeents, which tends to depress the yields obtainable on acceptances.

The volume of trading is probably one of the best measures of marketability. It is easier to dispose of a given amount of assets when the volume of trading is large than when it is small. The volume of trading in some of the money market instruments is much greater than that in others. At any given time, a holder of money market instruments is limited in the amount of such assets that can be liquidated or acquired in the market at prevailing market prices or yields. Since the volume of trading in Treasury bills and Federal funds is greater than the volume of trading in other money market instruments, a holder of such instruments may liquidate a relatively large amount.

The existence of these differences gives rise to a structure of money market rates, in place of a single money market rate of interest. The differentials among the various rates tend to change with variations in the supply of and demand for individual types of money market instruments.

Dr. Roosa has described the structure of money market rates in the following manner:*

*Roosa, op. cit., pp. 32-33.

The keystone of the entire structure is the discount rate of the Federal Reserve banks. Fluctuating around, though more often below, the dominant discount rate, is the weekly auction rate for Treasury bills. Loosely related to both are the dealer bid and offering rates on bankers' acceptances and on commercial paper, the latter somewhat higher, partly because such paper is usually several months longer in term and does not carry a bank name. Then comes the "one-year" rate on . . . [Federal obligations] . . . and along with that is the whole family of prevailing rates on currently outstanding . . . [Federal obligations] . . . in the under-five-year area. Rates on the various Government agency issues, bank lending rates on stock exchange collateral [to dealers and to customers] and the somewhat slower moving rate of great significance to quality business borrowers the country over, the "prime rate" of the leading money market banks — all these are a part of the money market.

To illustrate the basic principles of the rate structure, the structure of rates on October 7, 1960 is shown in the following tabulation:

REPRESENTATIVE MONEY MARKET RATES

Federal Funds:

Open	High	Low	Final
$2\frac{3}{4}\%$	3%	$2\frac{3}{4}\%$	3%

Call Loans to Dealers: On Governments .... $3\frac{3}{4}\%$-$4\frac{1}{2}\%$
Call Loans to Brokers: Stock Exchange Collateral .... 4%-$4\frac{1}{2}\%$

Time Loans
   30-90 days .... 4%-$4\frac{1}{2}\%$
   4-6 months .... 4%-$4\frac{1}{2}\%$
   Effective Aug. 24, 1960.

3-Month Treasury bills:
   Market yield 2.53%

Commercial Paper:
   4-6 months .... $3\frac{3}{8}\%$-$3\frac{7}{8}\%$
   Effective Sept. 30, 1960.

Bankers' Acceptances:
   30-90 days .... $3\frac{1}{8}\%$ @ 3%
   91-120 days .... $3\frac{1}{4}\%$ @ $3\frac{1}{8}\%$
   121-180 days .... $3\frac{3}{8}\%$ @ $3\frac{1}{4}\%$
   Effective Aug. 24, 1960.

Discount Rate:
   N. Y. Fed. Res. Bank 3%
   Effective Aug. 12, 1960.

Source: *The New York Times*, October 8, 1960, pp. 30 and 34.

The rate structure in the tabulation above departs only slightly from the generalizations stated above. First, all of the money market rates except those of Treasury bills and Federal funds are above rather than below the discount rate at the New York Federal Reserve Bank. Second, the position of the prime rate (4%-$4\frac{1}{2}\%$) in relation to the rate charged on call money lent to dealers in Federal obligations and lent on stock exchange collateral does not suggest an immediate change in the prime rate. If the rate structure departed considerably from what is considered typical, it would suggest that change in the prime rate and discount rates is imminent. Third, the effect of maturity is clearly evident in the rates on various maturities of bankers' acceptances and commercial paper.

Representative money market rates for the period 1940-1960 are portrayed in Figure 24-1. The structure of rates has changed very little over

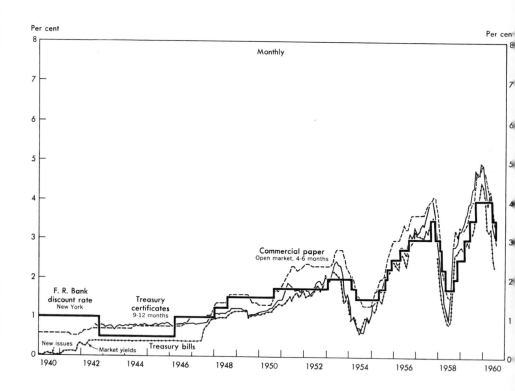

FIGURE 24-1   REPRESENTATIVE MONEY MARKET RATES, 1940-1960

Source: Board of Governors of the Federal Reserve System, "Historical Supplement to Federal Reserve Chart Book on Financial and Business Statistics," September 1960.

this period but the level of the rate structure has changed considerably. The chart shows how the rate structure was maintained during the period of war financing, and gradually the level of the rate structure became much more sensitive to business conditions. At the peaks, the discount rate was below other rates, whereas at the troughs the discount rate was above other rates.

The level of money market rates depends upon the state of business conditions, the state of expectations concerning future interest rates, the cost and inconvenience related to shifting into and out of money market instruments, and the interrelationships among money markets throughout the world. Generally, the level of interest rates rises during prosperity and falls during recessions. Money market interest rates tend to move over a wider range than capital market rates do, because the money market tends to serve as a temporary reservoir during a period of changing interest-rate expectations. The level of money market rates in relation to capital market rates depends upon the state of expectations as to future rates; this subject is covered in the latter part of the present chapter, which deals with the maturity structure of interest rates. Inasmuch as certain costs are incurred in the process of shifting from money to money market instruments, and there is an element of inconvenience in such shifts, money market instruments become unattractive below a certain level of money market rates. Furthermore, money markets throughout the world are interrelated, and when rates become relatively low in one country's market, funds tend to be shifted to markets in other countries, assuming freedom of movement. The shift of funds out of the United States to financial centers in other parts of the world during the latter part of 1960 is a case in point. Also, the effect of a given rise in the level of rates is greater when the level of market rates is low, and this tendency discourages temporarily the acquisition of some money market instruments. All of these factors tend to establish a floor below which money market rates will not be expected to fall. At very low rates, changes in the supply of money may have little or no effect on the level of money market rates. Additions to the money supply may simply flow into idle cash balances, there to await the return of a higher rate structure.

CAPITAL MARKET

As noted in the introduction to this chapter, the total system of financial markets may be broken down into two broad markets, the money market, and the capital market. Accordingly, the capital market is said to include the credit and equity market instruments that are not considered a part of the money market. Like the money market, the capital market is composed of many separate markets. Specifically, the capital market consists of the customers' loan market, the market for residential, commercial, and farm mortgages, the market for corporate, state and local government bonds, the market for long-term Federal obligations, and the market for equity market instruments.

Although brokers and dealers seek out and bring together suppliers and users of long-term funds, and match up the supply of and demand for long-term funds, the individual components of the capital market are not nearly as sensitive to change in demand and supply as are the individual money market components. Some of the markets for long-term funds are more regional than national. For example, mortgage lending rates are not uniform throughout the country, the rates even varying within a given region. One of the major reasons for these rate differentials is the absence of a well-organized secondary market for mortgages. The customers' loan market consists of literally thousands of local customers' loan markets. The customers' loan markets in New York City and other financial centers do involve firms on a nationwide basis, but most of the lending is restricted to local and regional customers. The pressures in these markets are reflected in the secondary market for government-underwritten mortgages and in the reserve position of commercial banks.

The markets for other long-term credit market instruments and the equity market instruments are of greater scope. The primary market for securities exchanges and the over-the-counter markets were fully described in previous chapters. At this stage of our study, it is necessary only to review in a cursory manner the over-all structure of the capital market and to note the level and structure of capital market rates (or yields) and their relationship to money market rates.

Supply of Capital Market Funds

The ultimate source of long-term funds is net saving, but only a part of total net saving constitutes effective supply of long-term funds. A portion of consumer saving flows directly into residential construction, durable consumer goods, and non-corporate firms. The remaining portion of consumer saving flows into cash balances, fixed-value redeemable claims, insurance and pension reserves, capital market instruments, and the reduction of liabilities. When saving is put to these uses, it flows into financial institutions, and the ultimate use of the savings depends upon the institutions' financial investment. The institutions themselves generate a small amount of saving through their retained earnings.

Almost all business net saving is used within the firms to build up both tangible and financial assets. Government saving is generally used to reduce outstanding debt, and the ultimate use of those savings depends upon the decisions of investors who have had part or all of their holdings of Federal obligations redeemed by the Treasury.

In order to estimate the flow of capital or the supply of capital market funds, it is necessary to estimate the increase in new capital, accumulated capital, and the savings of savings and loan associations, credit unions, mutual savings banks, life insurance companies, nonlife insurance companies, corporate pension funds, state and local retirement funds, investment companies, and commercial banks. It is also necessary to estimate the net flow of funds from the rest-of-the world sector and the direct flow of consumer savings into credit and equity market instruments. The problem is further complicated by the fact that each of the investor groups is free to invest a portion of these funds in money market instruments. Except for the commercial banks, it would be reasonable to expect most of the funds to flow into capital market instruments. Probably the most uncertain factor in the capital markets is the ultimate investment of funds that flow into the time deposits of commercial banks. Conceivably, commercial banks could allocate all of these funds to money market instruments. The rate structure and the demand for bank credit would be important considerations in the commercial banks' decisions as to investment.

Demand for Capital Market Funds

The demand for capital market funds is reflected in the issue of new security offerings and mortgages. As noted in previous chapters, there is a constant turnover of outstanding securities and mortgages as well as of net additions to the total stock of capital market instruments. Securities are issued by corporations, state and local governmental units, the Federal Government, and economic and political units in the rest of the world. Mortgages are issued by both individuals and firms.

The corporate demand for capital market funds is based upon the need to build up working capital and to add to plant and equipment. The forces leading to additional debt issues of state and local governments were discussed in Chapter 22, where it was pointed out that rapid population expansion and its concentration in urban and suburban areas have required that state and local governments provide additional facilities relating to education, highways, and other modes of transportation, public health and housing, sanitation, and police and fire protection. State and local government revenues have not been adequate to finance the large volume of capital outlays and at the same time meet the higher level of general expenditures. The Federal Government's demand for capital markt funds is determined by the changes in both the level and the composition of the Federal debt. To estimate the future level of capital market rates, it is necessary to predict the refunding policy of the Treasury and the relationship between revenues and expenditures. The volume of new issues in the United States by economic units in the rest of the world depends upon the condition of our capital market in relation to the condition of capital markets in other major countries.

The more important factors underlying demand for real estate mortgage financing are household or family formation, vacancies, demolitions, relative importance of multi-family dwelling units, family income, downpayment and maturity requirements, and expectations concerning all of these factors. The increase in consumer debt to finance consumer durable goods also absorbs capital market and money market funds.

The demand for capital funds is generally more stable than the demand for money market funds, but the principal components of the demand for capital funds may fluctuate considerably from year to year. Also, it must be recognized that part of the demand for funds may be shifted to the money market temporarily. Eventually, the long-term need for funds will probably be financed with long-term sources of funds. The flow of savings does not change much from year to year, so that the markets must be flexible. Otherwise, changes in economic conditions and corresponding credit demands would result in extreme strain in certain segments of the market and extreme ease in other segments. Flexibility is vital to efficient allocation of capital market funds and to the moderation of business fluctuations. Change in the level and structure of interest rates is a vital part of this flexibility.

Level and Structure of Capital Market Rates

The level and structure of capital market rates reflect the interaction of a complex variety of supply and demand forces. Certainly, the over-all economic conditions of the economy, the direction of change in business conditions, the state of expectations, and the nature and extent of government measures are underlying determinants of credit conditions and the level and structure of both money market and capital market rates. The structure of capital market rates covers a wide range because of the great variation in the degree of risk among the various types of capital market instruments. Also, there is great variety within a given class of capital market instruments. For example, corporate bonds may be assigned to as many as ten categories in terms of financial risk, and the variety among mortgages is so great that it is not possible to construct a meaningful index of mortgage rates.

A partial picture of the structure of capital market rates is presented in Figure 24-2, which shows that both the level and structure of rates have changed with the passage of time. However, there is a pattern to the changes that have occurred. With respect to bond yields, the relative position of each type of bond has not changed. The highest-quality state and local obligations are at the bottom of the rate structure, and the lower-quality corporate bonds are at the top of the structure. If gross yields on residential mortgages had been plotted on the same chart, the line would be above the corporate Baa line, reflecting risk, liquidity, and administrative costs. The yield on preferred stock parallels the yield on bonds. The structure of rates changed most radically with respect to yields on common stock. An analysis of this change is presented below. The narrowing spread between yields on state and local obligations and yields on taxable high-grade securities was discussed in Chapter 22.

The factors that explain the structure of capital market rates are almost identical to those discussed above with respect to the structure of money market rates. These factors include risk, maturity, tax status, legal status, and marketability. Assuming a high degree of certainty that income will be paid and principal will be redeemed, state and local obligations are at the bottom of the structure because of their favored tax treatment. The yield on long-term Federal obligations is relatively low because of the absence of risk, their acceptance as legal investments, and the volume of trading. Corporate bonds invoke varying degrees of financial risk; all corporate bonds are not legal investments; and the market is very thin for many corporate issues. Investors in corporate bonds require a premium to compensate for the less favorable investment characteristics.

The variations in the yield differential between the various types of capital market instruments reflect changes in the level and composition of output and state of expectations. Compare the yield differentials between the corporate Aaa and the corporate Baa bonds. The spread becomes greater during periods of recession and smaller during periods of prosperity. Looking only at the postwar period, the spread was relatively large during 1949, 1954, and 1958; and it was relatively small during mid-1948, early 1951, early 1953, and late 1956. A review of business cycles in the postwar period indicates a recession trough occurred in each of the former years, and cycle peaks occurred in the latter years. When investors are confident about the immediate future, they tend to reach out and acquire market instruments that involve slightly greater risk, and when they are uncertain about the immediate future, they tend to shift funds into market instruments that involve a lesser degree of financial risk.

Figure 24-2 shows that the actual level and relative position of the common stock yield has undergone extensive change in recent years. The decline in the level of the common stock yields indicates that prices of common stocks in general have been rising at a faster rate than the dividends paid on common stock. On the basis of maturity and financial risk, the stock yield should be higher than the bond yield. However, some of the other investment characteristics of equities have pulled the yields down below the bond yield. The organized securities exchanges provide a broad market for many equities. Although common stocks fluctuate over a much wider price range than bonds do, in the short run relatively large amounts of common stock may be sold quickly without serious effect on prices.

From the investor's point of view, dividends on stock have a tax advantage over interest receipts on credit market instruments. It will be recalled that institutional investors receive a dividend credit of 85 per cent in the calculation of the corporate income tax, whereas no credit is given on bond interest. Therefore, the effective tax on dividend income is lower than the effective tax on interest income. Also from the investor's point of view, the tax treatment accorded capital gains introduces a favorable investment characteristic. Since stocks offer much greater possibilities of capital gain, the demand for this type of asset tends to depress the yield on equities. Investors who are fortunate enough to select equities that appreciate considerably with the passage of time tend to keep their holdings in order to avoid payment of the capital gains tax. In other words, the relatively low capital gains tax attracts funds into equities, and at the same time discourages investors from realizing their capital gains. This situation tends to

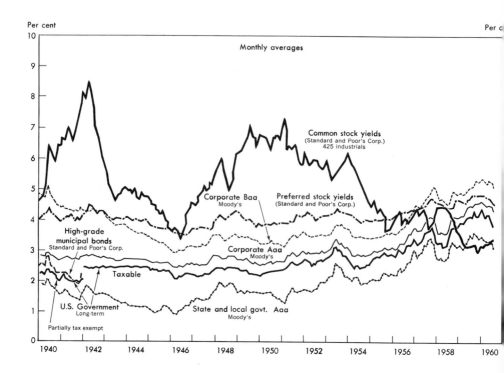

FIGURE 24-2   CAPITAL MARKET RATES, 1940-1960

Source: Reproduction of bond yield chart from Board of Governors of the Federal Reserve System, "Historical Supplement to Federal Reserve Chart Book on Financial and Business Statistics," September 1960; stock yields taken from Standard & Poor's *Security Price Index Record*, 1960 Edition, and *Current Statistics*, October 1960.

increase the demand for and reduce the floating supply of equities. There is also a tax consideration connected with the supply of corporate securities. Interest expense is deductible for tax purposes, which tends to make debt issues less costly than equity issues from the point of view of the issuer. The mix of corporate offerings has tended to depress yields on equities and to increase yields on debt issues.

Another factor accounting for the relatively low yields on common stock is expected growth in dividends. Investors assume that corporate earnings will improve and that higher dividends will be paid in the future. Although the yield based on present dividend and present price is low, the future yield based on future dividend and present price is expected to be higher. In some instances, the dividend income would have to increase at a phenomenal rate to justify the high market price of some stocks.

Many investors believe that the general level of commodity prices will continue to rise, so that they tend to adopt investment policies that incorporate some hedge against the possible loss of purchasing power. For many people, common stock investment is about the only possible method that can be adopted to hedge against inflation. Research proves that carefully selected and diversified common stock investment in the past would have offset much of the rise in the general level of prices.

Figure 24-2 indicates that the yield on common stocks was substantially lower than the yield on high-grade bonds between August, 1958 and early 1960. This comparison raises a very fundamental question: Is this a normal or an abnormal relationship? During the period covered by the chart, this relationship had prevailed only once before, in 1957. Additional insight into the question of whether the stock yield-bond yield relationship has undergone a fundamental change is provided by a historical review. The stock yield was lower than the bond yield for all but seven years during the period 1881-1900. One of the principal explanations for this imbalance was the fact that our financial system was still in its early stages of development. It was not adequate to cope with the tremendous flow of new debt issues, and the compensating factor was relatively high bond yields. The same relationship also prevailed in the late 1920's. Certainly 1928 and 1929 were not normal years; there was tremendous speculation in common stocks. During the 1930's the stock yield was lower than the bond yield intermittently, reflecting the inflow of foreign capital and the reduction or elimination of dividend payments. Our cursory review suggests that history does not support the contention that the yield relationship of 1959 and 1960 was normal. The argument that it was normal must rest on the assumption that a new era has come, and past relationships are no longer valid guides to future relationships. It is too early to take this stand.

RELATIONSHIPS BETWEEN MONEY AND CAPITAL MARKET RATES

Yields on Federal obligations over a period of time serve as a good frame of reference to illustrate the relationships between money and capital market rates. Figure 24-3 shows that interest rates on all maturities of Federal obligations tend to move generally in the same direction, with yields on shorter maturities moving over a wider range than yields on long maturities. Short and long-term rates tend to move up and down together for two reasons. First, demand schedules for funds in all maturity sectors tend to move up together during prosperity and tend to move down together during a recession. Second, professional investors carry on arbitrage operations when yields on securities in certain maturity sectors get out of line in relation to what is considered "normal." Professional investors conduct closely

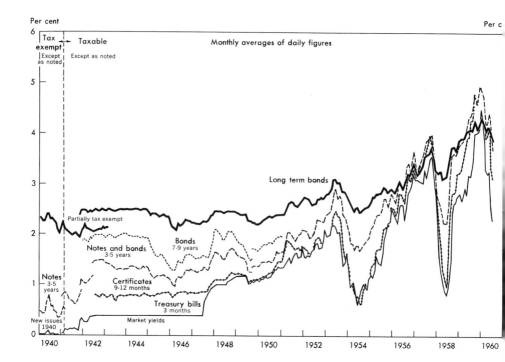

FIGURE 24-3   YIELDS ON U. S. GOVERNMENT SECURITIES

Source: Board of Governors of the Federal Reserve System, "Historical Supplement to Federal Reserve Chart Book on Financial and Business Statistics," September 1960.

timed sales and purchases in different maturity sectors; they tend to shift funds out of "overpriced" securities and into "underpriced" securities. In the short-run, these shifts may cause short and long-term yields to move in opposite directions. Third, substitutability or interchangeability as to market and maturity introduces much flexibility for suppliers and users of funds. These underlying factors tend to bring about a yield structure of short- and long-term rates that is considered appropriate considering the state of business conditions and of expectations as to prospective conditions and government policy. The maturity structure at any given moment is considered in the closing section of this chapter.

Arbitrage and substitutability are the factors underlying fluid movement of funds between various maturity sectors. The substitutability or interchangeability of different maturities exists on both sides of the money and capital markets. As an example, we shall consider lenders. The commerical banking system constitutes the hub of our financial system, and it is an established fact that commercial banks operate in almost all financial markets, both as lenders to the ultimate user and as lenders to other financial intermediaries. Non-banking financial intermediaries are very sensitive to yield differentials. They change their net flows in market and maturity in response to changes in the structure of yields. Individuals also shift funds in response to the same changes, as evidenced in October 1959 by the public's withdrawal of funds from savings institutions to invest in Treasury notes yielding 5 per cent. This action reduced the supply of long-term funds, and exerted upward pressure upon long-term yields, and particularly upon yields on mortgages.

Borrowers may be in a position to choose among various financial plans, and the structure of yields is one of the more important factors influencing final choice. Issuers attempt to design financial plans that will fit into a given market situation. They will attempt to market securities in the least costly maturity sectors, and the increased supply of such instruments tends to lower their prices and increase their yields. Whether or not high rates discourage borrowers from following through on their financial plans is open to question. That topic is considered in the closing chapter.

Obviously, there are links between the many individual markets comprising the money and capital markets. The yield structure serves as a signal device for the allocation of funds, just as the price structure serves as a signal device for the allocation of resources. However, there is widespread disagreement as to the degree of linkage and the speed with which funds are actually shifted among various market instruments and maturity sectors. The response of borrowers and lenders may be sluggish.

The position that one takes concerning the degree of fluidity among markets has an important bearing on his understanding of the mechanics of open market policy of the Federal Reserve. If there is a high degree of fluidity, then the initial effects in any maturity sector will permeate the entire structure of yields. On the basis of this assumption, it may be argued that open-market operations may be restricted to short-term Federal obligations. In fact, it may be argued that such operations are preferred because they minimize misinterpretation of open market measures. If there is not a high degree of fluidity among markets and maturity sectors, then it may be argued that open market operations should be conducted in all maturity sectors. Open market policy is discussed further in the chapters that follow.

MATURITY STRUCTURE OF INTEREST RATES

The maturity structure of interest rates may be shown in the form of a yield curve, with yield shown on the vertical axis and maturity shown on the horizontal axis. The yield curve is a snapshot picture. It portrays the yields as of a given moment in time. Obviously, comparable securities must be used in the construction of a yield curve. Federal obligations are commonly used in the construction of the curve, because they carry no financial risk and there are several maturity sectors.

The maturity structure of interest rates or the pattern of a yield curve may be explained to a major extent by reference to interest rate expectations. The continuous change in expectations leads to continuous change in the relationship between yields on short- and long-term credit market instruments. As the economy moves through the various stages of the business cycle, the yield curve undergoes continuous change. Three yield curves are shown in Figure 24-4. The smoothness of each yield curve implies perfect fluidity of funds among various maturity sectors and continuous adjustments in the market.

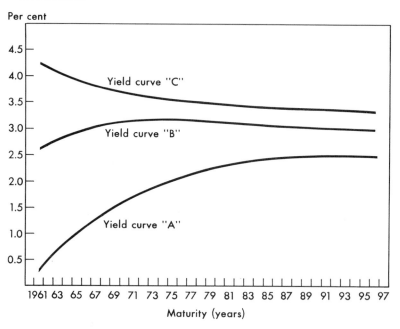

FIGURE 24-4   HYPOTHETICAL YIELD CURVES OF FEDERAL OBLIGATONS

Yield curve A may be typical of a recession period; yield curve C may be typical of a boom period; and yield curve B may be typical of a transition period in which the public's expectations are about evenly divided as to the future state of economic conditions. The pattern of a yield curve may be explained by an expectational theory of interest rates. The theory rests on the assumption that the elasticities of interest rate expectations are between zero and unity; in other words, the amount of revision in expectations resulting from a change in the level of rates is less than the amount of actual change.

Take the case of yield curve A for which the short-term yields are relatively low. It may be reasoned that the yield curve reflects the expectation that the level of interest rates — particularly long-term rates — will rise. That expectation may rest on the belief that the state of business conditions is going to improve or that the present level of rates is abnormally low. Given this state of expectations, investors will tend to avoid long-term securities in order to minimize future capital losses and to achieve maximum future interest income. In the meantime, investors tend to invest a proportionately large amount of funds in short-term credit market instruments, particularly Federal obligations. The excess demand for short-term credit market instruments tends to depress the yields on short-term obligations, and the lack of demand for long-term credit market instruments tends to increase the yields on long-term obligations. To the extent that borrowers' expectations are similar, they tend to shift part of their demand for short-term funds to the long-term market in order to minimize the cost of long-term capital. These forces are consonant with the forces set in motion by the suppliers of funds. There is a shift in the demand for funds to the long-term market, and a shift in the supply of funds to the short-term market. For a time, the spread between short- and long-term yields may be wide, and the yield curve will slope upward rather sharply.

The following quotation indicates what the structure of the market would be if funds were shifted among maturity sectors on a very carefully calculated basis.*

> If investors held identical expectations with complete certainty, the long-term rate for any specified period would become equal to the average of the expected short-term rates over that period. That is, neglecting compounding of interest, if the present rate for six-month loans were three per cent and this rate were expected to rise continuously to four per cent, five per cent, and six per cent, respectively, for the next three six-month periods, the current rate for a two-year loan would be about 4.5 per cent, the average of these rates. The reason for this is that the investor would have to be able to get the same return for investing for two years as he could obtain for investing now for six months and successively reinvesting in similar six-month contracts over the next two years. If this relationship did not hold, shifts of demand and supply would occur until it did prevail.

Yield curve C indicates that investors and borrowers expect long-term rates to fall. Perhaps the public expects a downturn in the state of business conditions. In this frame of mind, investors tend to shift funds to the long-term market to assure maximum future capital gains and interest income, and borrowers tend to shift their demand to the short-term market to minimize the cost of long-term funds. These forces tend to push short-

*Warren L. Smith, "Debt Management in the United States," Study Paper No. 19 in U.S. Joint Economic Committee, *Study of Employment, Growth, and Price Levels*, 86th Cong., 2nd sess. (Washington, D.C.: Government Printing Office, 1960), p. 82.

term rates above long-term rates. Another possible reason for a downward-sloping yield curve may be an excess issue of short and intermediate-term issues by the Treasury. For example, during 1958 and 1959 the interest-rate ceiling on newly issued Treasury bonds required that the Treasury raise almost all of its new funds and refund maturing issues by the issue of short and intermediate-term obligations. The excessive supply of securities in these maturity sectors caused the yields in these sectors to rise in relation to other yields, resulting in the rather strangely shaped yield curve, shown in Figure 24-5.

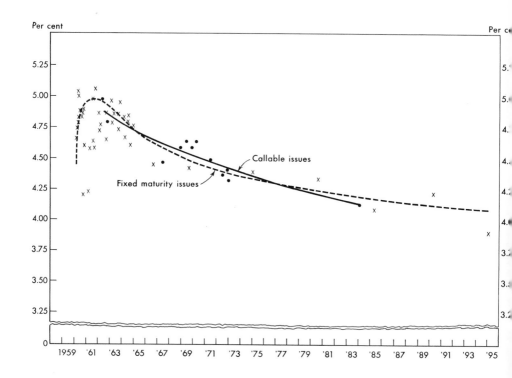

**FIGURE 24-5   YIELDS OF TAXABLE TREASURY SECURITIES, NOV. 30, 1959
(BASED ON CLOSING BID QUOTATIONS)**

Explanation: The points represent yields to call when prices are above par, and to maturity date when prices are at par or below. The smooth curves for two classes of points are fitted by eye. Market yields on bills other than those offered the latest week and on coupon issues for which an exchange offer has been made or which are due or callable in less than 3 months are excluded.

Source: *Treasury Bulletin*, December 1959, p. 54.

In the case of yield curve *B*, in which the short- and long-term yields are approximately equal, it may be assumed that borrowers and investors expect no change in the level of rates in the near future, or that their expectations are about evenly divided as to the direction of near-term changes in the level of rates. The yield curve shows short-term yields slightly below long-term yields, because borrowers tend to prefer long-term funds, which enable them to avoid frequent trips to the market, and investors tend to prefer short-term creidt market instruments, which help them to avoid loss of principal associated with future interest rate changes.

TYPES OF MARKETS FOR FEDERAL OBLIGATIONS

There are three types of markets for Federal obligations: free market, orderly market, and pegged market. A free market is one in which prices of outstanding Federal obligations are determined by natural forces of supply and demand; Federal Reserve and Treasury officials do not intervene in the market to influence the prices of Federal obligations. An orderly market is one in which monetary and Treasury officials buy and sell Federal obligations to prevent sharp fluctuations in prices. A pegged market is one in which monetary and Treasury officials tend to stabilize a given yield curve. Each of these markets is described in greater detail below.

In all three types of markets, the prices of Federal obligations are determined by the interaction of supply and demand. A pegged market is not a violation of the "law of supply and demand." Government officials simply influence either supply or demand in such a manner that the two functions or schedules always intersect at predetermined prices or yields. In other words, the prices or yields are administered. Such a policy may only continue as long as government officials adjust their holdings on the basis of price considerations.

The three markets may be differentiated according to the governing features of each. In a free market, monetary measures, regardless of their security price effects, are paramount. In an orderly market, price consideration may shift between flexible monetary measures and market conditions. In a pegged market, primary consideration at all times is the maintenance of a predetermined yield curve, and consequently a predetermined price structure.

Free Market

With some exceptions, the market for Federal obligations during the period between World War I and World War II may be considered a free market. During and immediately after World War I, a large amount of Federal obligations were unabsorbed by permanent holders. In such a situation a rapid change in the yield curve would be highly detrimental to the temporary holders and to the Treasury. However, in 1920 it was the opinion of Federal Reserve officials that conditions had changed and the market for Federal obligations did not preclude restrictive monetary measures. During the early 1920's, the prices of Federal obligations fluctuated over a wide range.

In a free market, monetary measures are carried out regardless of their effects on the market for Federal obligations. That does not mean that monetary officials would have no regard for security price effects; instead, security price effects would be secondary to other considerations. The term "free market" does not imply reckless actions taken by monetary officials. Since 1923, the purchase and sale of Federal obligations by Federal Reserve banks have been recognized as instruments of control, and the use of such open-market operations is permissible in a free market. When market considerations do not permit the use of monetary measures, it is doubtful if the market may be considered a "free" market.

Orderly Market

During the late 1930's Federal Reserve and Treasury officials became concerned with fluctuations in the prices of Federal obligations, because of the repercussive effects that sharp and wide swings in prices of Federal obligations had on the portfolios of commercial banks and on the capital markets in general. For instance, in March, 1937 the money market banks decreased their holdings of Federal obligations as a result of increased reserve requirements and withdrawals of balances by correspondent banks. The banks held Federal obligations in all maturity sectors, and they chose to sell the longer-term obligations in order to realize capital gains. The amount of selling depressed the price of long-term obligations, and other banks began to sell so as to realize capital gains while it was still possible to do so. Prices fell further, and more banks sold long-term obligations, not to realize profits, but to minimize future capital losses. From February to April the long-term yield increased from 2¼ per cent to 2¾ per cent. During this period, the Federal Reserve open market committee purchased long-term securities and sold short-term securities to moderate the decline in long-term yields and to promote an increase in the yield on short-term securities.

Market manipulation may be defended on the basis of public interest.

> By helping to maintain orderly conditions . . . the system can exert a steadying influence on the entire capital market, which is an essential part of the country's economic machinery, and disorganization in which would be a serious obstacle to the progress of economic recovery. . . . The System also has a measure of responsibility for safeguarding the large United States Government portfolio of the member banks from unnecessary wide and violent fluctuations in prices. The System cannot and does not guarantee any current prices of Government obligations, nor does it undertake to preserve for member banks such

profits as they may have on their Government securities, or to protect them against losses in this account.*

In early 1942, a pegged market was substituted for an orderly market. A policy statement of the Federal Open Market Committee on June 28, 1949, contained some indication that an orderly market was being reinstated by Federal Reserve authorities, and in early 1951 the actions of the Federal Open Market Committee became consistent with the criteria of an orderly market.

In the 1959 Hearings of the Joint Economic Committee, Federal Reserve officials were asked to indicate what constitutes disorderly conditions in the Government securities market. The following statement was submitted:

> The general conception of disorderly market conditions in the Government securities market envisions a situation in which selling "feeds on itself," that is, a situation in which a fall in prices, instead of eliciting an increase in the amount of securities demanded and a decrease in the amount supplied, elicits the reverse — a falling away of bids and a rise in both the number and the size of offerings. Temporarily, there is no price level which will clear the market. The presence of these technical conditions, however, may not always be enough to warrant finding of "disorderly conditions," for other factors which accompany them or cause them must be considered, and these other factors must be appraised in terms of the extent to which they affect or contribute to market psychology. In this regard, the Open Market Committee in arriving at its finding of "disorderly conditions" in July 1958 was influenced, not only by the rapid falling away of prices and the virtual absence of bids in the face of a multiplication of offerings, but also by the threat of almost certain failure in a major Treasury refunding operation and by the development of a highly precarious international, political, and military situation. These factors contributed importantly to a demoralized atmosphere in which potential buyers appeared unwilling for a time to commit at almost any price.
>
> It is thus evident that the problem of determining what constitutes disorderly conditions is a very difficult one. It is clear that price movement alone would not ordinarily justify a finding that a disorderly market exists (although such a movement would nevertheless require careful consideration of its causes and possible consequences). Even rapid price change, accompanied by minimal trading, might not constitute a disorderly market condition if increased offerings were not being pressed on the market and, most important, if the price adjustment were occurring in an atmosphere free of panic.
>
> In general, three conditions would ordinarily have to exist to justify a finding of disorder: Spiralling price changes that tend to "feed upon themselves"; a trading vacuum accompanied by a buildup in the number and size of offerings and by a disappearance of bids; and a disorganized market psychology. The emergence of such conditions might be caused by or be coincident with major international or domestic political developments or a Treasury financing operation. . . . This definition is, necessarily, general rather than precise; a determination that

*Federal Reserve System, *Annual Report of the Board of Governors*, 1939, p. 57.

disorder exists in a particular market situation must rest upon appraisal of the combination of circumstances at the time, rather than upon application of firm criteria.*

Pegged Market

The pegged market had its origin in the financing of World War II. In this type of market, the purchase and sale of Federal obligations by monetary and Treasury officials rest primarily on price or yield considerations. In a fully pegged market, there is general agreement on both rates and maturities, and every effort is made to maintain the structure.

In the pegged market of World War II, the long-term rate was set at 2½ per cent. Setting the rate at this level was defended by the following list of arguments:† (1) Natural market forces determined it, (2) It was lower than the long-term rate in England, (3) It was reasonably in line with rate then being paid by savings institutions, and (4) The establishment of a higher rate would have led to higher returns to private investors. The rate was not necessarily the equilibrium rate associated with "desired" savings and "desired" capital formation. The maturity of the long-term Federal obligations was set at 25 years. After much controversy among government officials, the short-term bill rate was set at ⅜ of 1 per cent, and the one-year certificate rate was set at ⅞ of 1 per cent. In terms of our earlier discussion of the maturity structure of interest rates, the World War II yield curve implied that investors expected the long-term rate to increase.

In a pegged market there exists the problem of whether or not the fact that the market is pegged should be communicated to the market. During the period of the pegged market, the Federal Reserve authorities wanted to make a formal statement, and Treasury officials favored a policy that would keep the market "guessing." In line with the position of the Federal Reserve officials, it was desired that the spread between short- and long-term rates be narrowed, because a pegged market implies no uncertainty as to future rates and therefore little or no logical justification for a relatively wide spread in the yield structure. Treasury officials believed, however, that it would be possible to inject some uncertainty into the market and thus facilitate the maintenance of a wide spread. Actually, as it turned out, the action of government officials confirmed the existence of a pegged market. In a pegged market (and this was true of the market in World War II), it is possible for investors to gain a "free ride" on the yield curve. In other words, investors may purchase Federal obligations with the intention of re-

*U.S. Joint Economic Committee, "Employment, Growth, and Price Levels," Hearings, Part 6A, 86th Cong., 1st sess. (Washington, D.C.: Government Printing Office, 1959), pp. 1278-1279.

†For a discussion of the establishment of rates and maturities for World War II financing, see Henry C. Murphy, *National Debt in War and Transition* (New York: McGraw-Hill Book Co., Inc., 1950), pp. 90-103.

sale at higher prices in the future. Obviously, monetary measures are subordinated in a pegged market.

QUESTIONS

1. Define "money market." Define "capital market." Indicate the similarities and differences between these markets.

2. List and describe the major money market instruments.

3. Describe the structure and operation of the market for Federal funds. What functions are performed by this market?

4. Contrast the interest rate theories of Ohlin and Keynes.

5. Look up the present structure of money market rates, and explain the differentials within the rate structure. Compare the rate structure with the one shown in the text. Why has the level of the rate structure changed? Are there any important changes in the structure?

6. Summarize briefly the supply of and demand for capital market funds.

7. Look up the present structure of capital market rates, and explain the differentials within the rate structure. Compare the rate structure with the one shown in the text. Why has the level of the rate structure changed? Are there any important changes in the structure?

8. Indicate the nature and extent of interrelationships of the money and capital markets. What are the implications?

9. What is meant by the maturity structure of interest rates?

10. Look up the present yield curve of Federal obligations. Explain its structure in terms of the expectational theory of interest rates.

11. List and define the three types of markets for Federal obligations. What type of market exists today? Is it likely to change? Explain.

12. Explain the interrelationships among national economic objectives, financial markets, and government financial policies.

ADDITIONAL READING

All of the money and banking texts listed at the end of Chapter 4, a large number of investment texts listed at the end of Chapter 12, and a large number of public finance texts listed at the end of Chapter 21 treat topics covered in Chapter 24.

Board of Governors of the Federal Reserve System. *The Federal Funds Market.* A study by a Federal Reserve System Committee. Washington, D.C.: Board of Governors of the Federal Reserve System, 1959.

Conrad, Joseph W. *Introduction to the Theory of Interest.* Berkeley: University of California Press, 1960.

Keynes, John Maynard. *The General Theory of Employment, Interest, and Money.* New York: Harcourt, Brace & Co., 1935.

Lutz, F. A., and L. W. Mints (eds.) *Readings in Monetary Theory.* Philadelphia: Blakiston Co., 1951.

Madden, Carl H. *The Money Side of the Street.* New York: Federal Reserve Bank of New York, 1959.

Money Market Essays. New York: Federal Reserve Bank of New York, 1952.

Nadler, Marcus, Sipa Heller, and Samuel S. Shipman. *The Money Market and Its Institutions.* New York: The Ronald Press Co., 1955.

Roosa, Robert V. *Federal Reserve Operations in the Money and Government Securities Markets.* New York: The Federal Reserve Bank of New York, 1956.

The Treasury and the Money Market. New York: Federal Reserve Bank of New York, 1952. Contains reprints of six articles that originally appeared in the *Monthly Review of Credit and Business Conditions* of the Federal Reserve Bank of New York and a reprint of an address.

Willis, Parker R. *The Federal Funds Market.* Boston: The Federal Reserve Bank of Boston, 1957.

Current data and observation on the money and capital markets are provided in the monthly publications of banks and investment dealers. Three of the more widely read are the *Monthly Review of Credit and Business Conditions* of the Federal Reserve Bank of New York, *the Federal Reserve Bulletin,* and the First National City Bank Monthly Letter, *Business and Economic Conditions.*

25: National economic objectives

GOVERNMENT policies imply the existence of national economic objectives toward which specific measures or actions may be directed and in terms of which the effectiveness of specific policy measures may be evaluated. It is only in relation to the pursuit of and the successful attainment of national economic objectives that government policies have real meaning. Therefore, it is necessary to identify the objectives and know what they entail before examining the role and influence of monetary and debt management policy.

The establishment of objectives is based on the assumption that if Federal Reserve and Treasury officials state that certain specific objectives are being sought, and if their actions are reasonably consistent with the achievement of these objectives, then these objectives have operational significance for the formulation, implementation, and evaluation of such policy. These officials base their statements on the Federal Reserve Act and the Employment Act of 1946. Using this approach, it is possible to establish the following national economic objectives: (1) a high and stable rate of employment; (2) a high degree of stability in the general level of prices; and (3) a high rate of growth in our national output and procurative capacity. This set of objectives is not set forth as all-inclusive. The existence of other objectives might be established by the method used in this chapter, or by other methods. However, these objectives have received most attention in recent years, as evidenced by the Joint Economic Committee's "Study of Employment, Growth, and Price Levels."*

Monetary and debt management measures are not the only means of achieving these goals; fiscal policies and many other government programs

*In 1959, the Joint Economic Committee was authorized and directed to conduct a complete study of an investigation into the problems of providing maximum employment and an adequate rate of growth, as well as maintaining price stability and preventing inflation. The Committee conducted nine sets of hearings, received testimony from over 100 witnesses, and sponsored 20 special study papers by consultants. There was much diversity of opinion among the witnesses, and both a majority and a minority report were submitted at the close of the study. The reports, hearings, and study papers provide a wealth of material on the subjects treated in this chapter, and the author has drawn upon these sources in writing this chapter.

are directly related to these objectives. Monetary policy is probably a necessary ingredient of any over-all program designed to achieve these objectives. There is some doubt as to whether or not debt management falls into the same category.

The establishment of these national economic objectives is not a very difficult task. It is much more difficult to define each objective. For example, each of the objectives listed above uses the word "high." What does "high" mean? None of the objectives refers to a time period. Are the objectives to be achieved year-in and year-out, or are they to be achieved in the long run? What is meant by "long-run"? Does the employment objective really mean that the rate of employment should not vary at all? What is a "high degree of stability"? What are the limits of acceptable deviation? What is meant by "employment"? Does "general level of prices" refer to consumer prices, wholesale prices, or a combination of the two? Assuming that there is general agreement on the meaning of each objective, are the objectives compatible in our contemporary free competitive enterprise economy? In other words, can the objectives be simultaneously achieved within the given institutional structure? If not, which should be modified or sacrificed?

These and other basic questions are considered in this chapter under four major headings: (1) national economic objectives in a free competitive enterprise system; (2) establishment of national economic objectives; (3) meaning and measurement of national economic objectives; and (4) degree of compatibility among national economic objectives.

NATIONAL ECONOMIC OBJECTIVES IN A FREE COMPETITIVE ENTERPRISE SYSTEM

Economic institutions are practices and organizations that have to do with the use of the means of production and the distribution and use of final products. The primary function of economic institutions is the allocation of the available economic resources among alternative economic wants. Individuals must balance their desires for leisure against their desires for economic goods; they must balance their wants for present goods against their wants for future goods; and, given their demands for present goods, they must balance their want satisfactions among a multitude of goods. Inasmuch as resources are scarce in relation to aggregate demand for final goods, it is necessary to economize in their use; that is, the system should be efficient. The system should achieve maximum total economic want satisfactions, given the social organization and distribution of income and wealth.

Economic justice requires that an economic system have a relatively stable monetary unit and provide jobs to those who want to and are able to work. In this sense, a high degree of stability in the general level of prices and a high and stable rate of employment are basic conditions or requirements of any satisfactory economic and social system. Why have employment and price stability been set forth formally as national economic objectives? The answer is found in the past weaknesses or failures of our free competitive enterprise system. In response to the Great Depression of the 1930's the people became so deeply concerned with the failure of the free competitive enterprise system to provide ample employment opportunities that this basic requirement was raised to that of a social goal or economic objective. The people could no longer take for granted that the American economy would provide a high and stable rate of employment, and it became necessary to set up an employment objective or aim for the nation. Although the idea that our free competitive enterprise system needs to have goals or objectives formally stated was a departure from past theory, a high and stable rate of employment was not a new idea. A similar reaction occurred in response to the protracted rise in the general level of prices. A high degree of stability in the level of prices could no longer be taken for granted. The time had come to establish this basic requirement of a satisfactory economic and social system as a social goal or national economic objective, and to formulate and implement national policies to attain this objective. In summary, past failures of our free competitive enterprise system led to the adoption of a high and stable rate of employment and a high degree of stability in the general level of prices as conscious aims or objectives toward which government programs of action should be directed.

The major piece of national legislation having to do with national economic objectives is the Employment Act of 1946. This Act states that government programs should foster and promote free competitive enterprise. In other words, they should be consistent with the institutional structure of the contemporary American economy. The Act implies that government should not go so far in promoting national economic objectives that substantial institutional changes are required. It is limited to programs that are consistent with free consumer choice, free occupational choice, entrepreneurial freedom, private property and the right of contract, a free and competitive price system, financial incentives, and functional distribution of income. Government must be a part of our economic institutions, but the majority of the American people do not want it to become the major part. The objectives of our system were originally defined in terms of the individual, and the Employment Act indicates that the role of government should not expand at the expense of reducing the role of the individual.

If experience demonstrates that the government cannot simultaneously create and maintain conditions that afford adequate employment opportunities and foster and promote free competitive enterprise, then the people will have to make a choice between successful achievement of the employment objective and maintenance of our existing economic institutional structure. Of course, before making this choice, the people will have to consider what constitutes a high and stable rate of employment. For example, does a 95 per cent rate of employment in the long run satisfy the objective? If not, must the rate be 96, 97, or 98 per cent? If 95 per cent is the highest rate of employment that can be sustained under our present institutional arrangements, then how much of a change in the structure would be necessary to lift the rate of employment to, say, 96 per cent? These and other questions must be given careful consideration before large-scale government programs are adopted.

Since 1914, our free competitive enterprise economic system has relied upon monetary measures to curb a rise in the general level of prices, but in recent years restrictive monetary policy has been subject to much criticism. Critics have asserted that the rise in the general level of prices during the postwar period was caused by several factors, many of which were not and could not be affected by monetary policy. The market forces of industry and labor were able to raise prices and wages in the absence of excess demand. Many labor-management contracts stretch over a period of two to three years, building into the system an automatic schedule of increases in wages and fringe benefits even during periods of recession. Also, strong shifts in the structure of demand led to excessive expansion in plant and equipment and generous labor-management agreements in certain segments of the economy. Given a lower than expected demand for the products of these industries, the firms' higher unit costs were not conducive to price reductions. The higher level of prices also resulted from the fact that many firms in service industries, in order to remain competitive in the market for resources, had to increase wages and salaries more than the real increases in factor productivity warranted. These firms passed some or all of the higher unit costs along to the public in the form of higher prices. Medical and dental service fees were also pushed up during this period, reflecting a shortage in the supply of such services as well as a long-run lag in postwar price adjustments.

On the basis of these and other institutional factors, the contemporary economy has a built-in inflationary bias, making it very difficult to maintain a given price level and nearly impossible to bring about a reduction in the general level of prices, especially when the adjustments in prices and costs are supposed to result from a reduction in aggregate demand. A reduction in aggregate demand tends to lead to contraction in the rate of employment and growth. If experience demonstrates that the more conventional government policies no longer operate effectively in curbing inflation, then the people must either rely on more direct government measures or must sacrifice the traditional requirement of a high degree of stability in the general level of prices.

Many economists question whether or not stability in the general level of prices is vital to our economic and social system. They believe a substantial conflict exists between this objective and high and stable rates of employment and growth. They suggest that it might be wiser to adopt measures to offset the injustice caused by a rising price level than to sacrifice growth and employment. It is reasoned that if a rising price level is accepted as a necessary condition, it will be much easier to preserve our present institutional structure. If the people insist on maintaining a high degree of stability in the general level of prices as a necessary objective, substantial institutional change might be necessary. Only the issues are raised at this time; the degree of compatibility among objectives is considered later in the chapter.

In a country whose population is growing, productive capacity and national output must increase to maintain the material standard of living and to provide jobs for a growing labor force. A rate of economic growth adequate to provide a high and stable rate of employment and maintenance of a given material standard of living can be considered a basic requirement of a satisfactory economic and social system. A lower growth rate would be unjust to the people. In this sense, employment, price stability, and economic growth are an "inseparable economic trinity."

Until recently, economic growth was not an economic objective. Individuals sought to improve their economic well-being and their combined activities produced growth in real gross national output. In his testimony before the Joint Economic Committee, Professor Milton Friedman of the University of Chicago stated that "there is no way in a free society to say in advance that one or another numerical rate of change is needed or desirable, or that a higher rate of change is better than a lower. . . . Whatever rate of change in the statistical aggregate results from the effort of free men to promote their own aspirations is the right rate."*

That economic growth is considered a national economic objective means that growth can no longer be taken for granted. Instead, it must be stated as an objective, and the government must pursue actively a host of growth-facilitating policies. Most economists specify a rate of growth very much in line with our historical experience on the ground that it will not require fundamental changes in our economic system. They want growth, but they want it to be consistent with the institutions of our free competitive enterprise system. A growth objective that requires a rate of growth no greater than our historical average rate of growth is viewed as a standard; that is, as something that should be achieved.

Some people believe that future economic growth can and should be greater than our historical averages. When stated in this manner, is

*U.S. Joint Economic Committee, "Employment, Growth, and Price Levels," Hearings, Part 9A, 86th Cong., 1st sess. (Washington, D.C.: Government Printing Office, 1959), pp. 3019-3020.

the objective in the same category as a high and stable rate of employment and a high degree of stability in the general level of prices? It would appear that some changes would have to be made to achieve a sustained rate of growth higher than, say, 3½ per cent. The "Staff Report on Employment, Growth, and Price Levels" minimized the necessity of change. It stressed three factors:*

> (1) In recent years, the total output of the economy has been well below its potential output. (2) So long as a major depression, like that of the 1930's, is avoided, the economy will probably grow in the future at a rate somewhat higher than the average rate for the past five decades. Making the least favorable assumptions about the future behavior of the factors determining growth, but still assuming no depression, it turns out that the economy will probably grow at a rate of 3.4 per cent every year. If somewhat more optimistic assumptions are fulfilled, the growth rate is likely to be 3.9 per cent per year. But to repeat, achievement of either rate requires that growth not be interrupted by severe or too frequent slumps in economic activity. (3) Actually, we can enjoy an even higher rate of growth, 4.5 per cent per year, if we try. Achievement of this rate of growth, which is considerably higher than the average of the past 50 years, requires no change in our economic way of life. It does, however, require that the Government actively pursue growth-facilitating policies, that it continually maintain an adequate level of aggregate demand, and that it promote increased resource mobility and competition.

The pursuit of growth-facilitating policies by the government will tend to speed up and direct future changes in the structure and operation of our economic system. Much discussion concerning the degree of compatibility between a rate of growth of this desired magnitude and other economic objectives has begged the more fundamental question, as to whether such an objective is consistent with maintenance of our free competitive enterprise system. It would appear that the fundamental issue has been avoided by making the assumption that the proposed government programs and policies will require no change in our economic way of life.

Even if a high rate of growth required fundamental changes in our economic way of life, the public might prefer the attainment of the growth objective. For example, if survival in the world economy depends upon the attainment of a "high" rate of growth, then the public would probably go along with the objective. Is it vital, or are other aspects of our total activities more important? The arguments or reasons underlying the need for a "high" rate of growth should be examined critically before approving programs or policies that require fundamental changes in our economic and political system.

Maintenance of confidence in the credit of the United States Gov-

*U.S. Joint Economic Committee, "Employment, Growth, and Price Levels," Staff Report, 86th Cong., 1st sess. (Washington, D.C.: Government Printing Office, 1960), p. xxvi.

ernment and a strong and dynamic financial system are vital aspects of our economic system. The role of the United States dollar in international trade and investment and the widespread ownership of Federal obligations among our private financial institutions make it imperative that credit in the United States Government be maintained. The importance of our private financial institutions has been stressed throughout this text. Private ownership of financial institutions is one of the fundamental characteristics of our free competitive enterprise system. Although these aspects of our system are not set forth as national objectives they are important things to consider in the formulation and implementation of policy. If and when the government programs and policies impair the credit of the United States Government or weaken the system of private financial institutions they might also be lifted to the status of national objectives. Until that time, their importance is taken for granted. Although many social scientists believe that a more equitable distribution of income should be one of our major economic objectives, public officials, who are vested with the responsibility of carrying out financial policies, have not publicly accepted it as an operational objective.

ESTABLISHMENT OF NATIONAL ECONOMIC OBJECTIVES

As noted in the introduction to this chapter, the establishment of national economic objectives is based upon the assumption that if Federal financial officials state that certain specific objectives are sought and if their actions are reasonably consistent with the achievement of these objectives, then these objectives have operational significance for the formulation, implementation, and evaluation of financial policies. Officials base such statements on existing national legislation.

National Legislation

In the Employment Act of 1946, Congress declared that:

> It is the continuing policy and responsibility of the Federal Government to use all practicable means consistent with its needs and obligations and other essential considerations of national policy, with the assistance and cooperation of industry, agriculture, labor, and state and local governments, to coordinate and utilize all its plans, functions, and resources for the purpose of creating and maintaining, in a manner calculated to foster and promote free competitive enterprise and the general welfare, conditions under which there will be afforded useful employment opportunities including self-employment, for those able, willing, and seeking to work, and to promote maximum employment, production, and purchasing power.[*]

[*]U.S. Senate Committee on Finance, "Investigation of the Financial Condition of the United States," Hearings, Part 3, 86th Cong., 1st sess. (Washington, D.C.: Government Printing Office, 1957), p. 1518.

The Employment Act states that "all practicable means" are to be used in achieving the purposes of the act. Federal Reserve and Treasury officials interpret this phrase to include monetary and debt management policy. Although the Act does not state explicitly that a high degree of stability in the general level of prices is an objective, officials have given this interpretation to the phrase "maximum purchasing power." For example, Chairman Martin of the Federal Reserve, in testimony before the Senate Committee on Finance stated that the Federal Reserve Act and the Employment Act of 1946 supply the Federal Reserve with a mandate to seek price stability in conjunction with economic growth.

Statements of Officials Responsible for Financial Policies

Study of officials' replies to questionnaires sent out by Congressional committees provide much insight into the national economic objectives that influence their actions. During the postwar period, the Chairman of the Board of Governors of the Federal Reserve System and the Secretaries of the Treasury have stated emphatically that their actions have been directed toward the attainment of employment, growth, and price level objectives. These officials have defended their actions in terms of these goals. However, they have admitted that employment, growth, and price stability are relative objectives, and the relative importance of a particular objective may vary with over-all economic, political, and social conditions.

A few selected statements of these officials are cited here to illustrate the operational significance of these objecties. Before the Senate Finance Committee, Chairman Martin of the Federal Reserve made the following statement:*

> The objective of the . . . (Federal Reserve) . . . System is always the same — to promote monetary and credit conditions that will foster sustained economic growth together wtih stability in the value of the dollar. This goal may be thought of in human terms and should be. The first part may be considered as concerned with job opportunities for wage earners; the latter as directed to protecting those who depend upon savings or fixed incomes, or who rely upon pension rights. In fact, however, a realization of both aims is vital to all of us. They are inseparable. Price stability is essential to sustainable growth. Inflation fosters maladjustments.

The Honorable Robert B. Anderson, then Secretary of the Treasury, made the following statement before the Joint Economic Committee:

"Our national economic objectives can be summarized under three broad headings: (1) continuity of employment opportunities for those able, willing, and seeking to work; (2) a high and sustainable rate of economic growth; and (3) reasonable stability of price levels. Each of these

*Ibid., p. 1262.

objectives is important; each is related to the others."* In this same general statement, the Secretary stated "that Government can make a most significant contribution to growth primarily by using its broad financial powers — fiscal, debt management, and monetary policies — to promote reasonable stability of price levels and relatively complete and continuous use of our economic resources." †

In reply to a question submitted by a member of the Joint Economic Committee, Treasury Secretary Anderson stated that:**

> . . . promotion of sustainable economic growth with stable prices and minimization of interest payments on the public debt are both important objectives of Treasury debt management. When these two objectives come into conflict, however, economic stabilization must be given a higher priority than minimization of interest costs. A number of observers believe that the primary or sole objective of debt management should be to promote sustainable economic growth with stable prices by countering inflationary and deflationary pressures in the economy. They argue that the Treasury should rely heavily on issues of long-term bonds during periods of economic expansion and on short-term financing during periods of economic contraction. It would be impossible to adhere strictly to this approach in practice, nor would it be desirable to do so. . . . Within the limits imposed by . . . important practical considerations, the Treasury does attempt to minimize reliance on short-term financing during periods of expansion, and it also attempts to handle its financing in a recession in a manner that will contribute to balance economic recovery.

MEANING AND MEASUREMENT OF NATIONAL ECONOMIC OBJECTIVES

Almost everyone will agree that the objectives established in the previous section of this chapter should be national economic objectives, but it is doubtful that they will agree on the meaning of each objective. In this section we shall review some of the technical and statistical problems relating to each of the objectives.

High and Stable Rate of Employment

There are differences of opinion as to the construction or interpretation of statistical measures of the labor force, employment, and unemployment. Also the qualitative aspects of both employment and unemployment are

*U.S. Joint Economic Committee, "Employment, Growth, and Price Levels," Hearings, Part 6A, 86th Cong., 1st sess. (Washington, D.C.: Government Printing Office, 1959), p. 1088.

† Ibid., p. 1092.

**U.S. Joint Economic Committee, "Employment, Growth, and Price Levels," Hearings, Part 10, 86th Cong., 1st sess. (Washington, D.C.: Government Printing Office, 1960), p. 3265.

important considerations in determining the seriousness of a given level of unemployment and the appropriateness of different policies to deal with unemployment. A recent statement of the Chamber of Commerce of the United States illustrates some of the problems connected with unemployment statistics.*

> Unemployment statistics lump together many diverse categories. They include some who are unemployable for one reason or another; some who are shopping around but are unwilling to accept employment at the wage rates their skills and experience can command on the market; others who are in the labor force temporarily (college students during the summer for instance); and still others who are voluntarily and temporarily out of work as they change from one job to a better one. . . . Unemployment totals give little indication of the numbers entering or leaving the labor force or the numbers moving into or out of employment. . . . They fail to include some workers involuntarily working less than full time. Unemployment statistics also include the involuntary unemployed, those who have lost their jobs as a result of seasonal and of cyclical fluctuations in economic activity, and many who have lost their jobs because of secular changes in the composition of final demand, in techniques of production, in composition of materials, in the location of economic activities. Some of these victims of secular change are in areas and industries where their labor is surplus, but can look forward to other jobs using their skills and experiences in other areas or other industries. Other victims are not so fortunate; the demand for their skills, in whatever area or industry, has declined, and they can only hope for renewed employment at a different occupation, which may require either retraining or reduction in their wage rates.

This statement illustrates why a single unemployment ratio is very unsatisfactory as a guide to public policy.

Unemployment is comprised of both cyclical and frictional unemployment. Cyclical unemployment is associated with business fluctuations. Frictional unemployment exists at all times; it includes unemployment associated with seasonal fluctuations, job shifting between occupations, industries, and areas, and the entrance of new workers into the labor force. Free occupational choice is a basic economic institution in our economy system and it is expected that workers will shift jobs in response to better job opportunities or higher incomes. A certain amount of frictional unemployment is involved in factor mobility. A recent study indicated that voluntary shifting from one job to another accounted for roughly 10 per cent of the unemployed during the 1955-1957 period.† Only 4 per cent of the labor force was involved in such job shifting, but there was a high rate of unemployment among those workers who shifted jobs. The study re-

*U.S. Joint Economic Committee, "Employment, Growth, and Price Levels," Hearings, Part 9B, 86th Cong., 1st sess. (Washington, D.C.: Government Printing Office, 1959), pp. 3146-3147.

†U.S. Joint Economic Committee, "Employment, Growth, and Price Levels," Staff Paper No. 6, "The Extent and Nature of Frictional Unemployment," Bureau of Labor Statistics, 86th Cong., 1st sess. (Washington, D.C.: Government Printing Office, 1959).

vealed that one in every three of the persons involved in such job shifts was unemployed in the process. It takes time for new members of the labor force to locate jobs. The study revealed that the continuing entry of new workers into the labor force, including those who re-entered after a period of absence, accounted for about 20 per cent of the unemployed during the period 1955-1957. Most of the new entrants found jobs after a relatively brief search. Seasonal fluctuations in employment accounted for an estimated 20 per cent of the unemployed during the same period. The percentage probably would have been higher had more data been available.

The importance of recognizing frictional unemployment in the formulation and implementation of financial policies is stressed in the B.L.S. study referred to above. It was stated that:

> The acceptance of the fact of an unavoidable minimum level of unemployment in our economy raises the inevitable question of what that level ought to be. Federal Government action to minimize unemployment without unduly stimulating inflationary pressures demands, as a prerequisite, as complete an understanding as possible of the nature of frictional unemployment. This is especially true since frictional unemployment is not a single form of unemployment, but rather a complex of many factors — economic, institutional, and personal.*

The problem is especially difficult when it is recognized that the present system of collecting employment and unemployment statistics does not measure directly the extent and nature of frictional unemployment. It appears that frictional unemployment may approach 3 per cent of the labor force, which means that the employment objective should not be set any higher than 97 per cent of the labor force.

The seriousness of a given rate of unemployment depends upon the turnover among the unemployed. It is obvious that workers involved in long-term unemployment experience adverse psychological effects and lose much income. All types of unemployment may lead to long-term unemployment. However, there is a tendency for unemployment associated with seasonal factors, voluntary job shifting, and new entrants into the labor force to be of shorter duration than structural and cyclical unemployment. The B.L.S. study reported that "unemployment lasting 15 weeks or over averaged 560,000 in 1957, or about 20 per cent of the unemployed total."† Concerning cumulative weeks of unemployment, it was reported that over 1.5 million workers experienced more than 26 weeks of unemployment in 1957.

The prescription to remedy unemployment depends upon the nature of as well as the extent of unemployment. If most of a given level of unemployment were of a frictional nature, financial policies would not have much effect in reducing it. Instead, the policies might lead to inflation

*Ibid., p. 2.
†Ibid., p. 5.

If a major portion of the unemployment represented involuntary unemployment associated with a general downturn in economic conditions, financial policies could be used to increase aggregate demand and reduce the rate of unemployment. If much of the unemployment were associated with long-term structural changes in the economy, financial policies might not be appropriate. More direct policies and programs might be necessary, especially in dealing with the problem of depressed areas.

There is no strong evidence of a distinct trend toward either a higher or lower rate of employment.* Between 1957 and 1960 the rate of employment averaged about 95.5 per cent of the labor force. During this period, the rate did not exceed 97 per cent, and at the trough of each of the postwar recessions it fell as low as or not lower than 93 per cent. If the employment objective is set at 96 per cent of the labor force, the economy will have to perform better in the future than it has in the past. Some persons assert that the rate of employment should be lower than this in order to facilitate stability in the general level of prices, to improve factor mobility, to encourage the workers who are employed to be more efficient, and to promote sounder long-term growth. The rebuttal to this point of view is to question whether or not stability in the general level of prices is an essential condition to a strong and growing economy and to question whether or not unemployment is the most desirable means of improving factor mobility, efficiency, and the rate of growth.

What happens if the employment objective is set at 96 per cent of the labor force, and our system provides jobs for only 95 per cent of the labor force? The answer to this fundamental question depends upon what was meant by the objective. Was the 96 per cent rate of employment a target to shoot for or was it a standard? It should be remembered that the employment goal first received attention during the Great Depression, when the rate of employment fell considerably below the historical average. To some people the high and stable rate of employment represents a target for the economy to shoot for, and if the economy fails to achieve it, drastic action is not necessary unless the actual rate falls far short of the goal. To others, the objective represents a standard or expectation, and failure to achieve that objective calls for positive action on the part of the government, even though the actual rate of employment may be as high as the historical rate. Officials charged with the formulation and implementation of policy tend to view the employment objective as a target, whereas many economists and liberal politicians tend to see it as a standard. It is not surprising that these two groups disagree on policy.

High Degree of Stability in the General Level of Prices

Three indexes are currently being used to measure change in the general level of prices: (1) the Consumer Price Index, (2) the Wholesale Price

*Ibid., p. 60.

Index, and (3) the gross national product implicit price deflator. The Consumer Price Index measures retail price trends of goods and services in the consumer sector. The Wholesale Price Index measures price trends of commodities in primary markets. The gross national product implicit price deflator measures change in the over-all price level of all final purchases in all sectors of the economy. The objective as stated above does not specify which price index should be used as a guide to policy.

The Consumer Price Index is probably the most frequently quoted index in discussions pertaining to the price level objective because of concern for the consumer. This index, which is compiled by the Bureau of Labor Statistics, is a statistical measure of changes in the prices of goods and services purchased by moderate-income families of urban wage earners and salaried clerical workers. The quantities and qualities of goods and services that go into the computation of this index are referred to as the "market basket." About 300 representative goods and services make up the "market basket," and each item is given an importance or weight in the index calculation equal to its importance in family spending, as determined by consumer spending patterns in 1951 and 1952. Both quantities and qualities are held constant, and change in the index measures only the effect of price changes. The computation of the index will be described in the following paragraph. A rise in the index means that retail prices, on the average, have risen; a fall in the index means that retail prices, on the average, have fallen. A change in the index does not mean that all prices have changed. During a given period, prices of individual goods and services may have risen, remained constant, or fallen. Inasmuch as the Consumer Price Index measures price trends of goods and services purchased by wage-earner and clerical-worker families, it is often referred to as the cost-of-living index. It is used as an automatic adjustment factor in many types of contracts, including labor-management contracts covering more than four million workers.

The Wholesale Price Index is a statistical*

> . . . measure of the general rate and direction of the composite of price movements in primary markets, and of the specific rates and directions of price movements for individual commodities and groups of commodities. The index is based on price quotations for approximately 2,000 commodities selected to represent all commodities sold on primary markets in the United States. All types of commodities, from raw materials to fabricated products are included in the index. . . . Basically, the same statistical method is used in computing the Wholesale Price Index and the Consumer Price Index. The individual price series are combined into the index by multiplying the value weight assigned each item by its current price relative, and summing to obtain

*U.S. Joint Economic Committee, "Economic Indicators," 1957 Historical and Descriptive Supplement, prepared by the Committee Staff and the Office of Statistical Standards, Bureau of the Budget, 85th Cong., 1st sess. (Washington, D.C.: Government Printing Office, 1957), p. 54.

the current aggregate. The current aggregates are totaled by product classes, subgroups, groups, and all commodities. The current index for each of these is obtained by dividing the current aggregate by the appropriate value weight in the base period.

The Wholesale Price Index is widely quoted and is used extensively to trace price trends in the long run.

The gross national product implicit price deflector is a statistical measure of change in the average price of the final goods and services comprising gross national product. The Department of Commerce calculates the deflator price index by combining a number of other indexes, including components of the Consumer Price Index and the Wholesale Price Index. The index is applied to gross national product in current dollars in order to adjust the data to reflect constant dollars; that is, constant dollars in terms of some base period. The index is widely used in aggregative analysis and is probably the most broadly representative price index.

Many difficulties are inherent in all three of the indexes. The sample data used to construct and measure change in an index are not as accurate as they might be. Changes in quality of products and services are not reflected in the indexes. Assuming that quality of goods and services is improving in the long run, an upward bias is introduced. Product substitution in response to price changes also introduces an upward bias. Buyers tend to avoid higher prices by switching their purchases to alternative lower-priced goods and services. There is a time lag in the inclusion of new products in the indexes. In spite of these and other limitations or difficulties, the indexes are reasonably accurate. However, since these indexes influence policy, it is important that the availability of new products and changes in quality be incorporated as soon as possible in order to correct for built-in upward bias in the indexes.

Figure 25-1 and the data in Table 25-1 show that movements in the Wholesale Price Index and the Consumer Price Index tend to parallel each other. However, in the short run, the two indexes may not move in the same direction. For example, during the January, 1951 through July, 1952 period, the Consumer Price Index continued to rise, but the Wholesale Price Index reversed its upward trend and declined. If the Consumer Price Index had been the sole guide to action, the policy might have been one of monetary restraint. If the Wholesale Price Index had been the guide to action, the policy might have been one of monetary ease. Instead of using either one of these approaches it would be wiser to analyze the price trends of major groups of commodities making up each index to gain insight into the sources of price changes. The data in Table 25-1 indicate a serious time lag in the computation of the G.N.P. deflator, which precludes its use as a guide to action. However, the G.N.P. deflator is probably the best index to use in the evaluation of policy. Although it would be possible to establish mechanical guides to action based upon one or a

TABLE 25–1
CHANGES IN THE PRICE LEVEL, 1945-1959
(1947-1949 = 100)

Date	Consumer price index	Wholesale price index	GNP[1] deflator
1945 — July	77.5	68.9	(2)
1946 — January	77.8	69.6	(2)
July	84.6	81.1	
1947 — January	91.9	92.3	93.8
July	95.0	95.3	96.2
1948 — January	101.3	104.5	100.6
July	104.3	105.5	103.2
1949 — January	102.7	102.8	102.9
July	101.4	98.0	101.2
1950 — January	100.6	97.7	101.4
July	102.9	103.0	104.1
1951 — January	108.6	115.0	109.9
July	110.9	114.2	111.4
1952 — January	113.1	113.0	112.7
July	114.1	111.8	113.7
1953 — January	113.9	109.9	114.1
July	114.7	110.9	114.6
1954 — January	115.2	110.9	115.4
July	115.2	110.4	115.5
1955 — January	114.3	110.1	116.1
July	114.7	110.5	117.3
1956 — January	114.6	111.9	119.0
July	117.0	114.0	121.5
1957 — January	118.2	116.9	123.7
July	120.8	118.2	126.0
1958 — January	122.3	118.9	127.3
July	123.9	119.2	127.9
1959 — January	123.8	119.5	129.0
July	124.9	119.5	(2)
September	125.2	119.7	(2)
Per cent change:			
July 1946 to July 1948.......	+23.3	+30.1	(2)[2]
July 1948 to July 1950.......	— 1.3	— 2.4	+ 0.9
July 1950 to July 1953.......	+11.5	+ 7.7	+10.1
July 1953 to July 1955.......	0	— 0.4	+ 2.4
July 1955 to July 1959.......	+ 8.9	+ 8.1	[3]+10.0

[1] 1st and 3rd quarter figures.
[2] Not available.
[3] Based on January, 1959.
Sources: Bureau of Labor Statistics and Department of Commerce.

combination of price indexes, Federal Reserve and Treasury officials have strongly resisted the efforts of some legislators to establish rigid guides to action.*

*See Lloyd W. Mints, Monetary Policy for a Competitive Society (New York: Mc-Graw-Hill Book Co., 1950), Chapters 6 and 8.

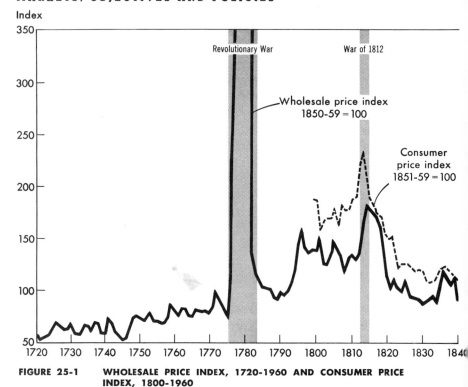

FIGURE 25-1   WHOLESALE PRICE INDEX, 1720-1960 AND CONSUMER PRICE INDEX, 1800-1960

Source: U.S. Joint Economic Committee, "Employment, Growth, and Price Levels," Hearings, Part 2, Statement of Ethel D. Hoover, Chief of the Commodities and Services Branch, Bureau of Labor Statistics, 86th Cong., 1st sess., Washington, D. C.: Government Printing Office, 1959, p. 395.

Figure 25-1 provides an historical framework within which to view the most recent inflationary period. The general level of prices more than doubled between 1940 and 1960, but this increase was not unusual compared with previous war periods, e.g., the Revolutionary War, the Civil War, and World War I. However, in previous postwar periods, the general level of prices eventually fell off sharply. It should be noted in Figure 25-1 that the Wholesale Price Index in 1930 was at the same level as it was in 1790. It was suggested in the "Staff Report on Employment, Growth, and Price Levels" that "we may view the sharp price rises of 1946-48 and 1950-53 with at least some equanimity, though this is not to say that they were in any sense desirable. The third period of so-called creeping inflation, however, beginning in mid-1955 . . . has caused much more concern because of the lack of any exceptional stress on the economy, and indeed, because the price indexes have continued to rise even in the face of relatively high unemployment and very low increases in output."* The price level objec-

*Op. cit., p. 106.

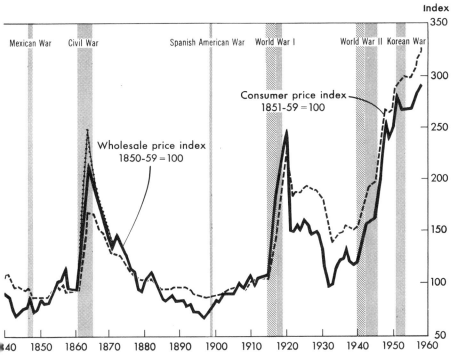

Index

350

Mexican War   Civil War   Spanish American War   World War I   World War II Korean War

300

Consumer price index
1851-59 = 100

250

Wholesale price index
1850-59 = 100

200

150

100

50

40 1850 1860 1870 1880 1890 1900 1910 1920 1930 1940 1950 1960

[1] Higher index Cotton at prewar importance.
[2] Lower index Cotton reduced in importance.

tive does not imply that the general level of prices should be forced down to its pre-World War II level. Instead, it means that the existing general level of prices should not be allowed to continue its almost constant rise. In other words, fluctuations in general level of prices should be held within narrow limits compared with past levels. Neither a major downward correction in the general level of prices nor a steady rise in the general level is desirable.

Stability in the general level of prices does not mean nor does it require stability in individual prices. A flexible price structure is relied upon to promote shifts in economic resources. Even during the recent inflationary period there was considerable flexibility in the price structure; the trouble was that it was almost all in an upward direction. A review of some of the major product groups reveals that price changes were not uniform during the 1947-1958 period. The price of services in the Consumer Price Index went up 50.7 per cent, whereas all items in the index went up 29.3 per cent. The Wholesale Price Index went up 23.7 per cent, but textile and farm products, respectively, went down 6.6 per cent and 5.1 per cent. On the other hand, metals and metal products went up 64.7 per cent. The major components of the G.N.P. deflator also show different percentage changes during this same period.

611

The effectiveness of monetary and debt management policies in restraining or reversing an upward trend in the general level of prices depends upon the cause or causes of inflation. Therefore, it is important to determine the cause or causes of a change in the level of prices as well as to recognize and measure the degree of change. Before moving on to the topic of economic growth, it is appropriate that we review briefly three of the more important theories of the inflationary process: (1) demand-pull, (2) cost-push, and (3) structural imbalances. Each is considered separately, but it must be realized that elements of each are involved in an actual inflationary process. However, certain elements may be more dominant than others, and it is important that the more dominant elements be uncovered and that appropriate policies be adopted.

The essential idea underlying the "demand-pull" theory of inflation is that the available purchasing power exceeds the quantity of available goods and services at the prevailing general level of prices. Assuming that economic resources are being used to nearly their full extent, it is not possible to increase the supply of goods and services in the short run, and equilibrium is restored by a rise in the level of prices. At equilibrium, the available purchasing power clears the market of the available supply of goods and services at the new prevailing level of prices. Assuming that prices of factor inputs and final goods and services are determined in impersonal, competitive markets and that prices are flexible in both directions, equilibrium is not disturbed by shifts in the composition of demand. Price increases in one sector are offset by price reductions in other sectors. If excess available purchasing power is the major cause of an inflationary process, aggregate fiscal and monetary policies are appropriate, but to the extent that the assumptions relating to market structure and operation are not consistent with reality, restrictive aggregate fiscal and monetary policies may have adverse effects on the rate of employment and the level of national output.

The essential idea underlying the "cost-push" theory of inflation is that both industry and labor groups tend to establish higher prices for their products and services than would be determined in impersonal, competitive markets. Various terms are applied to this type of inflationary process. The process may be referred to as "sellers" inflation to emphasize the fact that sellers initiate the price increases. The process may be referred to as "administered-price" inflation in view of the fact that sellers are able to administer their prices. Since the ability to establish or administer prices implies an element of market power, the process may also be referred to as "market-power" inflation. "Cost-push" inflation is most clearly indicated when prices of goods and services rise in spite of excess capacity or supply, and wage rates increase in spite of excess unemployment. The downward rigidity of wages and prices also reflects the influence of market power of industry and labor. This type of inflation cannot take place in the absence of an increase in available purchasing power. If aggregate demand does not increase sufficiently to support the higher prices for products and services, market power is weakened. Some people contend that aggregate fiscal and monetary policies are appropriate in dealing with this type of inflation. They contend that if labor and industry groups believe that supporting fiscal and monetary policies will not be adopted, those groups will not exercise excessively their market power. However, if those groups fail to restrain their market power, and restrictive fiscal and monetary policies are adopted to curb the increase in the general level of prices, the measures are likely to have adverse effects on the rate of employment and the level of national output. The nature of cost-push inflation suggests that direct measures will have to be adopted if aggregative fiscal and monetary policies are to be effective. Only a few of the possible measures are suggested. First, the government might participate in the setting of wages and prices in those sectors in which market power is excessive. Second, more rigorous antitrust enforcement might be used to reduce market power in selected industries. Third, more restrictive labor legislation might be adopted to curb industry-wide bargaining. Fourth, a reduction in trade barriers might be used to increase the degree of competition between the domestic and foreign markets.

The basic idea underlying the "structural imbalance" theory of inflation is "that an initial upward thrust of prices and wages can occur in particular sectors of the economy because of substantial and rapid shifts in demand toward those sectors, though aggregate demand in the economy is not excessive."* The theory rests on the assumptions of factor immobility and lack of downward flexibility in prices and wages. The theory holds that the factors of production cannot adjust quickly to shifts in demand, and the resulting market pressures lead to higher wages and prices in those sectors. A shift in demand implies that demand has declined in one or more sectors. Assuming impersonal, competitive markets, prices and wages would be expected to fall in those sectors in which demand is falling. However, the market power of both industry and labor tend to block reductions in prices and wages, and instead, the higher prices and wages tend to filter out to these sectors. In the contemporary American economy, flexibility in our wage and price structure is achieved by differential rates of increase in wages and prices rather than by a combination of increases and decreases in prices and wages.

The "Staff Report on Employment, Growth, and Price Levels" set forth the problem of dealing with types of inflation in a very succinct manner.†

> It is clear that the use of aggregative monetary and fiscal controls will result primarily in lowered output and employment with only small

*Staff Report, op. cit., p. 116.
†Ibid., p. 117.

effects on the level of wages or prices. If attempts are made by selective controls of some sort to halt the price rise in the particular sectors where demand pressures exist, there is danger that additional resources of labor and capital, which should be attracted into those sectors, will not be; in the long run, the allocating function of the pricing mechanism will be seriously impaired. Conceptually, the most appropriate policy would be to reduce the degree of downward inflexibility in the labor and product market. How this can be done without sacrificing other desirable objectives, however, is a most difficult question.

The review of the major theories of inflation emphasizes the fact that an inflationary process is a very complex phenomenon and there is no single policy that is best in all inflations. The discussion of monetary and debt management policies in the concluding chapter is based on the assumption that officials can determine when the use of such policies is appropriate.

Rate of Growth in National Output and Productive Capacity

The establishment of economic growth as an objective implies that the rate of growth can be measured. The objective, as stated above, indicates that the rate of change in national output and productive capacity are appropriate measures of economic growth.* Obviously, growth in national output should be measured in terms of constant dollars rather than in current dollars, which can be accomplished by the use of the gross national product implicit price deflator. Since part of the national output must be used to replace capital consumption, net national output is preferable to gross national output as an indicator of growth in productive capacity. However, the estimates of capital consumption are not wholly reliable, so that gross national product is used in practice. If attention is focused on growth in the industrial sector, the Federal Reserve Board's Index of Industrial Production is an appropriate measure of economic growth.

Economic growth is desirable for many reasons, a few of which are cited here. First, it enables the American people to achieve higher levels of consumption and to reduce poverty. Second, public services can be expanded without contracting private consumption. Third, it enables the United States to provide increased economic aid to the so-called underdeveloped nations and to expand trade with other countries.

Since our purpose in the following two chapters is to examine the financial policies in relation to our national economic objectives, it is appropriate that we present the basic factors underlying the level of national output. Output depends upon the quantity and quality of factor inputs

*It may be argued that "true" economic growth is that over and above the increase in national output resulting from change in population. The way in which growth is defined in this chapter implies that growth can come about simply from sustained employment and population growth. In fact the term "high rate of employment" is embodied in the growth concept. An alternative approach would be growth in output per unit of productive factors, given the optimum rate of employment of human resources.

(land, labor, and capital) and the manner in which the inputs are combined. During a given accounting period, the volume of national output equals the percentage of population constituting the labor force, times the population, times hours worked per worker, times output per man-hour. Future growth is related to improvement in the quality of the factor inputs and growth in population and the stock of capital goods. The percentage of population constituting the labor force and the number of hours worked per worker are expected to decline in the future.

Science, technology, education, training, and health of the people are basic elements in the growth process. In fact, the major portion of future economic growth is expected to result from improvement in the quality of inputs and the manner in which the inputs are combined. The expected growth in the size of the labor force will provide growth at the rate of 1 per cent per year and the remaining portion of growth will come about through improvement in efficiency. Improved quality of the inputs and improved combinations of the factor inputs are the basic factors underlying improvements in efficiency. The "attributes of human beings which have been 'produced' as a means to the production of economic goods" may be referred to as nonmaterial capital goods or intangible capital.* This aspect of capital has been one of the most important elements in past growth and it will probably be the most important element in future growth.†

How high must the rate of growth be to satisfy the growth objective? Studies indicate that the real gross national product of the American economy grew 4.3 per cent per year from 1839 through 1878; 3.7 per cent per year from 1879 through 1918; and 3.0 per cent per year from 1939 through 1959.** If the growth objective is a standard rather than a target, it can be assumed that most people would not favor an objective that would be incompatible with the institutions of our free society. In other words, government should neither force growth nor assume a predominant role in the growth process unless basic freedoms can be preserved in the process. Government should adopt policies that are designed primarily to foster and facilitate economic growth in the private sector of the economy. Essentially, this is the position held by officials who have been responsible for the formation and implementation of financial policies. The following

*Howard Bowen, *Toward Social Economy* (New York: Holt, Rinehart, and Winston, Inc., 1948), p. 89.

† The importance of intangible capital is underscored in the following: Soloman Fabricant, "Study of Economic Growth," in *39th Annual Report of the National Bureau of Economic Research* (New York: National Bureau of Economic Research, 1959), pp. 1-13; Soloman Fabricant, "Basic Facts of Productivity Changes," N.B.E.R. Occasional Paper No. 63 (New York: National Bureau of Economic Research, 1959); Howard Bowen, "Investment in Man: An Economist's View," *Social Service Review*, Vol. 33, June 1959, pp. 109-117.

**U.S. Joint Economic Committee, "Employment, Growth, and Price Levels," Staff Report, *op. cit.*, p. 23.

statement by the Honorable Robert B. Anderson, Secretary of the Treasury under the Eisenhower Administration, illustrates this point of view:* "In an economy in which major reliance is placed on individual initiative and decisions and in which the alternative uses of economic resources respond through the market mechanism, primarily to consumer demand, government can and should play only a facilitating, not a predominant role in the growth process."

Business fluctuations are a characteristic feature of our economic system, and it is not reasonable to expect a high rate of growth to occur year in and year out. This statement does not mean that the government should not attempt to moderate the magnitude and duration of business fluctuations; instead, it implies that the government should not attempt to eliminate business fluctuations. To do so would involve the loss or sacrifice of our basic economic freedoms. In other words, the "cost" is too great. Our economy has grown by staggering magnitudes in the past, and it is likely that future growth must also be of a staggering nature. It is generally agreed that the term "growth objective" refers to a certain average annual rate of economic growth. Probably the shortest period over which to judge growth performance is the length of the average cycle, which tends to range between 40 and 42 months.

As noted earlier in this chapter, the "Staff Report on Employment, Growth, and Price Levels" recommended a 4.5 per cent per year growth rate. The important question is whether this rate should be viewed as a target or as an expectation. If the economy grew at the rate of 4 per cent per year, would it be considered unsatisfactory? Compared with the past, it would not be unsatisfactory. In relation to the potential set forth in the "Staff Report," it would be. The officials charged with the responsibility for carrying out financial policies tend to judge the performance of the economy in relation to the past rather than to its potential.

The position of Dr. Leon H. Keyserling, former Chairman of the Council of Economic Advisers and President of the Conference on Economic Progress, provides a good illustration of a much more positive approach to economic growth. Dr. Keyserling set forth three great purposes of almost any economic system, including ours:†

> (1) To achieve steady and optimum economic growth in real terms. This means calling forth the maximum use of our productive capabilities, including manpower and brains, technology and science, and natural resources. . . . The whole history of economic progress has been founded upon the use of improved technology to increase produc-

---

*U.S. Joint Economic Committee, "Employment, Growth, and Price Levels," Hearings, Part 6A, 86th Cong., 1st sess. (Washington, D.C.: Government Printing Office, 1959), p. 1091.

†U.S. Joint Economic Committee, "Employment, Growth, and Price Levels," Hearings, Part I, 86th Cong., 1st sess. (Washington, D.C.: Government Printing Office, 1959), pp. 95-96.

tion and especially to increase production per capita. . . . (2) To apportion our total national production wisely, in accord with relative priorities of needs, so that we do not get what we need least at the expense of what we need most. . . . (2) To combine economic progress and efficient use of resources with economic justice, as the American people understand economic justice.

According to Dr. Keyserling:

> . . . the basic conditions for achieving these three great economic purposes may be stated fairly simply. I do not think that the desire or initiative or enterprise is lacking among our people and their various privately organized efforts to move consistently toward these three great purposes. Certainly, our public institutional devices and our system of free government are equal to their share of the task. However, the central economic condition for the accomplishment of these three great purposes, by no means yet achieved, is that there be a balanced development of (a) investment in the means of expanding production, and (b) the private and public consumption — meaning public demand for goods and services — at balanced growth rates which call forth maximum use of total resources and optimum economic growth.

Financial policies influence two important aspects of the growth process. Aggregate demand must be adequate to clear the market of the output resulting from higher productive capacity. Financial policies may be used to stimulate and support aggregate demand. The application of science and technology to production requires real capital formation. There must be saving and it must be invested in capital goods. Financial policies may promote increases in the available purchasing power to accommodate and facilitate secular growth and influence saving and its allocation into deserving capital projects.

COMPATIBILITY AMONG NATIONAL ECONOMIC OBJECTIVES

The growth and employment objectives are not only compatible, but they are also to some extent mutually supporting. A high rate of growth in national output and productive capacity requires an intensive use of all resources, including labor. However, it must be realized that economic growth does require temporary dislocation of employment and shifts of labor from declining industries, occupations, and areas to expanding industries, occupations, and areas. A high and stable rate of employment supports a high level of aggregate demand, which is favorable to the achievement of a high rate of growth in national output. However, overemphasis on achieving a high and stable rate of employment could impede growth if job shifting were discouraged or plant capacities so strained that productivity per worker and total output both declined.

The price level objective and the employment and growth objectives may not be compatible. The "Staff Report on Employment, Growth, and Price Levels" stated that three views of the relationship between growth and the price level were not substantiated by the Joint Economic Committee's study. The following summary is pertinent.

> We find that policies designed to stabilize the price level do not automatically promote economic growth. In fact, the present set of policy tools, applied with the objective of keeping prices stable, have been the major cause for the slowdown in growth. Second, we find that the promotion of growth will not suffice to halt the inflation. While it is true that an increase in final demand would have raised productivity in 1956 and 1957 and would have allowed the increase in productive capacity to be more fully utilized, it would have been impossible with the policy tools available to manage this increase in demand in such a way that it would not have added to the pressures on demand in those sectors in which prices were already rising. However, it does appear, with the benefit of hindsight, that the amount of growth that was surrendered for what at best was a small gain toward stabilizing the price level, was very large. Third, we find that inflation and growth are not separate problems.*

The Report of the Joint Economic Committee's "Study of Employment, Growth, and Price Levels" emphasized that the national economic objectives can be achieved simultaneously. However, the Report notes that the economy has failed to achieve them in recent years. According to the Report, "there has been more unemployment than usual in so-called good times. Although there has been an appreciable growth of productive capacity, we have not made full use of it, and total output has gone up at only a low rate. At the same time, consumer prices have gone up. Although there has been no serious and deep depression, sharp recessions have occurred."† Among the fundamental conclusions set forth in the Report, the following are pertinent: "It is possible with proper policies to achieve a high and sustained rate of economic growth, relatively full employment, without creeping or galloping inflation." Second, "Under present policies followed by the Administration, the Treasury, the Federal Reserve, and the Congress, we would have to choose between growth equal to our potential, on the one hand, or price level stability, on the other." Third, "In order to get a rate of growth close to our potential, we must reduce the inflationary bias of the economy so that we will not have to choose between growth, on the one hand, or stable prices on the other. We must then pursue programs of growth."**

Monetary officials have been queried about possible conflicts between price stability and other objectives. These officials tend to give priority to price stability if and when a choice is really necessary, on the assumption

---

*"Staff Report," op. cit., p. xxi.
† "Report," op. cit., p. 1.
**U.S. Joint Economic Committee, "Employment, Growth, and Price Levels," Report, 86th Cong., 2nd sess. (Washington, D.C.: Government Printing Office, 1960), pp. 2-3.

that price stability promotes employment and growth in the long run. They believe that sacrifice of price stability in the short run will lead to unemployment and a low rate of economic growth in the long run. In reply to a question concerning productivity, wage increases, and price stability, Chairman Martin of the Federal Reserve Board replied that "there should be no pressure on us to increase the money supply just to validate some imbalance which occurs in the economy."*

The failure to achieve simultaneously the national economic objectives during the postwar period supports the contention that the objectives are not wholly compatible. A reduction in the built-in inflationary bias would make the objectives less incompatible. However, is it possible to reduce concentrations of market power and increase the mobility of resources? It is much easier to specify changes that would be desirable, than it is to bring them about. For example, the institutions of collective bargaining should be encouraged to allow for the introduction of new technology, but how can that be accomplished? Certainly, a reordering in government expenditures would be helpful, but such an effort would require the elimination or reduction of various types of subsidy expenditures. The Federal tax system could be made more conducive to the successful achievement of the national economic objectives, but over-all revision of the system is most unlikely. If voluntary efforts fail to restrain groups that possess market power, is it practicable to set up hearing and fact-finding boards to participate in setting wages and prices? The tariff policy could be used to promote more effective competition between domestic and foreign firms. A vigorous antitrust program could be used to reduce some elements of market power, but progress along these lines is slow.

Until the built-in inflationary bias is reduced, how should the conflict between price-level stability and other economic objectives be resolved? The officials charged with carrying out financial policies will probably continue to give priority to maintaining reasonable stability in the general level of prices. If this decision on the part of financial officials precludes achievement of high and stable rates of economic growth and employment, it will tend to force needed legislation; that is, if the people really want to attain these other objectives. It has been suggested that stability in the general level of prices should not have priority over growth. It is asserted that a gradual rise in the general level of prices can be tolerated if the public's expectations of future changes in the general level of prices are inelastic. Under these conditions, the general level of prices could climb indefinitely, but how can officials be certain that the public's expectations will continue to be inelastic? If the expectations became elastic, the economy would experience hyperinflation.

*U.S. Senate Committee on Finance, "Investigation of the Financial Condition of the United States," Hearings, Part 3, 85th Cong., 1st sess. (Washington, D.C.: Government Printing Office, 1957), p. 1310.

QUESTIONS

1. What approach was used in this chapter in establishing national economic objectives?

2. Why is it necessary to establish national economic objectives in our free competitive enterprise system? Explain the establishment of the employment, price level, and growth objectives.

3. What is meant by a "high and stable rate of employment"? Indicate some of the problems of measurement.

4. Define "frictional" unemployment. What were the major findings of the Bureau of Labor Statistics?

5. What is meant by a "high degree of stability in the general level of prices"? Indicate some of the problems of measurement.

6. Describe the computation of a price index, and summarize the long-run movement in the consumer price index.

7. Name and describe briefly three popular theories of the inflationary process. Which theory best describes the most recent inflationary period?

8. What is meant by a "high rate of growth in our national output and productive capacity"? Indicate some of the problems of measurement.

9. "The growth and employment objectives are not only compatible, but to some extent are also mutually supporting." Explain.

10. Explain why the price-level objective and the employment and growth objectives may not be compatible.

11. "The national economic objectives can be achieved simultaneously." Write briefs for both the affirmative and the negative. Take a position and defend it.

ADDITIONAL READING

The Budget and Economic Growth. A statement of national policy. New York: Committee for Economic Development, 1959.

Defense Against Inflation. Policies for Price Stability in a Growing Economy, a statement of national policy. New York: Committee for Economic Development, 1958.

Domar, Evsey D. Essays in the Theory of Economic Growth. New York: Oxford University Press, 1957.

Economic Growth in the United States, Its Past and Future. A statement of national policy. New York: Committee for Economic Development, 1958.

Economic Report of the President. Washington, D.C.: Government Printing Office. See past and present reports

Egle, W. P. Economic Stabilization — Objectives, Rules, and Mechanisms. Princeton, N.J.: Princeton University Press, for University of Cincinnati, 1952.

Gordon, R. A. *Business Fluctuations*. New York: Harper & Bros., 1952.

Thorp, Willard, and Richard Quandt. *The New Inflation*. New York: Mc-Graw-Hill Book Co., Inc., 1959.

U.S. House of Representatives Subcommittee of the Committee on Government Operations. *Amending the Employment Act of 1946 to Include Recommendations on Monetary and Credit Policies and Proposed Price and Wage Increases*. 85th Cong.. 2nd sess. Washington, D.C.: Government Printing Office ,1958.

U.S. Joint Economic Committee. *Economic Report of the President*. Hearings and Report. Conducted each year and provide considerable data relating to goals and policy.

————. *Employment, Growth, and Price Levels*, Parts 1-10. Study papers 1-23; Staff Report; and Report of the Joint Economic Committee. Washington, D.C.: Government Printing Office, 1959, 1960. See the report for the titles of Parts and Studies.

————. *Relationship of Prices to Economic Stability and Growth*. Compendium of papers submitted by panelists, March 1958; hearings, July 1958; commentaries submitted by economists from labor and industry, November 1958; and hearings, February 1959. Washington, D.C.: Government Printing Office.

U.S. Senate Committee on Finance. *Investigation of the Financial Condition of the United States*. Hearings, Part 1-6. (Part 4 is an index to Parts 1-3); compendium of comments of the presidents of the Federal Reserve Banks; executives of corporations, officials of trade and business associations, professors, and economists in response to questionnaire; . . . Part 7 is an analysis of hearings by J. W. Ford, S. E. Harris, and W. F. Bennet; Parts 1-3, 85th Cong., 1st sess., 1957; Part 4, 1958; Parts 5 and 6 and compendium, 85th Cong., 2nd sess., 1958; Part 7, 1959. Washington, D.C.: Government Printing Office.

U.S. Senate Subcommittee of the Committee on Banking and Currency, *Employment Act Amendments*. Hearings on S. 64 and S. 2382 (bills to amend the Employment Act of 1946 to provide for its more effective administration; to bring an informed public opinion on price and wage increases which threaten economic stability, and to make relative stability of prices an explicit aim of Federal policy). 86th Cong., 2nd sess. Washington, D.C.: Government Printing Office, 1960.

26: Monetary and debt management measures, I

To complete our study of the framework within which monetary and debt management measures are carried out, we shall concentrate in the first part of this chapter on the structure of policy-formulating agencies. In the second part of the chapter we shall describe the various monetary and debt management measures and illustrate the initial impact of these measures upon the level and structures of interest rates and liquidity. In the concluding chapter we shall examine their influence on national economic objectives.

STRUCTURE OF POLICY-FORMULATING AGENCIES

The Federal Reserve System is charged by Congress with the statutory responsibilities of exercising general and selective monetary measures or controls. The original purposes of the System were to give the country an elastic currency, to provide facilities for discounting commercial paper, and to improve the supervision of commercial banks. Gradually, the purposes were expanded to include the objectives established in the previous chapter. The general monetary measures include open market operations, changes in legal reserve requirements, and discounting. The general monetary measures have their initial impact on the reserve position of commercial banks, influencing the availability, cost, and volume of bank credit. The measures are a key factor in the determination of the money supply and the level and structure of interest rates. The selective measures include changes in margin requirements on the extension of credit for the purchase and carrying of certain types of securities, and regulation of down payment and maturity terms of consumer loans, and particularly of consumer installment loans and residential mortgage loans. Only regulation of margin requirements was authorized in early 1961, but there was a strong possibility that Congress might restore regulation of consumer loans on a standby basis.

The Treasury is charged by Congress with statutory responsibilities associated with debt management. As noted earlier, debt management is the selection and timing of new issues of securities to raise new funds or to refund maturing or callable issues. The Secretary of the Treasury selects new issues from among different maturities of bills, certificates, notes, and bonds; he sets coupon rates on the latter three types of securities; and he makes decisions on many technical debt matters, including call options, down payment requirements, allotment percentages on cash issues, options on refunding, time intervals between announcement of new issues and the opening of subscription books, and the length of subscription periods. These and other decisions relating to debt management influence debt composition and the level and structure of interest rates. Debt management should be distinguished from fiscal policy, which determines whether or not there is a budget surplus or deficit and whether the total Federal debt is increasing or decreasing. Fiscal policy is one of the more important determinants of the framework within which debt management is conducted, and it is a responsibility of Congress.

In summary, the Federal Reserve System is the only monetary and credit agency having primarily monetary functions. However, the Treasury does exercise some functions of a monetary nature, particularly in the area of debt management. Although the Treasury has the primary responsibility for debt management, the Federal Reserve System exercises debt management functions through its open market operations. Obviously, monetary and debt management measures tend to influence a common set of economic variables. During World War II and up to early 1951, monetary policy was subordinate to debt demanagement policy. In March, 1951 there was a Treasury-Federal Reserve Accord that restored the independence of the Federal Reserve from the Treasury. It was agreed that monetary policy should play a coordinate rather than a subordinate role in debt management policy. Since the Accord, the Federal Reserve has not provided rigid market support for Federal obligations. As a minimum, debt management should not obstruct a flexible monetary policy. The preferred arrangement is mutual support.

Federal Reserve System

The Board of Governors of the Federal Reserve System is comprised of seven members appointed by the President and confirmed by the Senate. Each member serves a fourteen-year term, with expiration of terms so arranged that a vacancy occurs at two-year intervals. The Board exercises general supervision over the Federal Reserve Banks and branches; it appoints three of the nine directors at each Federal Reserve Bank; it approves appointments and salaries of the President and First Vice President of each Federal Reserve bank; it determines legal reserve requirements within the limits set by Congress; it determines maximum interest rates on time deposits; it determines margin requirements on the extension of credit for the purchase and carrying of certain types of securities; it reviews and determines discount rates charged by the Federal Reserve banks; and at times in the past it has had statutory authority to establish maximum terms on consumer credit and real estate credit transactions. All seven members of the Board are also members of the Federal Open Market Committee.

The Board of Governors of the Federal Reserve System is an independent agency within the structure of the Federal Government. It is not a part of any other government department. The Board reports directly to Congress and its funds are derived from assessments on Federal Reserve banks. The Chairman of the Board is designated by the President. In recent years there has been much discussion concerning the possibility of integrating the various agencies and departments exercising monetary functions. Since the scope of our study precludes discussion of this topic, let us merely mention that the suggestions range from an informal mechanism to a major reorganization of all of the affected agencies and departments. The possibility of a sweeping change in the structure is very remote.

The Federal Open Market Committee consists of the Board of Governors and five representatives of the Federal Reserve banks. In practice, Presidents of Federal Reserve banks are the representatives, and over the course of any three years, all Presidents serve at least a one-year term as a full member and a one-year term as an alternate member. Generally, all the Presidents attend the meetings whether they are members or not. The Committee's responsibility is to determine policy as it relates to open market operations.

The purchase and sale of Federal obligations by the individual Federal Reserve banks was not coordinated until 1923. In that year, a committee of five Governors of the Reserve banks was established for the purpose of regulating the sale and purchase of Federal obligations as an instrument of credit control; that is, open market operations were to be conducted with regard to existing credit conditions and in such a way as to accommodate commerce and business. In 1933, the composition of the Committee was modified to include all twelve Presidents of the Federal Reserve banks, and in 1935 the Committee took on its present structure. It might be noted at this point that market support of Federal obligations became part of policy in 1937. Until 1951, the policy was one maintaining the prices of outstanding Federal obligations at or above par. As part of the Federal Reserve-Treasury Accord in 1951, the policy was stated in terms of maintaining orderliness in the market for Federal obligation, and, since that time, prices of oustanding bonds have been permitted to seek their own levels even though the prices have had to drop well below par.

Both the Board of Governors and the Federal Open Market Committee consult with and receive recommendations from the Chairmen's Conference, which is composed of the Chairmen of the twelve Federal Reserve banks, and from the Presidents' Conference, which is composed of the Presidents of the twelve Federal Reserve banks. The Presidents' Conference is the more active of the two, having sub-committees working continuously on various aspects of the System's operations. The Board of Governors also receives advice and recommendations from the Federal Advisory Council, which is a formal organization within the System. The Council is composed of twelve members, each representing a Federal Reserve district. The Board of Directors of each Federal Reserve bank elects its representatives, and the Council serves as a medium through which the Board may have access to expressions of opinion from the banking community in each of the districts. The Council meets at least four times each year, and has the power of conferring directly with the Board of Governors on business conditions and of making recommendations on all aspects of the System's operations. Although the Federal Advisory Council, the Chairmen's Conference, and the Presidents' Conference do not make policy decisions, their recommendations are influential in shaping final policy decisions. The structure is such that the recommendations that originate in individual Federal Reserve banks tend to filter through various organizations before reaching the Board of Governors and the Federal Open Market Committee.

There are twelve Federal Reserve districts with a Federal Reserve bank in each district. Some districts also have branches in the larger cities. The Federal Reserve banks are bankers' banks, performing central banking functions in the public interest. Six of the nine directors are elected by the member banks, and the other three are appointed by the Board of Governors. The Chairman and Deputy Chairman of the Board of each Reserve bank are selected from the three directors appointed by the Board. Three of the elected directors are bankers and three come from nonfinancial firms. The composition of the Board of Directors is designed to reflect the viewpoints of individuals representing different economic backgrounds, contacts, and experiences.

The Reserve banks are the principal medium through which the credit policies and general supervisory powers of the System are exercised. They perform for member banks many of the services that member banks perform for the public. In addition, they serve as fiscal agents, depositaries, and custodians for the United States Treasury and other government agencies. The Reserve banks hold a large volume of Federal obligations, and in case of stringency in the Treasury's cash balance in the short run, the Reserve banks may purchase Federal obligations directly from the Treasury.

New York is the center of the money market and the government securities market, so that the Securities Department of the Federal Reserve Bank of New York is the operating arm of the Federal Open Market Committee. The Department is referred to as the trading desk and its activities are carried on for the System Account to assure that execution of policy conforms with the policy directives or objectives of the Committee. There is frequent consultation between the trading desk in New York and the staff in Washington, D. C.

The senior and junior officers who are involved in the operation of the System open market account conduct interviews with dealers in government securities each morning before the market opens. A manager of the Open Market Account has described these interviews as follows: "One [dealer] comes at 9:30 and the other comes at 9:45. Each remains approximately 15 minutes. They comment on the market . . . . Not all of us are there at one time . . . . Sometimes a representative from the Board staff, or perhaps the president of another Reserve bank who might happen to be in New York, or senior officer of such a bank, or a Treasury representative might be present. The dealer usually would be commenting on the type of business that was going on in the market since he had been there the preceding week. . . . It affords us as observers to the market and operating as far as the System open market is concerned and as advisor to the Treasury with, I think, a very helpful cross index, if you will, of opinion as to what is going on in the market. . . . As you can imagine, we have no information to volunteer unless it should be a technical question in response to Treasury finance or the like."* It was reported by Mr. M. J. Rossant in *Business Week* that "the dealers feel that they get some guidance from the discussion."† Mr. Rossant quoted one dealer as stating that "they never tell you if you are on the right track, but they sometimes drop a hint that you're way off target."

Given the structure of the Federal Reserve System, it would be very surprising, indeed, not to find differences in point of view among the Board of Governors, the Federal Open Market Committee, the Federal Advisory Council, the Boards of Directors of Reserve banks, and the Securities Department at the Federal Reserve Bank of New York. Late in 1959, the Chairman of the Board of Governors was asked to comment on this problem and a few selected quotations follow.** "In no case does the record of meetings of the Federal Open Market Committee indicate a difference of view as between the majority of the members from the Board of Governors and a majority of the members of the Federal Open Market Committee as to what monetary policy was currently most appropriate or as to whether

---

*U.S. Joint Economic Committee, "Employment, Growth, and Price Levels," Hearings, Part 6B, Testimony of Robert G. Rouse, Federal Bank of New York, 86th Cong., 1st sess. (Washington, D.C.: Government Printing Office, 1959), p. 1543.

† *Business Week*, July 12, 1958.

**U.S. Joint Economic Committee, "Employment, Growth, and Price Levels," Hearings, Part 10, 86th Cong., 1st sess. (Washington, D.C.: Government Printing Office, 1960), pp. 3388-3413.

current monetary policy should be effectuated through open market operations or through reductions in reserve requirements."*

On the problem of communication between a policy-making body and the people carrying out this policy, the Chairman said: "On only one occasion, in 1957, did a member criticize operations that had been carried on for the System Account on the grounds that they had departed from what the Committee intended when it issued its instructions. He stated that this reflected the inadequacy of the steps taken by the Committee to specify what it wanted, adding that he was certain that the management of the System Account felt that its actions were within the intent of the Committee, although he personally believed that they were not in accord with what the Committee had desired."†

Chairman Martin of the Federal Reserve Board indicated that the frequent joint discussions by Federal Reserve officials "undoubtedly have an influence on individual Reserve bank actions with respect to recommendations for discount rate change and on Board actions with respect to approval of recommended changes."** Chairman Martin indicated that there had been only a few occasions when the Board failed to adopt a discount rate recommendation made by a Reserve bank.‡ On the determination of lending policies of Federal banks, Chairman Martin pointed out that "in brief, each Federal Reserve bank determines its own lending policies, subject to statutory requirements and over-all supervision and regulation by the Board of Governors. The Federal Reserve Act authorizes the board of directors of each Reserve bank, subject to provisions of the law and orders of the Board, to extend to each member bank such credit accommodations as may be safely and reasonably made with due regard for the claims and demands of other member banks, the maintenance of sound credit conditions, and the accommodations of commerce, industry, and agriculture. Advances and discounts by the Reserve Banks are subject to such restrictions, limitations, and regulations as may be imposed by the Board. In its regulation A, relating to this subject, the Board has prescribed certain requirements and set forth certain general principles to be observed by the Reserve banks in making advances and discounts. As stated in a foreword to that regulation, the extension of credit assistance to member banks by the Reserve banks "is administered in the light of the basic objective which underlies all Federal Reserve credit policy, i.e., the advancement of the public interest by contributing to the greatest extent possible to economic stability and growth."§

To summarize the nature of the decision-making process within the

---

*Ibid., p. 3390.
† Ibid., p. 3391.
** Ibid., p. 3392.
‡ Ibid., p. 3393.
§ Ibid.

Federal Reserve System, the following statement by the Board of Governors is useful:*

> As to the general economic and credit situation and appropriate credit policy under particular circumstances, judgments among the individual participants in System policy formation may and do differ. There is no reason, however, for assuming that, among men selected for independence of thought and judgment, differences will generally crystallize by groups — the Board of Governors, the Reserve bank presidents, and the boards of directors of the Reserve banks. Nor is there any reason for assuming that the resulting System attitude with respect to the current credit problem and needed policy must be in some sense a negotiated compromise among these groups. Since the statutory changes of the early thirties affecting System decision making, experience in System policy formation indicates that policy positions reflect mainly the influence of individual leadership in reconciling different viewpoints and in pointing up current credit issues with the result that a consensus on policy action crystallizes. System policy experience shows, furthermore, that differences in judgment as to appropriate policies reflect primarily the special background and understanding of the policy problem on the part of individual participants in the policy formation process, and that the merging of differences of judgment into a common policy is necessarily a process of discussion and mutual understanding of the varying points of view.
>
> Differences of viewpoint among the individuals in responsible policy authority also arise sometimes as to the use, combination of use, and timing of use of the separate policy instruments. These differences again are subject to reconciliation through discussion and mutual understanding, with a decision representing the consensus of those having ultimate policy authority, but with the judgment of those in a consultative or advisory position being a factor taken into consideration in a final determination. The formulation of national credit policy is a complex process which needs as full an analysis as possible of all relevant facts as well as the benefit of viewpoints that represent differing economic backgrounds, contacts, and experience.

In summary, it may be stated that the decision-making process relating to the formulation and execution of policy introduces a major limitation to monetary policy. By having such a large number of persons involved in the final stages of the decision-making process, it is nearly impossible to secure agreement on a complicated set of monetary measures and timing instructions. In practice, the chief administrator must strive to secure agreement on a very general set of measures. One of the implications of the policy formation structure is that the final policy must be stated and the execution of the policy must be carried out rather simply.

---

*U.S. Joint Committee on the Economic Report, "Monetary Policy and the Management of the Public Debt," Replies to questions and other material for the use of the Subcommittee on General Credit Control and Debt Management, Part I, 82nd Cong., 2nd sess. (Washington, D.C.: Government Printing Office, 1952), pp. 298-299.

Treasury Department

In this section, we shall describe the agencies within the Treasury Department that have responsibility in the area of debt management, and shall describe the structure and use of advisory groups representing major segments of our financial system.

The Secretary of the Treasury has the responsibility for the over-all functioning of the Treasury Department. He is the chief fiscal officer and his foremost responsibility is to maintain confidence in the credit of the United States Government. However, he is a political appointee and is expected to shape policy decisions that are in line with the objectives of the incumbent administration. As noted in the previous chapter, the Secretaries of the Treasury in the postwar period have considered debt management as one of the measures that should be used to achieve our national economic objectives.

The policy decisions of the Treasury Department are also conditioned by the decisions of other government agencies, and especially of the Federal Reserve. If and when conflicts between the Treasury and other monetary authorities reach an impasse, action or threat of action by Congress has been adequate to restore a working relationship. For example, the Treasury-Federal Reserve Accord of 1951 could not have been achieved without the support of Congress.

The organization chart of the Department of the Treasury in early 1959 indicated that the Department's responsibilities pertaining to debt management were assigned to the Under-Secretary for Monetary Affairs, two Assistants to the Under-Secretary for debt management, Fiscal Assistant Secretary, and a Chief of the Debt Analysis Staff.*

> The Fiscal Assistant Secretary, under the general direction of the Under Secretary for Monetary Affairs, is responsible for the administration of the financing operations of the Treasury; preparation of estimates of the future cash position of the Treasury for use of the Department in its financing; direction of the distribution of funds between the Federal Reserve banks and other Government depositaries; preparation of calls for the withdrawal of funds from the special depositaries to meet current expenditures; . . . and direction of fiscal agency functions in general.†
>
> The Bureau of the Public Debt, in support of the management of the public debt, has responsibility for the preparation of circulars offering public debt securities, the direction of the handling of subscriptions and making of allotments, for the formulation of instructions and regulations pertaining to each security issue, the issuance of the securities and conduct or direction of transactions in those outstanding. The Bureau is responsible for the final audit and custody of retired securities, the maintenance of the control accounts covering all public

---

*Annual Report of the Secretary of the Treasury, Fiscal Year ended June 30, 1959, Washington, D.C., p. xii.

† *Ibid.*, p. 96.

debt issues, the keeping of individual accounts with owners of registered securities and authorizing the issue of checks in payment of interest thereon, and the handling of claims on account of lost, stolen, destroyed, or mutilated securities.

Under Bureau supervision many transactions in public debt securities are conducted through nationwide agencies, which are, principally, Federal Reserve banks, as fiscal agents of the United States, and their branches; selected post offices, financial institutions, industrial organizations, and others, approximately 23,000 in all, which cooperate in the issuance of savings bonds, and nearly 19,000 financial institutions that redeem savings bonds.*

The debt analysis staff provides technical assistance on matters relating to Treasury financing and debt management. The analysis provides an economic framework for the formation of policy. The Report of the Joint Economic Committee's study of Employment, Growth, and Price Levels recommended "that the Treasury set up an adequate marketing analysis and research staff upon whose advice it can largely rely and which is not influenced either in fact or in appearance by the advice of an organized group of customers."†

The United States savings bond program — with tens of millions of American bond owners — continues to be the keystone of the Treasury's efforts to manage soundly our public debt by attracting long-term savings into Government bonds. It also continues to be an important part of the Government's efforts to encourage the increased savings in all forms which are needed to finance soundly our growing economy. . . . The United States savings Bonds Division is a small Government staff which plans and directs the promotional activities of a large corps of volunteers. They consist of thousands of public-spirited men and women who serve voluntarily as a sales promotion force and as issuing agents. They have been primarily responsible for the success of the program over the years.**

Debt management in this area consists almost entirely of changing terms to fit changes in the level of interest rates being paid on comparable forms of financial investment. It is also possible that the Treasury may issue in the future a savings bond incorporating a price level hedge.

The Secretary of the Treasury uses advisory committees, representing various private groups or organizations within the financial system, to assist Treasury officials in interpreting the potential market demand for new securities among various types of investor classes and among different maturities. The advisory committees also discuss marketing techniques and probable interest rates on prospective debt issues. The committees enable the Treasury to conduct a quick, yet comprehensive, survey of potential market demand close to the time of financing. In 1959, the Treasury was using five

*Ibid., pp. 111-112.
† U.S. Joint Economic Committee, "Employment, Growth, and Price Levels," Report, op. cit., p. 38.
**Ibid., pp. 159-160.

formally organized advisory committees, representing the following financial groups or organizations: Investment Bankers Association, American Bankers Association, mutual savings banks, savings and loan associations, and life insurance companies. The American Bankers association and the Investment Bankers Association advisory committees reflect the opinions of dealers and bankers who are in daily contact with literally thousands of investors in every part of the country. The American Bankers Association's advisory committee provides the Treasury with an up-to-date "feel" on commercial banks' current investment requirements and practices. This service is especially important because the commercial banks perform an "underwriting" function in the sale of Federal obligations. As noted earlier, commercial banks resell many of the securities they purchase at the time of issue. The use of these two committees probably represents the most practical and efficient way of ascertaining current investment practices and needs of all investor classes. The activities of the other three advisory committees are more limited, except as they apply to their own respective investor classes.

Our discussion of these advisory committees is based on selected quotations of Treasury Secretary Anderson, who described for the Joint Economic Committee the structure and operation of the Treasury's advisory committees.*

> The committees are invited to meet by the Secretary of the Treasury and a time schedule is worked out which is mutually agreeable. . . . Committee membership is determined exclusively by its parent body, as is the selection of the chairman. Committee members come to Washington at their own expense and they assume full responsibility for any staff work, financial arrangements, minutes, and reports. With the exception of the savings and loan advisory group (which was initiated in 1958) all of the advisory committees had their origin during the World War II period, for all practical purposes, and have been very helpful to the Treasury ever since.†
>
> When the advisory groups come to the Treasury they begin their meetings with a review of the background of the forthcoming financing by Treasury staff members. This review is helpful in bringing the committee members up to date on relevant factual material so that the committee's time is not wasted. These oral presentations to the committees are based on publicly available information . . . the briefing serves the important function for consolidation and integration of publicly available information. There is, therefore, no inside information, but all members do have a common factual basis for their analysis. After these briefing sessions, each committee meets by itself, with no Treasury employee present, to discuss the problems thoroughly and to work out recommendations.**
>
> Advisory committee recommendations are presented orally in the case of the Investment Bankers Association and in written summary by

*U.S. Joint Economic Committee, "Employment, Growth, and Price Levels," Hearings, Part 10, op. cit., pp. 3284-3293.

† Ibid., p. 3285.

**Ibid.

the American Bankers Association group in terms of what might be called a majority report. The meetings of both of these groups with the Secretary, the Under Secretary, and other Treasury officials are informal. Strong minority positions with regard to types of securities to be offered, interest rates, exact maturity dates, and many other aspects of the forthcoming financing are typically presented. This may be handled by the chairman of the committee on behalf of the minority or by a spokesman selected by the chairman. Individual members of the committee are always encouraged by their own chairman and Treasury officials to express independent positions as freely as possible, and a typical meeting will find many such expressions.*

Meetings with [the] three other formally organized advisory groups . . . are usually different in scope from those with the ABA and IBA committees. Their financing recommendations are often rather general. As a result, they largely focus on expressions of interest in various maturity areas and discussion as to the way in which the current demand for Government securities, or lack thereof, relates to the general economic environment in which the Treasury financing is to take place. . . .†

The Treasury's own analysis of the factors which lead up to each financing decision is a composite of many points of view. The Treasury staff itself is constantly reviewing past financings in a critical way. . . . The Federal Reserve System actively participates in the construction of the framework on which the Secretary's ultimate decision is based. This is true of the staff of the Board of Governors itself as it gathers background information that is in many cases just as important for debt management as for monetary policy. It is true also of the staff of the Federal Reserve Bank of New York in its unique role as an observer on an hour-by-hour basis of the operations of the Government securities market. It is true also of each of the Federal Reserve Banks throughout the country, not only in terms of interpretation of regional differences in the market for Governments, but even more importantly in terms of the experience which the Reserve banks have gained as fiscal agents for the Treasury Department in the actual management of each financing operation once the Treasury policy decision has been made.**

The composite of all of these expressions, together with independent expressions through correspondence or personal contact by individual participants or observers in the market, helps to form the fabric from which the eventual decision on financing is made. Finally, of course, each decision is made personally by the Secretary of the Treasury and that decision is announced to the public within a few hours at the most after it has been reached. If his decision happens to be quite similar to the advice of one or more committees, it is more likely to reflect their support of action he was already seriously considering rather than the acceptance of advice.‡

The Report of the Joint Economic Committee's "Study of Employment, Growth, and Price Levels" took the position that "the Treasury places

*Ibid., pp. 3286-3287.
†Ibid., p. 3287.
**Ibid., p. 3288-3289.
‡Ibid., p. 3289.

too much reliance concerning both the length and rate of maturities on the advice it seeks from its customers."* The American Bankers Association provided a list of its recommendations to the Treasury for the period 1952-1959. Some members of the Joint Economic Committee expressed concern with the finding that 83 of the 103 specific recommendations were accepted by the Treasury, and in almost 60 per cent of the cases the advice was accepted as given.† To the majority of the Committee, this acceptance indicated an amazing degree of "conscious parallelism" between the recommendations of the customers of the Treasury and its decisions on the interest rate and maturity of its issues. As noted above, the majority report encouraged the formation of an expanded marketing analysis and research staff within the Treasury Department. It must be realized that if the Treasury contacted a larger number of its customers on an individual basis, the well-informed respondents would probably make similar recommendations.

Joint Participation of the Federal Reserve and Treasury

The previous discussion emphasizes the fact that the Federal Reserve and the Treasury are interested in the same background information. Furthermore, monetary measures and debt management measures affect a common set of variables. Therefore, joint participation in the decision-making process is vital. The nature of the joint participation in recent years was described by the Secretary of the Treasury in reply to the following questions: Does the Treasury participate in the formulation of monetary policy? If so, in what ways? Is any such participation sufficient to insure coordination of monetary, budgetary, and debt management policies for achieving public economic policy objectives?**

> The Treasury does not, of course, participate directly in the formulation of monetary policy. The Federal Reserve System is an agency created by and responsible to the Congress. Independence of Federal Reserve from the executive branch, in principle and in practice, is highly desirable.
>
> Nevertheless, the necessity for coordination of national economic policies is recognized, and to this end a number of informal arrangements have been established for exchange of ideas and information. When occasion warrants, the President, the Chairman of the Board of Governors of the Federal Reserve System, and Secretary of the Treasury, the Chairman of the Council of Economic Advisors, and the economic assistant to the President meet for an informal discussion of economic trends and developments.
>
> Frequent consultation occurs between Treasury and Federal Reserve officials. The Chairman of the Board of Governors and I [Secre-

*Op. cit., p. 37.
† Ibid., pp. 37-38.
**U.S. Joint Economic Committee, "Employment, Growth, and Price Levels," Hearings, Part 6C, 86th Cong., 1st sess. (Washington, D.C.: Government Printing Office, 1959), pp. 1720-1721.

tary of Treasury] usually have lunch together each Monday. On each Wednesday, the Under Secretary for Monetary Affairs and several members of the senior Treasury staff usually join the Chairman of the Board of Governors, plus at least one other Board member, and their senior staff people for lunch. At these meetings, there is a free interchange of ideas and information concerning the state of the economy, credit and debt management problems, and other matters of mutual interest. In addition, we confer frequently on many other occasions, either in person or by telephone.

These arrangements have worked out well in practice. The important point is that as we carry out our respective responsibilities, both the Treasury and the Federal Reserve have the opportunity for full knowledge of each other's views. The final decisions, however, are made solely by the responsible agency.

So long as there is basic agreement as to our national economic objectives and as to the means of achieving these objectives, these informal arrangements would appear to be sufficient for insuring the necessary degree of coordination between debt management and monetary policies. Any attempt to formalize relationships between the Federal Reserve and the executive would run the serious risk of impairing the independence of the monetary authorities. Indeed, complete centralization of authority over monetary, budgetary, and debt management policies is impossible — and, in my judgment, undesirable — under our form of government.

MONETARY AND DEBT MANAGEMENT MEASURES

Monetary Measures

Monetary measures are classified generally in terms of their initial impact. General monetary or credit measures influence initially the reserve position of member banks. Selective monetary or credit measures influence initially particular types of financial or credit transactions. General measures are often referred to as indirect measures, and selective measures, as direct measures. The general monetary measures are "indirect" in the sense that they influence the cost, availability, and supply of bank credit; the specific effects work themselves out in the free financial markets. In other words, the initial impact of general monetary measures is broad and general. It must be realized that the structure and operation of our financial markets are such that certain sectors or groups within sectors are affected more than others by general monetary measures. To the extent that officials know that the ultimate effects of general monetary measures are allocated unevenly in our free financial markets, the difference between general and selective credit controls is not as great as it appears on the surface.

The fundamental guide to the implementation and evaluation of general monetary policy is the level of free reserves or net borrowed reserves, which is defined in terms of the difference between aggregate member bank excess reserves and aggregate member bank borrowings from Federal Reserve banks, the latter of which are in the form of discounts and advances. If aggregate member bank excess reserves exceed aggregate member bank borrowings from Federal Reserve banks, the difference represents free reserves. If aggregate member bank borrowings from Federal Reserve banks exceed aggregate member bank excess reserves, the difference represents net borrowed reserves, also referred to as negative free reserves. Generally, free reserves exist during recessions, and net borrowed reserves exist during prosperity. During the transition period, the level of free reserves is gradually reduced and replaced by net borrowed reserve position The distribution of the reserves is an important consideration.

As noted in Chapter 6, many factors influence the level of member bank reserves, making it necessary for Federal Reserve officials to offset various types of transactions as well as to promote desired changes in the level of member bank reserves. The terms "defensive" and "dynamic" have been coined by Federal Reserve Officials to help clarify the distinction between these two responsibilities of the Federal Reserve System. The defensive side of the System's duties consist of "defending against those seasonal, regional, or perhaps accidental causes of sudden stringency that arise in the process of issuing currency, or clearing checks, or meeting net flows of funds among regions (or vis-a-vis other countries), for example, and which might by unhappy coincidence aggravate, or even ignite, a financial and economic crisis."[*]

The dynamic side of the Federal Reserve System's duties relate to the positive use of monetary measures to achieve national economic objectives. The defensive and dynamic responsibilities of the System are carried out simultaneously.

The interrelationship of these two responsibilities are summarized very succinctly by Dr. Roosa.[†]

> In practice, the defensive and the dynamic responsibilities of the System are carried out side by side, day by day, and most operating arms of the System are involved to some degree in each. The provision of currency, the processing and crediting of checks for collection, the expediting of wire transfers of deposit balances among banks and of Government securities among investors, the calling and disbursement of funds for the United States Treasury, the settlement of the United States balance of payments with other countries, and a variety of other receipts and disbursements of funds for foreign governments and central banks — all of these and other operations, though primarily defensive in character, nonetheless frequently are of real importance in the implementation of dynamic policy. And from the other side, the three main instruments of positive policy — reserve requirements, discounting, and open market

[*]Robert V. Roosa, "Federal Reserve Operations in the Money and Government Securities Markets," Federal Reserve Bank of New York, 1956, p. 8.
[†]Ibid., p. 9.

operations — very frequently play a part in meeting the Federal Reserve's defensive responsibilities.

The defensive and dynamic responsibilities of the System are carried out in terms of their effects on the reserve positions of member banks.*

> Defensively, the System's job might be seen, when stripped of complicating details, as that of keeping a given volume of reserves in being and helping with the economical distribution of that given total. Dynamically, the job is to vary the quantity of reserves (after allowing for seasonal variations) by such amounts, and through such methods, as to make the banking system, and the money market as well, an active force in the economy — promoting growth, resisting depression, and limiting inflation. That means inescapably that the Federal Reserve System, as it varies the volume of bank reserves for policy purposes, will also have some influence of its own upon the cost and availability of credit. Moreover, the Federal Reserve and the Treasury are necessarily market influences because of the large part they must play in determining the supply of secondary reserve assets. Consequently their actions, and expectations concerning them, become a part of the matrix of supply and demand forces that the money market continually is resolving into "going" rates of interest for the various kinds of money market instruments.

The manner in which flexible monetary policy was carried out in the decade of the 1950's clearly indicated that the basic economic philosophy of the Federal Reserve was one of minimum intervention with basic market forces. The Federal Reserve had the power to buy and sell all maturities of Federal obligations, but in practice it restricted itself primarily to the purchase and sale of short-term Federal obligations. The Federal Reserve had the power to promote a secular increase in member bank reserves by the purchase of publicly held Federal obligations, but in practice it restricted itself to gradual reductions in legal reserve requirements. It did not request an expansion in selective measures. The economic philosophy of the Federal Reserve was founded primarily on two basic principles. First, the level and structure of interest rates should be influenced only by controlling the total supply of money and credit. Second, the determination of the interest-rate structure and specific allocation of credit should be handled through the operation of our free money and capital markets. These principles were compromised in early 1961. Open market operations were expanded to include Treasury notes and bonds, the maturity of some of which exceeded five years. The policy aimed to "nudge" down long-term rates on Federal obligations and at the same time maintain the level of short-term rates.

In the application of these principles, the Federal Reserve has restricted its open market operation to short-term Federal obligations on the assumption that such a policy leads to a stronger market for longer-term obligations. It is assumed that dealers in Federal obligations would be more

*Ibid., pp. 13, 14.

reluctant to assume positions and make markets in intermediate- and long-term Federal obligations if open market operations were conducted in all maturities. This assumption can be criticized on the ground that the market for long-term obligations is inherently a thin market and it is questionable whether any policy short of a pegged market could lead to a stronger market in long-term Federal obligations. The position of dealers in Federal obliga-tions depends primarily on the broad interest rate movements and related expectations. It is possible that open market operations in long-term maturities might be misinterpreted by the market, but that would depend on whether the Federal Reserve officials had judged market psychology correctly at the time of the action.

A strong case for general monetary measures and minimum interven-tion can be built upon the machinery relating to the decision-making process. As noted in the discussion of the structure and operation of policy formulat-ing agencies, policy decisions, and especially those related to open market operations, involve a large number of persons with different points of view. Would it be possible to reach agreement on a complicated set of general and selective monetary measures that would require deliberate intervention in the free markets? Can agreement be reached on measures that would not only influence the level of a given rate structure, but also modify the rate structure in a deliberate manner? Until the policy formation process is modified, it is likely that the Federal Reserve will have to continue to rely primarily on general monetary measures and restrict its open market operations primarily to short maturities.

The fundamental guide to the implementation of selective monetary measures is the rate of change in selected types of credit transactions. Margin requirements are changed in the light of speculative activity in the securities markets, and the degree to which credit is being used to finance speculative transactions. Selective consumer credit measures may be desirable when consumer credit extensions approach or reach a non-sustainable rate of change. In other words, selective consumer credit controls may be used to reduce or eliminate spurts, that might otherwise lead to instability. To the extent that the causes of inflation are selective, it is reasonable to use selective measures in dealing with the problem even if this method does require some interventions with the free market process. Of course, the administrative problems connected with selective controls must be studied.

Debt Management Measures

There are two basic considerations in debt management policy. First, there is a debt composition that is optimal in terms of national economic ob-jectives. Second, there are shifts in debt composition that are conducive to the achievement of national economic objectives. One of the problems in debt management is to achieve a balance between these two considerations.

In theory, debt management officials should move toward the optimal debt composition, but at the same time they should promote marginal changes in response to changes in economic conditions. To restate these considerations in a slightly different manner, the composition of debt may be used as a built-in or automatic stabilizer, and shifts in debt composition may be used as a discretionary measure. The present state of knowledge does not permit determination of the optimal composition of the Federal debt. The major unanswered question is whether the long-run problem of our economy is unemployment or inflation. The Federal debt provides a large store of purchasing power. The problem for debt management during a period of threatened inflation is to prevent the use of various debt holdings as a source of expenditure. During inflation, it would be desirable to have the holders of debt view their respective holdings as investments, not liquid assets. However, if the problem were one of inadequate aggregate demand, it would be desirable for the holders of the debt to view their respective holdings as liquid assets. If the long-run problem is one of inflation, it would be agreed generally that the debt composition in early 1961 was not optimal. It must also be realized that optimal debt composition is related to many other economic variables, and to the extent that these change, shifts in debt composition would be necessary to achieve the new optimum.

There are three basic variables in debt management: ownership, the level and structure of interest rates, and maturity. These variables are inter-related. For example, change in ownership may be encouraged by a change in the maturity of newly offered securities. If the Treasury refunded notes by offering to exchange Treasury bonds, it would be expected that the holders of maturing notes would not prefer the newly offered bonds. Furthermore, some investors not holding the maturing notes would desire to invest in the new bonds. Prior to the exchange, shifts in ownership of the notes would probably occur, and the newly issued bonds would be acquired by long-term investors. A change in the stipulated rate of interest on newly offered securities may also be used to promote a change in the pattern of ownership of Federal obligations. For example, the issue of a 5 per cent note in 1959 attracted a large amount of funds from investors who had not invested in marketable Federal obligations before that time. However, there is a limit to the use of high-interest rates to bring about changes in the composition of the debt, because minimization of interest costs is an important consideration in the final determination of debt management policy. These examples do not exhaust by any means the interrelationships among debt management variables.

Changes in debt composition influence initially the portfolios of different investor classes, and the effects of these changes may be analyzed in terms of interest-rate and liquidity effects. However, before analyzing the influence of these effects on the level and composition of private income-generating expenditures, marginal changes in debt composition will be examined.

WAYS OF PROMOTING CHANGES IN DEBT COMPOSITION: A change in the composition of the debt is not dependent upon a change in the total amount of Federal debt. To emphasize this point, the discussion of marginal changes in debt composition rests on the assumption that there is no change in the amount of Federal debt. Given this assumption, there are at least five ways in which a change in debt composition can be brought about.

First, the Treasury may initiate change in debt composition at the time of normal refunding by manipulating the maturity, interest coupon, and characteristics of new issues, in relation to the maturing issues.

Second, the Treasury may bring about change in debt composition by shifts in the holdings of United States Government investment accounts, hereafter referred to as accounts. The shifts may be either "automatic" or "discretionary." Automatic shifts consist of the investment and disinvestment of funds flowing into and out of the accounts. Given the assumption of no change in the volume of debt, a net flow of funds into the accounts or the payment of interest on debt held by these accounts requires an increase in the debt holdings of the accounts and a decrease in the debt holdings of the public. A net flow of funds out of the accounts requires opposite shifts. There are alternative methods to choose from in accomplishing these transactions, and it is possible to influence both the level and the composition of publicly held debt. Discretionary shifts are the investments of the accounts when there is neither a net inflow or net outflow of funds. For example, the Treasury may redeem some special issues held by the accounts and offer newly issued securities to the public. The proceeds from the sale of these securities may be used to purchase outstanding public marketable securities for the accounts. The Treasury may sell marketable securities held by the accounts and may issue special obligations to the accounts. In summary, the accounts provide a channel through which the Treasury can enter the market as buyer and seller of outstanding securities. It is possible by discretionary management of the investment accounts to influence the level and structure of interest rates and the liquidity position of various investor classes. However, Secretaries of the Treasury have not carried out discretionary shifts on many occasions, and similar shifts may be accomplished more effectively through Federal Reserve open market operations.

As noted above, a third way in which debt composition may be changed is by open market operations of the Federal Reserve system. The Federal Reserve may simultaneously purchase long-term obligations and sell short-term obligations. This operation would tend to shift debt from investor classes holding long-term obligations to those holding short-term obligations. Such a shift would affect the interest-rate structure as well as the liquidity position of various investor classes. In this case the expected interest-rate changes would be reduction in long-term yields and an increase in short-term yields. There would be a net increase in liquidity because investors in long-term securities would have increased their state of liquidity by more than investors in short-term securities had reduced their state of liquidity. The Federal Reserve may also change their total holdings of Federal obligations. Net market sales are limited by the Reserve banks' holdings of Federal obligations, and net market purchases are limited by the holdings of gold certificates and the volume of debt liabilities. The net sales or purchases may be spread out over all maturities or concentrated in a particular maturity sector. Obviously, the composition of the Federal Reserve banks' portfolio of Federal obligations is a determinant of the degree of freedom or flexibility.

A fourth way in which the composition of the debt may be changed is by the sale or redemption of non-marketable obligations. Assuming that the sale of non-marketable bonds is continuous, net sales permits a reduction in the amount of marketable debt. If redemptions exceed sales, it is necessary for the Treasury to offer marketable obligations. A change in the balance between marketable or non-marketable obligations makes it possible to influence the composition of the marketable portion of the debt.

A fifth way in which the composition of the debt may be changed is by a transfer of ownership of outstanding marketable obligations without any Treasury or Federal Reserve action. In the final analysis, the amount of such shifting is dependent, to some extent, upon Treasury action. If the Treasury issues securities that are well tailored to the needs of the original purchaser, the likelihood of investors liquidating their securities prior to maturity is lessened in relation to the situation that might exist if there were no regard for the long-run investment requirements of particular investment classes. However, Treasury officials would not want to compartmentalize the debt to such an extent that shifts were not possible. A reasonable amount of autonomous shifting is desirable. For example, the commercial banks expanded their loans almost $12 billion in 1959, but the banks raised most of the funds for this lending by selling government obligations to the non-bank public. In a statement before the Joint Economic Committee, the Chairman of the Board of Governors of the Federal Reserve System explained the shift as follows:*

> The banks performed an intermediary service by obtaining funds from savers, to whom they transferred investment securities, and by passing the funds on to others who had a need to borrow. This flow of funds from savers to banks to borrowers did much to assure that the need for credit was met without a dangerous increase in the money supply. It did, however, bring about an increase in the turnover or

*U.S. Joint Economic Committee, "January 1960 Economic Report of the President," Hearings, 86th Cong., 2nd sess. (Washington, D.C.: Government Printing Office, 1960), p. 164. The full text of the statement is reprinted in Federal Reserve Bulletin, February 1960, pp. 126-132.

rate of use of the existing money supply and, by so doing, produced much the same economic and financial effect as would have been produced by a modest increase in the money supply without the accompaniment of a faster rate of use. . . . The banks, in effect, drew out of the market, from individuals and corporations not engaged in lending, the funds to meet the specialized credit demands of borrowers — as, for instance, many small business concerns —who could not themselves have raised funds in the market because their needs were unsuitable for general market participation.

EFFECTS OF CHANGES IN DEBT COMPOSITION. Changes in debt composition or ownership may affect the actual or required reserves of commercial banks, the level and structure of interest rates, and the supply and velocity of circulation of money. Their influence upon the level and composition of income-generating private expenditures is discussed in the following chapter.

Exclusive of the "automatic" shifts resulting from a net flow of funds either into or out of the United States Government investment accounts there are four basic types of shifts in debt ownership: (1) between Federal Reserve banks and commercial banks, (2) between Federal Reserve banks and non-bank investors, (3) between commercial banks and non-bank investors, and (4) between different classes of non-bank investors. In this discussion, no distinction will be made as to the manner in which the shifts are brought about. It is sufficient to mention that shifts may occur from autonomous transfers in the market, open-market operations by the Federal Reserve, and discretionary Treasury action. Abbreviated balance sheets or T-accounts are used to trace the effects of various types of shifts in debt ownership. Each transaction is assumed to be $100.

A shift or transfer of government obligations between Federal Reserve banks and commercial banks is generally considered the typical open-market operation, and it is the first case we shall examine. Assume that the Federal Reserve banks sold securities and the commercial banks purchased those securities by drawing against reserve balances. The effects of the shift are illustrated in the following abbreviated balance sheets:

Before shift:

Federal Reserve Banks

Government securities	400	Reserves of M.B.	200
		F. R. notes	200

Commercial Banks

Reserves with F.R.B.	200	Demand deposits	1200
Government securities	800		
Cash (F.R. notes)	200		

After shift:

Federal Reserve Banks

Government securities	300	Reserves of M.B.	100
		F.R. notes	200

Commercial Banks

Reserves with F.R.B.	100	Demand deposits	1200
Government securities	900		
Cash (F.R. notes)	200		

The net effects on the accounts of commercial banks are a reduction in their reserves with Federal Reserve banks and an increase in their holdings of government obligations. To the extent that reserves are reduced, the lending power of the banks is contracted. If banks were loaned up at the time, a reduction in their reserves would lead to a contraction in their loans and deposits by an amount equal to the reciprocal of the reserve ratio times the decrease in reserves. If commercial banks discounted commercial paper or arranged advances secured by government obligations, contraction in loans would not be necessary. However, the higher level of discounts and advances would exert pressure. A shift of securities from commercial banks to Federal Reserve banks would have the opposite effects.

A transfer of government obligations between Federal Reserve banks and non-bank investors will be examined next. Assume that Federal Reserve banks sold securities and non-bank investors purchased the securities by drawing against their demand deposits. The effects of the shift are illustrated in the following abbreviated balance sheets.

Before shift:

Federal Reserve Banks

Government securities	400	Reserves of M.B.	200
		F.R. notes	200

Non-bank Investors

Demand deposits	1,000	
Government securities	400	

Commercial Banks

Reserves with F.R.B.	200	Demand deposits	1,000
Government securities	800		

After shift:

Federal Reserve Banks

Government securities	300	Reserves of M.B.	100
		F.R. notes	200

Non-bank Investors

Demand deposits	900	
Government securities	500	

Commercial Banks

Reserves with F.R.B.	100	Demand deposits	900
Government securities	800		

The net effects on the accounts of commercial banks are a reduction in both the volume of demand deposits and the reserves of commercial banks, and the net effect on the accounts of non-bank investors is a substitution of a non-money asset for money. If commercial banks were loaned up at the time of transfer, further contraction would be necessary unless the reserves with Federal Reserve banks were built up.

A transfer from Federal Reserve banks to non-bank investors is more restrictive than a shift from Federal Reserve banks to commercial banks because, in the former case, the effective supply of money is actually decreased. The maximum restrictive effect is achieved by substituting debt for otherwise active balances. Generally, investor classes that purchase the greatest volume of goods and services, such as individuals and nonfinancial corporations, would have the more active balances. To the extent that transfers of debt to financial institutions absorb funds that otherwise would be invested in new privately offered securities, these shifts are also restrictive. However, if idle balances are replaced by government securities, the net effects are not appreciable.

The opposite shift, one from non-bank investors to Federal Reserve banks, may be traced in the abbreviated balance sheets shown above. Non-bank investors substitute money for government obligations. Commercial banks' reserves at Federal Reserve banks are increased by the same amount, and the increases in the level of free reserves put the commercial banks in a position to increase their loans and investments. A shift in ownership of Federal obligations from non-bank investors to Federal Reserve banks is expansive. The maximum expansive effects are expected when Federal obligations are removed from the portfolios of the non-bank investor classes that are most likely to increase the level of income-generating expenditures. The reduction in the holdings of financial institutions is at least one step removed from income-generating expenditures.

A transfer between commercial banks and non-bank investors is next to be examined. Assume that commercial banks sold securities and non-bank investors purchased them. The effects are illustrated in the following abbreviated balance sheets:

Before shift:

Commercial Banks

Reserves with F.R.B.	200	Demand deposits	1,000
Government securities	600		
F.R. notes	200		

Non-bank Investors

Demand deposits	1,000	
Government securities	400	
F.R. notes	200	

After shift:

Commercial Banks

Reserves with F.R.B.	200	Demand deposits	900
Government securities	500		
R.F.R. notes	200		

Non-bank Investors

Demand deposits	900	
Government securities	500	
F.R. notes	200	

The net effects are a substitution of government securities for money in the portfolios of non-bank investors, and a reduction in both the assets and liabilities of commercial banks.

A shift in ownership between different classes of non-bank investors affects neither the supply of money nor the reserves of commercial banks. Some non-bank investors reduce their holdings of money and increase their holdings of Federal obligations, whereas the opposite is true for some other non-bank investors. Therefore, the most that can be expected from such shifts is a change in the structure of interest rates and in degree of liquidity in the portfolios of different investor classes.

A shift of Federal obligations from, say, state and local governments, nonfinancial corporations, and individuals, to non-bank financial intermediaries provides a source of spendable funds to nonfinancial economic units. Rather than issue their own securities, non-bank investors liquidate previously acquired government obligations in the open market, and use the proceeds to purchase nonfinancial assets, preferably newly produced capital and consumers' goods.

In summary, shifts may be ranked in terms of their expansive effects: (1) shift from non-bank investors to Federal Reserve banks, preferably from nonfinancial investors; (2) shift from non-bank investors to commercial banks, preferably from nonfinancial investors; (3) shift from commercial banks to Federal Reserve banks; and (4) shift from non-bank, nonfinancial investors to non-bank, financial investors. The ranking would be reversed if it were in terms of restrictive effects.

The last type of shift to be considered is one resulting from a net flow of funds into or out of the United States Government investment accounts. Assume that payments to the investments accounts are made by checks drawn by business firms. The initial effects of a net flow of funds into the accounts are illustrated in the following abbreviated balance sheets.

Before payment to the accounts:

Non-bank Investors

Demand deposits	1,000	
Government securities	400	

Commercial Banks

Reserves with F.R.B.	200	Demand deposits	1,000
Government securities	800		

Federal Reserve Banks

Government securities	300	Reserves of M.B.	200
		Treasury deposits	100

Investment Accounts

Government securities	200	

After payment to the accounts:

Non-bank Investors

Demand deposits	900	
Government securities	400	

Commercial Banks

Reserves with F.R.B.	100	Demand deposits	900
Government securities	800		

Federal Reserve Banks

Government securities	300	Reserves of M.B.	100
		Treasury deposits	200

Investment Accounts

Government securities	200	
Treasury balances	100	

The effects of the payment to the accounts are a reduction in the volume of demand deposits and reserves of commercial banks, and an increase in the cash assets of the investment accounts. Assuming a constant volume of Federal debt, the increased holdings of the investment accounts would be offset by an equal reduction in some other segment of the debt. The net effects depend upon Treasury action with respect to reduction in publicly held debt. Assume in all illustrations to follow that payment for publicly held government securities is made by drawing on Treasury accounts at Federal Reserve banks. Assume that the holdings of the banks are reduced. The net effects of the entire series of transactions are illustrated in the following abbreviated balance sheets:

Federal Reserve Banks

Government securities	200	Reserves of M.B.	100
		Treasury deposits	100

Investment Accounts

Government securities	300	

The net effects of the entire series of transaction are as follows: (1) the volume of demand deposits is reduced; (2) reserves of member banks are reduced; (3) the Federal Reserve banks' holdings of government securities

645

are reduced; and (4) the investment account's holdings of government obligations are increased.

Assume that the holdings of commercial banks are reduced. The net effects are shown below:

Commercial Banks

Reserves with F.R.B.	200	Demand deposits	900
Government securities	700		

Federal Reserve Banks

Government securities	300	Reserves of M.B.	200
		Treasury deposits	100

Investment Accounts

Government securities	300	

The net effects of the entire series of transactions are as follows: (1) the volume of demand deposits is reduced; (2) reserves of member banks remain unchanged; (3) commercial banks' holdings of government obligations are reduced; and (4) the investment accounts' holdings of government obligations are increased.

Assume that the holdings of non-bank investors are reduced, non-bank investors deposit checks in their deposit balances, and the checks are cleared through the Federal Reserve. The net effects are shown below:

Non-bank Investors

Demand deposits	1,000	
Government securities	300	

Commercial Banks

Reserves with F.R.B.	200	Demand deposits	1,000
Government securities	800		

Federal Reserve Banks

Government securities	300	Reserves of M.B.	200
		Treasury deposits	100

Investment Accounts

Government securities	300	

The net effects of the entire series of transactions are as follows: (1) the volume of demand deposits is unchanged; (2) the financial position of Federal Reserve banks and commercial banks is unchanged; (3) non-bank investors' holdings of government securities are decreased; and (4) the investment accounts' holdings of government securities are increased.

In summary, the shifts may be ranked in terms of their restrictive effects: (1) reduce holdings of Federal Reserve banks; (2) reduce holdings of commercial banks; and (3) reduce holdings of non-bank investors, preferably those who are likely to hold additional idle balances. If there were a net flow of funds out of the investment accounts, the volume of publicly held debt would have to be increased unless other tax revenues were adequate. The reader is asked to trace through the opposite effects and rank the alternative transactions in terms of their restrictive and expansive effects.

QUESTIONS

1. Describe the structure of the Board of Governors of the Federal Reserve System and indicate its responsibilities.

2. Describe the structure of the Federal Open Market Committee and indicate its responsibilities.

3. Describe the Board of Directors of a Federal Reserve bank and indicate its responsibilities.

4. Describe the structure and role of the Chairmen's Conference and the Presidents' Conference.

5. Summarize the influence of the structure of the Federal Reserve System upon the over-all decision-making process. What are the implications?

6. Describe the pertinent agencies within the Treasury Department that have responsibility in the formulation of debt policy.

7. Discuss the structure and role of advisory committees in the formulation of debt management policies. What is your opinion of these advisory committees?

8. Explain how Federal Reserve and Treasury policies are coordinated. Should any changes be made? Explain.

9. Distinguish between "direct" and "indirect" monetary measures.

10. What is the fundamental guide to the implementation and evaluation of general monetary measures? What is the present level of net borrowed or net free reserves?

11. What is meant by the "defensive" and "dynamic" policies?

12. In recent years, what has been the basic economic philosophy of Federal Reserve officials? Do you agree with this philosophy?

13. What are the arguments for and against the policy of restricting open-market operations to the short end of the market? What is your opinion of recent policy?

14. What constitutes "debt management measures"? What are the basic variables?

15. Describe some ways in which the debt composition may be changed.

16. Trace the effects of the following changes in debt ownership: (1) shift between Federal Reserve banks and commercial banks; (2) shift

between commercial banks and non-bank investors; and (3) shift between government investment accounts and non-bank investors.

ADDITIONAL READING

Additional reading for Chapter 26 will be found at the end of Chapter 27.

27: Monetary and debt management measures, II

MONETARY and debt management measures may contribute to the achievement of our national economic objectives by affecting basic determinants of the level of private income-generating expenditures. Among the economic variables so affected are the availability of credit, the degree of liquidity, and the level and structure of interest rates. Also, the adoption of positive measures to achieve national economic objectives generally has a favorable influence on the state of expectations. For example, the adoption of restrictive measures to promote stability in the general level of prices tends to diminish the strength of expectations relating to inflation. It should be recognized at the outset that the economic variables mentioned above are interrelated and influence the level of private income-generating expenditures simultaneously. However, for the purpose of this chapter, each variable is discussed separately.

All other things being equal, a high rate of economic growth and a high stable rate of employment are promoted by increasing the availability of credit and the degree of liquidity, and by having interest rates at their lowest possible level. A high degree of stability in the general level of prices may require at times the imposition of restrictions on the availability of credit, a reduction in the degree of liquidity, and a relatively high level of interest rates. One of the basic problems in carrying out monetary and debt management policies is the achievement of a proper balance between short-run and long-run considerations. In response to criticism that policies are too restrictive in terms of growth and employment objectives, monetary and debt management officials reply that their short-run policies tend to promote, in the long run, sustainable growth in productive capacity, gross national product, and the rate of employment. They contend that in the absence of these short-run restrictive policies, the rise in the general level of prices would eventually bring about severe contractions in the rate of employment and the level of output. Conjecture is predominant in both positions.

AVAILABILITY OF CREDIT

The reserve position of commercial banks is the major target of Federal Reserve policy, and the availability of credit is dependent upon this factor. It was pointed out in the previous chapter that various monetary and debt management measures may be used to influence the reserve position of commercial banks, and in the process the measures also influence the degree of liquidity and the level and structure of interest rates. Generally, the effects of a change in the lending ability of commercial banks are more direct than effects resulting from changes in liquidity and interest rates.

As a general rule, credit restraint is more effective than credit ease. Monetary and debt management officials may make bank credit more freely available, but they cannot bring about an automatic increase in the volume of requests for bank credit. However, an increase in the availability of bank credit may alert potential borrowers to the possibility that loan requests will be approved and thereby induce prospective borrowers to file loan requests. Also, an improved reserve position encourages the banks to seek earning assets in the form of investments. However, an increase in bank credit effected through the money and impersonal capital market may have a less direct effect on the level of production than an increase in bank credit effected through customers' loans.

Restriction on bank lending during a period featured by excess demand for bank credit may have immediate effects on further increase in the volume of bank credit and on the quality of outstanding bank credit. In this situation the initiative rests with the banks; the borrowers are already in the banks and increasing numbers are approaching the banks.

Assume that there is a strong demand for bank credit and monetary and debt management officials fear the consequences of further increases in the volume of bank credit at this time. As noted in the previous chapter, the degree of strain will be indicated by the level of net borrowed reserves. Inasmuch as commercial banks view their borrowings from Federal Reserve banks as temporary, there is a limit to the creation of additional bank reserves, and unless additional bank reserves can be built up, the commercial banks are prompted to hold their loans and investments at or near present levels. The banks may be able to change the proportion of loan assets by shifting some of their investments to non-bank investors. Firms and individuals borrowing from commercial banks may be informed that their present loans are under review, that only the higher quality loans may be renewed, and that only a few of the outstanding loans may be increased. Some of the lower-quality loans may not be renewed at the end of the loan period, allowing the bank to shift bank credit to new borrowers who show greater promise of growth in the future and provide greater safety to the banks.

It should be recognized that commercial banks supply extensive credit to intermediaries, so that when the availability of bank credit is restricted, the availability of many other forms of credit is also restricted. Finance companies may be adversely affected. Nonfinancial firms may have to tighten up on trade credit.

During a period of credit restraint, further increases in the volume of bank credit usually occur. The restrictive effects are measured by comparing the rate of increase in bank credit with the rate of increase that would have taken place in the absence of credit restraint. Although the measurements are based on pure conjecture, it is clear that the restrictive effects of credit availability do slow down the rate of expenditures financed by credit.

LIQUIDITY EFFECTS

Monetary and debt management measures may be used to promote changes in the volume, composition, and ownership pattern of financial assets, and may thereby affect the degree of liquidity. Also, changes in the level and structure of interest rates affect the value of outstanding assets, both financial and nonfinancial. It is assumed that the level and composition of private income-generating expenditures are influenced by liquidity. An increase in liquidity is conducive to an increase in private expenditures, and a decrease in liquidity introduces a restraining factor in the flow of private spending. Inasmuch as liquidity effects are not equally distributed or effective among sectors, the composition of spending may be affected. There is a dearth of empirical studies dealing with the influence of liquidity on private expenditures, so that the actual impact of changes in liquidity is unknown.

VOLUME OF LIQUID ASSETS. Money is the most liquid of all assets. Money market instruments, fixed-value redeemable claims, and United States savings bonds are close substitutes for money. Capital market instruments and physical assets are less liquid, because the markets for such assets are relatively thin and the prices of long-term assets are subject to widespread fluctuations as a result of changes in the level of interest rates. Monetary and debt management officials may bring about an increase in the supply of money, money market instruments, United States savings bonds, and fixed-value redeemable claims, and thereby bring about an increase in amount of liquidity. The availability of near-money assets encourages some economic units to reduce their holdings of money and to increase their holdings of near-money assets. In the process, the money is transferred to economic units that desire to increase their holdings of money. The reduction of liquidity among the former group of economic units is probably less than the increase in the liquidity among the latter group of economic units. The creation of near-money assets permits a more economical use of an existing stock of money. The net increase in liquidity prompts an increase in the level of private income-generating expenditures. It is alleged that the creation of near-money assets tends to reduce the effectiveness of restrictive financial measures, which is probably true in the early stages of a restrictive policy, but eventually the creation of near-money assets slows down and merely matches an equal increase in the volume of saving. This matter is discussed further in the closing section of this chapter.

COMPOSITION OF ASSETS. The composition of the public's holdings of Federal obligations determines the liquidity associated with a given amount of debt. A shift from long-term to short-term securities or a reduction in the public's holdings of Federal obligations may be used to increase liquidity. It is assumed that the increase in liquidity of the ex-holders of long-term obligations is greater than the reduction in the liquidity of the new holders of short-term debt. A shift from short-term to long-term obligations or an increase in the public's holdings of Federal obligations may be used to reduce liquidity. It is assumed that the increase in the liquidity of ex-holders of short-term obligations is less than the reduction in the liquidity of the new holders of long-term obligations.

In terms of practical policy decisions, one of the major unknowns is the extent to which economic units may be induced to shift from cash into long-term obligations, and thereby be induced to reduce their expenditures. Another unknown is the extent to which the ex-holders of short-term Federal obligations may be encouraged to use their additional cash balances to finance additional expenditures on goods and services.

CAPITALIZED VALUE OF ASSETS. We now focus our attention on the change in liquidity associated with changes in the value of outstanding assets, both financial and nonfinancial. The following assumptions underly this discussion. First, a reduction in the market value of outstanding assets tends to discourage their sale in the market, and introduces an element of greater caution in future spending decisions. Second, an increase in the market value of outstanding assets tends to have the opposite effects. Although changes in the capitalized value of assets are brought about by changes in the level and structure of interest rates, it is appropriate to analyze the effects in terms of the public's liquidity.

The capitalized value or present value of an asset is affected by the size of the periodic payments, the length of time over which payments are received, and the current interest rate with allowance for risk. For example, take the case of an asset which is expected to pay out $5 per year for an infinite period, e.g., a perpetuity is assumed. Assume that the current interest rate with allowance for risk is 5 per cent. The present value or capitalized value of a perpetuity may be calculated as follows:

$$\text{Present value} = \frac{\text{size of each payment}}{\text{current interest rate with allowance for risk}}$$

Substituting the values above in this formula, the present value of the asset is $100.

Take an asset that is expected to yield $5 per year for an finite period, say 20 years, at which time the owner of the asset is to receive $100. The asset has the characteristics of a bond contract. The determination of this asset's present value requires calculation of the present value of the periodic payments and the present value of the principal that is to be repaid at the end of the payment period. The applicable formulas are as follows (current interest rate with allowance for risk is shown as i and the number of payment periods is shown as n):

$$\text{Present value of periodic payments} = \frac{\text{Amount of one payment}}{i} - \frac{\text{Amount of one payment}}{i\,(1+i)^n}$$

$$\text{Present value of principal} = \frac{\text{Principal}}{(1+i)^n}$$

The two formulas may be combined into one. In practice, bond tables may be used to secure an answer.

The formulas indicate that an increase in the current interest rate reduces the capitalized value, and an increase in the amount of periodic payment enlarges the capital value. The longer the time over which payments are to be made, the greater the change in capitalized value, given a change in the current interest rate. The effect of a change of 1 per cent in the current interest rate depends on the absolute level of interest rates at the time of the change. For example, assume that an income of $60 is expected to continue for an infinite number of years. If the rate of interest is 4 per cent, the capitalized value is $1,500. If the rate of interest rises to 5 per cent, the capitalized value falls from $1,500 to $1,200. Assume the same facts, except that the rate of interest is only 2 per cent. At a 2 per cent rate, the capitalized value of the annual income is $3,000. If the rate of interest rises to 3 per cent, the capitalized value falls to $2,000. In the first case the capitalized value fell $300, but in the latter it fell $1,000.

Professor Samuelson has suggested that capitalization be analyzed in terms of the flow of out-payments as well as that of in-payments.* His analysis rests on the assumption that investors, such as financial institutions, are primarily concerned with their respective "disposable" real income with the passage of time. This assumption appears reasonable in view of bank examination policy and state insurance laws, which permit institutions to value a large proportion of their credit market instruments at amortized values. Using the term "disposable" real income over time, Professor Samuelson sets down a general rule that relates the weighted average time period of disbursements to the weighted average time period of receipts, and shows that when the former exceeds the latter, an increase in interest rates

* "The Effect of Interest Rate Increase on the Banking System," *American Economic Review*, Vol. xxxv, March 1945, pp. 16-27.

will not affect present value as adversely as suggested by the capitalization formulas shown above. Applying this theory of present value to a relatively realistic model of our banking system, Professor Samuelson demonstrates that an average doubling of all interest rates would cause capital values, as he uses the term, to fall by only 3 per cent. If operating expenses and dividend policy remained constant, and the higher level of rates remained in effect, the 3 per cent drop in capital values could be replaced in less than three years' time. It must be noticed that capital losses are not realized unless the securities are actually liquidated during the period of adjustment. If the banks incurred large deposit withdrawals, the weighted average time period of disbursements would be changed, and the present values would be affected appreciably in the Samuelson model. Losses would be minimized by restricting liquidations to short-term government obligations. The implication of this line of reasoning is that the institutions are not necessarily "locked in" by moderate changes in the level of interest rates.

INTEREST-RATE EFFECTS

Interest-rate effects are analyzed in terms of relationships in which the rate of interest is a determinant. It should be pointed out at the outset that empirical evidence is woefully lacking on the degree of strength of interest-rate effects. However, it is possible to analyze the nature and direction of the effects. Before considering individual relationships, the theoretical foundation of interest-rate policy is set out.

Theoretical Foundation of Interest-Rate Policy

As a theoretical foundation of monetary and debt-management policies as they pertain to interest-rate effects, it is interesting to note that the classical theory of the rate of interest severely limits the scope of interest-rate policy. The proponents of the classical theory did not recognize the level of interest rates as a determinant of the level of output; instead, they viewed the level of interest rates only as a determinant of the composition of output. Other things being equal, a reduction in the demand for capital or loanable funds would cause the level of interest rates to fall, but a reduction in the demand for capital or loanable funds would not lead to a reduction in the level of output, because, as the classicists assumed, the volume of saving was equally sensitive to a change in the level of interest rates. The lower level of interest rates would discourage some saving and encourage additional consumption expenditure. Therefore, the fall in investment would be matched by an increase in consumption.

Within the classical framework, assume an autonomous change in the volume of saving, i.e., there is a change in one or more of the determinants of the supply schedule of saving. Perhaps the change in the schedule was brought about by a change in custom, self-control, or family affection. An increase in the volume of net national saving out of a given level of national income would cause the rate of interest to fall, other things remaining equal. The reduction in the rate of interest would lead to an increase in the amount of capital funds demanded. Assuming that capital funds flow into capital expenditures, the increase in capital expenditures would match or offset the decrease in consumption expenditure. No change would occur in the level of output, but a change would occur in the composition of output. Within such a theoretical framework, interest-rate policy as a determinant of the level of national output and employment would have no place.

Within the framework of the Keynesian and Swedish theoretical formulations there is no direct relationship between the volume of saving and the rate of interest. Instead, the volume of saving is dependent primarily upon the level of income. As for the relationship between interest and volume of investment, the theories are very much the same. However, empirical data suggest that only certain types of investment are sensitive to a change in the level of interest rates.

The absence of a direct relationship between the rate of interest and the volume of saving has important policy implications. It means that the rate of interest may affect the level of output. This was not possible in the classical theory of the rate of interest. In the Keynesian and Swedish theoretical formulations, an increase in the rate of interest, other things being equal, tends to reduce investment expediture and the level of output. Assuming a relatively constant relation between the level of income and the volume of saving, saving tends to fall as the level of national income declines. Therefore, it is possible for a higher interest rate to discourage investment and lead to a lower volume of saving.

In terms of practical considerations, interest-rate policy cannot be relied upon as the sole means of affecting the level of income-generating expenditures. However, it is doubtful if over-all policy measures can be effective without flexibility in the level and structure of interest rates. Generally, Federal Reserve and Treasury officials do not deliberately fix interest rates at high levels. It was pointed out in Chapter 24 that the level and structure of interest rates are determined by the interaction of the demand for and the supply of loanable funds. During a boom period, demand for credit tends to increase more than the supply of credit, bringing about an increase in the level of interest rates.

If the volume of current saving is not sensitive to small changes in the rate of interest, if idle balances are worked down to a minimum, and if bank lending is restricted, interest rates are bound to rise. The monetary and debt management officials could hold the level of interest rates down by supplying additional bank reserves, but this method would require the elimination or sacrifice of general monetary measures as a means of promoting reasonable stability in the general level of prices.

Effect on Savers

Saving is defined as the excess of current receipts over current expenditures. The aggregate volume of saving in an accounting period is equal to the difference between gross saving and dissaving, and it is dependent upon the decisions of all economic units. It may be recalled that the consumer sector accounts for the major portion of both gross and net national saving.

The volume of saving is affected by many factors other than interest rates, such as the level of employment, income, and output, the distribution of income, the age distribution of the population, the rate of growth of income, and the state of expectations as to future employment, income, output, and the general level of prices. These factors are interrelated. It is very difficult to go beyond a mere listing of factors. Much of what has been written about the rate of interest and its affect on saving has generated more light than heat. Empirical evidence is vital, but mostly impossible to obtain. Even if a statistical relationship could be established between the rate of saving and the level of interest rates, it might be caused by the influence of other common factors. Certainly, the effect of interest rates on the rate of saving is less important than that of other factors listed above.

As noted in the previous chapter, flexible monetary and debt management measures may be used to bring about changes in the level and structure of interest rates. The effect of such changes on the amount of credit supplied and demanded depends upon the respective elasticities of supply and demand schedules. It will be recalled from the principles of economics that elasticity is the sensitivity of one economic variable to a change in another economic variable. Applied to the supply of funds in a particular market, the elasticity of supply gives an indication as to how sensitively the suppliers of funds respond or react to change in the rate of interest paid on those funds. If suppliers of funds supply considerably more funds when the rate falls, then the elasticity of supply is high. If they supply only slightly more funds when the rate falls, then the elasticity of supply is low. If the supply of funds is unaffected by a change in the rate, then the elasticity of supply is perfectly inelastic, or zero. If the supply of funds is infinite at a given rate, then the elasticity of supply is perfectly elastic, or infinity. If the change in the supply of funds is exactly proportional to a change in the rate, then the elasticity of supply is unit elasticity. An elasticity between zero and one is inelastic, and elasticity between one and infinity is elastic. The state of expectations is an important determinant of elasticity. If an increase in the level of rates is considered as temporary and it is expected to decline in the near future, the higher rates may bring about a substantial increase in the volume of loanable funds, but if the increase is considered as merely a prelude to further increases, then the initial increase may bring about a decrease rather than an increase in the volume of loanable funds. In the first case, the supply of funds may be elastic; in the second, the supply of funds may be negatively elastic.

CONSUMER SAVING. Before considering the effect of a change in the level and structure of interest rates on consumer saving, we should review the theory of consumer saving as formulated by the Chairman of the Board of Governors of the Federal Reserve System.*

> Consumer saving, like the saving of other sectors, is equal, on the investment side, to purchases of tangible assets plus the financial component — net acquisition of financial assets less net increase in debt. Purchases of tangible assets are part of domestic capital formation and the Nation's investment. The financial components of investment taken together are the consumer sector's net financial investment, or saving in financial form, and represent the net amount of funds made available to other sectors.
>
> These two components of sector investment can be expected to react differently to changes in interest rates. Purchases of tangible assets would be expected to respond negatively to a rise in interest rates, to the extent that they respond at all. Interest is a cost of investment; and as costs rise, the amount of investment tends to decline. Even if this effect is small, especially in the consumer sector, as seems likely, clearly a rise of interest rates does not encourage such investment.
>
> On the other hand, consumers' saving in financial form would be expected to respond positively to changes in interest rates. A rise in interest rates tends to encourage the acquisition of assets and discourage the incurrence of debt. Both tendencies would be reflected in a rise of saving in financial form.

The effect of change in the level of interest rates on the volume of consumers' saving in financial form depends upon the consumers' motives underlying current spending and saving habits. If a consumer's goal is to achieve a certain amount of accumulated financial assets, a rise in the level of interest rates may permit a reduction in current saving if the higher level of rates is expected to prevail in the future and if there is no change in the length of the intended saving period. On the other hand, a higher level of interest rates may encourage some consumers to increase their current saving and encourage others to save for the first time. The shift of accumulated saving from one financial form to another in response to rate differentials indicates that many consumers are concerned with the rate return on saving. As noted in earlier chapters, the savings and life insurance institutions are competing vigorously for saving, which has led to a growing public awareness of rate differentials on various types of financial assets. However, evidence is lacking as to whether higher interest rates induce consumers as

*U.S. Joint Economic Committee, "Employment, Growth, and Price Levels," Hearings, Part 10, op. cit., p. 3356.

a group to save a larger percentage of their incomes. It seems reasonable that there is a fringe group of consumers who would attempt to save for the first time or save more than in the past in response to relatively attractive rates.

Interest income is more likely to be saved than other types of income because much of it is not actually paid out to the saver unless a specific request for payment is made. Generally, the saver allows the interest to accrue to realize compound interest on accumulated saving. Although the change in saving resulting from higher interest income may be small, the direction of the effect does lend support to flexible monetary and debt management measures.

Since the aggregate volume of consumer saving in an accounting period is equal to the difference between gross saving and dissaving, it is also necessary to analyze the response of consumers in their role as borrowers. This matter is analyzed in a later section, but it might be pointed out here that restraint on the availability of credit may moderate the amount of consumer expenditure being financed by borrowing. Also, in transactions in which interest expense is an important component of total cost, rising rates, especially if considered as temporary, may prompt some consumers to delay mortgage indebtedness. The delay in moving ahead with new home construction slows down consumer dissaving, which leads to a higher level of net saving.

SAVING BY FINANCIAL AND NONFINANCIAL FIRMS. A corporate firm saves when it pays out in dividends less than it earns. For financial firms, interest income is the main source of income, and higher interest rates lead to an increase in net earnings. At the same time, economic units having to pay higher interest costs on borrowed funds may have to reduce other expenditures to meet higher interest expense or shift the additional costs to other economic units. Assuming that the dividend policy of financial firms is relatively stable in the short run, financial firms tend to retain more earnings during a period of rising interest rates. It is reasonable to assume that the marginal propensity to save is greater for financial firms than for many of the economic units who bear the incidence of higher interest expense.

As noted above, rising interest rates accompany a general tightening on the reserve position of commercial banks. If nonfinancial firms are unable to secure additional bank credit because of the effect of monetary and debt management measures on the availability of bank credit, they are likely to offset this lack by holding back an immediate increase in dividends, with the result that level of net saving by nonfinancial firms tends to increase. Retained corporate earnings are more likely to flow into physical investment than the dividend income that would have been received by stockholders. Additional investment should lead to a larger flow of goods and services.

Effect on Borrowers

It should be recognized that borrowers are affected by changes in the level and structure of interest rates as well as by change in the availability of credit. During a period of credit restraint, a borrower's loan request may be refused by two or three lenders, which may so discourage him that he postpones the search for borrowed funds to a later period. Borrowers know that funds will become available during a period of credit ease. In this case, the higher level of interest rates was not the deterrent; instead, the funds simply were not available to the borrower. In this section, our attention will be focused on the influence of a higher level of interest rates, assuming that borrowers are able to get their loan requests approved. However, in the real world, it must be realized that the availability of credit and the level of interest rates influence borrowers simultaneously, and it is very difficult to measure with any degree of precision the influence of each factor. The absence of empirical data has led to considerable diversity of opinion as to the realtive importance of these factors. It is generally agreed that the availability of funds and the provisions of loan agreements are probably more important than the stated rate of interest.

Other things being equal, a fall in the level of interest rates would be expected to bring about an increase in the demand for investment goods, and a rise in the level of interest rates would be expected to bring about a decrease in demand for investment goods.*
The effects of a change in the level and structure of interest rates depends upon the elasticity of the demand for investment funds, which can be expected to vary considerably among economic units in the different sectors of the economy. It is reasonable to assume that the ratio of interest expense to total costs would be one of the more important factors underlying the degree of elasticity.

There are other factors in addition to the rate of interest that affect expenditures on additional investment, and these other factors are seldom static or unchanging. The influence of change in these other factors may offset a change in the rate of interest; in fact, they may offset it to such an extent that expenditures on additional investment may actually rise during a period of rising rates, and fall during a period of falling rates. Furthermore, the effects of a change in the level of interest rates upon the level of investment expenditures may be very slow in taking effect, especially upon major investment projects. Some individuals may take months in planning new home construction; business firms must plan their investment expenditures over a one- or two-year period; and it takes time to change investment plans. If such lags are very important, monetary measures may get out of phase with the cycle, and be disturbing rather than corrective.

*It was pointed out earlier that the guiding criterion used by the Federal Reserve in determining whether a nonfinancial transaction is investment or not is the "acquisition of an asset that yields services over time, that is, beyond the current accounting period."

CONSUMER BORROWERS. The effect of higher interest rates on consumer borrowers depends on the nature of consumer borrowing. Interest rates probably have little or no effect on borrowing to finance durable consumer goods for three reasons. First, many consumers do not know the effective interest cost that is being charged by sellers and lenders. Second, an increase in the rate of interest has only a slight effect on the size of the periodic payments. Third, a change in down payment and maturity may be used to obscure the higher interest rates.

Speculative factors tend to be predominant in borrowing to finance securities transactions, and small changes in the level of interest rates cannot be expected to have much effect on this form of borrowing.

The level of interest rates is an important consideration in the financing of one- to four-family mortgage credit, because the ratio of interest expense to total cost is significant. Assume that a mortgage has the following terms: principal is $10,000; maturity is 20 years, and the loan is amortized on a monthly basis. If the rate of interest is 4 per cent, monthly payments will be $60.60, but if the rate of interest is 6 per cent, the monthly payment will be $71.64. The increase in the monthly payment may discourage some persons from going ahead with new construction, assuming that interest rates will fall in the near future. Some may reconsider their buying or building plans, and may have to scale down their plans to fit the higher monthly payments associated with a given amount of mortgage credit. To the extent that the mortgage payment period may be lengthened, the size of the monthly payments may be adjusted downward to offset the higher interest costs.

In the above example, lengthening the maturity to 30 years would reduce the monthly payment from $71.64 to $59.96. However, this move has the effect of locking the consumer into a long-term commitment at a time when interest rates are relatively high. There is little doubt that higher interest rates influence the volume of mortgage credit. In fact, the critics of flexible monetary policy build much of their case on the ground that the effect of higher interest rates is concentrated to a major extent on residential mortgage credit, i.e., it is too selective or discriminatory in its effects.

BUSINESS BORROWERS. The analysis of business financing in Chapter 16 indicated that in the corporate nonfinancial business sector, approximately 75 per cent of total uses of funds is capital expenditure, and approximately one-third of total sources of funds is obtained from external sources. The percentages are even higher in the case of the non-corporate, nonfinancial business sector. The data show that a substantial amount of business expenditure is in the form of capital outlays, and that much of this expenditure is financed with borrowed funds. It is reasonable to assume that businesses would not borrow to finance investment unless that rate of expected return exceeded or equaled the cost of the funds. The difference between return and cost depends on the profitability of the projects and the rate of interest. A change in the level and structure of interest rates affects not only the cost of borrowed funds but also expectations as to profitability. The relationship implies that a change in the level of rates would have its greatest effect on those businesses in which interest costs are significant and profit margins are relatively low.

Entrepreneurs tend to evaluate investment projects in terms of achieving maximum profits, by comparing the present value of the expected future returns from various projects with their costs. If the present value of a project is greater than cost, the investment decision may be undertaken. The present value of the expected future returns is determined by discounting the stream of future income at an appropriate discount rate, which is comprised of three elements: (1) pure rate of interest as represented by the interest rate on a Treasury security of comparable maturity; (2) an allowance for lender's risk to cover the uncertainty of investment income or repayment of principal; and (3) an allowance for the firm's risk to cover the uncertainties of the particular project. The composition of the discount rate is an important consideration in determining the influence of a higher level of interest rates on investment decisions. The allowance for the firm's risk may be so high that a change of 1 or 2 per cent in the level of interest rates may have little effect on capital budget decisions. Many firms use a pay-back criterion, which involves the number of years in which a project is supposed to pay for itself. A pay-back period of four years implies a very high discount rate. In areas of economic activity in which there is a low degree of uncertainty and a long pay-back period, the level of pure interest rates is an important consideration, and a change in the level of rates can be expected to affect decisions. In practice, as well as in theory, the interest rate is more important in housing, industrial construction, railroads, public utilities, and public facilities than in other sectors of the economy. Space limitations do not permit us to review the empirical evidence relating to the degree of sensitivity of business investment to the rate of interest.*

In recent years, economists have tended to give more weight to the influence of the level of interest rates on some of the important components of business investment.** This change in emphasis has led some economists to recommend a long-term, low-interest rate policy at all times, and has led others to recommend that long-term rates be lowered as rapidly as possible when output begins to decline.

*For a short review of the theory of expenditure elasticities and empirical studies on the effects on private expenditures of a change in the general level of interest rates, see Warren L. Smith, "Debt Management in the United States," Study Paper No. 19 in U.S. Joint Economic Committee, "Study of Employment, Growth, and Price Levels," 86th Cong. 2nd sess. (Washington, D.C.: Government Printing Office, 1960), pp. 92-98.

**See "Controversial Issues in Recent Monetary Policy: A Symposium," *The Review of Economics and Statistics*, Vol. XLII, No. 3 (August 1960), particularly the papers of Alvin H. Hansen, pp. 255-265, and Paul A. Samuelson, pp. 263-269.

FINANCIAL MEASURES AND FINANCIAL
INTERMEDIARIES*

It will be recalled that non-bank financial institutions (hereafter referred to as financial intermediaries) have been and are continuing to grow more rapidly than commercial banks. Since financial intermediaries are not directly controlled by Federal Reserve or Treasury officials, the increase in the relative importance of financial intermediaries has raised some fundamental questions. Have the changes in the structure of the financial system made financial policies more or less effective? This question is very difficult to answer because so many changes have also occurred in the structure of the nonfinancial sectors, particularly in the direction of built-in inflationary forces. The mix of financial measures has also undergone change, and open market operations have become the most important financial measure. It is no easy task to pinpoint and rank the causes underlying the supposed decline in the effectiveness of financial measures. Some students of this subject conclude that their effectiveness has declined, whereas others conclude just the opposite. Another question concerns the issue of equity. Do commercial banks absorb an undue share of the burden of restrictive financial measures? To state it differently, are financial measures equitable in their effects on the various types of financial institutions? Questions such as these suggest the possibility that the structure of financial measures may have to be changed to improve both their effectiveness and their equity.

To facilitate the evaluation of the present mix of financial measures and their influence on the total financial system, we shall review the basic relationships among commercial banks, financial intermediaries, and the nonfinancial public. One of the more important relationships has to do with credit creation by financial intermediaries. Following this discussion,

---

*This section of the chapter is based on ideas developed in the following articles and books: J. G. Gurley and E. S. Shaw, "Financial Aspects of Economic Development," *American Economic Review*, XLV, September 1955, pp. 515-538; Gurley and Shaw, "Financial Intermediaries and the Saving-Investment Process," *Journal of Finance*, XI, May 1956, pp. 257-276; Gurley and Shaw, "Reply to Communication of J. M. Culbertson," *American Economic Review*, XLVIII, March 1958, pp. 132-138; Gurley and Shaw, *Money in a Theory of Finance* (Washington, D.C.: The Brookings Institution, 1960); J. M. Culbertson, "Intermediaries and Monetary Theory: A Criticism of the Gurley-Shaw Theory," *American Economic Review*, XLVIII, March 1958, pp. 119-131; John G. Gurley, "Statement before U.S. Joint Economic Committee," in U.S. Joint Economic Committee, "Employment, Growth, and Price Levels," Hearings, Part 4, 86th Cong., 1st sess. (Washington, D.C.: Government Printing Office, 1959), pp. 847-887; Gurley, "Liquidity and Financial Institutions in the Postwar Period," Staff Paper No. 14 in U.S. Joint Economic Committee, "Study of Employment, Growth, and Price Levels," 86th Cong., 1st sess. (Washington, D.C.: Government Printing Office, 1960); Donald Shelby, "Some Implications of the Growth of Financial Intermediaries," *Journal of Finance*, XIII, December 1958, pp. 527-541; Richard S. Thorn, "Nonbank Financial Intermediaries, Credit Expansion, and Monetary Policy," *Staff Papers*, International Monetary Fund, VI, November 1958, pp. 369-383; Eugene A. Birnbaum, "The Growth of Financial Intermediaries as a Factor in the Effectiveness of Monetary Policy," *Staff Papers*, International Monetary Fund, VI, November 1958, pp. 384-426.

the effectiveness and equity of financial measures will be considered. The closing section of the chapter is devoted to the position of Chairman Martin of the Board of Governors of the Federal Reserve System on the question of regulation of financial intermediaries.

Credit Creation by Financial Intermediaries

Legal reserve requirements are imposed against commercial banks' deposit liabilities, and the major portion of their reserves must be held on deposit with Federal Reserve banks at all times. Similar reserve requirements are not imposed against the liabilities of financial intermediaries. However, in practice the financial intermediaries maintain deposits in commercial banks and currency in their vaults to satisfy in part their liquidity needs; these assets may be viewed as their reserves. In a sense, a certain amount of the legal reserves held at Federal Reserve banks represents reserves of intermediaries. For example, if their demand deposits represent 5 per cent of their liabilities, and if the banks' legal reserve requirement were 20 per cent, then 1 per cent of the intermediaries' liabilities would be in the form of legal reserves at Federal Reserve banks. If the banks' legal reserve requirement were 10 per cent, then ½ of 1 per cent of the intermediaries' liabilities would be held in the form of legal reserves.

Nonfinancial firms, governmental units, and consumers must also hold a certain portion of their assets in the form of money in order to satisfy the transaction motive, and these economic units may also hold additional amounts of money to satisfy precautionary and speculative motives. It has been pointed out previously that many types of financial assets, and particularly fixed-value redeemable claims, may also be held to satisfy precautionary and speculative motives. In addition, fixed-value redeemable claims are a very attractive investment outlet to consumers who desire safety of principal and a reasonable rate of return. In our discussion of the money market, it was pointed out that many economic units are willing to exchange money for money market instruments when money market rates are sufficiently attractive. Of course, all economic units are limited in volume of exchange by the need to hold minimum cash balances for transactions. Shifts from demand deposits and currency to fixed-value redeemable claims and money market instruments represent economizing of a given stock of money. In other words, some economic units are willing to reduce their holdings of money to accommodate the money needs of other economic units, and in the process near-money assets are created. If, in the short run, there is a reasonably stable relationship among the public's preferences for money, money market instruments, and fixed-value redeemable claims, then it may be argued that expansion in the volume of money market instruments and fixed-value redeemable claims is dependent upon concurrent expansion in the stock of money. A large autonomous shift from demand deposits to other financial assets would imply that the public was holding a large volume of idle cash balances. The inflationary effects of such behavior are not dependent upon the existence of financial intermediaries. However, if the intermediaries did not exist, the public would have to purchase marketable instruments, the liquidity of which would not be as high as the intermediaries' liabilities.

If Federal Reserve and Treasury officials tend to hold down or minimize the public's holdings of idle cash balances, then the expansion of credit through the financial intermediaries may be restricted to the amount of net saving flowing through the financial intermediaries. As net saving flows into the intermediaries sector, the ownership of existing demand deposits is transferred to that sector. Setting aside a small amount of the demand deposits for reserve, the sector transfers the ownership of the remaining demand deposits to other sectors. The supply of money is unchanged, but the saving-investment process has created additional highly liquid assets.

The credit creation process can be illustrated by the following example. Assume that a person exchanges a demand deposit for a fixed-value redeemable claim, say a savings deposit in a savings bank. Assuming that the bank's policy is to hold 5 per cent of its liabilities in the form of demand deposits, the savings bank is now in a position to increase its loans and investments by an amount equal to 95 per cent of its new or primary deposit. In the process, the bank transfers the demand deposit to an economic unit desiring to increase its expenditures. The net effects of the entire series of transactions are: (1) no change in the volume of demand deposits; (2) change in ownership of demand deposits; (3) the demand deposit is transferred from an idle cash balance to an active cash balance; (4) change in the volume of fixed-value redeemable claims; and (5) change in the total amount of credit. It will be recalled from our discussion of expansion of commercial bank credit that bank loans and investments create deposits and these deposits tend to circulate or to be transferred within the commercial banking system. The recipients of the loans and investments of financial intermediaries also receive their loans in the form of demand deposits, but the deposits are not newly created. However, as loans and investments of financial intermediaries lead to additional exchanges of demand deposits for intermediaries' liabilities, the non-bank financial institutions can expand credit further. Although empirical data are not available, it would seem reasonable to assume that the return flow of deposits to financial intermediaries probably offsets the amount of their reserve ratio, implying that non-bank financial institutions may expand loans and investments by an amount approximately equal to the increase in their liabilities. For example, assume the following: (1) $10 active balance generates initially an additional $10 of G.N.P.; (2) disposable income is 6/10 of G.N.P.; (3)

personal saving is 1/10 of disposable income; and (4) personal saving bears a 5:1 ratio between fixed-value redeemable claims and demand deposits. Under these assumptions, the return flow would be 0.5, which is approximately equal to the reserve ratio of the financial intermediaries (.05 times 10 = 0.5).

A simple formula may be used to illustrate further the total increase in financial assets associated with a given change in the amount of commercial banks' legal reserves. The following assumptions are made: (1) financial assets consist of demand deposits and fixed-value redeemable claims; (2) the public's marginal ratio of fixed-value redeemable claims to demand deposits is known and remains unchanged; and (3) there is no change in the amount of currency outstanding. The formula is:

$$FA = \frac{R\,(1+a)}{r_d + r_d\,r_f}$$

The meanings of the symbols are as follows:

FA Change in financial assets
R   Amount of change in legal reserves
a   Public's marginal ratio of fixed-value redeemable claims to demand deposits
r_d Legal reserve ratio against demand deposits
r_f Financial intermediaries' ratio of demand deposits to liabilities

Substituting the following values into the formula, the total increase in financial assets and its composition may be determined:

$$R = \$5 \quad a = .75 \quad r_d = .20 \quad r_f = .05$$

On the basis of these assumptions, the amount of financial assets held by all non-bank sectors may be expected to increase approximately $42. The approximate changes in financial assets may be summarized in the form of changes to abbreviated balance sheets: (Assume that the change in commercial banks' legal reserves was due to open market purchases by Federal Reserve banks):

Commercial Banks

Government bonds	−5	Demand deposits	+25
Reserve	+5		
Loans	+25		

Financial Intermediaries

Demand deposits	+1	Fixed-value redeemable claims	+18
Loans	+17		

Up to this point nothing has been said about time deposits of commercial banks. It will be recalled that the legal reserve requirement against time deposits is lower than the legal reserve requirement against demand deposits. However, the legal reserve requirement against time deposits is greater than the product of the reserve ratio of financial intermediaries times the legal reserve ratio against demand deposits. If the public's preference ratio for time deposits in commercial banks falls, and the preference ratios for other fixed-value redeemable claims increase, the public will carry out exchanges of financial assets. In the process, the total amount of credit is increased; time deposits are converted into demand deposits. If the commercial banks are fully loaned up at the time of change, then commercial banks must reduce their loans and investments, thereby reducing demand deposits, or else they must build up their legal reserves to support the higher volume of demand deposits. In the former case, the reduction in bank credit offsets partially the previous increase in credit created by the financial intermediaries. In the latter case, total credit increases by an amount equal to the amount of time deposits shifted to financial intermediaries. For a discussion of a formula that includes the public's marginal ratio of commercial bank time deposits to demand deposits as an additional component, refer to the article cited below.*

Effectiveness of Financial Measures

The growth and development of financial intermediaries do not necessarily preclude effective use of the present mix of financial measures. The potential ineffectiveness of financial measures is related to potential exchanges of demand deposits and time deposits in commercial banks for the liabilities of financial intermediaries. Although Federal Reserve and Treasury officials do not have the power to control directly either the public's preference ratios for various types of financial assets or the reserve ratios of financial intermediaries, the use of open market operations does represent an indirect control measure over the financial intermediaries.

The ownership and maturity patterns of Federal obligations and the manner in which they may be changed were examined earlier, and it was demonstrated that open market operations may affect almost all financial institutions. It may be recalled that open market operations are conducted through dealers in government securities, and all financial institutions buy and sell Federal obligations through dealers. It is generally recognized that control over money alone is less effective in influencing the level of private-income generating expenditures than control over money plus Federal obligations. This control could be carried one step further to include all credit market instruments. However, since Federal obligations involve all maturity sectors and almost all financial institutions, open market operations in Federal obligations are probably adequate. It would appear that the basic issue is not whether or not additional measures must be added to the existing arsenal of financial measures; instead, it is whether or not the present arsenal of financial measures is being used most effectively in terms of the present structure and operation of the financial system. If "return flows" and "marginal preference ratios" are to be affected, additional measures would be needed.

*Shelby, op. cit., pp. 528-534.

Two issues are involved, and space precludes an intensive treatment of either. One concerns the possibility that financial measures may have to be used to reduce the stock of money during an inflationary period to offset the credit creation of financial intermediaries. In other words, the velocity of circulation may increase to such an extent that the policy calls for a reduction in the stock of money. This policy could be particularly severe on commercial banks in terms of growth. The other issue concerns open market operations. There is general agreement among Federal Reserve officials that open market operations should be restricted primarily to short-term obligations. This policy, which is referred to as the "bills only" policy, was adopted to avoid the possibility of creating unwarranted expectations among dealers and investors, to encourage the development of a stronger market for Federal obligations, and to place major reliance on the market for the determination of the interest rate structure and the allocation of credit.

The Federal Reserve officials defend their policy on the ground that the effects of open market operations in short-term Federal obligations permeate all maturity sectors. Critics of the "bills only" policy point out that the market for Federal obligations has not been strengthened, and the allocation of credit has not been appropriate in terms of our national economic objectives. They suggest that the Federal Reserve abandon the "bills only" policy and substitute a policy that permits intervention in any or all maturity sectors of the market. It is argued that such a policy may be used to minimize undesirable speculative activity in Federal obligations and to affect directly the determination of interest rates in all maturity sectors. Major reliance would still be placed on the purchase and sale of short-term obligations to achieve desirable money market conditions. To state the positions differently, the Federal Reserve officials continue to place major emphasis on the effects of policy on the monetary or banking system, whereas the critics of Federal Reserve policy place major emphasis on the effects of policy on the total financial system. As noted earlier, it is very difficult under the present administrative structure of the Federal Reserve System to reach agreement on open market operations when all maturity sectors are involved. Supposedly, officials would have to reach agreement on a desired interest rate structure and measures to achieve this structure.*

Direct control over financial intermediaries could be achieved by establishing legal reserve requirements for some of the more important institutions. For example, the institutions could be required to hold legal reserves equal to a certain percentage of their liabilities. Conceivably, the reserves could be held in the form of deposit balances at commercial banks, and a regulatory body, say the Board of Governors of the Federal Reserve System, could have discretion as to the exact legal reserve ratios. If officials

*Open market operations in early 1960 indicated a slight departure from the "bills" doctrine.

believed that financial intermediaries were providing an excessive amount of funds to non-financial firms and consumers, the legal reserve ratios could be increased, immobilizing a larger percentage of the institutions' assets and reducing the profit margin on a given volume of assets. The reduction in the profit margin would restrain the institutions from increasing the rate of return paid to "depositors," which would tend to discourage further exchanges of liabilities of commercial banks for liabilities of financial intermediaries. To encourage more investment by financial intermediaries, the legal reserve requirements could be lowered. Would such a set of controls be either necessary or desirable? As to necessity, the previous discussion suggests a negative response. Effective control of commercial bank credit does not require that all banks be member banks. As long as the major segment of the commercial banking system is subject to credit restraint, the remaining portion must adjust to what the other banks are doing. In the process the non-member banks must adopt loan and investment policies similar to those being followed by member banks. The same reasoning may be applied to the financial system, assuming that idle cash balances are not outstanding. After a certain point, the financial intermediaries must adjust themselves to keep in step with the commercial banking system.

Equity of Financial Measures

The previous discussion suggests that the strong preferences for liabilities of financial intermediaries will continue, and that in the long run the relative importance of the commercial banks in terms of total financial assets will continue to decline. This prospect raises a fundamental question as to whether the regulation of commercial banks reflects a basic difference between commercial banks and financial intermediaries or whether the present state of regulation over the financial system is discriminatory. It must be admitted that commercial banks are distinctly different from other financial institutions in the sense that they have the ability of creating the most liquid of all financial assets, namely money. However, there is not much difference between time deposits of commercial banks and other fixed-value redeemable claims, and herein lies an element of discrimination. The commercial banks are closely regulated as to payment of interest on time deposits, whereas the majority of non-bank financial institutions are not so regulated. The regulation of financial intermediaries deals primarily with loans and investments. As proven during the years 1958-1960, consumers tend to exchange time deposits of commercial banks for other higher-yielding financial assets during a period of rising interest rates. When the level of rates falls, re-exchanges are unlikely. One possible solution to discrimination against time deposits in commercial banks would be to segregate savings banking entirely from commercial banking by establishing departments similar to trust departments in commercial banks. Assets would be segregated, and the departments would hold reserves in the form of demand deposits with commercial banks.

Another way of reducing discrimination would be to remove the interest rate ceiling on time deposits, allowing commercial banks to change rates in line with competitive conditions in the money and capital markets. The negative arguments with respect to this proposal were considered earlier, in Chapter 8.

Another alternative would be for the Federal Reserve officials to choose to use lower required legal reserves rather than the acquisition of Federal obligations as a means of providing reserves to commercial banks in the long run. It may be argued, on the other hand, that the Federal Reserve officials should purchase Federal obligations, because that action would assure Federal Reserve banks of maximum profits and prevent a profit windfall to commercial banks. Federal Reserve officials tend to favor a reduction in the legal reserve ratio, but they do not defend their choice of measures on the basis of commercial banks' earnings. If they were to do so, the uproar set up by certain members of Congress would be deafening. However, it does appear that a case could be built for a deliberate choice of the lower legal reserve ratio on the ground that the additional profit potential tends to offset the discrimination inherent in the present mix of financial measures.

Position of the Federal Reserve System

Questions dealing with regulation of non-bank financial institutions were submitted to Federal Reserve officials by the Joint Economic Committee: "Would it be desirable to give the Federal Reserve System or some other Federal agency authority to control the lending activities of institutional lenders e.g., life insurance companies, mutual savings banks, savings and loan associations?" "What specific controls would be desirable?"*

It seems appropriate to conclude this study of our financial system by quoting the reply of Chairman Martin of the Federal Reserve System to these two important questions. Part of the Chairman's response to the questions serves as a good review of the operation of the total financial system. The author concurs with the position taken by the Chairman.

> The primary function of most nonbank financial institutions is to serve as a conduit for savings. In general, these financial institutions operate by gathering together part of the current income stream not used by receivers to finance current, primarily consumption expenditures, and make these gathered funds available to finance outlays principally for investment goods (including houses and consumer durables) by other individuals, by businesses, and by governments. So

*U.S. Joint Economic Committee, "Employment, Growth, and Price Levels," Hearings, Part 6C, 86th Cong., 1st sess. (Washington, D.C.: Government Printing Office, 1959); answers and questions on pp. 1783-1784.

long as these intermediaries limit their activities to channeling the current savings stream, there would appear to be no more need to control their lending activities than there would be to establish allocations for the use of any of the community's savings.

In time of increasing demand for institutional funds, financial intermediaries may attempt to supplement their inflows of savings by selling financial claims acquired earlier or by borrowing. Because the relationship of these intermediaries to savers (policyholders, depositors, and shareholders) is a fiduciary one, the financial community tends to regard continuing large resort to bank borrowing to supplement saving inflows as undesirable. Prudent management requires that intermediaries support their investment operations by their savings accumulations rather than by borrowings especially borrowing of short-term funds.

Occasionally, suppplementary funds are needed to accommodate short-term fluctuations in savings inflows, particularly since so large a share of investment outflows is determined by commitment arrangements made earlier. For some institutions, such as savings and loan associations, specific governmental programs have been created to moderate the impact of unforeseen contingencies and to even out flows of funds as between local mortgage markets. For other institutions, borrowing or "warehousing" arrangements with commercial banks have been developed to equalize temporary discrepancies between savings flows and investments. There would clearly be a hazard to national economic stability if financial intermediaries as a group built up a large current indebtedness in a period of strong demands for funds which then had to be liquidated out of their savings inflow in the succeeding period. This process could lead to excessive long-term lending and investment on the basis of short-term funds in prosperity periods and unduly sharp curtailment in periods of recession.

To the extent that nonbank financial intermediaries depend on supplements from the banking system, they are subject, of course, to the same credit restraints limiting all bank credit expansion. In attempting to borrow from the banks, intermediaries must compete with other borrowers for whatever total of credit is available.

To the extent that supplementary funds are obtained from sources other than the commercial banking system by selling financial claims, additional inflationary pressures can be created, but only in the sense of any other factor tending to increase the turnover or rate of use of the existing money supply. In attempting to sell assets, financial intermediaries are limited — perhaps to an even greater degree than other investors — by unwillingness to suffer losses in asset values in a period of rising interest rates and declining values for outstanding financial claims.

To the extent that the Federal Government or one of its agencies provides facilities for leading to, or taking over the assets of, savings institutions, there will be an impact on the market for securities. The effect on the credt situation would be similar to that of financing through the securities market corresponding changes in other governmental expenditures.

Inflation is not, however, a necessary consequence when financial intermediaries attract funds from the banking system, either by offering higher returns for savings or by selling financial claims to banks.

The restraint on deposit growth at a time when economic conditions necessitate such restraint requires banks to make appropriate adjustments in their lending and investing activities. The competitve efforts of nonbank intermediaries, of course, may change the structure of lender-borrower relationships, and these shifts may work to increase the rate of use of the active money supply and possibly even the money supply itself. These developments, however, would be affecting the formation of monetary policy, and presumably would be taken into account.

To some extent the lending activities of nonbank institutions may add in other ways to inflationary pressures in the short run. This may occur if resource limitation is more intense in capital goods industries, for the bulk of institutional lending is to finance investment activities which place their greatest demands on capital goods lines.

The "near-money" nature of the liabilities of various nonbank financial institutons may induce holders of these liabilities to spend more freely out of current incomes than they would if the liabilities they held had a greater degree of risk. This would be true also if savers held short-term marketable Government securities or other liquid assets of this type. As a consequence, changes in the public's holdings of such liquid assets need to be taken into consideration in determining credit and monetary policies directed toward maintaining a supply of money appropriate for sustained growth.

In one sense, the growth of nonbank financial intermediaries may have made the economy more responsive to the exercise of monetary policy during economic expansion. An important part of the flows through intermediaries are of contractual nature and not readily available for diversion by individual savers to finance inflationary or speculative outlays. These contractual flows tend to be relatively stable, and their allocation to investment outlets tends to follow fairly regular and to some extent predictable patterns. As an increasing share of the savings flow becomes contractual, erratic movements in capital markets tend to be reduced and monetary policy can be applied more effectively.

QUESTIONS

1. What economic variables are influenced by monetary and debt management policies?

2. Explain how monetary and debt management policies affect the availability of credit. Explain how the availability of credit affects the achievement of national economic objectives.

3. Explain how monetary and debt management policies affect the degree of liquidity. Explain how changes in the degree of liquidity affect the achievement of national economic objectives.

4. What is meant by the "capitalized value of assets"? Summarize Samuelson's point of view with respect to capitalization.

5. What is the theoretical foundation of interest rate policy?

6. Explain how monetary and debt management policies affect the level and structure of interest rates. Explain how changes in the level and

structure of interest rates affect the achievement of national economic objectives.

7.   What influence has the growth of non-bank financial institutions had on the nature of and effectiveness of monetary and debt management policies?

ADDITIONAL READING

All of the money and banking texts listed at the end of Chapter 4, and references listed at the end of Chapter 25 treat topics covered in Chapters 26 and 27.

Board of Governors of the Federal Reserve System. *Annual Reports, Federal Reserve Bulletin*. Washington, D.C.: Board of Governors of the Federal Reserve System. The following reprints are available, as of early 1961: "Influence of Credit and Monetary Measures on Economic Stability," "Federal Financial Measures for Economic Stability," "Open Market Operations in Long-term Securities," "Public Debt Management," "The Government Securities Market," "Capital Markets and Money and Bank Credit," "Monetary Policy for Economic Growth." See recent *Federal Reserve Bulletin* for additional information.

————. *The Federal Reserve System — Purposes and Functions*. Washington, D.C.: Board of Governors of the Federal Reserve System, 1954.

Commission on Money and Credit, (sponsored by C.E.D., Ford Foundation, and Merrill Center for Economics). The Commission is examining the American financial system in terms of how well it performs in terms of national economic objectives. Research studies and recommendations of the Commission are bound to provide a wealth of new information on our financial systems.

Goldenweiser, E. A. *American Monetary Policy*. C.E.D. study. New York: McGraw-Hill Book Co., Inc., 1951.

Managing the Federal Debt. A Statement of National Policy. New York: Committee for Economic Development, 1954.

Mints, Lloyd W. *Monetary Policy for a Competitive Society*. New York: McGraw-Hill Book Co., Inc., 1950.

National Objectives and the Balance of Payments Problem. A Statement of National Policy. New York: Committee for Economic Development, 1960.

The Review of Economics and Statistics, Vol. XLII, No. 3, August 1960. Twelve authors contributed to a symposium, "Controversial Issues in Recent Monetary Policy."

Smithies, Arthur, and J. Keith Butters (eds.). *Readings in Fiscal Policy*. Homewood, Ill.: Richard D. Irwin, Inc., 1955.

Sayers, R. S., *Central Banking after Bagehot*. New York: Oxford University Press, 1957.

United States Monetary Policy. Background papers and *Final Report of the Fourteenth American Assembly*. New York: The American Assembly, 1958.

U.S. Joint Economic Committee Subcommittee on Monetary, Credit, and Fiscal Policies. *Monetary, Credit, and Fiscal Policies*. Compendium of materials (collection of statements submitted to the Subcommittee by

Government officials, bankers, economists, and others, November 1949); hearings (conducted during September, November, and December 1949), January 1950; report of the Subcommittee, January 1950.

————. *General Credit Control, Debt Management, and Economic Mobilization.* Materials prepared by the staff of the Joint Committee on the Economic Report. Committee print, January 1951.

————. Subcommittee on General Credit Control and Debt Management. *General Credit Control and Management of the Public Debt.* Questions (prepared by staff of the subcommittee. Committee print, October 1951.)

————. *Monetary Policy and the Management of the Public Debt.* Replies to questions and other material for use of the Subcommittee, February 1952; hearings (conducted in March 1952), May 1952; and report of the Subcommittee, July 1952 (Senate Doc. No. 163).

U.S. Joint Economic Committee Subcommittee on Tax Policy. *Federal Tax Policy for Economic Growth and Stability.* Papers submitted by panelists appearing before Subcommittee, November 1955; hearings conducted in December 1955 (January 1956); report of the Subcommittee, December 1955.

————. Subcommittee on Economic Stabilization. *Conflicting Official Views on Monetary Policy,* April 1956. Hearings, June 1956; *Monetary Policy: 1955-56,* Hearings, January 1957.

————. Subcommittee on Fiscal Policy. *Federal Expenditure Policy for Economic Growth and Stability.* Papers submitted by panelists appearing before the Subcommittee, November 1957; Hearings, January 1958; and Report, January 1959.

U.S. Senate Committee on Banking and Currency. *Federal Reserve Policy and Economic Stability,* 1951-1957. Report to the Committee, prepared by Asher Achinstein, 85th Cong., 2nd sess. Washington, D.C.: Government Printing Office, 1958.

Index